T0137808

Communications in Computer and Information Science 815

Commenced Publication in 2007
Founding and Former Series Editors:
Alfredo Cuzzocrea, Xiaoyong Du, Orhun Kara, Ting Liu, Dominik Ślęzak,
and Xiaokang Yang

Editorial Board

Simone Diniz Junqueira Barbosa
*Pontifical Catholic University of Rio de Janeiro (PUC-Rio),
Rio de Janeiro, Brazil*
Phoebe Chen
La Trobe University, Melbourne, Australia
Joaquim Filipe
Polytechnic Institute of Setúbal, Setúbal, Portugal
Igor Kotenko
*St. Petersburg Institute for Informatics and Automation of the Russian
Academy of Sciences, St. Petersburg, Russia*
Krishna M. Sivalingam
Indian Institute of Technology Madras, Chennai, India
Takashi Washio
Osaka University, Osaka, Japan
Junsong Yuan
Nanyang Technological University, Singapore, Singapore
Lizhu Zhou
Tsinghua University, Beijing, China

More information about this series at http://www.springer.com/series/7899

Guangtao Zhai · Jun Zhou
Xiaokang Yang (Eds.)

Digital TV and Wireless Multimedia Communication

14th International Forum, IFTC 2017
Shanghai, China, November 8–9, 2017
Revised Selected Papers

 Springer

Editors
Guangtao Zhai (iD)
Shanghai Jiao Tong University
Shanghai
China

Xiaokang Yang
Jiao Tong University
Shanghai
China

Jun Zhou
Shanghai Jiao Tong University
Shanghai
China

ISSN 1865-0929   ISSN 1865-0937 (electronic)
Communications in Computer and Information Science
ISBN 978-981-10-8107-1   ISBN 978-981-10-8108-8 (eBook)
https://doi.org/10.1007/978-981-10-8108-8

Library of Congress Control Number: 2018931876

© Springer Nature Singapore Pte Ltd. 2018
This work is subject to copyright. All rights are reserved by the Publisher, whether the whole or part of the material is concerned, specifically the rights of translation, reprinting, reuse of illustrations, recitation, broadcasting, reproduction on microfilms or in any other physical way, and transmission or information storage and retrieval, electronic adaptation, computer software, or by similar or dissimilar methodology now known or hereafter developed.
The use of general descriptive names, registered names, trademarks, service marks, etc. in this publication does not imply, even in the absence of a specific statement, that such names are exempt from the relevant protective laws and regulations and therefore free for general use.
The publisher, the authors and the editors are safe to assume that the advice and information in this book are believed to be true and accurate at the date of publication. Neither the publisher nor the authors or the editors give a warranty, express or implied, with respect to the material contained herein or for any errors or omissions that may have been made. The publisher remains neutral with regard to jurisdictional claims in published maps and institutional affiliations.

Printed on acid-free paper

This Springer imprint is published by Springer Nature
The registered company is Springer Nature Singapore Pte Ltd.
The registered company address is: 152 Beach Road, #21-01/04 Gateway East, Singapore 189721, Singapore

Preface

The present book includes extended and revised versions of papers selected from the 14th International Forum of Digital TV and Wireless Multimedia Communication (IFTC 2017), held in Shanghai, China, during November 8–9, 2017.

IFTC is a summit forum in the field of digital TV and multimedia communication. The 2017 forum was co-hosted by SIGA, the China International Industry Fair 2017 (CIIF 2017), and co-sponsored by Shanghai Jiao Tong University (SJTU) and the IEEE BTS Chapter of Shanghai Section. The 14th IFTC served as an international bridge for the exchange of the latest research advances in digital TV and wireless communication around the world as well as the relevant policies of industry authorities. The forum also aims to promote technology, equipment, and applications in the field of digital TV and multimedia by comparing the characteristics, frameworks, significant techniques and their maturity, and by analyzing the performance of various applications in terms of scalability, manageability, and portability and discussing the interfaces among various networks and platforms.

The conference program included invited talks delivered by six distinguished speakers from China, Switzerland, and Hong Kong SAR, as well as oral sessions of 11 papers and a poster session of 35 papers. The topics of these papers range from audio/image processing to image and video compression as well as telecommunications. This book contains 46 papers selected from IFTC 2017. We would like to thank the authors for contributing their novel ideas and visions that are recorded in this book.

November 2017

Guangtao Zhai
Jun Zhou
Xiaokang Yang

Organization

General Co-chairs

Xiaokang Yang   Shanghai Jiao Tong University, China
Ping An   Shanghai University, China
Guangtao Zhai   Shanghai Jiao Tong University, China

Program Chairs

Jun Zhou   Shanghai Jiao Tong University, China
Jia Wang   Shanghai Jiao Tong University, China
Jiantao Zhou   University of Macau, SAR China
Liquan Shen   Shanghai University, China

International Liaisons

Weisi Lin   Nanyang Technological University, Singapore
Patrick Le Callet   Nantes University, France
Byeungwoo Jeon   Sungkyunkwan University, South Korea
Lu Zhang   INSA de Rennes, France

Finance Chairs

Yi Xu   Shanghai Jiao Tong University, China
Lianghui Ding   Shanghai Jiao Tong University, China

Publications Chairs

Yue Lu   ECNU, China
Qiudong Sun   Shanghai Second Polytechnic University, China

Award Chairs

Changwen Chen   SUY Buffalo, USA
Wenjun Zhang   Shanghai Jiao Tong University, China

Publicity Chairs

Xiangyang Xue   Fudan University, China
Dingxiang Lin   Shanghai Institute of Visual Art, China

Industrial Program Chairs

Yiyi Lu	China Telecom Shanghai Branch, China
Yongjun Fei	Giant Interactive Group Inc., China
Guozhong Wang	Shanghai University, China

Arrangements Chairs

Cheng Zhi (Secretary-General)	SIGA, China
Xiao Wei	Shanghai Jiao Tong University, China

Contents

Machine Learning

Quality Assessment

Social Media

Telecommunications

Video Surveillance

Virtual Reality

Computer Vision

Image Compression

Image Processing

Text Extraction from Mail Images with Complex Background

Qingqing Wang[1](✉), Xiao Tu[2], Shujing Lu[2], and Yue Lu[1,2]

[1] Department of Computer Science and Technology, East China Normal University,
Shanghai 200062, China
qqwang0723@163.com, ylu@cs.ecnu.edu.cn
[2] ECNU-SRI Joint Lab for Pattern Analysis and Intelligent,
Shanghai Research Institute of China Post Group, Shanghai 200062, China

Abstract. A novel method is proposed for text extraction from mail images with complex background. Firstly, wavelet transform and Laplacian operator are applied to generate the features of regions which are obtained by dividing input image with sliding window. Then, support vector machine (SVM) is utilized to classify these regions into texts and non-texts according to the features. *Bootstrap* strategy is used to build the training database. Finally, connected components analysis (CCA) is employed to merge text regions into text candidates which can be processed by following steps to get the delivery address. Experimental results involving 534 mail images show the effectiveness and robustness of the proposed method, and comparison results with other methods demonstrate the advantages of the selected features.

Keywords: Text extraction · Mail images · Wavelet transform · SVM

1 Introduction

Text extraction is of great importance in the community of pattern recognition. It has been studied for decades and continues to be attractive because of its applications in broad fields, such as content-based image analysis, image retrieval, text detection in video frames and scene images and so on. Several approaches have been well developed, including CCA-based methods [20], edge-based methods [9,19], texture-based methods [13], and learning-based methods [8,16]. Particularly, text detection in scene images has attracted intensive attentions in recent years [2,6,7,11,17]. Among these methods, the Maximally Stable Extremal Region (MSER) based ones [4,10,12,18] achieved the best performance before 2015, but afterwards, the deep learning based ones [1,3,5] play a dominate role in these field. However, these methods are not suitable for mail images. The existing methods usually detect all of the text in images, but in mail images, only a certain kind of texts is the target. For example, the extraction of forwarding address in mail images is the first step of automatic address recognition, which is significantly important for the automation of post system. Besides, the

© Springer Nature Singapore Pte Ltd. 2018
G. Zhai et al. (Eds.): IFTC 2017, CCIS 815, pp. 3–11, 2018.
https://doi.org/10.1007/978-981-10-8108-8_1

MSER and deep learning based methods don't work well in mail images due to the resolution and blur problems. Other challenges of text extraction in mail images are presented as follows: (1) the image resources include many kinds of mail images such as envelope mails, flat mails, and parcel mails etc. and the data is rare; (2) some of them have backgrounds like magazine or book covers and plastic bags with printed patterns. Text extraction is greatly interfered by these complicated backgrounds; (3) texts in background need to be pruned as many as possible; (4) an effective method must be robust for size, alignment, skew, font and hand-writing text because forwarding addresses in mail images are some kind of arbitrary. Directed by these requirements, a novel method is proposed for text extraction from mail images with complex background.

2   Proposed Method

We propose a wavelet transform and SVM based method in this paper to extract text from mail images. Firstly, the 2D wavelet transform is utilized to extract features from pathes of the input images. Then SVM classifier is used to classify them into text or non-text. Finally, the connected component analysis is performed to locate target text areas. The flowchart of proposed method is shown in Fig. 1.

2.1   Feature Extraction

Firstly, a series of regions are obtained by dividing input mail image with a sliding window of size 50 by 50. Then 2D wavelet transform is executed on each region respectively. As a result, one low-frequency sub band S closed to the original image and three high-frequency sub bands HH (diagonal), HL (vertical), and LH (horizontal) are obtained as shown in Fig. 2. Next, HE is calculated as the enhanced high-frequency sub band as:

$$HE_{ij} = \alpha\sqrt{HL_{ij}^2 + LH_{ij}^2 + HH_{ij}^2} \qquad (1)$$

where $\alpha \geq 1$ is the enhancement coefficient, and we set it to 1.1 in this work. Laplacian operator is used to detect edge points in HE and the filter is as shown in equation

$$\nabla = \begin{bmatrix} 0 & 1 & 0 \\ 1 & -4 & 1 \\ 0 & 1 & 0 \end{bmatrix} \qquad (2)$$

Let t denote the computational result which corresponds to the gradient amplitude of pixel (i, j). If $t > T$ is satisfied, the pixel is regarded as an edge point. Here T is a threshold and t is defined as

$$t = |4 * f(i, j) - f(i - 1, j) - f(i + 1, j) - f(i, j + 1) - f(i, j - 1)| \qquad (3)$$

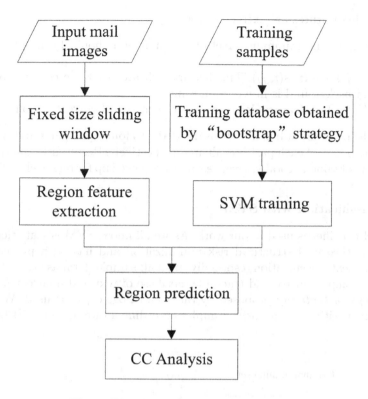

Fig. 1. Flowchart of the proposed method

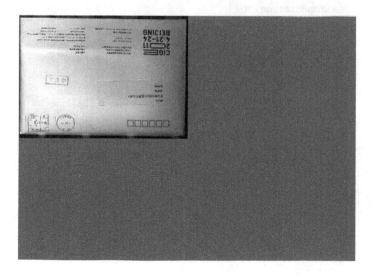

Fig. 2. Result of wavelet transform

The following features are extracted from S:

- $min(s(i,j))$. The minimum pixel of a text region should be in an apposite range;
- $max(s(i,j)) - min(s(i,j))$. This feature indicates that the contrast between text and background is in a certain range;
- $\frac{1}{N}\sum s(i,j)$. This feature demonstrates the energy of current region.

In high-frequency sub band, HE is divided into four equal parts and the number of edge points of each part is evaluated respectively. Resultantly, another four features are obtained. Totally, seven features are picked up for region classification.

2.2 Classification with SVM

The SVM classifier is used in our work. As we all know, SVM is statistics-based and in the theory of structural risk minimization and has been proved to be effective in text classification, especially in small sample database case. In order to build a comprehensive and tractable database of text and non-text patterns, the strategy of *bootstrap* proposed by Sung and Poggio [14] is used. We firstly select some positive and negative samples according a rate of about 5:1 from the

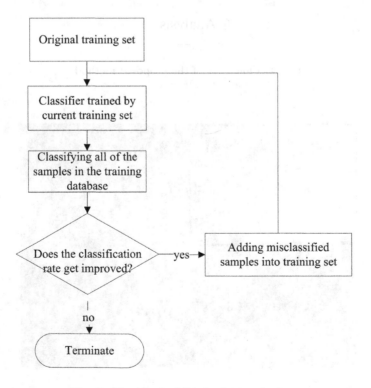

Fig. 3. Flowchart of the *bootstrap* strategy

training set. These samples are used to train a primal SVM classifier, which is then used to classify the rest of training samples. Next, the misclassified samples are picked out and used to train the primal SVM classifier. This procedure is repeated until the classification accuracy become steady. The procedure is shown in Fig. 3. At first the training set is composed of 342 positive samples and 63 negative samples, which achieve a classification accuracy of 72%. And finally 881 positive samples and 1401 negative samples are included in the training set, and the accuracy is elevated to 81%. The Radial Basis Function (RBF) kernel is used for SVM since it achieves the best performance when comparing to other kernel functions. Some important parameters such as c, which is used to trade off misclassification of training examples against simplicity of the decision surface, and γ, which can be seen as the inverse of the radius of influence of samples selected as support vectors, are chosen by the well-known ten-fold cross-validation, as shown in Fig. 4. The classification result of SVM is shown in Fig. 5.

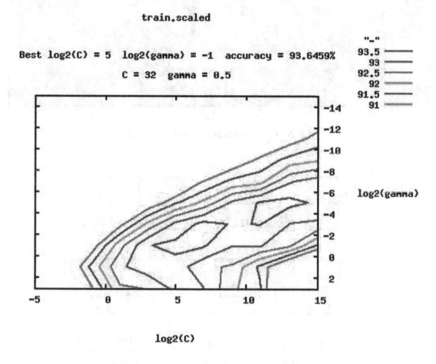

Fig. 4. Ten-fold cross-validation for parameter selecting

2.3 Connected Component Analysis (CCA)

The run-based CCA method [15] is used to merge connected text regions. In this method, only one-pass scan is needed to find all the runs and represent their relationships with trees. The input images are scanned from up to bottom,

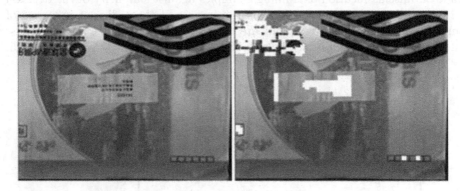

Fig. 5. Classification result of SVM

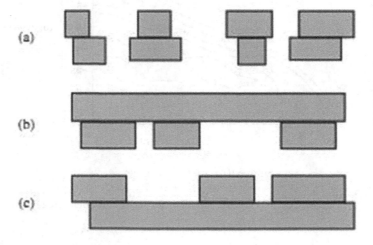

Fig. 6. Connected runs. (a)1-1 connected (b)1-n connected (c)n-1 connected

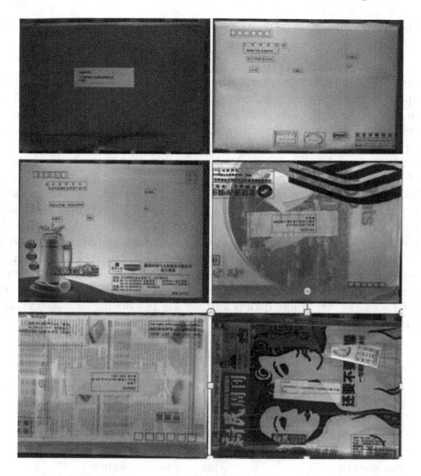

Fig. 7. Extraction results

and there are three connection types for runs between two adjacent lines, which is described in Fig. 6. Finally, each tree corresponds to a connected component. If connected components A and B satisfy $A \cap B \neq \varnothing$ & $A \bigcup B < T$, where T is a threshold, they will be grouped together, and the final extraction results are shown in Fig. 7.

3 Experiments

The following conditions are defined for an accurately extracted mail image:

- All the texts belonging to address are located;
- Rectangles containing address texts are restrain the address texts exactly;
- One address text should belong to only one rectangle.

And the extraction rate is defined as

$$ER = \frac{number\ of\ accurately\ extracted\ images}{total\ number\ of\ tested\ images} \quad (4)$$

Experiments are conducted on five kinds of mail images to evaluate the performance of the proposed method, including white envelopes with stickers (addresses are written or printed on the stickers), white envelopes without stickers (addresses are directly written or printed on the the envelope), yellow envelopes with stickers, flat mails and packages. In this mail images, backgrounds of the flat mails and packages are the most complex, which is shown in the last row of Fig. 6.

The extraction results are listed in Table 1. As we can see, our method is capable of extracting address texts from mail images with complex background. Furthermore, the proposed method is robust to size, alignment, skew, font and hand-writing texts. We also compare the proposed wavelet-Laplacian based feature with Sobel, Robert, Laplacian and Canny in Table 2. As is shown, our wavelet-Laplacian method gives a extraction rate of 84%, which is higher than those given by other resolutions. The result may be caused by the fact that wavelet-Laplacian gives more details for text and less details for non-text, while other resolutions give fine details for both text and non-text.

Table 1. Recognition accuracies (%) on the cropped datasets

Type of mail images (amount)	Accurately extracted images	ER (extraction rate)
White envelope with sticker (91)	87	95.60%
White envelope without sticker (50)	41	82%
Yellow envelope with sticker (71)	69	97.18%
Flat mails (290)	238	82.07%
Packages (32)	31	96.87%
Total (534)	466	87.27%

Table 2. Performance comparison of methods for edge points extraction

	Proposed method	Robert	Laplacian	Sobel	Canny
ER	84%	78%	78%	77%	4%

4   Conclusions

A new approach combining the advantages of wavelet, SVM and CCA is proposed to extract text from mail images with complex background. Gray level information and edge information are extracted from the low and high frequency sub bands of wavelet, respectively. Then, SVM and CCA are used to predict text location in the mail images. Experimental results on five kinds of mail images demonstrate the effectiveness and robustness of the proposed method.

References

1. He, P., Huang, W., He, T., Zhu, Q., Qiao, Y., Li, X.: Single shot textdetector with regional attention. In: International Conference on Computer Vision (2017)
2. He, T., Huang, W., Qiao, Y., Yao, J.: Accurate text localization in natural image with cascaded convolutional text network. arXiv:1603.09423 (2016)
3. He, T., Huang, W., Qiao, Y., Yao, J.: Text-attention convolutional neural networks for scene text detection. IEEE Trans. Image Process. **25**, 2529–2541 (2016)
4. Iqbal, K., Yin, X., Yin, X., Ali, H., Hao, H.: Classifier comparison for MSER-based text classification in scene images. In: International Joint Conference on Neural Networks, pp. 1–6 (2013)
5. Jiang, Y., Zhu, X., Wang, X., Yang, S., Li, W., Wang, H., Fu, P., Luo, Z.: R2CNN: Rotation region CNN for orientation robust scene text detection. arXiv:1706.09579v2 (2017)
6. Koo, K., Kim, D.: Scene text detection via connected component clustering and nontext filtering. IEEE Trans. Image Process. **22**(6), 2296–2305 (2013)
7. Liao, M., Shi, B., Bai, X, Wang, X., Liu, W.: Textboxes: a fast textdetector with a single deep neural network. In: The 31th AAAI Conference on Artificial Intelligence, pp. 4161–4167 (2017)
8. Lienhart, R., Wernicke, A.: Localizing and segmenting text in images and videos. IEEE Trans. Circuits Syst. Video Technol. **12**(4), 256–268 (2002)
9. Liu, C., Wang, C., Dai, R.: Text detection in images based on unsupervised classification of edge-based features. In: The 18th International Conference on Document Analysis and Recognition, pp. 610–614 (2005)
10. Neumann, L., Matas, J.: Real-time scene text localization and recognition. In: IEEE Conference on Computer Vision and Pattern Recognition, pp. 3538–3545 (2012)
11. Pan, Y.F., Hou, X., Liu, C.L.: A hybrid approach to detect and localize texts in natural scene images. IEEE Trans. Image Process. **20**(3), 800–813 (2011)
12. Shi, C., Wang, C., Xiao, B., Zhang, Y., Gao, S.: Scene text detection using graph model built upon maximally stable extremal regions. Pattern Recogn. Lett. **34**(2), 107–116 (2013)
13. Shivakumara, P., Trung, Q.P., Tan, C.L.: A robust wavelet transform based technique for video text detection. In: The 10th International Conference on Document Analysis and Recognition, pp. 1285–1289 (2009)
14. Sung, K., Poggio, T.: Example-based learning for view-based human face detection. IEEE Trans. Pattern Anal. Mach. Intell. **20**(1), 39–51 (1998)
15. Tu, X., Lu, Y.: Run-based approach to labeling connected components in document images. In: The 2th International Workshop on ETCS, pp. 206–209 (2010)
16. Ye, Q., Gao, W., Wang, W., Zeng, W.: A robust text detection algorithm in images and video frames. In: IEEE ICICS-PCM, pp. 802–806 (2003)
17. Yi, C., Tian, Y.: Text string detection from natural scenes by structure-based partition and grouping. IEEE Trans. Image Process. **20**(9), 2594–2605 (2011)
18. Yin, X., Yin, X., Huang, K., Hao, H.: Robust text detection in natural scene images. IEEE Trans. Pattern Anal. Mach. Intell. **36**(5), 970–983 (2014)
19. Zhang, J., Kasturi, R.: Text detection using edge gradient and graph spectrum. In: The 20th International Conference on Pattern Recognition, pp. 3979–3982 (2010)
20. Zini, L., Destrero, A., Odone, F.: A classification architecture based on connected components for text detection in unconstrained environments. In: The 6th IEEE International Conference on Digital Object Identifier, pp. 176–181 (2009)

A Quantitative Analysis System of Pulmonary Nodules CT Image for Lung Cancer Risk Classification

Vanbang Le[1], Yu Zhu[1(✉)], Dawei Yang[2], Bingbing Zheng[1], and Xiaodong Ren[1]

[1] School of Information Science and Engineering,
East China University of Science and Technology, Shanghai, China
lebang2018@gmail.com, zhuyu@ecust.edu.cn, 1130072360@qq.com,
13248255186@163.com
[2] Department of Pulmonary Medicine, Shanghai Respiratory Research Institute,
ZhongShan Hospital, Fudan University, Shanghai, China
yang_dw@hotmail.com

Abstract. To improve the classification performance for lung nodule, we proposed a lung nodule CT image feature extraction method. The approach designed multi-directional distribution features to represent nodules in different risk stages effectively. First, the reference map is constructed using integral image, and then K-Means approach is performed to clustering the reference map and calculate its label map. The density distribution map of lung nodule image was generated after calculate the gray scale density distribution level for each pixel. An exponential function was designed to weighting the angular histogram for each components of the distribution map. Then, quantitative measurement was performed by Random Forest classifier. The evaluation dataset is the lung CT database which provided by Shanghai Zhongshan Hospital (ZSDB), the nodule risk categories were AAH, AIS, MIA, and IA. In the result the AUCs are 0.9771, 0.9917, 0.9590, 0.9971, and accuracy are 0.7478, 0.9167, 0.7450, 0.9567 for AAH, AIS, MIA and IA respectively. The experiments show that the proposed method performs well and is effective to improve the classification performance of pulmonary nodules.

Keywords: Lung CT image · Gray scale density distribution · Angular histogram
Exponential weighting · Nodule classification

1 Introduction

CT (Computerized Tomography) imaging can significantly improve the clinical diagnosis rate of lung cancer patients [1]. Improving the level of early diagnosis and identification of small lung adenocarcinoma has been always an important topic for imaging studies. In the field of clinical medicine, ground-glass opacity (GGO) grows to ground-glass nodule (GGN) and appears as a tiny cloudy region in the CT image [2]. By measuring the tiny region of GGN at a high resolution, the area can be divided into three types: pure GGN (pGGN), mixed GGN (mGGN) or so-called part-solid nodule (PSN)

© Springer Nature Singapore Pte Ltd. 2018
G. Zhai et al. (Eds.): IFTC 2017, CCIS 815, pp. 12–24, 2018.
https://doi.org/10.1007/978-981-10-8108-8_2

and solid nodule (SN). When the pGGN showed a clear edge density, translucent, non-solid nodules at the opposite edge are less clear than the part-solid nodule with regard to the low-energy region [3].

The quantitative methods are mainly used a combination of image features and classifiers for the classification and recognition of lung nodules. There are several features, namely 2D shape-based, 3D shape based [4], context feature [5], density distribution feature [6]; the common classifiers are ANN [7], CNN [8], deep learning [9].

Lee et al. [10] performed a quantitative analysis of preoperative CT imaging metrics to distinguish invasive adenocarcinoma from AIS, MIA, and proved that 75th percentile CT attenuation value and entropy feature as independent predictors, and with a ROC curve of 0.780. Most of the previous work did not consider the prediction as Atypical Adenomatous Hyperplasia (AAH) with other categories for lung adenocarcinomas. For the diversity and complexity of GGNs, more effective and quantitative CT image feature expressions are essential for the prediction of lung nodules histopathological diagnosis.

Maldonado et al. [6] proposed the CT value density distribution calculation method, firstly, collecting the image block set (block sizes as 9×9) from nodule CT images, then using Affinity propagation clustering approach to classified the correlation matrix of image block set. After that, scanning the testing nodule image, calculating the density level for pixels and exporting the feature vector were implemented respectively. Finally, through analysis the components of feature vector, the difference categories of pulmonary nodules was recognized. Foley et al. [11] also used CT density distribution features to characterize the nodule image for 264 and 294 cases of Mayo Clinic cohort and National lung screening trial study, respectively. The categories of dataset are AIS, MIA, and IA. The results shown Sensitivity of 95.4% (95% CI: 75.1%–99.7%) and specificity of 96.8% (95% CI: 82%–99.8%), and a sensitivity of 98.7% (95% CI: 91.8%–99.9%) and specificity of 63.6% (95% CI: 31.6%–87.6%) in the training and independent validation set.

In 2011, the International Association for the Study of Lung Cancer (IASLC), the American Thoracic Society (ATS) and the European Respiratory Society (ERS) proposed a new international multidisciplinary classification system for lung adenocarcinoma [4]. According to the classification criteria, we organized a structured Chinese lung CT dataset provided by Shanghai ZhongShan Hospital (ZSDB) in this paper. There are 595 PET/CT sets in ZSDB dataset with the pathological definition. These nodules (4 mm < diameter < 32 mm) are divided into four categories: Atypical Adenomatous Hyperplasia (AAH); Adenocarcinoma In Situ (AIS); Minimally Invasive Adenocarcinoma (MIA); and Invasive Adenocarcinoma (IA), while the degree of risk of these classes is increasing. Early classification of lung adenocarcinomas from AAH to IA will have great significance for clinical auxiliary diagnosis and have great significance in improving the 5-year survival rate.

To optimize the lung adenocarcinoma classification effect and improve the clinical significance, this article proposes an effective lung CT image density distribution features. First, we conducted lesion segmentation based on unsupervised clustering for ZSDB database. Then, we proposed a nodule image feature of weighted gray scale angular density distribution. The remainder of this paper is organized as follows: In Sect. 2, we introduce the materials preparation briefly. In Sect. 3, we formulate the proposed framework of weighted gray scale angular density distribution feature extraction, which includes unsupervised feature representation and pattern recognition models. In Sect. 4, we present the experimental results according with the process in Sect. 3 and show the analysis of the results. Section 5 concludes the paper.

2 The Lung CT Dataset Provided by Shanghai ZhongShan Hospital (ZSDB)

In ZSDB database contains four categories as AAH, AIS, MIA and IA nodule classes, the sample number per class are 92, 157, 158, and 188 samples, respectively. The dataset was collected from radiology data of 350 patients. All nodules have been pathologically defined by four clinical experts in Shanghai Zhongshan Hospital. These nodules (4 mm < major length diameter < 32 mm) are divided into four categories: AAH, IAS, MIA, and IA. In ZSDB, the edges for each lung nodule was marked by clinician of Shanghai Zhongshan hospital and saved as XML files. The imaging parameters of ZSDB are the following: Electric parameters as 500 mA, 120 kV, the size of the image as 512 × 512; Type: PET/CTQSZLXX; Protocol: 10.1 CT CHEST; Pixel Spacing: 0.703125 mm; Slice Thickness: 0.625 mm. In ZSDB, the database informations are shown in Table 1.

Table 1. The information of ZSDB

Classes	Sample number	Ages (Years, Y)	Gender (Male, F; Female, F)	Gray scale (HU)	Diameter (mm)
AAH	092	63.5 ± 8.5	F:M = 25%:75%	−810.95 to −6.24	4.12 to 13.93
AIS	157	57 ± 21	F:M = 67%:33%	−869.56 to −453.33	4.82 to 20.88
MIA	158	56 ± 22	F:M = 77%:23%	−845.01 to 33.61	4.05 to 30.75
IA	188	58 ± 27	F:M = 51%:49%	−450.63 to 18.87	5.57 to 31.67

3 Methods

The frame work of the proposed method was shown in Fig. 1.

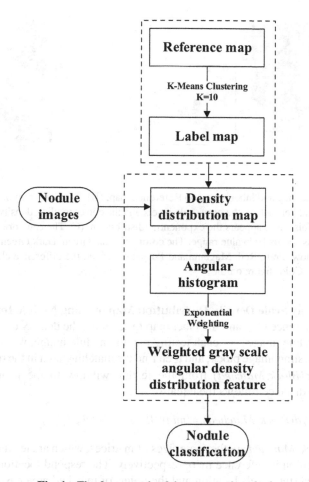

Fig. 1. The frame work of the proposed method

3.1 Lung Nodule Image Feature Extraction

3.1.1 Reference Map Construction and Labeling

We proposed an image gray scale density distribution calculation method based on *reference map*. The Reference map was defined by an integration image, with sizes of (w, h) and its value ranged from -824 to 176 (HU). The value range was set up by manually. There are consulted the opinion of radiologist. The minimal and maximal could be the value of the ranged for lung nodule image. In which the value of upper left point is stand for the lowest value (-824 HU), and the maximum value (176 HU) was located at the lower right point. After that, K-Means (K = 10) method was performed the clustering process for the reference map. Figure 2 shows the visualization of reference map, the histogram image, and the label map.

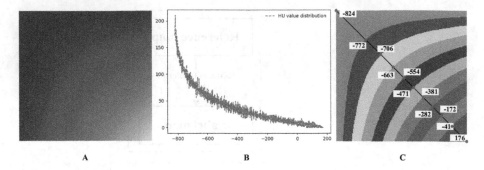

Fig. 2. Reference map and label map. (A) Reference map; (B) The histogram of reference map. The horizontal and vertical are the gray scale levels and the corresponding density distribution in reference map. This curve appears the exponential distribution. (C) The categories resulted from clustering process and its HU value range. The colors of Lime Green, Dark Green, Cyan, Dodger Blue, Navy, Yellow, Peru, Red, Magenta and Purple described the difference classes from 1 to 10, respectively. (Color figure online)

3.1.2   The Gray Scale Density Distribution Map of Lung Nodule Image

We used the reference map and the label map to calculate the density distribution level for pixels of nodule image. For each testing pixel in nodule image, we selected neighbourhood as a testing image block, and then find the matching area in the reference map. The distance $d(Block, Matched)$ from the testing window to the matching area is minimum. The distance follows the equation:

$$d(Block, Matched) = min\|Block - Matched\|_2 \tag{1}$$

Where *Block, Matched* are the same sizes of matrices, which are testing image block and matched region in reference map, respectively. The respond location in label map of Matched area (the pixels location and the points of matched area have a one-to-one correspondence) will be within a category region, or in cross-region of two categories, which the labels are continuous value. Therefore, we calculated the round value of the average value of the correspond region as the density distribution level of the testing pixels.

The density distribution map of nodule image (D) is follows:

$$D(i,j) = \{g_{i,j} | i \in [0, w], j \in [0, h]\} \tag{2}$$

Where $g_{i,j}$ is the gray scale density distribution level of the non-zero pixel in nodule image (zero pixels result as -1). These values described the difference solidly degree of the pixels in lung nodule image.

3.1.3   Extraction the Gray Scale Angular Density Distribution Feature Based on Exponential Weighting

In Sects. 3.1.1 and 3.1.2, we proposed a 10-level grey scale density distribution map to describe nodule images. This type of feature map is insufficient to reflect the directional distribution information for solid or partly solid elements in a lung nodule. However, the elemental directional distribution of a nodule is also important to more effective features. To solve this problem, we propose an angular density distribution feature based on exponential weighting. The calculation steps are as follows:

Step 1: Calculate the centroid of the nodule image, then translate the location of the pixels to the centre of the lung nodule image.

Step 2: Split the grey scale density distribution map D into a 10 sub-label map. Transform the location of the pixels in a sub-label map from plan coordinates to angular coordinates.

Step 3: Extract the exponential-weighted grey scale angular density distribution feature for the sub-label map;

Step 4: Sequence the components that are exported from the sub-label maps in Step 3 to generate the feature vector of the lung nodule image.

We defined the angle step as θ and the bin number as $B = \dfrac{360}{\theta}$. The dimension of the feature vector is

$$dims = \frac{360}{\theta} \times K = B \times 10 \tag{3}$$

Choosing the number of bins is also directly related to the nodule size. When the bin spacing is too small, the number of pixels in the bins is rather small and will reduce the distinction between the bins, so we chose minimum angle step to evaluate the proposed method as 30.

The local centre $(\bar{x}, \bar{y})$ of the nodule image is:

$$(\bar{x}, \bar{y}) = \left(\frac{\sum_{x=1}^{h} x(L_{x,y} > 0)}{\sum (L_{x,y} > 0)}, \frac{\sum_{y=1}^{w} y(L_{x,y} > 0)}{\sum (L_{x,y} > 0)} \right) \tag{4}$$

where L is label map, which the value ranged is from 1 to 10. The new centroid after translation to the centre of the nodule image will be used as the original point to calculate the density distribution for all bins.

We resolved D into 10 *sub-label maps (S)*. An example for the transformation to the angular coordinate system of the local (x, y) in the sub-label map k is shown in Fig. 3. After translation of the image centroid $(\bar{x}, \bar{y})$, the local pixel (x, y) was transformed to (r, α). In this example, the angle step is $\theta = 30^{o}$ and bins $= 12$.

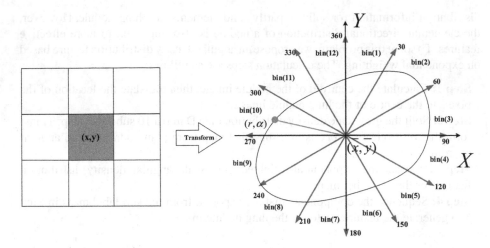

Fig. 3. Example of the transformation to the angular coordinate system with angle step $\theta = 30$. The blue line shows the region of the lung nodule. (Color figure online)

In the transformation, the angle α was calculated by the following:

$$\alpha = \arg \cos \left(\frac{y}{\sqrt{(x - \bar{x})^2 + (y - \bar{y})^2}} \right) \tag{5}$$

In the sub-label map k, the feature component in $f_{k_{bin}}$ for the *bin(b)* direction (where the correlation between α and b is $\dfrac{180 \times \cos(\alpha)}{\theta \times \pi} \in (b - 1, b)$ is as follows:

$$f_{k_{bin}} = \underbrace{\sum \sum |(r, \alpha)_{k,bin}|}_{\text{Angular histogram of density distribution}} \times \underbrace{w_{\text{exponential}}}_{\text{weighted}} \tag{6}$$

The angular histogram shows the spatial distribution for pixels of the nodule image in different directions. We analysed statistically the number of pixels of the different directions on the same sub-label map so that the feature vector shows the spatial distribution relative to the nodule centre of these pixels. The image pixel $(r, \alpha)_{k,bin}$ belongs to the direction *bin(b)* in sub-label map k. In this way, the weighted $w_{\text{exponential}}$ is the exponential function to the amplitude of mean location in the direction of *bin = b*. The average coordinate of the pixels in direction *bin(b)* is

$$\left(x_{average}, y_{average} \right) = \left(\frac{\sum_x x}{n}, \frac{\sum_y y}{n} \right),$$ where (x, y) is pixel in the direction b of sub label

map k, and n is pixel number in this region ($n = \sum_x \sum_y |(x, y)|$). Therefore, the weighted $w_{\text{exponential}}$ is as follow:

$$w_{exponential} = \exp\left(-\sqrt{\frac{3 \times \left(x^2_{average} + y^2_{average}\right)}{\max(x_{average}, y_{average})^2}} + \xi\right) \tag{7}$$

where ξ is the repair parameter. Parameter ξ adjusts the value of the weight for the small nodules (nodules where the pixel coordinates are close to zero). The commonly selected value of ξ in these experiments is from 0.001 to 0.1. This weight has been shown to enhance the effect of the pixels that are closer to the centre and reduce the effect of the pixels on the borders at the same time. In addition to the selection of angle step, θ depends on the size of the nodule image. In this way, a bigger step is a smaller image, and vice versa.

Finally, the normalized exponential weighting angular density distribution feature F_G was extracted as follows:

$$F_G = \left\{100 \times \frac{f_{k_{bin}}}{\sum_k \sum_{bin} f_{k_{bin}}} | k \in [1, K], bin \in [1, B]\right\} \tag{8}$$

The factors were computed to difference direction for each sub label map. All of components are sequencing and construct the weighted gray scale angular density distribution feature of nodule image. The feature is used to characterize the risk level of pulmonary nodule. We have taken the concept of the density distribution and its calculation from the method of Maldonado et al. [11–13], and we optimized that concept. The method present by Maldonado et al. [11–13] mainly based on the collected image blocks to extract the density distribution feature of nodule image. The image block set which randomly collected from pulmonary nodule image. The histogram distribution of overall image blocks is not stable. The gray scale density distribution of lung nodule image may not achieve the optimal results. Moreover, that was the lack of robustness to process for different database.

In the proposed method, the reference map generated based on the integration image was used instead of the distance matrix of image cells. The HU range covers overall values of the grey scale, which range from the value of the air to the calcification region in the lung CT image. The histogram of the reference map is more even and smooth than the distance matrix, and it basically obeys an exponential distribution. In this paper, the calculated density distribution of the nodule image will achieve the optimal result. The density distribution calculated from the labelled reference map is unified for different datasets. We also calculated the spatial relationship between the factors of feature vectors.

3.2   Lung Nodule Image Classification

For the nodule classification, the quantitative measurement was performed by the well-known Random Forest classifier. The Area under curve of the receiver operating characteristic (AUC) value and Cross-validation Score are used to evaluate the training parameters [13]. The AUC of ROC curve is computed using the Sensitivity and 1-Specificity, where:

$$Sensitivity = \frac{TP}{TP + FN} \qquad (9)$$

$$Specifity = \frac{TN}{TN + FP} \qquad (10)$$

Cross-validation scoring to multi-class using *Accuracy* parameter, which as:

$$Accuracy = \frac{TP + TN}{TP + FP + TN + FN} \qquad (11)$$

Where:

TP (True Positive rate)   = correctly classified positive cases;
TN (True Negative rate) = correctly classified negative cases;
FN (False Negative)   = incorrectly classified positive cases; and
FP (False Positive)   = incorrectly classified negative cases:

4   Experimental

4.1   Weighted Gray Scale Angular Density Distribution Feature Extraction

We set three types of the angle step are (30°, 60°, 90°). The features extracted using the proposed method are named as the exponential weighting based feature (Ew). The different angle steps constructed 3 sets of weighted angular density distribution feature, such as Ew-30, Ew-60 and Ew-90. The features have difference responses to the identification process of nodule image set.

The characterization process using the proposed method of the segmented nodule image are shown in Fig. 4. The meaning of these colors is the same as the color code in Fig. 2. The features of AAH, AIS, MIA were mainly composed of lower density levels, these factors corresponded to the GGO regions of nodule images. Otherwise, the nodules of the IA category have a large number of higher density level components. The result accorded with the radiologic characteristics since IA nodule images are composed of a large area of the solid region.

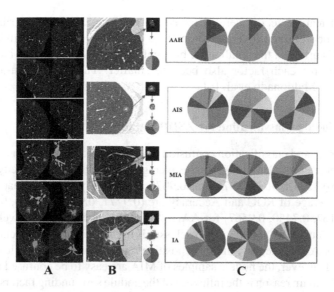

Fig. 4. Pulmonary nodule image segmentation and characterization process for ZSDB database. (A), (B): Nodule image segmentation and characterization. The example for 4 nodule cases, i.e., AAH (1st row), AIS (2nd row), MIA (3rd row), and IA (4th row); (C): The gray scale density distribution feature of nodule image, rows 1st to 4th are the features of AAH, AIS, MIA, IA, respectively.

The schematic image of exponential weighted gray scale angular density distribution is shows in Fig. 5. There are 6 types of features computed from the segmented nodule shown in Fig. 5 (C) to (II). The proposed feature vectors are able to describe the spatial correlation between pixels in nodule image. The different distribution and

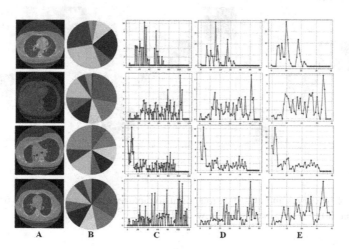

Fig. 5. Lung nodule angular histogram exponential weighted features extraction. (A) source image of the pulmonary nodule, the red line is the nodule region; (B) normalization of density distribution feature vector; (C) to (E) are Ew-30, Ew-60, Ew-90, respectively. (Color figure online)

dimension of feature vector were extracted from the same density distribution map. Variant bins or weighted function can make a difference to the amplitude of vector factors. In this process, the smaller the bins gets, the longer the vector increases and the amplitude for each factor also become smaller. That a more in-depth study compared with Maldonado et al. [6].

4.2   Lung Nodule Classification for ZSDB Database

The ROC curves and classification confusion matrix to multi classes with 6 features for ZSDB dataset are provided in Fig. 6. The average of Sensitivity, Specificity, AUC and Accuracy are 0.8704, 0.9697, 0.9715 and 0.9075, respectively. In the evaluation to multi-classes, the average of ROC and Accuracy are (0.9771, 0.9917, 0.9590, 0.9971), and (0.7478, 0.9167, 0.7450, 0.9567) for AAH, AIS, MIA, and IA, respectively. The true positive rate (Sensitivity) of AIS and IA classes is higher than the others classes. At the same time, for AAH category, the false positive rate is lower than the classes of AIS, MIA and IA. However, the nodule samples of MIA are easy to be confused with AIS or IA classes. The main reason is the influence of the nodule surrounding factors of vascular vessel. The experiment results shown the high performance for early cancer detection process.

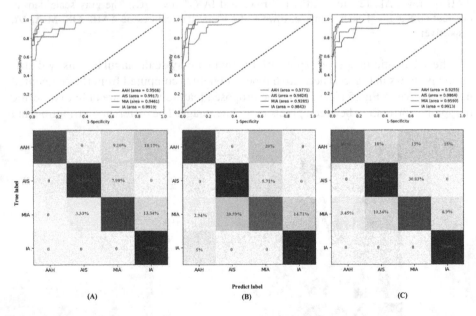

Fig. 6. The ROC curves and classification confusion matrix to multi classes with 6 features for ZSDB dataset. (a) to (f) are the result of Ew-30, Ew-60, Ew-90, respectively.

5   Conclusion

For the pulmonary nodule risk classification problem, we proposed an image characterization method based on gray scale density distribution. We designed a clustered integral image (sizes as 200×200, HU value range from -824 to 176) based on K-means algorithm ($K = 10$) to extract the gray scale density image of nodules. We calculated the various angular histogram features with weighted with exponential distribution function for each nodule image in ZSDB dataset and generated the evaluation feature vector set. This method can distinguish the nodule categories into AAH, AIS, MIA and IA with high precision, the result shows the efficient performance of the proposed method. The experimental result shows the greatly robustness of the proposed method for different lung CT image dataset.

The experimental results above provide a great reference value in clinical diagnosis as well as the development of electronic diagnostic systems that detect early stage lung cancer for patients in China or Asia region. It has great significance to support radiologists in performing clinical diagnosis for lung cancer patients and increasing their survival rate when detecting first-stage lung cancer areas in time. The further work will concern about more effective feature extraction algorithms for proper representation of nodules in the feature space and improve the performance of classification.

Acknowledgements. The authors greatly appreciate the financial supported by Zhongshan Hospital Clinical Research Foundation No. 2016ZSLC05, No. 2016ZSCX02, National Key Scientific and Technology Support Program No. 2013BAI09B09 and Natural Science Foundation of China No. 81500078.

References

1. Emil, J.B., Neil, M.R., Ryan, Z.: Appendicitis: the impact of computed tomography imaging on negative appendectomy and perforation rates. Am. J. Gastroenterol. **93**, 768–771 (1998)
2. Goo, J.M., Park, C.M., Lee, H.J.: Ground-glass nodules on chest CT as imaging biomarkers in the management of lung adenocarcinoma. Am. J. Roentgenol. **196**, 533–543 (2011)
3. Noriyuki, S., Hidetake, Y., Masatoshi, K., et al.: Volumetric measurement of artificial pure ground-glass nodules at low-dose CT: comparisons between hybrid iterative reconstruction and filtered back projection. Eur. J. Radiol. **84**, 2654–2662 (2015)
4. El-Baz, A., Nitzken, M., Khalifa, F., et al.: 3D shape analysis for early diagnosis of malignant lung nodules. In: Biennial International Conference on Information Processing in Medical Imaging, pp. 772–783 (2011)
5. Jacobs, C., van Rikxoort, E.M., Twellmann, T., et al.: Automatic detection of subsolid pulmonary nodules in thoracic computed tomography images. Med. Image Anal. **18**, 374–384 (2014)
6. Maldonado, F., Duan, F., Raghunath, S.M., et al.: Noninvasive computed tomography–based risk stratification of lung adenocarcinomas in the National Lung Screening Trial. Am. J. Respir. Crit. Care Med. **192**, 737–744 (2015)
7. Zhu, Y., Tan, Y., Hua, Y., et al.: Feature selection and performance evaluation of support vector machine (SVM)-based classifier for differentiating benign and malignant pulmonary nodules by computed tomography. J. Digit. Imaging **23**, 51–65 (2010)

8. Li, W., Cao, P., Zhao, D., Wang, J.: Pulmonary nodule classification with deep convolutional neural networks on computed tomography images. Comput. Math. Methods Med. (2016)

9. Setio, A.A.A., Ciompi, F., Litjens, G., et al.: Pulmonary nodule detection in CT images: false positive reduction using multi-view convolutional networks. IEEE Trans. Med. Imaging **35**, 1160–1169 (2016)

10. Son, J.Y., Lee, H.Y., Lee, K.S., et al.: Quantitative CT analysis of pulmonary ground-glass opacity nodules for the distinction of invasive adenocarcinoma from pre-invasive or minimally invasive adenocarcinoma. PLoS ONE **9**, e104066 (2014)

11. Foley, F., Rajagopalan, S., Raghunath, S.M., et al.: Computer-aided nodule assessment and risk yield risk management of adenocarcinoma: the future of imaging? Semin. Thorac. Cardiovasc. Surg. **28**, 120–126 (2016)

12. Yeh, Y.-C., Kadota, K., Nitadori, J.-I., et al.: International Association for the Study of Lung Cancer/American Thoracic Society/European Respiratory Society classification predicts occult lymph node metastasis in clinically mediastinal node-negative lung adenocarcinoma. Eur. J. Cardiothorac. Surg. **49**, 9–15 (2016)

13. Bose, S., Pal, A., SahaRay, R., Nayak, J.: Generalized quadratic discriminant analysis. Pattern Recogn. **48**, 2676–2684 (2015)

A Fast Fabric Image Matching and Retrieval Algorithm Based on Locality-Sensitive Hashing and Visual Word

Xueqin Zhang$^{(\boxtimes)}$, Yuanyuan Liu, and Yifan Wei

Institute of Information Science and Technology,
East China University of Science and Technology, Shanghai, China
zxq@ecust.edu.cn

Abstract. In order to meet the demands of designers in rapid fabric image retrieval, this paper proposes a fabric image matching algorithm based on Locality-Sensitive Hashing and visual word. The algorithm extracts the SIFT features of fabric images, which are clustered by K-Means to form the bag of visual words. According to the clustering results, feature histogram of each image can been calculated. At last, it realizes the fabric image matching and retrieval by E2LSH algorithm. Experiments show that the algorithm realizes the high detection accuracy in rapid fabric image matching and reach μs level for single image matching time.

Keywords: Fabric image · SIFT feature · K-Means clustering
E2LSH

1 Introduction

Costume designers usually have four kinds of demands when selecting the fabric in gallery: finding the target fabric they need, obtaining the same fabric category with similar patterns, getting space distribution and color to give them inspiration, and retrieving the desired fabric rapidly. But this case is extremely difficult and time-consuming for massive gallery with manual operation. Computer vision and image intelligence analysis technology provides the possibility for this application.

The SIFT feature of image is widely used in the feature-based image matching algorithm. But because of its high dimension, image matching with SIFT feature needs high computational complexity and storage space. BOF (Bag-of-Feature) based matching method is introduced by Sivic [1] from text to image. It extracts the original feature descriptor of the image and obtains the visual word bag BOW (Bag-of-Word) through some algorithms such as K-Means clustering etc. Then the new image feature descriptor (visual word histogram) with lower dimension can be constructed with the BOW. Exact Euclidean Locality-Sensitive Hashing (E2LSH) [2] is a fast-nearest neighbor search algorithm for

© Springer Nature Singapore Pte Ltd. 2018
G. Zhai et al. (Eds.): IFTC 2017, CCIS 815, pp. 25–35, 2018.
https://doi.org/10.1007/978-981-10-8108-8_3

massive high dimensional data proposed by Datar. It can implement the image pre-classification by hash function to make the similarity probability of the hash value of two highly similar data high, thus decrease the number of matching images and improves the retrieval speed.

By analyzing the characteristics of fabric image, based on the methods above, this paper proposes a new combination algorithm named SKE (SIFT + K -Means + E2LSH). First, the SIFT feature vector of the image in gallery is extracted. All the SIFT feature vectors are clustered by K-Means to generate the bag of word. Then the shape feature histogram of each image can be calculated using clustering result. Finally, E2LSH algorithm is used to realize the image matching and retrieval. The speed of image retrieval reaches the μs level. Experiment verified the high precision and the fast matching and retrieval speed of SKE algorithm.

2   Algorithm Introduction

2.1   SIFT Algorithm

SIFT algorithm [3], proposed by Lowe in 2004, is based on the invariant feature of image, which consists of two parts: feature point detection and feature description.

Feature Point Detection. Suppose an image is $I(x, y)$, then its Gaussian image in different scale space is:

$$L(x, y, \sigma) = G(x, y, \sigma) \otimes I(x, y) \tag{1}$$

where σ is the spatial scale factor of the scale space, and $G(x, y, \sigma)$ is two-dimensional Gaussian function, which is defined as:

$$G(x, y, \sigma) = \frac{1}{2\pi\sigma^2} e^{-(x^2+y^2)/2\sigma^2} \tag{2}$$

To obtain the efficient feature points, the Laplace operator (LOG) is replaced by a Gaussian difference (DOG) operator, which is defined as:

$$D(x, y, \sigma) = (G(x, y, k\sigma) - G(x, y, \sigma)) \otimes I(x, y) \tag{3}$$

DOG scale space pyramid is shown in Fig. 1. In the $3 \times 3 \times 3$ Stereo neighborhood of the DOG scale space pyramid, the non-maximum value is suppressed. The feature point, which is larger or smaller than the previous scale, the next scale and the 26 neighborhood values around the scale, is selected as candidate feature point. To improve the anti-noise performance and stability, the candidate points with low contrast and unstable edge feature points need to be removed.

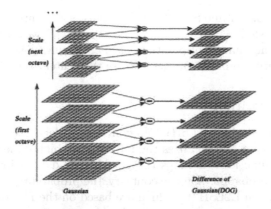

Fig. 1. DOG pyramid of scale space

Feature Descriptor. (1) The main direction of the feature point

Taking the feature point as the center, select the square neighborhood of 16 $s\times$16 s (s for the feature point scale). Then, the equations, which calculate gradient values and gradient direction of all pixels of the neighborhood in the x and y direction are shown as Eqs. 4 and 5. The gradient histogram is obtained by counting the direction of the pixels in the neighborhood. The peak of the gradient histogram represents the main direction of the neighborhood gradient of the key.

$$m(x,y) = \sqrt{(L(x+1,y) - L(x-1,y))^2 + (L(x,y+1) - L(x,y-1))^2} \quad (4)$$

$$O(x,y) = \tan^{-1}(L(x,y+1) - L(x,y-1))/(L(x+1,y) - L(x-1,y)) \quad (5)$$

(2) Generate a feature descriptor

Taking the feature point as the center, the direction of the feature point is the main direction. The 16 $s \times$ 16 s square neighborhood is divided into 4×4 subfields, and calculating the gradient cumulative values in 8 directions for each sub-region. For each feature point, a feature descriptor with 128 dimensions is got.

2.2 K-Means Clustering Algorithm

As a simple unsupervised learning algorithm, assuming the size of the database is M, then the steps of K-Means algorithm are as follows [4]:

Initialization: Set the number of clusters K

Step 1: Randomly choose K data points as the cluster centers, named C_k, ($k = 1, 2..., K$);

Step 2: Calculate the Euclidean distance of other data points to the center C_k, distinguish these points to some class which has the smallest Euclidean distance to some C_k;

Step 3: Re-calculate the clustering center according to the new class formed in Step 2, and update the cluster centers C_k;

Step 4: Repeat Step 2 and Step 3, until the clustering center no longer changes or the threshold $SSE = \sum_{k=1}^{K} \sum_{x_i=NUM_k} ||x_i - C_k||^2$ varies in a given area. Here, MUM_k is the number of points in each clustering class;

Step 4: Clustering process finished, derive the center points C_k^*.

2.3   E2LSH Algorithm

Locality Sensitive Hashing (LSH) [5], which is widely used to solve image retrieval of large scale. LSH realizes the reduction of high-dimension of features by a list of hash functions. It maps the neighboring data points into one hash bucket by a large probability, on the contrary, the probability is relatively small. The hash functions in E2LSH [6], which are based on the $P-$stable distribution is defined as Eq. 6:

$$h_{c,b}(v) = \left\lfloor \frac{c \cdot v + b}{w} \right\rfloor \tag{6}$$

where $\lfloor . \rfloor$ is an operator about round down v is the original data c is a vector which has the same dimension with v. Its each dimension is an independent variable selected from p-stable b is a random number in the range $[0, w]$. w is the interval size, which decides the number of hash bucket. The range of w usually is from -2 to -6.

Since the weak resolution of one hash function, in E2LSH, a series of h function are usually randomly selected. Assume the number is l. The function set is defined as $\varsigma = \{g : S \to U^l\}$, where, $g(v) = (h_1(v), h_2(v), \ldots, h_l(v))$. For each data point v, in the dataset, its dimension is reduced to l and vector $a = (a_1, a_2, \ldots, a_l)$ is formed by $g(v)$.

Moreover, to speed up the retrieval process, adopt the other two hash functions: main hash function h_1 and sub-hash function h_2 with Eqs. 7 and 8. Then the data points with the same values of h_1 are classified into the same hash table, and the data points with the same values of h_2 are classified into the same hash bucket in one hash table. The values of h_1 and h_2 are the index value of the hash table and the hash bucket.

$$h_1(a) = ((\sum_{i=1}^{l} r_i' a_i) \bmod prime) \bmod tablesize \tag{7}$$

$$h_2(a) = (\sum_{i=1}^{l} r_i'' a_i) \bmod prime \tag{8}$$

where r_i' and r_i'' is a random number. $tablesize$ is the size of the hash table, that is, the number of data points. $prime$ is a large prime. In general, its value is $2^{35}-5$.

3   Fabric Image Retrieval Based on SKE

The image retrieval process based on SKE (SIFT+K-Means+E2LSH) is: Extracting the SIFT feature of the image in gallery firstly, and then all the SIFT feature vectors are clustered by K-Means to obtain the visual words. Based on the visual words, the feature histogram of each image is obtained. Finally, build the index of each image and realize image retrieval by E2LSH algorithm. Fabric image retrieval based on SKE algorithm consists of two parts: training phase and testing phase.

1. Training phase

Initialize: Set the number of images M in the fabric gallery, K is a constant

Step 1: Extract the SIFT feature vector $T = \{t_1, t_2, \cdots, t_n\}, t \in R^d$ of each image, n is the number of feature points of each image, and get the set of feature vector $AT = \{T_1, T_2, \cdots, T_M\}$ of all images. Where, $t \in R^d$, $d = 128$;

Step 2: Do K-Means clustering on AT, obtain vectors $W = \{w_1, w_2, \cdots, w_K\}$, $w \in R^d$, w constitute the basic bag of visual word;

Step 3: Calculate the Euclidean distance between t_i and $w_i (i = 1, 2, \cdots, K)$, according to the cumulative frequency f_i on w, get the feature histogram v of each image, where the formula of f_i and v are expressed as:

$$f_i = \{w_1, w_2, \cdots, w_K\}(\sum_{j=0}^{K} L_{i,j} = N_i)$$

$$v = \{f_1, f_2, \cdots, f_K\}$$

where, $L_{i,j}$ is the frequency which indicates that the i-th eigenvector appears on the j-th basic bag of visual word.

Step 4: Apply the hash function $g(v)$ on v to obtain the l-dimension vector $a_t = (h_1(v), h_2(v), \ldots, h_l(v)), l < K$. Here, a simple threshold function is used as hash function considering the computational complexity;

Step 5: Calculate the main hash $h_1(a_t)$ and sub-hash value $h_2(a_t)$ of each image by Eqs. 7 and 8, and assign the image to the corresponding hash bucket in a hash table.

2. Test phase:

Step 1: Extract the SIFT feature vector of test image, and get $Q = \{q_1, q_2, \ldots, q_n\}, q \in R^d$;

Step 2: Get the feature histogram v of test image with the same method above;

Step 3: Apply the hash function $g(v)$ on v to obtain the l-dimension vector $a_q = (h_1(v'), h_2(v'), \ldots, h_l(v')), l < K$;

Step 4: Calculate the main hash $h_1(a_q)$ and sub-hash value $h_2(a_q)$ of test image, and assign the image to the corresponding hash bucket in a hash table;

Step 5: Match the test image with the images in the hash bucket, calculate the similarity with KNN algorithm and output the approximate images.

The flow of SKE algorithm is shown in Fig. 2:

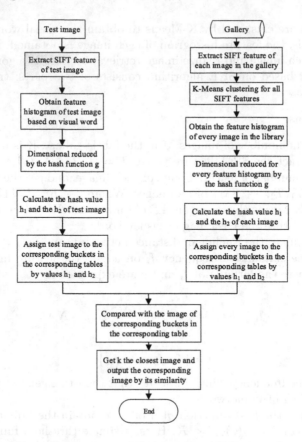

Fig. 2. Image retrieval flow based on SKE algorithm

4   Experiments and Results

4.1   Experiment Data and Environment Description

The fabric images, used in the experiment, are from one clothing company. In this dataset, there are 10,000 samples. The patterns include lace, leopard, wave point, square, stripe, geometry, flower, swallow gird. The description of dataset is shown in Table 1:

Table 1. Fabric library description

Number of images	Lace	Leopard	Wave point	Square	Stripes	Geometry	Flower	Swallow gird
Train gallery	1587	757	1427	1900	1622	762	1395	550
Test gallery	30	30	30	30	30	30	30	30

In the experiment, the development environment is Visual Studio 2010. OpenCV2.4.11 is used as open source library for image processing. The OS is Windows 7. The CPU is 1.7 GHZ and memory is 8 GB RAM.

4.2   Evaluation Indicator

Subjective and objective indicators are adopted to evaluate the matching results. The Subjective indicator relies on expert score, and the objective indicator is detection accuracy.

1. Objective evaluation indicators

$De\_acc = NumDect/NumOut$

Where, De_acc is the Detection accuracy. $NumDect$ is the number of images which's category are correctly detected. $NumOut$ is the output number of images. Here $NumOut = 50$.

2. Subjective evaluation indicators

As the similarity evaluation of fabric image has strong subjectivity, according to the investigation on designer, subjective evaluation indicators, named Sub_score are designed by considering pattern shape, color, fabric type and spatial distribution. The evaluation indicators are shown in Table 2.

Table 2. The subjective evaluation indicators

	Selfsame	Quite similarities	Similarities	Difference	Quite difference
Shape	0.5	0.38	0.24	0.12	0
Color	0.2	0.15	0.1	0.05	0
Fabric type	0.15	0.12	0.08	0.04	0
Spatial distribution	0.15	0.12	0.08	0.04	0

Comparing the object and subject indicator, the former is much stricter to ensure the same one and the same kind of images are found. The latter is more in line with human visual characteristics. It helps to get the similar images which can give the designer inspiration. In the later experiments, three experts were invited to participate in subjective scoring.

4.3   Experimental Results and Analysis

Parameters of SKE Algorithm. In SKE algorithm, the parameters in SIFT part, are *Octave, layers, edge_thresh, peak_thresh*; In K-Means part, it is K. And in E2LSH part, it is w. Experiments verified that the optima *Octave, layers,* edge_thresh and peak_thresh are 5, 4, 18, 0.18 respectively when the K is 400 and the w is -4. Considering the length of the article, the experiment data are no long listed.

Experiment 1. This experiment verifies the validity of the SKE algorithm by comparing the SIFT, SK (SIFT + K-Means) algorithm and SKL (SIFT + K-Means + LSH) algorithm with SKE. The subjective and objective evaluation indexes are considered at the same time. The matching results of the first 50 fabric image in different algorithm are shown in Table 3.

Table 3. The match results of fabric image in different algorithm

	De_acc(%)				Sub_score				Matching time(sec)			
	SIFT	SK	SKL	SKE	SIFT	SK	SKL	SKE	SIFT	SK	SKL	SKE
Lace	46.7	72.6	71.4	86.44	0.68	0.83	0.8	0.93	12900	227.2	0.66	0.65
Leopard	89.5	83.4	81.13	87.03	0.92	0.94	0.86	0.91	12100	170.9	0.88	0.84
Wave point	79.5	84.3	78.8	94.14	0.84	0.91	0.85	0.97	8300	101.5	0.88	0.86
Square	83.8	76.2	58.26	75.68	0.86	0.86	0.86	0.9	13300	111.3	0.80	0.78
Stripe	51.9	95.7	99.72	94.34	0.72	0.92	1	0.98	7300	190.8	0.53	0.57
Geometry	15.6	50.1	14.73	78.29	0.45	0.73	0.52	0.7	10200	207.05	0.71	0.72
Flower	72.6	88.3	69.8	90.27	0.83	0.95	0.85	0.93	11700	164.7	0.65	0.61
Swallow grid	88.7	84.9	60.6	78.13	0.88	0.89	0.79	0.93	14900	158.5	0.78	0.73
Average	66	79.44	66.81	*85.54*	0.77	0.88	0.81	*0.91*	11300	166.5	0.74	*0.72*

From the Table 3, it can be seen that the detection accuracy of the SKE algorithm is above 85.54%. Compared with SIFT, SK and SKL algorithms, the accuracy of SKE is increased 6%, 18.7% and 19% respectively. The subjective score of SKE algorithm is above 0.91. The subjective score of SIFT, SK and SKL is 14%, 3% and 10% lower than SKE algorithm respectively. For the matching speed, the SKE algorithm is similar to SKL. But compared with the SIFT and SK algorithm, the speed is increased by 15694 and 231 times respectively. The average matching time between single image is only 72 μs. The speed is six orders of magnitude faster than the speed of the SIFT algorithm, four orders of magnitude faster than the speed of SK algorithm. It meets the requirements of online real-time matching.

Experiment 2. This experiment tests retrieval speed by increasing the number of gallery and verifies the superiority of SKE algorithm in speed. The result is shown in Table 4.

Table 4. The retrieval time of SKE algorithm

	Retrieval time (sec)				
	2000	5000	10000	30000	50000
Lace	0.53	0.61	0.65	0.93	1.52
Leopard	0.55	0.61	0.84	0.88	1.43
Dot	0.48	0.58	0.86	0.89	1.37
Square	0.50	0.61	0.78	0.93	0.81
Stripe	0.50	0.61	0.57	1.02	0.70
Geometry	0.52	0.60	0.72	0.95	0.85
Flower	0.53	0.61	0.61	0.87	0.81
Swallow grid	0.52	0.62	0.73	0.87	0.90
Average	**0.52**	**0.61**	**0.72**	**0.92**	**1.05**

The retrieval time on different size of galleries is 0.52, 0.61, 0.72, 0.92, 1.05 respectively. And the increasing trend of retrieval time is slow as shown in Fig. 3. So, with the increase in the number of images in the gallery, the superiority of SKE algorithm will become more and more obvious.

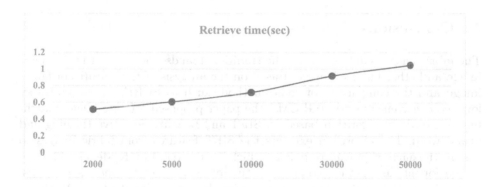

Fig. 3. The matching time trend of output first 50 match image

The section shows the first 50 matching results for eight different types of fabric images are more intuitive about matching results as shown in Table 5.

In the Table 5, it gives the samples of the matching result on three kinds of fabric by showing the results more intuitive. The first one in the result is the same as the testing image. The other ones are the similar images. It can be seen that SKE algorithm can find the same fabric image as well as the similar ones.

Table 5. The matching result of fabric image in different type

Test image	Output image									

5   Conclusions

The fabric image is different from the traditional landscape image, the character image and other kinds of image. Based on the analysis of the features of fabric image and the comparison of some methods such as SURF, Canny and gray level co-occurrence matrix (GLCM), the paper proposed a fabric image matching and retrieval algorithm based on SIFT and Locality-Sensitive Hashing and visual word. The algorithm extracts the SIFT features from fabric images to ensure the amount of feature points, which are clustered by K-Means to reduce dimensionality and get the common feature of images to form the visual words. According to the results, each image's feature histogram is calculated. With the help of E2LSH algorithm and hash coding, the dimensionality of feature vectors is reduced further. The image matching number decreases by establishing the hash table and the hash bucket. By setting the hash index, the retrieval speed is further accelerated. The algorithm can not only help designers find the exact fabric at once, but also can recommend the similar fabrics and meet the needs of real-time retrieval.

References

1. Delaitre, V., Laptev, I., Sivic, J.: Recognizing human actions in still images: a study of bag-of-features and part-based representations. In: British Machine Vision Conference, BMVC 2010, Aberystwyth, UK, pp. 1–11 (2014). https://doi.org/10.5244/C.24.97
2. Datar, M., Immorlica, N., Indyk, P., Mirrokni, V.S: Locality-sensitive hashing scheme based on p-stable distributions. In: Twentieth Symposium on Computational Geometry, vol. 34, pp. 253–262. ACM (2004). https://doi.org/10.1145/997817.997857
3. Liao, K., Liu, G., Hui, Y.: An improvement to the SIFT descriptor for image representation and matching. Pattern Recogn. Lett. **34**(11), 1211–1220 (2013). https://doi.org/10.1016/j.patrec.2013.03.021
4. Jégou, H., Douze, M., Schmid, C., Pérez, P.: Aggregating local descriptors into a compact image representation. In: Computer Vision and Pattern Recognition. IEEE Press, San Francisco, pp. 3304–3311 (2010). https://doi.org/10.1109/CVPR.2010.5540039
5. Li, L., Yan, C.C., Ji, W., Chen, B.W., Jiang, S., Huang, Q.: LSH-based semantic dictionary learning for large scale image understanding. J. Vis. Commun. Image Representation **31**, 231–236 (2015). https://doi.org/10.1016/j.jvcir.2015.06.008
6. Zhang, R., Wei, F., Li, B.: E2LSH based multiple kernel approach for object detection. Neurocomputing **124**, 105–110 (2014). https://doi.org/10.1016/j.neucom.2013.07.027

Research on Surface Color Difference of Solar Cells Based on Support Vector Machine

Jing Zhang and Tangyou Liu[✉]

College of Information Science and Technology, Donghua University,
Shanghai 201620, China
liuty@dhu.edu.cn

Abstract. As a clean and renewable energy, solar has great development and utilization value. The production instability will affect the solar cells' photoelectric conversion efficiency, so it is necessary to classify color difference cells. Currently, color difference classification is still detected by manual method, which is low efficient and depends on subjectivity and experience and hard to meet the production requirements, so it's urgent to find a new method to detect and classify color difference automatically. This paper introduces an effective way to achieve that by us-ing SVM. Using HSI model to calculate hue, saturation and intensity color histograms, 12 color feature vectors are extracted from the histograms. After experiments and simulation analyses, some feature vectors in these 12 features are as input vectors to SVM. After training the train set, the result of prediction set classification can be predicted and the accuracy rate can reach 94.79%, which shows that this method is effective.

Keywords: Solar cell · Color difference · Histogram
Color feature · SVM

1 Introduction

Nowadays, as a typically clean and renewable energy, solar energy has great value for development and utilization [1]. With the development of science and technology, the producing cost of solar cell has decreased, and the production of solar cell is increasing rapidly. However, the unstable factors in the production links cause color distribution uneven, namely color difference. The quality of solar cells directly affect the photovoltaic components' reliability and efficiency. One reason of low efficiency is color difference of solar cells, because different color has different to electric transformation efficiency. In addition, color difference affects the appearance of solar cells, which also affect the selling price. Using solar cells with different conversion efficiency would affect the whole conversion efficiency [2]. In the industrial production of solar cells, whether color difference exist or not is one effective and important way to evaluate the quality. So the color difference detection and classification of the solar cells before utilization is essential. The color difference detection is still using manual methods now, which costs low and is easy to implement, but relies on operator's experience

© Springer Nature Singapore Pte Ltd. 2018
G. Zhai et al. (Eds.): IFTC 2017, CCIS 815, pp. 36–45, 2018.
https://doi.org/10.1007/978-981-10-8108-8_4

too much. Because there aren't group of standards, manual way brings lots of detection problems. The efficiency is difficult to meet the requirements of the production. Therefore, it is necessary to find a new and efficient method for color difference detection and classification of solar cell.

Typical figures with and without color difference are shown in Fig. 1, in which, the image color of Fig. 1a is uniform, in other words, is without color difference, the images color of Fig. 1b, c and d isn't uniform, in which, the Fig. 1b image exist some massive brighter block, the Fig. 1c image is too bright and the color of the left part of Fig. 1d image is different with color of the right part, in other words, with color difference. However, the difference of most cell color is very little, a judgment whether with color difference or without color difference in a cell interior depend on operator's experience and hasn't a uniform standard, so it is urgent to find a uniform standard.

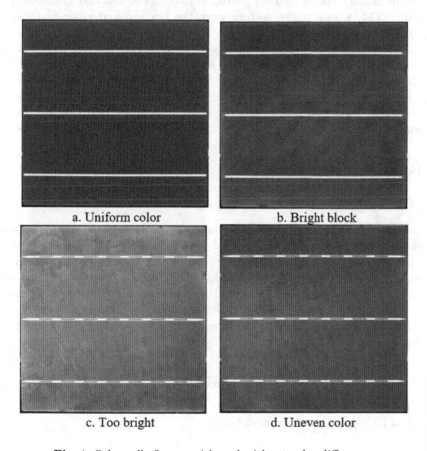

a. Uniform color   b. Bright block

c. Too bright   d. Uneven color

Fig. 1. Solar cells figures with and without color difference.

In this study, a 5 million pixel industrial camera is used for image acquisition. After image preprocessing such as removing the other parts in the images than the cells, choose an appropriate color model for transformation, and then extract the color feature, finally using classification algorithm to analyze, and using it to find whether the solar cell color difference or not.

Jingjing Wang et al. used SVM and histogram for classifying lip color [3]. They divided range [0, 1] of each HSI channel into five intervals, and counted the number of pixels falling into each interval on every HSI component value. If the number of pixel is more than 50%, this interval would be divided into five intervals again. They got at least 15 dimensions to be histogram feature vectors, which were used as SVM input vectors. In the study of ship detection, Morillas et al. divided the high-resolution ship image detection process by block, then feature extraction and SVM classification [4]. The color features were the mean and standard deviation of each image block extracted RGB, HSV and CIE Lab color space, followed by SVM training and component. Kavitha and Suruliandi classify the dermoscopy images into melanoma and non-melanoma by using SVM, whose input vectors were the texture and color features [5]. They used color histograms to extract the color features in RGB, HSV and OPP color spaces, where each space was divided into $8 \times 8 \times 8 = 512$ bins, and each bin as a feature vector for SVM. Xu et al. utilized spectra coupled with color features before LS-SVM to determine sugar content of fragrant pears [6]. They extracted the means, standard deviation and coefficient of variation of four measured quantities which were the sugar content of pear, L *, a *, and b * components of CIELAB space for using them to train the LS-SVM to classify.

2   Feature Extraction

2.1   Color Model Conversion

The original solar cell image is RGB model, and color processing usually needs to convert to other color model. RGB, HSV, HSI, LAB, YUV, CMYK are common color models. In this study, the HSI model, which uses Hue, Saturation and Intensity to describe the environment's color [7], is used because it comes from human visual perception, and being natural and intuitive for human senses so it's suitable for the solar cells color difference detection. First thing to do is to convert the RGB model to HSI model after image preprocessing. The relationship between HSI and RGB is as follows [8]:

$$
\begin{cases}
H = \begin{cases} \theta, & B <= G \\ 360 - \theta, & B > G \end{cases}, \quad \theta = \arccos \frac{[(R-G)+(R-B)]}{2\sqrt{(R-G)^2 + (R-B)(B-G)}} \\
S = 1 - \frac{3}{(R+G+B)}[\min(R,G,B)] \\
I = \frac{1}{3}(R+G+B)
\end{cases}
\tag{1}
$$

In order to avoid interference, the pixels of solar cells' grids need to be eliminated by making the pixels values zero which are ignored during converting to HSI model. The results of Formula (1) is float data, which needs to be integer by rounding for convenience. The ranges of H, S, and I are [0, 359], [0, 99], [0, 255].

2.2 Color Feature Extraction

After RGB model is transformed to HSI model, an image is transformed to 3 images, but it is still difficult to judge whether an image with or without color difference. In order to judge it conveniently, it is necessary to extract same color features from the 3 images of HSI model. For extracting color features, the 3 component histograms of HSI model are plotted and shown on Fig. 2. Figure 2a show a H component histogram of an image without color difference, there is a single and almost symmetrical peak, the spread of frequency is narrow, in fact, so are S and I component histograms of images without color difference, but H, S and I component histograms of images with color difference are not, as shown on Figs. 2b and c, the H, S, I component histograms of images with color difference may be single peaks and symmetry or not, and the spread of frequency in histogram is more extensive.

According to these features of histograms, same color features for classifying whether an image is with color difference. Taking I component histogram for example, as shown in Fig. 2d, where max stands for abscissa of peak position, I_w means the full width at half maximum frequency, I_{left} is the left width at the 10% maximum frequency, I_{right} means the right width of it. I_{w10} equals to I_{left} + I_{right}, namely width of the 10% maximum frequency. And I_{offset} equals to absolute value of $I_{left} - I_{right}$. Therefore, there are 4 features of I component, namely I_{max}, I_w, I_{w10}, I_{offset}. On the same way, H_{max}, H_w, H_{w10}, H_{offset}, S_{max}, S_w, S_{w10} and S_{offset}, total 12 color features, can be extracted.

2.3 Preliminary Selection of Color Features

There are 12 color features being extracted above, while they are not always being needed, it's necessary to be analysed and selected. H_{max} is peak location of hue component, it shows the dominant hue of an image, no matter what value it is, as long as the interior color of a picture is consistent, there is no color difference, so H_{max} is irrelevant for color difference and can be deleted from the feature vectors. On the same way, S_{max} is peak location of saturation histogram, which may be irrelevant for color difference. I_{max} means the peak location of intensity, when the value is large, the image is brighter. In essence, the solar cell has a high reflectivity of light and low absorption rate and the photoelectric conversion efficiency is low, which shows that I_{max} is a relatively important value.

H_{w10}, S_{w10} and I_{w10} are the widths at the 10% maximum frequency of HSI, these values are large if the image colors are widely distributed. They directly reflect the color distribution and should be closely related to color difference. H_{offset}, S_{offset} and I_{offset} show the symmetry of histograms, there are lots of

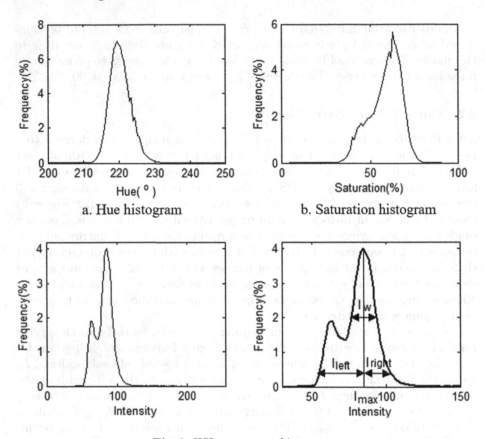

a. Hue histogram   b. Saturation histogram

Fig. 2. HSI component histogram.

image with color difference which value of H_{w10}, S_{w10}, and I_{w10} are small, but value of H_{offset}, S_{offset} and I_{offset} are large, so the 3 color features may help identifying color difference. H_w, S_w and I_w are width at half maximum frequency of HSI histogram, and they are important indexes for single peak figure, but the histograms of images of solar cells must be single peaks, so these features may be effective, or be repeated with H_{w10}, S_{w10}, and I_{w10}, which need to be confirmed later. According to the above preliminary analysis, this paper intend to use H_w, H_{w10}, H_{offset}, S_w, S_{w10}, S_{offset}, I_{max}, I_w, I_{w10}, I_{offset}, these 10 color features to identify and detect the internal color difference of solar cells.

3   Classification Method

3.1   Euclidean Distance

The distance is a common way to measure the similarity of two images at home and abroad. The distance includes Euclidean distance, Chernov distance, Hausdorff distance, Mahalanobis distance and Bhattachayya distance [9].

In practical applications, different kinds of distance vary greatly in different ways. Euclidean distance is widely used in a variety of image processing fields because of its simplicity and efficiency.

$$d(x,y) = \sqrt{\sum_{k=0}^{n}(x_k - y_k)^2}. \tag{2}$$

Euclidean distances is shown in the above formula, x_k and y_k represent the features of two pictures. The larger the d(x,y), the smaller similarity between the two pictures, and the greater difference. However, this method is too simple and not suitable for the complex situation of this study. Because the units of the 10 color features selected above to identify and detect the internal color difference of solar cells are different. Variables with different units should not be put together to measure and compare. So the following method is considered.

3.2 SVM

Support vector machine is a kind of new machine learning method based on statistical learning theory, which can achieve the idea of structural risk minimization. It uses the training error as the constraint condition to optimize problem, and minimizes the confidence range as the optimization target. In the solution of non-linear, over-learning, dimension disaster and local minima etc., it shows many unique advantages [10].

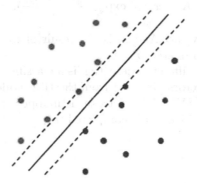

Fig. 3. Linear classification diagram.

To find a classification hyperplane in n-dimensional space is to classify the points in the space, generally speaking, the distance between a point and the hyperplane can be expressed as accuracy of classification and prediction.

SVM is for maximizing this interval value. Figure 3 shows the linear classifier, where the dotted line is called Support Vector. The classified method of SVM is to transform the input space into a high-dimensional space by the nonlinear transformation defined by inner product function. Finding the generalized optimal classification surface in this space makes it possible to correctly separate the two types of data points as much as possible at the same time. And it makes the separated two kinds of data points farthest away from the classification surface [11]. The classification hyperplane equation is shown in Formula (3):

$$W^T X + b = 0. \tag{3}$$

X is the input vector, W is the weight vector, and b is the offset [12]. The performance of SVM is related to the choice of kernel function. The prediction function of linear kernel is simple and speed is fast. The support vectors of the nonlinear classifier in the high-dimensional space will be very much, and the classification speed is much lower than linear classifier. The generalization of linear SVM is guaranteed, while nonlinear, such as Gauss kernel, is possible to be over learning [13].

RBF kernel function can map samples to high dimensional space. Compared with polynomial kernel function, RBF needs less parameters, and the number of kernel parameters directly affects the complexity of function. RBF kernel function has a wide convergence domain, and it is widely used kernel functions, whether it is low-dimensional or high-dimensional, small or large samples, RBF kernel functions are applicable. The RBF kernel function is as follows:

$$K(x, x_i) = \exp(-\frac{(\|x - x_i\|)^2}{\sigma^2}). \tag{4}$$

x is the input eigenvalue. And x_i is the result of the eigenvalue x. σ is the radial basis function parameter, $\sigma > 0$.

The essence of color difference detection is a classification problem on mathematics. The feature vectors obtained from the HSI model histogram are taken as the input vectors of SVM. The data set is mapped into a high-dimensional space, where linear classification is completed [14].

4   Result

192 solar cells images are collected in this experiment. Using Lib-SVM toolbox of MATLAB and setting C-SVC as the type and liner kernel as the kernel function, this paper divides 192 preprocessed cell images into two subsets randomly, one is as training set and the other as prediction set. Both the training set and the prediction set has 96 cells, of which 62 cells are with color difference and 34 cells without color difference. Using SVM's train function and predict function to

achieve training and prediction results. The following groups of feature vectors are selected from H_w, H_{w10}, H_{offset}, S_w, S_{w10}, S_{offset}, I_{max}, I_w, I_{w10}, I_{offset}, which has higher accuracy, as shown in Table 1:

Table 1. Feature vectors selection using liner kernel SVM.

H_w	✓			
H_{w10}	✓	✓	✓	✓
H_{offset}	✓	✓	✓	✓
S_w	✓	✓	✓	✓
S_{w10}	✓	✓	✓	
I_{max}	✓	✓		
I_w	✓	✓	✓	✓
I_{w10}	✓	✓	✓	
I_{offset}	✓	✓	✓	✓
Accuracy	93.75%	94.79%	94.79%	92.78%

According to the experiment result, it basically conforms to the above analysis. When Hw10, H_{offset}, S_w, S_{w10}, I_w, I_{w10} and I_{offset} are selected as the input of the support vector machine, the classification accuracy can be 94.79%, which is the best effect of these combinations of feature vectors. The accuracy of other combinations can also reach more than 90%.

The simulation of SVM training whose kernel function is linear kernel by using matlab as follows:

```
*
optimization finished, #iter = 65
nu = 0.665300
obj = −114.099424, rho = 3.501558
nSV = 66, nBSV = 62
Total nSV = 66
Accuracy = 94.7917% (91/96) (classification)
```

The number of iterations is 65, the kernel function type parameter is 0.67, the minimum value of quadratic programming is −114.1. The offset number of decision function is 3.5, the number of standard support vectors is 66 and support vector on boundary is 62, the total number of support vectors is 66.

However, using the same characteristic vectors as above, the kernel function of SVM using RBF kernel function instead of linear kernel function, whose classification accuracy using the same feature vectors as above is 64.58%, which is lower then linear kernel function. The simulation results of RBF kernel SVM training is as shown in Table 2:

Table 2. Feature vectors selection using RBF kernel SVM.

H_w	✓			
H_{w10}	✓	✓	✓	✓
H_{offset}	✓	✓	✓	✓
S_w	✓	✓	✓	✓
S_{w10}	✓	✓	✓	
I_{max}	✓	✓		
I_w	✓	✓	✓	✓
I_{w10}	✓	✓	✓	
I_{offset}	✓	✓	✓	✓
Accuracy	92.71%	92.71%	92.71%	89.58%

It can be seen that the highest accuracy of RBF kernel classification is 92.71%, which is lower than the linear kernel in this study.

5   Conclusions

In this paper, an efficient and accurate method for solar cells color difference detection is proposed. The histogram features of each component of HSI model are extracted, and are used as input vectors of SVM. Using the RBF kernel SVM can reach a lower classification accuracy then liner kernel, so using the liner kernel is reasonable. The experimental results show that the accuracy of this method can reach 94.79%, which can effectively realize the detection and classification of solar cells color difference.

References

1. Duenas, S., Perez, E., Castan, H., et al.: The role of defects in solar cells: control and detection defects in solar cells, 301–304 (2013)
2. Du, J., Zhang, X., Hu, Q.: An automatic condition detection approach for quality assurance in solar cell manufacturing processes. IEEE Robot. Autom. Lett. **2**(3), 1825–1831 (2017)
3. Zheng, L., Li, X., Yan, X., Li, F., Zheng, X., Li, W.: Lip color classification based on support vector machine and histogram. In: 3rd International Congress on Image and Signal Processing, Yantai, pp. 1883–1886 (2010)
4. Morillas, J.R.A., Garcia, I.C., Zolzer, U.: Ship detection based on SVM using color and texture features. In: 2015 IEEE International Conference on Intelligent Computer Communication and Processing (ICCP), Cluj-Napoca, pp. 343–350 (2015)

5. Kavitha, J.C., Suruliandi, A.: Texture and color feature extraction for classification of melanoma using SVM. In: 2016 International Conference on Computing Technologies and Intelligent Data Engineering (ICCTIDE 2016), Kovilpatti, pp. 1–6 (2016)
6. Xu, H., Ying, Y.: Spectra coupled with color features to determine sugar content of fragrant pears using LS-SVM. In: IEEE/SICE International Symposium on System Integration (SII), Kyoto, pp. 197–201 (2011)
7. Zhang, C., Wang, P.: A new method of color image segmentation based on intensity and hue clustering. In: Proceedings 15th International Conference on Pattern Recognition, ICPR-2000, Barcelona, vol. 3, pp. 613–616 (2000)
8. Gonzalez, R.C., Woods, R.E.: Digital Image Processing. Publishing House of Electronics Industry, Beijing (2010)
9. Yu, Z., Chen, W., Guo, X., Chen, X., Sun, C.: Analog network-coded modulation with maximum Euclidean distance: mapping criterion and constellation design. IEEE Access **5**, 18271–18286 (2017)
10. Yin, Z., Liu, J., Krueger, M., Gao, H.: Introduction of SVM algorithms and recent applications about fault diagnosis and other aspects. In: 2015 IEEE 13th International Conference on Industrial Informatics (INDIN), Cambridge, pp. 550–555 (2015)
11. Osuna, E., Freund, R., Girosit, F.: Training support vector machines: an application to face detection. In: Proceedings of IEEE Computer Society Conference on Computer Vision and Pattern Recognition, San Juan, pp. 130–136 (1997)
12. Demir, B., Bruzzone, L.: Fast and accurate image classification with histogram based features and additive kernel SVM. In: IEEE International Geoscience and Remote Sensing Symposium (IGARSS), Milan, pp. 2350–2353 (2015)
13. Ajay, A., Dixon, K.D.M., Sowmya, V., Soman, K.P.: Aerial image classification using GURLS and LIBSVM. In: 2016 International Conference on Communication and Signal Processing (ICCSP), Melmaruvathur, pp. 0396–0401 (2016)
14. Pooja, A., Mamtha, R., Sowmya, V., Soman, K.P.: X-ray image classification based on tumor using GURLS and LIBSVM 2016 International Conference on Communication and Signal Processing (ICCSP), Melmaruvathur, pp. 0521–0524 (2016)

Video Background Modeling Algorithm of Low Complexity Based on the Minimum Second Derivative

Anlun Zhang$^{(\boxtimes)}$, Guowei Teng, Guozhong Wang, and Haiwu Zhao

School of Communication and Information Engineering,
Shanghai University, Shanghai 200444, China
anlunz@126.com

Abstract. The coding of scene videos such as surveillance videos, conference videos, is becoming a hot spot of research in recent years. The key technology of this kind of video coding is to create one or more background images as a long-term reference frame in the process of encoding accurately and efficiently. This paper proposes a video background modeling algorithm of low complexity based on the minimum second derivative. Firstly, estimating the wave characteristics of the function according to its second derivative; after that, getting the stability of every pixel by using second-order difference to fit the second derivate of pixels in the time domain; finally, extracting the steadiest value of every pixel during the training period in the basis of threshold value, then take it as the corresponding background model value. The experiment results indicate that compared with AVS2, it saves 9.83% on BD-rate and improves 0.37 dB on BD-PSNR, compared with the background modeling algorithm of AVS2-S, this algorithm not only effectively improved the problem of foreground pollution, but also reduces the algorithm complexity.

Keywords: Video coding · AVS2 · AVS2-S · Background modeling
Second-order difference

1 Introduction

At present, scene video occupies a very important position in people's life. As important video applications in the information age, surveillance video and conference video are increasingly becoming the largest video system. Effectively transferring, storing, analyzing and identifying these massive videos, which are collected by a large number of cameras, is facing major challenges [1]. The biggest feature of scene video is that the camera angle is fixed, there is a lot of almost constant background information in video. Therefore, by distinguishing the foreground and background of video, the establishment of high quality background model can eliminate a large amount of background redundant information, improve the compression efficiency of video [2].

In order to meet the requirement of scene video compressing, Chinese AVS working group developed a scene video coding standard named AVS-S with

© Springer Nature Singapore Pte Ltd. 2018
G. Zhai et al. (Eds.): IFTC 2017, CCIS 815, pp. 46–54, 2018.
https://doi.org/10.1007/978-981-10-8108-8_5

independent intellectual property rights in 2008 [3], which make the compression efficiency of scene video obviously enhanced. Background modeling is also integrated into the next-generation standard AVS2, which named AVS2-S. However, both of them face the challenge of high complexity. Therefore, the research of video background modeling algorithm with low complexity and high efficiency has important application value.

The purpose of video coding is to minimize the redundancy in video data, use as few data as possible to characterize video, so as to achieve the effect of compressed video. The scene video has a stable background information as a special kind of video. For example, sports events venues long-term change, scene in the plants, the climate showed regular changes and so on. And these background areas are exposed to varying degrees with the movement of foreground objects.

In scene video, relatively fixed background information increases video encoded data volumes, hence a reasonable background model is needed as a long-term reference frame in video coding to replace adjacent frames as reference images for frame prediction and eliminate the redundant information generated by the background to achieve the purpose of improving compression efficiency. As a result, a high quality background model is the key to ensure coding efficiency.

The rest of the paper is organized as follows. An overview for related works is presented in Sect. 2. Statistical analysis is displayed in Sect. 3. Section 4 introduces the background modeling algorithm particularly. Section 5 shows the overall algorithm. Experimental results are given in Sect. 6. Paper is concluded in Sect. 7.

2   Related Works

Recently, many background modeling algorithms have been proposed to improve coding efficiency of scene video, which can be roughly classified into two categories: using original frame as background frame and training to generate background frame.

A simple background modeling method is to select a frame from the original sequence as a long-term reference frame. In [4], the author proposes selecting a frame as a special reference frame for high quality coding, but this method does not achieve the ideal compression effect for that the background of each frame is covered by the different degrees of the foreground movement object in video, simply choosing a frame as a background model is not universal.

Another approach uses training to generate a background model. In contrast to the former, the method of training the background frame can provide a higher quality background model, this background model usually fills the background area of the original frame that is obscured by the foreground object, and is therefore more suitable as a long-term reference frame in the video encoding process.

A good video background modeling algorithm must first ensure the quality of the background image, but also to reduce the computational complexity as much as possible while ensuring the background quality. There are two aspects to reducing complexity: one is to reduce the complexity of the model calculation, which is determined by the specific modeling algorithm; the other is to shorten the training cycle. A certain video sequence, the longer the training cycle, the number of frames that can take advantage of the long-term reference frame is less, and the two compete with each other. In some algorithms, although the training cycle can improve the quality of the background model to a certain extent, the coding efficiency does not achieve the desired result because the number of frames that can be encoded with the long-term reference frame is too small. So how to balance the complexity of the algorithm and the background model of the contradictory relationship between the current video background modeling algorithm is facing the main problem.

In [5], Zhang et al. proposes an algorithm based on sectional weighted sliding average, which is adopted by AVS2-S as the standard background modeling algorithm. The algorithm can increase the efficiency of video coding by about double, but two weighted mean arithmetic also results in high complexity of the algorithm. Similarly, [6] proposes a background modeling algorithm based on Gaussian Mixture Model (GMM), the algorithm is also confronted with the problem of high algorithm complexity due to the introduction of a large number of operational parameters. In [7], Takamura and Shimizu proposes an algorithm of median modeling in time domain, this algorithm selects the appropriate pixel points from the original image to form the background model, avoids the complicated multiplication and division operation, and effectively solves the problem of high complexity. However, the change of training frame number in this algorithm has different effect on the compression efficiency of different video series, it is impossible to determine a proper training perimeter, which makes the practical application of the algorithm not significant.

In this paper, according to the trend of the inter-pixel pixel difference, selecting the most stable pixel in the training cycle to form the background model. In the process of generating high-quality background model while reducing the complexity of the algorithm, in the selection of the training cycle is also more flexible, whether it is short cycle or long period have achieved a good compression effect.

3   Observation and Statistical Analysis

In order to generate the background model, the foreground and background of video need to be distinguished. Usually, in the video process, the moving object is considered as the foreground, while the long fixed area is considered to be the background. This is reflected in the data, that the pixel value in the background region can remain unchanged for a long time. Because of foreground objects and external noise interference, even the pixel values of the background region will fluctuate, but relative to foreground area pixel point, the change of background pixel point is significantly smoother. Therefore, the background model can be generated by determining the most stable pixel points in video.

In the analog signal, the pixel located in (x, y), its value in the time domain can be considered as discrete functions associated with t, which is shown in formula (1),

$$p(x, y) = f[(x, y), t] \tag{1}$$

The first derivative and second derivative of f[(x, y), t] are shown in formula (2) and formula (3).

$$\frac{\partial f}{\partial t} = \lim_{\Delta t \to 0} \frac{f[(x, y), t + \Delta t] - f[(x, y), t]}{\Delta t} \tag{2}$$

$$\frac{\partial^2 f}{\partial t^2} = \lim_{\Delta t \to 0} \frac{\frac{f[(x,y),t+\Delta t]-f[(x,y),t]}{\Delta t} - \frac{f[(x,y),t]-f[(x,y),t-\Delta t]}{\Delta t}}{\Delta t} \tag{3}$$

For digital signal, the upper formula is equivalent to the gradient of the two-dimensional discrete function [8]. Using difference to approximate the derivative, expressions of the first derivative and the second derivative can be rewritten as follow,

$$\frac{\partial f}{\partial t} = f[(x, y), t + \Delta t] - f[(x, y), t] = p_{n+1}(x, y) - p_n(x, y) \tag{4}$$

$$\begin{aligned}\frac{\partial^2 f}{\partial t^2} &= f[(x, y), t + \Delta t] - f[(x, y), t] - f[(x, y), t] - f[(x, y), t - \Delta t] \\ &= [p_{n+1}(x, y) - p_n(x, y)] - [p_n(x, y) - p_{n-1}(x, y)]\end{aligned} \tag{5}$$

p_n(x,y) stands for the pixel which located in (x, y) in n_{th} frame. From formula (4), formula (5) we can see that make a second frame difference for the pixel in time domain can approximate its second derivative. The results of the second frame difference can reflect the change trend of the pixel point function in the time domain. The traditional three-frame differential method takes three consecutive frames of images, and sets the frame difference of two adjacent frames to get the characteristic information of the moving target [9]. This paper extends the three frame difference method to the whole time domain, As shown in Fig. 1, Select a certain length of video sequence as a training frame, for each pixel point, calculate its absolute difference diff of the pixel points corresponding to adjacent frames without considering the change direction, as shown in formula (6), then calculate absolute difference of the adjacent difference, denoted as d-diff, as shown in formula (7).

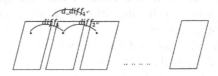

Fig. 1. Process of calculating the stationary parameter d-diff

$$diff_n(x, y) = |p_{n+1}(x, y) - p_n(x, y)| \qquad (6)$$

$$d - diff_n(x, y) = |diff_{n+1}(x, y) - diff_n(x, y)| \qquad (7)$$

$diff_n(x,y)$ represents the degree of change in pixels, while d-diff$_n$ indicates how fast the pixel changes. When d-diff$_n$ = 0, the current point may be the inflection point of the function. When d-diff$_n$ = 0 is true at any time for a while, the original function changes at constant speed. There are two types of functions that change at a constant rate, linear function and constant function. For the pixels of the video sequence that can only be the second case. So we can determine whether the current pixel point is stable based on the value of d-diff$_n$.

Denote th-diff as a minimum constant, when d-diff$_n \leq$ th-diff, the current pixel point is stable, otherwise denote it as a wave point. To illustrate it more visually, this paper select two pixels in sequence BasketballDrill randomly and draw the variation trend of its d-diff in 100 frames, which is shown as below (Figs. 2 and 3).

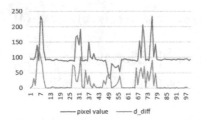

Fig. 2. Changing curve of pixel on (192,208)

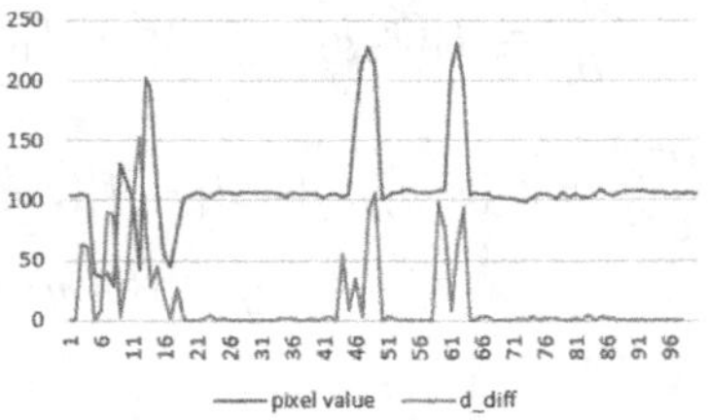

Fig. 3. Changing curve of pixel on (400,160)

It can be seen from the figure that the value of pixels for different positions is uncertain. So it's hard to set a stable value for pixels. But for different pixel points, when it reaches a steady state, almost all of its d-diff are less than a minimum, and d-diff is basically the same as the pixel value. Therefore, it is possible to judge the stationary state of pixel values according to its changes.

4   Proposed Algorithm

The idea of this algorithm is to find the stationary pixel value of each pixel in the training cycle, and take it as the value of the corresponding point in the background model. The key to the algorithm is to set a reasonable sentence to determine the degree of change of pixels.

From the above, th-diff is set to determine whether the current point is stationary. In theory, th-diff should be 0, but even a smooth state is difficult to meet the condition for the actual video is subject to foreground objects and noise interference. So we take th-diff = 3 as decision condition based on statistical experiment. Set another parameter th-weight to determine whether the current point has reached an absolute plateau, it stands for the consecutive stable frames of the pixel. When the value of th-weight is too small, it is easy to generate a situation where the persistent foreground object is misjudged as the background, while when it is too large, the stable weight can never be reached for the pixel point of the entire training cycle, which make it meaningless to set this parameter. Figure 4 shows that the change direction of the BD-rate of the sequences in Table 1 according to th-weight.

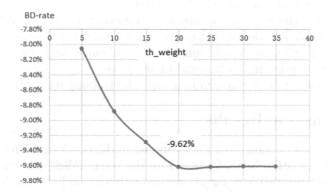

Fig. 4. Relation curve of th-weight and the average BD-rate

As shown in the figure, when th-weight = 20, the average BD-rate of test sequences comes up to maximum.

Table 1. Test sequences

Video resolution	Test sequences
832 × 480	BasketballDrill
	Johnny
1280 × 720	Fourpeople
	KristenandSara
	Vidyo1
1920 × 1080	Cactus

5 Overall Algorithm

According to the above analysis, the detail steps of the algorithm are presented as follows:

Step one: initialize the background model value BGP to the pixel value of the corresponding point in the first frame training frame;

Step two: calculates the absolute difference between the current frame pixels and the adjacent frames corresponding to the pixels, denoted as diff;

Step three: calculate the absolute difference of adjacent diff; denoted as d-diff.

Step four: set a threshold th-diff as smooth threshold, when d-diff$_n$ ≤ th-diff, make the stable weight of the current pixel point plus one, otherwise, compare temporary stationary weight weight-temp with the stable weight, if and only if weight > weight-temp, assign weight to weight-temp, record the pixel value of the current point, at the same time, weight is zero, to make sure weight-temp always be the current maximum stable weight;

Step five: set th-weight as an absolute stationary threshold. When weight reach th-weight, tt is believed that the change of pixels has reached an absolute plateau. The training process is completed in advance, and the current pixel point is the corresponding background model point;

Step six: cycle step two to step four until the training set is over.

6   Experimental Results

To evaluate the performance of the proposed background modeling algorithm, the proposed algorithm is implemented on the recent AVS2 reference software (RD16.1). Sequences with different motion activities and texture features are tested. Testing conditions of the experiment is shown in Table 2. The QP of background frames is set refer to evaluation parameters in [10]. To ensure the reliability of the contrast experiment with AVS2-S meanwhile to present the advantages of the algorithm in the selection of training frame length, the experiment uses 120 and 50 as the training frame length.

Table 2. Test conditions

Configuration	Description
GOP size	8
QP of I frame	27,32,38,45
Intra period	0
Background QP	QPI-9
Search range	64

As shown in Fig. 5, The background modeling obtained by the background modeling algorithm of this paper is more closely related to the background of the original image than the model algorithm of the AVS2-S and effectively eliminate the foreground pollution of the background image in AVS2-S modeling algorithm. Table 3 records coding efficiency of this algorithm compared with AVS2, AVS2-S. It can be seen from this that compared with AVS2, the algorithm in this paper increases the average BD-PSNR by 0.37 dB and the average BD-rate of video is 9.83%, Compared with the monitoring class AVS2-S, video's average BD-rate saved 2.78%.

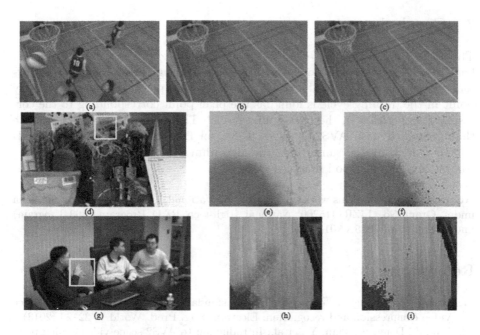

Fig. 5. (a)(d)(g): original frame, (b)(e)(h): the background model generated by the AVS-S algorithm, (c)(f)(j): the background model generated by MSD

Table 3. Experimental test results

N = 120	Proposal vs. AVS2		Proposal vs. AVS2-S	
Sequences	BD-rate (%)	BD-PSNR (dB)	BD-rate (%)	BD-PSNR (dB)
Basketballdrill	−16.38	0.70	−6.34	0.14
Johnny	−5.86	0.17	−0.59	0.01
Fourpeople	−11.42	0.47	−2.29	0.06
KristenaandSara	−14.86	0.51	−2.67	0.07
Vidyo1	−4.20	0.15	−2.45	0.08
Cactus	−4.99	0.13	−0.8	0.01
Average	−9.62	0.36	−2.52	0.06
N = 50	Proposal vs. AVS2		Proposal vs. AVS2-S	
Sequences	BD-rate (%)	BD-PSNR (dB)	BD-rate (%)	BD-PSNR (dB)
Basketballdrill	−14.91	0.60	−4.78	0.18
Johnny	−8.81	0.26	−3.63	0.09
Fourpeople	−11.45	0.49	−2.79	0.11
KristenaandSara	−14.92	0.53	−2.92	0.09
Vidyo1	−5.30	0.16	−1.07	0.04
Cactus	−4.99	0.13	−0.8	0.01
Average	−10.03	0.37	−3.04	0.10

7 Conclusion

This paper presents a low-complexity video background modeling algorithm based on the minimum second derivative. By judging the stability of the current pixel point and the stable weight of the current point, the most stationary point in the training cycle is found as the pixel point corresponding to the corresponding position in the background model. The experiment results indicate that compared with AVS2, it saves 9.83% on BD-rate and improves 0.37 dB on BD-PSNR, at the same time, the algorithm has advantages in computing complexity and has good practical value

Acknowledgment. This work is supported by National Science Foundation of China under Grant No. 14ZR1415200. National High-tech R&D Program (863 Program) under Grant No. 2015AA015903.

References

1. Huang, T., Zhang, X., et al.: IEEE 1857 standard for high efficiency surveillance video compression and recognition. Electron. Eng. Prod. World **7**, 22–26 (2013)
2. Yan, J., Dong, S., Tian, Y., et al.: Introduction to AVS2 scene video coding techniques. ZTE Commun. **1**, 010 (2016)
3. Zhang, X., Zhang, L., Liang, L., et al.: AVS video coding standard technology in face of surveillance applications. China Secur. Prot. **5**, 38–42 (2011)
4. Tiwari, M., Cosman, P.C.: Selection of long-term reference frames in dual-frame video coding using simulated annealing. Signal Process. Lett. IEEE **15**, 249–252 (2008)
5. Zhang, X., Huang, T., Gao, W., et al.: An efficient coding scheme for surveillance videos captured by stationary cameras. Proc. SPIE Int. Soc. Opt. Eng. **7744**, 77442A1–77442A10 (2010)
6. Paul, M., Lin, W., Lau, C.T., et al.: McFIS: Better I-frame for video coding. In: International Symposium on Circuits and Systems, DBLP, pp. 2171–2174 (2010)
7. Takamura, S., Shimizu, A.: Simple and efficient H.265/HEVC coding of fixed camera videos. In: IEEE International Conference on Image Processing, pp. 804–808. IEEE (2016)
8. Sonka, M., Hlavac, V., Boyle, R.: Image processing, analysis, and machine vision. J. Electron. Imaging **14**(82), 685–686 (2014)
9. Liu, H., Dai, J., Wang, R., et al.: Combining background subtraction and three-frame difference to detect moving object from underwater video. In: Oceans, pp. 1–5 (2016)
10. Dong, S., Tian, Y., Huang, T.: Performance evaluation for AVS2 scene video coding techniques. In: IEEE International Conference on Multimedia Big Data, pp. 411–414. IEEE Computer Society (2015)

Human Pose Estimation via Deep Part Detection

Xiangyang Wang[✉], Jiacheng Hu, Yusu Jin, Zhi Liu, Xiaoqiang Zhu,
Qiuyu Zhu, and Haiwu Zhao

School of Communication and Information Engineering,
Shanghai University, Shanghai 200444, China
{wangxiangyang,hjc1028,xqzhu,zhaohaiwu}@shu.edu.cn,
iejinyusu@gmail.com, {liuzhi,zhuqiuyu}@staff.shu.edu.cn

Abstract. In this paper, we propose to treat human pose estimation as an object detection problem. Specifically, the human pose is determined by the location of different body parts, different body parts are taken as different objects and a deep Convolutional Neural Network (CNN) is trained to detect these parts. We take advantage of the recently proposed fast and accurate deep object detector, SSD (Single Shot MultiBox Detector) to train a human body part detection model. We also propose to train a human body orientation model, with which to distinguish the left from the right of the body limbs. By combining body orientation and body part detection, we design a simple yet efficient human pose estimation method, which infers the location and category of the joints and link them together to form a whole pose. Experimental results show that, compared with other part detection based human pose estimation approaches, our method achieves better results on two public human pose estimation datasets.

Keywords: Human pose estimation · Object detection
SSD (Single Shot MultiBox Detector)

1 Introduction

Human pose estimation aims at locating the human parts or joints in an image. It is a challenge computer vision problem because of different clothes, limb orientation or self-occlusion, severe body deformations and various camera angles. Human pose estimation has many important applications, such as human-computer interaction, virtual reality, action recognition, etc.

With the successful development of Deep Convolutional Neural Networks (CNN) in image classification and object detection, currently, state-of-the-art human pose estimation results are all achieved by taking advantage of CNN [1–7]. "DeepPose" proposed by Toshev et al. [1] regress the whole image without prior. Later works combine CNN with graphical models [2, 4], or consider the body structure [3, 5]. Hourglass Network [7] is a state-of-the-art architecture for human pose estimation which is inspired by residual block [8] and fully convolutional network for image segmentation [9]. Most of these CNN based pose estimation methods can be seen as body pose regression, that is, the input is the whole image and the output is the heatmap of all joints.

© Springer Nature Singapore Pte Ltd. 2018
G. Zhai et al. (Eds.): IFTC 2017, CCIS 815, pp. 55–66, 2018.
https://doi.org/10.1007/978-981-10-8108-8_6

Recently, SSD (Single Shot MultiBox Detector) [11], a fast object detection method using a single deep neural network has been proposed. It outperforms the state of the art Faster R-CNN model [10]. In [12], Faster R-CNN is used for human body part detection and pose estimation.

In this work, we treat human pose estimation as an object detection problem. Specifically, the human pose is determined by the location of different body parts, such as head, torso, upper arm, lower arm, upper leg and lower leg. Different body parts are taken as different objects, and a deep convolutional neural network (CNN) is trained to detect these parts. We take advantage of the fast and accurate deep object detector, SSD (Single Shot MultiBox Detector) [11], as our part detector. Then, based on the detected body parts, we design a simple yet efficient pose estimation method, which infers the location and category of the joints and link them together to form a whole pose.

During the training of the part detector, we do not distinguish the left and right limbs. So, we cannot directly apply widely used criterions to evaluate our pose estimation method. To improve and accurately evaluate our results, we further train a human body orientation model to identify left or right of the body parts. Experiments show that, by combining body orientation and body part detection, we achieve better results than other part-detection based pose estimation method.

2   Human Pose Estimation via Body Part Detection

2.1   Body Part Detection via SSD

SSD is a recently proposed fast and accurate deep object detection architecture. SSD [11] discretizes the output space of bounding boxes into a set of default boxes over different aspect ratios and scales per feature map location. The network combines predictions from multiple feature maps with different resolutions to naturally handle objects of various sizes.

SSD detects objects without proposal generation, and encapsulates all computation in a single network. SSD outperforms Faster R-CNN in both speed and accuracy in object detection [11].

In this paper, we treat the body part, head, upper arm, lower arm, upper leg and lower leg as 5 different objects, a SSD is trained to detect these parts. Because the ground truth of the human pose dataset [13, 14] are usually joint coordinates and categories, so we must construct body part bounding box ground truth from these joint coordinates.

To acquire ground truth of body part bounding box for training the part detector, we generate the rectangle box with the two joint coordinates of the same part. For example, we use the joints of shoulder and elbow from the same side to construct the bounding box for upper arm. To make the bounding box tightly contain the whole limb, we assume that if the ratio between the width and height is less than 0.3, the shorter side is extended to be 0.3 times of the longer side. We then resize the box to be 1.2 times larger, which leads to better detection performance. In this way, we can train our part detection model.

2.2 From Body Part to Human Pose

The goal of human pose estimation is to acquire the joint coordinates and link them sequentially. So, after locating the body parts, we need to get the joint coordinates from these detected body parts. We can apply the body part detection results for pose estimation. Specifically, we can compute the two joints of one part from the detected part location rectangle box.

When we have trained the part detector with SSD, we use it to detect human body parts to get part location boxes with categories. Next, if the width-height ratio of a box is less than 0.5, then we can confirm that the location of the part is horizontal or upright (Fig. 1(a)), we will choose the center of the shorter edge of the rectangle box as the two joints of this part. Otherwise, if the width-height ratio of a box is larger than 0.5, it is likely to be a square, and the part will be located along the diagonal of this box. In this case, we crop out this image patch and compute the gradient along its two diagonal lines, to determine the part is from upper-right to bottom-left (Fig. 1(b)), or upper-left to bottom-right (Fig. 1(c)). Figure 1 shows these three cases.

(a)   (b)   (c)

Fig. 1. Different cases of part detection results. (a) horizontal or upright, (b) upper-right to bottom-left, (c) upper-left to bottom-right

When all the joints are obtained, the last step is to link them up to form a whole human pose. We need to link upper arm with lower arm to get the whole arm, and link upper leg with lower leg for the whole leg.

Because, during training the part detector, our model cannot distinguish left from right, so we link the top point of the lower leg with the bottom point of the upper leg that is the nearest one from it. Then the center of the line is seen as the knee. Besides, we label the top point of upper leg as hip, and the bottom point of the lower leg as ankle. In this way we can get the three joints of the leg. Arm is linked in the same way.

2.3 The Body Orientation Model

Although we can estimate the human pose by the above method, but we cannot distinguish the left limb from right limb, and the left joints from right joints. So, we propose to train a specific model to detect human body orientation. By combining the information of body orientation and body part location, we can distinguish the left or right joints.

2.3.1   The Dataset of Body Orientation

We construct a body orientation dataset by our own. Because our goal is to combine the information of body orientation with body part location to optimize the pose estimation results, so we select images from two human pose dataset, MPII human pose dataset [13] and Leeds Sports Pose dataset [14]. In addition, we add the images usually used for pedestrian detection that is the INRIA person dataset [15]. We label approximate 27K images, each image contains more than one human body. Among these images, 4/5 of these are used for training, and 5K images are used for testing which are also used as test data for body part detection with SSD.

We train a SSD detector to detect the four body orientations that is front, back, left and right.

2.3.2   Human Pose Estimation with Body Orientation Model

For a testing image containing a human body, we can acquire the joints such as head, shoulder, elbow, wrist, hip, knee and ankle. Then we need to distinguish left or right of these joints.

Take the shoulder joints for instance. After the two upper arms are detected, we get the two joint coordinates of the two shoulders. We then confirm the left or right according to the body orientation. If the body orientation is front, then the one with the smaller x coordinate is treated as the right shoulder, while the other is the left shoulder. If the body orientation is back, then the one with the smaller x coordinate is the left should while the other one is the right shoulder.

If only one shoulder joint is detected, and the body orientation is left or right, then the joint is seen as corresponding left or right shoulder. If only one shoulder joint is detected and the body orientation is front, it is usually due to the occlusion of arm or failure in detection, in this case we need to infer the left or right of this shoulder according to the head location. If the x coordinate of this shoulder joint is less than the x coordinate of the head, the detected joint is treated as right shoulder. Otherwise, it should be the left shoulder.

The other joints, elbow, wrist, knee and ankle, are of the same principle. In this way, we can get the 14 body joints, including head, left shoulder, right shoulder, left ankle and right ankle.

3   Experimental Results

To evaluate our methods, we test it on two public human pose estimation datasets, The MPII human pose dataset [13], and Leeds Sport Dataset and its extension (LSP) [14]. In the following, we will show our results on human body part detection and pose estimation, and will further illustrate our method and compare it with other human pose estimation approaches.

We use a modified version of Caffe [16] to train the SSD model. All our experiments are run on a computer with i7-7700 CPU and GTX1070 GPU.

3.1   Results on MPII Human Pose Dataset

The MPII dataset contains 25000 images, with about 40000 human bodies. Its annotation includes 16 joints (head, left and right shoulder, etc.) and the corresponding coordinates. To get the location and categories of the body parts for training, we use the way described in Sect. 2 to construct 5 body part (head, upper arm, lower arm, upper leg and lower leg) ground truth box as the annotation file. In practice, there are 17000 images containing enough annotations, so we use these images and their joints annotation to generate corresponding body part annotation. The SSD network is trained as body part detector. Among these images, 4/5 of them are used for training and the other 1/5 for testing.

Next, we need to make the xml format annotation files needed by SSD, and set some network parameters for training. In our experiments, we finetune the original SSD model (based on VGG model), the initial learning rate is set as 0.00004, the number of class is 6 including 5 body part and 1 background. The maximal iteration is 100000, the model is tested every 20000 iterations.

Figure 2 shows our body part detection results on MPII dataset. We can see that the AP (Average Precision) of every category is increase with the iterations. In Table 1, we compare our result with that use of Faster R-CNN for body part detection [12]. Our SSD based detection outperforms other two Faster R-CNN based body part detectors.

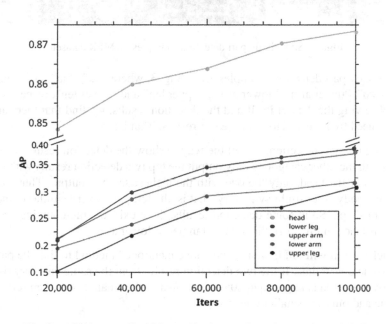

Fig. 2. AP (Average Precision) of body part detection results on MPII

Table 1. Comparison of the part detection results

AP (%)	Lower leg	Upper leg	Lower arm	Upper arm	Head
Faster RCNN	23.8	20.0	13.3	22.5	54.7
Multi-branch Faster RCNN	32.4	30.3	18.1	30.5	74.3
SSD	38.1	30.8	31.8	37.1	87.3

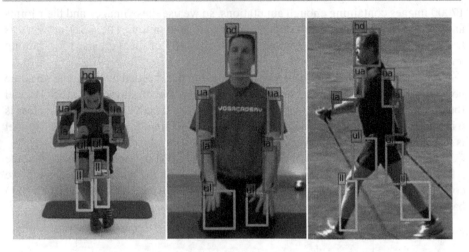

Fig. 3. Some body part detection examples on MPII dataset

Some body part detection examples are in Fig. 3, where "hd", "ua", "la", "ul", "ll" imply "head", "upper arm", "lower arm", "upper leg" and "lower leg", respectively.

By observing the dataset itself and the detection results, we find that there are two problems need to be solved to improve our results. That is:

(1) During the part detection, we set the way to show the detection results as: except head, all the other categories only output the top two detection results with highest score. For the head, only the one with the highest score is output. Thus, because human body is left-right symmetry, that is, the left part is very similar to the right part in shape. So in some detection results, there exist double-counting problem. For instance in Fig. 4(a), the blue rectangle for lower arm.

In such case, it will fail if we use the above mentioned method to link the parts. So we add some constraints. If the two detection results from the same category overlap, and the overlap area is larger than 80% of the area of the smaller box, then remove the larger one and only the smaller one is kept.

(a)   (b)

Fig. 4. (a) the double-counting problem during part detection, (b) example of fault detection (Color figure online)

(2) When use the trained SSD model for body part detection, there exist fault detection. For instance in Fig. 4(b).

In Fig. 4(b), the left lower leg is wrongly detected as left lower arm, so that the lower arm of the other side is not rightly detected. To avoid such confusion, we set the following constraint.

When linking lower arm with upper arm, if the distance between upper arm and lower arm is larger than 1.5 times of the length of the head in this image, then kept upper arm while remove lower arm. This is because in our body part detection the recognition accuracy of upper arm is high than that of lower arm. The way to link lower leg with upper leg follows the same principle.

With these improvements, we optimize the pose estimation and acquire better results. Figure 5 shows some of our pose estimation results on MPII dataset.

3.2   Results on LSP Dataset

We also test on another human pose estimation dataset, Leeds Sport Dataset and its extension (LSP) [14]. LSP dataset contains 2000 images, 14 body joint annotations are given for each image. LSP extended dataset contains 10000 images. In our experiments we use these 10000 image for training and the other 2000 images for testing. The size of the images in LSP is small, and the number of images is still not large enough for training, so we enlarge the original dataset. We resize each image 2 times larger, that is the width and height of each image is enlarged 2 times. The corresponding joint coordinates are multiplied 2 in annotations. Consequently, we have 20000 images for training and 4000 for testing. Some examples of the detection and pose estimation results on LSP are shown in Fig. 6.

Fig. 5. Some of our pose estimation results on MPII dataset.

Fig. 6. Some examples of the detection and pose estimation results on LSP

3.3 Human Body Orientation Model and PCP Evaluation Results

The human body orientation detection results are shown in Table 2 and Fig. 7.

Table 2. Human body orientation detection result (AP)

AP	Front	Back	Left	Right
Body Orientation	0.85	0.83	0.64	0.65

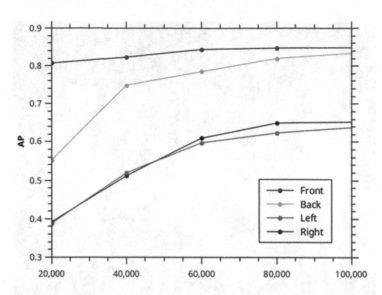

Fig. 7. AP (Average Precision) of human body orientation detection

We can see that our body orientation detection model have high recognition accuracy with respect to front and back cases, however lower accuracy on left and right orientations. This is due to two reasons. First, in the three training datasets most of these images are of front or back orientation. That is, we have enough training data for front and back orientation, on the other side, fewer images for left and right orientation training. Second, because the two datasets, MPII and LSP, are mainly used for human pose estimation, the human poses vary largely, various poses exist in the images. So, during the construction of our body orientation dataset, we lack a uniform criterion to define the left and right body orientation, we have to recognize them subjectively. So the learned common features for left and right orientation will decrease accordingly, which leads to lower recognition accuracy than that of front and back.

Because in MPII and LSP dataset, most of the human bodies are of front and back orientation, while left and right orientations only occupy a small portion, so, although our orientation model cannot recognize left and right orientation accurately, it has high accuracy on front and back. Still, our trained body orientation model takes good effect for the pose estimation task.

According to the method illustrated in Sect. 2, we combine the human body part detection with body orientation detection to get the coordination and category of the 14 joints (whose left and right can be distinguished), which we use as the predicted joints. We use PCP (Percentage of Correct Parts) to evaluate our whole human pose estimation method.

PCP is a criterion used to evaluate the human pose estimation results. With the predicted joints and the ground truth joints, PCP will connect the corresponding category among predicted joints and ground truth joints, and then compute their distance. If the distance is less than 0.5 times of this part, it assumes that the body part is correctly detected.

Table 3 shows the PCP comparisons. Our method outperforms other detection based human pose estimation approaches.

Table 3. Comparisons of human pose estimation on LSP dataset (PCP)

Method	Head	Torso	Upper arm	Lower arm	Upper leg	Lower leg	Average
Andriluka [13]	74.9	80.9	46.5	26.4	67.1	60.7	55.7
Dontone [17]	79.2	81.6	45.1	24.7	66.5	61.0	55.5
Yang [18]	79.3	82.9	56.0	39.8	70.3	67.0	62.8
Pishchulin [19]	78.1	87.5	54.2	33.9	75.7	68.0	62.9
Wei [12]	87.4	84.9	47.5	34.6	72.6	74.2	63.0
Ours	86.3	88.5	51.9	45.3	69.3	69.4	**64.6**

4 Conclusions

In this paper, we propose to treat human pose estimation as object detection problem, in this way we can take advantage the fast and accurate deep object detection approach for our task. We apply the recently proposed state-of-the-art deep object detector, SSD, to train a human body part detection model. Compared with other method, such as Faster R-CNN, the detection speed and accuracy are all improved. We design a human pose estimation method based on part detection.

Because our human body part detection model cannot distinguish the left from the right limbs, we propose to train a human body orientation model. With the detected body orientation information, we can infer the left or right of the body limbs. We construct a body orientation dataset containing about 27K samples. The experimental results show that, compared with other part detection based human pose estimation approaches, our method achieves better results on two public human pose estimation datasets.

Acknowledgements. This work was supported by the National Natural Science Foundation of China under Grants 61171144 and 61402277, and Innovation Program of Shanghai Municipal Education Commission (grant no. 15ZZ044). We also thank NVIDIA Corporation for their GPU donation.

References

1. Toshev, A., Szegedy, C.: DeepPose: human pose estimation via deep neural networks. In: Proceedings IEEE Conference Computer Vision Patern Recognition, pp. 1653–1660 (2014)
2. Tompson, J.J., Jain, A., LeCun, Y., Bregler, C.: Joint training of a convolutional network and a graphical model for human pose estimation. In: Proceedings Advances in Neural Information Processing Systems, pp. 1799–1807 (2014)
3. Bulat, A., Tzimiropoulos, G.: Human pose estimation via convolutional part heatmap regression. In: Leibe, B., Matas, J., Sebe, N., Welling, M. (eds.) ECCV 2016. LNCS, vol. 9911, pp. 717–732. Springer, Cham (2016). https://doi.org/10.1007/978-3-319-46478-7_44
4. Chu, X., Ouyang, W., Li, H., Wang, X.: Structured feature learning for pose estimation. In: Proceedings IEEE Conference Computer Vision Pattern Recognition, pp. 4715–4723 (2016)
5. Wei, S.-E., Ramakrishna, V., Kanade, T., Sheikh, Y.: Convolutional pose machines. In: Proceedings IEEE Conference Computer Vision Pattern Recognition, pp. 4724–4732 (2016)

6. Insafutdinov, E., Pishchulin, L., Andres, B., Andriluka, M., Schiele, B.: DeeperCut: a deeper, stronger, and faster multi-person pose estimation model. In: Leibe, B., Matas, J., Sebe, N., Welling, M. (eds.) ECCV 2016. LNCS, vol. 9910, pp. 34–50. Springer, Cham (2016). https://doi.org/10.1007/978-3-319-46466-4_3

7. Newell, A., Yang, K., Deng, J.: Stacked hourglass networks for human pose estimation. In: Leibe, B., Matas, J., Sebe, N., Welling, M. (eds.) ECCV 2016. LNCS, vol. 9912, pp. 483–499. Springer, Cham (2016). https://doi.org/10.1007/978-3-319-46484-8_29

8. He, K., Zhang, X., Ren, S., Sun, J.: Deep residual learning for image recognition. In: CVPR (2016)

9. Long, J., Shelhamer, E., Darrell, T.: Fully convolutional networks for semantic segmentation. In: Proceedings of the IEEE Conference on Computer Vision and Pattern Recognition, pp. 3431–3440 (2015)

10. Ren, S., He, K., Girshick, R., Sun, J.: Faster R-CNN: towards real-time object detection with region proposal networks. In: Advances in Neural Information Processing Systems, pp. 91–99 (2015)

11. Liu, W., Anguelov, D., Erhan, D., Szegedy, C., Reed, S., Fu, C.-Y., Berg, A.C.: SSD: single shot multibox detector. In: Leibe, B., Matas, J., Sebe, N., Welling, M. (eds.) ECCV 2016. LNCS, vol. 9905, pp. 21–37. Springer, Cham (2016). https://doi.org/10.1007/978-3-319-46448-0_2

12. Wei, K., Zhao, X.: Multiple-branches faster RCNN for human parts detection and pose estimation. In: Chen, C.-S., Lu, J., Ma, K.-K. (eds.) ACCV 2016. LNCS, vol. 10118, pp. 453–462. Springer, Cham (2017). https://doi.org/10.1007/978-3-319-54526-4_33

13. Andriluka, M., Pishchulin, L., Gehler, P., Schiele, B.: 2d human pose estimation: new benchmark and state of the art analysis. In: CVPR (2014)

14. Johnson, S., Everingham, M.: Clustered pose and nonlinear appearance models for human pose estimation. In: BMVC (2010)

15. Dalal, N., Triggs, B.: Histograms of oriented gradients for human detection. In: Computer Vision and Pattern Recognition (CVPR), vol. 1, pp. 886–893 (2005)

16. Jia, Y., Shelhamer, E., Donahue, J., Karayev, S., Long, J., Girshick, R., Guadarrama, S., Darrell, T.: Caffe: convolutional architecture for fast feature embedding. In: Proceedings of the 22nd ACM International Conference on Multimedia (2014)

17. Dantone, M., Gall, J., Leistner, C., Van Gool, L.: Human pose estimation using body parts dependent joint regressors. In: IEEE Conference on Computer Vision and Pattern Recognition (CVPR), pp. 3041–3048 (2013)

18. Yang, Y., Ramanan, D.: Articulated human detection with flexible mixtures of parts. IEEE Trans. Pattern Anal. Mach. Intell. 35(12), 2878–2890 (2013)

19. Pishchulin, L., Andriluka, M., Gehler, P., et al.: Poselet: conditioned pictorial structures. In: IEEE Conference on Computer Vision and Pattern Recognition, Portland, USA, pp. 588–595 (2013)

Polarization Based Invisible Barcode Display

Qi Chen[✉] and Yuanchun Chen

Institute of Image Communication and Information Processing,
Shanghai Jiao Tong University, Shanghai, China
{chen-qi1997,chenyuanchun}@sjtu.edu.cn

Abstract. QR Codes (Quick Response) have become a fast and effective
way to convey information. Users can get access to a website, a picture,
a phone number or any other information they are interested in simply
by scanning the QR Codes. However, QR Codes are meaningful only to
the mobile devices and naked-eye users can only see a permutation of
black dots. The traditional QR Codes mode leads to spatial waste on
the screen and makes the screen not appealing. This paper presents a
new QR Codes embedding in system based on polarization and Spacial-
temporal psychovisual modulation (STPVM). Using the fusion feature
of human visual system (HVS), we separate the users' view from the
smartphone camera view and make the QR Codes totally transparent
to human. At the same time, it can also be detected by the smartphone
camera. Based on this system, we can realize many applications such as
real-time advertisement of the merchandise shown on sceen inserted into
a film etc. This paper shows a prototype system of invisible QR Codes
aiming to proof and validate the theory of the system and this system
can be improved in future works.

Keywords: QR Codes · Visual invisible · Polarization
STPVM · Detectable QR Code

1 Introduction

1.1 General Introduction to QR Codes

Since Denso Wave invented QR Code in 1994 for the automotive industry in
a Toyota subsidiary [1], the QR Code® has run into every aspect of our life.
When you get in a shopping mall, receive a recipe in restaurant, get access
to a hyperlink of a website or even ask for a girl's account, you can't help
noticing the convenient black and white squares. This two dimensional barcodes
can be read optically and have vast benefits. The first benefit comes from its
convenience. Users can turn on their camera and scan the QR Codes to get
access to corresponding descriptions and pictures or even link to videos all in
a flash on the portable devices, this can free users from complex and clumsy
materials. QR Codes are high-density encoded and can convey huge amount of
information within quite little area, take version 40-L symbols as example, the

© Springer Nature Singapore Pte Ltd. 2018
G. Zhai et al. (Eds.): IFTC 2017, CCIS 815, pp. 67–77, 2018.
https://doi.org/10.1007/978-981-10-8108-8_7

maximum character storage capacity is 7089 numeric or 2953 bytes [2]. Another benefit is QR Codes have strong stability and can be encrypted to enhance security [3]. In a word, QR Codes have greatly changed our life and are still very promising in many fields. However, QR Codes have one shortage that is often criticized: the black and white picture has to take up enough space to be detected by the smartphone, which causes meaningless view for HVS and may cover some important information.

1.2 Present Ways to Improve the Outlook of QR Codes

As QR Codes become more and more common, people have several attempts to improve the abovementioned shortage [4]. Methods are mainly the following four categories as shown in Fig. 1

(a) Manually Designed   (b) Visual Lead

(c) Icon Overlaid   (d) Fluorescent material

Fig. 1. Four present types of methods to improve QR Codes appearance (Color figure online)

(a) Use colorful dots instead of the to compose QR Codes (b) Use colorful bits to give a visual lead of icon for users. (c) Replace the center of the QR Code with the icon picture so that users can know what they are scanning at. (d) Codes are created from tiny nanoparticles, combined with blue and green fluorescence ink, and the invisible code can be seen under infrared laser light and can be scanned in the traditional manner, using a code scanner application on a smartphone [5].

1.3 Our Work

This paper provides a new method to display the QR codes that can both enhance the visual appearance for human visual system [6] and give the

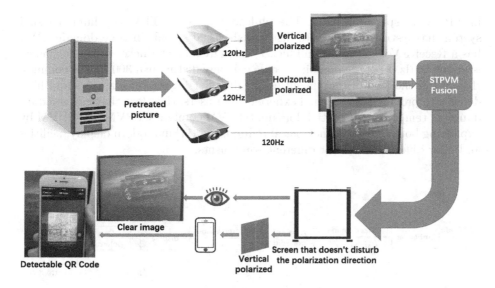

Fig. 2. Working mechanism

smartphone camera a clear and detectable QR Code view [7]. The method puts emphasis on the fusion of signals and uses the character of human visual system to cancel out the QR Codes for naked-eye users. Our system is based on the idea of separating the naked-eye view and camera view by polarization [8]. We put a horizontal polarized polaroid and a vertical polarized polaroid in front of two projectors. The two projectors are showing the QR Code and the opposite of the QR code in gray field. Then with modulation coefficients [9] adjusted to the projector view, we can realize that the QR codes are cancelled out in naked-eye system and the mobile camera with polarization film can detect the QR code of one of the projectors. Then throughout our experiment, we find that there is deviation in the cancellation of the QR Code and naked-eye users [10] can also see some remaining and ghosting of the QR Code. Since the correlation from gray value to brightness value is nonlinear [11] and our PC deals with the picture in gray value and HVS perceives the picture in brightness value. The computing code should be converted from gray space to brightness space. But only adjusting the modulation coefficients will make the system lack of applicability to different pictures or even videos [12]. By studying the mechanism of HVS, we found that a steady image is composed by continuous integration in light field [13]. We can use spatial-temporal psychovisual modulation (STPVM) to finally form two different view for the naked-eye users and the smartphone camera with polarization film. STPVM is a new information display technology by combining the temporal psychovisual modulation (TPVM) [14] and spatial psychovisual modulation (SPVM)[15]. TPVM enables a single display to generate specific view for different viewers by extend traditional time division multiplexing technology using the peculiarity of HVS mentioned above. SPVM extends the idea of fusion in TPVM to spatial domain. The philosophy behind TPVM is human visual system has restricted ability to distinguish visual signal. In time domain, HVS has a Receive Velocity limit and flicker fusion frequency. Flicker fusion frequency is about 60 Hz. In space domain, people can only distinguish 300 PPI in common [16]. While modern display facilities usually offer higher refresh rates and high density to provide better visual experience for users, therefore they cause redundancy in temporal and spatial domain. STPVM combines TPVM and SPVM by exploiting both temporal and spatial redundancy [17] in modern display facilities and offer different views for different equipments.

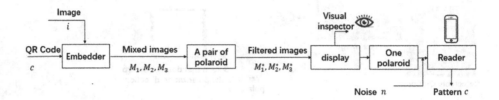

Fig. 3. Communication model

2   Proposed Invisible QR Code Scheme

2.1   Working Mechanism

Figure 2 shows the working mechanism of our proposed invisible QR Code scheme. This proposed invisible QR Code scheme can be realized by three steps.

QR Codes Embedding. The signal transferred from PC to projectors has been pretreated and three projectors are showing pictures of origin image, image with QR Code and image with the negative of QR Code. The pictures are with specific coefficients and filtered by polaroid to make the visual appearance perfect. Through this way, we embed the QR Codes into the origin image.

STPVM Fusion. The system uses STPVM fusion to give naked-eye users an unambiguous image by the psychovisual modulation algorithm [18]. It can give modulation weights to the pictures from the projector, making the fusion and cancellation of the QR Codes been calculated. Also the computing of gray field values should be changed to brightness field because there is a nonlinear correspondence between the brightness and gray values for out projector [19].

QR Codes Extraction. To extract the QR Codes from the screen, we put a thin polarization film whose polarization direction is the same as the image with QR Codes, in front of the smartphone camera. Then the QR Codes is not cancelled out on the screen for the camera. Through experiment we can adjust the coefficient of three pictures to make the QR Codes more detectable as well as the naked-eye view more clean and clear [20].

2.2 Communication Model

Figure 3 shows the communication model of invisible QR Codes based on polarization and STPVM. Assume that f_d is the flicker fusion frequency of HVS, $f_c = \mathbf{j} \, f_d$ is the refresh rate of the three projectors. And assume the input image **I** and QR Code **C** are all in $\mathbf{w} \in \mathbb{R}^N$ range. **N** is the resolution of **I** and obviously the QR Code we embed is smaller than our image **I**, so we need to pad the QR Code with gray picture to the same size as **I**. Then We define the views of our system. The naked-eye users' view is denoted as Y_0 [21], the smartphone camera view is denoted as Y_1, the display frames for the projectors are denoted as X_1, $X_2 \ldots X_{3\mathbf{j}}$, each projector is broadcasting **j** frames simultaneously on the same screen. Before experiment we have adjusted the position of three projectors so that they project on the exactly same area on the screen. Then we can know that the naked-eye view Y_0 can be calculated as:

$$Y_0 = \sum_{i=1}^{\mathbf{j}} X_i. \tag{1}$$

In this experiment, we take **j** as 2 because the projectors have the refresh rate of 120 Hz. And the modulation weights of the polaroid are between 0 and 1. When totally transparent it is 1 and when totally blocked it is 0. Then we can apply the thought of SPVM and have the following nonnegative matrix factorization (NMF):

$$Y_k = \sum_{i=1}^{k} X_i W_k^i. \tag{2}$$

This matrix factorization is nonnegative because the modulation weights varies from 0 to 1, and the frames of X_1, X_2 is larger than zero in brightness field [13]. k is the number of projectors, in this paper we will take k as 3 to simplify the problem. Then we try to solve the matrix equation with nonnegative constraints:

$$(Y_0 \; Y_1) = (X_0 \; X_1 \; X_2) \begin{pmatrix} W_1^0 & W_1^1 \\ W_2^0 & W_2^1 \\ W_3^0 & W_3^1 \end{pmatrix}. \tag{3}$$

Only getting the lightness value being positive, the weight W ranges from 0 to 1 and they are restricted within the equation above does not lead to a confirmed result. It can only give a range of solution and may take quite a long time in computation [14]. So in practical system, we can approximately treat

W as 0 or 1 instead of 0 to 1. Then considering the system, we can find that W_1^0, W_2^0, W_3^0, W_1^1 and W_3^1 is set to 1 and W_2^1 is set to 0 because of the polarization. We then get a quicker solution as follows:

$$\begin{pmatrix} W_1^0 & W_1^1 \\ W_2^0 & W_2^1 \\ W_3^0 & W_3^1 \end{pmatrix} = \begin{pmatrix} 1 & 1 \\ 1 & 0 \\ 1 & 1 \end{pmatrix}. \tag{4}$$

So we simplified the problem into a least-square problem as follows and is much easier to evaluate:

$$\min_{X_1, X_2} \left\{ ||Y_0 - X_0 - X_1 - X_2|| + ||Y_1 - X_0 - X_1|| \right\}.$$

To find the solution of least-square problem we also have to deal with matrix inversion and need to correct repeatedly through experiment. In this paper, we only give a guideline of the range of solution. Assuming the naked-eye view $Y_0 = \mathbf{I}$ and smartphone camera view is $\mathbf{C}$, we let $X_0 = \mathbf{I}$, $X_1 = \mathbf{C}$, X_2 be the negative of X_1 in brightness field. In this case we can ideally display the pure image $\mathbf{I}$ for naked-eye users and QR Codes detected for smartphone camera.

2.3   QR Codes Model

Zones of 2-D Matrix QR Codes. The main purpose of this paper is to give a proposed scheme to embed QR Codes and to extract them from the fusion picture. So we need to figure out the structure of QR Codes and know how to deal with the QR Codes so that the presulfided QR Code can be detected by smartphone camera and convey information. The QR Codes are composed by the five main zones shown in Fig. 4. Zones like format information, data and error-correction area and version information contains information separately and are grouped into various functions. Especially in the third zone the QR Code can deal with error correction and the distortion compensation. Also there is a quiet zone in the QR Code area, carrying no data just to separate the QR Code from the surrounding words.

Error Correction Method. As mentioned above in the model of QR Code, we know that the QR Code permits certain range of error both because of it has a error correcting arithmetic and the quiet zone allows some error space while fusing with SPVM [22]. Before generating the correction codewords and to correct the error, we may first need to break up the data codewords to simplify the arithmetic. The main method to generate the error correction codewords is Reed-Solomom Error through polynomial long division, and using Galois Field Arithmetic to calculate and generate the error correction codewords. After rapid calculation we can generate and interleave the codewords with the data blocks to generate the detectable QR Codes [23].

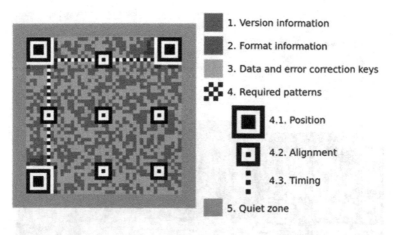

Fig. 4. Zones of 2-D matrix QR Codes

3 System Design and Results

Since QR Codes were invented, great changes have taken place in the outlook, storage capacity, detectability and many other features of QR Codes. But there are rarely effective attempts to reduce the huge meaningless space of QR Codes for HVS. The four main methods to improve the appearance of QR Codes mentioned above only focus on how to maintain the space and to make the QR Codes less meaningless for human visual system. This paper manages to find another way to solve this problem: to separate the information for naked-eye users from the information smartphone camera should detect. We use a pair of vertical and horizontal polarized polaroid to present the QR Codes and the negative of QR Codes, making the QR Codes cancelled out for naked-eye users. Then we give the camera a polarization film to detect QR Codes and make the two channels separated. This paper develops a prototype system of invisible QR Codes based on polarization and combined with STPVM. The system uses three Optoma DLP$^{®}$ IS500 projectors with 120 Hz refresh rate and an IR emitter. The system design is as shown in Fig. 5. Two of the projectors are each filtered by a horizontal and a vertical polaroid. The system is written in C++ language in Microsoft Visual Studio 2010. SDKs of NVIDIA$^{®}$ 3D vision, CEGUI and DirectX are used to support the functions of the system. Given that the critical fusion flicker frequency of HVS is 60 Hz, our three 120 Hz display projectors can emit two frames and fuse them into one picture for HVS simultaneously.

3.1 Embed QR Code

Our system uses two projectors P_1, P_2 to embed the QR Code, and uses the other projector P_3 to give naked-eye users an unambiguous picture. To embed QR code, we attach a thin polarization film to the camera of users smartphone and the polarization direction of the film is horizontal. Then we put a horizontally

Fig. 5. System design

polarized polaroid in front of projector P_1, and a vertically polarized polaroid in front of projector P_2. Because the polaroid can block all of the light signal in vertical polarization direction and can pass all of light signal in the same polarization direction, the naked-eye view is the SPVM fusion of the image I and the cancelled out of the QR Code. So the QR Code is successfully embedded into the image I. To make sure our system can provide a clear view for naked-eye users, we take the following two steps:

(1) We adjust the coefficient of the picture I and the QR Code C so that the QR code is totally counteracted by the negative of C in the gray field.
(2) Considering the corresponding relationship between the brightness space and the gray space, we should convert the computing of gray scales to brightness space thus naked-eye users can have an unambiguous view in the brightness space [24].

3.2   Read QR Code

Since we have a horizontally polarized film in front of our smartphone camera, which is the same as projector P_1 and vertical to projector P_2. Due to the character of polaroid, the camera can only detect the signal from projector P_1 and P_3. Then the camera view is a composed view of P_1 and P_3 and the QR Code can be detected as shown in Fig. 2. To make the QR Code more detectable, we shall find the range of solution to the matrix equation II.4 that can maximize the weight W_1^1 on condition that the naked-eye users can still have a clear view (Fig. 6).

Fig. 6. Results

4 Conclusion

The paper introduces a prototype system of invisible QR Codes realized by polarization and spatial-temporal psychovisual modulation (STPVM). Considering the fusion feature of HVS, we attempt to break the tradition method to improve the appearance of QR Code and make it more functional and commercially valuable. We separate the view of naked-eye users and mobile device cameras by

SPVM and polarization, making the naked-eye users see a clear image without QR Code and the smartphone detect the QR Code without being disturbed by the image.

References

1. Denso.ADC, QR Code essentials (2011). Accessed 12 Mar 2013
2. Qrcode.com. Information Capacity and Versions of the QR Code. http://www.qrcode.com/en/about/version.html
3. Agarwal, R., Chen, Z., Kloosterman, F., Wilson, M.A., Sarma, S.V.: A novel nonparametric approach for neural encoding and decoding models of multimodal receptive fields. Neural Comput. **28**(7), 1356–1387 (2016). https://doi.org/10.1162/NECO_a_00847
4. Samretwit, D., Wakahara, T.: Measurement of reading characteristics of multiplexed image in QR Code. In: 2011 Third International Conference on Intelligent Networking and Collaborative Systems, Fukuoka, pp. 552–557 (2011). https://doi.org/10.1109/INCoS.2011.117
5. BBC.com. Invisible QR codes to combat counterfeit goods. http://www.bbc.com/news/technology-19569933
6. Chen, Y., Liu, N., Zhai, G., Gao, Z., Gu, K.: Information security display system on android device. In: 2016 IEEE Region 10 Conference (TENCON), Singapore, pp. 1634–1637 (2016). https://doi.org/10.1109/TENCON.2016.7848294
7. Zhai, G., Wu, X.: Multiuser collaborative viewport via Temporal Psychovisual Modulation [applications corner]. IEEE Signal Process. Mag. **31**(5), 144–149 (2014)
8. Fang, W., Zhai, G., Yang, X.: A flash light system for individuals with visual impairment based on TPVM. In: 2016 7th International Conference on Cloud Computing and Big Data (CCBD), Macau, China, pp. 362–366 (2016). https://doi.org/10.1109/CCBD.2016.077
9. Wu, X., Zhai, G.: Image/information display system and method based on temporal psycho-visual modulation. U.S. Patent Application 14/128,509, filed 21 June 2012
10. Min, X., Zhai, G., Gu, K.: Visual attention on human face. In: 2015 Visual Communications and Image Processing (VCIP), Singapore, pp. 1–4 (2015). https://doi.org/10.1109/VCIP.2015.7457922
11. Lan, F., Zhai, G., Gao, Z., Yang, X.: Live demonstration: screen piracy protection using saturation laser attack and TPVM. In: 2016 IEEE International Symposium on Circuits and Systems (ISCAS), Montreal, QC, p. 2376 (2016). https://doi.org/10.1109/ISCAS.2016.7539067
12. Min, X., Zhai, G., Hu, C., Gu, K.: Fixation prediction through multimodal analysis. In: 2015 Visual Communications and Image Processing (VCIP), Singapore, pp. 1–4 (2015)
13. Hu, C., Zhai, G., Gao, Z., Min, X.: Simultaneous triple subtitles exhibition via Temporal Psychovisual Modulation. In: 2014 IEEE 9th Conference on Industrial Electronics and Applications (ICIEA), pp. 944–947. IEEE (2014)
14. Wu, X., Zhai, G.: Temporal Psychovisual Modulation: a new paradigm of information display [exploratory DSP]. IEEE Signal Process. Mag. **30**(1), 136–141 (2013). https://doi.org/10.1109/MSP.2012.2219678
15. Gao, Z., Zhai, G., Hu, C.: The invisible QR Code. In: ACM International Conference on Multimedia (MM 2015), pp. 1047–1050. ACM, New York (2015)

16. Chen, Y., et al.: Movie piracy tracking using temporal psychovisual modulation. In: 2017 IEEE International Symposium on Broadband Multimedia Systems and Broadcasting (BMSB), Cagliari, Italy, pp. 1–4 (2017). https://doi.org/10.1109/BMSB.2017.7986217
17. Hu, C., Zhai, G., Gao, Z.: Visible light communication via Temporal Psycho-Visual Modulation. In: ACM International Conference on Multimedia (MM 2015), pp. 785–788. ACM, New York (2015)
18. Gao, Z., Zhai, G., Hu, C., Min, X.: Dual-view medical image visualization based on spatial-temporal psychovisual modulation. In: The International Conference on Image Processing (ICIP). IEEE (2014)
19. Min, X., Zhai, G., Gao, Z., Gu, K.: Visual attention data for image quality assessment databases. In: 2014 IEEE International Symposium on Circuits and Systems (ISCAS), Melbourne VIC, pp. 894–897 (2014)
20. Gao, Z., Zhai, G., Hu, C.: DEMO: the invisible QR Code. In: 2014 IEEE International Conference on Multimedia and Expo (ICME). IEEE (2015)
21. Sutheebanjard, P., Premchaiswadi, W.: QR-code generator. In: 2010 Eighth International Conference on ICT and Knowledge Engineering, Bangkok, pp. 89–92 (2010). https://doi.org/10.1109/ICTKE.2010.5692920
22. Hu, C., Zhai, G., Gao, Z., Min, X.: Simultaneous dual-subtitles exhibition via Spatial Psychovisual Modulation. In: 2014 IEEE International Symposium on Broadband Multimedia Systems and Broadcasting, Beijing, pp. 1–4 (2014). https://doi.org/10.1109/BMSB.2014.6873483
23. Li, D., Zhai, G., Yang, X., Hu, M., Liu, J.: Perceptual information hiding based on multi-channel visual masking. Neurocomputing (2017)
24. Chen, Y., et al.: Quality assessment for dual-view display system. In: 2016 Visual Communications and Image Processing (VCIP), Chengdu, pp. 1–4 (2016). https://doi.org/10.1109/VCIP.2016.7805459

Security Thread Detection in Passport Using Improved Template Matching

Lei Wang[1,2(✉)], Menghan Hu[1], Duo Li[1], Zhaohui Che[1], and Xiaoliang Zhang[1,2]

[1] Institute of Image Communication and Information Processing, Shanghai Jiao Tong University, Shanghai, China
Sd1588860@163.com
[2] Shanghai Mite Speciality & Precision Printing Co., Ltd., Shanghai, China

Abstract. In recent years, passport has been paid more and more attention. Passport is not only a certificate of the passport holders, but also involves the international anti-terrorism situation. Passport security thread, as a security feature which is the most direct and easy to identify, is generally used by national passports. However, in the passport manufacturer, the current inspection method of the passport security thread is manual inspection. Computer vision can be applied in this aspect for automatic inspection through some systems or machines. This paper proposes that a custom-built computer vision system can utilize the reflected light to collect images, and detect the buried security thread with the relative high accuracy. After analysis, the detection of the security thread can be considered as a class of the object detection. On account of the gorgeous page's pattern around the security thread in passport, the most of object detection algorithms are failed to complete this task. Taking both accuracy and detection speed into account, in this work, we develop an improved algorithm based on the traditional SURF operator to achieve security line detection in passport. After verification on a sample set containing 134 samples, this approach has been a certain ability to detect the security thread with the accuracy of 84.33%.

Keywords: Passport image processing · Corner detection · Passport quality
Object detection

1 Introduction

Under the tendency of economic globalization, passport which customs utilize to check traveler's legal identity, as one of the documents in international travel, plays an important role in people's identification. According to the matter that [1] mentioned, the international community had also focused the quality of passport, including the quality of anti-counterfeiting features, since the world was shocked by 911 event in 2001. After the "9.11" happened, the situation of international terrorism had been becoming increasingly serious. More developed countries have applied some unique anti-counterfeiting technologies or improved the quality of these features present to fight against the terrorism. Following the statement of [2], it is not difficult to find that a part of manufacturers had utilized computer vision to ensure the quality control of products.

© Springer Nature Singapore Pte Ltd. 2018
G. Zhai et al. (Eds.): IFTC 2017, CCIS 815, pp. 78–90, 2018.
https://doi.org/10.1007/978-981-10-8108-8_8

The technology of computer vision is definitely not limited to some fields. There are a lot of aspects which are available to be associated with this technique, such as agriculture and food industry, light industry, public transport, public security. [3, 4] introduced that the use of automatized inspections in agriculture and industry had become a way of the analysis of product quality. In [4], a system for apple surface defect detection was designed by this technique. [5] was presented as an example of light industry. The application of computer vision can effectively avoid the risk that the visual inspection led to. From [6, 7], the technology likewise promoted the intelligent level of public utility, and not only enhanced the efficiency but also ensured the safety of people. Furthermore, the paper [8] shows that computer vision is combined with other technology for measuring the line scale, such as laser interferometer. Nevertheless, application of computer vision to the process of manufacturing passport is substantially less extensive than it to the other fields. The most relevant application is only the identification of the security thread in the banknotes involved in [9].

According to my work experience, the overall quality of the passport is divided into appearance quality, functional quality and anti-counterfeiting features quality. For e-passports, the RFID chip and personal information page represent the passports' functionality. In terms of manufacturers and customs, they are more concerned about the quality of passport anti-counterfeiting features. On account of the security line that is a visible effect, it can be easily identified security feature, and this feature is fairly difficult to imitate. The quality of the security thread is particularly more important than others. As the security line is buried in the paper and the paper is printed, the contrast of the security thread is difficult to highlight from the other areas of printing. Because of the demand for stacked paper, the security thread is required to drift on a large scale in a certain release region. Hence making the safety line's positioning will be a great challenge.

In essence, we can deem that the detection of security thread is a problem of object detection. On the basis of paper [10–13], there are several algorithms or methods for object detection, which are respectively based on multi-modal images using genetic programming, image reconstruction with PCA, geometric invariant moment, SURF and Superpixels. However, since security line is not highlighted on the image, the conventional template matching algorithm may not be available.

Therefore, the objectives of this paper are: (1) preparing passports or its semi-finished products and setting up computer vision equipment for passport detection; (2) developing improved template matching algorithm to detect the security thread of e-passport; (3) verifying our developed algorithm and verification on a small sample-data set.

2   Materials and Methods

2.1   Passport Sample Preparation

Through the support of the passport manufacturer, we obtained a part of the passport of the finished product with the semi-finished product. The production process of the sample is consistent with the production process of the passport product. At the moment, the processes are listed in the following figure. The passport of the general production process: (1) papermaking; (2) printing; (3) cutting; (4) binding. The subdivision of each process is shown in Fig. 1.

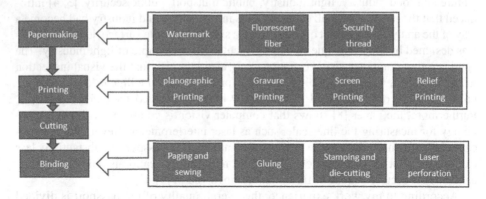

Fig. 1. Flow chart of e-passport's process.

Papermaking includes watermarks, security thread and fluorescent fibers introduced in [14]. Printing includes offset printing involved in [15] and is used to the main pattern of printing on the sample, gravure printing, screen printing and letterpress printing. Binding includes paging, sewing, gluing, stamping, die-cutting and laser perforation (just in the process of e-passport) introduced in [16]. Among above, paging and sewing process is done together, and stamping and die-cutting in the same process is completed. Since the passport consists of multiple pages, we select the inner page containing the security thread as the sample, and it only passes through the process (1) and (2). The inside page without cutting, we call it "sheet 1". Thus, the sample exhibits a larger size which is about 780 mm * 555 mm, and the printed pattern is intertwined with the security line, and it is not particularly noticeable under the reflected light.

2.2   Custom-Built Computer Vision System

At present, the passport manufacturer already has a set of custom-built computer vision detection system. This system consists of color linear array CCD camera introduced in [17, 18], light source, front-end computer containing image acquisition card, signal box and server. Camera, light source, front-end computer composed of the core unit of image acquisition and processing. The camera is connected to the front-end computer with the Camera-Link wire involved in [19, 20]. Signal box is to control the signal interaction between the cameras of system and the sensors of mechanical platform. The server is used to return the processing results and to control the overall detection system. The interaction between the server and the front-end computer relies on Gigabit Ethernet. The following is a schematic diagram of the system in Fig. 2 and the real object images of the components for the version system in Fig. 3.

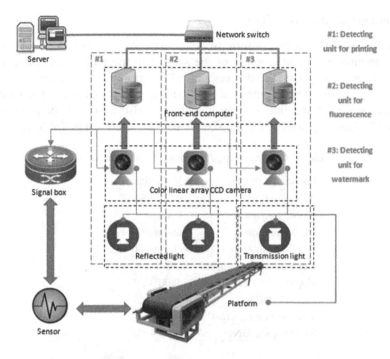

Fig. 2. Schematic diagram of inspection system.

Fig. 3. The components for the version system including color linear array CCD camera, Light source, Signal box, Server and front-end computer.

2.3 Passport Image Acquisition

We use the above detection platform to obtain a certain number of sample images. In order to ensure that the flatness of the sample in the process of collecting the sample, the conveying speed of the mechanical platform was appropriately reduced, and the machine speed was controlled at 1.7 sheets per second. Simultaneously, the main parameters of the linear array camera are also adjusted for adapting the velocity of adjusted platform and the size of sample, as shown in Table 1.

Table 1. Camera settings for passport image acquisition.

Camera parameters	Value/Status
Exposure time	90.00 uSec
SYNC frequency	1 Stuck
CCD direction	Internal/forward
Region of interest	(1,1) to (4096,1)
Number of line samples	1024
Upper threshold	3600
Lower threshold	400
Total analog gain (dB)	−0.8 −0.8
System gain (DN)	4096 4096

Using the above parameters to configure the camera and mechanical platform, a number of samples are collected. As the sheet format is relatively large, using the two cameras to collect the sample for ensuring the higher image resolution, we choose images from one of the cameras. The sample image is shown in Fig. 4. We had used these images to create a final perfect match template for the security line detection.

It is obvious that the sample image contains the complex patterns of offset, and the entire security line is almost hard to find. For the reason that the pattern of passport, it is difficult to distinguish the detected security line. The position of the security thread is near the page number 13 of the passport. The security thread runs through the entire image from top to bottom.

Fig. 4. Sample image.

In order to present the security line more clearly, we intercept a local image for displaying the security line as shown in Fig. 5. It shows a partial plot of the sample, and the texture of the security line can be found, but it is still blurred since the thread is entirely buried into the interlayer of the sheet.

Fig. 5. The partial image of the sample.

2.4 Security Thread Detection

To accurately find the security thread in the passport, we develop an improved template matching approach based on the traditional speeded up robust features (SURF) [21]. The SURF descriptor is developed from the scale invariant feature transform, and it calculates the corner points in the integral passport images and template using Hessian matrix.

$$H(I(x, y)) = \begin{bmatrix} \partial^2 f / \partial x^2 & \partial^2 f / \partial x \partial y \\ \partial^2 f / \partial x \partial y & \partial^2 f / \partial y^2 \end{bmatrix} \tag{1}$$

where, H and I(x,y) represent the Hessian matrix and integral image, respectively.

Meanwhile, since the low offset of the overall captured images, compared to the traditional algorithm, we add some image geometry operations to the SURF process to speed up the processing of the image and the registration between template and sample, such as shrinking the scale, utilizing the outer frame of the overall pattern to initial registration. After the completion of the SURF process, the image of sample will be restored to the initial proportion for contrasting template. This operation will not affect the overall extraction of the safety line and the image is extracted efficiently.

The description of improved template matching algorithm in this study is given in Algorithm 1.

$$\text{Gray} = 0.2989 \times R + 0.5870 \times G + 0.1140 \times B \qquad (2)$$

where, R, G and B denote the red, green and blue channels of passport image, respectively; Gray is the transformed gray passport image.

Algorithm 1. improved template matching algorithm used in the current work

Step 1: load the original passport image
Step 2: convert the original RGB image into the gray image using equation (2)
Step 3: crop one region inclusive of security thread to form the initial template manually
Step 4: recruit two experts to eliminate security thread to generate the final perfect template
Step 5: enhance the final perfect template using the Gaussian filter
Step 6: search the SURF corner points in the final perfect template
Step 7: import the original passport image set
Repeat
Step 8: enhance one selected original passport image using the Gaussian filter
Step 9: yield the SURF corner points in one detected passport image
Step 10: conduct the template matching operation between the perfect template and original image
Step 11: carry out matrix subtraction between two matched image region
Step 12: label the detected security thread in the original passport image
Until: reach a stopping criterion (here is number of imported passport images)
Step 13: evaluate the performance of the improved template matching algorithm

---

As described in Algorithm 1, to generate the final perfect template, we use the Photoshop CS6 software (Adobe Systems Inc., San Jose, CA) to eliminate the security thread in the initial cropped template. Figure 6(b) displays the final perfect template. As shown in Fig. 6, we can clearly observe that the security thread (in red rectangular box in Fig. 6(a)) has been entirely wiped in Fig. 6(b).

Fig. 6. Initial cropped template (a) and final perfect template (b). (Color figure online)

After creating the final perfect template, the template matching operation is conducted throughout the input passport image, and then, we obtain the binary cropped image (Fig. 7) by carrying out the subtraction operation between the located region and final perfect template.

Fig. 7. One example of binary cropped image.

Subsequently, we statistically analyze the binary cropped image by using the equation below

$$\vec{y} = \sum_{x} I(x, y) \tag{3}$$

where, $\vec{y}$ is the sum vector of image $I(x,y)$ in y direction.

One of the results of statistical analysis is demonstrated in Fig. 8.

As shown in Fig. 8, the location of security thread can be easily found by calculating the maximum value in the Y-axis.

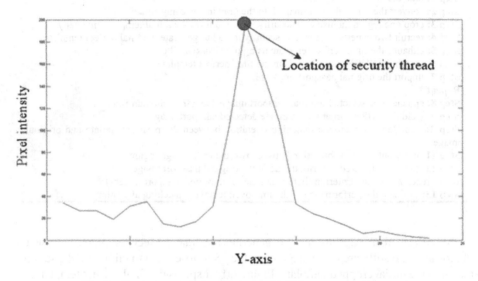

Fig. 8. Typical statistical analysis result of binary cropped image.

According to the simple summary above all, the general process of this detection can be divided into six stages, followed by the pre-production of samples, sample image acquisition, preprocessing of the images, creating perfect matching template, improved SURF algorithm processing, and outputting image to determine the security thread position in the region of inspection. Pre-production contains the papermaking and two kinds of offset printing. The sample images were captured from custom-built platform. There are two steps such as binarized and cropped including the preprocessing of the images. Creating matching template was based on estimating the security line of the image collected. By Hessian matrix, improved SURF calculates the corner points in the integral passport images and template. Outputting image from the subtraction operation between the located region and final perfect template, relies on the statistical characteristics to determine the position of the security line. The flow of the detection is shown in Fig. 9.

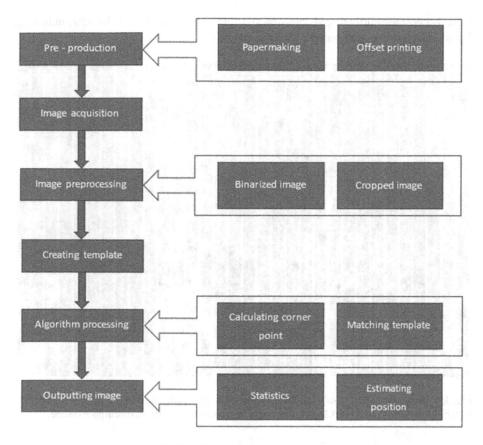

Fig. 9. The flow of the detection.

All programs are implemented in the MATLAB 2014b software (The MathWorks, Inc., Natick, MA).

3   Results and Discussion

3.1   Security Thread Detection

In order to verify the performance of our algorithm, the passports are first produced via the procedure presented in Fig. 1 according to the Chinese national standards. Afterwards, the passports are placed in the platform (Fig. 2), and the passport images are captured by the CCD camera under the white light illumination. The fusion of signal box and server as well as front-end computer enables our passport computer vision system acquire images in real time. The camera settings listed in Table 1 make the good quality of obtained passport images.

By using the proposed SURF based template matching algorithm, the testing results on a total of 134 passport images are shown in Fig. 10. We can find that the overall accuracy of the proposed security thread detection algorithm on this database is 84.33%, indicating that a small proportion of security threads are ignored.

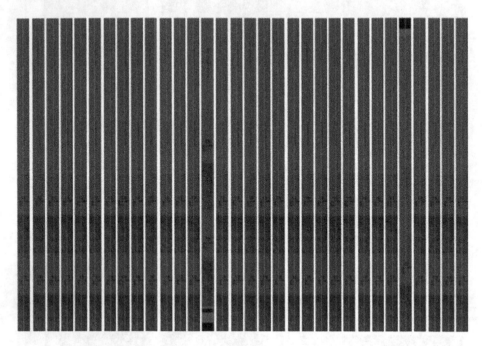

Fig. 10. Some detection results of security thread in passport image using improved template matching algorithm (red lines indicate the detected security thread). (Color figure online)

3.2   Discussion

Subsequently, we discuss and analyze the above-mentioned results of the security thread detection. The focus of the discussion will be the sample where the mistake occurred in the detection. The faults in the detection are divided into the following three cases.

1. The results of sample number 2, 10, 17, 21 were unsatisfactory so that the position of the security line was not correctly determined. The reason for this fault may be caused by disturbances from the pattern of sheet's edge. This case shows that we produced the template existing a certain flaw.
2. The case of 14th sample was that the detection did not detect the security thread, but we thought that template matching was correct since the detection found the correct area of inspection. The reason that led to this result is that some problems happened when the sample image has been binarized and cropped.
3. The 28th sample would be listed as the correct sample, because the security thread was found. However, in the process of the templates match, our template matching misregister to the top of the original image. This case also shows that we need to make collect more templates and collect more samples to enrich the detail of template's position in future research.

As above, the most important point of improvement in the future is how to improve the quality of the template, thus obtaining a relatively perfect template of security line. Through the following method, it is the most possible to obtain a perfect security line template adopted to practical application. We can collect a number of less perfect templates in the passport production process, to calculate the probability through one by one detected. But this process will increase the time of inspection and system processing cost. Provided that the capacity of system's hardware can be increased, this method is still available.

4 Conclusion

In the contemporary world, passports have become important documents for people walking around the world. The quality of passports, especially the quality of passport anti-counterfeiting features, reflects the exclusivity of 'nation card' and it is rather related to the global anti-terrorism situation. It is not difficult to imagine how fake passports have a great threat to a country. The development of automatic inspection is not only the trend of the transformation and upgrading of manufacturing, but also becomes the core of the quality control of products. This paper proposes an approach for detecting security thread to control the position of this line in the passport.

The image processing method is implemented in MATLAB software to detect the offset or defect of this anti-counterfeiting feature. In this research, we have attempted to design the prefect template for the security thread of passport's sheet on a small sample set, and had achieved the high accuracy of the full buried security thread segmentation in passport in the case of the reflected light, reaching more than 80%. In the specialty print industry, the consequence is a great leap to detect the security thread.

By improving the use of the SURF operator and the template matching method, the security line in the image can be detected in the small sample set, although this line has a certain difficulty of detection. Nevertheless, it is unavoidable that the results are unsatisfactory, such as, the printing pattern and security line are mixed; the original image preprocessing results in processing results are not ideal; image matching template is not enough comprehensive, but the application of this method presents practical significance. Then, the future research can be done by making finer templates (printing same pattern on non-security line paper for the perfect template), enriching template matching methods, and optimizing the original image preprocessing approach. We also can try deep learning for distinguishing the actual defect of the security line and the situation of abnormal template matching. In the near future, this approach will be improved again on the basis of this algorithm, and collecting a series of samples to enlarge this sample set for verifying algorithm can be utilized to estimate the detection capability and stability of this method. The popularity of this inspection method, will bring the quality of passport manufacturers to enhance tremendously, but also achieve the upgrading of manufacturing automation.

Acknowledgements. The authors would like to acknowledge the financial support from the National Science Foundation of China under Grant Nos. 61422112, 61371146, and 61221001, and the China Postdoctoral Science Foundation funded project (No. 2016M600315).

References

1. Wang, Q.: Application of digital watermarking technology in passport security. China Anti-Counterfeiting Rep. **6**, 22–23 (2003)
2. Zhi, C.J.: Automatic Detection System of Print Defects Based on Machine Vision. Guangdong University of Technology (2011)
3. Gomes, J.F.S., Leta, F.R.: Applications of computer vision techniques in the agriculture and food industry: a review. Eur. Food Res. Technol. **235**(6), 989–1000 (2012)
4. Li, Q., Wang, M., Gu, W.: Computer vision based system for apple surface defect detection. Comput. Electron. Agric. **36**(2), 215–223 (2002)
5. Kumar, A.: Computer-vision-based fabric defect detection: a survey. IEEE Trans. Ind. Electron. **55**(1), 348–363 (2008)
6. Messelodi, S., Modena, M., Zanin, M.: A Computer Vision System for the Detection and Classification of Vehicles at Urban Road Intersections. Springer, London (2005)
7. Reyin, B.U., Dedeo, L.Y., et al.: Computer vision based method for real-time fire and flame detection. Pattern Recogn. Lett. **27**(1), 49–58 (2006)
8. Luo, P.F., Pan, S.P., Chu, T.C.: Application of computer vision and laser interferometer to the inspection of line scale. Opt. Lasers Eng. **42**(5), 563–584 (2004)
9. Pilania, E.: Recognition of fake currency based on security thread feature of currency (2016)
10. Bhanu, B., Lin, Y.: Object detection in multi-modal images using genetic programming. Appl. Soft Comput. **4**(2), 175–201 (2004)
11. Malagonborja, L., Fuentes, O.: Object detection using image reconstruction with PCA. Image Vis. Comput. **27**(1–2), 2–9 (2013)
12. Rizon, M., Yazid, H., Saad, P., et al.: Object detection using geometric invariant moment. Am. J. Appl. Sci. **3**(6), 1876–1878 (2006)
13. Lopezdelacalleja, M., Nagai, T., Attamimi, M., et al.: Object detection using SURF and superpixels. J. Softw. Eng. Appl. **06**(9), 511–518 (2013)
14. Tang, A.: Characteristics of fluorescence fibers and their application in anti-counterfeiting paper production. Paper Sci. Technol. (2007)
15. Wang, X.: The color control technique of the offset printing image. Packag. Eng. (2005)
16. Xin, F.L.: Research on High Quality Laser Punching Technology. Beijing Industrial University (2006)
17. Chen, W.T., Liu, Y.G., Chao, X.L.: Color excursion and correction of parallel color linear array CCD camera. Semicond. Optoelectron. **27**(4), 478–480 (2006)
18. Zhu, X.Y., Hu, X.L.: Intelligent high-speed linear array color CCD camera, CN 103916643 A (2014)
19. Jian-Jun, Y.U., Zhi-Yong, W.U.: Application of CameraLink to video control system. OME Inf. **28**(5), 42–45 (2011)
20. Shen, G.: The system of video image collection and transmission based on CameraLink. Microcomput. Inf. (2011)
21. Bay, H., Ess, A., Tuytelaars, T., et al.: Speeded-up robust features (SURF). Comput. Vis. Image Underst. **110**(3), 346–359 (2008)

Joint Denoising and Enhancement
for Low-Light Images via Retinex Model

Mading Li, Jiaying Liu$^{(\boxtimes)}$, Wenhan Yang, and Zongming Guo

Institute of Computer Science and Technology,
Peking University, Beijing 100871, People's Republic of China
liujiaying@pku.edu.cn

Abstract. Guided by the Retinex model, image decomposition based low-light image enhancement methods attempt to manipulate the estimated illumination and project it back to the corresponding reflectance. However, the L2 constraint on the illumination often leads to halo artifacts, and the noise existed in the reflectance map is always neglected. In this paper, based on the Retinex model, we introduce a total variation optimization problem that jointly estimates noise-suppressed reflectance and piece-wise smooth illumination. The gradient of the reflectance is also constrained so that the contrast of the final enhancement result can be strengthened. Experimental results demonstrate the effectiveness of the proposed method with respect to low-light image enhancement.

Keywords: Low-light images · Joint denoising and enhancement
Retinex model

1 Introduction

Images captured under low-light conditions suffer from many degradations, such as low visibility, low contrast, and high-level noise. Although these degradations can be somewhat alleviated by professional devices and advanced photographic skills, the inherent cause of the noise is unavoidable and can not be addressed at the hardware level. Without sufficient amount of light, the output of camera sensors is often buried in the intrinsic noise in the system. Longer exposure time can effectively increase the signal-to-noise ratio (SNR) and generate a noise-free image, however it breeds new problems such as motion blur. Thus, low-light image enhancement technique at the software level is highly desired in consumer photography. Moreover, such technique can also benefit many computer vision algorithms (object detection, tracking, *etc.*) since their performance highly relies on the visibility of the target scene.

However, this is not a trivial task, for that images captured under low-light conditions have rather low SNRs, which means the noises are highly intensive

This work was supported by National Natural Science Foundation of China under contract No. 61472011 and Microsoft Research Asia Project under contract No. FY17-RES-THEME-013.

© Springer Nature Singapore Pte Ltd. 2018
G. Zhai et al. (Eds.): IFTC 2017, CCIS 815, pp. 91–99, 2018.
https://doi.org/10.1007/978-981-10-8108-8_9

(a) Observed low-light image

(b) Our enhancement result   (c) Close-ups

Fig. 1. (a) The observed low-light image. (b) The enhancement result of the proposed method. (c) Close-ups from top to bottom correspond to the input image, the enhancement result of the classic histogram equalization algorithm, and that of the proposed method. We can observe that the input image has low visibility and contrast. Intensive noise hidden in the observed image is revealed by histogram equalization. The proposed method generates visually pleasing results with better details and less noise.

and may dominate over the image signals. Thus, low-light image enhancement algorithms need to tackle not only the low visibility, but also the high-level noises, in addition to low contrast (as illustrated in Fig. 1).

An intuitive way to enhance low-light images is to directly amplify the illumination. However, relatively bright areas may be saturated and some details might be lost through the operation. Histogram equalization (HE) based methods [1,2], which aim to stretch the dynamic range of the observed image, can mitigate the problem to some extent. Nevertheless, their purpose is to enhance the contrast other than adjusting the illumination. Thus, results of these methods may be over- or under-enhanced. Furthermore, HE based methods neglect the intensive noise hidden in low-light images.

Some researchers [3,4] noticed that the inverted low-light images look like haze images. Dehazing methods are therefore applied and the dehazing result is inverted once more as the enhancement result. A joint-bilateral filter is applied in [4] to suppress the noise after the enhancement. Li *et al.* [3] attempted to further improve the visual quality by segmenting the observed image into super-pixels and adaptively denoising different segments via BM3D [5]. Although these methods can generate reasonable results, a convincing physical explanation of their basic model has not been provided. Moreover, the order of enhancing and denoising has always been a problem. Performing enhancement method before denoising may result in noise amplification, which increases the difficulty of denoising. On the other hand, enhancement results may be somewhat blurred after denoising.

Retinex theory [6] has been studied extensively in the past few decades, which assumes that images can be decomposed into two components, namely reflectance and illumination. Single-scale Retinex [7] and multiscale Retinex [8] are the pioneering studies in this field. They manipulate the illumination component and treat the reflectance as the final output. Wang *et al.* [9] proposed a bright-pass filter to decompose the observed image into reflectance and illumination, and attempted to preserve the naturalness while enhancing the image details. Based on the bright-pass filter proposed in [9], Fu *et al.* [10] fused multiple derivatives of the estimated illumination to combine different merits into a single output. The method proposed in [11] refines the initial illumination map by imposing a structure-aware prior. Nevertheless, due to the lack of constraint on the reflectance, these methods often amplify the latent intensive noise that exists in low-light images.

Although the logarithmic transformation is widely adopted for the ease of modeling by most Retinex based algorithms, a recent work [12] argues that the logarithmic transformation is not appropriate in the regularization terms since pixels with low magnitude dominate over the variation term in the high magnitude areas. Thus, a weighted variational model is proposed in [12] in order to impose better prior representation in the regularization terms. Even though this method shows rather impressive results in the decomposition of reflectance and illumination, the method is not suitable for the enhancement of low-light images as the noise often appears in low magnitude regions.

In this paper, instead of performing image enhancement and denoising separately, we present an optimization function designed for joint denoising and enhancement for low-light images. The rest of the paper is organized as follows: Sect. 2 introduces the proposed optimization problem that simultaneously estimates a noise-suppressed reflectance and a smoothed illumination map. Low-light enhancement results and analysis are presented in Sect. 3. Finally, Sect. 4 concludes the paper.

2   The Proposed Method

In this section, we propose a new optimization function that simultaneously estimates the reflectance $\mathbf{R}$ and the illumination $\mathbf{L}$ of the input image $\mathbf{I}$:

$$\operatorname*{argmin}_{\mathbf{R},\mathbf{L}} \|\mathbf{R} \circ \mathbf{L} - \mathbf{I}\|_F^2 + \alpha \|\nabla \mathbf{R}\|_F^2 + \beta \|\nabla \mathbf{L}\|_1 + \omega \|\nabla \mathbf{R} - \mathbf{G}\|_F^2, \qquad (1)$$

where α, β, and ω are the coefficients that control the importance of different terms. The operator $\circ$ denotes element-wise multiplication. $\| \cdot \|_F$ and $\| \cdot \|_1$ represent the Frobenius norm and ℓ_1 norm, respectively. In addition, ∇ is the first order differential operator, and $\mathbf{G}$ is the adjusted gradient of $\mathbf{I}$, which will be discussed in Eq. (2). The role of each term in the objective (1) is interpreted below:

- $\|\mathbf{R} \circ \mathbf{L} - \mathbf{I}\|_F^2$ constrains the fidelity between the observed image $\mathbf{I}$ and the recomposed one $\mathbf{R} \circ \mathbf{L}$;
- $\|\nabla\mathbf{R}\|_F^2$ enforces the spatial smoothness on the reflectance $\mathbf{R}$, for that noise is often observed in the reflectance image;
- $\|\nabla\mathbf{L}\|_1$ corresponds to the total variation sparsity and considers the piece-wise smoothness of the illumination map $\mathbf{L}$;
- $\|\nabla\mathbf{R} - \mathbf{G}\|_F^2$ minimizes the distance between the gradient of the reflectance $\mathbf{R}$ and that of the observed image $\mathbf{I}$, so that the contrast of the final result can be strengthened.

As for the matrix $\mathbf{G}$, it is designed as the adjusted version of $\nabla\mathbf{I}$. The formulation of $\mathbf{G}$ is given as follows,

$$\mathbf{G} = \mathbf{K} \circ \nabla\hat{\mathbf{I}}, \tag{2}$$

$$\mathbf{K} = (1 + \lambda e^{-|\nabla\hat{\mathbf{I}}|/\sigma}), \tag{3}$$

where

$$\nabla\hat{\mathbf{I}} = \begin{cases} 0, & \text{if } |\nabla\mathbf{I}| < \varepsilon, \\ \nabla\mathbf{I}, & \text{otherwise.} \end{cases} \tag{4}$$

Specifically, after suppressing small gradients (i.e., the noise), $\nabla\hat{\mathbf{I}}$ is amplified by the factor $\mathbf{K}$ that decreases with the increment of the gradient magnitude. Note that this amplification factor makes less adjustment in areas with higher gradient magnitude, while areas with lower gradient magnitude are strongly enhanced. So that after the amplification, the adjusted gradient $\mathbf{G}$ tends to have similar magnitude. Further, λ controls the degree of the amplification; σ controls the amplification rate of different gradients; ε is the threshold that filters small gradients. Images with higher noise levels often need a larger ε. In our experiments, parameters λ, σ, and ε are all set as 10. For each observed image, matrix $\mathbf{G}$ only needs to be calculated once.

The optimization problem (1) can be effectively solved by the alternating direction minimization technique [13]. By substituting $\nabla\mathbf{L}$ in the third term with an auxiliary variable $\mathbf{T}$, the objective (1) can be rewritten in the following equivalent form:

$$\underset{\mathbf{R},\mathbf{L},\mathbf{T}}{\operatorname{argmin}} \|\mathbf{R} \circ \mathbf{L} - \mathbf{I}\|_F^2 + \alpha\|\nabla\mathbf{R}\|_F^2 + \beta\|\mathbf{T}\|_1 + \omega\|\nabla\mathbf{R} - \mathbf{G}\|_F^2, \text{ s.t. } \mathbf{T} = \nabla\mathbf{L}. \tag{5}$$

By introducing a Lagrange multiplier $\mathbf{Z}$ to remove the equality constraint, we have the augmented Lagrangian function of (5):

$$\mathcal{L}(\mathbf{R}, \mathbf{L}, \mathbf{T}, \mathbf{Z}) = \|\mathbf{R} \circ \mathbf{L} - \mathbf{I}\|_F^2 + \alpha\|\nabla\mathbf{R}\|_F^2 + \beta\|\mathbf{T}\|_1 \\ + \omega\|\nabla\mathbf{R} - \mathbf{G}\|_F^2 + \Phi(\mathbf{Z}, \nabla\mathbf{L} - \mathbf{T}),$$ (6)

where $\Phi(\mathbf{Z}, \nabla\mathbf{L} - \mathbf{T}) = \langle \mathbf{Z}, \nabla\mathbf{L} - \mathbf{T}\rangle + \frac{\mu}{2}\|\nabla\mathbf{L} - \mathbf{T}\|_F^2$ and $\langle\cdot,\cdot\rangle$ represents the matrix inner product. μ is a positive scalar. The equivalent objective function can be solved by iteratively updating each variable while regarding other variables that have been estimated in the previous iteration as constants.

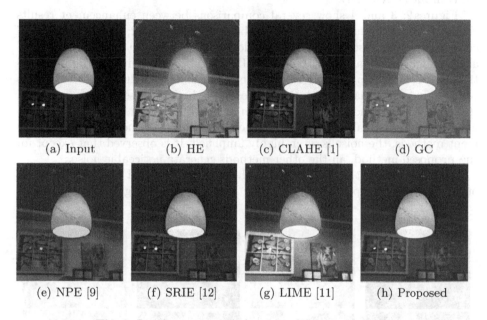

(a) Input   (b) HE   (c) CLAHE [1]   (d) GC

(e) NPE [9]   (f) SRIE [12]   (g) LIME [11]   (h) Proposed

Fig. 2. Results comparison between different methods.

3 Experimental Results

In this section, we demonstrate low-light image enhancement results. All experiments are conducted in MATLAB R2015b on a PC running Windows 10 OS with 16G RAM and 3.5 GHz CPU. In our experiments, the parameters α, β, and ω are empirically set as 0.001, 0.01, and 0.01, respectively.

After the estimation of the illumination $\mathbf{L}$ and the reflectance $\mathbf{R}$, the gamma correction operation is applied in order to adjust the illumination. And the final enhancement result $\mathbf{I}'$ is generated by:

$$\mathbf{I}' = \mathbf{R} \circ \hat{\mathbf{L}}^{\frac{1}{\gamma}},$$ (7)

where $\hat{\mathbf{L}}$ is the normalized $\mathbf{L}$, and γ is empirically set as 2.2.

We compare the proposed method with several state-of-the-art methods, including histogram equalization (HE), contrast limited adaptive histogram equalization (CLAHE) [1], gamma correction (GC), naturalness preserved enhancement algorithm (NPE) [9], simultaneous reflectance and illumination estimation (SRIE) [12], and low-light image enhancement via illumination map estimation (LIME) [11]. HE and CLAHE use the MATLAB built-in functions. GC is performed by $\mathbf{L}^{\gamma}$ with $\gamma = 5$. The codes of NPE, SRIE, and LIME are downloaded from the authors' websites. Test images come from LIME's website. In this work, we assume that each color channel has its own illumination and reflectance. Thus the proposed method is performed on different channels of the RGB input individually.

Figures 2, 3 and 4 show several comparisons between enhancement results generated by different methods. As can be observed in Fig. 2, CLAHE and SRIE cannot effectively restore the details hidden by the insufficient illumination. SRIE also generates halo artifacts. GC and LIME significantly improve the illumination, yet some parts of their results are over-enhanced. Although NPE shows comparable performance with the proposed method in these noise-free images, they fail to handle noisy cases. As shown in Fig. 3, the noise hidden in very low-light condition is really intense. After being processed by most of the enhancement methods, the noise is often highly amplified. It is observed that except for the proposed method, all the other methods generate noticeable noise.

We also provide the comparison of the proposed method with the results of other methods post-processed by BM3D [5]. As shown in Fig. 5, BM3D success-

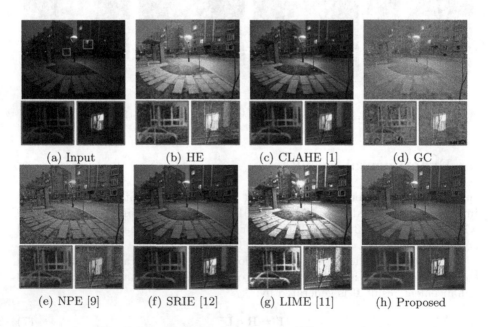

(a) Input   (b) HE   (c) CLAHE [1]   (d) GC

(e) NPE [9]   (f) SRIE [12]   (g) LIME [11]   (h) Proposed

Fig. 3. Results comparison between different methods.

Fig. 4. Comparison between different enhancement methods. (a)–(h): The input image, HE, CLAHE, SRIE, GC, LIME, NPE, and the proposed method.

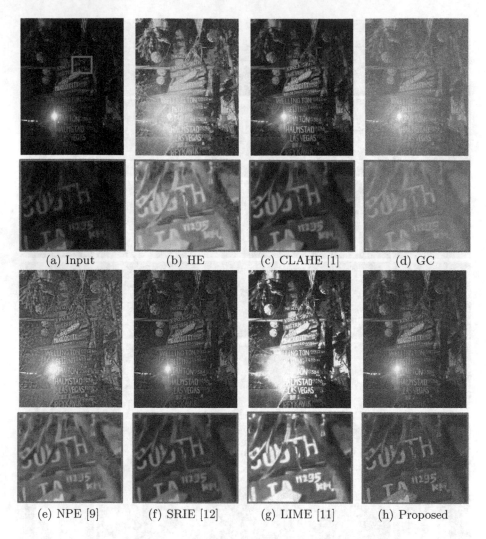

Fig. 5. Comparison of denoising results with the proposed method. (a) is the input image; (b)–(g) are enhancement results with a denoising procedure performed by BM3D with the denoising parameter $\sigma = 30$; (h) is the result obtained by the proposed method.

fully smoothes most of the amplified noise, but some details of the input image are also lost. By contrast, our result looks sharper and contains less noise.

4   Conclusion

The well-established Retinex model for intrinsic image decomposition faces challenges when being applied to low-light image enhancement due to the ignorance of the noise term. In this paper, we attempt to correct this point by introducing a noise term into the classic model. The new model naturally leads to a joint estimation for the reflectance and the illumination of the observed image. Specifically, the constraint on the gradient of the reflectance preserves the contrast of the final enhancement result. Experimental results show that our method can produce visually pleasing results for images captured under low-light situation.

References

1. Pizer, S.M., Johnston, R.E., Ericksen, J.P., Yankaskas, B.C., Muller, K.E.: Contrast-limited adaptive histogram equalization: speed and effectiveness. In: Proceedings of the Conference on Visualization in Biomedical Computing, pp. 337–345 (1990)
2. Abdullah-Al-Wadud, M., Kabir, M.H., Dewan, M.A.A., Chae, O.: A dynamic histogram equalization for image contrast enhancement. IEEE Trans. Consum. Electron. **53**(2), 593–600 (2007)
3. Li, L., Wang, R., Wang, W., Gao, W.: A low-light image enhancement method for both denoising and contrast enlarging. In: Proceedings of IEEE International Conference on Image Processing, pp. 3730–3734, September 2015
4. Zhang, X., Shen, P., Luo, L., Zhang, L., Song, J.: Enhancement and noise reduction of very low light level images. In: Proceedings of IEEE International Conference Pattern Recognition, pp. 2034–2037, November 2012
5. Dabov, K., Foi, A., Katkovnik, V., Egiazarian, K.: Image denoising by sparse 3-D transform-domain collaborative filtering. IEEE Trans. Image Process. **16**(8), 2080–2095 (2007)
6. Land, E.H., et al.: The Retinex Theory of Color Vision. Citeseer (1977)
7. Jobson, D.J., Rahman, Z., Woodell, G.A.: Properties and performance of a center/surround retinex. IEEE Trans. Image Process. **6**(3), 451–462 (1997)
8. Jobson, D.J., Rahman, Z., Woodell, G.A.: A multiscale retinex for bridging the gap between color images and the human observation of scenes. IEEE Trans. Image Process. **6**(7), 965–976 (1997)
9. Wang, S., Zheng, J., Hu, H.M., Li, B.: Naturalness preserved enhancement algorithm for non-uniform illumination images. IEEE Trans. Image Process. **22**(9), 3538–3548 (2013)
10. Fu, X., Zeng, D., Huang, Y., Liao, Y., Ding, X., Paisley, J.: A fusion-based enhancing method for weakly illuminated images. Signal Process. **129**, 82–96 (2016)
11. Guo, X., Li, Y., Ling, H.: Lime: low-light image enhancement via illumination map estimation. IEEE Trans. Image Process. **26**(2), 982–993 (2017)
12. Fu, X., Zeng, D., Huang, Y., Zhang, X.P., Ding, X.: A weighted variational model for simultaneous reflectance and illumination estimation. In: Proceedings of IEEE International Conference on Computer Vision and Pattern Recognition, pp. 2782–2790, June 2016
13. Lin, Z., Liu, R., Su, Z.: Linearized alternating direction method with adaptive penalty for low-rank representation. In: Proceedings of Annual Conference on Neural Information Processing Systems, pp. 612–620 (2011)

Terahertz Security Image Quality Assessment by No-reference Model Observers

Menghan Hu[1(✉)], Xiongkuo Min[1], Wenhan Zhu[1], Yucheng Zhu[1], Zhaodi Wang[1], Xiaokang Yang[1], and Guang Tian[2]

[1] Shanghai Institute for Advanced Communication and Data Science,
Shanghai Key Laboratory of Digital Media Processing and Transmission,
Shanghai Jiao Tong University, Shanghai 200240, People's Republic of China
humenghan@sjtu.edu.cn

[2] BOCOM Smart Network Technologies Inc., Shanghai 200433, People's Republic of China

Abstract. To provide the possibility of developing objective image quality assessment (IQA) algorithms for THz security images, we constructed the THz security image database (THSID) including a total of 181 THz security images. Subsequently, the existing no-reference IQA algorithms, which were 5 opinion-aware approaches viz., NFERM, GMLF, DIIVINE, BRISQUE and BLIINDS2, and 8 opinion-unaware approaches viz., QAC, SISBLIM, NIQE, FISBLIM, CPBD, S3 and Fish_bb, were executed for the evaluation of the THz security image quality. The statistical results demonstrated the superiority of Fish_bb over the other testing IQA approaches for assessing the THz image quality with PLCC (SROCC) values of 0.8925 (−0.8706), and with RMSE value of 0.3993. The linear regression analysis and Bland-Altman plot further verified that the Fish_bb could substitute for the subjective IQA. Nonetheless, for the classification of THz security images, we tended to use S3 as a criterion for ranking THz security image grades because of the relatively low false positive rate in classifying bad THz image quality into acceptable category (24.69%). Interestingly, due to the specific property of THz image, the average pixel intensity gave the best performance than the above complicated IQA algorithms, with the PLCC, SROCC and RMSE of 0.9001, −0.8800 and 0.3857, respectively. This study will help the users such as researchers or security staffs to obtain THz security images of good quality. Currently, our research group is attempting to make this research more comprehensive.

Keywords: Terahertz security image quality assessment · THz image database
THz imaging technique · Blind image quality assessment
THz security device

1 Introduction

Recently, terahertz (THz) imaging technique is rapidly developing worldwide, spurred by its powerful capability of acquiring useful data in respect to physics, chemistry, biology and medicine [1, 2]. In contrast to the other imaging approaches, owing to the prominent merits of THz imaging technique such as low photon energy and high transparency [3], THz imaging technique has been extensively studied as an analysis tool in almost all basic and applied domains such as biological diagnosis [4] and security

© Springer Nature Singapore Pte Ltd. 2018
G. Zhai et al. (Eds.): IFTC 2017, CCIS 815, pp. 100–114, 2018.
https://doi.org/10.1007/978-981-10-8108-8_10

inspection [5]. Nonetheless, the current THz imaging devices require several seconds to collect one image, and therefore, the ultimate THz image quality is significantly influenced by the variations of environmental factors and the performances of equipment [6]. According to the previous researches, the present THz imaging systems always generate the THz images of sufficient low quality [7, 8], which in turn affects the detection or prediction accuracies and hinders the extension of THz imaging technique to the large scale applications. Hence, the assurance of THz image of good or acceptable quality is an indispensable procedure during the practical applications.

The use of objective image quality assessment (IQA) method can provide an efficient solution to quantitatively evaluate the THz image quality, thus allowing the subsequent improvement of the THz image quality in hardware or software [9]. IQA is extremely important for the numerous image and video processing tasks [10], aiming to automatically examine image quality in agreement with human quality judgments [11] or task requirements. The existing objective IQA approaches are in general classified into three categories, which are full-reference, reduced-reference and no-reference or blind methods, depending on the accessibility of reference images [12, 13]. Nowadays, IQA has been widely used in many multimedia applications inclusive of image compression and video transmission [14]. In terms of THz imaging technique, IQA can be used as a criterion for assessing the performance of imaging system, optimizing image acquisition and processing modules, and monitoring the working conditions of imaging components. For the reason that it is highly hard to capture the perfect reference THz images in the real world THz imaging, the no-reference IQA algorithms are recommended for the further analysis in this study.

For IQA of specific image modalities, Chow and Paramesran summarized the IQA algorithms for various medical image types containing magnetic resonance image, computed tomography and ultrasonic image [15]. Like natural images, the IQA algorithms for these specific image modalities can also be applied to optimize imaging protocol [16] and improve detection accuracy [17]. Very limited research work has been conducted on the design of IQA algorithms to assess THz image quality. Fitzgerald et al. calculated the modulation transfer function from the amplitude of optical transfer function to verify the spatial resolution of THz image [9]. Hou et al. computed the mean square error of the peak values of time domain in a column's pixel to evaluate THz image quality [6]. However, their researches are not comprehensive, and therefore, the further studies are urgently needed.

There are some publications using IQA for assessing security image quality in specific modalities. Long and Li leveraged five image features viz., sharpness, brightness, resolution, head pose and expression to evaluate the NIR face image quality [18]. Wu et al. developed IQA software for monitoring the performance of X-ray security screening system [19]. A similar research was reported in a research paper by Irvine et al. [20]. This team of investigators presented an IQA protocol to quantitatively evaluate the X-ray image quality for baggage screening. IQA algorithms were also applied as measures to identify whether the biometric samples were fake or real [21–23]. Nevertheless, to the best of our knowledge, there is no publication in respect to IQA of THz security image.

Thus, the objectives of the current work are to: (1) establish the THz security image database (THSID) and give the corresponding mean opinion scores (MOSs) for each image in proposed database; (2) adopt the existing no-reference IQA algorithms for the evaluation of the THz security images and automatically classify the THz security images into two grades; and (3) discuss the significance of IQA approach in the development of THz imaging technique and forecast the future research tendency.

2   Methods

2.1   THz Security Image Database (THSID)

THSID contains a total of 181 THz security images with the resolution of 127×380. To generate THSID, four volunteers were invited to stand in the THz device, and imaged with various legal goods such as bracelet or illegal substances such as hammer each time. A raw THz image is a three-dimensional image cube, which can be revealed in Fig. 1. The two-dimensional THz image used in this paper is extracted from the three-dimensional THz image cube by combining the maximum pixels in the Z direct into the new two-dimensional plane.

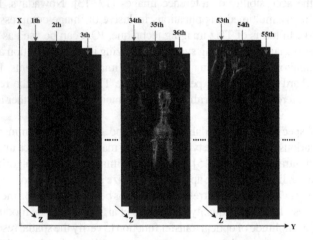

Fig. 1. One sample for the explanation of three-dimensional image cube.

Some source THz security images are presented in Fig. 2.

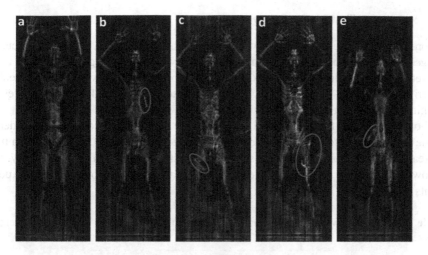

Fig. 2. Some source THz security images in THSID: (a) volunteer without any objects; (b) volunteer carrying mineral water in right chest; (c) volunteer taking knife in left pocket; (d) volunteer carrying hammer in right pocket; and (e) volunteer carrying plier in left abdomen. (Red circles are used to highlight the regions of legal or illegal substances) (Color figure online)

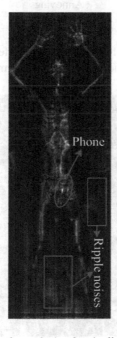

Fig. 3. One THz image example for the analysis of main distortion type in THz security images. (Red circle and rectangles are applied for highlighting the illegal target and ripple noises respectively) (Color figure online)

2.2 Subjective Test Methodology

Before the subjective experiments, we analyzed main distortion types in THz security images. Figure 3 shows one THz image with the volunteer taking phone in the right pocket, and the ripple noises caused by the unstable imaging device and changeable experimental factors make this target to be detected unidentified by human eyes or imaging processing algorithms.

For THz images, from the above analysis, these global ripple noises are considered as the major factors to seriously deteriorate THz security image quality, which in turn decrease the detection accuracy of security inspection equipment. Consequently, the following subjective evaluation criteria (Table 1) are proposed for subjective experiments.

Table 1. Subjective evaluation criteria using five-grade scale for image quality assessment of THz security image.

Score	Quality	Level of overall noise
5	Excellent	Acceptable
4	Good	Unacceptable, but not annoying
3	Fair	Slightly annoying
2	Poor	Annoying
1	Bad	Very annoying

With respect to each grade, the corresponding reference THz images (Fig. 4) are selected by two experts for conducting the double-stimulus method [24].

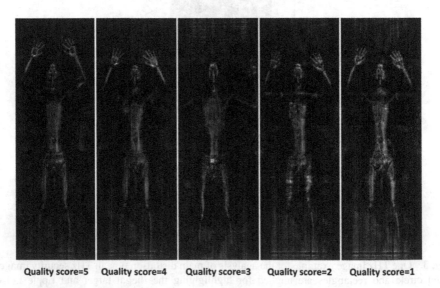

Quality score=5   Quality score=4   Quality score=3   Quality score=2   Quality score=1

Fig. 4. Five reference THz security images for each grade presented in Table 1.

A total of 15 observers including 2 experts and 13 subjects having no related expertise were recruited to assess the quality of THz security images. Prior to tests, the objective and procedure of this experiment were individually introduced to all observers in detail. The experiments were carried out under the normal indoor illumination of about 2400 lx. The testing images were displayed in the 23 inches LED monitor with the resolution of 1920×1080, and the viewing distance was set to 2–2.5 screen heights. After the experiments, the mean opinion scores (MOSs) of THz security images in THSID were obtained by the following equation.

$$MOS_j = \sum_{i=1}^{N} u_{i,j}/N_i \tag{1}$$

where N_i and $u_{i,j}$ denote the number of observers and the score of image j assigned by ith observer, respectively.

Figure 5 demonstrates the statistical distribution of MOSs.

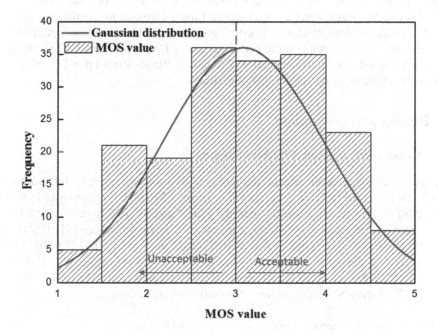

Fig. 5. Histogram of MOS values for THz security images in THSID.

As shown in Fig. 5, the distribution of MOSs in THSID follows the Gaussian distribution, ensuring the comprehensive examination of the used IQA algorithms.

Furthermore, the THz images whose MOSs are below and up 3 are regarded as the bad and acceptable categories, respectively. Because we are more concerned with is that whether the THz image quality could meet the inspector's acceptability or final applicable requirements in practical applications. Subsequently, the k-means clustering was utilized to classify the THz images into two categories using IQA features.

2.3   No-reference IQA Algorithms and Performance Metrics

A total of 13 no-reference IQA algorithms were executed in this study for evaluating the THz image quality. They are 5 opinion-aware approaches viz., NFERM [25], GMLF [26], DIIVINE [27], BRISQUE [28] and BLIINDS2 [29], and 8 opinion-unaware approaches viz., QAC [30], SISBLIM [31], NIQE [32], FISBLIM [33], CPBD [34], S3 [35], Fish_bb [36] and Sin [37]. Notice that the opinion-aware IQA methods used in this work employed natural images to establish the regression models.

In order to calculate the performance metrics, the monotonic logistic function of five parameters $\{\beta_1, \beta_2, \beta_3, \beta_4, \beta_5\}$ was first leveraged to fit the MOSs estimated by IQA algorithms, and the equation below was afterwards used to map the fitted objective scores to the subjective scores.

$$\text{Mapped Quality}(x) = \beta_1\left(1/2 - 1/\left(1 + e^{\beta_2(x-\beta_3)}\right)\right) + \beta_4 x + \beta_5 \qquad (2)$$

where Mapped Quality and x are mapped objective score and its original score.

Subsequently, three metrics viz., Pearson Linear Correlation Coefficient (PLCC), Spearman Rank-Order Correlation Coefficient (SROCC) and Root Mean Squared Error (RMSE) were used to examine the performances of IQA algorithms on THz security images. Moreover, the linear correlation plot and the Bland-Altman plot [38] were also used to check the effectiveness of IQA algorithms.

3   Results and Discussion

3.1   No-reference IQA for THz Security Images

The statistical data regarding the performances of five opinion-aware no-reference IQA methods is presented in Table 2. As shown in Table 2, BRISQUE was promising for the estimation of THz security images with the PLCC and SROCC as well as RMSE of 0.8001 and −0.7560 as well as 0.5309, respectively. The performances of DIIVINE and NFERM were slightly inferior to that of BRISQUE, with nearly 0.0277 (0.0312) and 0.0113 (0.0132) decrement (increment) in PLCC (RMSE), respectively. Both GMLF and BLIINDS2 did not yield desired results for the prediction of THz security images with the PLCC (RMSE) values below (beyond) 0.3500 (0.8000).

Table 2.   Performance metrics of five opinion-aware blind IQA methods for THz security image database. (The superior results are highlighted in boldface)

Criteria	IQA				
	NFERM	GMLF	DIIVINE	BRISQUE	BLIINDS2
	score	out	q	qualityscore	predicted_score
PLCC	0.7888	0.3298	0.7724	**0.8001**	0.2929
SROCC	0.5539	−0.2904	−0.7271	**−0.7560**	−0.2660
RMSE	0.5441	0.8356	0.5621	**0.5309**	0.8463

Table 3 summarizes performance metrics of seven opinion-unaware no-reference IQA algorithms for THSID database. As shown in Table 3, Fish_bb gave the best predictions than the other IQA approaches for assessing THz image quality, with PLCC (SROCC) values of 0.8925 (−0.8706), and with RMSE value of 0.3993. The performances of QAC, S3 and SISBLIM were comparable with that of Fish_bb, which produced the PLCC (SROCC) values of 0.8280 (0.7985), 0.8716 (−0.8560) and 0.8186 (−0.7915), and with RMSE values of 0.4963, 0.4339 and 0.5083, respectively. NIQE, FISBLIM, CPBD and SINE resulted in low PLCC (SROCC) and high RMSE values for the assessment of THz security image quality (below 0.5600 (0.4600) and beyond 0.7300, respectively). In contrast, Fish_bb achieved the slightly superior overall performance to S3, with the PLCC (SROCC) values of 0.8925 (−0.8706) versus 0.8716 (−0.8560), and with RMSE value of 0.3993 versus 0.4339 (Table 3).

Table 3. Performance metrics of eight opinion-unaware blind IQA methods for THz security image database. (The superior results are highlighted in boldface)

Criteria	IQA							
	QAC	SISBLI M	NIQE	FISBLI M	CPBD	SINE	S3	Fish_bb
	q	score3	quality	ss	metric_c pbd	noise_S D	s31	sh1
PLCC	**0.8280**	**0.8186**	0.4451	0.5512	0.2052	0.3457	**0.8716**	**0.8925**
SROCC	**0.7985**	**−0.7915**	−0.4025	−0.4501	0.1122	−0.3907	**−0.8560**	**−0.8706**
RMSE	**0.4963**	**0.5083**	0.7926	0.7385	0.8663	0.8305	**0.4339**	**0.3993**

Figure 6 visualizes the distributions of the estimated and reference MOSs. As shown in Fig. 6, for QAC, SISBLIM, S3 and Fish_bb, the scatter plots of predicted against reference MOSs clearly revealed that a majority of the THz image samples were mainly close to the line of perfect match (slope = 1) and within the 95% confidence intervals. The vertical distances between the upper and lower 95% confidence intervals were 1.61, 1.67, 1.50 and 1.42 for QAC, SISBLIM, S3 and Fish_bb respectively, indicating that Fish_bb performed better than the other algorithms for THz images in THSID database. In the case of linear regression analysis, Fish_bb was further verified to outperform QAC, SISBLIM and S3 with determination coefficients (R^2) of 0.80 versus 0.68, 0.67 and 0.76.

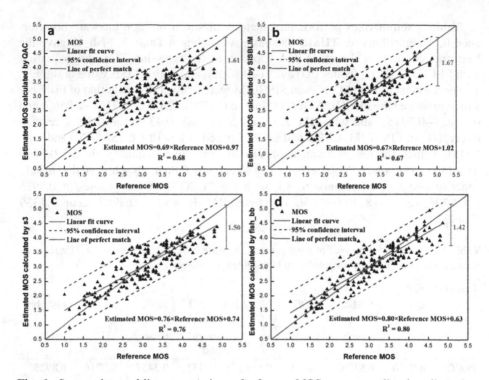

Fig. 6. Scatter plots and linear regressions of reference MOSs versus predicted quality using QAC (a), SISBLIM (b), S3 (c) and Fish_bb (d).

The Bland-Altman plot of reference and Fish_bb estimated MOS is demonstrated in Fig. 7. It could be observed that the distribution of points in Bland-Altman plot in Fig. 7 was quite similar to that in Fig. 6(d). Approximately 93.9% of data points located within the limits of agreement of 0.7848 and −0.7848 and the majority of points were dispersed around the line of perfect agreement, which further indicated that the Fish_bb objective IQA algorithm could substitute for the subjective IQA.

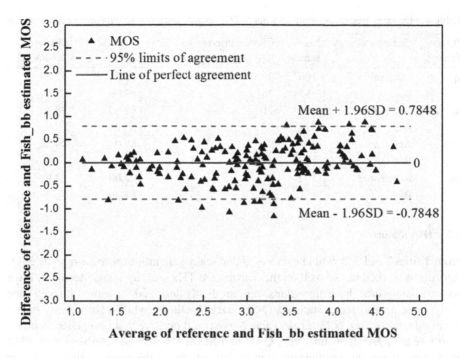

Fig. 7. Bland-Altman plot ($N = 181$ image samples) of the difference against average for THz IQA using subjective evaluation and Fish_bb objective IQA algorithm.

3.2 Classification of THz Security Images

In real world applications, we are more concerned with is that whether the THz image quality could meet the inspector's acceptability or final applicable requirements. Table 4 summarizes the unsupervised classification results of THz security image quality based on four IQA algorithms. The four IQA features viz., q, score3, s31 and sh1 achieved the overall classification accuracies of 77.35%, 78.45%, 79.56% and 83.98%, respectively. Although sh1 estimated by Fish_bb yielded the best classification result, 26 THz images of bad quality were classified as images of acceptable quality (Table 4). This illustrated that 26 THz images of bad quality would display on the screen for inspectors when 81 images of bad quality were generated by THz device. In this sense, we preferred to choose s31 calculated by S3 as a criterion to screen the THz images of bad quality with relatively low false positive rate of 24.69% (Table 4).

Table 4. Unsupervised classification results of THz security image quality using four IQA features.

IQA feature	Quality category	No. of sample	Classification result		Accuracy/%	Overall accuracy/%
			Acceptable	Bad		
q	Acceptable	100	85	15	85.00	77.35
	Bad	81	26	55	67.90	
score3	Acceptable	100	91	9	91.00	78.45
	Bad	81	30	51	62.96	
s31	Acceptable	100	83	17	87.00	79.56
	Bad	81	20	61	75.31	
sh1	Acceptable	100	97	3	97.00	83.98
	Bad	81	26	55	67.90	

3.3 Discussion

From Tables 2 and 3, it could be observed that many general-purpose no-reference IQA algorithms worked not so well on the constructed THz security image database. It was not surprising since those algorithms were implicitly designed for natural images, especially these natural scene statistics (NSS) based methods, while THz security images largely deviated from NSS. From Table 3, we could observe that two general-purpose no-reference IQA algorithms viz., QAC and SISBLIM worked relatively well. QAC performed quality-aware clustering, in which patches of the same quality level were clustered. During the training procedure of QAC, noisy images were used, and thus there could be clusters of noisy patches. Noisy patterns of natural images and THz images were very similar. This might be the reason why QAC performed relatively well. Similarly, SISBLIM also contained a module estimating noise. Besides these two algorithms, two sharpness algorithms viz., S3 and Fish_bb also worked relatively well. As illustrated in Fig. 4, it can be observed that high-quality THz security images have clean background, and the whole image is relatively smooth except for the target. Nonetheless, in THz images of low quality, the whole image is quite noisy and sharp. Consequently, sharpness algorithms can have low quality scores for THz images of high quality and high quality scores for THz images of low quality (data not shown), which is contrary to natural images. This reversed phenomenon has no effect on the final predictive ability of sharpness algorithm.

We tried to develop a new IQA algorithm to evaluate the THz image quality; however, the average pixel intensity of THz image achieved the good performance with the PLCC, SROCC and RMSE of 0.9001, −0.8800 and 0.3857, respectively, outperforming the Fish_bb and S3. The possible reason for this might be due to the fact that the THz images were to some extent similar to the binary images. The subjects perceived the white pixels in THz images as the noises, thus making the average pixel intensity work well. Hence, in terms of assessing noise level in THz images, the average pixel intensity could be used instead of the complicated IQA algorithms. In practice, the new subjective evaluation criteria were urgently required to obtain MOS values that could reflect both the noise level and perceived quality in region of interest (e.g. the regions containing illegal substances).

Actually, we were not sure that whether the THz display mode used in this work was better than the other display modes or not. For example, we could also use the cross profile of maximum average pixel intensity in Z direction to be displayed in the viewing screen for security staffs. Therefore, there existed two possible research contents for the further study: the first is to devise a rule (this rule could be an IQA algorithm) to confirm one best THz display mode for commercial applications and scientific researches, and the second is to design a series of IQA approaches for subjective and objective quality assessment of THz image (these algorithms could be developed on the basis of three-dimensional or two-dimensional THz images).

The possible application perspectives of the IQA of THz image quality could refer to commercial applications and scientific researches. For commercial applications, as shown in Fig. 8, the IQA indicator can guarantee THz security images of good quality displaying on the screen via reshoot or shooting parameters reset. With respect to scientific researches, we can use the IQA indicator as a criterion to assist in developing new THz security image processing algorithms such as THz image enhancement for THz imaging device (Fig. 8).

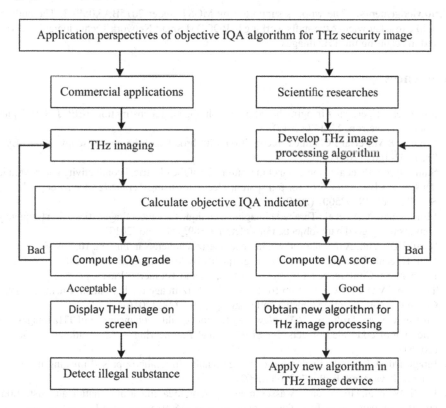

Fig. 8. Role of THz IQA algorithms in the overall THz security imaging system.

4 Conclusion

In this paper, we constructed the THz security image database (THSID) inclusive of 181 THz security images with the resolution of 127 × 380. The results of statistical metrics demonstrated that the Fish_bb objective IQA algorithm outperformed the existing no-reference IQA algorithms viz., NFERM, GMLF, DIIVINE, BRISQUE, BLIINDS2, QAC, SISBLIM, NIQE, FISBLIM, CPBD and S3, with PLCC (SROCC) values of 0.8925 (−0.8706), and with RMSE value of 0.3993. The linear regression analysis and Bland-Altman plot further verified that the Fish_bb could substitute for the subjective IQA. In respect to the classification of THz security images, S3 was preferred to be applied as an indicator for screening THz security image grades because of the low classification rate in classifying bad THz image quality into acceptable category. However, we found that the average pixel intensity could give the best performance than the above complicated IQA algorithms. Therefore, the average pixel intensity could be used as the indicator to evaluate the noise level of THz image in the practical application.

Acknowledgements. The work is supported by MOST under 2015BAK05B03. The authors would like to acknowledge the staffs working in BOCOM Smart Network Technologies Inc., who assisted in acquiring the THz images.

References

1. Shi, J., et al.: Terahertz imaging based on morphological reconstruction. IEEE J. Sel. Topics Quantum Electron. **23**, 1–7 (2017)
2. Fischer, B.M., et al.: Chemical recognition with broadband thz spectroscopy. Proc. IEEE **95**, 1592–1604 (2007)
3. Sung-Hyeon, P., et al.: Non-contact measurement of the electrical conductivity and coverage density of silver nanowires for transparent electrodes using Terahertz spectroscopy. Meas. Sci. Technol. **28**, 025001 (2017)
4. Moldosanov, K.A., et al.: Terahertz imaging technique for cancer diagnostics using frequency conversion by gold nano-objects. Ferroelectrics **509**, 158–166 (2017)
5. Suzuki, D., et al.: A flexible and wearable terahertz scanner. Nat. Photon. **10**, 809–813 (2016)
6. Hou, L., et al.: Enhancing terahertz image quality by finite impulse response digital filter. In: International Conference on Infrared, Millimeter, and Terahertz Waves, pp. 1–2 (2014)
7. Trofimov, V.A.: New algorithm for the passive THz image quality enhancement. In: SPIE Commercial + Scientific Sensing and Imaging, p. 98560L (2016)
8. Trofimov, V.A., Trofimov, V.V.: New way for both quality enhancement of THz images and detection of concealed objects. In: SPIE Optical Engineering + Applications, p. 95850R (2015)
9. Fitzgerald, A.J., et al.: Evaluation of image quality in terahertz pulsed imaging using test objects. Phys. Med. Biol. **47**, 3865 (2002)
10. Hanli, W., et al.: Image quality assessment based on local linear information and distortion-specific compensation. IEEE Trans. Image Process. **26**, 915–926 (2017)
11. Sheikh, H.R., et al.: A statistical evaluation of recent full reference image quality assessment algorithms. IEEE Trans. Image Process. **15**, 3440–3451 (2006)

12. Gu, K., et al.: Blind quality assessment of tone-mapped images via analysis of information, naturalness, and structure. IEEE Trans. Multimed. **18**, 432–443 (2016)
13. Gao, F., Yu, J.: Biologically inspired image quality assessment. Signal Process. **124**, 210–219 (2016)
14. Gu, K., et al.: The analysis of image contrast: from quality assessment to automatic enhancement. IEEE Trans. Cybern. **46**, 284–297 (2016)
15. Chow, L.S., Paramesran, R.: Review of medical image quality assessment. Biomed. Signal Process. Control **27**, 145–154 (2016)
16. Noferini, L., et al.: CT image quality assessment by a Channelized Hotelling Observer (CHO): application to protocol optimization. Phys. Med. Eur. J. Med. Phys. **32**, 1717–1723 (2016)
17. Hellen-Halme, K., et al.: Comparison of the performance of intraoral X-ray sensors using objective image quality assessment. Oral Surg. Oral Med. Oral Pathol. Oral Radiol. **122**, 784–785 (2016)
18. Jianfeng, L., Shutao, L.: Near infrared face image quality assessment system of video sequences. In: Proceedings of the Sixth International Conference on Image and Graphics, pp. 275–279 (2011)
19. Wu, W., et al.: Image quality assessment software of security screening system. In: 42nd Annual IEEE International Carnahan Conference on Security Technology, pp. 107–111 (2008)
20. Irvine, J., et al.: Perceived X-ray image quality for baggage screening. In: IEEE Applied Imagery Pattern Recognition Workshop, pp. 1–9 (2015)
21. Galbally, J., et al.: Image quality assessment for fake biometric detection: application to iris, fingerprint, and face recognition. IEEE Trans. Image Process. **23**, 710–724 (2014)
22. Pravallika, P., et al.: SVM classification for fake biometric detection using image quality assessment: application to iris, face and palm print. In: 2016 International Conference on Inventive Computation Technologie, vol. 1, pp. 55–60 (2016)
23. Selvi, J.A.G., et al.: Fake biometric detection using image quality assessment: application to iris, fingerprint recognition. In: 2th International Conference on Science Technology Engineering and Management, pp. 98–103 (2016)
24. ITU-R BT: Methodology for the subjective assessment of the quality of television pictures (2015)
25. Gu, K., et al.: Using free energy principle for blind image quality assessment. IEEE Trans. Multimed. **17**, 50–63 (2015)
26. Xue, W., et al.: Blind image quality assessment using joint statistics of gradient magnitude and Laplacian features. IEEE Trans. Image Process. **23**, 4850–4862 (2014)
27. Moorthy, A.K., Bovik, A.C.: Blind image quality assessment: from natural scene statistics to perceptual quality. IEEE Trans. Image Process. **20**, 3350–3364 (2011)
28. Mittal, A., et al.: No-reference image quality assessment in the spatial domain. IEEE Trans. Image Process. **21**, 4695–4708 (2012)
29. Saad, M.A., et al.: Blind image quality assessment: a natural scene statistics approach in the DCT domain. IEEE Trans. Image Process. **21**, 3339–3352 (2012)
30. Xue, W., et al.: Learning without human scores for blind image quality assessment. In: IEEE Conference on Computer Vision and Pattern Recognition, pp. 995–1002 (2013)
31. Gu, K., et al.: Hybrid no-reference quality metric for singly and multiply distorted images. IEEE Trans. Broadcast. **60**, 555–567 (2014)
32. Mittal, A., et al.: Making a "Completely Blind" image quality analyzer. IEEE Signal Process. Lett. **20**, 209–212 (2013)
33. Gu, K., et al.: FISBLIM: A Five-Step Blind Metric for quality assessment of multiply distorted images. In: 2013 IEEE Workshop on Signal Processing Systems, pp. 241–246 (2013)

34. Narvekar, N.D., Karam, L.J.: A no-reference image blur metric based on the cumulative probability of blur detection (CPBD). IEEE Trans. Image Process. **20**, 2678–2683 (2011)
35. Vu, C.T., et al.: S-3: a spectral and spatial measure of local perceived sharpness in natural images. IEEE Trans. Image Process. **21**, 934–945 (2012)
36. Vu, P.V., Chandler, D.M.: A fast wavelet-based algorithm for global and local image sharpness estimation. IEEE Signal Process. Lett. **19**, 423–426 (2012)
37. Zoran, D., Weiss, Y.: Scale invariance and noise in natural images. In: IEEE 12th International Conference on Computer Vision, pp. 2209–2216 (2009)
38. Carkeet, A., Goh, Y.T.: Confidence and coverage for Bland-Altman limits of agreement and their approximate confidence intervals. Stat. Methods Med. Res. 1–16 (2016)

Spatial-Temporal Recurrent Residual Networks for Video Super-Resolution

Wenhan Yang, Jiaying Liu, and Zongming Guo[✉]

Peking University, Beijing 100871, People's Republic of China
guozongming@pku.edu.cn

Abstract. In this paper, we propose a new video Super-Resolution (SR) method by jointly modeling intra-frame redundancy and inter-frame motion context in a unified deep network. Different from conventional methods, the proposed Spatial-Temporal Recurrent Residual Network (STR-ResNet) investigates both spatial and temporal residues, which are represented by the difference between a high resolution (HR) frame and its corresponding low resolution (LR) frame and the difference between adjacent HR frames, respectively. This spatial-temporal residual learning model is then utilized to connect the intra-frame and inter-frame redundancies within video sequences in a recurrent convolutional network and to predict HR temporal residues in the penultimate layer as guidance to benefit estimating the spatial residue for video SR. Extensive experiments have demonstrated that the proposed STR-ResNet is able to efficiently reconstruct videos with diversified contents and complex motions, which outperforms the existing video SR approaches and offers new state-of-the-art performances on benchmark datasets.

Keywords: Spatial residue · Temporal residue
Video super-resolution · Inter-frame motion context
Intra-frame redundancy

1 Introduction

Video super-resolution (SR) aims to produce high-resolution (HR) video frames from a sequence of low-resolution (LR) inputs. It is modeled as restoring the original scene $\mathbf{x}_t$ from its several quality-degraded observations $\{\mathbf{y}_t\}$. Typically, the observation can be modeled as

$$\mathbf{y}_t = \mathbf{D}_t\mathbf{x}_t + \mathbf{v}_t, t = 1, \ldots, T. \tag{1}$$

Here $\mathbf{D}_t$ encapsulates various signal quality degradation factors at the time instance t, *e.g.*, motion blur, defocus blur and down-sampling. Additive noise during observation at that time is denoted as $\mathbf{v}_t$. Generally, the SR problem, *i.e.*,

Z. Guo—This work was supported by National Natural Science Foundation of China under contract No. U1636206.

© Springer Nature Singapore Pte Ltd. 2018
G. Zhai et al. (Eds.): IFTC 2017, CCIS 815, pp. 115–127, 2018.
https://doi.org/10.1007/978-981-10-8108-8_11

solving out $\mathbf{x}_t$ in Eq. (1), is an ill-posed linear inverse problem that is rather challenging. Thus, accurately estimating $\mathbf{x}_t$ demands either sufficient observations $\mathbf{y}_t$ or proper priors on $\mathbf{x}_t$.

All video SR methods can be divided into two classes: reconstruction-based and learning-based. Reconstructed-based methods [1,4,5] craft a video SR process to solve the inverse estimation problem of (1). They usually perform motion compensation at first, then perform deblurring by estimating blur functions in $\mathbf{D}_t$ of (1), and finally recover details by local correspondences. The hand-crafted video SR process cannot be applicable for every practical scenario of different properties and perform not well to some unexpected cases.

In contrast, learning-based methods handle the ill-posed inverse estimation by learning useful priors for video SR from a large collection of videos. Typical methods include recently developed deep learning-based video SR methods [8–10] and give some examples of non-deep learning approaches. In [8], a funnel shape convolutional neural network (CNN) was developed to predict HR frames from LR frames that are aligned by optical flow in advance. It shows superior performance on recovering HR video frames captured in still scenes. However, this CNN model suffers from high computational cost (as it relies on time-consuming regularized optical flow methods) as well as visual artifacts caused by complex motions in the video frames. In [9,10], a bidirectional recurrent convolutional network (BRCN) was employed to model the temporal correlation among multiple frames and further boost the performance for video SR over previous methods.

However, previous learning-based video SR methods that learn to predict HR frames directly based on LR frames, suffer from following limitations. First, these methods concentrate on exploiting between-frame correlations and does not *jointly* consider the intra- and inter-frame correlations that are both critical for the quality of video SR. This unfavorably limits the capacity of the network for recovering HR frames with complex contents. Second, the successive input LR frames are usually highly correlated with the whole signal of the HR frames, but are not correlated with the high frequency details of these HR images. In the case where dominant training frames present slow motion, the learned priors hardly capture hard cases, such as large movements and shot changes, where neighboring frames distinguished-contributed operations are needed. Third, it is desirable for the joint estimation of video SR to impose priors on missing high frequency signals. However, in previous methods, the potential constraints are directly enforced on the estimated HR frames.

To solve the above-mentioned issues, in this work, we propose a unified deep neural network architecture, **S**patial **T**emporal **R**ecurrent **Res**idual **Net**work (STR-ResNet), to *jointly* model the intra-frame and the inter-frame correlation in an end-to-end trainable manner. Compared with previous (deep) video SR methods [8–10], our proposed deep network model does not require explicit computation of optical flow or motion compensation. In addition, our proposed model unifies the convolutional neural networks (CNNs) and recurrent neural networks (RNNs) which are known to be powerful in modeling sequential data. Combining the spatial convolutional and temporal recurrent architectures enables our model to capture spatial and temporal correlations jointly. Specially, it models spatial and temporal correlations among multiple video frames jointly. The temporal residues of HR frames are predicted based on input LR frames along with their temporal residues to further regularize estimation of the spatial residues. This architectural choice enables the network to handle the videos containing complex motions in a moving scene, offering pleasant video SR results with few artifacts in a time-efficient way. Extensive experiments on video SR benchmark datasets clearly demonstrate the contribution of each component to the overall performance.

2   Spatial-Temporal Recurrent Residual Networks for Multi-frame SR

In this section, a basic network structure – SRes-CNN for spatial residual learning for single image SR is presented in formulation. Then, we construct a new proposed STR-ResNet by stacking and connecting the basic component – SRes-CNN for joint temporal learning is elaborated.

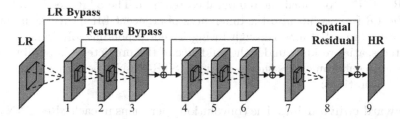

Fig. 1. The bypass structure and spatial residual learning in the proposed SRes-CNN. The *feature bypass* connection forwards the feature maps output from a previous layer (1st/4th) to a later one (4th/7th). The *LR bypass* from the LR frame to the last layer (9th) makes the network focus on predicting the residue, the high frequency component of a frame.

2.1   Architecture of SRes-CNN

Single frame SR aims to reconstruct an HR frame from a single LR frame. Some recent deep learning based SR methods [13–15] propose to use a CNN model to extract features from LR frames and then map them to HR ones. In our paper, we propose a new CNN architecture – Spatial Residual CNN (SRes-CNN) – to learn spatial residue between HR and LR frames. Specifically, SRes-CNN contains nice layers, including six convolutional layers, three bypass connections and three element-wise summations, as shown in Fig. 1. The bypass connections forward the feature maps output from the i-th layer ($i = 1, 4$ for the SRes-CNN we use in the experiments) to the $(i + 2)$-th layer directly. Then, the feature maps output from the $(i + 2)$-th and i-th layers are fused as input to the next

$(i + 3)$-th convolution layer. To focus on predicting the high-frequency components, SRes-CNN also establishes a bypass connection from the input LR frame to the penultimate layer. Note that, these two kinds of bypass connections play different roles in STR-ResNet. The first "long-range" one directly forwards an input LR frame to its penultimate layer (the 7th one). The other bypass connections provide a coarse-to-fine refinement. For example, the feature maps of the 1st layer correspond to the low-level features directly extracted from the LR image, and then the feature maps of the 3rd and 5th layers therefore concentrate on capturing the enhanced details of HR features. Besides, the bypass connections also make constructing a deeper network possible and speed up the training process [13].

2.2   Architecture of STR-ResNet

We now elaborate how the STR-ResNet exploits inter-frame correlation by connecting multiple SRes-CNNs with convolutions and how it incorporates temporal residual information for multi-frame SR. The intuition of choosing the architecture is to propagate information across multiple frames recurrently in order to capture the temporal context. STR-ResNet uses recurrent units to connect several SRes-CNNs to embed the temporal correlation. The STR-ResNet takes not only the LR frames but also the differences of adjacent LR frames as inputs. It reconstructs an HR frame through fusing its corresponding LR frame and the predicted spatial residue, under the guidance of the predicted temporal residues among adjacent frames. As shown in Fig. 2, STR-ResNet performs following six types of operations:

1. **Forward convolution.** The convolution operations in each SRes-CNN component for single frame SR.
2. **Recurrent convolution.** To propagate information across adjacent frames and restore lost information from the adjacent frames, STR-ResNet performs recurrent convolutions (the gray arrows between frames as shown in Fig. 2) to

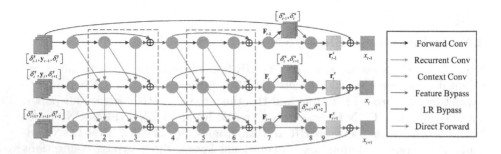

Fig. 2. The architecture of the STR-ResNet. It has a two-layer structure, which includes spatial and temporal residuals jointly in a unified deep framework.(Color figure online)

propagate the features of the i-th layer of the adjacent $(t-1)$-st and $(t+1)$-st frames (defined as $\mathbf{C}^a_{(t-1,i)}$ and $\mathbf{C}^a_{(t+1,i)}$) to the i-th layer of the t-th frame (defined as $\mathbf{C}^{r,p}_{(t,i)}$ and $\mathbf{C}^{r,n}_{(t,i)}$.)

3. **Context convolution.** With the similar intuition of transmitting complementary information among frames, the context convolution (the light-green arrows between frames as shown in Fig. 2) propagates the features of the $(i-1)$-th layer of the adjacent $(t-1)$-st and $(t+1)$-st frames (defined as $\mathbf{C}^a_{(t-1,i-1)}$ and $\mathbf{C}^a_{(t+1,i-1)}$) to the i-th layer of the t-th frame (defined as $\mathbf{C}^{c,p}_{(t,i)}$ and $\mathbf{C}^{c,n}_{(t,i)}$.)

4. **Temporal residue embedding.** In the 8th layer, we first predict the temporal residues (the green rectangles between the 7-th and 8-th layers as shown in Fig. 2). In the training, these outputs are constrained by the loss function to regress the ground-truth temporal residues, which will be presented more clearly in the next subsection. Then, we concatenate the predicted temporal residues with the output feature maps from the 7th layer to generate the output feature maps of the 8th layer.

5. **Feature bypass.** The operation to transmit the features output from the 1st/4th layers and combine them with the output of the 3rd/6th layers respectively.

6. **LR bypass.** It bypasses the LR frames to the output of the 8th layer, which generates the estimated HR details of frame t.

7. **Feed forward.** The operation to propagate the feature maps to the subsequent unit.

Among these operations, the recurrent and context convolutions are only deployed in the 2nd, 3rd, 5th and 6th layers of SRes-CNNs as shown in Fig. 2 (b). All the recurrent connections transmit outputs of layers (2nd, 3rd, 5th and 6th) on the t-th frame to their corresponding layers (2nd, 3rd, 5th and 6th) of the adjacent $(t-1)$-th and $(t+1)$-th frames. All the context connections transmit from a previous layer (1st, 2nd, 4th and 5th) of the t-th frame to their corresponding next layer (2nd, 3rd, 5th and 6th) of the adjacent $(t-1)$-th and $(t+1)$-th frames. After all these convolutions, an element-wise summation operation is employed to fuse these convolution outputs and produce a new feature map. The outputs of the five convolutional operations and the fusion are formulated as follows,

$$
\begin{aligned}
\mathbf{C}^f_{(t,i)} &= \mathbf{W}^f_i * \mathbf{C}^a_{(t,i-1)} + \mathbf{B}^f_i, \\
\mathbf{C}^{c,p}_{(t,i)} &= \mathbf{W}^{c,p}_i * \mathbf{C}^a_{(t-1,i-1)} + \mathbf{B}^{c,p}_i, \\
\mathbf{C}^{c,n}_{(t,i)} &= \mathbf{W}^{c,n}_i * \mathbf{C}^a_{(t+1,i-1)} + \mathbf{B}^{c,n}_i, \\
\mathbf{C}^{r,p}_{(t,i)} &= \mathbf{W}^{r,p}_i * \mathbf{C}^a_{(t-1,i)} + \mathbf{B}^{r,p}_i, \\
\mathbf{C}^{r,n}_{(t,i)} &= \mathbf{W}^{r,n}_i * \mathbf{C}^a_{(t+1,i)} + \mathbf{B}^{r,n}_i, \\
\mathbf{C}^a_{(t,i)} &= \max\left(0, \mathbf{C}^f_{(t,i)} + \mathbf{C}^{c,p}_{(t,i)} + \mathbf{C}^{c,n}_{(t,i)} + \mathbf{C}^{r,p}_{(t,i)} + \mathbf{C}^{r,n}_{(t,i)}\right),
\end{aligned}
\tag{2}
$$

where $i = 2, 3, ..., 6$, and $\mathbf{W}$ and $\mathbf{B}$ are filters and biases, respectively. The superscripts f, c, r and a denote the unit type – forward convolution, context convolution, recurrent convolution and element-wise summation aggregation. The superscripts p, n denote the direction of the convolution, from the previous frame or the next frame. The subscript (t, i) denotes that the operation is performed on the i-th layer of the t-th frame. Consequently, $\mathbf{C}^f_{(t,i)}$, $\mathbf{C}^{c,p}_{(t,i)}$, $\mathbf{C}^{c,n}_{(t,i)}$, $\mathbf{C}^{r,p}_{(t,i)}$ and $\mathbf{C}^{r,n}_{(t,i)}$ are the outputs of the forward convolution, context convolution from the previous frame, context convolution from the next frame, recurrent convolution from the previous frame and recurrent convolution from the next frame in the i-th layer of the t-th frame respectively. $\mathbf{C}^a_{(t,i)}$ performs an element-wise summation overall all the five outputs, for combining the predictions from the current frame and adjacent frames. A ReLU unit is then connected subsequently. The responses of previous layers are as follows,

$$\mathbf{C}^a_{(t,i)} = \mathbf{C}^f_{(t,i)}, \text{ for } i = 1, 4, 7, 9. \tag{3}$$

For the 8st layer, we try to predict the temporal residues of HR frames and utilize them as parts of the features to estimate the spatial residues,

$$\delta^{\mathbf{x}}_t = \mathbf{W}_\delta * \mathbf{C}^a_{(t,7)} + \mathbf{b}_\delta, \mathbf{C}^a_{(t,8)} = \left[\mathbf{C}^a_{(t,7)}, \delta^{\mathbf{x}}_t \right]. \tag{4}$$

With the help of context and recurrent convolutions as well as the temporal residue constraints, the STR-ResNet captures the inter-frame motion context propagated from adjacent frames for video SR.

2.3   Training STR-ResNet

To learn meaningful features and capture some consistent motion contexts between frames, STR-ResNet shares its parameters among different frames. That is, for all $\mathbf{C}^f_{(t,i)}$, $\mathbf{C}^{c,p}_{(t,i)}$, $\mathbf{C}^{c,n}_{(t,i)}$, $\mathbf{C}^{r,p}_{(t,i)}$, and $\mathbf{C}^{r,n}_{(t,i)}$, their parameters $\left\{ \mathbf{W}^f_i, \mathbf{B}^f_i \right\}$, $\{\mathbf{W}^{c,p}_i, \mathbf{B}^{c,p}_i\}$, $\{\mathbf{W}^{c,n}_i, \mathbf{B}^{c,n}_i\}$, $\{\mathbf{W}^{r,p}_i, \mathbf{B}^{r,p}_i\}$ and $\{\mathbf{W}^{r,n}_i, \mathbf{B}^{r,n}_i\}$, are decided by the unit type, denoted by superscript, and layer depth, and have nothing to do with the frame number.

For training STR-ResNet, provided with LR video frames $\{\mathbf{y}^g_t\}$ and HR frames $\{\mathbf{x}^g_t\}$, we minimize the Mean Square Error (MSE) between the predicted frames and the ground truth HR frames:

$$\min_{\mathbf{\Theta}} \sum_{t=1}^{9} \lambda_t \|\widehat{\mathbf{x}}_t \left(\mathbf{y}^g_t, \mathbf{\Theta} \right) + \mathbf{y}^g_t - \mathbf{x}^g_t\|^2_F + c \sum_{t=1}^{9} \|\widehat{\delta^{\mathbf{x}}_t} \left(\mathbf{y}^g_t, \mathbf{\Theta} \right) + \mathbf{x}^g_t - \mathbf{x}^g_{t-1}\|^2_F, \tag{5}$$

where

$$\mathbf{\Theta} = \left(\mathbf{W}^f, \mathbf{B}^f, \mathbf{W}^{c,p}, \mathbf{B}^{c,p}, \mathbf{W}^{c,n}, \mathbf{B}^{c,n}, \mathbf{W}^{r,p}, \mathbf{B}^{r,p}, \mathbf{W}^{r,n}, \mathbf{B}^{r,n} \right), \tag{6}$$

$\mathbf{x}^g_0 = \mathbf{x}^g_1$ and $\{\lambda_i, i = 1, 2, ..., 8, 9\}$ are the weighting parameters that control the relative importance of these terms. c is set to 0.1 to play a role but not the dominant one. We set $n_T = 9$ as the step/recurrence number following the default setting in the previous RNN-based video SR method [9].

3 Experiments

3.1 Experiments Setting

The compared single image SR baselines include Bicubic interpolation and super-resolution convolution neural network (SRCNN) [13]. The compared video SR baselines include a commercial software video enhancer (VE)[1], 3DSKR [18], Draft SR [8] and BRCN [9]. To evaluate the effectiveness of our method, we simulate the degradation process and enlarge the generated LR images to their original scales. Peak Signal to Noise Ratio (PSNR) is chosen as the metric. The testing scaling factor is chosen as 4. In the simulation of degradation, the LR frames are generated by blurring HR frames with a 9×9 Gaussian filters with blur level 1.6.

For training our STR-ResNet, we use 300 collected video sequences, sampled uniformly from 30 high-quality 1080p HD video clips as our training set[2,3]. We use 6 HDTV sequences (*Tractor, Sunflower, Blue Sky, Station, Pedestrian, Rush Hour*) downloaded from the Xiph.org Video Test Media (see footnote 2) as the testing set, which are commonly used high quality video sequences for video coding testing. To reduce the memory storage needed in the training phrase, we crop these frame groups into 75,000 overlapped patch groups as the input of training. Each patch group contains 9 adjacent patches in the temporal domain with the same location in the spatial domain. Similar to [13], the size of the spatial window of each patch group is set to 33×33 and the spatial stride is set to 11.

The proposed STR-ResNet uses the following parameters: all convolutions have a kernel size of 3×3 and a padding size 1; the layer type and number are set as mentioned above; the channel size of the intermediate layers is set to 64. We employ stochastic gradient descent[4] to train the whole network. The training strategy is standard: learning rates of weights and biases of these filters are set to 0.0001 initially and decrease to 0.00001 after 2.5×10^5 iterations (about 37 epochs). We stop the training in 3×10^5 iterations (about 44 epochs). The batch size is set to 6.

3.2 Objective Evaluation

Tables 1 shows PSNR results of compared video super-resolution methods on the testing image set. The proposed method and the BRCN method are evaluated

---

[1] http://www.infognition.com/videoenhancer/.

[2] **Xiph.org Video Test Media [derf's collection]**, https://media.xiph.org/video/derf/.

[3] **Dataset from Harmonic Inc.**, http://www.harmonicinc.com/resources/videos/4k-video-clip-center.

[4] http://caffe.berkeleyvision.org/tutorial/solver.html.

with 9 adjacent frames as inputs. For Draft Learn, we report its results in two cases: (1) taking 31 adjacent LR frames (Draft31) as its input; (2) taking 5 adjacent LR frames (Draft5) as its input. For 3DSKR, the HR estimation is generated based on adjacent 5 LR frames. From the result, one can observe that even compared with the recent Draft Learning and BRCN, our proposed STR-ResNet achieves a significant performance gain over them. In particular, the average gain over the second best BRCN is as high as 0.56 dB. VE and 3DKR achieve better reconstructed results than Bicubic. However, their PSNR results are lower than very recent single image SR methods, such as SRCNN and A+, which only make use of the intra-frame spatial correlation.

Table 1. PSNR results among different methods for Video SR (scaling factor: 4). The bold numbers denote the best performance.

Video	Bicubic	SRCNN	VE	3DSKR	Draft	BRCN	STR-ResNet
Tractor	31.10	32.13	31.27	32.27	30.34	33.23	**33.85**
Sunflower	37.85	38.69	37.55	37.57	36.43	39.28	**40.02**
Blue Sky	28.77	30.16	29.19	29.74	30.92	31.40	**32.23**
Station	33.35	34.38	33.36	34.80	33.22	35.20	**35.63**
Pedestrian	33.51	34.55	33.60	33.91	31.78	34.95	**35.22**
Rush Hour	38.17	38.90	37.96	37.49	36.22	39.86	**40.30**
Average	33.79	34.80	33.82	34.30	33.15	35.65	**36.21**

3.3   Subjective Evaluation

Figures 3 visualize the SR results of different methods. Bicubic generates blurred results. SRCNN generate sharper results. However, without exploiting the temporal correlation, some visually important features are blurred, such as the brand text in Fig. 3. In contrast, video SR methods, such as 3DSKR and Draft Learning, generate results with richer details. But 3DSKR may suffer from inaccurate motion estimation and generate block artifacts, and Draft Learning produces granular artifacts in smooth regions, where optical flow estimation is unreliable. Due to RNN's strong capacity of modeling complex motions, BRCN and our method present rather sharp results. Especially, the proposed STR-ResNet recovers details with a very natural look (Figs. 4 and 5).

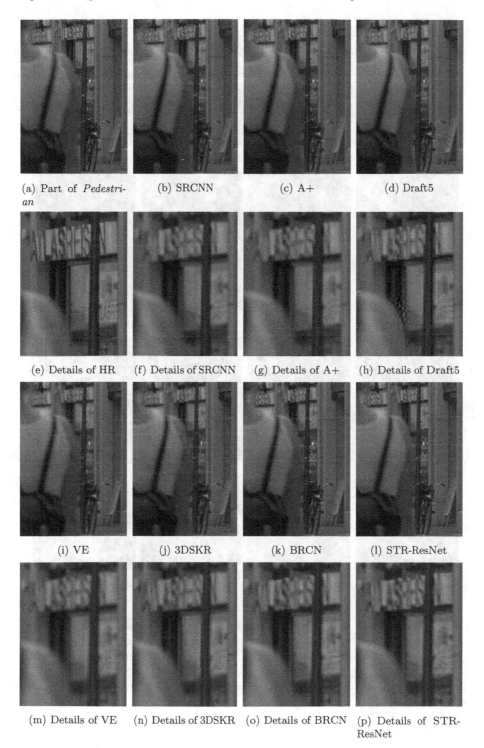

(a) Part of *Pedestrian*   (b) SRCNN   (c) A+   (d) Draft5

(e) Details of HR   (f) Details of SRCNN   (g) Details of A+   (h) Details of Draft5

(i) VE   (j) 3DSKR   (k) BRCN   (l) STR-ResNet

(m) Details of VE   (n) Details of 3DSKR   (o) Details of BRCN   (p) Details of STR-ResNet

Fig. 3. The reconstruction results of *Pedestrian* with different methods (enlarge factor: 4×).

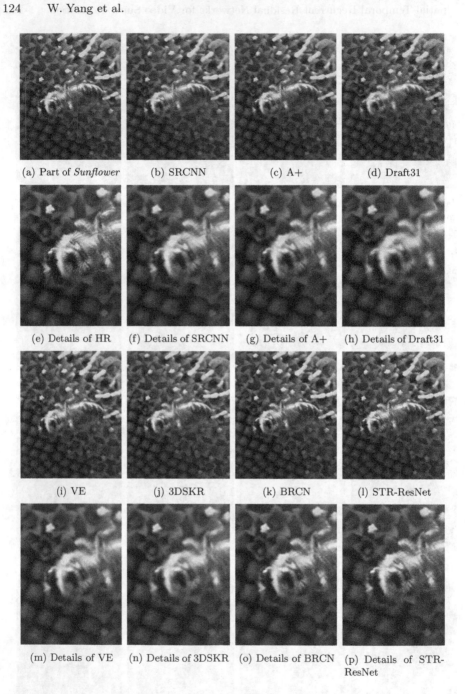

(a) Part of *Sunflower*   (b) SRCNN   (c) A+   (d) Draft31

(e) Details of HR   (f) Details of SRCNN   (g) Details of A+   (h) Details of Draft31

(i) VE   (j) 3DSKR   (k) BRCN   (l) STR-ResNet

(m) Details of VE   (n) Details of 3DSKR   (o) Details of BRCN   (p) Details of STR-ResNet

Fig. 4. The reconstruction results of *Sunflower* with different methods (enlarge factor: 4×).

(a) Part of *Tractor*   (b) SRCNN   (c) A+   (d) Draft31

(e) Details of HR   (f) Details of SRCNN   (g) Details of A+   (h) Details of Draft31

(i) VE   (j) 3DSKR   (k) BRCN   (l) STR-ResNet

(m) Details of VE   (n) Details of 3DSKR   (o) Details of BRCN   (p) Details of STR-ResNet

Fig. 5. The reconstruction results of *Tractor* with different methods (enlarge factor: 4×).

4   Conclusion and Future Work

In this paper, we proposed a novel Spatial-Temporal Recurrent Residual Network (STR-ResNet) for video super-resolution. This network simultaneously models high frequency details of single frames, the differences between high resolution (HR) and low resolution (LR) frames, as well as the changes of these adjacent detail frsames. To model intra-frame correlation, a CNN structure with bypass connections is constructed to learn spatial residual of a single frame. To model inter-frame correlation, STR-ResNet estimates the temporal residue implicitly. Extensive experiments have demonstrated the effectiveness and efficiency of our method for video SR.

References

1. Liu, C., Sun, D.: On bayesian adaptive video super resolution. IEEE Trans. Pattern Anal. Mach. Intell. **36**(2), 346–360 (2014)
2. Baker, S., Kanade, T.: Super-Resolution Optical Flow (1999)
3. He, H., Kondi, L.P.: An image super-resolution algorithm for different error levels per frame. IEEE Trans. Image Process. **15**(3), 592–603 (2006)
4. Kanaev, A.V., Miller, C.W.: Multi-frame super-resolution algorithm for complex motion patterns. Opt. Express **21**(17), 19850–19866 (2013)
5. Omer, O.A., Tanaka, T.: Region-based weighted-norm approach to video super-resolution with adaptive regularization. In: Proceedings of IEEE International Conference Acoustics, Speech, and Signal Processing, pp. 833–836 (2009)
6. Farsiu, S., Robinson, M.D., Elad, M., Milanfar, P.: Fast and robust multiframe super resolution. IEEE Trans. Image Process. **13**(10), 1327–1344 (2004)
7. Rudin, L.I., Osher, S., Fatemi, E.: Nonlinear total variation based noise removal algorithms. Physica D **60**(1–4), 259–268 (1992)
8. Liao, R., Tao, X., Li, R., Ma, Z., Jia, J.: Video super-resolution via deep draft-ensemble learning. In: Proceedings of IEEE International Conference Computer Vision, pp. 531–539 (2015)
9. Huang, Y., Wang, W., Wang, L.: Bidirectional recurrent convolutional networks for multi-frame super-resolution. In: Proceedings of Annual Conference on Neural Information Processing Systems, pp. 235–243 (2015)
10. Huang, Y., Wang, W., Wang, L.: Video super-resolution via bidirectional recurrent convolutional networks. IEEE Trans. Pattern Anal. Mach. Intell. **99**, 1–1 (2017)
11. Wu, W., Zheng, C.: Single image super-resolution using self-similarity and generalized nonlocal mean. In: IEEE International Conference of IEEE Region, pp. 1–4 (2013)
12. Dong, W., Zhang, L., Shi, G.: Centralized sparse representation for image restoration. In: Proceedings of IEEE International Conference Computer Vision, pp. 1259–1266 (2013)
13. Dong, C., Loy, C.C., He, K., Tang, X.: Image super-resolution using deep convolutional networks. In: Proceedings of IEEE European Conference Computer Vision (2014)
14. Wang, Z., Liu, D., Yang, J., Han, W., Huang, T.: Deep networks for image super-resolution with sparse prior. In: Proceedings of IEEE International Conference Computer Vision, pp. 370–378 (2015)

15. Yang, W., Feng, J., Yang, J., Zhao, F., Liu, J., Guo, Z., Yan, S.: Deep edge guided recurrent residual learning for image super-resolution. arXiv:1604.08671
16. Kim, J., Lee, J.K., Lee, K.M.: Deeply-recursive convolutional network for image super-resolution. In: Proceedings of IEEE International Conference Computer Vision and Pattern Recognition, pp. 1637–1645 (2016)
17. Timofte, R., De Smet, V., Van Gool, L.: A+: adjusted anchored neighborhood regression for fast super-resolution. In: Proceedings of IEEE Asia Conference Computer Vision (2014)
18. Takeda, H., Milanfar, P., Protter, M., Elad, M.: Super-resolution without explicit subpixel motion estimation. IEEE Trans. Image Process. **18**(9), 1958–1975 (2009)
19. Jia, Y., Shelhamer, E., Donahue, J., Karayev, S., Long, J., Girshick, R., Guadarrama, S., Darrell, T.: Caffe: convolutional architecture for fast feature embedding. In: ACM International Conference on Multimedia, pp. 675–678 (2014)
20. Dong, C.: Image super-resolution using deep convolutional networks. IEEE Trans. Pattern Anal. Mach. Intell. **38**(2), 295–307 (2016)
21. Kim, J., Lee, J.K., Lee, K.M.: Accurate image super-resolution using very deep convolutional networks. In: Proceedings of IEEE Internetional Conference Computer Vision and Pattern Recognition, pp. 1646–1654 (2016)
22. Lai, W.-S., Huang, J.-B., Ahuja, N., Yang, M.-H.: Deep Laplacian pyramid networks for fast and accurate super-resolution. ArXiv e-prints
23. Timofte, R., Smet, V.D., Gool, L.V.: Semantic super-resolution: when and where is it useful? Comput. Vis. Image Underst. **142**, 1–12 (2016)

Depth Image Denoising via Collaborative Graph Fourier Transform

Rong Chen, Xianming Liu$^{(\boxtimes)}$, Deming Zhai, and Debin Zhao

School of Computer Science and Technology, Harbin Institute of Technology,
Harbin 150001, China
csxm@hit.edu.cn

Abstract. Depth maps offer partial geometric information of a 3D scene, and thus have been widely used in various image processing and computer vision task. However, due to the limitation of capturing devices, depth images usually suffer from noises. How to remove noises containing in depth images become an important problem, which will benefit many practical applications. Depth image denoising is ill-posed, whose performance largely relies on the prior knowledge of depth images. In this paper, we propose a patch-wise depth image denoising algorithm which exploits intra-patch and inter-patch correlations represented by graph. Specifically, we first cluster similar patches in a depth map, and then stack them together into a 3D group. For each patch, a fully-connected 2D graph is built to model the intra-patch correlation among pixels. Furthermore, the employ the inter-patch correlation, we construct 1D fully connected graph, in which each node represents a patch in the collected group. Finally, a collaborative filtering based on 3D graph Fourier transform (GFT) is conducted on the 3D patch group. We conduct shrinkage of the transform coefficients to get the denoised patches. Experimental results demonstrate that our proposed approach outperforms state-of-the-art image denoising methods in both objective results and subjective visual quality.

Keywords: Graph Fourier transform · Graph signal processing
Depth image denoising

1 Introduction

Depth maps can be simply obtained at present, leveraging on the advances in depth sensing technologies such as Microsoft Kinect. Acquired depth maps can be used for advanced imaging applications, such as depth-image-based rendering (DIBR) [1]. However, caused by the limitation of hardware, the obtained result suffers a series of problems, such as blurred edge, low resolution and loss of local depth information. Thus the reconstruction of depth maps from their corrupted versions remains important in depth map processing.

Since image restoration is an inverse problem, which is intrinsically ill-posed, it is necessary to find appropriate image priors. Various image prior have been

© Springer Nature Singapore Pte Ltd. 2018
G. Zhai et al. (Eds.): IFTC 2017, CCIS 815, pp. 128–137, 2018.
https://doi.org/10.1007/978-981-10-8108-8_12

proposed, such as total variation (TV) [2] and sparsity prior [3]. TV regularization can effectively remove the noise artifacts but often oversmooth the images due to the piecewise constant assumption. Sparsity-based regularization assuming that natural images can be sparsely represented using a few atoms of an appropriate over-complete dictionary, has successfully been used in a wide range of image restoration problems [4–6]. Due to the advances in graph signal processing (GSP) [7,8], a relatively simple but useful new prior—graph Laplacian regularizer, has been presented. Graph Laplacian regularizer can describe the underlying structure of the graph-signal, which relies on the graph Laplacian matrix of a constructed graph. For image restoration problem, one can interpret an image (or image patch) as a graph-signal residing on a finite graph G, where pixels can be viewed as the vertices of graph, and the correlation between two adjacent pixels is represented by edge weight. Given a defined graph, graph Laplacian regularization has been prensented for various inverse imaging problems, such as denoising [9,10], deblurring [11], super-resolution [12], and interpolation [13,14].

Notice the fact that different from typical RGB color images, a depth image is a per-pixel map (depth value measures the physical distance between objects in the 3D scene and the capturing camera). In other words, depth images consist of sharp boundaries and smooth interior surfaces, due to the textural information of objects are not captured, and hence piecewise smooth (PWS). In this paper, we use the graph-signal smoothness prior, which was shown to perform particularly well when restoring piecewise smooth signal [15–17], to propose an novel 3D collaborative filtering in graph Fourier transform (GFT) domain. More specifically, for depth image denoising, we first cluster similar patches and stack them together into 3D groups. Then for each group, we can construct a full-connected graph describing the correlations among all the pixels. Next, we transform each 2D patch to a GFT domain, where the GFT matrix can be computed from the constructed graph. And then, we apply a 1D transform across the grouped patches in the same way. Finally, by using the smoothness prior in the 3D GFT domain, we can formulate an iterative quadratic programming problem, which has a closed form solution.

As our contribution, we propose a novel image denoising approach based on a 3D collaborative filtering in GFT domain. Different from other collaborative transform methods, like BM3D [18], we use GFT on weighted graph, which is signal dependent. Note that BM3D use the Discrete Cosine Transform (DCT), which is a fixed transform without signal adaptation and the edge weight describing correlation between each adjacent pixels is assumed to be 1. Like DCT, projecting a signal onto GFT is a simple linear operation, but GFT can describe the unique underlying structure of signal on each patch and can be used for signal adaptive processing. Experimental results demonstrated that our proposed denoising method can outperform state-of-the-art image denoising methods in both objective and subjective evaluations noticeably.

The rest of the paper is organized as follows. In Sect. 2, the proposed image denoising algorithm is developed and described in detail. The experimental results are presented in Sect. 3 and conclusions are drawn in Sect. 4.

2   The Proposed Method

The proposed method is inspired by that the graph-signal smoothness prior can achieve particularly performance for piecewise smooth signals (such as depth map) restoration. We first introduce the definition of a weighted graph. Next, we interpret a graph-signal smoothness in the graph frequency domain. Finally, we propose a new 3D collaborative filtering in graph Fourier transform domain using graph-signal smoothness prior.

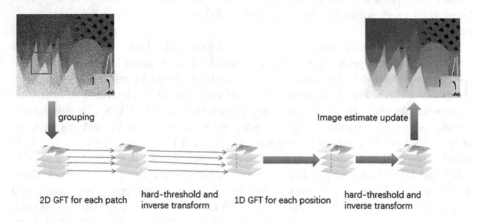

Fig. 1. Illustration of our depth images denoising method for one iteration. At stage $t+1$, we first cluster similar patches from the current result $\mathbf{x}_t$ and stack them together into 3D groups. After 2D transform for each patch, perform 1D transform for each position. Finally, averaging each reconstructed patch, we update the estimate image $\mathbf{x}_{t+1}$.

2.1   Signal on Weighted Graph

A graph is conventionally defined as $\mathcal{G} = (\mathbf{V}, \mathcal{E}, \mathbf{W})$, where $\mathbf{V}$ is a set of vertices connected with corresponding edges $\mathcal{E}$. $\mathbf{W}$ is a adjacent matrix, with $W_{i,j}$ as the weight of the edge connecting vertices i and j. We only consider undirected graphs [19], which means $\mathbf{W}$ is symmetric weighted adjacency matrices, i.e., $W_{i,j} = W_{j,i}$. Here, weights are also assumed non-negative, i.e., $W_{i,j} \geq 0$.

Specially for image patch signal, we can view each pixel in the $n \times n$ patch as a vertex in a graph $\mathcal{G}$, then connect it to all other vertices in the patch, with $W_{i,j}$ as the weight modeling the similarity between pixels i and j, resulting a full-connected graph. The weight $W_{i,j}$ can be computed using Gaussian kernels [19]:

$$W_{i,j} = \exp\left(-\frac{\|x_i - x_j\|_2^2}{\sigma^2}\right). \tag{1}$$

where $\|x_i - x_j\|_2^2$ measures the square of the difference in intensity between two pixels i and j as a model of similarity. The constant σ controls the sensitivity of the similarity when defining the weight based on intensity difference. With such a constructed graph, we can interpret an image patch $\mathbf{x}$ as a graph-signal to the respected graph $\mathcal{G}$.

2.2   Graph-Signal Smoothness

With the constructed graph, we can similarly define the degree matrix $\mathbf{D}$, which is a diagonal matrix, with ith diagonal element as the sum of all elements in the ith row of $\mathbf{W}$, $i.e.$,

$$D_{i,i} = \sum_j W_{i,j}. \tag{2}$$

A graph Laplacian matrix is defined as,

$$\mathbf{L} = \mathbf{D} - \mathbf{W}. \tag{3}$$

Note that the graph Laplacian can be used to describe the total variation of the signal with respect to the graph [16,17], $i.e.$, given $\mathbf{L}$, the squared variations of the signal $\mathbf{x}$ with the underlying $\mathcal{G}$ can be described using the *graph Laplacian regularizer* $\mathbf{x}^T \mathbf{L} \mathbf{x}$:

$$\mathbf{x}^T \mathbf{L} \mathbf{x} = \frac{1}{2} \sum_{(i,j) \in \mathcal{E}} (x_i - x_j)^2 W_{i,j}. \tag{4}$$

It shows that $\mathbf{x}^T \mathbf{L} \mathbf{x}$ is small if the values of $\mathbf{x}$ at vertices i and j is similar with a connecting edge, or the edge weight $W_{i,j}$ is small when connecting vertex pair (i, j) with dissimilar value. Thus $\mathbf{x}$ is imposed to be smooth when minimizing the graph Laplacian regularizer with respect to the graph. For instance, if there is an edge between pixel $\mathbf{x}_i$ and $\mathbf{x}_j$, the smoothness prior will not over-smooth during optimization when the weight $W_{i,j}$ is small.

2.3   Graph Fourier Transform

Since $\mathbf{L}$ is symmetric and positive definite, it has a set of orthogonal eigenvectors $\{\mathbf{u}_i\}_{i=1,\cdots,n}$, with corresponding non-negative eigenvalues $0 = \eta_1 \le \eta_2 \le \cdots \le \eta_n$. We define $\mathbf{U} = [\mathbf{u}_1, \mathbf{u}_2, ..., \mathbf{u}_n]$ as the eigen-matrix. Then, the *graph Fourier transform* (GFT) matrix [20] is defined as $\mathbf{F} = \mathbf{U}^T$. A graph-signal $\mathbf{x}$ can be transformed to the graph frequency domain via:

$$\boldsymbol{\alpha} = \mathbf{F} \mathbf{x}. \tag{5}$$

It can be interpreted as *frequency* of signal $\mathbf{x}$ on a given graph $\mathcal{G}$. We employ the GFT for the reason that there always have a DC component (with a eigenvalues

$\eta_1 = 0$), which facilitates the restoration of PWS images where most regions are smooth. As shown in [15–17], PWS signals can be well approximated as linear combinations of low graph frequencies for appropriately constructed graphs, due to the high frequency components are most likely caused by noise.

Thus, for an observed pixel patch $\mathbf{x}_0$, we can effectively suppress noise by developing the following unconstrained quadratic programming problem:

$$\mathbf{x}^* = \arg\min_{\mathbf{x}} \|\mathbf{x} - \mathbf{x}_0\|_2^2 + \lambda \mathbf{x}^T \mathbf{L} \mathbf{x}. \tag{6}$$

where λ is a weighting parameter. The l_0-norm fidelity term computing the difference between the noisy observation $\mathbf{x}_0$ and the denoised $\mathbf{x}$, and $\mathbf{x}^T \mathbf{L} \mathbf{x}$ is a prior term. For a given graph Laplacian matrix L, (6) has a closed-form solution:

$$(\mathbf{I} + \gamma \mathbf{L})^{-1} \cdot \mathbf{x}_0. \tag{7}$$

Later, we will propose a collaborative filtering in graph Fourier transform domain.

2.4 Collaborative Filtering in GFT Domain

Having defined the GFT, we propose an effective collaborative linear filter for PWS image denoising. First, we cluster similar patches in a image and stack them together into 3D groups. Next, for a group, 3D collaborative linear filtering includes the following steps:

- Transform each 2D patch to a graph Fourier transform (GFT) domain using (5).
- Perform a hard threshold on the transform coefficients to attenuate noise.
- Invert the 2D GFT to produce estimates of all patches.
- Apply a 1D transform across the grouped patches (for the corresponding position of each patch) in the same way.

Finally, image updates by returning the outcomes of the patches to their original positions. Since the patch estimates can overlap, we may obtain many different estimates for each pixel which need to be averaged. Figure 1 illustrates the process of one iteration in our method. We experimentally found that only need to iterate several times to get good results.

This collaborative filtering in graph Fourier transform domain perform particularly well when deal with the 3D groups of piecewise smooth image. It can exploit both intra-patch correlation and inter-patch correlation characterized by these groups. The proposed 3DGFT can thus recover the image structures shared by grouped patches, while retaining the unique details of each individual patch.

3   Experimental Results

In this section, we present experimental results to show the superior performance of our depth images denoising algorithm. The depth images tested in experiment are selected from Middlebury Stereo dataset. We make a comparisons between the proposed approach and other leading methods and further demonstrate the effectiveness of 3DGFT. Specially, the PSNR and SSIM results are used to measure the objective performances. Local image details are also provided to show subjective comparisons.

3.1 Parameters Setting

First, we discuss the parameters setting in our proposed scheme. The weight parameters of Gaussian kernels σ in (1) is setted as $\sigma = 0.2\,(\sigma_n + \max\,(\max\,(Dis)))$, where σ_n is the noise variance and Dis is intensity difference matrix of the patch. The threshold $th1$ and $th2$ represent the hard-thresholding of the 2D and 1D transform coefficients respectively. As per the rule from [21], we set set as $th_i = \sigma_i\sqrt{2\log{(n^2k)}}$, where σ_i is specially set for 2D and 1D transform, n is the patch size, and k is the number of similar patches. The the number of iterations $Niter$ controls the denoising level, we observe in experiments that $Niter = 4$ is enough for well performing, and larger $Niter$ only result over-smooth.

3.2 Objective Quality

We compare denoising performance of our approach with three other competing methods: Block-Matching 3D (BM3D) [18], Nonlocal Graph-based Transform (NLGBT) [21], Optimal Graph Laplacian Regularization (OGLR) [17]. NLGBT and OGLR are both graph-based approach for depth image denoising and achieved leading performance. The test depth maps were corrupted by additive white Gaussian noise (AWGN), with the σ ranging from 10 to 40, then recovered by 3DGFT and the competing methods. The objective performance (PSNR and SSIM) of ten test images using above methods are presented in Table 1. We can see that, NLGBT and OGLR achieved more competitive performance than BM3D. Moreover, our 3DGFT achieved the best objective results among the four methods, and outperformed OGLR by up to 1.86 dB (baby3, $\sigma = 30$).

3.3 Subjective Quality

Subjective quality comparison is also made among different denoising methods. The reconstructed versions of depth maps for *Teddy* are shown in Fig. 2 respectively. It can be seen that, the depth maps denoised by our proposed approach can smooth the surface while preserve clean sharp edges. The BM3D method produced a competitive result but tends to blur along the edges. NLGBT provided sharper transitions than BM3D, however, it generates many artifacts. OGLR shows a performance close to that of ours, though it failed to remove all the noise. More details are shown in Fig. 3, where two cropped fragments of test image (*baby3*) are presented for comparison.

Table 1. Performance comparison in PSNR (top, in dB) and SSIM (bottom). In each cell, results of four denoising methods are presented. From Left to right: BM3D [18], NLGBT [21], OGRL [17], GFT3D (proposed). The best results among the four methods are highlighted in each cell.

Images	σ = 10				σ = 20				σ = 30				σ = 40			
	BM3D	NLGBT	OGRL	Ours	BM3D	NLGBT	OGRL	Ours	BM3D	NLGBT	OGRL	Ours	BM3D	NLGBT	OGRL	Ours
cones	40.133	42.743	42.735	**42.951**	35.049	36.827	37.415	**38.296**	32.346	32.968	34.144	**34.801**	30.582	30.358	31.477	**32.192**
	0.984	**0.988**	**0.988**	**0.988**	0.960	0.967	**0.969**	**0.969**	0.938	0.939	**0.947**	0.942	0.916	0.911	**0.923**	0.913
teddy	40.987	41.966	42.481	**42.621**	35.887	36.785	37.481	**38.487**	32.969	33.531	34.506	**35.994**	31.066	30.756	32.136	**33.618**
	0.986	0.986	0.987	**0.988**	0.970	0.968	0.968	**0.971**	**0.951**	0.947	0.950	0.948	0.931	0.926	**0.935**	0.924
bowling2	42.108	44.024	44.228	**45.409**	36.567	38.124	38.933	**39.961**	33.433	34.583	35.616	**36.858**	31.703	31.097	33.274	**33.625**
	0.990	0.992	0.991	**0.993**	0.976	0.978	0.977	**0.981**	0.959	0.960	0.958	**0.961**	0.939	**0.959**	0.947	0.936
baby3	40.999	42.432	42.230	**43.673**	35.299	36.771	36.896	**38.193**	32.195	33.065	33.808	**35.666**	30.162	30.283	31.314	**32.744**
	0.990	0.990	0.988	**0.992**	0.974	0.976	0.970	**0.977**	**0.959**	0.958	0.954	**0.959**	**0.944**	0.942	0.937	0.937
rocks2	41.604	43.521	43.636	**44.090**	35.924	38.137	38.477	**39.844**	32.993	34.624	35.370	**36.608**	31.027	30.609	32.828	**33.673**
	0.987	0.988	0.988	**0.989**	0.971	0.937	0.937	**0.974**	0.955	**0.956**	0.952	0.951	0.935	**0.955**	0.939	0.928
midd1	42.050	43.156	43.704	**44.544**	36.518	37.739	38.306	**39.497**	33.844	34.051	35.232	**35.838**	32.091	31.047	32.760	**33.341**
	0.988	0.990	0.987	**0.992**	0.970	0.974	0.967	**0.976**	0.952	**0.954**	0.948	**0.954**	0.924	**0.942**	0.923	0.923
lampshade1	42.879	44.001	45.070	**45.811**	37.504	38.452	39.527	**39.948**	34.927	35.140	36.133	**36.459**	33.189	32.802	33.705	**33.955**
	0.990	0.991	0.990	**0.993**	0.973	0.978	0.974	**0.979**	0.958	**0.959**	0.956	0.955	0.936	**0.960**	0.940	0.932
flowerpots	42.860	44.504	44.691	**45.574**	36.944	39.076	39.811	**40.678**	33.730	35.080	36.279	**37.708**	32.149	31.936	33.617	**34.402**
	0.989	0.991	0.985	**0.992**	0.973	0.981	0.966	**0.982**	0.952	**0.966**	0.943	0.962	0.925	**0.961**	0.928	0.940
plastic	45.693	45.659	46.263	**46.618**	40.560	40.480	41.305	**41.549**	37.956	37.096	38.520	**38.886**	36.141	35.446	36.130	**36.613**
	0.993	0.992	0.991	**0.993**	**0.982**	0.980	0.976	0.979	**0.971**	0.962	0.961	0.958	0.955	**0.960**	0.948	0.938
tsukuba	42.936	44.008	44.207	**44.955**	37.765	38.327	39.072	**40.145**	34.752	35.209	35.763	**36.531**	32.985	32.808	33.483	**33.820**
	0.983	0.987	0.979	**0.989**	0.963	0.963	0.947	**0.969**	0.935	**0.948**	0.912	0.940	0.906	**0.936**	0.887	0.920

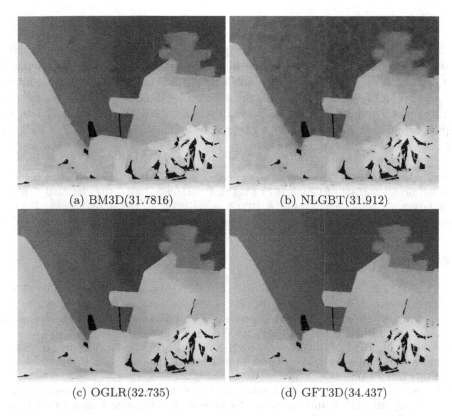

(a) BM3D(31.7816)   (b) NLGBT(31.912)

(c) OGLR(32.735)   (d) GFT3D(34.437)

Fig. 2. Comparison of tested methods in visual quality on *teddy* at $\sigma = 35$. The corresponding PSNR value are also given as references.

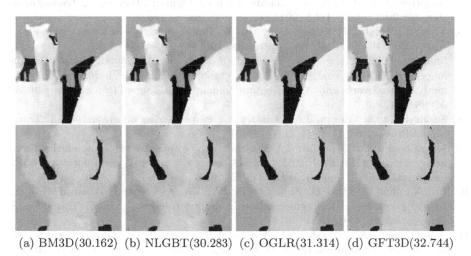

(a) BM3D(30.162) (b) NLGBT(30.283) (c) OGLR(31.314) (d) GFT3D(32.744)

Fig. 3. Comparison of tested methods in visual quality on *baby* at $\sigma = 40$. Two cropped fragments of each image are presented for comparison.

4   Conclusions

In this paper, we presented a 3-D Graph Fourier Transform Domain Collaborative Filtering (3DGFT) denoising algorithm and applied it to depth maps restoration. It provides new insight on jointly exploiting 3D collaborative filtering and graph Laplacian regularizer prior for image denoising. The experimental results on corrupted depth images shows that the 3DGFT approach can achieve highly competitive performance to other state-of-the-art denoising methods, in both PSNR and visual quality.

Acknowledgements. This work is supported by the Major State Basic Research Development Program of China (973 Program 2015CB351804), the National Science Foundation of China under Grants 61502122 and 61672193, and in part by the Fundamental Research Funds for the Central Universities (Grant No. HIT. NSRIF. 2015067).

References

1. Tian, D., Lai, P.L., Lopez, P., Gomila, C.: View synthesis techniques for 3D video. Proceedings of SPIE, vol. 7443, 74430T–1 (2009)
2. Rudin, L.I., Osher, S., Fatemi, E.: Nonlinear total variation based noise removal algorithms. Phys. D **60**(1–4), 259–268 (1992)
3. Aharon, M., Elad, M., Bruckstein, A.: K-SVD: an algorithm for designing overcomplete dictionaries for sparse representation. IEEE Trans. Signal Process. **54**(11), 4311–4322 (2006)
4. Dong, W., Zhang, L., Shi, G.: Centralized sparse representation for image restoration. In: 2011 IEEE International Conference on Computer Vision (ICCV), pp. 1259–1266. IEEE (2011)
5. Dong, W., Zhang, L., Shi, G., Wu, X.: Image deblurring and super-resolution by adaptive sparse domain selection and adaptive regularization. IEEE Trans. Image Process. **20**(7), 1838–1857 (2011)
6. Yang, J., Wright, J., Huang, T.S., Ma, Y.: Image super-resolution via sparse representation. IEEE Trans. Image Process. **19**(11), 2861–2873 (2010)
7. Shuman, D.I., Narang, S.K., Frossard, P., Ortega, A., Vandergheynst, P.: The emerging field of signal processing on graphs: extending high-dimensional data analysis to networks and other irregular domains. IEEE Signal Process. Mag. **30**(3), 83–98 (2013)
8. Sandryhaila, A., Moura, J.M.: Discrete signal processing on graphs. IEEE Trans. Signal Process. **61**(7), 1644–1656 (2013)
9. Kheradmand, A., Milanfar, P.: A general framework for kernel similarity-based image denoising. In: 2013 IEEE Global Conference on Signal and Information Processing (GlobalSIP), pp. 415–418. IEEE (2013)
10. Liu, X., Zhai, D., Zhao, D., Zhai, G., Gao, W.: Progressive image denoising through hybrid graph laplacian regularization: a unified framework. IEEE Trans. Image Process. **23**(4), 1491–1503 (2014)
11. Kheradmand, A., Milanfar, P.: A general framework for regularized, similarity-based image restoration. IEEE Trans. Image Process. **23**(12), 5136–5151 (2014)
12. Hu, W., Cheung, G., Li, X., Au, O.C.: Graph-based joint denoising and super-resolution of generalized piecewise smooth images. In: 2014 IEEE International Conference on Image Processing (ICIP), pp. 2056–2060. IEEE (2014)

13. Mao, Y., Cheung, G., Ortega, A., Ji, Y.: Expansion hole filling in depth-image-based rendering using graph-based interpolation. In: ICASSP 2013, pp. 1859–1863 (2013)
14. Mao, Y., Cheung, G., Ji, Y.: Image interpolation for DIBR viewsynthesis using graph fourier transform. In: 3DTV-Conference: The True Vision-Capture, Transmission and Display of 3D Video (3DTV-CON 2014), pp. 1–4. IEEE (2014)
15. Hu, W., Cheung, G., Kazui, M.: Graph-based dequantization of block-compressed piecewise smooth images. IEEE Signal Process. Lett. **23**(2), 242–246 (2016)
16. Pang, J., Cheung, G., Hu, W., Au, O.: Redefining self-similarity in natural images for denoising using graph signal gradient. In: APSIPA ASC, December 2014
17. Pang, J., Cheung, G., Ortega, A., Au, O.: Optimal graph Laplacian regularization for natural image denoising. In: IEEE International Conference on Acoustics, Speech and Signal Processing, April 2015
18. Dabov, K., Foi, A., Katkovnik, V., Egiazarian, K.: Image denoising by sparse 3-D transform-domain collaborative filtering. IEEE Trans. Image Process. **16**(8), 2080–2095 (2007)
19. Shuman, D., Narang, S., Frossard, P., Ortega, A., Vandergheynst, P.: The emerging field of signal processing on graphs: Extending high-dimensional data analysis to networks and other irregular domains. IEEE Signal Process. Mag. **30**(3), 83–98 (2013)
20. Liu, X., Cheung, G., Wu, X., Zhao, D.: Random walk graph laplacian-based smoothness prior for soft decoding of JPEG images. IEEE Trans. Image Process. **26**(2), 509–524 (2017)
21. Hu, W., Li, X., Cheung, G., Au, O.: Depth map denoising using graph-based transform and group sparsity. In: IEEE International Workshop on Multimedia Signal Processing, Pula, Italy, October 2013

How to Efficiently Identify Real and Pseudo 4K Video Contents?

Maoshen Liu$^{(\boxtimes)}$, Junfei Qiao, Li Wu, and Huiqing Zhang

Beijing Key Laboratory of Computational Intelligence and Intelligent System,
Faculty of Information Technology, Beijing University of Technology,
Beijing 100124, China
LMSbjut@163.com

Abstract. In this paper we address the problem of how to identify real 4K video contents from pseudo ones which were generated using complicated image post-processing technologies such as upsampling or super-resolution (SR). Two individual sets of 22 4K video sequences and 6 popular SR algorithms were collected for conducting this research. Despite the superior performance of current SR methods, they still not reach the perfect level since SR image reconstruction is a severely ill-posed problem and details are hard to be entirely recovered. This implies the reconstructed images based on SR methods do not conform to the natural scene statistics (NSS) model. According to this, we explore the difference of the locally normalized luminances' distributions between real 4K video sequences and SR-generated pseudo 4K video sequences. It was shown by extensive tests that simple statistical features can be fused to form a good classifier for separating real 4K video contents from pseudo versions. Experimental results demonstrate that the proposed classier consumes less than a quarter of a second for a 4K video frame and the accuracy of classification is beyond 90%. *abstract* environment.

Keywords: Real 4K video identification · Pseudo 4K video
Super-resolution (SR) · Natural scene statistics (NSS) · Classification

1 Introduction

The next-generation TV is the Ultra High Definition Television (UHDTV) which receives growing attention during the recent years. As a natural evolution of the present High Definition Television (HDTV) and 3DTV formats, the UHDTV standard is capable of providing the users with advanced visual experiences in a more realistic and immersive way. The UHDTV standard introduces two new formats, namely 4K and 8K. In comparison to the HDTV of 2K resolution (1920 × 1080), the UHDTV has greater spatial resolution, respectively 4 and 16 times of the HDTV resolution, i.e. 3840 × 2160 and 7680 × 4320. Furthermore, in the UHDTV standard, higher temporal resolution, wider dynamic

---

M. Liu—This work was supported in part by National Natural Science Foundation of China under Grants 61533002 and 61703009.

© Springer Nature Singapore Pte Ltd. 2018
G. Zhai et al. (Eds.): IFTC 2017, CCIS 815, pp. 138–146, 2018.
https://doi.org/10.1007/978-981-10-8108-8_13

range, larger bit depth, enhanced colorimetry, and more are also included as compared with the previous HDVT format.

Due to the supplied high fidelity content, the UHDTV has many practical applications, for example, home theater or large-scale public events like ceremony or sports. Further, the UHD image/video contents are also needed in the lately hot virtual reality (VR)-related 360° panoramic view. Despite numerous requirements of the UHDTV, the real UHD video sequences are far less than sufficient to meet such a great number of demands, mainly because the UHD video capture devices are extremely expensive. Instead, plenty of pseudo UHD video streams are produced by using advanced super-resolution (SR) techniques to upsample HD video streams, for the purpose of compensating for the lack of real UHD video contents.

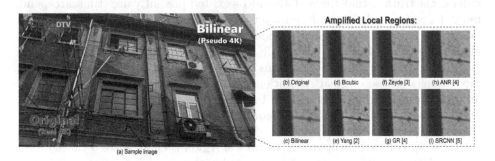

Fig. 1. Comparison of a real 4K video frame and its associated pseudo frames generated using seven SR technologies: (a) Sample image; (b) Representative amplified local region map in the real 4K frame; (c)–(i) Amplified local region maps in upsampled pseudo 4K frames.

Nonetheless, as shown in Fig. 1(a), we compare a real 4K video frame with its corresponding pseudo one which is created with the classical 'Bilinear' upsampling technology[1]. By zooming in the sample image, differences can be found at some edge and textural regions; that is, some details are removed in the pseudo 4K video frame as compared with its associated real 4K frame. The human visual system (HVS) is supposed to be heavily adapted for perceiving structural information from a given image scene [1]. This implies the difference errors between real and pseudo 4K videos affect the users' quality of experience (QoE). So, accurately identifying and choosing the real UHD video contents beforehand to be presented to end-users is greatly significant, otherwise it will be irresponsible to or even cheat consumers. Manual selection seems a good solution but it is inevitably a time-consuming, labor intensive, and oftentimes expensive task, and thus a fast and valid automatic way is highly desirable. This paper tries to solve this problem by proposing a natural scene statistics (NSS)-based classifier. We only concentrate on 4K since real 4K videos are not sufficient currently, let alone 8K videos.

---

[1] More advanced upsampling or SR methods will be discussed later.

The design principle behind our proposed classification model is that the distribution of locally normalized luminances of a real 4K video frame conforms to certain statistical regulation, while SR-generated pseudo 4K frames breaks this regulation. Experiments show that our classifier implements efficiently and effectively.

The remainder of the paper is outlined below. In Sect. 2, the NSS-based classifier is described in detail. In Sect. 3, the validation is conducted via a comparison between our proposed classifier and relevant methods. In Sect. 4, we conclude the whole paper.

2   Classifier

Despite the abroad propaganda concerning advanced visual experiences of 4K videos, the truth is that the real 4K videos existed presently are still scarce, and more 4K videos will be produced after consuming a great amount of time and labor. Therefore, a straightforward idea emerging in our minds is to deploy SR algorithms for upsampling existing 2K video sequences. As shown in Figs. 1(b)–(i), we compare amplified local regions of a real 4K image and seven '×2' upsampled images whose original resolution is 2K. We label the local region to be amplified using a colorful square in Fig. 1(a). The latter seven images are created applying representative SR algorithms, including classical 'Bilinear' and 'Bicubic', popular Yang [2] and Zeyde [3], and recent GR [4], ANR [4] and SRCNN [5]. For easy comparison, each local region is enlarged to 5 times based on the 'Nearest' interpolation. As compared with the original local region map in Fig. 1(b), upsampled local region maps in Figs. 1(c)–(i) present obvious loss of details. Even the powerful CNN based SRCNN method cannot well address this difficulty. When applied to enjoyment, pseudo 4K video contents very possibly degrade the users' QoE, which encroaches on consumers' rights. So a classifier is needed for the judgment of real and pseudo 4K videos beforehand. Moreover, a good classifier can also serve as the HVS for evaluating and optimizing SR methods and finally lead to further performance improvement.

A natural solution resorts to the popular NSS model. To specify, given an input image, imposing one local non-linear operation on log-contrast luminance is able to eliminate local mean displacements from zero log-contrast and to normalize the local variance of log-contrast [6]. This step is what the decorrelating function does, which was shown to effectively model the contrast-gain masking process in the early study of HVS [7]. Supposing the input image $I(x, y)$, the above-mentioned process is implemented via local mean removal and divisive normalization:

$$\tilde{I}_{x,y} = \frac{I_{x,y} - U_{x,y}}{V_{x,y} + \Delta} \tag{1}$$

where x and y are the indices in the horizontal and vertical directions, respectively; Δ indicates a small fixed number to remove the division-by-zero; $U_{x,y}$ and $V_{x,y}$ are local mean and variance maps, defined as

$$U_{x,y} = \sum_{a=-A}^{A} \sum_{b=-B}^{B} W_{a,b} \times I_{x+a,y+b} \tag{2}$$

$$V_{x,y} = \sqrt{\sum_{a=-A}^{A} \sum_{b=-B}^{B} W_{a,b} \times (I_{x+a,y+b} - U_{x,y})^2} \tag{3}$$

where $W = \{W_{a,b} | a = -A, -A+1, ..., A; b = -B, -B+1, ..., B\}$ is a 2D circularly-symmetric Gaussian weighting function; A and B are both assigned as 3. For convenience, we denote $\tilde{I}_{x,y}$ as the mean subtracted contrast normalized (MSCN) coefficients. Thereafter, as for natural images, the histogram of MSCN coefficients is close to the Gaussian-like appearance, while the introduction of blur distortion, the main problem caused by SR technologies, reshapes the histogram toward a more Laplacian distribution. We provide in Fig. 2 the MSCN coefficients' distributions of the original real 4K video frame stated above and upsampled frames which are produced by applying three SR methods (including classical 'Bilinear', popular Zeyde [3] and state-of-the-art SRCNN [5]) to the 2K frame. One can easily find that, as compared with the real 4K MSCN histogram of a long tail, other three have clear cut-off points.

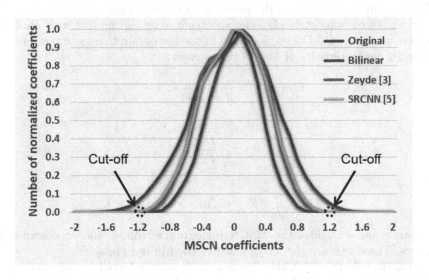

Fig. 2. Comparison of MSCN coefficients' histograms of a real 4K frame and three pseudo upsampled frames generated using 'Bilinear', Zeyde [3], and SRCNN [5].

As shown in Fig. 2, a threshold may estimate the cut-off value and thus identify the real and pseudo 4K videos. But it was viewed from considerable samples that the cut-off value is changed in a wide scope with varied video contents. This means a constant threshold cannot work well and a content-aware thresholding technology is required. Instead, we consider another solution

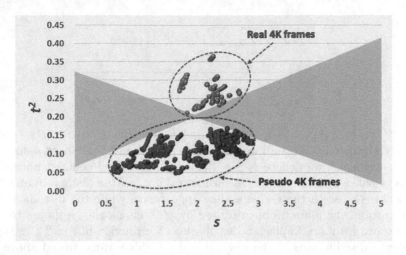

Fig. 3. Distribution of the used two features on real 4K frames (blue points) extracted from SJTU 4K Video Sequences [9] and associated pseudo 4K frames (red points) upsampled using six SR methods. (Color figure online)

as follows. Broadly speaking, the generalized Gaussian distribution (GGD) has a good ability to well catch a broader spectrum of histogram statistics. Based on this, the zero-mean GGD is exploited to fit the histogram thanks to the generally symmetric characteristics of MSCN parameters [8]:

$$h(z; s, t^2) = \frac{s}{2c\Gamma(1/s)} e^{-(|z|/c)^s} \tag{4}$$

where

$$c = t\sqrt{\frac{\Gamma(1/s)}{\Gamma(3/s)}} \tag{5}$$

and

$$\Gamma(\phi) = \int_0^\infty \theta^{\phi-1} e^{-\theta} d\theta, \quad \text{when } \phi > 0. \tag{6}$$

The parameter s decides the MSCN histogram's 'shape' and t^2 describes its variance. These two are the whole features used in our classifier.

A publicly SJTU 4K Video Sequences [9] were selected in this work. This dataset is composed of 15 video sequences of resolution 3840×2160 and the corresponding 4500 frames. Six SR algorithms (except 'Bilinear') were applied to these 4500 frames by first downsampling to 2K before upsampling to the original resolution, thereby to form 27000 pseudo 4K frames. We plan to observe the distribution of the used two features on the aforesaid 31500 frames. To ensure readers convenient to recognize clearly, one frame was chosen from every 10 frames and exhibited in Fig. 3 for comparison. The x- and y-axes individually refer to s and t^2. The blue and red points are respectively associated to real and pseudo 4K frames. One can see that blue and red points are apparently isolated

Table 1. Classification performance on the testing UHD video dataset [10].

Algorithms	Stream 1	Stream 2	Stream 3	Stream 4	Stream 5	Stream 6	Stream 7	Overall
MBBM [11]	91.4%	85.7%	85.7%	84.8%	85.7%	85.7%	85.7%	86.5%
JNB [12]	99.5%	86.9%	85.7%	79.5%	85.7%	85.7%	85.7%	87.2%
CPBD [13]	85.7%	100%	100%	64.8%	85.7%	100%	85.7%	75.1%
FISH [14]	100%	85.7%	85.7%	85.7%	85.7%	85.7%	85.7%	88.1%
FISH$_{bb}$ [14]	85.7%	85.7%	85.7%	85.7%	85.7%	85.7%	85.7%	85.7%
LPC-SI [15]	85.7%	85.7%	85.7%	85.7%	85.7%	85.7%	85.7%	85.7%
ARISM [16]	100%	100%	100%	100%	100%	100%	100%	100%
Propose classifier	60.7%	100%	100%	100%	95%	100%	94.5%	91.7%

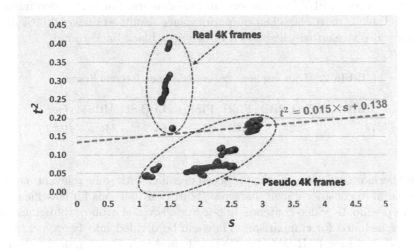

Fig. 4. Distribution of the used two features on the testing UHD video dataset [10]. Blue and red points are associated to real and pseudo 4K frames respectively. The green straight dash line is the proposed linear classifier. (Color figure online)

from each other. Here we consider the simple linear classifier. In Fig. 3, we plot all candidate straight lines which have the perfect classification performance, just as the golden region labeled. We can find that the used two features have a good ability to separate real and pseudo 4K video contents.

3 Validation

For validation, we first define the classification performance to be

$$P = \frac{\sum_i (M_i \odot N_i)}{\sum_i (N_i \odot N_i)} \times 100\% \tag{7}$$

where i is the frame index; $M = \{+1, -1\}$ is the result of classifier where $+1$ and -1 mean real and pseudo 4K frames; $N = \{+1, -1\}$ is the ground truth; $\odot$ is the XNOR operator. A good classifier is wished to obtain a P value close to 100%. As can be observed from Fig. 3, there exist a few straight lines that have attained the 100% classification performance on the SJTU 4K Video Sequences [9] and each line can serve as a classifier. We collected other seven 4K video streams from another entirely novel UHD video dataset [10] for testing the classifier. There include 600 frames in each video stream and 4200 frames in total. Similarly, we prepare the real and pseudo 4K videos which involve totally 29400 frames. We compute the two features on each frame and plot the distributions in Fig. 4. The green straight dash line is the proposed classifier, which has the optimal performance on the testing UHD video dataset among candidate straight lines belonging to the golden region in Fig. 3. This classifier is defined as $t^2 = 0.015 \times s + 0.138$. The classification performance of the proposed classifier reaches to 91.7% on the overall performance. For each video frame, as listed in Table 1, most classification performance results are beyond 90% except the first video stream which shows a beauty in a black background.

Table 2. Mean implementation efficiency (second/frame).

MBBM	JNB	CPBD	FISH	FISH$_{bb}$	LPC-SI	ARISM	Our
14	17	23	0.78	45	61	346	0.22

Furthermore, we compare the proposed classifier with some relevant methods. It is natural to consider image sharpness/blurriness methods for classification of real and pseudo 4K video contents. In our work, seven sharpness/blurriness measures are included for comparison. They can be divided into two types. One is composed of classical MBBM [11], JNB [12], and CPBD [13] models; the other is composed of state-of-the-art FISH [14], FISH$_{bb}$ [14], LPC-SI [15], and ARISM [16] models. In addition, general-purpose NR-IQA, such as [17–21] can also be used for this work. But due to space constraints, them will be compared later. Note that these seven measures are not classifiers but sharpness/blurriness predictors, and thus a proper threshold is required to modify each of above measures to be a classifier. Akin to the proposed classifier, we use the real and pseudo 4K video streams from the SJTU 4K Video Sequences to find the optimal threshold for each measures mentioned above. Based on the optimal threshold, the classification performance values of the seven measures above are respectively 87.3% for MBBM, 86.8% for JNB, 89.1% for CPBD, 89.5% for FISH, 89.5% for FISH$_{bb}$, 85.7% for LPC-SI, and 85.7% for ARISM. Different from the proposed classifier, there is no golden threshold which achieves the perfect classicization performance. We directly use the optimal thresholds trained on the SJTU 4K Video Sequences to modify these seven measures to be classifiers. Next, we also examine the classicization performance of these seven measures on the UHD video dataset, and the results can be found in Table 1. For easy comparison, we highlight the best performed classifier in boldface. One can see that the proposed classifier has acquired the better overall performance than those seven measures compared. And moreover, we further make comparisons on each of seven video streams and report the results in Table 1. It can be observed that, in six video streams, our proposed classifier has achieved the highest results. Besides the effectiveness, the efficiency also plays an important role in practical applications. Therefore, we implement the proposed classifier and seven competing measures on the UHD video dataset and tabulate the mean computational times in Table 2. The test is conducted using a computer with 3.2 GHz CPU processor, 16 GB memory and MATLAB R2014b. Obviously, our classifier is of significant efficiency as compared with other seven testing measures, and particularly reaches to real-time computation for a UHD video frame of size 3840 × 2160.

4   Conclusion

In this paper, we have investigated into a new and important problem which concerns the discrimination of real and pseudo 4K video sequences. On the basis of natural scene statistics, a new classifier has been proposed. Our proposed classifier implements by first applying an input image with local mean removal and divisive normalization and extracting two features about shape and variance from it, followed by a linear classifier. Experiments confirm the efficiency and efficacy of the proposed classifier, as compared to popular sharpness/blurriness-based classifiers. Further, note that our classifier works invalidly in the video stream which displays a beauty in a black background. So the future work will focus on content-adaptive thresholding methods for modification.

References

1. Wang, Z., Bovik, A.C., Sheikh, H.R., Simoncelli, E.P.: Image quality assessment: from error visibility to structural similarity. IEEE Trans. Image Process. **13**(4), 600–612 (2004)
2. Yang, J., Wright, J., Huang, T.S., Ma, Y.: Image super-resolution via sparse representation. IEEE Trans. Image Process. **19**(11), 2861–2873 (2010)
3. Zeyde, R., Elad, M., Protter, M.: On single image scale-up using sparse-representations. In: Boissonnat, J.-D., Chenin, P., Cohen, A., Gout, C., Lyche, T., Mazure, M.-L., Schumaker, L. (eds.) Curves and Surfaces 2010. LNCS, vol. 6920, pp. 711–730. Springer, Heidelberg (2012). https://doi.org/10.1007/978-3-642-27413-8_47
4. Timofte, R., De Smet, V., Van Gool, L.: Anchored neighborhood regression for fast example-based super-resolution. In: International Conference on Computer Vision, pp. 1920–1927, December 2013
5. Dong, C., Loy, C.C., He, K., Tang, X.: Image super-resolution using deep convolutional networks. IEEE Trans. Pattern Anal. Mach. Intell. **38**(2), 295–307 (2016)
6. Ruderman, D.L.: The statistics of natural images. Netw. Comput. Neural Syst **5**(4), 517–548 (1994)
7. Carandini, M., Heeger, D.J., Movshon, J.A.: Linearity and normalization in simple cells of the macaque primary visual cortex. J. Neurosci. **17**(21), 8621–8644 (1997)

8. Sharifi, K., Leon-Garcia, A.: Estimation of shape parameter for generalized Gaussian distributions in subband decompositions of video. IEEE Trans. Circuits Syst. Video Technol. **5**(1), 52–56 (1995)
9. Song, L., Tang, X., Zhang, W., Yang, X., Xia, P.: The SJTU 4K video sequence dataset. In: QoMEX, pp. 34–25, September 2013. http://medialab.sjtu.edu.cn/web4k/index.html
10. http://ultravideo.cs.tut.fi/#testsequences
11. Marziliano, P., Dufaux, F., Winkler, S., Ebrahimi, T.: A no-reference perceptual blur metric. In: Proceedings IEEE International Conference on Image Process, vol. 3, pp. 57–60, September 2002
12. Ferzli, R., Karam, L.: A no-reference objective image sharpness metric based on the notion of just noticeable blur (JNB). IEEE Trans. Image Process. **18**(4), 717–728 (2009)
13. Narvekar, N.D., Karam, L.J.: A no-reference image blur metric based on the cumulative probability of blur detection (CPBD). IEEE Trans. Image Process. **20**(9), 2678–2683 (2011)
14. Vu, P., Chandler, D.: A fast wavelet-based algorithm for global and local image sharpness estimation. IEEE Signal Process. Lett. **19**(7), 423–426 (2012)
15. Hassen, R., Wang, Z., Salama, M.: Image sharpness assessment based on local phase coherence. IEEE Trans. Image Process. **22**(7), 2798–2810 (2013)
16. Gu, K., Zhai, G., Lin, W., Yang, X., Zhang, W.: No-reference image sharpness assessment in autoregressive parameter space. IEEE Trans. Image Process. **24**(10), 3218–3231 (2015)
17. Gu, K., Zhai, G., Yang, X., Zhang, W.: Using free energy principle for blind image quality assessment. IEEE Trans. Multimed. **17**(1), 50–63 (2015)
18. Gu, K., Zhou, J., Qiao, J., Zhai, G., Lin, W., Bovik, A.C.: Noreference quality assessment of screen content pictures. IEEE Trans. Image Process. **26**(8), 4005–4018 (2017)
19. Gu, K., Zhai, G., Lin, W., Yang, X., Zhang, W.: Learning a blind quality evaluation engine of screen content images. Neurocomputing **196**, 140–149 (2016)
20. Gu, K., Zhai, G., Yang, X., Zhang, W.: Hybrid no-reference quality metric for singly and multiply distorted images. IEEE Trans. Broadcast. **60**(3), 555–567 (2014)
21. Zhai, G., Wu, X., Yang, X., et al.: A psychovisual quality metric in free-energy principle. IEEE Trans. Image Process. **21**(1), 41–52 (2012)

Design of Embedded Intelligent Video Processing Device Based on TMS320DM368

Lixin Shi, Yang Li, Bin Fu, Mengxiang Zhang, and Jianling Hu[✉]

School of Electronic and Information Engineering,
Soochow University, Suzhou 215006, Jiangsu, China
jlhu@suda.edu.cn

Abstract. An embedded intelligent video processing system based on TI TMS320DM368 processor and cloud service is designed and demonstrated in this paper. The proposed system can be used for video image acquisition, pre-processing, compression and etc. For different video applications, the system can request corresponding video analysis functions to the cloud server and perform proper operations based on the return values. The whole system includes five parts: the core TMS320DM368 processing module, video capture and display module, storage module, network communication module and USB interface module with wireless network extension function. The Linux operating system transplantation and driver development is fulfilled. And a framework of the face recognition system based on the cloud service is proposed.

Keywords: Intelligent video processing · Embedded system
Cloud service · TMS320DM368

1 Introduction

Intelligent video processing technology has a very wide range of applications, from sensor, computer vision, digital image processing to pattern recognition. Generally, the separation of background and object in video image is firstly implemented using the image analysis technologies. Then, target detection, target recognition, target location and target tracking will be completed [1]. In practical applications, video processing terminals need to process a large amount of raw video data. At the same time, some applications request high real-time performance, which poses a challenge to the video processing terminal.

Embedded system is widely used because of its advantages such as specificity, compact system, low power consumption, and low cost. Intelligent video processing terminal based on embedded system will be one of the hot spots of video application in the future. However, with the demands growth of image processing and the complexity of the processing algorithms, the burden of embedded devices in processing data is also increasing rapidly [2]. In recent years, with the development of computer and Internet technology, the rapid development of

© Springer Nature Singapore Pte Ltd. 2018
G. Zhai et al. (Eds.): IFTC 2017, CCIS 815, pp. 147–158, 2018.
https://doi.org/10.1007/978-981-10-8108-8_14

cloud computing technology provides a good solution to deal with the limitations that the embedded systems meet with in computing large amounts of data.

In this paper, a set of embedded video processing terminal system is designed, which can connect to internet to use cloud services. The video processing terminal completes the basic work of image processing, such as video capture, preprocessing and compression. And the other more complex video processing services can be handled by the cloud server. This design reduces the computational and storage requirements of the video processing terminals and improves the versatility of video processing terminals.

2   System Framework

According to the requirement of the system, the embedded video processing terminal can not only capture the video data, but also be capable of processing the original video data. Its functions include video preprocessing, ROI extraction, target detection, data compression and so on. In some applications with relatively simple functions, the video processing terminal can independently accomplish the desired video image processing task. And in other applications with complex task, the cloud server can provide special cloud service according to the specific requirements and assist embedded video processing terminal to achieve the goal. However, even in such applications, the local terminal still needs the ability to analyze and process the original video data, so as to reduce the pressure of application development and data transmission [3]. Figure 1 shows the framework of a cloud service based video processing system, which includes embedded video processing terminal and cloud server.

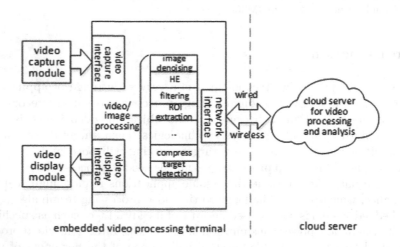

Fig. 1. The framework of cloud service based video processing system

TMS320DM368 produced by TI is used as the core processor in the embedded terminal, which is integrated with ARM9 processor core and two video image co-processors (HDVICP, MJCP) engines. And its working clock rate is 432 MHz. ARM is usually in charge of the management and control of peripheral interface, man-machine interface, network communication and so on. Meanwhile, the video image co-processor is responsible for the implementation of various video encoding and decoding algorithms [4]. This design scheme not only has the ability of high-speed processing of multimedia signals, but also has powerful capability to manage various peripherals. Moreover, the chip is relatively cheap and its power consumption is low, which meets the design requirements of the system very well.

Firstly, video image data is captured by camera and transmitted through the interface to the embedded terminal; Secondly, the terminal will complete a series of video processing according to the task requirements, such as video preprocessing (image denoising, histogram equalization (HE), filtering), region of interest (ROI) extraction, image compression, target detection etc. Thirdly, the processed images are transmitted to the cloud sever via wired or wireless networks, which can be the compressed video data or the extracted ROI. Then, the cloud server provides customized services based on different applications. Lastly, the processing result is returned to the terminal and displayed at the terminal. The embedded terminal has good applicability and scalability, which can connect to cloud server and realize various video applications, such as face recognition, intelligent video surveillance, video server and so on.

3   Hardware Design of Embedded Video Processing Terminal

According to the tasks that the embedded video processing terminal needs to accomplish, modularity design is adopted. The whole system can be divided into five parts: the core TMS320DM368 processing module, video capture and display module, storage module, network communication module and USB interface module with wireless network extension function. The block diagram of the terminal hardware platform is shown in Fig. 2.

3.1   Configuration Logic

The ARM can boot from either asynchronous EMIF (One NAND/NOR) or from ARM ROM, as determined by the setting of the device configuration pins BTSEL[2:0]. The ARM ROM boot loader (RBL) executes when the BTSEL[2:0] pins indicate a condition other than the normal ARM EMIF boot. The RBL of DM368 supports 7 distinct boot modes: NAND Boot mode, MMC0/SD0 Boot mode, UART0 Boot mode, USB Boot mode, SPI0 Boot mode, EMAC Boot mode and HPI Boot mode. The proposed video processing terminal adopts NAND boot mode with data width of 8 bits, which is implemented by controlling the status of BRSEL and AECFG pins during power up sequence. The configuration of BRSEL and AECFG is shown in Table 1.

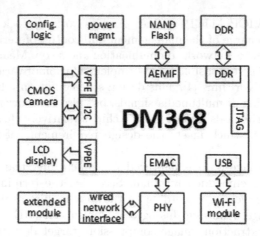

Fig. 2. The block diagram of the terminal hardware platform

Table 1. Configuration of bootloader

Pins	Config	Description
BTSEL[2:0]	000	NAND Boot mode
AECFG[2:0]	000	8-bit NAND

3.2   Video Capture and Display Module

OV7725 CMOS image sensor is selected as the video image acquisition sensor in the embedded video processing terminal. The OV7725 sensor has an image array of 664 × 490 pixels for a total of 325360 pixels, of which 640 × 480 pixels are active (307200 pixels), and it supports the following image sizes: VGA, QVGA, and any size scaling down from CIF to 40x30. OV7725 is connected with the VPFE interface of DM368. The system also supports high-definition input in order to meet the high definition (HD) video application.

LCD is used to display the video and graphical user interface (GUI) and is connected to the VPBE interface of DM368. Also, the terminal uses SN74AVCH16T245GR voltage conversion chip to enhance the drive capability of the DM368 VPBE.

3.3   Storage Module

When the video processing terminal works, the nonvolatile memory devices are needed to store data such as UBL, U-Boot, Kernel, file systems and so on. NAND Flash that the system selected is MT29F16G08FAAWC:A, which is produced by Micron Corporation and has 2G-byte capacity with data width of 8 bits. The NAND Flash is connected to the AEMIF interface of DM368.

Meanwhile, the DDR2 chip, MT47H64M16HR-3:E produced by Micron is selected as the external extension of the dynamic storage space, which has

1G-bit capacity with data width of 16 bits. The on-chip DDR2 controller interface of DM367 is used to access the MT47H64M16HR-3:E.

3.4 Network Communication Module

The communication module has a role of data transmission between the embedded video processing terminal and the external equipment. The designed terminal provides two ways to access the network: wired connection and wireless connection.

The Ethernet Media Access Controller (EMAC) and the Management Data Input/Output (MDIO) are integrated in DM368. EMAC provides an efficient interface between the device and the network. And it supports both 10 Mbps and 100 Mbps in either half- or full-duplex mode. The EMAC controls the flow of packet data from the device to the PHY. However, it belongs to the data link layer, so it is necessary to use a physical layer interface chip to realize network communication. The designed terminal selects KS8001L as the physical layer interface chip.

In order to improve the flexibility of the system and support various applications, the terminal provides both the USB interface and the WiFi extension module. The DM368 integrates USB interface controller to support USB2.0 high speed devices and can work under host and OTG mode. In this system, USB interface works under host mode, and it can supply power to slave device.

The terminal hardware platform is shown in Fig. 3.

Fig. 3. The terminal hardware platform

4   Software Transplantation and Development

TI provides a Digital Video Software Development Kit (DVSDK), which includes the following components: Linux kernel 2.6.32, boot loaders, drivers and sample applications. There are three steps in the process of transplanting operating system: (1) building server platform and cross-compiler environment; (2) modifying and compiling user boot loader (UBL) and universal boot loader (U-Boot), and burning into NAND Flash; (3) cutting, building and transplanting kernel and file system.

4.1   Transplanting UBL and U-Boot

TI provides the source code of UBL and U-Boot. So we only need to make some functional changes according to the designed system. The modification of UBL includes: (1) setting the clock of DM368 at 432 MHz; (2) adjusting the PLL divider to set the DDR working clock as 216 MHz; (3) configuring the PLL1 to output CLKOUT0 at 24 MHz to support the camera module; (4) reconfiguring registers according to the pin usage of the designed circuit. Then, the modified code can be compiled to generate the ubl.bin file.

During the developing process, due to the kernel file "uImage" needs to be downloaded via TFTP, and the file system "rootsf" is loaded via NFS. Therefore, after the completion of U-Boot, startup parameters and kernel boot mode are set through the serial console, and tftp is used to burn the kernel and file system to the embedded system. So, the U-boot parameters such as bootargs, bootcommand contained in the dm368evm.h file should be modified, then the code should be re-compiled to generated the u-boot.bin file.

4.2   Linux Kernel Clipping and Transplanting

According to the boot sequence, kernel should be loaded after execution of U-Boot. TI's DVSDK package contains the reference code of Linux kernel, which needs to be modified and cut according to the designed system. For the designed video processing system, under the "/arch" directory, only "arm", "um" and "x8" three folders are retained and others are deleted. Furthermore, delete all files beginning with "march" except "mach-davinci" under "/arch/arm" directory. The codes about UART, EMAC, USB and other needed interface should be kept, then the kernel should be compiled to generate the kernel image file "uImage".

4.3   Driver Development

V4L2 (Video for Linux2) is used as the video image acquisition module to obtain the image data collected by the camera module. There is no corresponding driver for OV7725 in the Linux2.6.32 kernel version, so the driver for OV7725 access should be developed. OV7725 driver mainly includes initializing function, register reading and writing function, configuration function, camera controlling function and other functions. The driver is compiled into the kernel directly. After the loading of kernel, the camera device node will be generated, which can be accessed by API to obtain the acquired image data.

The system selects RT3070 wireless network card provided by Ralink company as the Wi-Fi module, which is connected to the system through USB interface. RT3070 supports two working modes: STA (station) and SoftAP (Access Point). When compiling the kernel, the wireless module and the Ralink RT3070 driver need to be selected and compiled into the kernel. Also the wireless network tools "Wireless tools", "Wpa_supplicant", and "Openssl" should be transplanted.

4.4 System Boot Process

The system boot process is shown in Fig. 4.

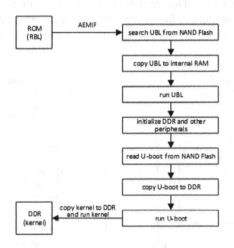

Fig. 4. Boot process of DM368

The core architecture of DM368 is ARM926EJS, and its boot process is composed of phases: RBL, UBL and U-Boot. After power-on reset, DM368 will determine the UBL boot mode and data width information according to the status of BTSEL and AECFG pins. This system uses NAND Flash boot mode with data width of 8 bits. So after power-on reset, the RBL will be executed. Firstly, RBL searches and reads UBL from NAND Flash and copies it to the DM368 internal 14 KB RAM addressed from 0x10020 then jump to the entry point of UBL. After that, UBL begins to execute in RAM, complete the initialization of PLL, DDR and other hardware peripherals. U-Boot is searched and read from the NAND Flash, and copied to the DDR memory addressed from 0x81080000. Then, jump to this address and begin to execute U-Boot. U-Boot re-initializes the CPU and other peripherals, copies the kernel to the DDR, start kernel and load root file system.

5   Application Development

Based on the designed embedded video processing terminal, a demo system of face recognition based on cloud service is constructed. The demo system takes the members of author's lab as the test objects for testing the performance of the embedded video processing terminal.

5.1   Architecture of Face Recognition System Based on Cloud Service

The basic workflow of the demo system based on cloud services mainly includes the following steps: (1) Video capture and image preprocess; (2) Face detection; (3) Construction of face recognition library; (4) Face recognition; (5) Results display. Among them, the embedded terminal mainly implements video capture image preprocess , face detection and results. At the same time, the cloud server is responsible for constructing face recognition library and providing face recognition services [5]. Figure 5 shows the working flow chart of the demo system.

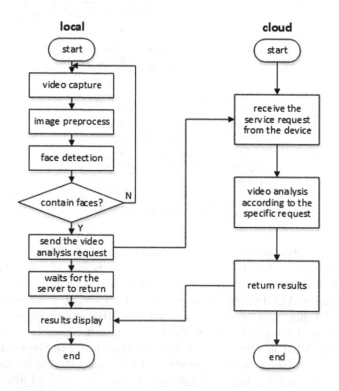

Fig. 5. The flow chart of face recognition demo system

5.2   Video Image Acquisition

In this paper, the V4L2 specification is used to realize the video capture through OV7725 [6]. Figure 6 shows the flow chart of video capture.

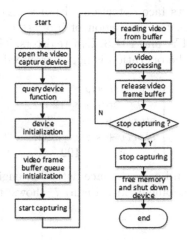

Fig. 6. The flow chart of video capture

As shown in Fig. 6, the process of the video capture is as follows: (1) After the open of video capture device, the relevant information of the capture device is obtained through the VIDIOC_QUERYCAP command, the legality of the device needs to be judged, and the functions supported by the device should be confirmed; (2) Setting the format of the video, including the image size and data format; (3) The video frame buffer is allocated in the kernel space and the user space respectively using the VIDIOC_REQBUFS command and malloc () function, and then mmap () function is called to establish the mapping relation of the memory between two spaces. After the video frame address is pushed into the buffer queue through the VIDIOC_QBUF command, the video capture can be started; (4) After acquiring one frame of video is captured, get one video frame address from the buffer queue through the VIDIOC_DQBUF command. Then, copy video data to the user space and release the frame address for subsequent acquisition; (5) Once the user's command of stopping video capture is received, the VIDIOC_STREAMOFF command is called to stop the video capture, and munmap () function is called to release the memory map; (6) Finally, the video capture device is switched off.

5.3   Face Detection

The video processing sub-system (VPSS) of DM368 contains HW face detection engine, which provides capabilities to detect multiple faces on the quarter video graphics array (QVGA) image/video frame. Since the size of the original video acquired by OV7725 is 640*480, it is necessary to scale the original video before face detection. The face detection engine can detect faces with face inclination $+/-45°$, face direction $+/-30°$ in vertical direction and $+/-60°$ in horizontal direction, with a maximum detection count of 35 faces. It allows a configurable minimum face size of 20–40 pixels. The accuracy of detection rate is close to 100%. The engine supports face detection within a region of interest as specified by the user. Settings for the region of interest are accomplished by the FD_STARTX, FD_STARTY, and FD_SIZEX registers. The following conditions must be ensured, or else the operation is not guaranteed:

$$\begin{cases} 0 \leq startx \leq 160 \\ 0 \leq starty \leq 120 \\ startx + sizex \leq 320 \\ starty + sizey \leq 240 \\ sizey = 192 \end{cases} \tag{1}$$

This system controls and calls the face detection engine contained in VPSS through the IPNC development kit. Figure 7 shows the workflow for face detection.

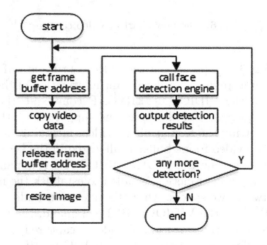

Fig. 7. The flow chart of face detection

As shown in Fig. 7, the steps of face detection loop are as follows: (1) Get the video frame address, and copy video data to the user space, and release the video frame address; (2) according to the requirements of VPSS face detection engine on the input image size, scale the original video image; (3) call face detection engine for face detection; (4) output the results of the face detection to the application; (5) repeat until it receives the command of exiting application.

The design takes some members of author's lab as the test objects, and the authors' results of the original images and face detection are shown in Fig. 8.

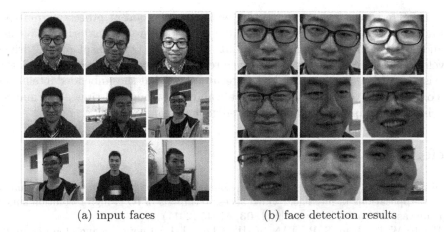

(a) input faces   (b) face detection results

Fig. 8. Input face and face detection results

From the results of face detection, we can see that the system can locate the human face accurately and realize the face detection function as expected.

5.4 Face Recognition Based on Cloud Service

Many cloud platforms in domestic and overseas support face recognition services, such as Face++, Tencent excellent map, Microsoft cognitive services. We can choose one of the cloud platform and process standard service application in the development of cloud based face recognition system [7].

The workflow of the system contains two aspects of local and cloud platforms. The general process is as follows: (1) Local: First, the image data is captured through camera module and the image is preprocessed, the face detection engine is then requested for face detection and send the video analysis request to the cloud service platform through the network, which can be the face recognition library construction or face recognition. Waiting for the server to return the video analysis result. Finally, the following analysis and display will be executed. (2) Cloud: first, the platform receives the service request from the terminal, analyzes and processes the video according to the specific request (face recognition library construction or face recognition). Finally, the processing results will be return back to the embedded video processing terminal through the network.

The results show that the face recognition based on cloud service is flexible and successful, which achieves the expected design specification.

6   Conclusion

An embedded intelligent video processing terminal system based on TI's TMS320DM368 processor is designed, which supports cloud platform connection. It combines the advantages of embedded system with low cost, simple and the characteristics of cloud computing with virtual, good at processing massive data. The development of the whole intelligent video processing terminal system includes the hardware design, assembling, debugging, OS transplant and driver development. The framework of the face recognition system based on cloud service is established and tested. The test results show that the embedded intelligent video processing terminal system is stable and has strong real-time performance, which could be applied in different intelligent video processing scenarios.

References

1. Shen, P., Yang, G., Zhang, L., Xiao, X., Zhang, X., Chang, Q., Yu, G.: Development and applications of intelligent video access terminals of IOT: high resolution smart cameras. Internet Things Technol. **03**, 41–45 (2011)
2. Hsieh, W.-H., Kao, S.-P., TAN, K.-H., Chen, J.-L.: Energy-saving cloud computing platform based on micro-embedded system. In: International Conference on Advanced Communication Technology, pp. 739–743 (2014)
3. Bera, S., Misra, S., Rodrigues, J.J.P.C.: Cloud computing applications for smart grid: a survey. IEEE Trans. Parallel Distrib. Syst. **26**(5), 1477–1494 (2015)
4. Zhang, M.: Design and Implementation of Embedded Face Recognition System Based on Cloud Service. Soochow University (2017)
5. Lu, J., Chen, J., Yang, Z.: Cloud computing-based embedded face recognition system construction and research. Comput. Meas. Control **24**(4), 146–148 (2016)
6. Qin, Z., Cao, J.: Design of high speed IP camera based on TMS320DM365. Electron. Des. Eng. **19**(10), 121–124 (2011)
7. Dobrea, D.-M., Maxim, D., Ceparu, S.: A face recognition system based on a Kinect sensor and Windows Azure cloud technology. In: International Symposium on Signals Circuits and Systems, pp. 1–4 (2013)

Machine Learning

Reverberation Level Recognition by Formants Based on 10-Fold Cross Validation of GMM

Sai Ma[1(✉)], Haiyan Li[2], Hui Zhang[3], and Xi Xie[1]

[1] Key Laboratory of Media Audio and Video, Communication University of China,
Ministry of Education, Beijing, China
{saima,cici.xie}@cuc.edu.cn
[2] School of Animation and Digital Arts, Communication University of China,
Beijing, China
hyli@cuc.edu.cn
[3] School of Science, Communication University of China, Beijing, China
zhanghui0931@cuc.edu.cn

Abstract. Formants can reflect the resonance feature of the vocal tract, which form the spectral components of speech signal, and are closely related to speech intelligibility. Reverberation has an influence on formants, and Reverberation Time (RT) and Direct-to-Reverberant energy Ratio (DRR) are the primary parameters for reverberation strength judgement. Given some selected RT, cluster reverberant speech signals at different DRR by formants in order to achieve the purpose of recognizing reverberation level. Train formants of the reverberant speech signals using Gaussian Mixture Model (GMM), and verify the efficiency via 10-fold cross validation, and choose frequently used MFCC as comparison. Experiments prove formants can be used as an index for reverberation level recognition with satisfactory efficiency.

Keywords: Reverberation · Formant
Direct-to-Reverberant energy Ratio · Cross validation
Gaussian Mixture Model

1 Introduction

The sound is produced by the vocal tract, which can be viewed as a filter that spectrally shapes the flow wave coming from the vocal cord. Voiced sound is generated when the vocal cord is in the voicing state, which means that vocal cord is tensed and vibrating periodically, and vocal tract filter is excited by periodic pulses, resulting in a speech waveform that is quasi-periodic; whereas unvoiced sound (e.g., consonant) is generated when the vocal cord is in the unvoiced state, which implies that vocal cord is not vibrating, and vocal tract filter is excited by aperiodic source, resulting in a random speech waveform [1, 2]. In this research, we focus on voiced speech.

The vocal tract is an acoustic space where source sounds for speech propagate. Voiced speech relies on strengthening or weakening of the spectral components of source sounds by resonances of the air column in the vocal tract.

© Springer Nature Singapore Pte Ltd. 2018
G. Zhai et al. (Eds.): IFTC 2017, CCIS 815, pp. 161–171, 2018.
https://doi.org/10.1007/978-981-10-8108-8_15

The intelligibility of voiced speech is determined by a few peak frequencies of vocal tract resonances, which are called formants. In the voiced speech production, the vocal tract forms a closed tube in which multiple reflections of sound waves give rise to the formants (F1, F2 and F3) [3,4]. Generally, the spectrum of speech signal decreases with 6 dB/octave, so the energy is mainly concentrated in the first three formants.

When speech signals propagate in an enclosed environment, they are distorted by the features of room acoustics, including room dimensions, reflection path and sound absorption of the enclosure that make them reverberate. Reverberation not only has an important influence on perceived speech intelligibility [5,6], but also affects many other applications, e.g. the performance of automatic speech recognition (ASR) system [7], the academic, psycho-educational, and psychosocial achievement of children [8], and cochlear implant users [9]. Therefore, it is of great practical significance to recognize reverberation level which has become a research focus of recent years. [10] assess the reverberation level by speech harmonic features, but only to determine reverberation exist or not. [11] utilize clarity index C50 to estimate reverberation intensity of speech, however, C50 is not as close as formants to speech intelligibility.

The image-source model (ISM) [12] represents an essential practical application for reverberant speech signal processing technologies. Numerous reverberation parameters can be predicted from room impulse response (RIR), which is the transfer function between sound source and microphone generated with the ISM, e.g. Direct-to-Reverberant energy Ratio (DRR) [13] and Reverberation Time (RT) [14], which are significant indicators of room reverberation characteristics. DRR is the energy ratio between direct and reverberant speech signals that is an important cue to sound source distance, and RT is defined as the time for the sound to die away to a level 60 decibels below its original level, which is the primary property of an acoustic environment.

In this paper we propose a recognition method of reverberation level based on formants. We cluster the reverberant speech signals by the first three formants under different DRR at some given RT to verify the validity and feasibility of formants in reverberation level recognition, and select MFCC for comparison. The paper is organized as follows: the reverberant speech databases include synthesized voiced speech and vowel EH are described in Sect. 2. In Sect. 3, we introduce the algorithm structure of our research, and experiments are done in Sect. 4. Conclusions are drawn in Sect. 5.

2   Database Illustrations

2.1   Room Reverberation Property

We use ISM to generate different RIRs. RT is roughly a function of the room size (for reflection constant) but not the Source-Microphone Distances (SMDs), taking three different RTs, (e.g. 300 ms, 600 ms and 1000 ms). Table 1 illustrates a number of SMDs which make the DRR span from 15 to 0 dB, where the room dimensions (length * width * height) = 9 * 4 * 6 m^3. Therefore, 18 room impulse responses are generated.

Table 1. SMD and corresponding DRR

RT = 300 ms		RT = 600 ms		RT = 1000 ms	
SMD (m)	DRR (dB)	SMD (m)	DRR (dB)	SMD (m)	DRR (dB)
0.174	15.0403	0.101	15.0083	0.072	15.0710
0.262	12.0170	0.151	12.0281	0.105	12.0789
0.387	9.0259	0.217	9.0200	0.155	9.0290
0.578	6.0290	0.315	6.0321	0.219	6.0517
0.857	3.0026	0.456	3.0044	0.314	3.0279
1.275	0.0030	0.647	0.0183	0.466	0.0196

2.2 Synthesized Voiced Speech

An estimator was proposed for recognizing reverberation level that is suitable for male speech; therefore, speech signals with female pitch are the research interest of this study. Based on our previous work, we have three sets of Linear Prediction (LP) coefficients (according to LP analysis order 12, 20, 28), and implementing an all-pole filter treated as Vocal Tract Model (VTM), respectively [15]. For female voiced speech signals, the all-pole filters are excited with a periodic pulse train wherein consecutive pulses are separated by the pitch period. Synthesis over a range of pitch frequencies, e.g. 150, 200, 250, 300, 350 Hz, is conducted to cover most of the range of female even children pitch [16,17].

To make each synthesized voiced speech long enough (e.g. around 5 s), the entire file would have only the active speech, and no pauses. There would be a total of 3 * 5 = 15 files. The all-pole filters have zero-state at time zero. We omit the onset and decay of the all-pole filter from the synthesized signals, for e.g., by starting to collect samples from the all-pole filter only after running it for 50 ms and stop collecting samples from it at time = 4.55 s.

2.3 Synthesized Vowel EH

We select vowel EH for a phonetic instance of our research, because EH first three formant locations are similar to the synthesized vocal tract resonance properties. Female EH parameters are shown in Table 2 [18].

We use formants to synthesize the vowel EH. There are three sets of empirical formulas for calculating formant bandwidth from frequency [19,20], and we choose the most accurate one for the first three formants,

$$B1 = 15 * (500/F1)^2 + 20 * (F1/500)^{\frac{1}{2}} + 5 * (F1/500)^2, \qquad (1)$$

$$B2 = 22 + 16 * (F1/500)^2 + 12000/(F3 - F2), \qquad (2)$$

$$B3 = 25 * (F1/500)^2 + 4 * (F2/500)^2 + 10 * F3/(F_\alpha - F3), \qquad (3)$$

Table 2. Female vowel EH parameters

Pitch F0/Hz	F1/Hz	F2/Hz	F3/Hz
223	610	2330	2990

where, $F_\alpha = 3700$ for female, $F_\alpha = 3400$ for male.

With the above procedure, 15 * 18 = 270 reverberant voiced speech files are synthesized, and the same as 18 reverberant EH. We only use the first 3 s of the reverberant voiced speech, and make the reverberant EH between 2.5 and 3 s.

3   Algorithm Description

Reverberant speech signals are classified into different categories according to DRR, and a target vector is created for each class. For reverberant speech signals, we extract their features together with the target vectors to construct the whole dataset, and divide it into training and test subset. The whole algorithm structure is described in Fig. 1.

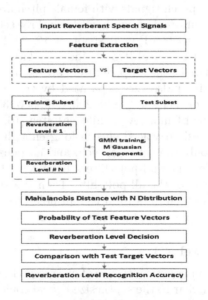

Fig. 1. Algorithm structure of reverberation level recognition system

Suppose there are n reverberation levels, by GMM (M components) [21,22] training we can obtain each component of nth category probability density,

$$g_n(x_n | u_{ni}, \Sigma_{ni}), \lambda_n = \{\omega_{ni}, \mu_{ni}, \Sigma_{ni}\}, i \in M \qquad (4)$$

Mahalanobis Distance (MD) [23] is used to measure the distance from an observation to a distribution. Test subset is $Y=\{y_1,\cdots,y_l\}$, the MD from l^{th} sample to i^{th} distribution of nth category is,

$$MD_{lni} = \sqrt{(y_l - \mu_{ni})^T \Sigma_{ni}^{-1}(y_l - \mu_{ni})}, \tag{5}$$

and the corresponding probability is defined as,

$$P_{lni} = e^{-MD_{lni}}, \tag{6}$$

then, the probability of lth sample belongs to n^{th} category is a weighted sum of P_{lni},

$$P_{ln} = \sum_{i=1}^{M} \omega_{ni} P_{lni}, \tag{7}$$

last, reverberation level decision of lth sample is,

$$Level_l = argmax\{P_{l1}, P_{l2}, \cdots, P_{ln}\}. \tag{8}$$

We use 10-fold cross validation [24], and select two features, formants and MFCC, for recognition comparison.

4 Experiments

4.1 Feature Extraction

Formants and MFCC were selected for comparison, and we focus on formants. Extract formants by LP analysis of the reverberant speech signals, which are the peaks of LP envelope. Autocorrelation has a lower Normalized Mean Square Error (NMSE) [15]; therefore, we should choose appropriate LP analysis order.

Log Spectral Distortion Comparison. The Log Spectral Distortion (LSD) is a distance index (expressed in dB) between two spectra. LSD between spectra $\hat{s}(\omega)$ and $s(\omega)$ is defined as,

$$D_{LS} = \sqrt{\frac{1}{2\pi} \int_{-\pi}^{\pi} \left| 10log_{10} \frac{\hat{s}(\omega)}{s(\omega)} \right|^2 d\omega}, \tag{9}$$

which is commonly used to measure the quality of LP analysis estimated spectral envelope. Take the three VTMs in Sect. 2 as 'true' envelope which are not affected by pitch frequency, then calculate LSD between them and synthesized voiced speech LP envelope for different LP analysis order under all pitch excitation signals, the results are in Fig. 2.

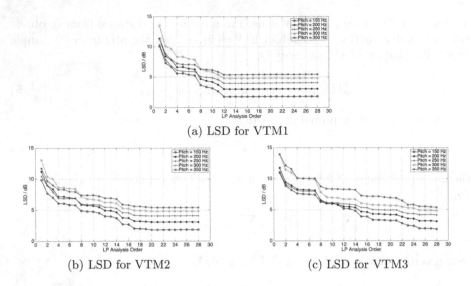

(a) LSD for VTM1

(b) LSD for VTM2   (c) LSD for VTM3

Fig. 2. Relation between LSD and LP analysis order

Poles and Formants Relation. According to [25] conclusion, the separated formants often beyond a critical distance of 3~3.5 Bark, we roughly classify the frequency domain into three regions: less than 1000 Hz, between 1000 and 2500 Hz, and larger than 2500 Hz based on the three VTMs and the parameters of vowel EH. The true formant within every region should be the pole that is closer to unit circle of the all-pole filter [26]. The relations between poles and formant locations are verified by analysis of the speech frame that is used to obtain the VTMs, and the results are shown in Fig. 3.

From the analysis above, LP analysis order 20 is a balance of performance and complexity; therefore, it is the one we use in the following experiments. However, there would still be spurious formants, we just treat them as formant noise.

4.2   10-Fold Cross Validation

The following experiments were accomplished using MATLAB 2011b on a Dell Vostro 220 s desktop with 2.6 GHz Pentium (R) Dual-Core E5300 processor and 2 GB of RAM. Here, the iteration time is defined as the time it takes to process once 10-fold cross validation.

Reverberant Voiced Speech. Divided the synthesized reverberant voiced speech into 3 groups on the basis of reverberation time, e.g. RT = 300 ms, RT = 600 ms and RT = 1000 ms. Compared the reverberation level recognition accuracy and iteration time by formants and MFCC via 10-fold cross validation of GMM, and repeated the validation for 100 times to get the average results that are illustrated in Table 3.

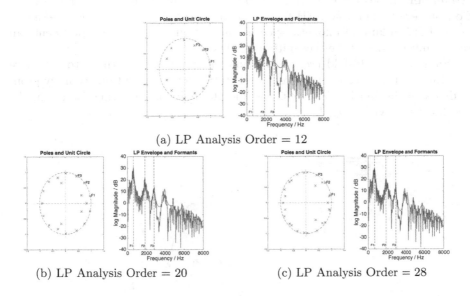

(a) LP Analysis Order = 12

(b) LP Analysis Order = 20   (c) LP Analysis Order = 28

Fig. 3. Relation between poles and formant locations

Table 3. Reverberant voiced speech formants and MFCC recognition comparison

RT/ms	Pitch/Hz	Formants		MFCC	
		Accuracy	Iteration time (s)	Accuracy	Iteration time (s)
300	150	0.9549	43.5601	0.9999	100.1873
	200	0.9835	54.9392	0.9976	99.8640
	250	0.9554	50.8653	0.9984	99.2490
	300	0.9835	57.8943	0.9964	98.9740
	350	0.9551	48.7711	0.8647	89.4056
600	150	0.9571	41.1120	0.9993	96.8098
	200	0.9489	52.4283	0.9957	95.2712
	250	0.8948	41.1763	0.9977	97.4577
	300	0.9459	53.3419	0.9955	97.7033
	350	0.9454	42.0021	0.8847	86.2560
1000	150	0.8996	43.5204	0.9996	93.2313
	200	0.9065	49.3599	0.9968	93.4008
	250	0.9071	39.7112	0.9964	95.0175
	300	0.9284	52.6712	0.9962	93.8167
	350	0.8957	38.5617	0.9021	81.2714

Reverberant Vowel EH. In the same way, executed the 10-fold cross validation on reverberant vowel EH for reverberation level recognition. Furthermore,
vowel EH is a kind of phonetic speech, and the outcome of the experiment can
reflect much more of the recognition validity.

Similarly, the 10-fold cross validation was repeated 100 times to get more
accurate result; we can obtain the reverberation level recognition accuracy probability distribution by formants, and did the polynomial fitting for them, the
results are shown in Fig. 4.

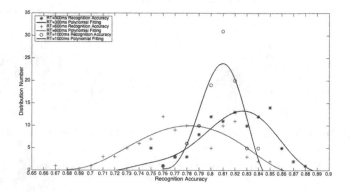

Fig. 4. Formants recognition accuracy probability distribution

Obviously, the probability distribution obeys a t-distribution, thus we calculated the recognition accuracy confidence interval of 90% confidence level, and
made a comparison between formants and MFCC together with the iteration
time that is illustrated in Table 4.

Table 4. Reverberant vowel EH formants and MFCC recognition comparison

RT/ms	Formants		MFCC	
	Confidence interval time (s)	Average iteration time (s)	Confidence interval time (s)	Average iteration time (s)
300	0.8138 ± 0.0494	16.9203	0.8073 ± 0.0278	54.9472
600	0.7721 ± 0.0600	16.7084	0.8232 ± 0.0298	54.4518
1000	0.8017 ± 0.0267	16.0381	0.8075 ± 0.0173	54.4817

We can see that the recognition accuracies based on formants are almost
the same as MFCC; however, the time consumptions are much lower. Clearly,
formants provide a satisfactory recognition efficiency.

5   Conclusions

We extracted the formants by LP analysis on the reverberant speech signals. It was difficult to prevent spurious formants; however, minority of them did not heavily influence the recognition accuracy, we treated them as accompany noise. LP analysis order was a compromise between performance and complexity. From LSD comparison we can see, order 20 and 28 has lower LSD than order 12 for the first two VTMs, and order 28 was smaller for the third one. Besides, consider the relation between poles and formant locations, the coincidence of order 12 LP envelope and spectrum was not high, and order 28 LP envelope existed a spurious formant at the fourth peak although it was not needed, and order 28 had a bigger computation than order 20 visibly. Therefore, order 20 was selected for our experiments.

Reverberation affects formants mean that there will be a shift of formant locations, i.e. formant frequencies, which will change according to different reverberation level. From the analysis mentioned above, formants could be used as a cue for reverberation level recognition, and its efficiency is much better than MFCC that is the commonly used feature in speech signal processing applications. In addition, formants can indicate the resonance characteristics of the vocal tract, which is closely related to speech intelligibility. The results of this study could be combined with the research area of dereverberation and objective speech intelligibility assessment.

From Table 3 we can see, MFCC recognition accuracy decreased dramatically at high pitch, i.e. 350 Hz, meanwhile, formants were more stable. As we known, part of female and some children, much less music or instruments, pitch frequencies may be higher than 350 Hz, which means it was more reliable to recognize reverberation level by formants. The present results are based on synthesized voiced speech and selected vowel, which should be extended to speech, music and even musical instruments applications in the future.

Acknowledgments. The authors thank Prof. W.-Y. Chan and Prof. S.-Y. Yu for their guidances for this research.

References

1. Deliyski, D.D.: Acoustic model and evaluation of pathological voice production. In: 3rd Conference on Speech Communication and Technology EUROSPEECH, Berlin, Germany, pp. 1969–1972 (1993)
2. Abberton, E.R.M., Howard, D.A., Fourcin, A.J.: Laryngographic assessment of normal voice: a tutorial. Clin. Linguist. Phonetics **3**, 281–296 (1989)
3. Benesty, J., Sondhi, M.M., Huang, Y. (eds.): Springer Handbook of Speech Processing. Springer, Heidelberg (2008). https://doi.org/10.1007/978-3-540-49127-9
4. Stevens, K.N.: Acoustic Phonetics. MIT, Cambridge (1998)
5. Nábělek, A.K., Letowski, T.R., Tucker, F.M.: Reverberant overlap- and self-masking in consonant identification. J. Acoust. Soc. Am. **86**(4), 1259–1265 (1989)

6. Kokkinakis, K., Loizou, P.C.: The impact of reverberant self-making and overlap-masking effects on speech intelligibility by Cochlear Implant Listeners (L). J. Acoust. Soc. Am. **130**(3), 1099–1102 (2011)
7. Kinoshita, K., Delcroix, M., Yoshioka, T., et al.: The REVERB challenge: a common evaluation framework for dereverberation and recognition of reverberant speech. In: IEEE WASPAA, pp. 1–4 (2013)
8. Crandell, C.C., Smaldino, J.J.: Classroom acoustics for children with normal hearing and with Hearing Impairment, Language, Speech, and Hearing Services in Schools. Am. Speech Lang. Hear. Assoc. **31**, 362–370 (2000)
9. Hazrati, O., Loizou, P.C.: The combined effects of reverberation and noise on speech intelligibility by cochlear implant listeners. Int. J. Audiol. **51**(6), 437–443 (2012)
10. Niessen, M.E., Krijnders, J.D., Boers, J., et al.: Assessing the reverberation level in speech. In: 19th International Congress on Acoustics, Madrid, 2–7 September 2007
11. Parada, P.P., Sharma, D., Naylor, P.A.: Non-intrusive estimation of the level of reverberation in speech. In: IEEE ICASSP (2014)
12. Allen, J.B., Berkley, D.A.: Image method for efficiently simulating small-room acoustics. J. Acoust. Soc. Am. **65**(4), 943–950 (1979)
13. Jeub, M., Nelke, C., Beaugeant, C., et al.: Blind estimation of the coherent-to-diffuse energy ratio from noisy speech signals. In: 19th European IEEE Signal Processing Conference, pp. 1347–1351 (2011)
14. Lehmann, E.A., Johansson, A.M., Nordholm, S.: Reverberation-time prediction method for room impulse responses simulated with the image-source model. In: IEEE Workshop on Applications of Signal Processing to Audio and Acoustics, pp. 159–162 (2007)
15. Ma, S., Xie, X.: Blind estimation of spectral standard deviation from room impulse response for reverberation level recognition based on linear prediction. Commun. Comput. Inform. Sci. **685**, 231–241 (2017)
16. Lee, S., Potamianos, A., Narayanan, S.: Acoustics of childrens speech: developmental changes of temporal and spectral parameters. J. Acoust. Soc. Am. **105**(3), 1455–1468 (1999)
17. Traunmüller, H., Eriksson, A.: the Frequency Range of the Voice Fundamental in the Speech of Male and Female Adults. Also in Perilus (2008)
18. Peterson, G.E., Barney, H.L.: Control methods used in a study of the vowels. J. Acoust. Soc. Am. **24**(2), 175–184 (1952)
19. Fant, G.: Vocal tract wall effects, losses, and resonance bandwidths. STL-QPSR **13**(2–3), 28–52 (1972)
20. Fant, G.: The vocal tract in your pocket calculator. STL-QPSR **1**, 001–019 (1985)
21. Reynolds, D.: Gaussian Mixture Model. Encyclopedia of Biometrics, pp. 659–663. Springer Science and Business Media, LLC, Boston (2009). https://doi.org/10.1007/978-0-387-73003-5
22. Dempster, A., Lair, N., Rubin, D.: Maximum likelihood from incomplete data via the EM algorithm. J. Roy. Stat. Soc. **39**, 1–38 (1977)
23. Xiang, S., Nie, F., Zhang, C.: Learning a Mahalanobis Distance Metric for data clustering and classification. Pattern Recogn. **41**(12), 3600–3612 (2008)

24. Kohavi, R.: A study of cross-validation and bootstrap for accuracy estimation and model selection. In: Proceedings of the 14th International Joint Conference on Artificial Intelligence, vol. 2(12), pp. 1137–1143. Morgan Kaufmann, San Mateo (1995)
25. Chistovich, L.A.: Center Auditory Processing of Peripheral Vowel Spectral. J. Acoust. Soc. Am. **77**, 789–805 (1985)
26. Rabiner, L.R.: Theory and Application of Digital Speech Processing, 1st edn. Pearson (2010). Chapter 9

Pedestrian Detection Using ACF Based Fast R-CNN

Lixue Zhuang[✉], Yi Xu, and Bingbing Ni

School of Electronic Information and Electrical Engineering,
Shanghai Jiao Tong University, Shanghai 200240, China
{qingliang,xuyi,nibingbing}@sjtu.edu.cn

Abstract. Accurate and efficient performance is an important requirement for pedestrian detection. In this paper, we propose a novel detection framework named as ACF Based Fast R-CNN (ABF-CNN). The
ABF-CNN consists of a ACF proposal generation part and a Fast R-
CNN detection network. The motivation to use the Aggregated Channel
Features (ACF) is due to its real-time efficiency and effective performance. To achieve high accuracy, we further propose to make use of
the deep learning method Fast-RCNN. Furthermore, in order to solve
the problem that CNN based methods have difficulty in hard negative
mining, we propose to integrate Online Hard Example Mining (OHEM)
training strategy into our detection framework. By thoroughly analyzing
and optimizing each step of pedestrian detection pipeline, we develop an
accurate detection framework with low computational complexity. The
experimental results demonstrate that our framework achieves state-of-
the-art performance on Caltech pedestrian dataset with 17% miss rate.

Keywords: ACF · Fast R-CNN · OHEM · Caltech
Pedestrian detection

1 Introduction

Pedestrian detection [1,2] is an important research problem and has attracted a
lot of attentions due to its diverse real-world applications, such as robotics [3],
person re-identification [4] and intelligent surveillance [5]. It aims to predict the
bounding boxes of all the pedestrians in an image. Generally, the main process
of pedestrian detection methods can be decomposed into two parts: proposal
generation and proposal classification.

Traditional methods [1,6,7] usually use a sliding window strategy to traverse
multiple locations of the image to generate proposals. Then they apply support
vector machine (SVM) or decision trees to classify the proposals based on hand-
crafted features. Therefore, exploring features that can discriminate pedestrians
from backgrounds is the main focus of these methods. A variety of features
have emerged with the development of research, such as Haar-like features [8],
Histogram of Oriented Gradient (HOG) [6], SIFT features [9] and so on. Later,

© Springer Nature Singapore Pte Ltd. 2018
G. Zhai et al. (Eds.): IFTC 2017, CCIS 815, pp. 172–181, 2018.
https://doi.org/10.1007/978-981-10-8108-8_16

Dollar et al. proposed Aggregated Channel Features (ACF) [1] to combine three kinds of channels: LUV color channels, normalized gradient magnitude channel, and histogram of oriented gradients channels on 6 directions. Then they extract the pixel sum in each block in each channel as features and feed them into AdaBoost decision trees to do classification. Due to the simplicity and efficiency, ACF becomes one of the most popular pedestrian detection method.

On the other hand, with the development of deep learning, several works [2, 10, 11] based on CNN show promising performance in many computer vision tasks, such as image classification, segmentation and object detection. R-CNN becomes a pioneering work in object detection field. In R-CNN, selective search [12] method is used to generate category-independent proposals, CNN network is used to extract a fixed-length feature vector for each proposal and the SVM classifier is used to classify the proposals. Although the R-CNN outperforms many traditional methods, its speed is limited for the need for proposal generation and CNN feature extraction for each proposal. This method is expensive and time-consuming. To solve this problem, SPPNet [13] and Fast R-CNN [2] methods have been proposed. In SPPNet, spatial pyramid pooling is introduced to allow the computation of CNN feature extraction once per image. Therefore the detection speed is increased by an order of magnitude. Based on SPPNet, Fast R-CNN further propose the ROI pooling and multi-task learning of class classification and bounding box regression. With multi-task loss, the Fast R-CNN network can be trained end to end and get the probability and locations of bounding boxes simultaneously. However, the limitation of Fast R-CNN is still the proposal generation part. Selective search takes about 2 s to generate proposals for a typical 500 × 300 images. This step takes as much time as the detection network. Moreover, since the selective search step generate ~2000 proposals for each image, it also brings a big computational burden to the CNN classification network.

To address this issue, we propose to apply Aggregated Channel Features (ACF) method for proposal generation. One of our motivation is to accelerate the proposal generation speed. Due to the simple design of multiple channel features and AdaBoost decision trees, the detection rate of ACF method can reach 20–30 FPS. In contrast, Selective Search takes about 2 s for one image. The other motivation is to reduce the number of proposals from thousands level to hundred level so that saving the computation cost of classification network. Selective Search method is based on grouping super-pixels to generate proposals which is more suitable to generate category-independent candidates. In contrast, ACF detector can be trained to specifically detect pedestrians. Compared with Selective Search method, ACF can produce fewer and higher quality candidate boxes which is more helpful to pedestrian detection.

At the same time, because of the imbalanced quantity of easy and hard examples in most training dataset, hard negative mining becomes important for boosting detection. However, due to the technical difficulty in training the CNN network with stochastic gradient descent (SGD), Fast R-CNN discard the step of hard negative mining. Therefore, in order to achieve faster training and higher accuracy, we propose to integrate Online Hard Example Mining (OHEM) [14] training strategy into our detection framework.

The rest of this paper is organized as follows. In Sect. 2, we first review the Fast R-CNN network and the Aggregate Channel Features (ACF) method, then describe our improved ACF and introduce how to apply Online Hard Example Mining (OHEM) into our detection framework. Experimental results on the popular Caltech pedestrian detection dataset are shown in Sect. 3. Finally, we give a conclusion of this paper in Sect. 4.

2   Methodology

In this section, we will introduce our proposed detection framework ACF Based Fast R-CNN (ABF-CNN) in detail. The framework of ABF-CNN is shown in Fig. 1. It consists of two parts: the ACF proposal generation part and the Fast R-CNN detection network. Compared with the original Fast R-CNN method [2], we propose to use the ACF method rather than selective search to extract proposals. In addition, we also make some improvement on ACF. The improved ACF achieve higher recall rate which ensuring the accuracy of the whole detection framework. At the same time, we propose to apply Online Hard Example Mining (OHEM) training strategy into our detection framework. In the following We will give a detailed introduction to each part.

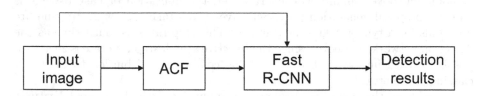

Fig. 1. Framework of pedestrian detection method ACF based Fast R-CNN

2.1   Fast R-CNN

In this section, we will briefly introduce the Fast R-CNN framework which is shown in Fig. 2. Fast R-CNN can be roughly divided into four steps: proposal generation, feature map generation, ROI pooling and network classification. In the first step, selective search method generate object-like proposals by grouping super-pixels. In the second step, given an input image, the Fast R-CNN network produce a feature map by a convolutional neural network. Then, for each proposal, the ROI pooling layer projects it onto the feature map and pool the region of interest (ROI) region into a fixed size feature vector. Finally, the feature vector of each proposal is fed into several fully connected layers which give class probability and bounding boxes locations.

The original Fast RCNN is tailored for generic object detection rather than pedestrian detection. Therefore, it choose selective search to generate proposals.

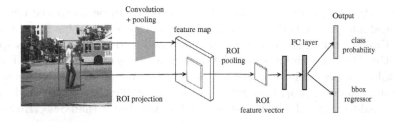

Fig. 2. Framework of Fast RCNN method

Generally, Selective search method extract ~2000 proposals for a 500 × 300 image and each image takes about 2 s. However, it is not necessary to generate all object-like proposals for pedestrian detection which will increase the computational complexity for the network. And selective search takes too much time for each image.

In order to solve these problem, we propose to apply the ACF algorithm instead of selective search to generate proposals for the framework. Next we will briefly introduce the ACF algorithm in Sect. 2.2.

2.2 Aggregated Channel Features

Given an input image I, ACF compute channels by linear or non-linear transformation of I as:

$$f = \Omega(I), \tag{1}$$

where Ω is a channel generation function, f is a registered map of the input image. ACF compute ten channels: LUV color channels, a gradient magnitude channel and histogram of oriented gradients channels of 6 directions. After obtaining the channels, ACF extract the sum of pixels values in each block of each channel as features. Then AdaBoost decision trees are trained over these features in boosting manner. The classifier is learned by four stages, where the number of trees in each stage are 64, 256, 1024 and 4096. In each stage, some hard negatives are extracted and added to the training set to improve the performance of detector. Finally, the illustration of ACF algorithm is shown in Fig. 3.

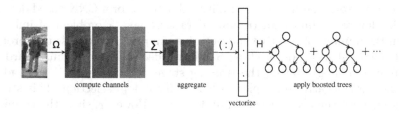

Fig. 3. Illustration of ACF method

Due to the simple design of ACF features, they can be computed efficiently by integral images. Thus the speed of ACF can achieve 20–30 fps for 640 × 480 image. Besides, the ACF detector can be trained to detect pedestrians specifically rather than generic objects. The candidate boxes extracted by ACF are of high-quality for pedestrian detection. Compared with Selective Search algorithm, ACF generates fewer proposals but has a higher recall rate. And the ACF detector have real-time speed which is about 40–60 times faster than Selective Search. Therefore, in this paper, we utilize the ACF method to generate proposals for the detection framework.

2.3   Improved Aggregated Channel Features

The proposal generation part plays a vital role in obtaining high recall rate for the whole detection framework. Once the pedestrian is missed in the proposal generation part, it can not be restored in the subsequent Fast R-CNN network. Therefore improving the recall rate of ACF algorithm is key point. The most direct way is to reduce the threshold of ACF detector. However, from our numerous experimental results, the improvement caused by reducing threshold is not satisfactory. Therefore, we propose a novel strategy to improve the recall rate of ACF detector. As stated in Sect. 2.2, the ACF classifier is learned by four stages. Each stage utilize hard negative mining strategy to accumulate the training set. The motivation of hard negative mining is to reduce the false positives rate and improve the accuracy of the ACF detector. However, this strategy will reduce the recall rate of the detector as more examples are rejected by the detector. In our detection framework, the proposals generated by ACF will continued to be classified by the Fast R-CNN network. The false positives can be rejected by the CNN network. Therefore, increasing the recall rate of ACF is more beneficial for the whole detection framework. For this reason, we propose to reduce the training stages and the number of decision trees to achieve a high recall rate on pedestrians. We propose a 3-stage cascaded ACF detector to generate proposals for the CNN network. In each stage, the detector combines 64, 256 and 1024 decision trees. The detailed experiment results will be shown in Sect. 3.1.

2.4   Online Hard Example Mining

It is well known that the training data plays an important role for the performance of detector, whether it is a traditional detector or a CNN based detection network. However, almost all training data sets have a problem of imbalance between the number of positive and negative samples. To address this problem, many traditional methods, such as SVM and decision trees, utilize hard negative mining strategy during the training stage. The key idea is to gradually select the hard negative examples rather than random selection. This strategy shows good performance in the field of detection. However, since the training of CNN network are always accompanied by stochastic gradient descent (SGD), it is difficult to apply hard example mining during the training of CNN network. Therefore many CNN-based methods ignore the hard negative mining strategy.

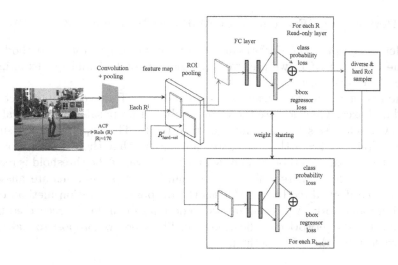

Fig. 4. Illustration of online hard example mining method

To address this problem, we propose to apply the Online Hard Example Mining strategy in our detection framework. OHEM can accelerate the convergence of the network by selecting better training samples. The illustration of online hard example mining algorithm is shown in Fig. 4. Instead of using read-only network, we achieve online hard example mining by alternately setting the whole network between "test" phase and "train" phase. In each training iteration, the network is set to "test" phase firstly and forward propagate all the proposals generated by ACF detector. Then by sorting the loss values we select the hard examples as the next batch of training data. In this way, we select the hard examples that are easily misjudged by the network rather than randomly selecting some samples as the training data. After that, the network is set to "train" phase and utilize the selected hard training examples for a forward and backward propagation. Experimental results show that OHEM strategy is of great help for accelerating the training and convergence of network. The detailed experiment results will be shown in Sect. 3.2.

3   Experimental Results

we investigate the performance of our proposed detection framework on the public Caltech pedestrian dataset. It consists of approximately 10 h of 640×480 30 Hz videos. The 10 h data is made up of 11 videos where the first 6 videos are used for training and the other 5 videos are used for testing. The standard Reasonable Caltech training set consists of 4250 frames with $\sim 2 \times 10^3$ annotated pedestrians. And the Caltech testing set contains 4024 frames with 1014 pedestrian bounding boxes.

3.1 Performance Evaluation of ACF and Improved ACF

In order to compare the performance of the proposal generation method ACF and the improved ACF, we use two strategies to conduct multiple experiments on the Caltech test set.

The first strategy is reducing the threshold of ACF detector to extract more candidate boxes. We calculate the total number of proposals and the recall rate on the Caltech test set under different thresholds. The experimental results is shown in Table 1. From this table, we can observe that the recall rate of ACF proposal generation method can not achieve 90% even if the threshold is reduced to −120. Therefore, there will be a large number of pedestrians are missed in the first step if we directly use ACF as the proposal generation method of our detection framework. And these missed pedestrians can not be recovered in the subsequent CNN network classification step. Therefore, we propose to make some improvements to the ACF method.

Table 1. Statistics of ACF proposals under different thresholds

Threshold	−10	−20	−30	−40	−50	−60
Number of proposals	11,769	20,558	35,149	58,144	92,178	142,083
Recall rate	80.1%	83.1%	85.3%	87.2%	87.6%	88.2%
Threshold	−70	−80	−90	−100	−110	−120
Number of proposals	212,951	309,936	439,037	621,671	831,448	1,057,504
Recall rate	88.5%	89.2%	89.5%	89.5%	89.6%	89.6%

The second strategy is to reduce the ACF training stages. The original classifier of ACF is learned by four stages, where the number of decision trees in each stage are 64, 256, 1024 and 4096. In each stage, some hard negative examples will be added to the training set to improve the accuracy of the classifier of next stage. In contrast, we propose to reduce the training stages of ACF. In this paper, we propose a 3-stage cascade ACF detector where the number of decision trees in subsequent stage are 32, 64, 1024, respectively. Specifically, we eliminate the last training stage of the original ACF detector. To evaluate the performance of our improved ACF, we also reduce its threshold and compare the results with that of the original ACF detector. The detailed results are shown in Table 2.

As can be seen from the table, as the lower the threshold, the recall rate of the ACF detector can reach more than 94%. At the same time, as the threshold decreases, the number of proposals will be significantly increased. Excessive proposals will cause a computational burden on the subsequent CNN network classification. Therefore, considering the accuracy and efficiency of the whole detection framework, we choose to set the threshold to −20. Under this threshold, there are approximately 170 candidate boxes per image and the recall rate is still as high as 94%.

Table 2. Statistics of improved ACF proposals under different thresholds

Threshold	-1	-10	-20	-30	-40	-50
Number of proposals	56,879	287,049	647,875	1,134,397	1,738,359	2,385,575
Recall rate	91.9%	93.3%	93.8%	94.0%	94.0%	94.1%
Threshold	-60	-70	-80	-90	-100	$-$
Number of proposals	2,984,878	3,394,890	3,552,328	3,580,557	3,582,573	$-$
Recall rate	94.1%	94.1%	94.1%	94.1%	94.1%	$-$

3.2 Performance Evaluation of OHEM

As mentioned in Sect. 2.4, when using Online Hard Example Mining (OHEM) strategy during the training phase, each iteration requires two forward propagation and one backward propagation which increase the complexity of one forward propagation over normal training strategy. Therefore, OHEM strategy takes more time than normal training strategy in each iteration. However, using OHEM strategy can speed up the convergence of the network and reduce the number of training iterations. The performance of networks trained by normal strategy and OHEM strategy is shown in Table 3.

Table 3. Comparisons of miss rates after different training iterations

Iterations	1k	2k	3k	4k
Miss rate (OHEM)	24%	22%	20%	19%
Miss rate (normal)	35%	31%	28%	26%
Iterations	5k	6k	7k	10k
Miss rate (OHEM)	17%	17%	17%	22%
Miss rate (normal)	25%	23%	21%	17%

From this table, we can observe that the network trained by OHEM strategy tends to converge after 5000 iterations, while the network trained by normal strategy require 10000 iterations to converge gradually. The training of network is conducted a single NVIDIA GTX TITAN GPU with 12 GB memory. From the perspective of time-consuming analysis, the network with OHEM takes 1120 ms while the normal network needs 800 ms in each iteration. But when taking into account of the number of iterations, using online hard negative example mining (OHEM) strategy to train network can save up to 30% times than normal training strategy. Besides, we find that the miss rate of OHEM after 10k training iterations is larger than that after 7k training iterations. This is because over-training leads to over-fitting on the training dataset.

Finally, we compare the performance of our proposed detection framework with the state-of-the-art methods on Caltech dataset. In our detection framework, the threshold of improved ACF is set to -20 and the Fast R-CNN network

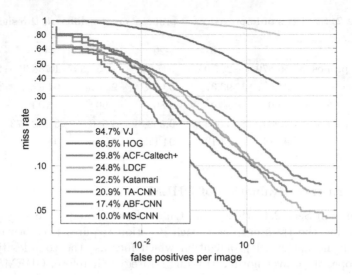

Fig. 5. Miss rate curve of pedestrian detection algorithm ACF based Fast R-CNN

is trained by OHEM strategy. The comparison result is shown in Fig. 5. Our proposed ACF Based Fast R-CNN (ABF-CNN) framework achieves 17% miss rate with shows comparable performance with the state-of-the-art methods. Besides, our ABF-CNN method reduce ~13% miss rate effectively compared with ACF method that resulting in a significant performance gain.

4   Conclusion

In this paper, we propose a novel pedestrian detection framework which named as ACF Based Fast R-CNN (ABF-CNN). In the framework, the proposed improved ACF effectively accelerate the detection and reduce the computation complexity of the network. And by integrating OHEM strategy, the network training has been accelerated significantly. In conclusion, our framework enables a accurate and fast solution for pedestrian detection. The experimental results demonstrate that our framework achieves state-of-the-art performance on Caltech pedestrian dataset with 17% miss rate.

Acknowledgments. The work was supported by State Key Research and Development Program (2016YFB1001003). This work was also supported by NSFC (U1611461, 61502301, 61527804, 61671298) and STCSM17511105401, China's Thousand Youth Talents Plan, 111 project, and the Shanghai Key Laboratory of Digital Media Processing and Transmissions.

References

1. Dollar, P., Appel, R., Belongie, S., et al.: Fast feature pyramids for object detection. IEEE Trans. Pattern Anal. Mach. Intell. **36**(8), 1532–1545 (2014)
2. Girshick, R.: Fast R-CNN. In: Proceedings of the IEEE International Conference on Computer Vision, pp. 1440–1448 (2015)
3. Ribeiro, D., Mateus, A., Miraldo, P., et al.: A real-time deep learning pedestrian detector for robot navigation. In: 2017 IEEE International Conference on Autonomous Robot Systems and Competitions (ICARSC), pp. 165–171. IEEE (2017)
4. Li, W., Zhao, R., Xiao, T., et al.: DeepReID: deep filter pairing neural network for person re-identification. In: Proceedings of the IEEE Conference on Computer Vision and Pattern Recognition, pp. 152–159 (2014)
5. Wang, X., Wang, M., Li, W.: Scene-specific pedestrian detection for static video surveillance. IEEE Trans. Pattern Anal. Mach. Intell. **36**(2), 361–374 (2014)
6. Dalal, N., Triggs, B.: Histograms of oriented gradients for human detection. In: IEEE Computer Society Conference on Computer Vision and Pattern Recognition, CVPR 2005, no. 1, pp. 886–893. IEEE (2005)
7. Xu, R., Zhang, B., Ye, Q., et al.: Cascaded L1-norm Minimization Learning (CLML) classifier for human detection. In: 2010 IEEE Conference on Computer Vision and Pattern Recognition (CVPR), pp. 89–96. IEEE (2010)
8. Chen, X., Kundu, K., Zhu, Y., et al.: 3D object proposals for accurate object class detection. In: Advances in Neural Information Processing Systems, pp. 424–432 (2015)
9. Lowe, D.G.: Distinctive image features from scale-invariant keypoints. Int. J. Comput. Vis. **60**(2), 91–110 (2004)
10. Girshick, R., Donahue, J., Darrell, T., et al.: Rich feature hierarchies for accurate object detection and semantic segmentation. In: Proceedings of the IEEE Conference on Computer Vision and Pattern Recognition, pp. 580–587 (2014)
11. Li, J., Liang, X., Shen, S.M., et al.: Scale-aware fast R-CNN for pedestrian detection. arXiv preprint arXiv:1510.08160 (2015)
12. Uijlings, J.R.R., Van De Sande, K.E.A., Gevers, T., et al.: Selective search for object recognition. Int. J. Comput. Vis. **104**(2), 154–171 (2013)
13. He, K., Zhang, X., Ren, S., Sun, J.: Spatial pyramid pooling in deep convolutional networks for visual recognition. In: Fleet, D., Pajdla, T., Schiele, B., Tuytelaars, T. (eds.) ECCV 2014. LNCS, vol. 8691, pp. 346–361. Springer, Cham (2014). https://doi.org/10.1007/978-3-319-10578-9_23
14. Shrivastava, A., Gupta, A., Girshick, R.: Training region-based object detectors with online hard example mining. In: Proceedings of the IEEE Conference on Computer Vision and Pattern Recognition, pp. 761–769 (2016)

Deep Face Recognition Using Adaptively-Weighted Verification Loss Function

Fan Qiu[1], Weiyao Lin[1(✉)], Xin Liu[2], Haoyang Yu[2], and Hongkai Xiong[1]

[1] Department of Electronic Engineering,
Shanghai Jiao Tong University, Shanghai, China
wylin@sjtu.edu.cn
[2] ShenZhen Tencent Computer System Co. Ltd., Shenzhen, China

Abstract. Face recognition plays a critical role in surveillance and security systems. Due to the large appearance variation of human faces, the dissimilarity among faces for the same person may be quite large. This leads to unstable results. To improve the stability and reliability of face recognition, this paper proposes a novel deep-based approach by introducing an adaptively-weighted verification loss function. The proposed loss function can properly enlarge the margin between positive face pairs and negative face pairs from the global perspective, thus obtain a more reliable recognition model by minimizing the dissimilarity between same-person faces and maximizing the dissimilarity between different-person faces. Experiments on the benchmark LFW and YTF datasets demonstrate that the proposed approach can obtain the state-of-the-art performances for face recognition.

Keywords: Face recognition · Deep learning · Verification loss
Adaptively weighted

1 Introduction

Face Recognition System (FRS) plays a critical role in several fields such as security, image database, surveillance, etc. With the appearance of more and more surveillance cameras, the demand for face recognition system has increased. Traditional methods [8–10] would use hand-crafted feature vectors to represent face images. However these methods cannot meet the actual needs in the real world. Recently, by using deep-based methods, the performance of face recognition began to reach the stage of practical application. As one of the deep-based methods, Deep Convolution Neural Network (DCNN) is wildly adopted to extract compact feature vectors from face images which contain identity information. [1, 5–7, 14]

The target of deep-based methods is to obtain a general and discriminative feature. Most existing works can be categorized into following: (1) Generating synthetic data and enlarging the size of the training dataset. [18, 19] (2) Designing suitable DCNN's structure for face recognition problem. [5, 16] (3) Proposing a

© Springer Nature Singapore Pte Ltd. 2018
G. Zhai et al. (Eds.): IFTC 2017, CCIS 815, pp. 182–192, 2018.
https://doi.org/10.1007/978-981-10-8108-8_17

novel loss function to train the neural network. [1,2,6] Among these methods, the loss functions have a great impact on the results. In this paper, we focus on the design of the loss functions.

In each training iteration, hundreds of face images are fed into the network. However, existing methods [1,2,6] only consider the relationship between two or three face images. The global information is ignored. Therefore, to cover the problem, we propose to consider the relationship from a global perspective. It will increase the stability and reliability by taking more face images into account.

Assuming there are several positive face pairs and negative face pairs, each face pair generates a feature distance which can represent the similarity of two face image. We use the positive distance to denote the feature distance between the positive face pair. The negative distance is used for the negative face pair. In Fig. 1, each red point denotes the positive distance and the black one denotes the negative distance. A threshold is manually selected to obtain a verification result. We argue that the distributions of the pair distances should be considered. The two distributions of the positive distances and negative distances should be apart. A margin between the positive distances and negative distances exists. From the global perspective, the margin need to be enlarged.

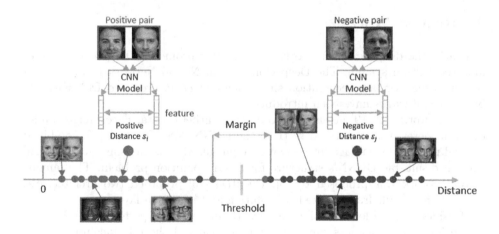

Fig. 1. The distributions of the pair distances. Each point denotes a pair distance. There is a margin between the positive distances and negative distances. Larger margin improves the stability and reliability.

Thus an adaptively-weighted verification loss function is proposed. We first minimize the covariance of the distributions. The essence of minimizing covariance is to add weights into the verification loss. Thus to further generalize the idea, different weights are merged adaptively into the verification loss. The margin between the positive distances and negative distances can be enlarged by the adaptively-weighted verification loss function.

In this paper, we propose a novel deep-based approach by introducing an adaptively-weighted verification loss function. Our main contributions are summarized as follows.

- We propose an adaptively-weighted verification loss function. The proposed loss function increase the stability of face recognition from a global perspective.
- We introduce three different methods to add weights into the verification loss. The margin between the positive distances and negative distances can be enlarged.
- We propose a novel deep-based approach by introducing an adaptively-weighted verification loss function. The proposed approach can obtain the state-of-the-art performances for face recognition.

The rest of this paper is organized as follows. Section 2 provides the related work. Section 3 demonstrates the framework of the proposed approach. Details of the proposed loss function are explained in the Sect. 4. Experiments and results will be demonstrated in Sect. 5. Finally, conclusions are discussed in the last section.

2   Related Works

Recently, the deep neural networks have greatly promoted the performance of face recognition system. The Deep Convolution Neural Network has become a powerful tool for face recognition since Taigman *et al.* proposed DeepFace [2]. Soon several works have been introduced.

Some works [18,19] attempted to create synthetic data. Face images under different poses were generated to train the DCNN. [18] Hu *et al.* [19] combined several parts of face image into a new face image. Meanwhile, some works [5,16] proposed suitable DCNN's structure for face recognition problem. The famous VGG network was proposed by [5]. DeepID3 [16] proposed two architectures which were rebuilt from stacked convolution and inception layers.

Besides, a good loss function can greatly increase the performance. Facenet [6] designed a triplet loss function which considered the relationship between three face images. The feature vectors extracted from the same person's images should be close. While those from different person's images should be apart. Meanwhile, DeepID [1] utilized the verification loss for the training phase. The verification loss takes two face images into account. Depending on whether the face images come from the same person or different people, the distance between them will be minimized or maximized. Based on feature space, the center loss function [14] was proposed employed to push each feature vector close to its class center.

The design of the loss function is quite important for the performance. Along this line, this paper proposes a novel loss function from the global perspective. Compared to the triplet loss or verification loss, several image pairs instead of one image pair are taken into account.

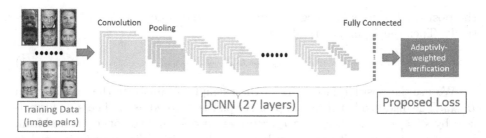

Fig. 2. The Framework of our proposed method. Positive and negative face pairs are used to train the deep convolution neural network (DCNN). A novel adaptively-weighted verification loss is proposed.

3 Overview

Our goal is to obtain a stable face recognition system. Thus we propose a novel deep-based approach by introducing an adaptively-weighted verification loss function. The framework of our proposed approach is shown in Fig. 2.

Lots of face images are used in the proposed approach. Face image pairs are randomly generated as the training data. To fully utilize the data, we adopt a deep convolution neural network (DCNN) to extract feature vector. The DCNN consists of several convolution layers, pooling layers and fully connected layers. A well trained DCNN can extract compact and representative feature vectors for face images. As mentioned earlier, loss function plays a critical role in the training phase. Thus we propose a novel adaptively-weighted verification loss to train the DCNN. The details of the proposed loss will be introduced in the following section.

4 Adaptively-Weighted Verification Loss

The proposed loss function is targeted at face verification problem. Positive face pairs and negative face pairs exist in the face verification problem. DCNN is used to extract feature vectors from the face images. General objective of loss functions is to obtain generalized and discriminative features from the face images.

We achieve this goal from a more global perspective. Figure 1 demonstrates the motivation. For face verification problem, there are several positive face pairs and negative face pairs. The margin between positive pairs and negative pairs is significant for face verification results. Larger margin allows more choices for the threshold, which will increase the stability and reliability.

To enlarge the margin, the covariances of the positive distances and negative distances are minimized respectively. The adaptively-weighted verification loss function is further proposed to generalize the idea.

The training dataset totally contains N_p positive face pairs and N_n negative face pairs. The proposed loss function is represented as L_{conv}. The covariances of the positive distances and negative distances are denoted as C_p and C_n respectively. Then the L_{conv} is formalized by

$$L_{conv} = C_p + C_n. \tag{1}$$

We use the positive face pairs as the example to illustrate the loss function L_{conv}. The distance between one positive pair is denoted as s_i. The s_i is formalized by $s_i = \|x_{ir} - x_{il}\|$. x_{il} and x_{ir} represent two feature vectors extracted from the positive face pair. The mean value μ_p of the positive distances is denoted as

$$\mu_p = \frac{1}{N_p} \sum_{i=1}^{N_p} s_i. \tag{2}$$

Thus the covariance of the positive distances is represented in Eq. 3

$$C_p = \frac{1}{N_p} \sum_{i=1}^{N_p} (s_i - \mu_p)^2. \tag{3}$$

Similarly, the covariance of the negative distances is formalized by Eq. 4

$$C_n = \frac{1}{N_n} \sum_{j=1}^{N_n} (s_j - \mu_n)^2. \tag{4}$$

The s_j denotes the negative distance and the μ_n represents the mean value of the negative distances. By minimizing the covariances of the positive distances and the negative distances respectively, the margin is enlarged.

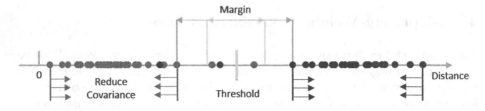

Fig. 3. The motivation behind the proposed loss function. The covariances of the pair distances (positive pair and negative pair) are reduced to enlarge the margin.

A loss function is used as the training objective. Through the gradient descent algorithm, the DCNN is well trained by minimizing the loss function. The gradients of the proposed loss function with respect to the feature vectors x_{il} and x_{ir} are formalized as

$$\frac{\partial L_{conv}}{\partial x_{ir}} = \frac{4}{N_p} (s_i - \mu_p)(x_{ir} - x_{il}), \tag{5}$$

$$\frac{\partial L_{conv}}{\partial x_{il}} = -\frac{4}{N_p}(s_i - \mu_p)(x_{ir} - x_{il}). \tag{6}$$

Figure 3 demonstrates the effect of the proposed loss function. From Eq. 5, the proposed loss function will push each positive pair distance s_i close to the mean value of the positive distances μ_p. Each negative pair distance s_j is pushed close to the mean value of the negative distances μ_n too. The second part $(x_{ir} - x_{il})$ of the gradient is same with the gradient of the verification(L2) loss function. Thus the first part $(s_i - \mu_p)$ can be treated as weights, and the adaptively-weighted verification(AWV) loss function L_{AWV} is further proposed.

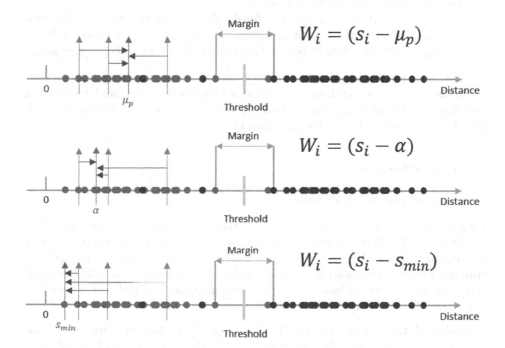

Fig. 4. The intuitive explanations for three kinds of adaptively-weighted methods. Each pair distance (red points) will be pushed close to the mean value μ_p, the fixed value α or the minimum value s_{min} respectively in different methods. The covariance of the distribution is reduced and the margin between the positive and the negative distances is enlarged. (Color figure online)

The gradients of the AWV loss function with respect to the feature vectors x_{il} and x_{ir} are denoted as

$$\frac{\partial L_{AWV}}{\partial x_{ir}} = \frac{4}{N_p}W_i(x_{ir} - x_{il}), \tag{7}$$

$$\frac{\partial L_{AWV}}{\partial x_{il}} = -\frac{4}{N_p}W_i(x_{ir} - x_{il}). \tag{8}$$

We still attempt to enlarge the margin between positive pairs and negative pairs. And we propose three adaptively-weighted methods for the AWV loss function.

- The basic one has been explained in the previous pages. The weight W_i is set to the difference between the pair distance s_i and mean value μ_p. Through gradient descent algorithm, each pair distance s_i will be pushed close to the mean value. And the covariance of the pair distances is minimized.
- The mean value is replaced by a fixed value α. The weight W_i is set to the difference between the pair distance s_i and the fixed value α. We can manually manipulate the pair distances to be close to a fixed value. By setting proper value α, the margin can be increased.
- In the positive pair distances, the fixed value is replaced by the minimum value s_{min} of the positive pair distances. The weight W_i is denoted as $W_i = s_i - s_{min}$. And the weights W_j for negative pairs are set to $W_j = s_i - s_{max}$.

The intuitive explanations are shown in Fig. 4. Three adaptively-weighted methods are proposed to illustrate the idea of adaptively-weighted verification loss function. By merging weights into the verification loss, the margin between positive distances and negative distances is enlarged.

5   Experiments

5.1   Implementation Details

Preprocessing. Generally, we follow the same strategy used in Wu's method [14]. The faces in the images will be detected by the method proposed by Felzenszwalb et al. [12]. When the detection fails, we discard the image from training set. Then the facial landmarks are detected by Xiong et al. [13]'s method. Based on the five facial landmarks, the face images are aligned and cropped to 112 X 96 RGB images.

Training data. We use the CASIA-WebFace [7] dataset to train the neural network. It contains 493,456 face images of 10,575 identities, which is public to researchers and wildly used dataset. All images in the dataset are applied the preprocessing algorithm. The images are horizontally flipped for data augmentation. The scale of CASIA-WebFace dataset is smaller compared to [5] (2M) and [6] (200M).

Detailed settings in Training. We implement our approach by using the Caffe [4] framework. The deep residual-structure convolution neural network provided by Wu [14] is adopted. Same training parameters are used with Wu's method [14]. The weights of the softmax loss and the adaptively-weighted verification loss are set to 1 and 0.005 respectively.

Testing dataset. The proposed methods are evaluated on the two famous datasets Labeled Faces in the Wild (LFW) [3] and YouTube Faces (YTF) [17], which have been widely used for face recognition in recent years. [2,6,9,10,15]

(a) Examples in LFW dataset.

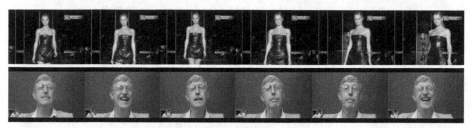

(b) Examples in YTF dataset.

Fig. 5. Some examples of testing datasets. In LFW dataset, there are several positive face pairs and negative face pairs for testing. And in YFT dataset, each subject contains one or several video clips. The objective is to recognize whether two video clips captured from the same person or not.

- The LFW dataset contains 13233 web-collected images from 5749 different identities, with large variations in pose, expression and illumination. There are total 3000 positive pairs and 3000 negative pairs for experiments.
- The YTF dataset contains 3,425 videos of 1,595 different people. An average of 2.15 videos are available for each subject. The shortest clip duration is 48 frames, the longest clip is 6,070 frames, and the average length of a video clip is 181.3 frames. And the results are reported on 5,000 video pairs (Fig. 5).

5.2   Results and Discussions

We evaluate the face verification result by the standard protocol of unrestricted with labeled outside data [11]. We compare results of four methods: (1) Simply applying the softmax loss function to train the DCNN (softmax only); (2) Minimizing the covariance of the distribution and using the differences between each distances and the mean value as the weights (mean-weighted); (3) Manually replacing the mean value and adopting $W_i = s_i - \alpha$ as the weights (manually weighted); (4) Pushing each positive distance to the minimum value and each negative distance to the maximum value (minimum-weighted).

We also compare our results with state-of-the-art methods on both LFW and YTF datasets: DeepFace [2], FaceNet [6], DeepID [1] and Center Loss [14].

The results of our proposed method and several comparison methods are presented in Table 1. The source code of the center loss is provided by the author. For a fair comparison, we use the center loss to train the network by ourselves. And other results are referred from their own paper respectively.

Table 1 shows the verification accuracy of different methods. From the accuracy results, we can see that: (1) Our approach has obviously improved results

Table 1. Accuracy results on LFW and YTF datasets.

Method	Images	Acc. on YTF	Acc. on LFW
DeepFace [2]	4M	91.4%	97.35%
FaceNet [6]	200M	95.1%	99.63%
DeepID [1]	0.4M	–	98.70%
Center Loss [14]	0.5M	93.7%	98.51%
Softmax only	0.5M	90.9%	97.1%
Mean-weighted (μ_p)	0.5M	93.5%	98.91%
Manually weighted (α)	0.5M	92.7%	98.87%
Minimum-weighted (s_{min})	0.5M	93.9%	98.96%

than the result of softmax only. This indicates that proper weighted verificaiton loss can effectively improve the performance by enlarging the threshold margin.(2) Improvements are obtained by our approach compared with other methods except the Facenet. This demonstrates the effectiveness of our approach. (3) A much larger training dataset is used by Facenet than ours. The size of the training data has much impact on the performance. Our approach achieve a comparable result by using much less training data.

5.3   Discussions About Three Weighted Methods

The performance of three weighted methods are shown in Table 1. Figure 6 shows the ROC curves of different methods, which includes the three different weighted methods, softmax only and the center loss approach. Due to the lack of data and hardware, we cannot realize the Facenet, DeepID and DeepFace approaches.

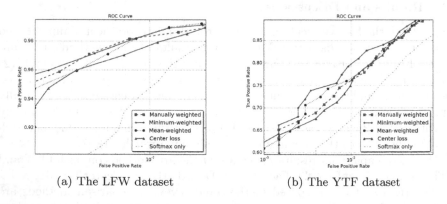

(a) The LFW dataset   (b) The YTF dataset

Fig. 6. ROC curves for different methods.

From Table 1 and Fig. 6, we can observe: (1) The proposed approach have larger AUC area than the center loss and softmax only methods. This indicates that the proposed approach have more stability and reliability. (2) The minimum-weighted method have better performance than the mean-weighted method. This demonstrates that minimum-weighted method can effectively enlarge the margin and increase the stability. (3) For the manually weighted method, the weights have been set several times with different values. However the best result is still inferior to the mean-weighted and minimum-weighted methods. This implies that it is not easy to manually set good weights for the proposed approach.

6 Conclusion

In this paper, the main target is to achieve stable and reliable results for the face verification problem. An novel adaptively-weighted verification loss is proposed. For different face pairs, different weights are merged into the verification loss adaptively. The margin between the positive and negative face pairs is enlarged. Experiments have shown the effectiveness of the proposed method. The stability and reliability increase due to the larger margin.

Acknowledgement. This work is supported by Tencent Research Grant, National Science Foundation of China (61471235, 61720106001), and Shanghai "The Belt and Road" Young Scholar Exchange Grant (17510740100).

References

1. Sun, Y., Chen, Y., Wang, X., et al.: Deep learning face representation by joint identification-verification. In: Advances in Neural Information Processing Systems, pp. 1988–1996 (2014)
2. Taigman, Y., Yang, M., Ranzato, M.A., et al.: Deepface: closing the gap to human-level performance in face verification. In: Proceedings of the IEEE Conference on Computer Vision and Pattern Recognition, pp. 1701–1708 (2014)
3. Huang, G.B., Ramesh, M., Berg, T., et al.: Labeled faces in the wild: a database for studying face recognition in unconstrained environments. Technical Report 07–49, University of Massachusetts, Amherst (2007)
4. Jia, Y., Shelhamer, E., Donahue, J., et al.: Caffe: convolutional architecture for fast feature embedding. In: Proceedings of the 22nd ACM International Conference on Multimedia, pp. 675–678. ACM (2014)
5. Parkhi, O.M., Vedaldi, A., Zisserman, A.: Deep face recognition. In: BMVC, vol. 1(3), p. 6 (2015)
6. Schroff, F., Kalenichenko, D., Philbin, J.: Facenet: a unified embedding for face recognition and clustering. In: Proceedings of the IEEE Conference on Computer Vision and Pattern Recognition, pp. 815–823 (2015)
7. Yi, D., Lei, Z., Liao, S., et al.: Learning face representation from scratch. arXiv preprint arXiv:1411.7923 (2014)
8. Turk, M.A., Pentland, A.P.: Face recognition using eigenfaces. In: IEEE Computer Society Conference on Computer Vision and Pattern Recognition, 1991, Proceedings CVPR 1991, pp. 586–591. IEEE (1991)
9. Chen, D., Cao, X., Wen, F., et al.: Blessing of dimensionality: high-dimensional feature and its efficient compression for face verification. In: Proceedings of the IEEE Conference on Computer Vision and Pattern Recognition, pp. 3025–3032 (2013)

10. Chen, D., Cao, X., Wang, L., Wen, F., Sun, J.: Bayesian face revisited: a joint formulation. In: Fitzgibbon, A., Lazebnik, S., Perona, P., Sato, Y., Schmid, C. (eds.) ECCV 2012. LNCS, vol. 7574, pp. 566–579. Springer, Heidelberg (2012). https://doi.org/10.1007/978-3-642-33712-3_41
11. Huang, G.B., Learned-Miller, E.: Labeled faces in the wild: Updates and new reporting procedures. Dept. Comput. Sci., Univ. Massachusetts Amherst, Amherst, MA, USA, Technical report, 14–003 (2014)
12. Felzenszwalb, P.F., Girshick, R.B., McAllester, D., et al.: Object detection with discriminatively trained part-based models. IEEE Trans. Patt. Anal. Mach. Intell. **32**(9), 1627–1645 (2010)
13. Xiong, X., De la Torre, F.: Supervised descent method and its applications to face alignment. In: Proceedings of the IEEE Conference on Computer Vision and Pattern Recognition, pp. 532–539 (2013)
14. Wen, Y., Zhang, K., Li, Z., Qiao, Y.: A discriminative feature learning approach for deep face recognition. In: Leibe, B., Matas, J., Sebe, N., Welling, M. (eds.) ECCV 2016. LNCS, vol. 9911, pp. 499–515. Springer, Cham (2016). https://doi.org/10.1007/978-3-319-46478-7_31
15. Cao, X., Wipf, D., Wen, F., et al.: A practical transfer learning algorithm for face verification. In: Proceedings of the IEEE International Conference on Computer Vision, pp. 3208–3215 (2013)
16. Sun, Y., Liang, D., Wang, X., et al.: Deepid3: face recognition with very deep neural networks. arXiv preprint arXiv:1502.00873 (2015)
17. Wolf, L., Hassner, T., Maoz, I.: Face recognition in unconstrained videos with matched background similarity. In: CVPR, pp. 529–534 (2011)
18. Masi, I., Trần, A.T., Hassner, T., Leksut, J.T., Medioni, G.: Do We Really Need to Collect Millions of Faces for Effective Face Recognition? In: Leibe, B., Matas, J., Sebe, N., Welling, M. (eds.) ECCV 2016. LNCS, vol. 9909, pp. 579–596. Springer, Cham (2016). https://doi.org/10.1007/978-3-319-46454-1_35
19. Hu, G., Peng, X., Yang, Y., et al.: Frankenstein: learning deep face representations using small data. arXiv preprint arXiv:1603.06470 (2016)

Exudate Detection in Fundus Images via Convolutional Neural Network

Guo Li, Shibao Zheng[✉], and Xinzhe Li

Shanghai Key Labs of Digital Media Processing and Transmission,
Institute of Image Communication and Network Engineering,
Shanghai Jiao Tong University, Shanghai 200240, China
sbzh@sjtu.edu.cn

Abstract. Exudate detection in fundus images is an important task for the screening of people with diabetic retinopathy. In this paper, Convolutional Neural Network (CNN) is used to detect the exudates in fundus images. An auxiliary loss for classification is designed to better train the CNN architecture. Besides, we use a boosted training method to improve and speed-up the CNN training. The trained model has been evaluated on our own annotated dataset and three public available databases, obtaining an AUC of 0.98, 0.96, 0.94, 0.91 respectively.

Keywords: Exudate detection · Convolutional Neural Network
Multi-task learning · Boosted training

1 Introduction

Diabetic retinopathy (DR) is the leading cause of blindness among middle-aged people. Early diagnosis of DR and timely treatment can keep patients with a fairly good quality of vision, so periodic examination is recommended for people with diabetes [1]. However, in many areas, especially for rural areas, the ophthalmologists are too few to meet the demand of large number of diabetic patients. Thus, computer-aided screening systems that help easing the burden on ophthalmologists are in great demand. In this paper, we focus on the detection of exudates, since exudates are one of the most obvious clinical signs that indicate the presence of DR. They usually appear as white or yellow structures in fundus images and have varying sizes. However, some other bright structures such as the reflections and the optic disk usually interfere with the detection of exudates. As illustrated in Fig. 1, the reflections always exist at the boundary or in the area around main blood vessels.

In recent years, deep convolutional neural networks (DCNN) have been widely used in the field of semantic segmentation [2]. Jonathan et al. [3] used fully convolutional network for pixel-wise prediction and proposed a novel skip architecture to combine the low level features with high level features to balance the location accuracy and semantics. Instead of bilinear interpolation in [3], deconvolutional network was proposed in [4]. Olaf et al. [5] took advantage of both skip architecture in [3] and deconvolution in [4] to design a network named "U-Net" which won the ISBI challenge 2015 for the segmentation of neuronal structures.

© Springer Nature Singapore Pte Ltd. 2018
G. Zhai et al. (Eds.): IFTC 2017, CCIS 815, pp. 193–202, 2018.
https://doi.org/10.1007/978-981-10-8108-8_18

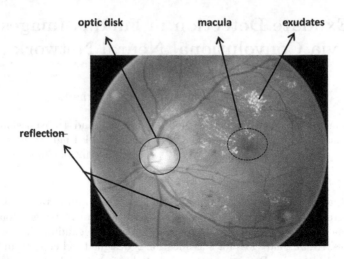

Fig. 1. A fundus image with exudates, including the optic disk, reflection and the macula.

In this paper, the U-Net [5] for neuronal membranes segmentation is transferred to the exudate detection. We design a multi-task DCNN network based on this architecture to predict the class label of every pixel. Compared to this architecture, our main contributions are summarized below.

(1) We add an auxiliary training loss to promote the training process of the network. Actually, the contracting path of U-Net which contains pooling layers aims at capturing context while the expanding path with deconvolution operations propagates the context information to higher resolution layers to locate the object. In order to make the network learn the context information faster and better, we propose an auxiliary binary classifier output that takes into account features from layers before each pooling layer and unpooling layer. This output indicates whether the input image contains exudates. Additionally, the features from the penultimate layer with the highest level of semantic information are also used to train the classifier. Due to the limited data, we resize these layers to a same size of 2×2 instead of using the whole feature maps which would introduce more parameters to the DCNN. The architecture is illustrated in Fig. 2.
(2) Considering the unbalanced training data, we adopt a dynamic weight assigning method from Mark et al. [6] during training process. For the fundus images, the regions with exudates are very small comparing to the whole image, which makes the positive samples far less than the negative data. Thus, the DCNN is more likely to classify test data as normal images. The boosted training method will make the "hard" samples with larger weights to be more concerned during training phase, which can improve and speed-up the training process.

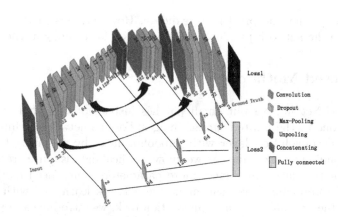

Fig. 2. Details of the DCNN architecture containing convolutional layers, dropout layers, max-pooling layers, unpooling layers, concatenating layers and a fully connected layer. The number of channels is denoted on the bottom of the box. The width or height is provided at the top of the box.

Moreover, the deconvolution layers in the original U-Net architecture are replaced by unpooling layers. The network is trained on the e-optha EX [7] database and tested on other two databases including DIARETDB1_v2 [8] and our own annotated Kaggle subset, obtaining an AUC (Area Under the Curve) of 0.96 and 0.98 respectively.

The rest of this paper is organized as follows. Related work on exudate detection in fundus images are reviewed in Sect. 2. The details of our method are presented in Sect. 3. Section 4 presents the details of the experiments. Conclusion and future work are discussed in Sect. 5.

2 Related Work

Researches on the automatic detection of exudates in fundus images can be roughly divided into two categories, unsupervised classification methods and supervised ones [1]. Methods including morphological operation, region growing and thresholding are mainly used in the unsupervised methods which do not need any label information. Walter et al. [9] leveraged the high contrast of exudate lesions to get the candidates, then used the morphological techniques to obtain the boundaries of exudates. For the supervised methods, machine learning methods are always used for candidates selection. Zhang et al. [7] first removed the dark and bright regions similar to exudates to get the candidates, then used a list of handcrafted features including textural features and contextual features to train a random forest classifier. Similarly, naive bayes classifier and SVMs are trained with colour information and wavelet analysis result of the candidates in [10]. Prentasic et al. [11] used a sliding-window approach to train a 10-layers DCNN with patches whose labels are determined by the center pixel of the corresponding patch, obtaining a probability map where the pixel value indicates the probability that the pixel is an exudate. However, this method was quite slow because the network predicted only one pixel for running a whole patch.

3   Proposed Method

Unlike the U-Net [5], we put small patches instead of the whole image into the DCNN due to the limited fundus images. For the network architecture, we replace the deconvolution layer with unpooling layer by repeating the data of the corresponding feature map. As we know, medical data is quite precious while the deconvolution layer introduces more parameters which need more training samples. The unpooling layer can make the network learn well with few data. Other than the original loss for segmentation task, we introduce a auxiliary loss for classification task.

3.1   Network Details

The network for segmentation contains two max-pooling layers, two unpooling layers and two corresponding concatenating layers. Before each pooling layer and unpooling layer, convolution layer is used twice. Besides, each convolution layer is followed by a ReLU activation layer. In order to reduce overfitting, we also use dropout layers. The loss for segmentation task is computed below.

$$Loss1 = -\frac{1}{M} \sum_{m=1}^{M} [t_m \log p_m + (1 - t_m) \log(1 - p_m)], \tag{1}$$

$$M = patch\_weight * patch\_height * batch\_size, \tag{2}$$

where t_m is the reference pixel label of the pixel with index of m and p_m is the assigned pixel probability score of the pixel whose index is m. For the auxiliary task, we use the feature maps both from the low level and high level. These feature maps are pooling to the same size of 2×2 and then are concatenated, finally connected to a fully connected layer with 2 nodes for binary classification. The second loss indicated by $Loss2$ is also Softmax loss.

$$Loss2 = -\frac{1}{N} \sum_{n=1}^{N} [t_n \log p_n + (1 - t_n) \log(1 - p_n)], \tag{3}$$

where t_n is the reference pixel label of the patch with a index of n and p_n is the assigned pixel probability score of the patch whose index is n. N is the batch size. At last the total loss is computed as follows:

$$Loss = \lambda_1 * Loss1 + \lambda_2 * Loss2, \tag{4}$$

where λ_1 and λ_2 are hyper-parameters. Figure 2 illustrates an overview of the network architecture with the omission of the ReLUs.

3.2 Dynamic Weights Assigning

In this experiment, we assign a weight to each training sample when computing the value of loss function. So the Eq. (1) is re-formulated as follows:

$$Loss1 = -\frac{1}{M} \sum_{m=1}^{M} w_m * [t_m \log p_m + (1 - t_m) \log(1 - p_m)], \tag{5}$$

where w_m is the weight of the training sample with the index of m. From the Eq. (5), we can infer that the sample with higher weight value would contribute more to the updating of the network parameters. Thus, we assign higher value to the samples that have a larger classification errors, which makes the network more concerned on these "hard" samples during the next training epoch. The boosted training procedure is described by Algorithm 1.

Algorithm 1. Dynamic Iterative Algorithm for training DCNN

Input: $F^0(x)$: initial score function of network; N: number of training samples; x_i: training sample, $i \in [1, N]$; y_i: ground truth corresponding to x_i; *epoch*: the total training epoch; *iter_interval*: the interval epoch for updating the weights
Output: optimal $F^*(x)$
 1: initial $t = 0$;
 2: **for** each $i \in [1, N]$ **do**
 3:     $w_i^0 = 1$;
 4: **end for**;
 5: **repeat**
 6:     Train the network for *iter_interval* epoches, $t = t + 1$, get $F^t(x)$;
 7:     Classify each training sample, obtaining p_i^t;
 8:     Compute the L1 loss $l_i^t = |p_i^t - y_i|$;
 9:     Compute the new weight $w_i^t = N * \dfrac{l_i^t}{\sum_{n=1}^{N} l_n^t}$;
10: **until** $(t * iter\_inteval >= epoch)$

---

4   Experimental Results

4.1   Datasets

Four public datasets including e-optha EX [7], DIARETDB1_v2 [8], HEI-MED [10], Messidor [12] are used in this paper. Besides, we select 30 images with exudates and 50 normal images from the Diabetic Retinopathy Detection challenge database from Kaggle [13]. Then an expert annotates the exudates in pixel-wise level. Table 1 summarizes the four public databases and our own database. Positive images mean images with exudates while negative images are equal to images without exudates.

4.2   Preprocessing

Before training, the black border of fundus images are removed using the thresholding method. Besides, images with various sizes are all resized to the same resolution of 512×512. As stated in [9], the green channel of the original color image appears most contrasted. We use Contrast Limited Adaptive Histogram Equalization (CLAHE) method to enhance the contrast of the exudates and non-exudates on the green channel. Ten thousand of patches with size of 48×48 are randomly selected from each image of the e-optha EX dataset and thus we obtain 470 thousand samples for training and evaluation. About 11% of them has at least one exudate pixel. Like other tasks in deep learning, data normalization is also performed on the input patches.

4.3   Training

In our experiment, we initialize the parameters of convolutional layers in the distribution of glorot uniform. The dropout ratio is set to be 0.2. The learning rate is 0.01. The kernel size is 3 and the stride size is 2. As we focus on the performance of exudate segmentation, the value of λ_1 should be larger than λ_2. By tuning the parameters, the pair of (10,1) achieves the best performance. The ratio of data for validation is 0.1. Max epoch for training is 130. For the dynamic assigning weights method, we update the parameters after every 5 epochs. About 20 min is cost for each epoch on a GPU with the type of NVIDIA TITAN X. During testing phase, we use sliding window method with a stride of 10 pixels to predict the patches, then average the overlayed pixels, and finally get a output probability map, which costs 10 s for a 512×512 image.

4.4   Evaluation Results

We train on the e-optha EX database and test on the other three public datasets and our annotated Kaggle subset. Figure 3 shows the results of 2 images from the HEI-MED database. We use the image level and pixel level evaluation, respectively indicating the performance of classification and detection. Two indictors including sensitivity and specificity are computed using four elements which are true positive (TP), false positive (FP), true negative (TN), false negative (FN). A pixel or image with exudate is called a TP when the prediction is exudate, FN otherwise. While a TN pixel or image means that a normal pixel or image is truly referenced to be an pixel or image without lesion. An FP pixel or image

Table 1. Description of four public databases and our annotated kaggle subset.

	e-optha EX	DIARETDB1_v2	HEI-MED	Messidor	Kaggle subset
Positive Number	47	38	54	226	30
Negative Number	35	51	115	974	50
groundTruth	pixel-wise	roughly pixel-wise	pixel-wise	image-wise	pixel-wise

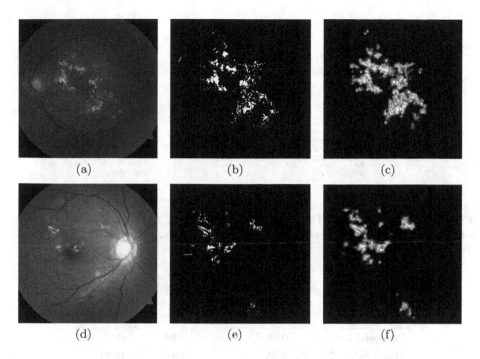

(a)   (b)   (c)

(d)   (e)   (f)

Fig. 3. Left column: color fundus images from HEI-MED. Middle column: ground truth images. Right column: output of the DCNN

is regarded as an exudate pixel or image while its true label is normal. The formulations are as followed:

$$sensitivity = \frac{TP}{TP + FN},$$ (6)

$$specificity = \frac{TN}{TN + FP}.$$ (7)

For the pixel level evaluation, we test on our own annotated 30 images and HEI-MED database. Every image gets a series of sensitivity and specificity numbers due to different threshold. We average the results of total images in each database respectively and get two ROC curves about the two databases. The corresponding AUC is 0.97 and 0.91 which are illustrated in Fig. 4(a).

For the image level evaluation, we first get the image level probability, i.e. a probability that image contains at least one exudate, by computing the maximum of the values in the output probability map. Then we also use Eqs. (6) and (7) to evaluate the performance. We apply it to the three public database including DIARETDB1_v2, HEI-MED, Messidor and our own Kaggle subset. The AUC value are 0.96, 0.94, 0.91, 0.98 respectively. The resulting ROC curves are given on Fig. 4(b). We compare our results with other different methods proposed by [7,10] which are illustrated in Table 2. Similarly, Zhang et al. [7] trained on e-optha EX and tested on the other three public available databases. Our result is

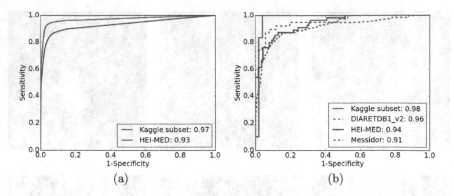

Fig. 4. The ROC curves and AUC values of our method. (a) Evaluated on the kaggle subset and HEI-MED at pixel level. (b) Evaluated on kaggle subset and three public databases at image level.

Table 2. Comparison of AUC on three public databases.

	DIARETDB1_v2	HEI-MED	Messidor
Proposed method	**0.96**	**0.94**	0.91
Zhang et al. [7]	0.95	0.94	**0.93**
Giancardo et al. [10]	0.93	0.94	0.90

slightly better than them on DIARETDB1_v2. However, there exists some hyper-parameters that depend on the test dataset in their method. For example, when testing on DIARETDB1_v2, they adjusted the coefficients of spatial calibration because the field of view (FOV) angle in e-optha EX dataset is different from that of DIARETDB1_v2. Another method proposed in [10] trained and tested on a same database using the leave-one-out cross-validation. From Table 2, we can see that our method is all better than them on the three databases. Moreover, the performance of this method decreases when training is done on one database and testing on a different database. For example, the AUC value is 0.84 when training on Messidor and testing on HEI-MED, which shows the relatively low robustness of the method.

4.5   Performance of Boosted Training and Auxiliary Loss

Owning to the boosted training method, the accuracy of validation data during training phase is improved which is illustrated in Fig. 5(a). At the first 5 epoches, the two accuracies are the same. Once the weights are re-assigned, the accuracy of the boosted training is higher than that of the regular training. From Fig. 5(b), we can see that the training loss of the multi-output network is decreasing faster than that of the single-output architecture, which illustrates that the auxiliary loss is helpful for training.

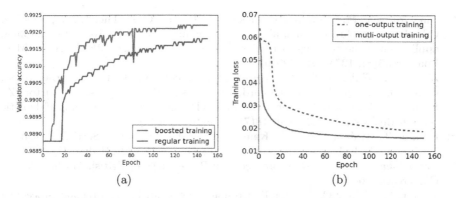

(a)   (b)

Fig. 5. (a) The accuracies of two different training method during training phase. (b) The training loss for segmentation task of two architectures during training phase.

5   Conclusion

In this paper, a CNN-based method for exudate detection on the fundus images has been introduced. The skip architecture in the network makes the model obtain good location and context information at the same time. Compared to the deconvolution layer, the unpooling layer still can maintain a good performance while reducing the number of parameters of DCNN. An auxiliary loss can speed up the training process and make the network easier to converge. Boosted training is proved to be very efficient in the DCNN training with fundus images. The good performance on the three public available databases shows the robustness of our method regardless of the various image quality and noise like reflections and artifacts. The method is simple and can be transferred to the detection of other diabetic retinopathy like hemorrhages and microaneurysms.

Acknowledgment. This work was supported in part by National Natural Science Foundation of China (61671289, 61221001, 61771303).

References

1. Oliver, F., Rajendra, A.U., Kwan, N., Jasjit, S.S.: Algorithms for the automated detection of diabetic retinopathy using digital fundus images: a review. J. Med. Syst. **36**, 145–157 (2012)
2. LeCun, Y., Bengio, Y., Hinton, G.: Deep learning. Nature **521**(7553), 436–444 (2015)
3. Long, J., Shelhamer, E., Darrell, T.: Fully convolutional networks for semantic segmentation. arXiv:1411.4038 [cs.CV] (2014)
4. Hyeonwoo, N., Seunghoon, H., Bohyung, H.: Learning deconvolution network for semantic segmentation. arXiv:1505.04366v1 [cs.CV] (2015)
5. Ronneberger, O., Fischer, P., Brox, T.: U-Net: convolutional networks for biomedical image segmentation. In: Navab, N., Hornegger, J., Wells, W.M., Frangi, A.F. (eds.) MICCAI 2015. LNCS, vol. 9351, pp. 234–241. Springer, Cham (2015). https://doi.org/10.1007/978-3-319-24574-4_28

6. van Grinsven, M.J.J.P., van Ginneken, B., Hoyng, C.B., Theelen, T., Sánchez, C.I.: Fast convolutional neural network training using selective data sampling: application to hemorrhage detection in color fundus images. IEEE Trans. Med. Imaging **35**(5), 1273–1284 (2016)

7. Zhang, X., Thibault, G., Decencirere, E., Marcotegui, B., Lay, B., Danno, R., Cazuguel, G., Quellec, G., Lamard, M., Massin, P., Chabouis, A., Victor, Z., Erginay, A.: Exudate detection in color retinal images for mass screening of diabetic retinopathy. Med. Image Anal. **18**(7), 1026–1043 (2014)

8. Kauppi, T., Kalesnykiene, V., Kamarainen, J.-K., Lensu, L., Sorri, I., Uusitalo, H., Pietila, J., Kalviainen, H., Uusitalo, H.: The DIARETDB1 diabetic retinopathy database and evaluation protocol. In: Proceedings of British Machine Vision Conference (2007)

9. Walter, T., Klein, J.C., Massin, P., Erginay, A.: A contribution of image processing to the diagnosis of diabetic retinopathy detection of exudates in color fundus images of the human retina. IEEE Trans. Med. Imaging **21**(10), 1236–1243 (2002)

10. Giancardo, L., Mseriaudeau, F., Karnowski, T.P., Li, Y., Garg, S., Tobin, K.W., Chaum, E.: Exudate-based diabetic macular edema detection in fundus images using publicly available datasets. Med. Image Anal. **16**(1), 216–226 (2012)

11. Prentasic, P., Loncaric, S.: Detection of exudates in fundus photographs using deep neural networks and anatomical landmark detection fusion. Comput. Methods Programs Biomed. **137**, 281–292 (2016)

12. MESSIDOR: Methods for evaluating segmentation and indexing techniques dedicated to retinal ophthalmology. http://www.adcis.net/en/Download-Third-Party/Messidor.htmlindex-en.php

13. Kaggle: diabetic retionpathy detection challenge. https://www.kaggle.com/c/diabetic-retinopathy-detection

The Statistic Modeling of Eye Movement Viewing S3D Images

Chi Zhang[1,2], Jun Zhou[1,2(✉)], and Shoucheng Zhu[3]

[1] Institute of Image Communication and Network Engineering,
Shanghai Jiao Tong University, Shanghai 200240, China
zhoujun@sjtu.edu.cn
[2] Shanghai Key Lab of Digital Media Processing and Transmissions,
Shanghai Jiao Tong University, Shanghai 200240, China
[3] Shanghai Yanan High School, Shanghai 200336, China

Abstract. Nowadays, more and more families are willing to buy 3D TV to improve their watching experience. Stereo perception produced by watching 3D images or videos brings strong immersive watching experience to users. However, accumulated vision fatigue confuses users a lot after watching 3D TV for a long time. When watching 3D images, controlled by past recognition experience and visual attention mechanism, gaze point of two eyes is changing among different objects which have different depth of field. The eye movement in this changing process is called vergence. Vergence can be defined as movement of our eyes in opposite directions to locate the area of interest on the fovea and accommodation as alteration of the lens to obtain and maintain the area of interest focused on the fovea. So the more frequently the vergence process occurs, the more uncomfortable we feel. We expect to obtain several eye movement patterns, which can be considered as some typical visual attention patterns, by building a top-down recognition and visual attention model and then applying some clustering methods to find them. So we use an eye tracker to record eye movement data and then model it as a bayesian network model. The generative model is based on beta process and we build an Autoregression-HMM model to describe the relationship between latent eye movement patterns and eye movement data. To uncover parameters which represent different eye movement patterns in this model, we use MCMC method to calculate them with iterative computations. In this work, some different latent patterns existed in the sequential eye movement data can be revealed. After analyzing these patterns, we are able to find out some similarities and differences of visual attention models between different people watching the same image or between different images viewed by the same one. These conclusions can help to improve quality of 3D image thus lessening the users' vision fatigue when watching 3D TV. This work also will contribute to understanding the relationship between visual attention, visual model and visual discomfort. A regression method can be applied to discover more specific conclusions in further research.

Keywords: Beta process · Hidden Markov chain · Bayes network
Clustering

© Springer Nature Singapore Pte Ltd. 2018
G. Zhai et al. (Eds.): IFTC 2017, CCIS 815, pp. 203–214, 2018.
https://doi.org/10.1007/978-981-10-8108-8_19

1   Introduction

As stereo 3D display technology gets more and more sophisticated, films and televisions with stereoscopic 3D (S3D) technology are becoming more and more popular. Among all different types of S3D display technologies which are mainly distinguished by glasses type, polarized glasses are the mainstream in 3D TV market. Two images produced with a few small differences are displayed on TV screen and then filtered by the polarized glasses. Eventually, as the polarized angles are different between two lenses, left eye receives the picture which can only pass through the left lens and so do the right one. Each picture then falls on central foveal region on the retina and the small difference between two images on the retina is called binocular parallax [1]. Some related regions (such as vision neural V1 region) in our brain becomes active and then the binocular parallax information will be divided into two parts and they will be transmitted to cerebral cortex through different neural circuits. They merge together here to reconstruct an image with depth of field [2]. What's mentioned above is the generation process of stereo 3D vision.

Studies have revealed that visual attention is influenced by two main input sources: bottom-up visual attention driven by low-level saliency image features and top-down visual attention driven by cognitive process which includes viewing task and context scene [3]. The latter one is the dominant way in viewing process. In view of this, we are curious about how our cognitive system works and whether there are some typical viewing patterns existing in the process of watching S3D images, and what is the relationship between eye movement patterns and visual discomfort.

Since eye movement is controlled by some unknown latent variables which are related with visual attention in brain, so different eye movement patterns are considered as manifestations of visual attention model. There are already several visual attention models brought up from different perspective and the aspects they lay particular emphasis on are also different. The categorization factors include bottom-up versus top-down models, spatial versus spatio-temporal models, overt versus covert attention, space-based versus object-based models, features, stimuli and task type, evaluation measures, data sets and so on [4]. Our work mainly focuses on the top-down cognitive process so we design the experiment carefully for the purpose of minimizing the influence of bottom-up visual attention process.

Graphical model is one of the typical methods to describe visual attention process. A graphical model is a probabilistic framework in which a graph denotes the conditional independence structure between random variables. The model treats eye movement data as a time series. Since there are hidden variables influencing the generation of eye movement, some previous researches such as Hidden Markov Models and Dynamic Bayesian Network have been conducted in the last 15 years. Salah [5] proposed an approach for attention and applied it to hand-written digit and face recognition. Their model includes attentive level, intermediate level and associative level. Liu [6] proposed a set of novel features and adopted a Conditional Random Field (CRF) to combine these features for salient object detection. Harel [7] introduced Graph-Based Visual Saliency (GBVS). They extract feature maps at multiple spatial scales then built a fully connected graph over all grid locations of each feature map. Weights between two nodes are assigned proportional to the similarity of feature values and their spatial distance. Avraham and Lindenbaum [8] introduced the Extended saliency model by utilizing a graphical model approximation to extend their static saliency model based on self-similarities. Pang [9] presented a stochastic model of visual attention based on the signal detection theory account of visual search and attention. They proposed a dynamic Bayesian network to predict where humans typically focus in a video scene. Their model consists of four layers. Chikkerur [10] proposed a Bayesian graphical model in which attention emerges as the inference. Pattern classification models have also been used in modeling visual attention by learning models from recorded eye-fixations or labeled salient regions. Kienzle [11] introduced a nonparametric bottom-up approach for learning attention directly from human eye tracking data. The model consists of a nonlinear mapping from an image patch to a real value. A support vector machine was trained to determine the saliency using the local intensities. Peters and Itti [12] trained a simple regression classifier to capture the task-dependent association between a given scene and preferred locations to gaze at while human subjects were playing video games.

Compared with several modeling methods mentioned above, our model combines some features of them. The model is of top-down driven and hierarchical structure. In view of the infinite possibilities of eye movement patterns, Beta Process is a proper stochastic process to describe eye-movement patterns existed in data sequence. According to [13], Beta Process can be generated through Indian Buffet Process.

In this paper, we investigated the modeling of eye movement using an BP-AR-HMM method. In Sect. 2, we present a hierarchical probability graphical model to represent the generation process of eye movement. Then we set prior to this model reasonably. Section 3 describes detailed information of experiment environment and several steps of processing eye movement data after collecting it. Section 4 presents a few visualized clustering results of eye movement patterns. Then we show the comparison of different eye movement patterns when watching images of high and low quality. Finally we presents the exploration of visual attention models in one subject and in different subjects. We conclude the paper in Sect. 5.

2   Beta Process Autoregressive Hidden Markov Model

Our hierarchical model can be divided into two parts, AR-HMM model and Beta-Bernoulli process. After introducing the structure of each part, we give prior distributions to all the parameters used in our model.

2.1   Autoregressive-Hidden Markov Model

Eye movement data at one moment is generated by an eye movement pattern with the possibility called emission possibility, and the transitions between different eye movement states obey the possibility called transition probability. Due to eye movement data is a kind of time series, we adopt Hidden Markov Model to describe the relationship between latent variables in brain and eye movement data. Hidden Markov Model is based on the Markov assumption that the current state has and only has a relationship with the previous one. The formula can be written as $z_t|z_{t-1} \sim \pi_{z_{t-1}}$, $\mathbf{y}_t|z_t \sim F(\theta_{z_t})$, $F(\cdot)$ is a kind of exponential family of distribution, π_k is transition distribution of certain state, θ_k is the emission parameter of state k, However, it's obvious that the recognition mechanism is very complicated so the Markov assumption seems too loose and rough for the mechanism. To achieve a balance of accuracy and computation complexity, we add first-order autoregressive to describe this process in a better way. The formula can be written as:

$$\mathbf{y}_t = \sum_{l=1}^{r} A_{l,z_t}\mathbf{y}_{t-l} + \mathbf{e}_t(z_t) = \mathbf{A}_k\tilde{\mathbf{y}}_t + \mathbf{e}_t(z_t)$$

$$\tilde{\mathbf{y}}_t = [\mathbf{y}_{t-1}^T \cdots \mathbf{y}_{t-r}^T]^T$$

$$\mathbf{A}_k = [A_{1,k} \cdots A_{r,k}]$$

$\mathbf{A}_k$ as the set of lag matrices, $r = 1$ for computing convenience, $\theta_k = \{\mathbf{A}_k, \Sigma_k\}$ to describe all the parameters of state k.

2.2   Beta-Bernoulli Process

At the top level of the model, we adopt Beta process as a prior distribution providing the flexibility of discovering new patterns after new eye movement data is observed. At the middle level, in view of the conjugate relationship between Beta process and Bernoulli process, we adopt Bernoulli process to describe whether feature k exists in sequence i. We define a subset of eye movement patterns $\{\theta_1, \theta_2, ...\}$, and then associate each time series i with a certain subset of patterns via a binary feature vector $\mathbf{f}_i = [f_{i1}, f_{i2}, ...]$, $f_{ik} = 1$ implies that time series i exhibits pattern k.

2.3   Model Overview and Prior Specification

The Beta-process-based graphical model can couple several time series such as left and right eye movement sequences. We name our model BP-AR-HMM for short. Figure 1 shows the overview of this graphical model.

A Beta process (BP) random measure, $B = \sum_{k=1}^{\infty} \omega_k \theta_k$, defines an infinite set of coin-flipping probabilities ω_k, one for each behavior θ_k. Beta process can be constructed from Poisson process (stick-breaking Beta process and Possion process).

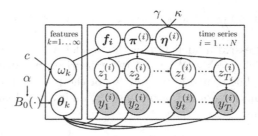

Fig. 1. BP-AR-HMM graphical model. For clarity, the feature-inclusion probabilities, ω_k, and AR parameters, θ_k, of the Beta process base measure $B \sim BP(c, B_0)$ are decoupled. The Bernoulli process X_i of time series i are represented in terms of feature vectors $\mathbf{f}_i$ indexed over the θ_k, here $f_{ik}|\omega_k \sim Bernoulli(\omega_k)$. The $\mathbf{f}_i$ can be used to define feature-constrained transition distributions $\pi_j^{(i)}|\mathbf{f_i}, \gamma, \kappa \sim Dir([\gamma, ..., \gamma, \gamma + \kappa, \gamma, ..., \gamma] \odot \mathbf{f_i})$, $\pi^{(i)}$ can be written in terms of transition weights $\eta^{(i)}$. The state evolves as $z_t^{(i)}|z_{t-1}^{(i)} \sim \pi_{z_{t-1}^{(i)}}^{(i)}$

$B \sim Beta(\alpha, B_0)$ is a positive levy process, and the levy measure relies on parameters α and B_0. B_0 is called base measure on the measurable space Θ. One time series is related with a Bernoulli process realization, $X_i|B \sim BeP(B)$. B, an atomic measure, is a collection of unit-mass atoms on Θ located at some subset of the atoms in B. Particularly, $f_{ik} \sim Bernoulli(\omega_k)$ is sampled independently for each atom θ_k in B. $X_i = \sum_k f_{ik}\delta_{\theta_k}$, that is the outcome of an infinite coin-flipping sequence based on the BP-determined coin weights. The conjugacy of the Beta process to the Bernoulli process allows for an analytic predictive distribution for a feature vector based on the feature vector observed so far. This predictive distribution can be described via the Indian buffet process, short for IBP, under certain parameterizations of BP [14].

The prior for transition distribution $\boldsymbol{\pi}^{(i)} = \{\pi^{(i)}\}$ is defined on an infinite-dimensional state space but restricted to a finite subset by $\mathbf{f}_i$. Because normalized gamma random variables can generate Dirichlet-distributed probabilities mass function, for each sequence i, we define a doubly-infinite collection of random variables:

$$\eta_{jk}^{(i)}|\gamma, \kappa \sim Gamma(\gamma + \kappa\delta(j, k), 1) \qquad (1)$$

Here $\delta(j, k) = 0$ when $j \neq k$, $\delta(j, k) = 1$ when $j = k$. The hyperparameters γ, κ control Markovian state switching probabilities. We define transition distribution by using transition weight variable $\boldsymbol{\eta}^{(i)}$:

$$\pi_j^{(i)} = \frac{[\eta_{j1}^{(i)} \eta_{j2}^{(i)} \cdots] \odot \boldsymbol{f}_i}{\sum_{k|f_{ik}=1} \eta_{jk}^{(i)}} \qquad (2)$$

where $\odot$ denotes Hadamard vector product. The generative process can also be written as this:

$$\pi_j^{(i)}|\mathbf{f_i}, \gamma, \kappa \sim Dir([\gamma, ..., \gamma, \gamma + \kappa, \gamma, ..., \gamma] \odot \mathbf{f_i}) \qquad (3)$$

This equation is an equivalent representation of the above one and the proof can be referred in [15].

As for autoregressive model part of this model, we set a conjugate matrix-normal inverse-Wishart (MNIW) prior (west harrison bayesian forecasting and dynamic models). The dynamic parameters of the prior is represented as $\theta_k = \{\mathbf{A_k}, \Sigma_k\}$. $\mathbf{A_k}$, a matrix normal prior, and Σ_k, an inverse Wishart prior, can be represented like this:

$$
\begin{aligned}
\Sigma_k | n_0, S_0 &\sim IW(n_0, S_0) \\
\mathbf{A_k} | \Sigma_k, M, L &\sim \mathcal{MN}(\mathbf{A_k}; M, \Sigma_k, L)
\end{aligned}
\tag{4}
$$

with n_0 the degrees of freedom, S_0 the scale matrix, M the mean dynamic matrix and L a matrix that together with Σ_k defines the covariance of A_k.

We use MCMC sampler to do the posterior inference. In this process, we refer to the split-merge and birth-death algorithm brought up by [16]. In one iteration of the sampler, each latent variable is visited and assigned a value by drawing from the distribution of that variable conditional on the assignments to all other latent variables as well as the observation.

3   Experiment

To get enough original eye movement data, twenty-four observers with normal or corrected-to-normal vision participated in the study (9 women and 15 men, with ages between 21 to 27, and with a mean age of 23.6). All of the subjects had normal stereo vision as tested using the vision tests (VTs) recommended in ITU-BT.1438 [17]. A 47-inch polarized HD 3D display (LG 47LA6600) was used to display the S3D images to the human subjects. All of the S3D images were input to the 3D display in Top-and-Bottom format. Each observer was comfortably arranged to view the display at a viewing distance of about 1.76 m (that is 3 times of the screen height distance) with a passive polarized glass.

The remote eye tracker used in our experiments was a Tobii X120. It can be used to track eye movements with the freedom of head movement with head-motion speed limit lower than 35 cm/s in a $44 \times 22 \times 30$ cm (Width × Height × Depth) track box [18]. The eye tracker was positioned and configured to the central front of the standalone 3D display using the assistance of a laser level meter. The sampling rate of the eye tracker was fixed at 60 Hz. The eye tracker records each gaze position, but cannot provide absolute gaze direction. The accuracy, which is defined as the average difference between the real stimuli position and the measured gaze position, is typically $0.5°$ under 60 Hz for monocular. And the precision for monocular is typically $0.22°$ that describes the standard deviation of successive samples [19].

After collecting eye movement data, the distance between eye fixation point and display can be calculated by using trigonometry method conveniently and accurately [20]. We are curious about whether the changes of depth plane on which the two eyes' fixation point lands have some typical features or patterns.

So we input eye movement time series and depth of field information sequence into this BP-AR-HMM model to see if the model can get the sequence data clustered and allocate each time step a cluster label.

From a more detailed perspective, after running the program, the MCMC algorithm will iteration over and over again. Hundreds of seconds later, all the parameters tend to be stable and they change within a very small range. So we set a runtime limitation to our program which is properly set to 300 s according to our experience. Due to split-merge and birth-death algorithm, in every iteration, some existed eye patterns may "dead" and some new patterns may be created. We assume that there are 20 patterns in one subject's eye movement data in the initial state and the number of patterns in the last iteration will be our final result when countdown clock hits zero.

4   Results and Discussion

In order to make it convenient and explicit to compare between different results, we show all the results and analysis only about one original image. This way also avoid the bottom-up attention machanism's influence driven by low-level image features.

4.1   Visualizaiton Representation of Eye Movement Patterns

Firstly, we input the subject A's depth sequence and intersection coordinates sequences of left & right eyesight and screen of watching the original image to the model. Figure 2 shows how the different 16 kinds of patterns change over time.

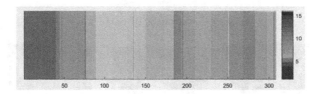

Fig. 2. Eye movement patterns with depth sequence of subject A

Compared with the result above, the result of another input which exclude the depth sequence has fewer patterns but very similar spectra structure, as shown in Fig. 3.

To show different eye movement patterns in a visualized way, we select pattern 1 (1–25 sampling point), pattern 4 (45–75 sampling point) and pattern 12 (197–209, 231–250, 283–297 sampling point) for example and draw the left eye and right eye's scanpath during these periods.

It's not difficult to make out the differences between pattern 1, 4 and 12 in Figs. 4, 5, 6 and 7. Interest zone and scan path are always the focus of attention.

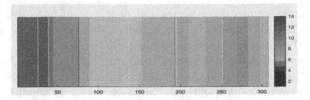

Fig. 3. Eye movement patterns without depth sequence of subject A

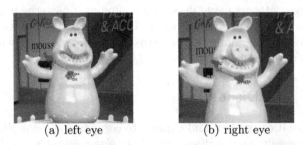

(a) left eye   (b) right eye

Fig. 4. Scan paths of pattern 1

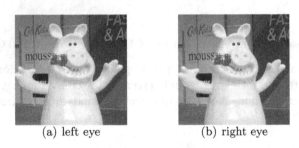

(a) left eye   (b) right eye

Fig. 5. Scan paths of pattern 4

(a) 197-209   (b) 231-250   (c) 283-297

Fig. 6. Left eye paths of pattern 12

The interest zone in Pattern 1 is more scattered and the saccade path between two interest zone is longer than pattern 4. The unique feature of pattern 12 is more reflected in the vertical direction, concentrated fixation zones separated by long-distance saccade. Specially, three different periods of pattern 12 show fairly

(a) 197-209	(b) 231-250	(c) 283-297

Fig. 7. Right eye paths of pattern 12

strong correlation between them such as the location of interest zone. These conclusions prove our model's validity.

4.2   Shifting S3D Images

We shifted two images to get more negative disparity for more out of screen effect, which will cause more visual discomfort. Thus, it can help to study the correlation between image quality and eye movement patterns watching the same S3D content but different depth range.

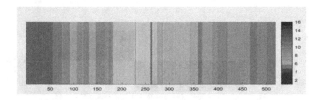

Fig. 8. Eye movement patterns when watching the low-quality image

The result reveals that there are two more patterns in this series and the spectra structure is totally different from the one in Fig. 3. In Fig. 8, patterns change more frequently and last for a shorter time which can be explained by accumulation of visual discomfort.

4.3   Multi-sequence Input

For further discussion, we input two sequences which include four time series (A's left eye, A's right eye, B's left eye, B's right eye's eye movement series) to see whether there are some regular recognition patterns in one person or whether there are some common patterns between different people.

Two Subjects Watching the Same Image. Figures 9 and 10 show subject A's and B's eye movement pattern spectra. Figure 11 shows which patterns are common and which patterns are particular in another way. Grey color lump means the pattern existed in this series before the last iteration but now it doesn't exist.

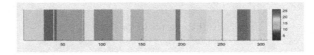

Fig. 9. Subject A's eye movement patterns

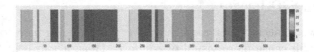

Fig. 10. Subject B's eye movement patterns

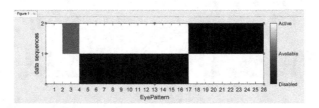

Fig. 11. Common eye movement patterns of A and B

One Subject Watching Two Different S3D Images. Figures 12 and 13 show different eye movement patterns existed in the process of watching image1 and image2. Compared with the Fig. 11 shown above, Fig. 14 shows more common eye movement patterns and the proportion is approximately equal to 40%.

So we find out the fact that common patterns do exist among different people in recognition process. But the conclusion of one subject watching different images indicates more valuable information. Once some recognition patterns has formed, people prefer to use these patterns to observe new things and get information about new things.

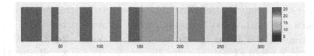

Fig. 12. Subject C's eye movement patterns in image1

Fig. 13. Subject C's eye movement patterns in image2

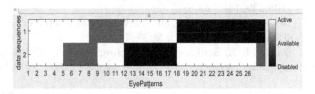

Fig. 14. Subject C's common eye movement patterns

5 Conclusion

Our model can be used to extract eye movement patterns of a few different subjects when they watch the same 3D image or video. By analyzing these patterns, we can improve the quality of this 3D image or video purposefully so that it can be visual-comfort for most people. The model can also help to brain science research and recognition & learning research by establishing a dataset of eye movement patterns and then analyzing common and particular eye movement patterns in it.

Acknowledgments. Thanks for Micheal C Hughes's open source project NPBayes toolbox on github. Our program's realization is based on his work. The work for this paper was supported by NSFC under 61471234 and 61527804, and MOST under Contact 2015BAK05B03.

References

1. Ponce, C.R., Born, R.T.: Stereopsis. Curr. Biol. **18**(18), R845–R850 (2008)
2. Yano, S., Emoto, M., Mitsuhashi, T.: Two factors in visual fatigue caused by stereoscopic HDTV images. Displays **25**(4), 141–150 (2004)
3. Torralba, A., Oliva, A., Castelhano, M.S., Henderson, J.M.: Contextual guidance of eye movements and attention in real-world scenes: the role of global features in object search. Psychol. Rev. **113**(4), 766–86 (2006)
4. Borji, A., Itti, L.: State-of-the-art in visual attention modeling. IEEE Trans. Patt. Anal. Mach. Intell. **35**(1), 185–207 (2012)

5. Salah, A.A., Alpaydin, E., Akarun, L.: A selective attention-based method for visual pattern recognition with application to handwritten digit recognition and face recognition. IEEE Trans. Patt. Anal. Mach. Intell. **24**(3), 420–425 (2002)
6. Liu, T., Yuan, Z., Sun, J., Wang, J., Zheng, N., Tang, X., Shum, H.Y.: Learning to detect a salient object. IEEE Trans. Patt. Anal. Mach. Intell. **33**(2), 353–367 (2011)
7. Harel, J., Koch, C., Perona, P.: Graph-based visual saliency. In: Advances in Neural Information Processing Systems, pp. 545–552 (2007)
8. Avraham, T., Lindenbaum, M.: Esaliency (extended saliency): meaningful attention using stochastic image modeling. IEEE Trans. Patt. Anal. Mach. Intell. **32**(4), 693 (2010)
9. Pang, D., Kimura, A., Takeuchi, T., Yamato, J., Kashino, K.: A stochastic model of selective visual attention with a dynamic Bayesian network. Technical report of IEICE PRMU 108:139–144 (2008)
10. Chikkerur, S., Serre, T., Tan, C., Poggio, T.: What and where: a Bayesian inference theory of attention. Vis. Res. **50**(22), 2233–47 (2010)
11. Kienzle, W., Franz, M.O., SchLkopf, B., Wichmann, F.A.: Center-surround patterns emerge as optimal predictors for human saccade targets. J. Vis. **9**(5:7), 1–15 (2009)
12. Peters, R.J., Itti, L.: Beyond bottom-up: incorporating task-dependent influences into a computational model of spatial attention. In: IEEE Conference on Computer Vision and Pattern Recognition, pp. 1–8 (2007)
13. Thibaux, R., Jordan, M.I.: Hierarchical Beta processes and the Indian buffet process. J. Mach. Learn. Res. **2**(3), 564–571 (2007)
14. Ghahramani, Z., Griffiths, T.L., Sollich, P.: Bayesian nonparametric latent feature models. In: Bayesian Statistics, pp. 201–226 (2007)
15. Fox, E.B., Sudderth, E.B., Jordan, M.I., Willsky, A.S.: A sticky HDP-HMM with application to speaker diarization. Ann. Appl. Stat. **5**(2A), 1020–1056 (2011)
16. Hughes, M.C., Fox, E.B., Sudderth, E.B.: Effective split-merge monte carlo methods for nonparametric models of sequential data. Adv. Neural Inf. Process. Syst. **25**, 1295–1303 (2012)
17. ITU-R BT.1438: "Subjective Assessment of Stereoscopic Television Pictures" (2000)
18. Tobii®Technology: "Accuracy and Precision Test Method for Remote Eye Trackers," 7 February 2011
19. Tobii®Technology: "Accuracy and Precision Test Report: Tobii X120 Eye Tracker," June 2012
20. Ma, B., Zhou, J., Gu, X., Wang, M., Zhang, Y., Guo, X.: A new approach to create 3D fixation density maps for stereoscopic images. In: 3DTV-Conference: the True Vision - Capture, Transmission and Display of 3D Video, pp. 1–4 (2015)

Weld Defect Images Classification with VGG16-Based Neural Network

Bin Liu[✉], Xiaoyun Zhang, Zhiyong Gao, and Li Chen

Institute of Image Communication and Network Engineering,
Shanghai Jiao Tong University, Shanghai 200240, China
{beanleo,xiaoyun.zhang,zhiyong.gao,hilichen}@sjtu.edu.cn

Abstract. Using X-ray weld defect images for defects detection is a very significant method for non-destructive testing (NDT). Traditionally, this work should be done by skilled technicians who are time-consumed and easily influenced by the environment. Many efforts have been made on automatic classification. However their work either need manual features specified by technicians or get a low accuracy. Some datasets they used for testing are too small to validate the generative capacity. In this paper, we propose a VGG16 based fully convolutional structure to classify the weld defect image, which achieves a high accuracy with a relative small dataset for deep learning method. We choose a dataset with 3000 images for testing the generative capacity of our network, which is large enough compared to others methods. Using this method, we got a 97.6% test accuracy and 100% train accuracy through our network on two main defects. The time used for each patch is about 0.012 s, which is faster than others methods.

Keywords: Weld defect images · VGG16-based neural network
Different size image processing

1 Introduction

X-ray images based weld defect detection is very significant and frequently used in the NDT (Non-destructive testing) domain. It is about using x-ray to irradiate the area of material, which may contain defects, and get the x-ray images for further analyse. Using this method can avoid destructing the material while achieving the goal of defects detection. However, traditionally, this work needs to be done by skilled technicians, because of so many kinds of different defections [1] which are shown in Fig. 1. The technician may also be subjective and influenced by the environment. Therefore using computers which are more objective and cheaper to replace the human to classify the defect in this domain is one of the important research direction.

Many efforts have been made in the weld defect detection domain. Tong et al. [2] used a mathematical morphology and threshold method for weld defect images segmentation. Hassan [3] et al. used geometric features extracted from

© Springer Nature Singapore Pte Ltd. 2018
G. Zhai et al. (Eds.): IFTC 2017, CCIS 815, pp. 215–223, 2018.
https://doi.org/10.1007/978-981-10-8108-8_20

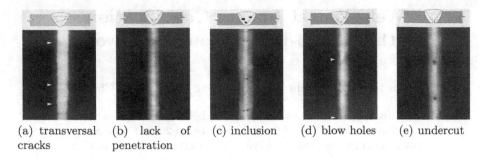

(a) transversal   (b) lack   of   (c) inclusion   (d) blow holes   (e) undercut
cracks   penetration

Fig. 1. Some examples of X-ray weld defect images

weld defect images as the input of ANN (artificial neural network) to realize classification. The methods used by the Tong and Hassan are traditional image feature extraction methods. These methods' performance changes easily due to different environments. In addition, machine learning methods have also been applied in this domain, for example [4,5], which both used SVM (support vector machine)for classification. However, some works of them are tested on a small scale dataset which cannot validate the generative capacity. What's more, all the methods mentioned before have to use handcraft features specified by skilled technicians. On the one hand, it needs more resource to design a weld defect extraction system. On the other hand, these features may be different and subjective due to different technicians.

The deep convolutional neural network has obtained a great success in the image classification domain in recent years. Its performance has been demonstrated by large scale image datasets like ImageNet [6], which contains more than 10 million images belonging to more than 20 thousands classes. The new deep neural networks like Alexnet [7], VGG [8], GoogLeNet [9] and ResNet [10] have performed better and better on reducing the top-1 error, which means the rate of error classification of images in 1000 categories. What's more, the ResNet has achieve a top-1 error of 19.38%, exceeding the professional technicians. Hence, it is reasonable to use deep convolutional neural network to practice the weld defect images classification task.

In this paper, we propose a deep learning based method to process the x-ray weld defect images and achieve a relatively better performance on a larger dataset with 15000 weld defect images. Besides that, the CNN [11] (convolutional neural network) structure we adopt enables automatic features extraction. We first use CNN as the feature extractor to extract the features from the defect image. Then we use 1×1 convolutional kernels to reduce the dimension to fit the classes and use mean-pooling kernels to mapping the output to the probability of each class. The 1×1 convolutional kernels and mean-pooling kernels together are called the fully convolutional structure in our experiment. After the mean-pooling, the output probability can be used for classification and back propagation (BP).

We will mainly discuss about the method used for weld defect images classification in Sect. 2. In Sect. 3, the result of the experiment will be shown, which is better than the traditional methods. Finally, in Sect. 4, we will give a brief conclusion of our paper.

2 Method

2.1 Overview Convolutional Neural Network Structure

In this section, we will give an overview of our VGG16 based network structure, which is shown in Fig. 2. In this figure, blue layers stand for convolution layers; red layers stand for max-pooling layers; brown layers stand for mean-pooling layers. The node placed on the top right corner of the overview structure is a fully connected layer which is replaced by a fully convolutional structure. The whole network structure can be modeled as a probability function shown in Eq. 1, whose output is a one dimension vector with elements equaling to the classes needed to be classified. Each element in the output vector stands for how much possible the input images can be classified to the corresponding class.

$$P = h_n(W_n h_{n-1}(...h_2(W_2 h_1(W_1 x + b_1) + b_2)) + b_n) \tag{1}$$

The different size input section in Fig. 2 stands for two scale input patches (a cropped section of the original images). There are totally two scale patches representing two kind of different scale defects in this structure. One of them is the transversal crack. The other is the blow hole or solid inclusion. Because blow wholes and solid inclusion are similar, they are seemed as the same defect in this structure and can be further divided with another classifier. The smaller defect as blow wholes or solid inclusion defect is represented by 128×128 size patches, while the larger defect transversal crack is represented by 256×256 patches.

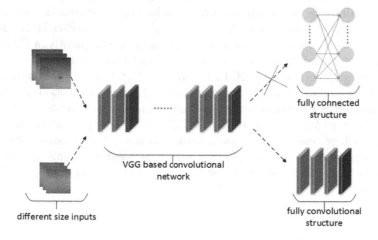

Fig. 2. Overview of VGG16 based neural network structure (Color figure online)

As for the middle part of the structure, VGG16 convolutional layers are serviced as a feature extractor. A CNN layer can extract the features automatically according to the different losses defined by costumer instead of using expensive skilled technicians. VGG structures have been convinced as a network with good generative capacity. Therefore, we adopt VGG16's convolutional layers as the feature extractor of our neural network model.

Traditional CNN structures are always followed by a fully connected layer as the classifier. Whereas the fully connected layer's scale should keep consistent with the size of input, we use convolutional layers and the mean-pooling layer structure mentioned in [12] to replace the fully connected layer. The final output of VGG16 structure is 256 feature maps. We adopt 1×1 convolutional to reduce the feature maps' dimension from 256 to 3 which is the classes of our defects. Finally, the mean-pooling operation is applied to these three feature maps to calculate the average of these three feature maps as the output.

2.2   The Detail of Fully Convolutional Structure and VGG16

A fully convolutional structure is used by us to solve the different size input question caused by different weld defects. Because of the different scale of weld defects, the weld defect has to be cropped into different sizes. Traditional fully connected layers function are shown in Eq. 2. It can be figure out that the first fully connected layer, which are feeded by the final feature maps from the last convolutional layer, must keep consistent with the dimension of the final feature maps, due to the matrix multiplication between W and x.

$$O = h(Wx + b) \tag{2}$$

A fully convolutional structure can ignore the consistent requirement. The principal is shown in Fig. 3, in which the input feature maps with different shape but the same channels is firstly get through 1×1 convolutional kernels. This operation will make the output feature maps having the channels same with the total classes. Then these channels pass through a mean-pooling layer and get a mean value vector having the same size of classes. Consequently, a CNN pluses a fully convolutional structure can solve the consistent question.

The overall structure of VGG16 is shown in Fig. 4, in which blue layers, red layers and yellow layers stand for convolutional layers, max-pooling layers and fully connected layers respectively. The input images size is set to $224 \times 224 \times 3$.

VGG16 is widely recognized as a CNN with good generative capacity. It uses the stack of small convolutional kernels instead of large ones to reduce the amount of parameters considerably compared to Alexnet. It only uses size 3×3 as its kernel size. And the last three layers are fully connected layers with size of 4096, which has been shown in Fig. 4.

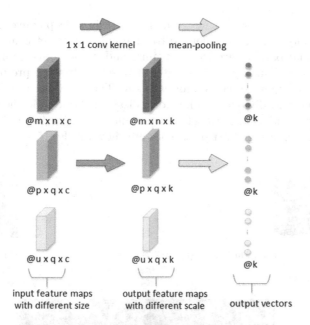

Fig. 3. Principal of fully convolutional structure

Fig. 4. Overall VGG16 neural network structure

3   Experiment and Result

3.1   Dataset Processing and Training Method

The weld defect x-ray image comes from [13], in which there are 63 images with 4k length and variable width. These defect x-ray images are well labels with position and defect classes. We choose two main flaws, blow holes or solid inclusion and transversal cracks, as defects to be classified. Three defects are manually cropped from the original images according to the labels and positions. Except the blow holes or solid inclusion and the transversal cracks, we also crop the patches without defects and label as none defect. In order to enable the network to classify defects in the different position of the patches, we crop each flaw in different positions like shown in Fig. 5. After the crop we can get 3000 128×128 patches with three different defects, one of which has no defect, and others 3000 images with 256×256 patch size. The different size of patches are based on the different size of defects.

These 3000 images are not large enough to train a deep convolutional neural network. We adopt Alexnet's method to enlarge the data set using rotation and flip. The original patches are rotate 3 times and flipped once to make the data set 4 times larger than the original patch data sets. After the pre-processing, we can get 15000 weld image patches for each size. These patches are then extracted the mean value and divided 256 for normalization. We divide the data set into train data set, validation data set and test data set with 9000, 3000 and 3000 images for further using. Part of patches are shown in Fig. 5.

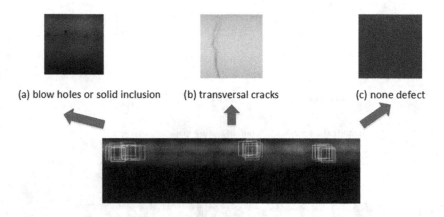

(a) blow holes or solid inclusion   (b) transversal cracks   (c) none defect

Fig. 5. The crop processing to produce defect patches

The neural network mentioned in method section is trained by these processed datasets. The network was trained with both 128×128 and 256×256 size images. When testing, any size of input patches is possible. We choosed 128×128 size patches for blow holes or solid inclusion defects, 256×256 size patches for solid inclusion defects and half of 256×256 and half of 128×128 size patches for none defect for testing. So there are totally 3000 images in testing set with different sizes. The input patches were in form of batch input whose size is 2 when training and validating the network. We used the adam gradient descent BP algorithm in our experiment and the initial learning rate was 5×10^{-5} decaying 0.93 per epoch to train the network. The loss function was the cross entropy loss which is usually used in images classification. We implemented this neural network by tensorflow platform on a GTX 980 GPU.

3.2   Experiment Result

The loss of our experiment is shown in Fig. 6. It has been smoothed by tensorboard, a plot tool of tensorflow, with a smooth factor of 0.97. The shadow part in the figure stands for real value, while the curve stands for the smoothed value. The real value fluctuation is unstable because we adopt a smaller batch size with 2 images, due to the limited computation resource. So we use the smoothed

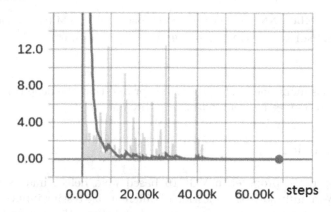

Fig. 6. The loss of the experiment

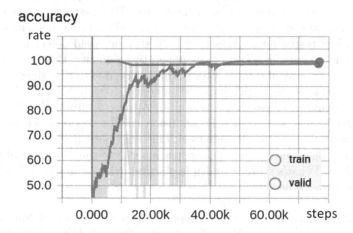

Fig. 7. The accuracy of train set and validation set during training processing

method to make the curves more readable. We can conclude from the figure that the network tend to convergence from the third epoch. And the cross entropy loss tend to zero with the steps increasing.

The accuracy curve of train set and validation set are shown in Fig. 7. Each point in accuracy curve stands for the right prediction rate of a batch of train or validation images. The accuracy curve adopts the same smooth processing as loss curve. We can see the accuracy of train set tend to 100% after 45k steps (10 epochs) as well as the validation set accuracy.

The test accuracy of 3000 weld defect testing images is 97.6%, which is better than the methods mentioned in [4,14]. A comparison of these methods is shown in Table 1. The time used for processing each patch is 0.012 s, which is also faster

Table 1. Comparison between different weld defects (SI&CR) detection methods

Name	MLP-ANN	SVM (Wang)	SVM (one vs. all)	SVM (one vs. one)	Ours
Accuracy	94.1%	99.1%	95.8%	97.0%	97.6%

than methods mentioned before. This has proved that the deep transfer learning is suitable for detecting weld defect in X-ray images.

4   Conclusion

In this paper, we proposed a VGG16 based weld defect images classification method. We mainly solve the question of different size testing inputs and accurate classification. By using fully convolutional structure, though we have to train the network using the same size input considering of the parallel processing, the defect images used for test can be variable size. This network achieve a testing accuracy on 3000 test images which have exceeded some methods as we know.

Our work is tested on a dataset with 3000 X-ray weld defect images, which is relatively large enough to prove the generative capacity. However, if offered a larger dataset, we may obtain a better performance, due to that the deep learning is a data driven scheme. In this paper we label the blow holes and solid inclusion as the same defect because they are similar. A more accurate classification that can distinguish blow holes from solid inclusion may be needed when we apply the neural network method to the practice. This may need a new specific network structure that designed for detail classification due to the similarity of these two kind of defects. What's more, a multiple classifier which can tell all kinds of weld defects may also be needed.

Acknowledgement. This work was supported in part by National Natural Science Foundation of China (61527804, 61301116, 61521062, 6113300961771306), Chinese National Key S&T Special Program (2013ZX01033001-002-002), the 111 Project (B07022), the Shanghai Key Laboratory of Digital Media Processing and Transmissions (STCSM 12DZ2272600).

References

1. EN ISO 6520-1. Welding and allied processes-classification of geometric imperfections in metallic materials-Part 1: Fusion welding (2007)
2. Tong, T., Cai, Y., Sun, D.: Defects detection of weld image based on mathematical morphology and thresholding segmentation. In: 2012 8th International Conference on Wireless Communications, Networking and Mobile Computing (WiCOM), pp. 1–4. IEEE (2012)
3. Hassan, J., Awan, A.M., Jalil, A.: Welding defect detection and classification using geometric features. In: 2012 10th International Conference on Frontiers of Information Technology (FIT), pp. 139–144. IEEE (2012)

4. Wang, Y., Guo, H.: Weld defect detection of X-ray images based on support vector machine. IETE Tech. Rev. **31**(2), 137–142 (2014)
5. Shao, J., Shi, H., Du, D., Wang, L., Cao, H.: Automatic weld defect detection in real-time X-ray images based on support vector machine. In: 2011 4th International Congress on Image and Signal Processing (CISP), vol. 4, pp. 1842–1846. IEEE (2011)
6. Russakovsky, O., Deng, J., Su, H., Krause, J., Satheesh, S., Ma, S., Huang, Z., Karpathy, A., Khosla, A., Bernstein, M., et al.: Imagenet large scale visual recognition challenge. Int. J. Comput. Vis. **115**(3), 211–252 (2015)
7. Krizhevsky, A., Sutskever, I., Hinton, G.E.: Imagenet classification with deep convolutional neural networks. In: Advances in Neural Information Processing Systems, pp. 1097–1105 (2012)
8. Simonyan, K., Zisserman, A.: Very deep convolutional networks for large-scale image recognition. arXiv preprint arXiv:1409.1556 (2014)
9. Szegedy, C., Liu, W., Jia, Y., Sermanet, P., Reed, S., Anguelov, D., Erhan, D., Vanhoucke, V., Rabinovich, A.: Going deeper with convolutions. In: Proceedings of the IEEE Conference on Computer Vision and Pattern Recognition, pp. 1–9 (2015)
10. He, K., Zhang, X., Ren, S., Sun, J.: Deep residual learning for image recognition. In: Proceedings of the IEEE Conference on Computer Vision and Pattern Recognition, pp. 770–778 (2016)
11. LeCun, Y., Bottou, L., Bengio, Y., Haffner, P.: Gradient-based learning applied to document recognition. Proc. IEEE **86**(11), 2278–2324 (1998)
12. Lin, M., Chen, Q., Yan, S.: Network in network. arXiv preprint arXiv:1312.4400 (2013)
13. Mery, D., Riffo, V., Zscherpel, U., Mondragón, G., Lillo, I., Zuccar, I., Lobel, H., Carraso, M.: GDXray: the database of x-ray images for nondestructive testing. J. Nondest. Eval. **34**, 42 (2015)
14. Mekhalfa, F., Nacereddine, N.: Multiclass classification of weld defects in radiographic images based on support vector machines. In: 2014 Tenth International Conference on Signal-Image Technology and Internet-Based Systems (SITIS), pp. 1–6. IEEE (2014)

Hardware Implementation and Optimization of Tiny-YOLO Network

Jing Ma, Li Chen(✉), and Zhiyong Gao

Institute of Image Communication and Network Engineering,
Shanghai Jiao Tong University, Shanghai, China
hilichen@sjtu.edu.cn

Abstract. Convolutional Neural Networks (CNNs) have achieved extraordinary performance in image processing fields. However, CNNs are both computational intensive and memory intensive, making them difficult to be deployed on hardware devices like embedded systems. Although lots of existing work has explored hardware implementation of CNNs, the crucial problem of either inefficient or incomplete still remains. Consequently, in this paper, we propose a design that is highly paralleled to perform efficient computation of CNNs. Furthermore, compared with previous work that rarely takes Fully-Connected (FC) layers into consideration, our work also does well in FC optimization.

We take Tiny-YOLO, an object detection architecture, as the target network to be implemented on an FPGA platform. In order to reduce computing time, we exploit an efficient and generic computing engine that has 64 duplicated Processing Elements (PEs) working simultaneously. Inside each PE, 32 MAC operations are executed in a pipeline manner for further parallelism. Then, for the purpose of reducing memory footprint, we take full advantage of data reusing and data sharing. For example, in our design, parallel PEs share the same input data and on-chip buffers are leveraged to cache data and weights for further reuse. Finally, we apply SVD to FC layers, which decreases 80.6% memory access and computing operations while maintaining comparable accuracy. With these optimizing approaches, our design achieves a detecting rate of over 20 FPS and gets a processing performance of 48 GMACS under 143 MHz working frequency.

Keywords: Object detection · Convolutional Neural Network · FPGA

1 Introduction

Object detection is a challenging task in computer vision, yet we are pleasant to see that Convolutional Neural Network (CNN) has led to impressive progress in this field. In recent 3 years, a number of successful CNN-based work for object detection sprang up. Object detection algorithms using Convolutional Neural Networks achieved state-of-the-art performance continuously. Among them, R-CNN [1], SPP-net [2], Fast R-CNN [3] and Faster R-CNN [4] are typically CNN

© Springer Nature Singapore Pte Ltd. 2018
G. Zhai et al. (Eds.): IFTC 2017, CCIS 815, pp. 224–234, 2018.
https://doi.org/10.1007/978-981-10-8108-8_21

methods based on the thought of region proposal, YOLO [5] and ssd [6] are end-to-end networks which directly predict bounding boxes. Research has shown that, in general, the former detects at a lower speed, but obtains higher accuracy, while the latter totally opposite [7]

Upon seeing the vast prospect of Convolutional Neural Network, researchers sought to make it into practical use, for example, applying it to embedded systems.

Previous work has proposed diverse acceleration models for CNN implementation. Peemen et al. viewed the issue as a bandwidth constrained problem and attempted to maximally exploit on-chip data reuse in their model [8]. Nevertheless, for the majority of object detection frameworks, they demand not only high memory bandwidth but also high computation resources. Subsequently, C. Zhang et al. put forward a roofline-model-based method to quantitatively analyze computing throughput and memory bandwidth of any potential solution of a CNN design [9]. Their proposal did well with convolutional layers, but fully-connected layers were not well studied. Similar design by [10] got the same limitation. Other work involves generic design for CNN, such as "Eyeriss" presented by Chen et al. [11].

In this paper, we devoted to deploy Tiny-YOLO on embedded FPGA platform. Our implementation design works for the entire flow (i.e., both convolutional layers and fully-connected layers). We assume that a trained model is already available and thus, weights can be directly picked to make an inference.

Specifically, main optimising efforts are as follows:

- **Generic PE model for calculation.** Our computing engine is flexible enough to handle with both CONV layers and FC layers. 64 identical PEs are included, each accomplishing up to 32 MAC operations in a pipeline manner.
- **Hardware Memory Hierarchy for data reuse.** Data and parameters are well organized so that they can be reused or shared.
- **Ping-pong buffer for task parallelism.** Two input buffers and two output buffers both work in a ping-pong manner. Data loading/storing and data computing tasks are conducted simultaneously, which greatly reduces whole processing time.
- **SVD for fully-connected layers.** Application of SVD to FC layers reduces 80.6% memory access as well as computing operations.

2   Tiny-YOLO Architecture

Tiny-YOLO, a unified CNN model proposed by Joseph et al. is fabricated by 9 Convolutional (CONV) layers and 3 FC layers, illustrated by Fig. 1. For all CONV layers, the kernel size is 3 and the stride is 1. Specifically, the first 6 CONV layers each has a 2×2 maxpooling layer following behind, which reduces the resolution of the features and makes the network robust against noise and distortion.

In the network, original 448×448 input image is divided into 7×7 grid cells. Each grid cell predicts 2 bounding boxes and a grid is only responsible for

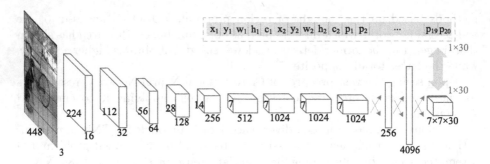

Fig. 1. Network structure of tiny-YOLO: 9 convolutional layers and 3 fully-connected layers. 30 values in dashed box refer to the contents of each output segment: 10 for location information and 20 for class probabilities.

objects whose central point falls inside it. To depict a bounding box, 5 parameters are required: coordinates (x, y), width w, height h and *confidence*. The last parameter *confidence* indicates whether the current bounding box contains an object and how accurate the location is, i.e. $confidence = Pr(Object) * IOU$.

Correspondingly, the 1470 dimensional output is grouped into 7×7 segments. There is a one-to-one correspondence between a grid cell and an output segment. As an example, the first segment represent the information of the first grid. Each segment contains 30 values, 10 for two bounding boxes and 20 for class probabilities. The latter, indicated by p_i, is a series of conditional probabilities, i.e. $p_i = P_r(Class_i|Object)$. Therefore, for a bounding box, the probability of the ith class would be indicated by $P_r(Class_i|Object) * Pr(Object) * IOU = P_r(Class_i) * IOU$.

3   System Design

In this section, we demonstrate the hardware architecture. A global system design is first given to state how memory and computing resources are organized to accomplish CNN inference. Then we go deeper to processing element (PE), which allows parallel computation.

3.1   System Architecture

In our design, CNN inference is conducted layer by layer since a layer's input is usually relied on the previous layer's output. The entire system is illustrated by Fig. 2.

Off-chip memory serves as a global storage for data and weights. We have 3 main areas in off-chip memory: parameter area, area for input data and area for output data. All weights and biases are prepared in parameter area before system starts to work. During the process of each layer, input data and output data will be stored in two data areas respectively.

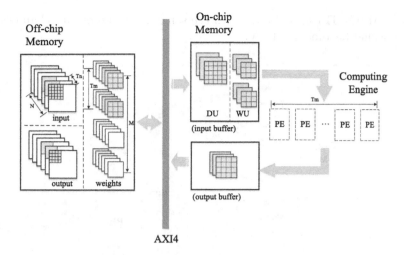

Fig. 2. System architecture. Major components are: Off-chip Memory, On-chip Memory, AXI4 data bus and Computing Engine (T_m PEs).

Input buffer and output buffer both belong to on-chip memory. Input buffer caches a portion of input data, as well as corresponding weights, which will be delivered to PEs for further computation. Then output buffer caches temporal results of these PEs. Data exchanging between on-chip memory and off-chip memory is accomplished through an AXI4 data bus.

Computing engine, made up of T_m duplicated PEs, is the key module for design acceleration. Each PE, completing 32 MAC operations, works for an independent output channel. Therefore, in our design, computation for T_m output channels runs in parallel. Detailed PE structure will be further introduced in Sect. 3.2.

For a layer which has N input channels and M output channels, each time on-chip input buffer caches a portion of data and weights from off-chip memory. The group of data is called a Data Unit (DU) in this paper and the related weights is called a Weight Unit (WU). A DU is of size $16 \times 16 \times T_n$ ($T_n < N$ in general cases), filtered by a $T_m \times 3 \times 3 \times T_n$ WU. In our design, T_n equals to 32 and T_m equals to 64, which fits PE structure perfectly. After rounds of processing by PEs, a $14 \times 14 \times T_m$ data block will be produced. This is a partial sum because DU does not cover all N channels. Therefore, DU and WU will be updated to next T_n channels till the last, and partial sums will be added together. Then added sums will be delivered off-chip without delay. Detailed updating sequence of DU and WU will be later discussed in Sect. 4.1.

3.2   PE Architecture

Computation in CNN is made up of numerous MAC operations. For a CONV layer with N input channels and M output channels, a result requires

$3 \times 3 \times N$ MACs. For an FC layer with the same input and output channels, the number would become $1 \times 1 \times N$.

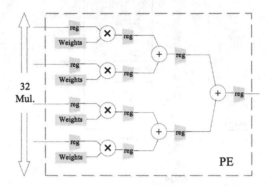

Fig. 3. PE structure

In this paper, we introduce a highly paralleled PE architecture that fits both CONV layers and FC layers. One PE is a function unit that accomplishes 32 MACs at a time. It has 32 multipliers and 31 adders, shown in Fig. 3. We feed PE with data across 32 input channels and thus, based on above analysis, it takes a PE $3 \times 3 \times N/32$ times to generate a result for CONV layers and $1 \times 1 \times N/32$ times for FC layers. PEs are pipelined so that new data can be accepted every 1 clock cycle.

MAC operations for different output channels are totally independent, that is why we exploit 64 identical PEs. There is a one-to-one correspondence between a PE and an output channel. To sum up, the entire computing engine is able to execute 32×64 MAC operations within a clock cycle, which accelerates data calculation by $2048\times$.

4   Dataflow

This section gives a description of data management, including how data is delicately arranged and how ping-pong working increases system parallelism.

4.1   Data Access Pattern

The computation and data access sequence is illustrated by Fig. 4. At first, we get a specific *DU* and related weights to execute the convolution operation, shown by step 1 and step 2. This generated partial sums. Then we have step 3, input data is changed to a newly DU. When step 3 covers all the input feature maps, all the partial sums are added together to generate a set of output pixels. Finally, step 4 and step 5 generate all the output values.

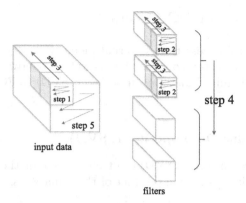

Fig. 4. Steps for data access and computation.

4.2 Ping-Pong Working Strategy

Our implementation uses ping-pong buffers for on-chip memory. Input buffer, shown in Fig. 2, is extended to $inbuf0$ and $inbuf1$. Similarly, output buffer is extended to $outbuf0$ and $outbuf1$.

Figure 5 shows the timing diagram of data transmission processes in ping-pong manner. Solid box indicates operations related with $inbuf0/outbuf0$ and dashed box indicates operations related with $inbuf1/outbuf1$. t_1 in Fig. 5 equals to the time of processing a DU (i.e. T_n channels), while t_2 equals to the time for all-channel processing (i.e. N channels). Obviously, there is a relationship that $t_2 = t_1 \times N/T_n$. Therefore, an output-level computing process actually includes N/T_n input-level computing processes. For input-level diagram, when loading data to $inbuf0$, computing with data from $inbuf1$ will be executed at the same time. Later, roles are exchanged so data from $inbuf0$ is computed and new data is loaded to $inbuf1$. In this way, we cover data loading time with computation. For output-level diagram, in a similar manner, we overlap data storing time and data computation time.

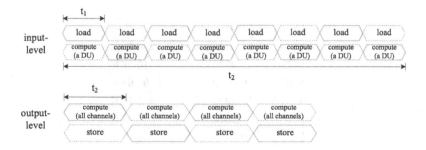

Fig. 5. Ping-pong working time graph of input buffers (input-level diagram) and output buffers (output-level diagram).

5   Optimization for FC Layers

Frequent and massive access from external memory is required for FC layers, which would increase energy consumption as well as bandwidth burden. In this section, we apply Singular Value Decomposition (SVD) to FC layers to alleviate the problem.

5.1   Singular Value Decomposition (SVD)

Singular Value Decomposition (SVD) is a factorization method that decomposes a rectangular matrix W into the product of three matrices:

$$W_{(m*n)} = U_{(m*k)} D_{(k*k)} V_{(k*n)}, \tag{1}$$

where D is a diagonal matrix, U and V are two orthogonal matrices. The key factor k equals to the rank of Matrix W.

Then,we replace the multiplication of U and D with W_1, replace V with W_2, and got the following decomposition:

$$W_{(m*n)} = W_{1(m*k)} W_{2(k*n)} \tag{2}$$

In this manner, the original W is separated into two smaller matrix. When calculating with W, replacing it with W_1 multiply W_2 would be a most helpful way to reduce computation complexity.

5.2   SVD for Tiny-YOLO

For a real-life Tiny-YOLO model, it is feasible to take k as 64. Table 1 demonstrates the comparison of both computing operations and weight size before and after SVD.

Table 1. MAC operations and weight size needed for each FC layer before and after SVD. A total amount for all three layers is also given to indicate the whole optimizing effects.

SVD	Layer	MAC operations	Weight size
No	FC1	12.85 M	200.70 K
	FC2	1.05 M	16.38 K
	FC3	6.02 M	94.08 K
	TOTAL	19.92 M	311.16 K
Yes	FC1	3.23 M	50.43 K
	FC2	0.28 M	4.35 K
	FC3	0.36 M	5.57 K
	TOTAL	3.87 M	60.35 K

As shown in Table 1, after applying SVD, both computation and weights of FC layers are greatly reduced, at a rate of 5.15×. However, since FC layers contribute most to total weight size but little to total computing operations, the optimizing effect on memory access will be much greater than on computing complexity.

6 Evaluation

6.1 Experimental Environment

Our design is implemented with Vivado HLS (v2017.1). Vivado HLS, developed by Xilinx, is a tool that enables hardware programing and simulation using C/C++/System C. After synthesis, it gives out resource report to evaluate hardware resource usage and timing analysis to asses performance. The design was built on VC707 board which has a Xilinx FPGA chip Virtex7 485t.

6.2 Experimental Results

Pictures are tested simultaneously by original YOLO and our system, the comparison is shown in Fig. 6. Figures in the first row are the results of original work and the second row displays ours. We can see that, in our work, dog, car, bird and aeroplanes are all detected and tagged correctly. Furthermore, our system obtains similar precision with original work, the difference is no more than 1%.

Fig. 6. Detecting results of original work and our implementation. First row was done by original work of darknet and second row was done by our implementation.

Our implementation uses 16 bit fixed-point data type for both data and parameters. It is widely accepted that designing in fixed-point leads to lower power usage and resource utilization [12] see Fig. 7. This remains true for our FPGA implementation, fixed-point implementation achieves similar performance, but has reduced latency, resource and power.

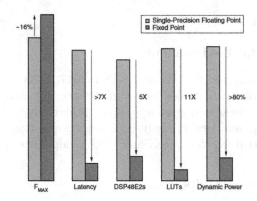

Fig. 7. Performance and resource usage of single-precision floating point and fixed point.

Vivado HLS supports arbitrary precision fixed-point data types. For a basic operation that contains a multiplication along with an add, we have Table 2 to indicate the differences in resource utilization.

For the same computation operations, fixed-point implementation requires much less DSP, LUT and FF, which are all limited but crucial resources for hardware design. The data type of our system is finally selected to be 16-bit fixed-point, we obtain comparable results while reducing resource utilization.

Table 2. Resouce utilization of floating point and fixed-point for the same operation.

Mul. & adder	DSP	LUT	FF
Floating point	5	393	387
32-bit fixed-point	3	66	238
16-bit fixed-point	1	0	75

Table 3 gives resource utilization report of our design. Approximately half of BRAMs and LUTs are used. The utilization percentage is suitable for hardware placement and routing.

Finally, we get a performance of 21 FPS at a rate of 143 MHz. Our system is much faster than running Tiny-YOLO on CPU, which needs approximately 0.97 s to process a single frame.

Table 3. FPGA resouce utilization.

Resource	BRAM_18K	DSP48E	FF	LUT
Total	1071	112	69014	163944
Available	2060	2800	607200	303600
Utilization	52%	4%	11%	54%

7 Conclusion

In this paper, we propose a system design for the implementation of Tiny-YOLO architecture on Xilinx FPGA board. A memory hierarchy is exploited in our design to enhance data reuse as well as to save memory access energy. And we introduce a highly paralleled computing engine which computes for multiple channels at the same time. Finally, we accomplished the real-time detecting system which has a performance of 21 fps at a working frequency of 143 MHz.

Acknowledgement. This work was supported in part by National Natural Science Foundation of China (61527804, 61301116, 61521062, 6113300961771306), Chinese National Key S&T Special Program (2013ZX01033001-002-002), the 111 Project (B07022), the Shanghai Key Laboratory of Digital Media Processing and Transmissions (STCSM 12DZ2272600).

References

1. Girshick, R., Donahue, J., Darrell, T., Malik, J.: Rich feature hierarchies for accurate object detection and semantic segmentation, pp. 580–587 (2013)
2. He, K., Zhang, X., Ren, S., Sun, J.: Spatial pyramid pooling in deep convolutional networks for visual recognition. IEEE Trans. Pattern Anal. Mach. Intell. **37**(9), 1904 (2014)
3. Girshick, R.: Fast R-CNN. Computer Science (2015)
4. Ren, S., He, K., Girshick, R., Sun, J.: Faster R-CNN: towards real-time object detection with region proposal networks. IEEE Trans. Pattern Anal. Mach. Intell. **39**(6), 1137–1149 (2017)
5. Redmon, J., Divvala, S., Girshick, R., Farhadi, A.: You only look once: unified, real-time object detection, pp. 779–788 (2015)
6. Liu, W., Anguelov, D., Erhan, D., Szegedy, C., Reed, S., Fu, C.Y., Berg, A.C.: SSD: single shot multibox detector, pp. 21–37 (2015)
7. Huang, J., Rathod, V., Sun, C., Zhu, M., Korattikara, A., Fathi, A., Fischer, I., Wojna, Z., Song, Y., Guadarrama, S.: Speed/accuracy trade-offs for modern convolutional object detectors (2016)
8. Peemen, M., Setio, A.A.A., Mesman, B., Corporaal, H.: Memory-centric accelerator design for convolutional neural networks. In: IEEE International Conference on Computer Design, pp. 13–19 (2013)
9. Zhang, C., Li, P., Sun, G., Guan, Y., Xiao, B., Cong, J.: Optimizing FPGA-based accelerator design for deep convolutional neural networks, pp. 161–170 (2015)

10. Motamedi, M., Gysel, P., Akella, V., Ghiasi, S.: Design space exploration of FPGA-based deep convolutional neural networks. In: Design Automation Conference, pp. 575–580 (2016)
11. Chen, Y.H., Krishna, T., Emer, J., Sze, V.: 14.5 eyeriss: an energy-efficient reconfigurable accelerator for deep convolutional neural networks. In: Solid-State Circuits Conference, pp. 262–263 (2016)
12. Finnerty, B.A., Ratigner, H.: Reduce power and cost by converting from floating point to fixed point (2017)

Offline Handwritten Chinese Character Recognition Based on New Training Methodology

Weike Luo and Guangtao Zhai[✉]

Department of Electronic Engineering,
Shanghai Jiao Tong University, Shanghai, China
{lwk9419,zhaiguangtao}@sjtu.edu.cn

Abstract. Deep learning based methods have been extensively used in Handwritten Chinese Character Recognition (HCCR) and significantly improved the recognition accuracy in recent years. Famous networks like GoogLeNet and deep residual network have been applied to this field and improved the recognition accuracy. While the structure of the neural network is crucial, the training methodology also plays an important role in deep learning based methods. In this paper, a new data generation method is proposed to increase the size of the training database. Chinese characters could be classified into different kinds of structures according to the radical components. Based on this, the proposed method segments the character images into sub-images and recombines them into new character samples. The generated database, including recombined characters and rotated characters, could improve the performance of current CNN models. We also apply the recently proposed and popular center loss function to further improve the recognition accuracy. Tested on ICDAR 2013 competition database, the proposed methods could achieve new state-of-the-art with a 97.53% recognition accuracy.

Keywords: Offline handwritten Chinese character recognition
Deep learning · Data generation · Center loss

1 Introduction

According to the types of input data, HCCR can be divided into online and offline recognition. For offline recognition, the main target is to extract the feature from the grayscale images and classify them into different categories. It plays an important role in mail sorting, handwritten notes reading and handwritten input on mobile devices. Due to its high practicality, this research has received content attention and plenty methods have been proposed to improve the recognition accuracy.

Nowadays, deep learning based methods have become more and more popular in this field. As shown in a recent report [1], all of the top-ranked methods are using deep neural networks. Among these works, the multi-column deep learning

© Springer Nature Singapore Pte Ltd. 2018
G. Zhai et al. (Eds.): IFTC 2017, CCIS 815, pp. 235–244, 2018.
https://doi.org/10.1007/978-981-10-8108-8_22

network (MCDNN) is believed to be the first successfully applied CNN model in HCCR [2]. The team of Fujitsu won the first place of the ICDAR 2013 by using an alternately trained relaxation convolutional neural network (ATR-CNN) [10]. After that, Zhong et al. [3] proposed a streamlined version of GoogLeNet [4] which is 19 layers deep and further improved the performance. Recently, Zhong et al. [9] applied the deep residual network [12] which is 34 layers deep and has become the state-of-the-art method.

While various CNN models have been proposed to improve the recognition accuracy, most of these methods only focus on the structure of neural network. The training methodology plays a crucial role in deep learning based methods. Existing works of training methodologies include new loss function, training data generation, the modification of back propagation algorithm, etc. Compared to traditional methods, convolutional neural networks provide a powerful solution to extract feature from raw images directly. Instead of designing complex methods for preprocessing, the current trend is to provide a large database for training which includes the generated samples. The input images are manually distorted and rotated to make the neural network more stable to the input data. Inspired by this, we design a new method to recombine the input images based on the structural information of the character. Most of the complex Chinese characters could be regarded to own specific structure like top-bottom structure and left-right structure. To generate new training samples, the original character image is first segmented into different parts according to the structure and then recombined within the same category to generate new samples. The rotated images are also generated for training. The total number of the generated data accounts for twice as big as the original database.

To further improve the performance, we also add the center loss function. As far as we know, most of the existing works in HCCR only use softmax layer to train the network. As current networks are designed to become deeper and deeper, simply using the softmax layer to train the network could not get an excellent result. Researchers start to design new loss functions to help the neural networks converge faster and get better performance. The center loss function is designed for classification which has a large number of categories. The extracted feature of the input images will be pulled towards the center of the category in the feature space. The whole network is jointly trained by softmax loss and center loss. As a result, while the inter-class distance trained by the softmax loss becomes large, the intra-class distance is reduced by the center loss. With a benefit of the intra-class distances and easy implementation, the center loss function soon becomes popular in face recognition.

The experiments are conducted on 2013 ICDAR competition database. The results show the proposed methods have 97.53% recognition accuracy and achieve the new state-of-the-art result.

To summarize, our main contributions are summarized as follows:

(1) We propose a new training data generation method based on the structural information of Chinese character. Compared to the previous character

generation methods, our methods could generate characters with different writing styles within the same category.

(2) We apply the center loss function to deep residual network in HCCR. The center loss significantly improves the training efficiency and recognition accuracy.

The rest of this paper is organized as follows: Sect. 2 introduces a previous data generation method in HCCR. The details of the proposed methods are described in Sect. 3. Section 4 presents the experimental results. The conclusion is shown in Sect. 5.

2   Related Work

Among the recent works, Chen et al. [6] are believed to be the first one to generate the new training data for deep learning based methods in HCCR. In their work, both local distortion and global distortion are added to the input character image. The local distortion is to add a small displacement to the grayscale input image including the X, Y coordinates and gray value. The global distortion is to rotate the image by a small random angle. Since then, plenty of works start to increase the size of training database. Most of the recently proposed methods use the rotated input images to improve the performance of the CNN model.

However, to keep the shape of the character, the displacement and rotation angle must be carefully designed and kept in a small range. Therefore, the generated samples are quite similar to the original ones. The methods only consider the displacements on the input images without making use of the relationship between the characters in the same category. The results show the influence of the generated data on the training is limited. To solve this problem, we design a novel method to generate new training data beyond single input image.

3   Proposed Method

3.1   Radical Region Based Data Generation

The size of the training database plays a key role in deep learning based methods. As shown in face recognition, the bigger database is more likely to get a higher recognition accuracy. Therefore, a great number of methods are proposed to increase the size of training database and make the network more stable to the distorted input. For HCCR, the input data is hard to be aligned without classifying the character. Compared to designing complex traditional methods for normalization, it is more efficient to provide various data to train the neural network. The proposed method is to generate data by recombining different radical regions of the character.

Chinese character, as the logogram, is composed of different radical components, which are the graphical components of the character. These radical components need to be written in certain regions. According to the position, Chinese character could be classified into different structures as shown in Fig. 1.

Structure of Chinese Character	Examples
Single-element Character	一 白 才
Left-right Structure	胡 跟 帆
Left-mid-right Structure	湖 摊 树
Top-bottom Structure	罗 李 昊
Top-mid-bottom Structure	爱 蒙 囊
Semi-enclosed Structure	句 床 司
Enclosed Structure	围 国 回
Pyramid structure	森 淼 晶

Fig. 1. The structural information of Chinese characters

Since different people write Chinese character in different writing styles, the samples would contain various kinds of distortion. To reduce or enlarge the radical components deliberately is one of the ways to make the handwritten character more beautiful. This is also one of the reasons why HCCR is more difficult than printed ones. Therefore, it is essential to generate enough data from samples, which contain different writing styles, to make the convolutional neural network more stable to different writing styles.

According to Fig. 1, the Chinese character could be divided into four categories: the single-element character, center-border character, the two-part character (top-bottom and left-right structure), the three-part character (pyramid, left-mid-right and top-mid-bottom structure). Each of the characters is firstly manually classified into the four categories based on the location of the radical components and then segmented into sub-images except for the single-element character as shown in Figs. 2 and 3. For example, the character with left-right structure is segmented into two parts: left region and right region. Then the segmented images are then recombined with the sub-images of the same character. After normalization, the generated images are resized to the original size for training.

Besides the recombined data, the rotated data is also created for training. For each data, including the original data and recombined data, the image is rotated by a small random angle between $-10°$ and $10°$ as shown in Fig. 4.

Therefore, the training database is composed of three parts: the original database, the recombined database and the rotated database. The size of the recombined database and rotated database is the same as the original database.

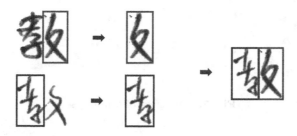

Fig. 2. An example of the left-right recombined data

Fig. 3. An example of the top-bottom recombined data

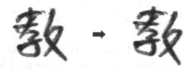

Fig. 4. An example of the rotated data

3.2 Center Loss

Softmax loss is the most widely used loss function in neural network. With current networks become deeper and deeper, simply using softmax loss shows its limitation. In order to get faster convergence and better results, plenty of loss functions have been proposed in the past few years.

The center loss is proposed to reduce the intra-class distances and make it easier to separate different classes [11]. High practicality and easy implementation make center loss soon become popular in face recognition. As far as we know, Yang et al. [13] was the first to apply center loss to HCCR and proposed a light CNN model. The effect of the center loss can be represented as Fig. 5. The star represents the center of the feature of the same category. It is believed that if the feature is tightly clustered around the center point, it will be easier for classification.

In training, the output feature $\mathbf{x}_i \in R^d$ of each input image i is pulled towards the center of each category $\mathbf{c}_{\mathbf{y_i}}$. Parameter d is the feature dimension while y_i represents the label of input image i. The formula of the center loss is shown as below:

Fig. 5. The effect of center loss

$$\mathcal{L}_c = \frac{1}{2} \sum_{i=1}^{m} \|\mathbf{x_i} - \mathbf{c_{y_i}}\|_2^2 \tag{1}$$

It is impossible to calculate the centers of categories in the whole database due to the limitation of memory. Thus, the center $\mathbf{c_{y_i}}$ is updated within the mini-batch in the training.

However, all of the feature will be pulled to the zeros if only center loss is used. In this way, the intra-class distance will be the smallest while the network could not classify the characters. Therefore, the center loss and softmax loss are jointly used in practice. The formula of the softmax loss could be represented as below:

$$\mathcal{L}_s = - \sum_{i=1}^{m} log \frac{e^{W_{y_i}^T x_i + b_{y_i}}}{\sum_{j=1}^{n} e^{W_j^T x_i + b_j}} \tag{2}$$

where n represents the number of class. $\mathbf{W}_j \in R^d$ is the jth column of the weights $\mathbf{W} \in R^{d \times n}$ in the last fully connected layer and $\mathbf{b} \in R^n$ is the bias term.

The whole loss function could be represented by the following equation. The parameter λ is used to balance the loss functions.

$$\mathcal{L} = \mathcal{L}_s + \lambda \mathcal{L}_c = - \sum_{i=1}^{m} log \frac{e^{W_{y_i}^T \mathbf{x_i} + b_{y_i}}}{\sum_{j=1}^{n} e^{W_j^T \mathbf{x_i} + b_j}} + \frac{\lambda}{2} \sum_{i=1}^{m} \|\mathbf{x_i} - \mathbf{c_{y_i}}\|_2^2 \tag{3}$$

3.3   Details of Implementation

In experiments, the deep residual network (DRN) is used for feature extracting. Compared to traditional CNN models, the DRN adopts residual learning to every few stacked layers which is realized by a residual building block defined as:

$$\mathbf{y} = \mathcal{F}(\mathbf{x}, \{W_i\}) + \mathbf{x} \tag{4}$$

The $\mathbf{x}$ and $\mathbf{y}$ are the input and output of the layers with the same dimension. Function $\mathcal{F}(\mathbf{x}, \{W_i\})$ represents the residual mapping to be learned and $\{W_i\}$ is the parameters to be optimized.

The whole network is the original 34 layers deep model [12] which is the most widely used one. Softmax loss and center loss are jointly used to train the network. To balance the softmax loss and center loss, the parameter λ is set as 0.008. The general architecture of the CNN is shown in Fig. 6

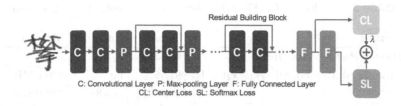

Fig. 6. A general architecture of the proposed network

Considering the influence of the image size on the recognition accuracy and the storage cost, the images are firstly shuffled and then resized into 120×120. We start with a learning rate of 0.02, divide it by 2 per 40k iterations. The maximum iteration is set to 550k. The training takes 2 days to get the best result. Input images are the grayscale images without any preprocessing and the whole network is an end-to-end method.

4   Experiment

4.1   Experimental Data

The databases come from the Institute of Automation of Chinese Academy of Sciences (CASIA) [5]. CASIA-HWDB 1.0 and CASIA-HWDB 1.1 are used for training with a total number of 2,678,424. All of the samples are in 3,755 categories of GB2312-80 level-1 set which covers most of the contemporary used characters. The test database is from the competition test database which contains 224,419 samples comes from 60 writers [7].

4.2   Experimental Results

We test the deep residual network (DRN), center loss (CL) and generated database (GD) separately. The experimental results show the proposed methods could further improve the performance of the current model. The best model improves the recognition accuracy by 0.28% compared to the original model as shown in Table 1.

Table 1. Results on Deep Residual Model

Method	Accuracy
DRN	97.29%
DRN + GD	97.43%
DRN + CL	97.41%
DRN + CL + GD	**97.53%**

Table 2. Results on ICDAR-2013 Offline HCCR Competition Database

Method	Accuracy	Ensemble	Memory
Human Performance [7]	96.13%	n/a	n/a
Traditional Method: DFE+DLQDF [1]	92.72%	no	120.0 MB
MCDNN [2]	95.79%	yes(8)	349.0 MB
ATR-CNN Voting [10]	96.06%	yes(4)	206.5 MB
HCCR-Gabor-GoogLeNet [3]	96.35%	no	27.77 MB
HCCR-Gabor-GoogLeNet-Ensemble [3]	96.74%	yes(10)	270.0 MB
CNN-Single [6]	96.58%	no	190.0 MB
CNN-Voting [6]	96.79%	yes(5)	950.0 MB
DirectMap-ConvNet [1]	96.95%	no	23.50 MB
STN-Residual-34 [9]	97.37%	no	92.30 MB
Proposed Method	**97.53%**	**no**	**124.8 MB**

Table 2 shows the comparison with current methods [9]. Both the recognition accuracy and the memory cost are shown in this table. There is only one end-to-end model in our proposed methods without any ensemble. The results show that the proposed methods could achieve new state-of-the-art performance on the test database.

We also compare the influence of the size of the generated data. The recombined data and rotated are tested separately in five groups. As shown in Fig. 7, the recombined data and the rotated data could further improve the performance of the current model. Both of them have a positive relationship with the recognition accuracy. However, too many generated data would influence the performance on the original database.

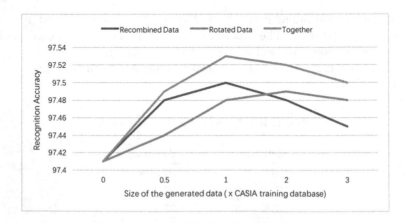

Fig. 7. The recognition accuracy with different size of generate database

4.3   The Recombined Database

The recombined database plays a key role in our methods. Compared to the rotated database, the recombined database is more effective as shown in Fig. 7. Figure 8 shows examples of the generated recombined database. The proposed method could get a good result even for some complex characters.

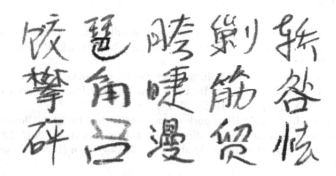

Fig. 8. Recombined database

However, due to the various writing styles, the recombined database also contains some invalid samples as shown in Fig. 9. Most of these samples are removed from the recombined database manually while a small percentage of these invalid samples are kept. We believe these invalid samples could still contribute to improving the performance for it could reduce the over-fitting problem.

Fig. 9. Invalid samples

5   Conclusion

In this paper, two training methods for offline HCCR are proposed to further improve the performance of the current model. A radical region based training data generation method is proposed to increase the size of the training data. The generated data could recombine samples with different writing styles. The center loss function is used in the residual model in HCCR. Both of the methods could improve the performance of current models on the ICDAR 2013 offline HCCR competition database. The best result comes to 97.53% which is the new state-of-the-art as we know.

The CASIA database also gives the human performance (96.13%) on it, which shows there is a limitation of this database. The wrong and similar characters are even impossible for human beings to recognize. By far, the performance of the neural network is far beyond the human performance. We will continue to improve the recognition accuracy until we find the real limitation of it. While deep CNN model is the key in HCCR nowadays, we believe the semantic meaning behind the character will become crucial in the future.

References

1. Zhang, X.Y., Bengio, Y., Liu, C.L.: Online and offline handwritten chinese character recognition: a comprehensive study and new benchmark. Pattern Recogn. **61**, 348–360 (2017)
2. Cireşan, D., Meier, U.: Multi-column deep neural networks for offline handwritten Chinese character classification. In: 2015 International Joint Conference on Neural Networks (IJCNN), pp. 1–6. IEEE (2015)
3. Zhong, Z., Jin, L., Xie, Z.: High performance offline handwritten Chinese character recognition using googlenet and directional feature maps. In: 2015 13th International Conference on Document Analysis and Recognition (ICDAR), pp. 846–850. IEEE (2015)
4. Szegedy, C., Liu, W., Jia, Y., et al.: Going deeper with convolutions. In: Proceedings of the IEEE Conference on Computer Vision and Pattern Recognition, pp. 1–9 (2015)
5. Liu, C.L., Yin, F., Wang, D.H., et al.: CASIA online and offline Chinese handwriting databases. In: 2011 International Conference on Document Analysis and Recognition (ICDAR), pp. 37–41. IEEE (2011)
6. Chen, L., Wang, S., Fan, W., et al.: Beyond human recognition: a CNN-based framework for handwritten character recognition. In: 2015 3rd IAPR Asian Conference on Pattern Recognition (ACPR), pp. 695–699. IEEE (2015)
7. Yin, F., Wang, Q.F., Zhang, X.Y., et al.: ICDAR 2013 Chinese handwriting recognition competition. In: 2013 12th International Conference on Document Analysis and Recognition (ICDAR), pp. 1464–1470. IEEE (2013)
8. Jia, Y., Shelhamer, E., Donahue, J., et al.: Caffe: convolutional architecture for fast feature embedding. In: Proceedings of the 22nd ACM International Conference on Multimedia, pp. 675–678. ACM (2014)
9. Zhong, Z., Zhang, X.Y., Yin, F., et al.: Handwritten Chinese character recognition with spatial transformer and deep residual networks. In: 2016 23rd International Conference on Pattern Recognition (ICPR), pp. 3440–3445. IEEE (2016)
10. Wu, C., Fan, W., He, Y., et al.: Handwritten character recognition by alternately trained relaxation convolutional neural network. In: 2014 14th International Conference on Frontiers in Handwriting Recognition (ICFHR), pp. 291–296. IEEE (2014)
11. Wen, Y., Zhang, K., Li, Z., et al.: A discriminative feature learning approach for deep face recognition. In: Leibe, B., et al. (eds.) ECCV 2016. LNCS, vol. 9911, pp. 11–26. Springer International Publishing, Heidelberg (2016). https://doi.org/10.1007/978-3-319-46478-7_31
12. He, K., Zhang, X., Ren, S., et al.: Deep residual learning for image recognition. In: Computer Vision and Pattern Recognition, pp. 770–778. IEEE (2016)
13. Yang, S., Nian, F., Li, T.: A light and discriminative deep networks for off-line handwritten Chinese character recognition. In: Youth Academic Conference of Chinese Association of Automation, pp. 785–790 (2017)

Video Saliency Detection by 3D Convolutional Neural Networks

Guanqun Ding and Yuming Fang[✉]

School of Information Technology, Jiangxi University of Finance and Economics,
Nanchang 330013, China
leo.fangyuming@gmail.com

Abstract. Different from salient object detection methods for still images, a key challenging for video saliency detection is how to extract and combine spatial and temporal features. In this paper, we present a novel and effective approach for salient object detection for video sequences based on 3D convolutional neural networks. First, we design a 3D convolutional network (Conv3DNet) with the input as three video frame to learn the spatiotemporal features for video sequences. Then, we design a 3D deconvolutional network (Deconv3DNet) to combine the spatiotemporal features to predict the final saliency map for video sequences. Experimental results show that the proposed saliency detection model performs better in video saliency prediction compared with the state-of-the-art video saliency detection methods.

Keywords: Video saliency detection · Visual attention
3D convolutional neural networks · Deep learning

1 Introduction

Saliency detection, which attempt to automatically predict conspicuous and attractive regions/objects in a given image or video, has been actively studied in the field of image processing and computer vision recently. Always considered as a preprocessing procedure, saliency detection can effectively filter out redundant visual information yet preserve important regions, and it has been widely used in a variety of computer vision tasks, such as object recognition [1], image retargeting [3] and summarization [2].

Over the past few years, many saliency detection methods have been proposed based on the characteristics of the Human Visual System (HVS). Saliency detection methods in general can be categorized as either human eye fixation prediction [3] approaches and salient object detection approaches [4]. The first one aims to identify salient locations where human observers fixate during scene view, and we call it as the eye fixation regions. The latter, salient object detection, focuses on predicting saliency values of pixels that determine whether the pixels belong to the salient object or not. In this paper, we focus on salient object detection task in video sequences.

© Springer Nature Singapore Pte Ltd. 2018
G. Zhai et al. (Eds.): IFTC 2017, CCIS 815, pp. 245–254, 2018.
https://doi.org/10.1007/978-981-10-8108-8_23

Recently, deep learning [4,9,10] has been successfully utilized in object detection, semantic segmentation, object tracking and saliency detection. Despite recent great progress in saliency detection for still images, spatiotemporal saliency detection for video sequences remains challenging and it is much desired to design effective video saliency detection models. It is not easy to extract the accurate motion information in video sequences, and thus the small and fast moving objects in video sequences are usually difficult to be captured. Furthermore, the semantic properties of a visual scene are typically related to salient objects and the context close to these objects in this scene. Thus, how to extract and combine the temporal information and high-level spatial features such as semantic cues is important to design effective video saliency detection models.

Currently, there are many video saliency detection models proposed for various multimedia processing applications [8,10–14,16]. For traditional video saliency detection models, they first extract spatial and temporal features to compute spatial and temporal saliency maps, respectively; then the final saliency map for video sequences is predicted by combining the spatial and temporal saliency maps with certain fusion method [13–16]. Most of these methods manually extract low level features such as color, luminance and texture for spatial saliency estimation. However, they might loss some important high-level features such as semantic information in video sequences. What's more, some existing methods attempt to use linear or nonlinear combination rules to fuse spatial and temporal information simply [8,13,14,16], which may ignore the intrinsic relationship due to the fixed weights used for the combination of spatial and temporal information.

In order to overcome these challenges, we adopt 3D convolutional and 3D deconvolutional neural networks to extract and fuse spatial and temporal features to build a effective video saliency detection model. In sum, the main contributions of the proposed method are summarized as follows:

(1) We propose a novel saliency detection model for video sequences based on 3D convolutional neural networks. We construct a 3D convolutional network (Conv3DNet), which can be used to extract spatiotemporal features efficiently for saliency map prediction of video frames.
(2) We devise a 3D deconvolutional network (Deconv3DNet) to learn saliency by fusing spatiotemporal features for the final saliency map calculation. Experimental results show that the proposed model outperforms other baseline methods on two large-scale datasets.

The rest of this paper is organized as follows: Sect. 2 give a detail description of the proposed deep saliency framework. Section 3 shows the comparison experimental results by using the state-of-the-art methods. Finally, we conclude this work in Sect. 4.

2   Proposed Method

The proposed model is demonstrated in Fig. 1. As we can see from this framework, the proposed method includes two components: the Conv3DNet for spatiotemporal feature learning and the Deconv3DNet for saliency learning by fusing spatiotemporal features. With three consecutive video frames (I_{t-1}, I_t, I_{t+1}) in Conv3DNet, the ground truth map G_t of video frame (I_t) in the training set is used to calculate the loss of forward propagation.

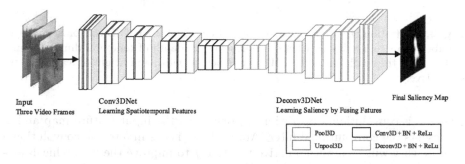

Input — Three Video Frames   Conv3DNet — Learning Spatiotemporal Features   Deconv3DNet — Learning Saliency by Fusing Fatures   Final Saliency Map

	Pool3D		Conv3D + BN + ReLu
	Unpool3D		Deconv3D + BN + ReLu

Fig. 1. Architecture of the proposed video saliency detection model. There are two components in the proposed model: Conv3DNet with three consecutive video frames for spatiotemporal feature learning, and Deconv3DNet for the final saliency learning.

For simplicity, we denote $d \times k \times k$ as the kernel/stride size for 3D convolutional layer, 3D pooling layer, 3D deconvolutional layer and 3D unpooling layer, where d represents the kernel/stride depth in temporal dimension and k stands for the spatial filter/stride size. Besides, we intend to employ $f \times h \times w \times c$ to indicate the output shape of 3D convolution and deconvolution layers, where f represents the number of input video frames; h, w, and c are the parameters for height, width and channels of video frames or feature maps.

2.1 The Spatiotemporal Stream Conv3DNet

As shown in Fig. 1, we construct a Conv3DNet including 5 group blocks, each of which consists of 3D pooling layer and 3D convolution layers with batch normalization and Relu (Rectified Linear Unites) operations. We design 5 group blocks for the proposed model, which would generate the feature maps with the size 7×7. The 3D convolutional operation is demonstrated in Fig. 2. It can be used to learn spatiotemporal features simultaneously for video sequences. Moreover, Du *et al.* demonstrated that 3D convolutional deep networks are useful and effective for learning spatiotemporal features [5].

Due to the stride of convolutional and pooling operations, the output feature maps will be down-sampled and become sparse. This is the reason that we use Deconv3DNet to learn high-level temporal and spatial features. The Conv3DNet takes three consecutive video frames (I_{t-1}, I_t, I_{t+1}) as the input for learning the coherence and motion information between video frames, which have significantly contribute to video saliency detection. The output feature map Y of convolutional operation can be denoted as follows:

$$Y = f(\sum w * X + b) \tag{1}$$

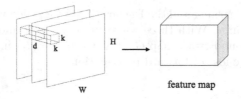

Fig. 2. Illustration of 3D convolutional operation. The kernel of 3D convolutional layer is cube with size $d \times k \times k$, where d represents the depth of temporal dimension and k stands for the spatial filter size. W and H denote width and height of feature maps, respectively.

where $*$ is convolutional operation, X denote as the input feature map and w represents the convolutional filter. After add a bias term b to the convolutional results, they will be input an active function f to improve the hierarchical non-linear mapping learning capability.

Existing studies have shown that the convolutional filter with homogenous parameters of $3 \times 3 \times 3$ is effective for either 2D convolutional networks [4,6] or 3D convolutional networks [5], thus we set 3D convolutional kernel as $3 \times 3 \times 3$ with strides $1 \times 1 \times 1$ in the proposed model. With direct extension of 2D max-pooling to the temporal field, many researches [5] have demonstrated that 3D max-pooling operation can work on multiple temporal samples. As can be seen from Fig. 1, the stride sizes of five 3D max-pooling layers are assigned as follows in the proposed method: $1 \times 2 \times 2$ for the first three max-pooling layers, $2 \times 2 \times 2$ for the last two max-pooling layers. We set these parameters for all 3D max-pooling layers as the above since we intend to learn more temporal features between video frames and do not expect to combine these temporal information at early stage.

2.2 The Deconv3DNet for Saliency Learning

As can be seen from Fig. 1, we adopt 3D deconvolutional and unpooling operations in the proposed Deconv3DNet to fuse spatiotemporal features for video sequences and up-sample the resolution of feature maps. Specifically, we design a Deconv3DNet containing 5 group operations, including a set of 3D deconvolutional layers, 3D unpooling layers and batch normalization layers. As shown in Fig. 1, we first provide a 3D unpooling layer, three 3D deconvolutional layers with batch normalization and Relu operation for the first and second group. Besides, we make use of one 3D pooling layer, two 3D deconvolutional layers for the last three groups, and all strides of the 3D unpooling layer are set as $1 \times 2 \times 2$ to upsample the spatial size of feature maps, while the temporal dimension is fixed to 1 since we aim to calculate the saliency map of unitary frame I_t.

At last, we utilize one extra 3D convolutional layer to generate the final saliency map with the size $224 \times 224 \times 1$ to keep high level saliency cues as much as possible. Here, we use Relu (Rectified Linear Unites) as the activation function of convolutional and deconvolutional layers. The square Euclidean error

Table 1. The basic information of four public datasets: DAVIS [22], SegTrackV2 [21], VOT2016 [18], USVD [13].

Datasets	Clips	Frames	Annotations
DAVIS [22]	50	3455	3455
SegTrackV2 [21]	14	1066	1066
VOT2016 [18]	60	21646	21646
USVD [13]	18	3550	3550

is used as the loss function. We denote (I, G) as a pair of training sampling, which consists of three frames (I_{t-1}, I_t, I_{t+1}) with the shape $h \times w \times 3$ and the corresponding ground truth map G_t of the video frame I_t. Besides, we denote S_t as the generated final saliency map. Because we intend to calculate saliency map of the single frame I_t, the goal of the proposed deep model is to optimize the following loss function on the mini-batch with size k:

$$L(S_t, G_t) = \frac{1}{k}\frac{1}{h}\frac{1}{w} \sum_{l=1}^{k}\sum_{i=1}^{h}\sum_{j=1}^{w} \parallel S_t(i,j) - G_t(i,j) \parallel_F^2 \qquad (2)$$

where $S_t(i,j)$ and $G_t(i,j)$ denotes the pixel value of saliency map S_t and ground truth map G_t.

Here, we adopt Adaptive Moment Estimation (Adam) [19] to optimize the proposed model. Adam is an optimization method that it uses the first moment estimation and second moment estimation of gradient to update the learning rate adaptively. During the training stage, all the parameters are learned by optimizing the loss function. More specifically, the loss function optimization aims to minimize the error between the saliency map generated by forward propagation and the corresponding ground truth map. In the test stage, the proposed model can predict the spatiotemporal saliency maps for any given video sequences without any prior knowledge by the trained model.

3 Experimental Results and Analysis

3.1 Database and Evaluation Criteria

In this study, we conduct the comparison experiments by using four public available benchmark video datasets: DAVIS [22], SegTrackV2 [21], VOT2016 [18], USVD [13]. We conclude the detailed information of these datasets in Table 1. DAVIS [22] contains 50 natural video clips in total with diverse visual content including sports, car drift-turn, animals and outdoor video sequences, with various typical challenges such as multi moving objects, low contrast and complex background. SegTrackV2 [21] consists of 14 video sequences with a variety of visual scenes and activities. VOT2016 [18] contains 60 video clips and 21646 corresponding ground truth maps with pixel-wise annotation of salient objects.

USVD [13] contains 18 video sequences with binary ground truth maps that segment salient objects accurately for each video frame.

In our experiments, we utilize two datasets of VOT2016 [18] and USVD [13] to train the proposed video saliency detection model. To test the proposed video saliency model, we adopt the other two datasets DAVIS [22] and SegTrackV2 [21] as the test data to evaluate the performance of the proposed method.

Similar with [16], we report the quantitative performance evaluation results based on three popular metrics: Pearson's Linear Correlation Coefficient (PLCC), Receiver Operating Characteristics (ROC) and Normalized Scanpath Saliency (NSS). PLCC is used to quantify the correlation and dependence, demonstrating statistical relationship between the saliency maps and ground truth maps. PLCC is commonly defined as follows:

$$PLCC(s, f) = \frac{cov(s, f)}{\sigma_s \sigma_f} \tag{3}$$

where $cov(s, f)$ denotes the covariance of saliency map s and ground truth map f; σ_s and σ_f stand for the standard deviation values of the saliency map s and ground truth map f, respectively. The range of PLCC values is [0,1]. Obviously, the lager PLCC value means the better performance of the saliency detection model.

In addition, ROC curve and area under ROC curve (AUC) are also used for evaluating the performance of saliency detection models. With the varied threshold, the ROC curve is plotted as the False Positive Rate (FPR) and True Positive Rate (TPR), which are defined as follows:

$$FPR = \frac{M \cap \bar{G}}{\bar{G}} \tag{4}$$

$$TPR = \frac{M \cap G}{G} \tag{5}$$

where M represents the binary mask of the saliency map generated by a series of varying discrimination thresholds on the saliency map; G denotes the binary ground truth map while $\bar{G}$ stands for the reverse of G. Generally, the lager AUC value means the better performance of saliency detection model.

As a widely adopted to evaluate the saliency detection method, NSS is defined by the response value at human fixation locations in the normalized saliency map with zero mean and unit standard deviation as:

$$NSS(s, g) = \frac{1}{\sigma_s}(s(g_i, g_j) - \mu_s) \tag{6}$$

where s and g denote the saliency map and corresponding ground truth map; (g_i, g_j) is the pixel location of the ground truth map; μ_s and σ_s represent the mean value and the standard deviation of the saliency map, respectively. Typically, the higher NSS value means better saliency detection model.

In our experiments, the proposed deep network of video salient object detection is implemented in Ubuntu operating system with the toolbox, Tensorflow library [23], an open source software for deep learning developed by Google. We use a computer with Intel Core I7-6900K*16 CPU (3.20 GHz), 64 GB RAM and Nvidia TITAN X (Pascal) GPU with 16 GB memory.

3.2 Performance Comparison

Furthermore, we compare the proposed approach against several existing video saliency detection methods including Fang [16], LGGR [14], MultiTask [4], RWRV [8], CE [17] and SGSP [13]. We show the quantitative experimental results in Table 2 on SegTrackV2 dataset [21] and Table 3 on DAVIS dataset [22], where the PLCC, AUC and NSS scores are collected from the mean value of 14 video sequences in SegTrackV2 dataset and 50 video sequences in DAVIS dataset, respectively.

Among these state-of-the-art approaches, Fang [16] is a Gestalt theory based saliency detection method; LGGR [14] uses local gradient flow optimization and global refinement for video saliency prediction; MultiTask [4] is a deep learning based salient object detection method for images, using multi-tasks of saliency detection and semantic segmentation; RWRV [8] predicts video saliency via random walk with restart method; CE [17] is a video saliency computation approach based on conditional entropy; SGSP [13] utilizes superpixel-level graph and spatiotemporal propagation method for saliency detection.

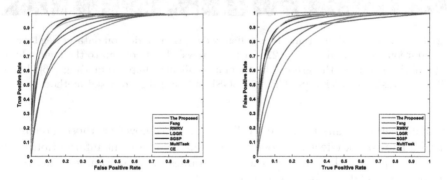

Fig. 3. ROC comparison of spatiotemporal saliency models on SegTrackV2 dataset [21] (left) and DAVIS dataset [22] (right).

We provide some visual saliency samples from different saliency detection models in Fig. 4 on SegTrackV2 [21] (first four rows) and DAVIS [22] (last four rows). It can be seen that the saliency map obtained from other existing methods contain some noises, as shown by the fact that some background regions are detected as the salient locations in some saliency maps generated from existing methods. Although the saliency maps of LGGR [14] and SGSP [13] have

Fig. 4. Comparison of different video saliency detection models on dataset SegTrackV2 [21] (first four rows) and DAVIS [22] (last four rows). First column to the final column: original video frames; the ground truth maps; saliency maps from Fang [16], LGGR [14], MultiTask [4], RWRV [8], CE [17], SGSP [13] and the proposed method.

relatively better results than the RWRV [8] method, however, those models still existing fatal block effect and loses some visually important information in the saliency map since they divided the video frames into block/super-pixel to calculate the local/globle feature contrast.

Meanwhile, From both Tables 2 and 3, we can observe that the proposed method can obtain better video saliency prediction performance than other related ones, as shown by the highest PLCC, AUC and NSS values among the compared models. We provide the ROC curves of all these methods in Fig. 3 on SegTrackV2 dataset [21] (left) and DAVIS dataset [22] (right) to demonstrate the better results of our model than other existing ones.

Table 2. Comparison of different video saliency detection models on SegTrackV2 [21].

Models	Fang	LGGR	MultiTask	RWRV	CE	SGSP	Proposed model
PLCC	0.5098	0.7133	0.7752	0.5831	0.4595	0.6452	**0.7838**
AUC	0.7936	0.8887	0.9099	0.8504	0.8257	0.8660	**0.9107**
NSS	2.5876	2.5895	3.0762	2.0302	1.8046	2.9739	**3.0830**

Table 3. Comparison of different video saliency detection models on DAVIS [22].

Models	Fang	LGGR	MultiTask	RWRV	CE	SGSP	Proposed model
PLCC	0.6720	0.6733	0.8138	0.4077	0.4985	0.7439	**0.8145**
AUC	0.9034	0.8735	0.9262	0.8282	0.8436	0.9114	**0.9325**
NSS	2.5904	2.4775	2.8294	1.6699	1.7874	2.7747	**2.9485**

4 Conclusion

In this paper, a novel salient object detection approach with 3D convolutional neural networks is proposed to effectively learn semantic and spatiotemporal features for video sequences. The proposed model mainly includes two components: the spatiotemporal stream Conv3DNet and the Deconv3DNet for saliency learning. The Conv3DNet consists of a series of 3D convolutional layers, which is proved to be effective to obtain spatiotemporal information between consecutive frames (I_{t-1}, I_t, I_{t+1}). The Deconv3DNet is designed to combine the spatiotemporal features from Conv3DNet to learn the final spatiotemporal saliency map for video. Experimental results have shown that there is great potential to build the video saliency detection model with 3D convolutional operation for effectively learning spatiotemporal features instead of time-consuming hand-crafted features.

Acknowledgments. This work was supported by NSFC (No. 61571212), and NSF of Jiangxi Province in China (No. 20071BBE50068, 20171BCB23048, 20161ACB21014, GJJ160420).

References

1. Rutishauser, U., Walther, D., Koch, C., Perona, P.: Is bottom-up attention useful for object recognition? In: IEEE Conference on Computer Vision and Pattern Recognition (2004)
2. Simakov, D., Caspi, Y., Shechtman, E., Irani, M.: Summarizing visual data using bidirectional similarity. In: IEEE Conference on Computer Vision and Pattern Recognition (2008)
3. Fang, Y., et al.: Saliency detection in the compressed domain for adaptive image retargeting. IEEE Trans. Image Process. **21**(9), 3888–3901 (2012)
4. Li, X., et al.: DeepSaliency: multi-task deep neural network model for salient object detection. IEEE Trans. Image Process. **25**(8), 3919–3930 (2016)

5. Du, T., Bourdev, L., Fergus, R., Torresani, L., Paluri, M.: Learning spatiotemporal features with 3D convolutional networks. In: IEEE International Conference on Computer Vision (2015)
6. Simonyan, K., Zisserman, A.: Very deep convolutional networks for large-scale image recognition. Computer Science (2014)
7. Krizhevsky, A., Sutskever, I., Hinton, G.E.: ImageNet classification with deep convolutional neural networks. In: International Conference on Neural Information Processing Systems (2012)
8. Kim, H., Kim, Y., Sim, J.Y., Kim, C.S.: Spatiotemporal saliency detection for video sequences based on random walk with restart. IEEE Trans. Image Process. **24**(8), 2552–2564 (2015)
9. Zhang, P., Zhuo, T., Huang, W., Chen, K., Kankanhalli, M.: Online object tracking based on cnn with spatial-temporal saliency guided sampling. Neurocomputing **257**, 115–127 (2017)
10. Huang, W., Ding, H., Chen, G.: A novel deep multi-channel residual networks-based metric learning method for moving human localization in video surveillance. Sig. Process. **142**, 104–113 (2017)
11. Fang, Y., Zhang, C., Li, J., Lei, J., Perreira, D.S.M., Le, C.P.: Visual attention modeling for stereoscopic video: a benchmark and computational model. IEEE Trans. Image Process. **26**(10), 1476–1490 (2017)
12. Fang, Y., Lin, W., Chen, Z., Tsai, C.M., Lin, C.W.: A video saliency detection model in compressed domain. IEEE Trans. Circuits Syst. Video Technol. **24**(1), 27–38 (2014)
13. Liu, Z., Li, J., Ye, L., Sun, G., Shen, L.: Saliency detection for unconstrained videos using superpixel-level graph and spatiotemporal propagation. IEEE Trans. Circuits Syst. Video Technol. **PP**(99), 1 (2016)
14. Wang, W., Shen, J., Shao, L.: Consistent video saliency using local gradient flow optimization and global refinement. IEEE Trans. Image Process. **24**(11), 4185–4196 (2015)
15. Wang, W., Shen, J., Porikli, F.: Saliency-aware geodesic video object segmentation. In: IEEE Conference on Computer Vision and Pattern Recognition (2015)
16. Fang, Y., et al.: Video saliency incorporating spatiotemporal cues and uncertainty weighting. IEEE Trans. Image Process. **23**(9), 3910–3921 (2014)
17. Li, Y., Zhou, Y., Yan, J., Niu, Z., Yang, J.: Visual saliency based on conditional entropy. In: Zha, H., Taniguchi, R., Maybank, S. (eds.) ACCV 2009. LNCS, vol. 5994, pp. 246–257. Springer, Heidelberg (2010). https://doi.org/10.1007/978-3-642-12307-8_23
18. Tomas, V., et al.: Pixel-wise object segmentations for the VOT 2016 dataset (2017)
19. Kingma, D.P., Ba, J.L.: Adam: a method for stochastic optimization. Computer Science (2014)
20. Ioffe, S., et al.: Batch normalization: accelerating deep network training by reducing internal covariate shift. In: International Conference on Machine Learning (2015)
21. Li, F., Kim, T., Humayun, A., Tsai, D., Rehg, J.M.: Video segmentation by tracking many figure-ground segments. In: IEEE International Conference on Computer Vision (2013)
22. Perazzi, F., Sorkine-Hornung, A., et al.: A benchmark dataset and evaluation methodology for video object segmentation. In: IEEE Conference on Computer Vision and Pattern Recognition (2016)
23. Abadi, M., Agarwal, A., Barham, P., Brevdo, E., Chen, Z., Citro, C.: Tensorflow: large-scale machine learning on heterogeneous distributed systems (2016)

Bit-Depth Enhancement via Convolutional Neural Network

Jing Liu[1(✉)], Wanning Sun[1], and Yutao Liu[2]

[1] Multimedia Institute, Tianjin University, 92 Weijin Road, Tianjin, China
jliu_tju@tju.edu.cn
[2] Department of Computer Science, Harbin Institute of Technology,
Harbin, China

Abstract. Nowadays, many monitors are able to display high dynamic range (HDR) images with high bit-depth for each quantized pixel, but most of the existing image and video contents are of low bit-depth. Therefore, bit-depth enhancement (BE) plays a key role in displaying a low bit-depth image in a high bit-depth monitor. Convolutional Neural Networks (CNNs) and Deep Learning (DL) have recently demonstrated impressive performance in generating realistic high-quality synthetic images, semi-supervised classification, and have been extended for video abstraction and so on. But CNNs or any other deep learning algorithm has not yet been applied to expand image bit-depth so far. In this paper, to fill the gap, we propose a novel algorithm to recover the high bit-depth images via deep convolutional neural network. By training the parameters of the neural networks, the model could learn to recover gradual transition areas and avoid the false contour artifacts, which are commonly seen with traditional bit-depth enhancement algorithms. The experimental results show that our proposed method achieves competitive performance compared with existing bit-depth enhancement methods in terms of PSNR and SSIM with greatly suppressed false contours.

Keywords: Bit-depth enhancement · Deep learning
Convolutional neural networks · High dynamic range imaging

1 Introduction

Image bit-depth is the number of bits used to represent each color of a rendered pixel. Bit-depth up-conversion plays a key role in the field of image enhancement. While there are many methods to convert high bit-depth images to lower bit-depth ones, the existing experimental results on bit-depth expansion are not satisfactory. When a low bit-depth image is shown in a higher bit-depth monitor directly, the value of each pixel are usually simply transformed, which often

This work is supported by the National Science Foundation of China under Grant (61701341, 61672193) and the Major State Basic Research Development Program of China (973 Program 2015CB351804).

© Springer Nature Singapore Pte Ltd. 2018
G. Zhai et al. (Eds.): IFTC 2017, CCIS 815, pp. 255–264, 2018.
https://doi.org/10.1007/978-981-10-8108-8_24

Fig. 1. Illustration of false contour artifacts. The left and right sub-images are zero padded high bit-depth image and ground-truth high bit depth image, respectively. Note false contours as well as chroma distortions are observed in the zero-padded image.

results in severe contouring effect in the smooth gradient area, degrading the image visual quality. Thus designing a good bit-depth enhancement method is of significant value to let low color bit-depth contents displayed on a high color bit-depth monitor.

The false contour artifacts caused by bit-depth quantization is shown in Fig. 1. When a high bit-depth image is quantized to low bit-depth version, and viewed on normal 8-bit monitors, it often suffers from low visual quality and have severe contouring effect, which is visually unpleasant. Meanwhile, the output of zero padded image has chroma distortions [1]. The colors of many quantized images are less bright than the raw images, especially when the pixel's luminance is high.

Recently, deep learning or more commonly known as deep structured learning or hierarchical learning emerges as a hot topic and draws lots of attention in multimedia processing field. It is a subset of machine learning, which aims at discovering the distributed representations of data, and transforming the input data to target data distribution. Numerous deep learning algorithms have been proposed to solve various computer vision problems, such as image classification [2], object detection [3], image retrieval [4], semantic segmentation [5] and human pose estimation [6], and achieved superior performance. The convolutional neural networks and deep learning algorithms could also be applied to traditional image processing problem such as single image super-resolution [7] and image inpainting [8]. They are especially powerful when it comes to dealing with large amounts of supervised datum and learning data representations in a greedy layer-wise framework compared with traditional machine learning methods.

However, to the best of our knowledge, the great power of deep learning methods has never been exploited to solve bit-depth enhancement problem, which is indeed a more difficult image restoration problem. Most of existing bit-depth enhancement algorithms are based on bottom-up calculation rather than machine learning. Widely used methods include multiplication-by-an-ideal-gain (MIG) [9], adaptive filter (ABDE) [10], maximum a posteriori estimation of AC Signal (ACDC) [11] and content adaptive image bit-depth expansion (CA) [1]. These algorithms either suffer from the contour artifacts, or over-blur the output image greatly, making some image content hard to recognize. By training the deep neural networks with large dataset, the proposed algorithm learns the distribution of data, and could transform low bit-depth images to realistic ones.

In this paper, we propose the framework of bit-depth enhancement via convolutional neural network (BE-CNN). Inspired by Christian Ledig's work [12], we adopt the most recently proposed Residential Energy Services Network (ResNet) [3] and train our model by gradient descending the perceptual loss [13]. Different from the pixel-wise mean square error (MSE) loss widely used in traditional methods, the perceptual loss is formulated as the difference between the feature map of VGG-19 [14] networks of the output image and the ground truth. Compared with the MSE loss, the perceptual loss could lead to more realistic output of high visual quality. The experimental results show that the proposed BE-CNN achieves competitive performance compared to existing bit-depth enhancement methods in terms of PSNR and SSIM, with greatly suppressed false contours.

The rest of the paper is organized as follows: we describe the proposed BE-CNN together with its network structure and training loss in Sect. 2. Then we exhibit the experimental validation of the whole method in Sect. 3. Finally, the conclusion of this paper is expressed in Sect. 4.

2 The Proposed Algorithm

2.1 Problem Formulation

Analogy to viewing a low-resolution picture on a high-resolution screen, when a low bit-depth image is displayed on an ordinary high bit-depth monitor, it would suffer from low visual quality. Inspired by the success of data representation with CNN, we aims to design a network to learn the intrinsic characteristics of natural images and automatically transform the low bit-depth image into high bit-depth version. In this paper, we propose the bit-depth enhancement framework via convolutional neural networks. We adopted the most recently proposed ResNet, which has significant better performance than previous AlexNet [2], VGGNet [14], GoogleNet [15] and so on. By training the proposed network with low bit-depth and ground truth high bit-depth image pair, the parameters can be automatically tuned to capture the characteristics of natural images and then used to generate high bit-depth images given low bit-depth ones.

To generate images of higher visual quality, we use the perceptual loss between the output image and ground truth, rather than the pixel-wise MSE. As illustrated by Justin Johnson et al. [13], when the parameters of network are gradient descended by the Euclidean distance of feature maps between the image pair, the output image could have better structure similarity and seems realistic, although the mean square error between them may be higher. The feature map is a high-level feature extracted from pretrained networks such as vgg-19 network. And compared with the previously used MSE loss, the contouring artifacts of the generated images of this method are significantly reduced.

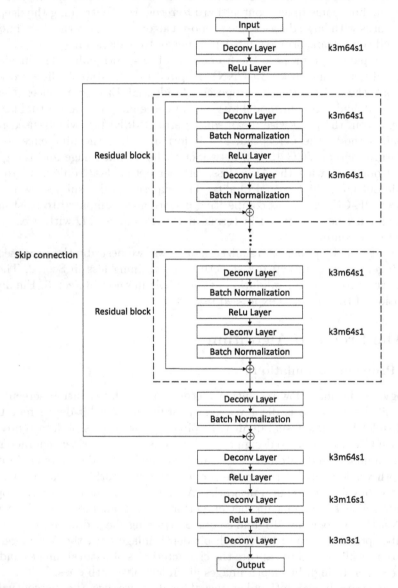

Fig. 2. Network structure of the proposed algorithm. The network has 5 residual blocks, each of which contains 2 deconvolutional layers. In this figure, the parameters of each deconvolutional layer are shown aside, most of which have 3 × 3 kernels (k), 64 feature maps (n) and 1 stride (s).

2.2 Network Structure

The network structure of the proposed algorithm is shown in Fig. 2. Inspired by the recently proposed Residential Energy Services Network (ResNet), we adopt the ResNet to solve the vanishing gradient problem when the network has too much layers. In this network, we add skip connections that shortcut two convolutional layers at a time and a connection bypassing the whole network. Each bypass gives rise to a residual block in which the convolution layers predict a residual that is added to the block's input tensor. This layer-skipping feedforward neural network could address the vanishing gradient, making it easier to train the whole network. We set 14 convolutional layers and 5 residual blocks in our proposed framework.

Besides, instead of using max pooling layers after each convolutional layer, the network uses batch normalization layers to make the network working more effective and efficient, as proposed by Ioffe et al. [16]. In addition, we replace the convolutional layers with deconvolutional layers to generate more realistic and of high visual-quality images. All the filter kernels of our deconvolutional layers are of the size of 3×3, and each layer has at most 64 feature maps with stride of 1 followed by batch-normalization layers and parametric ReLU. The fully connection layers are not used in this framework.

2.3 Loss Function

A proper loss function is essential in deep learning algorithms. The traditional machine learning algorithms typically train feed-forward convolutional neural networks using pixel-wise mean square error loss between the output and ground-truth images. But the results are always blurry and of low visual quality. When it come to recent parallel work, as illustrated by Justin Johnson et al. [13], it has been shown that defining and optimizing perceptual loss functions based on high-level features extracted from pretrained networks could generate high-quality images. Therefore, in the framework of BE-CNN we use Adam optimization [17] and gradient descend the perceptual loss to make the generated image more realistic. Compared with the previously used MSE loss, the contouring effect of the output image of this method is greatly suppressed. We formulate the perceptual loss as the average Euclidean distance between the feature maps of the pretrained VGG-19 network of output images and ground-truth as follows:

$$l_{VGG/i,j} = \frac{1}{W_{i,j}H_{i,j}} \sum_{x=1}^{W_{i,j}} \sum_{y=1}^{H_{i,j}} (\phi_{i,j}(groundtruth)_{x,y} - \phi_{i,j}(output)_{x,y})^2 \quad (1)$$

3 Experimental Results

We perform experiments on a 16-bit lossless version of the short animation film *Sintel*, which is downloaded from the Xiph.Org Foundation [18]. The dataset contains more than 20 thousand 16-bit images of the film, but many frames are almost the same. Therefore, we randomly select 1000 images of the them. Moreover, compared with natural photos, the details of animation images are sharper, while the gradual transition areas are smoother, which make it much more difficult to recover gradient areas with most details maintained. The images in the *Sintel* dateset contains various scenes, such as snowberg, town, sky, cave and so on. Some of them are illustrated as Fig. 3.

img1   img2

img3   img4

img5   img6

img7   img8

Fig. 3. Samples from the *Sintel* dataset.

The size of all the images in the dataset are 1024×436, and we cut them into 96×96 image blocks to train, which would reduce the training time and the memory demand significantly. The learning rate of the optimization is 1e-4, and the model is trained 8 epochs with the batch size of 20.

We evaluate the experimental results with two metrics. To assess the accuracy of the generated image, we calculate the peak signal to noise ratio (PSNR).

In addition, we compute the structural similarity index (SSIM) [19] between the output and the ground truth image to estimate the structure similarity. The PSNR and SSIM results of our experimental output and other methods, including zero padding (ZP), multiplication-by-an-ideal-gain (MIG) [9], bit replication (BR) [20], minimum risk based classification (MRC) [21], contour region reconstruction (CRR) [22] and content adaptive image bit-depth expansion (CA) [1], are presented as Table 1. The proposed algorithm could achieve competitive performance compared with others.

Table 1. SSIM and PSNR of different methods.

		ZP	MIG	BR	MRC	CRR	CA	CNN
img1	SSIM	0.6050	0.6076	0.6533	0.6970	0.7420	0.7921	**0.8998**
	PSNR	29.9607	30.7893	31.3501	32.1361	29.7761	33.6555	**35.1052**
img2	SSIM	0.9457	0.9423	0.9476	0.9551	0.9751	0.9687	**0.9792**
	PSNR	28.9566	32.2774	32.8358	33.0839	34.7606	35.8600	**36.4582**
img3	SSIM	0.9127	0.9102	0.9193	0.9317	0.9374	0.9388	**0.9625**
	PSNR	28.5716	31.7191	32.2785	33.8715	32.8341	34.1449	**35.2115**
img4	SSIM	0.5716	0.5758	0.6259	0.6580	0.8517	0.8904	**0.8988**
	PSNR	29.3621	30.0090	30.5698	31.2121	31.4495	34.6325	**35.9715**
img5	SSIM	0.9199	0.9160	0.9240	0.9382	0.9645	0.9602	**0.9665**
	PSNR	28.9096	30.8494	31.4078	32.2814	34.8448	**36.2888**	35.9674
img6	SSIM	0.7479	0.7506	0.7798	0.8396	0.5100	0.5662	**0.8655**
	PSNR	31.8946	33.0174	33.5782	35.2195	27.0242	30.6925	**37.9192**
img7	SSIM	0.6359	0.6375	0.6810	0.7859	0.5812	0.6761	**0.8889**
	PSNR	31.8092	33.1081	33.6689	35.4691	27.6567	31.9227	**37.3571**
img8	SSIM	0.9310	0.9301	0.9371	0.9435	0.9212	0.9271	**0.9576**
	PSNR	28.7563	31.8138	32.3726	33.4391	30.9861	33.2973	**34.7358**

Since traditional monitors and PDF could at most display 8-bit image in each channel, the enhanced 16-bit images are quantized to 8-bit for display. The subjective results are shown in Fig. 4. As is illustrated in the images, it is obviously that the algorithms of ZP, MIG, BR and MRC have dissatisfactory output, with severe contouring effect. Although the outputs of CRR and CA are the most smooth, some content may be too blurry to be seen, such as the shadow in the first set of output. But our proposed BE-CNN algorithm could reserve these details with greatly suppressed contouring artifacts. When the original images have gradual transition areas, as is shown in the second set of images, the BE-CNN could also recover the section, and avoid obvious false contouring artifacts. In the third set of images, which contain fine texture, the CA and CRR algorithms would significantly blur the details, while BE-CNN performs well.

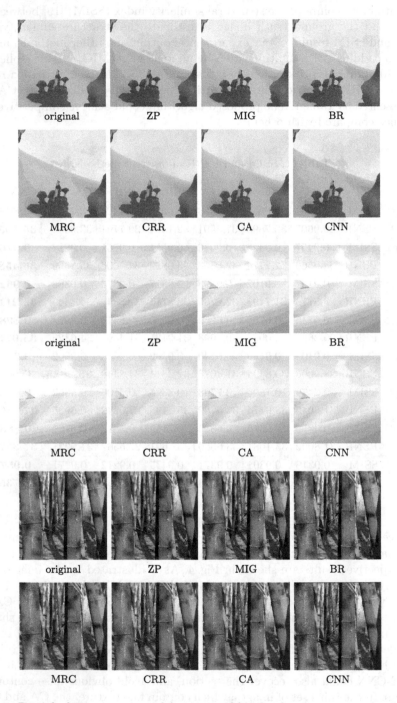

Fig. 4. Partial of images generated from several bit-depth enhancement algorithms.

4 Conclusion

In this paper, we propose an image bit-depth enhancement algorithm via convolutional neural network. The algorithm could increase the image bit-depth with high accuracy, greatly depressed contouring artifacts as well as keeping the original contents sharp. The proposed model have been trained and tested with a large dataset and the promising results demonstrate the superiority of the proposed algorithm.

References

1. Wan, P., Au, O.C., Tang, K., Guo, Y.: From 2D extrapolation to 1D interpolation: content adaptive image bit-depth expansion. In: IEEE International Conference on Multimedia and Expo, pp. 170–175 (2012)
2. Krizhevsky, A., Sutskever, I., Hinton, G.E.: Imagenet classification with deep convolutional neural networks. In: International Conference on Neural Information Processing Systems, pp. 1097–1105 (2012)
3. He, K., Zhang, X., Ren, S., Sun, J.: Deep residual learning for image recognition. In: Computer Vision and Pattern Recognition, pp. 770–778 (2016)
4. Wan, J., Wang, D., Hoi, S.C.H., Wu, P., Zhu, J., Zhang, Y., Li, J.: Deep learning for content-based image retrieval: a comprehensive study. In: The ACM International Conference, pp. 157–166 (2014)
5. Tsogkas, S., Kokkinos, I., Papandreou, G., Vedaldi, A.: Deep learning for semantic part segmentation with high-level guidance. Computer Science, pp. 530–538 (2015)
6. Ouyang, W., Chu, X., Wang, X.: Multi-source deep learning for human pose estimation. In: IEEE Conference on Computer Vision and Pattern Recognition, pp. 2337–2344 (2014)
7. Tseng, C.W., Su, H.R., Lai, S.H., Liu, J.C.: Depth image super-resolution via multi-frame registration and deep learning. In: Signal and Information Processing Association Summit and Conference, pp. 1–8 (2017)
8. Liu, M.: Image inpainting and super-resolution using non-local recursive deep convolutional network with skip connections. In: International Conference on Digital Image Processing, p. 104203A (2017)
9. Robert A Ulichney and Shiufun Cheung. Bit-depth increase by bit replication (2000)
10. Liu, C.H., Au, O.C., Wong, P.H.W., Kung, M.C., Chao, S.C.: Bit-depth expansion by adaptive filter. In: IEEE International Symposium on Circuits and Systems, pp. 496–499 (2008)
11. Wan, P., Cheung, G., Florencio, D., Zhang, C., Oscar, C.A.: Image bit-depth enhancement via maximum a posteriori estimation of AC signal. IEEE Trans. Image Process. **25**(6), 2896–2909 (2016)
12. Ledig, C., Theis, L., Huszar, F., Caballero, J., Cunningham, A., Acosta, A., Aitken, A.P., Tejani, A., Totz, J., Wang, Z., et al.: Photo-realistic single image super-resolution using a generative adversarial network. Computer Vision and Pattern Recognition, pp. 4681–4690 (2016)
13. Johnson, J., Alahi, A., Feifei, L.: Perceptual losses for real-time style transfer and super-resolution. In: European Conference on Computer Vision, pp. 694–711 (2016)

14. Simonyan, K., Zisserman, A.: Very deep convolutional networks for large-scale image recognition. In: International Conference on Learning Representations (2015)
15. Szegedy, C., Liu, W., Jia, Y., Sermanet, P., Reed, S., Anguelov, D., Erhan, D., Vanhoucke, V., Rabinovich, A.: Going deeper with convolutions. In: IEEE Conference on Computer Vision and Pattern Recognition, pp. 1–9 (2015)
16. Ioffe, S., Szegedy, C.: Batch normalization: accelerating deep network training by reducing internal covariate shift. In: International Conference on Machine Learning, pp. 448–456 (2015)
17. Kingma, D.P., Ba, J.L.: Adam: a method for stochastic optimization. In: International Conference on Learning Representations (2015)
18. Xiph.Org Foundation. Xiph.Org. https://www.xiph.org/ (2016). Accessed 16 May 2017
19. Wang, Z., Bovik, A.C., Sheikh, H.R., Simoncelli, E.P.: Image quality assessment: from error visibility to structural similarity. IEEE Trans. Image Process. **13**(4), 600 (2004)
20. Ulichney, R.A.: Pixel bit-depth increase by bit replication. Proc. SPIE Int. Soc. Opt. Engi. **3300**, 232–241 (1999)
21. Mittal, G., Jakhetiya, V., Jaiswal, S.P., Au, O.C., Tiwari, A.K., Wei, D.: Bit-depth expansion using minimum risk based classification. In: Visual Communications and Image Processing, pp. 1–5 (2013)
22. Cheng, C.H., Au, O.C., Liu, C.H., Yip, K.Y.: Bit-depth expansion by contour region reconstruction. In: IEEE International Symposium on Circuits and Systems, pp. 944–947 (2009)

Quality Assessment

Subjective Evaluation of Light Field Images for Quality Assessment Database

Liang Shan[1], Ping An[1(✉)], Deyang Liu[2], and Ran Ma[1]

[1] Key Laboratory of Advanced Displays and System Application,
Shanghai Institute for Advanced Communication and Data Science, Ministry of Education,
Shanghai University, Shanghai 200444, China
anping@shu.edu.cn

[2] School of Computer and Information, Anqing Normal University, Anqing 246133, China

Abstract. Light filed imaging is becoming popular for its diversity of post-processing and a wide range of applications. Various kinds of research about light field such as light field compression methods are coming out one after the other in recent years. For better evaluation of the quality of light field images and the performance of compression algorithm, the study on quality assessment of light field is in desperate need. In this paper, in order to establish a light field quality assessment database for the subsequent research, we propose a methodology of subjective evaluation for light field image and use a 2D objective evaluation method to verify the methodology. Results show that this methodology can be successfully used to assess the quality of light field content.

Keywords: Light field · Compression algorithm · Quality assessment
Subjective evaluation

1 Introduction

Light field (LF) images, also known as holoscopic images, integral images, or plenoptic images [1], which can be captured by LF camera. The concept of LF was firstly proposed by Gershun [2] in 1936. Then in 1991, Adelson [3] proposed the plenoptic function which has seven dimensions. After simplification, Levoy [4] used the theory that two spots in space can determine a straight line to propose a four-dimension plenoptic function:

$$L = L(u, v, x, y), \tag{1}$$

where uv and xy are two parallel planes, (x, y) and (u, v) are two points on two planes respectively, L is a ray of light that pass through the above two points.

There are many kinds of post-processing applications of LF images such as refocusing, depth of field, 3D image, 360-degree light field display [5], etc. However, the original raw image is Bayer array image that cannot be displayed normally. For obtaining LF image we should decode the original raw image. This process called light field decoding [6]. Lenslet image (shown in Fig. 1(a)) can be gotten from this process. Lenslet image is the raw image after demosaicing and devigneting. The

© Springer Nature Singapore Pte Ltd. 2018
G. Zhai et al. (Eds.): IFTC 2017, CCIS 815, pp. 267–276, 2018.
https://doi.org/10.1007/978-981-10-8108-8_25

decoded LF image called 4D LF and also called LF data structure (shown in Fig. 1(b)) which is a 15 × 15 stacked image structure. Each image presents one viewpoint and there exists a little parallax between two views. Figure 2 presents the overview diagram of the 4D LF decoding.

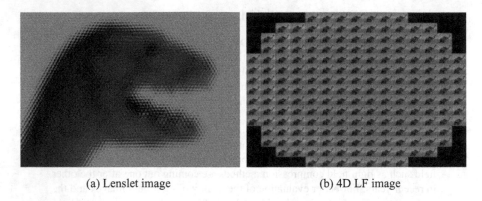

(a) Lenslet image   (b) 4D LF image

Fig. 1. Light filed image

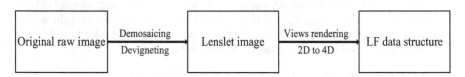

Fig. 2. Flow chart of LF decoding

The compression of LF images is a grand challenge in recent years. In January 2016, the ICME 2016 collected many kinds compression methods for LF imaging [7]. All of these methods can be classified into two groups. One group is lenslet image compression, the other is viewpoint image compression. The latest mainstream method of compression for viewpoints is pseudo-sequence method [8, 9] which is regarding each viewpoint image in LF data structure as a frame in a video sequence to compress. As for lenslet image compression, no matter image coding scheme or video coding scheme, it both has wider applicability than viewpoint image. So directly compressing lenslet image is still popular. Our team also did lots of work in this direction. In the aspect of lenslet image compression, [9, 10] talk about how to use Gaussian models to code the images, [11] use HEVC with kernel-based minimum mean square error estimation as the coding scheme. In another hand, [12] and [13] are both talks about LF rendered views coding in different prediction methods, and [14] use pseudo-sequence method to coding LF images.

The transmission may produce kinds of distortion. And how to evaluate different compression is also a challenge. Therefore, quality assessment of LF is a significant research direction. Unfortunately, there is almost no specialized quality evaluation method for LF contents. People usually use traditional 2D quality evaluation method such as PSNR or SSIM for verifying the performance of their compression scheme.

To solve this problem, an LF quality assessment database is needed. Current LF images databases are all used for the studies of LF compression or other LF processing like depth extraction, but we build an LF database for the study of LF quality evaluation.

There have been some recent studies on subjective evaluation. In [15], the authors proposed a subjective method for evaluating LF image compression algorithms, but what they chose or tested were three views and two refocus images, which could not fully reflect the quality of LF. In [16], the authors proposed a new approach to subjectively assess the quality of LF content, they used all the views to make an interactive user interface in which subjects of the test can choose any view to watch. But different subject may have different watching order. This will cause that the stimulation cannot be synchronized. In [17], the authors used an all-in-focus view to assess the quality of LF, then compared different 2D objective quality metrics. All-in-focus view equals the middle view of all the viewpoints, although it can give all the depth information of LF, the 2D image still cannot fully reflect the quality of LF. In [18], the authors compared two different subjective methodologies to assess LF content and then conclude that interactivity on the quality assessment of LF is very important.

In this paper, we propose a subjective evaluation method for LF images and compared the experimental results with one traditional objective method (PSNR), and based on this method, we build a basic LF quality assessment database.

The remainder of this paper is organized as follows. The details of the subjective test design are presented in Sect. 2. Then, the experimental results and the comparisons are discussed in Sect. 4, and the conclusions are drawn in Sect. 5.

2   Subjective Evaluation

2.1   Data Preparation

For building an LF quality assessment database, lots of LF images are needed. Our work is based on the Light-Field Image Dataset [19]. All the LF images in the dataset are shot by Lytro Illum, an LF camera. We choose six images (shown in Fig. 3.) from the dataset to build our database and use two of them (P1 and P2) as test materials for the subjective experiment to verify our method.

(a) P1   (b) P2   (c) P3

(d) P4   (e) P5   (f) P6

Fig. 3. Experiment contents

For each image, we use LF MATLAB toolbox function *LFDecodeLensletImage-Simple* (LFToolbox4.0) [6, 20] to decode the original raw image and add different kinds of distortion at lenslet image. The reason we use lenslet image is lenslet image is most likely to produce distortion no matter in compression or transmission. The type of distortion and the parameter are shown in Table 1. Then we continue to decode the distorted image to LF data structure. To avoid not fully reflect the quality of LF, we use all the viewpoints to make an animation that each view is one frame. The frame rate is set to 15 frames per second. And each one of these views is all-focus-view. The order of views is shown in Fig. 4.

Table 1. The types of distortion and parameters of each level

Distortion	Level 1	Level 2	Level 3	Level 4
Gaussian Blur (σ)	1	3	10	30
JPEG (QLs)	80	20	5	1
JPEG2000 (CRs)	50	500	2000	5000
White Noise (σ)	0.03	0.1	0.25	0.5

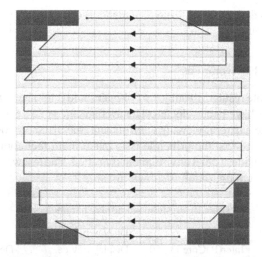

Fig. 4. The order of viewpoints to produce pseudo video sequence

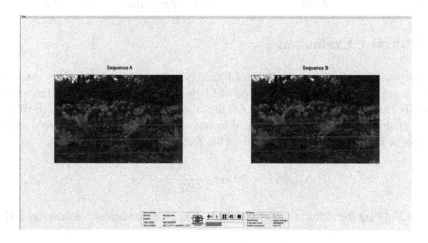

Fig. 5. Example of evaluation interface for DSCQS methodology

Two LF images for the subjective test, each one has four kinds of distortion [21], each distortion has four grades. In total of 4 × 4× 2 pairs of test animations.

The methodology selected for the test is based on Double Stimulus Continuous Quality Scale (DSCQS). Two animations in native resolution (625 × 434) are presented simultaneously in side by side fashion. We use MSU Perceptual Video Quality Tool as test play platform. The test user interface is shown in Fig. 5. One of the two animations is original video used as reference video, and be arranged on the screen randomly. All the pairs with the same kind of distortion are played in a random order. Each pair repeats twice. Each test of one subject has four sessions, before each session there is a training test, and the whole test time is about 25 min. The subjects were asked to rate the quality of both images on a discrete scale from 5 (Excellent) to 1 (Bad). The score can be rated after one decimal point.

2.2 Subjects and Environment

For collecting reliable results, 19 subjects (14 males and 5 females) whose age between 22 years to 35 years have been selected. The average age is 25 years.

In order to create a natural viewing environment, the distance from the monitor was determined by the subjects, the principle is to make them feel comfortable. To avoid interference from outside, a quiet environment is needed. The test was done in a windows OS computer whose configuration is shown in Table 2.

Table 2. System and display parameters

System parameters		Display parameters	
Processor	Inter(R)Core i3 550	Display device	Dell E2211Hb
Processor speed	@3.20 GHz	Screen Refresh Rate	60 Hz
RAM	8 GB	Screen Resolution	1920 × 1080

3 Objective Evaluation

The purpose of that we try to build an LF quality assessment database is to establish a research platform for quality evaluation of LF, including objective evaluation which is currently lack of specialized method. On the other hand, some existing objective evaluation methods for 2D images can help us to verify our proposed subjective method. We choose PSNR, which is computed on the Y channel as follow [7]:

$$PSNR_Y(k, l) = 10 \log_{10} \frac{255^2}{MSE(k, l)}, \tag{2}$$

where k and l are the index of viewpoints, the MSE for each view is computed as follow:

$$MSE(k, l) = \frac{1}{mn} \sum_{i=1}^{m} \sum_{j=1}^{n} [I(i,j) - R(i,j)]^2, \tag{3}$$

where m and n correspond to dimensions of each view. $I(i,j)$ and $R(i,j)$ are the values of pixel on the position (i,j) of individual evaluated and reference views respectively.

The PSNR_YUV value for each view is computed as follow:

$$PSNR_{YUV}(k, l) = \frac{6PSNR_Y(k, l) + PSNR_U(k, l) + PSNR_V(k, l)}{8}. \tag{4}$$

And average PSNR_X (X can be Y, U, V or YUV) is computed as follow:

$$PSNR_{X_{mean}} = \frac{1}{(K-2)(L-2)} \sum_{k=2}^{K-1} \sum_{l=2}^{L-2} PSNR_X(k, l), \tag{5}$$

where $K = 15$ and $L = 15$ represent the number of viewpoints.

4   Results

Outlier detection was performed according to the guidelines defined in ITU recommendation [22] Some outliers were detected and the relative scores were discarded. The Mean Opinion Score (MOS) was computed for each distortion condition j as follows:

$$MOS_j = \frac{1}{N} \sum_{i=1}^{N} m_{ij}, \tag{6}$$

where N is the number of participants and m_{ij} is the score for stimulus j by participant i.

Figure 6 gives the MOS against distortion level (as shown in Table 1) for test contents. From the figures, we can find something worthy of attention. We can see that the distortion level of compression distortion (JPEG and JPEG2000) is difficult to be distinguished, but the contents of white noise and Gaussian blur are easier to be evaluated. We consider adding more distortion level in the future work to complete the LF quality assessment database perfectly.

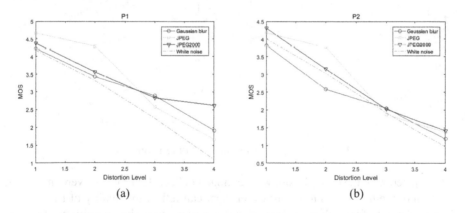

Fig. 6. MOS vs distortion level of test contents

We added the same level of distortion in the different image, so the curves of the two images are very similar. It's reasonable for our theory. But we still can find that scores of P2 are less than P1. It's probably because the texture complexity of P2 is lower than P1, and P1 is more colorful than P2. So how to select the scene of LF images is also a very important factor in building the database, because a complete database needs to cover enough information.

Figure 7 shows the objective method results. Apparently, these curves show similar trends with the subjective experiment. This proves that the proposed subjective methodology for building LF quality assessment database is feasible. However, we ought to know that objective measures should be tested by a subjective evaluation, so the PSNR cannot fully be validated our method, but it still can give us a proof that our method is logical and reasonable.

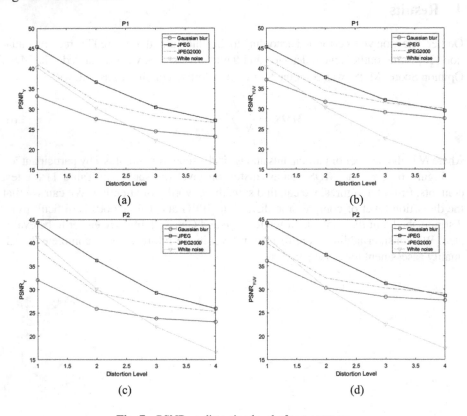

Fig. 7. PSNR vs distortion level of test contents

Compared with the related work we mentioned in Sect. 1, our work overcomes some defection of them. The result of our experiment can reflect the quality of LF contents reliably. Not only for evaluating the performance of compression algorithms, our work can also be used for the research of quality assessment.

5   Conclusion

In this paper, a subjective evaluation methodology for LF images is proposed, and database construction for LF quality assessment pave the way. In order to reflect the quality of LF images as comprehensive as possible, we use all of the all-in-focus views to produce pseudo video sequences as test data, then we use traditional 2D objective metric

PSNR to verify the proposed method. At last, how to use the result of the subjective experiment and the database to study new specialized objective evaluation method for LF images is the future work.

Acknowledgment. This work was supported in part by the National Natural Science Foundation of China under Grants 61571285 and U1301257, Construction Program of Shanghai Engineering Research Center under Grant 16dz2251300, and Shanghai Science and Technology Commission under Grant 17DZ2292400.

References

1. Conti, C., Soares, L.D., Nunes, P.: HEVC-based 3D holoscopic video coding using self-similarity compensated prediction. Signal Process. Image Commun. **42**, 59–78 (2016)
2. Gershun, A.: The light field. J. Math. Phys. **18**, 51–151 (1939). Moscow
3. Adelson, E.H., Bergen, J.R.: The plenoptic function and the elements of early vision (1991)
4. Levoy, M., Hanrahan, P.: Light field rendering. In: Proceedings of the 23rd annual conference on Computer graphics and interactive techniques, pp. 31–42. ACM (1996)
5. Jones, A., McDowall, I., Yamada, H., et al.: Rendering for an interactive 360 light field display. ACM Trans. Graph. (TOG) **26**(3), 40 (2007)
6. Dansereau, D.G., Pizarro, O., Williams, S.B.: Decoding, calibration and rectification for lenselet-based plenoptic cameras. In: Proceedings of the IEEE Conference on Computer Vision and Pattern Recognition, pp. 1027–1034 (2013)
7. ISO/IEC JTC 1/SC29/WG1 JPEG: "Grand challenge on light field image compression," Doc. M72022, Geneva, Switzerland, June 2016
8. Liu, D., Wang, L., Li, L., et al.: Pseudo-sequence-based light field image compression. In: IEEE International Conference on Multimedia & Expo Workshops, pp. 1–4. IEEE (2016)
9. Liu, D., An, P., Ma, R., et al.: 3D holoscopic image coding scheme using HEVC with Gaussian process regression. Signal Process. Image Commun. **47**, 438–451 (2016)
10. Liu, D., An, P., Du, T., et al.: An Improved 3D Holoscopic Image Coding Scheme Using HEVC Based on Gaussian Mixture Models, pp. 276–285 (2016)
11. An, P., Ma, R., Shen, L.: Three-dimensional holoscopic image coding scheme using high-efficiency video coding with kernel-based minimum mean-square-error estimation. J. Electron. Imaging **25**(4), 043015 (2016)
12. Liu, D., An, P., Ma, R., et al.: Scalable coding of 3D holoscopic image by using a sparse interlaced view image set and disparity map. Multimedia Tools Appl. **76**, 1–23 (2017)
13. Liu, D., An, P., Yang, C., et al.: Coding of 3D holoscopic image by using spatial correlation of rendered view images. In: IEEE International Conference on Acoustics, Speech and Signal Processing. IEEE (2017)
14. Yang, L., An, P., Liu, D., et al.: 3D Holoscopic Images Coding Scheme Based on Viewpoint Image Rendering (2016)
15. Viola, I., Řeřábek, M., Bruylants, T., et al.: Objective and subjective evaluation of light field image compression algorithms. In: 2016 Picture Coding Symposium (PCS), pp. 1–5. IEEE (2016)
16. Viola, I., Rerabek, M., Ebrahimi, T.: A new approach to subjectively assess quality of plenoptic content. In: Applications of Digital Image Processing XXXIX, SPIE 2016, (EPFL-CONF-221562), vol. 9971, pp. 99710X-1–99710X-13 (206)
17. Paudyal, P., Battisti, F., Sjöström, M., et al.: Toward the perceptual quality evaluation of compressed light field images. IEEE Trans. Broadcast. **63**(3), 507–522 (2017)

18. Viola, I., Řeřábek, M., Ebrahimi, T.: Impact of interactivity on the assessment of quality of experience for light field content. In: 2017 Ninth International Conference on Quality of Multimedia Experience (QoMEX), pp. 1–6. IEEE (2017)
19. Řeřábek, M., Yuan, L., Authier, L., et al.: EPFL light-field image dataset (2015)
20. Dansereau, D.G., Pizarro, O., Williams, S.B.: Linear volumetric focus for light field cameras. ACM Trans. Graph. **34**(2), 15:1–15:20 (2015)
21. Sheikh, H.R.: Image quality assessment using natural scene statistics (2004)
22. Assembly I T U R.: Methodology for the Subjective Assessment of the Quality of Television Pictures. International Telecommunication Union (2003)

Selection of Good Display Mode for Terahertz Security Image via Image Quality Assessment

Zhaodi Wang[1], Menghan Hu[1(✉)], Wenhan Zhu[1], Xiaokang Yang[1], and Guang Tian[2]

[1] Institute of Image Communication and Information Processing,
Shanghai Jiao Tong University, Shanghai, China
humenghan@sjtu.edu.cn
[2] BOCOM Smart Network Technologies Inc., Shanghai 200433, People's Republic of China

Abstract. In order to provide a good display performance for THz (terahertz) security image, we designed several display modes on the custom-built THz security image database (THSID). Based on our statistical analysis of THz images, a total of 4 candidate display modes are proposed, namely averaging the highest 1%, 10%, 20%, 30% pixel values in Z-axis for a coordinate *(x, y)*. In this paper, the subjective evaluation was first carried out, demonstrating that the second display mode, that was the averaging the highest 10% pixel values in Z-axis, got the greatest performance. Subsequently, to further support the result obtained by the subjective evaluation and the high throughout application requirement in real world, a total of 11 objective no-reference IQA (Image Quality Assessment) algorithms were implemented, including 4 opinion-aware approaches, viz. GMLF, NFERM, BLIINDS2, BRISQUE, and 7 opinion-unaware approaches viz. CPBD, FISBLIM, NIQE, QAC, SISBLIM, S3, Fish_bb. The results of objective evaluation show that the current objective IQA algorithms can hardly support the subjective evaluation. Even so, BLIINDS2 and CPBD perform relatively well for the chosen display mode above. A more suitable objective evaluation method need to be explored in the future study. This study will make some progresses on the display effect of THz image, which can promote the detection accuracy in the future applications.

Keywords: THz image database · THz imaging technique
THz image display mode · THz image quality assessment
Specific image quality

1 Introduction

In recent years, terahertz (THz) imaging technology is developing rapidly. In contrast to the traditional imaging approaches such as X-ray and visible light imaging, THz imaging technology has been proved to be a more promising and safer way for security check [1]. THz waves can penetrate plastic, ceramics, liquid and semiconductor, by which way a more reliable security check can be provided [2].

However, the down side of the THz technology is the time-consuming imaging process [3]. The present THz imaging devices need several seconds for one image, which means the quality of the THz image is significantly affected by the equipment and

© Springer Nature Singapore Pte Ltd. 2018
G. Zhai et al. (Eds.): IFTC 2017, CCIS 815, pp. 277–289, 2018.
https://doi.org/10.1007/978-981-10-8108-8_26

ambient noise. According to the previous study, the quality of the image generated by current THz imaging devices tends to be quite low [4, 5], affecting the detection accuracy adversely. Consequently, to ensure an acceptable imaging quality is imperative in the practical application. In order to make some improvement on the quality of current THz security image in the aspect of software, we propose several display modes, then use subjective and objective IQA to pick out a relatively good display mode for the ultimate purpose of the application.

The purpose of the image quality assessment (IQA) is to provide a quantitatively evaluation of the THz image quality, allowing the future improvement of the THz image quality in software and hardware [6]. IQA is divided into subjective and objective methods. The former makes a subjective qualitative evaluation of the image; the latter reflects the subjective perception of people by means of a mathematical model, and gives the results based on the numerical calculation [7–12]. IQA aims to make automatic assessment that consistent with task requirements or human judgments, which makes IQA a serviceable means for the numerous image processing tasks [13]. IQA provides a criterion for evaluating the imaging system, thus optimizing the image acquisition process and monitoring the working condition of the imaging modules. Currently, IQA has been applied widely in multi-media processing including video transmission and image compression [14]. However, IQA is seldom applicated in specific image processing, such as ultrasonic wave and CT. The application on THz image is only studied in paper [15] up to now.

In this study, we are going to: (1) denoise the THz security image to create enhanced images for the following analysis; (2) propose several good display modes based on the statistical data of subjective evaluation; (3) adopt the subjective IQA and the previous-proposed no-reference IQA algorithms for the evaluation of the THz security images in THSID to obtain the better display mode for safety inspection purpose; (4) discuss to the future research trend of THz imaging technique and image analysis.

2   Materials and Methods

2.1   THz Security Image Database (THSID)

THSID [15] is composed of 181 THz security images. Each image contains 200 vertical slices with a resolution of 127×380. Hence, the data structure of the obtained raw THz security image is three-dimensional, containing X-, Y- and Z-axes. Figure 1 clearly exhibits the three-dimensional THz security image. Due to this specific data structure, it is highly essential to extract the useful information from the image cube to display the informative two-dimensional image on the inspection screen, assisting security staffs in screening the illegal substances. To generate the THSID, four volunteers were invited. Each time they were imaged with various contraband such as knife and hammer, or with legal article such as bracelet and belt.

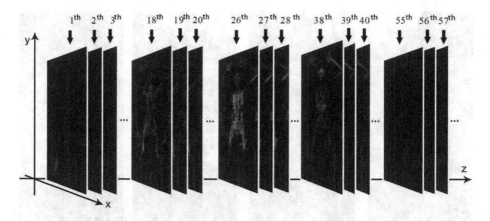

Fig. 1. A sample for three-dimensional raw THz image.

In this study, we design several display modes to extract two-dimensional image of good quality from the raw THz image cube.

2.2 Some Candidate Display Modes

The principle of the selection of the candidate THz security display modes is presented as follows: (1) enhancement of the difference between the slices with human body and the slices blank: owing to the limited performance of imaging device and the influence of the surrounding environmental factors (e.g. humidity and temperature), we use the contrast stretch transformation [16] for each slice of image cube in the THSID, as shown in Fig. 2; (2) determination of region of interest (ROI): considering the THz imaging principle, we need to confirm the range of the human body along Z-axis. To do this, we analyze the spatial distribution of pixel value, figure out the characteristics of the slices with human body and then find the set of consecutive slices that meet the requirements; (3) suppress the Gaussian noise and acquire the final THz images for display using the various selection threshold values.

The detailed descriptions of these three steps are presented below.

First, we enhance the difference between the slices with human body and the slices blank. Figure 2 shows the effect of contrast stretch transformation. As shown in Fig. 2(a) and (b), when subjected by the contrast stretch transformation, the body structure and background noise become clearer and lower, respectively. Whereas in Fig. 2(c) and (d), images without human body, it doesn't change much after the contrast stretch transformation. The above two phenomena can be also observed in their corresponding histograms (Fig. 2). This indicates the contrast stretch transformation can retain the necessary information to the extent that we want to use in the following analysis. Thus, the method of image enhancement is quite suitable for this study.

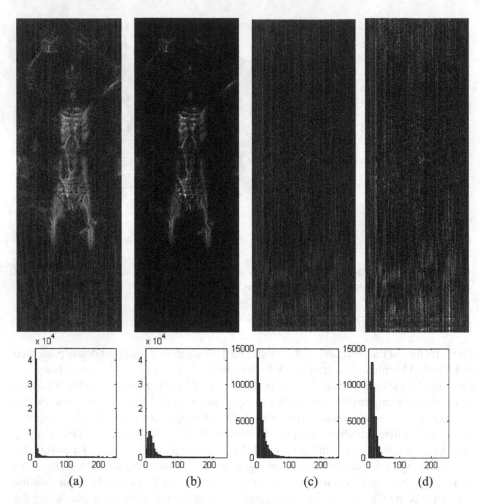

Fig. 2. The effect of contrast stretch transformation and the corresponding histogram: (a) The 25th slice from one image cube before contrast transformation; (b) the 25th slice from one image cube after contrast transformation; (c) the 60th slice from one image cube before contrast transformation; (d) the 60th slice from one image cube after contrast transformation.

Then, the region of interest (ROI) need to be determined. Figure 3 shows the spatial distribution of the pixel values for a certain cube of THz security image in THSID. The observation shows that human body occupies the range from 2 to 45 along the Z-axis in this THz image. Figure 4 shows the percentage of the number of pixels whose value is under 20.

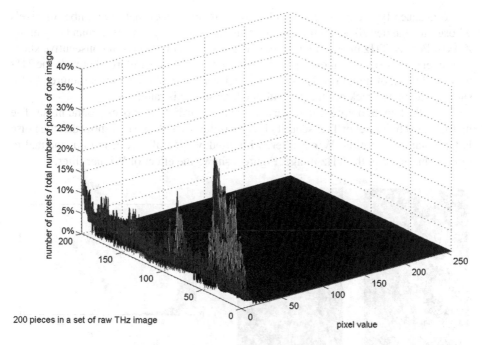

Fig. 3. Spatial distribution of pixel value.

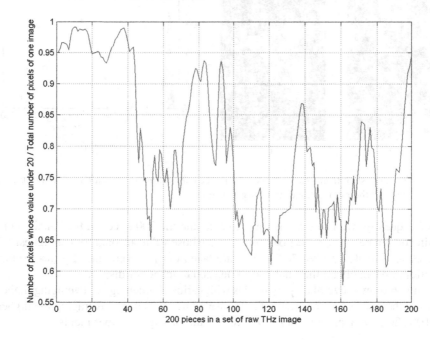

Fig. 4. The percentage of total number of pixels of image that number of pixels whose value is under 20.

Consequently, we consider to pick out continuous slices that the number of pixels whose value under 20 account for 90% or higher as the range of the human body along Z-axis. For one THz image cube, there may exist the multiple sets of consecutive slices that meet the restrictions above. This may due to the spectral similarity between the THz wave reflection of human body as well as device surface and the body structure. As for such situation, we pick out the set with the largest Z-axis range.

With the human body located, we analyze the distribution of background noise. The histogram of blank set of THz security images is fitted and the results show that the noise is Gaussian distribution. Winer filter, with window size of 3×3, is implemented to reduce this noise in the THz image. Figure 5 shows the effect of Winner filter.

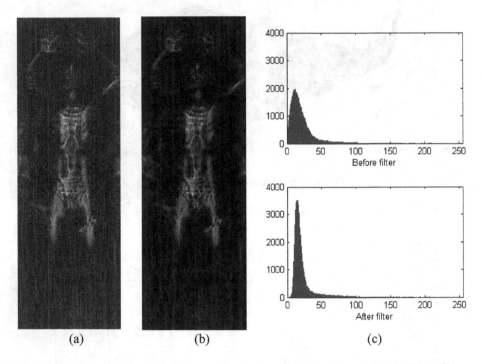

(a)   (b)   (c)

Fig. 5. The same slice from one THz security image cube before (a) and after (b) Winer filter is implemented and their corresponding histograms (c).

Subsequently, we use several ways to combine the 200 slices in the Z-axis. For a certain coordinate (x_0, y_0), the pixels on Z-axis whose value account for the highest 1%, 10%, 20%, 30%, 40%, 50%, 70%, 100% are taken out for averaging. By this average operation, we can obtain the final two-dimensional image for display.

Figure 6 shows several display modes with various percentage of averaging highest values in the Z-axis. We chose the first 4 display modes namely averaging the highest 1%, 10%, 20%, 30% pixel values in Z-axis for the subsequent experiments.

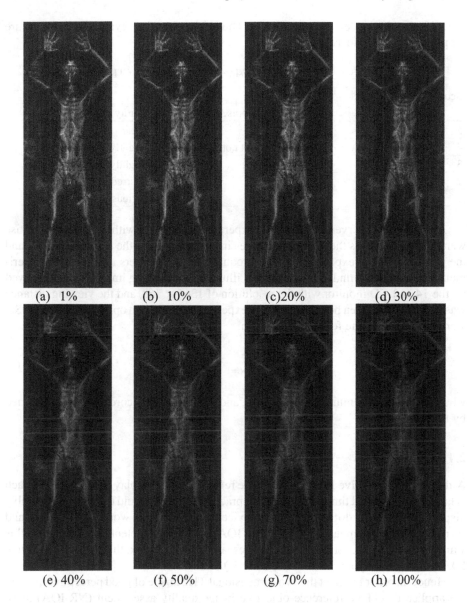

Fig. 6. Various display modes of THz security image with different thresholds.

2.3 Subjective IQA

The use of subjective IQA can help us to select the relatively good THz display mode from the candidate THz display modes.

For THz security image, the main factor that deteriorates THz security image quality is the background noise, which arises from the unstable device and the changeable environment. Background noise impacts the clarity of body structure in THz image, and in turn decreases the detection accuracy. Thus the subjective evaluation criteria are proposed, as shown in Table 1.

Table 1. Subjective evaluation criteria using five-grade scale for THz security image.

Score	Quality	Standards	
		Level of overall noise	Clarity of body structure
5	Excellent	Acceptable	Clear
4	Good	Unacceptable, but not annoying	Slightly clear
3	Fair	Slightly annoying	Slightly blurred
2	Poor	Annoying	Blurred
1	Bad	Quite annoying	Seriously blurred

A total of 10 observers containing 2 experts and 8 subjects without related expertise were invited to assess the quality of images in THSID. Before the test, the purpose and the procedure of the experiment were introduced to all observers in detail. The experiment was conducted under normal indoor illumination. Testing images were displayed on the 14 in. LCD monitor with the resolution of 1366×768, and the viewing distance was about 2–2.5 screen heights. After the experiments, the mean opinion scores (MOSs) were calculated by the following equation:

$$MOS_j = \sum_{i=1}^{N} \frac{\mu_{i,j}}{N_i} \tag{1}$$

where N_i denotes the number of observers, and $\mu_{i,j}$ denotes the score of image j assigned by the ith observer.

2.4   Objective IQA

Although the subjective IQA can select the relatively good display mode, this approach is labor-intensive and time-consuming. In practical use, we should calculate the suitable display mode for the different imaging devices in their various working conditions and surrounding environments. The objective IQA can offer the potential solutions for this situation. In addition, for the explorative research like this work, the results of objective IQA can further support that of subjective IQA.

Hence, in order to select the two-dimensional THz image of good perceptive quality, we applied the 11 no-reference objective image quality assessment (NR-IQA) algorithms as the merits. In the current work, 4 opinion-aware approaches, including GMLF [17], NFERM [18], BLIINDS2 [19], BRISQUE [20]; and 7 opinion-unware approaches viz. CPBD [21], FISBLIM [22], NIQE [23], QAC [24], SISBLIM [25], S3 [26], Fish_bb [27] were carried out for assessing the THz image quality.

To calculate the performance of these NR-IQA algorithms, the logistic function with 5 parameters was implemented to fit the MOSs estimated by no-reference IQA algorithms, as shown in Eq. 1. Subsequently, Eq. 1 was used to map the fitted objective scores to the subjective scores.

$$Mapped\ Quality\ (\mathrm{x}) = \beta_1 \left(\frac{1}{2} - \frac{1}{1 + e^{\beta_2(x-\beta_3)}} \right) + \beta_4 x + \beta_5 \tag{2}$$

Where *Mapped Quality* denotes the mapped objective score, and *x* denotes original score.

Then, Pearson Linear Correlation Coefficient (PLCC), Spearman Rank-Order Correlation Coefficient (SROCC) and Root Mean Squared Error (RMSE) were used to check the performance of IQA on THz images.

3   Results and Discussion

3.1   No-Reference IQA for Various Display Modes of THz Security Images

Figure 7 shows the MOSs of 4 display modes, with the average of 3.4167, 3.5227, 3.3317 and 3.1567, respectively. As shown in Fig. 7, we can observe that the most MOSs values of highest 20% and 30% are evenly distributed in the range from 1–5. This indicates that these two display modes are not acceptable for showing on the inspection screen. The second display mode, namely averaging the highest 10% value in Z-axis, gets the greatest MOSs among the 4 modes.

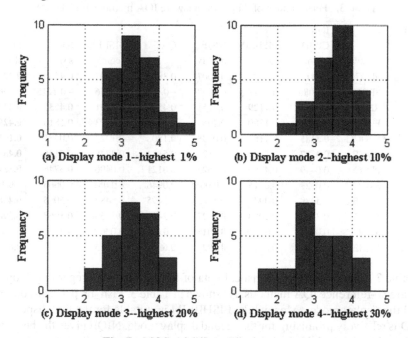

Fig. 7. MOSs of different display modes.

Table 2 shows the statistical data regarding the performance of 4 opinion-aware no-reference IQA methods. As shown in Table 2, NFERM is more suitable for the first display mode, whereas BLIINDS2 is relatively promising for the last 3 display modes.

Table 2. Performance of 4 opinion-aware IQA methods for THSID.

Criteria		IQA			
		GMLF	NFERM	BLIINDS2	BRISQUE
		out	score	predicted_score	qualityscore
1%	PLCC	0.3362	**0.6481**	0.5486	0.3590
	SROCC	−0.3031	**−0.0769**	0.0320	−0.2546
	RMSE	0.4692	**0.3794**	0.4165	0.4650
10%	PLCC	0.4291	0.2772	**0.4745**	0.4088
	SROCC	−0.0523	−0.0308	**−0.0517**	−0.1762
	RMSE	0.4727	0.5028	**0.4606**	0.4776
20%	PLCC	0.0473	0.3190	**0.5124**	0.5578
	SROCC	−0.0073	0.1916	**0.3510**	0.1431
	RMSE	0.5489	0.5208	**0.4719**	0.4561
30%	PLCC	0.1175	0.2337	**0.6687**	0.4079
	SROCC	0.0200	0.1485	**0.1600**	0.2254
	RMSE	0.6500	0.6364	**0.4867**	0.5976

Table 3. Performance of 7 opinion-unaware IQA methods for THSID.

Criteria		IQA						
		CPBD	FISBLIM	NIQE	QAC	SISBLIM	S3	Fish_bb
		metric	ss	quality	q	score3	s31	sh1
1%	PLCC	0.2413	**0.5595**	0.3007	0.3891	0.2807	0.4460	**0.4773**
	SROCC	−0.0869	**0.2777**	0.2077	−0.1315	0.3046	−0.1215	**0.1908**
	RMSE	0.4835	**0.4129**	0.4751	0.4589	0.4781	0.4533	**0.4378**
10%	PLCC	**0.4848**	0.1780	0.2054	0.1938	0.4203	0.1816	**0.4290**
	SROCC	**0.3185**	0.1162	0.0138	0.1808	0.1223	0.0331	**0.1515**
	RMSE	**0.4577**	0.5149	0.5121	0.5134	0.4748	0.5146	**0.4814**
20%	PLCC	0.0449	0.4366	0.1623	0.0121	0.0496	0.3746	**0.5518**
	SROCC	0.0927	0.0215	−0.0635	0.0946	−0.0515	0.0666	**−0.1096**
	RMSE	0.5489	0.4944	0.5422	0.5495	0.5488	0.5095	**0.4583**
30%	PLCC	0.3262	0.1004	**0.4527**	0.2415	0.3353	0.1968	**0.2980**
	SROCC	0.0715	−0.0346	**0.0015**	−0.1092	0.0369	−0.1326	**−0.1600**
	RMSE	0.6315	0.6513	**0.5927**	0.6353	0.6245	0.6418	**0.6258**

Table 3 demonstrates the statistical data of the performance regarding 7 opinion-unaware no-reference IQA methods. As shown in Table 3, Fish_bb performs quite well for all the display modes. Meanwhile, FISHBLIM is suitable for the first display mode. CPBD is relatively promising for the second display mode. NIQE gives the best prediction than the other opinion-unaware IQA algorithms for the last display mode.

From the results of objective IQA, because of the lack of the suitable objective IQA for THz image, we cannot get any support for subjective IQA from objective IQA. Even so, to some extents, CPBD and BLIINDS2 can give consistent results with the subjective

IQA. Therefore, in the future research, an objective evaluation algorithm applicable to THz image need to be explored.

3.2 Discussion

Tables 2 and 3 demonstrate that most of existing no-reference IQA algorithms get pretty bad performance for THz security images. Since the existing algorithms are based on natural image rather than specific image, it is not surprising to come to such a conclusion.

Actually, the further optimization can be made for the current display mode. After the observation of the THz security images, there are some major factors that damage the image quality, and in turn influence the accuracy of detection. One reason is the annoying noise. The difficulty of denoising lies in the almost inseparable image contents and noise, which is exactly the difference between the specific image and the natural image. The noises of THz security image mainly caused by unstable device, changeable environment, the reflection of human body and the materials they carried as well as the device surface. In the further study, we will try to analyze the distribution of noises from different resources, then denoise separately. The other reason is the body structure to be clarified. And as for that, we consider to strengthen the edge and weaken the internal structure slice by slice, so that the 3D location information of the human body can be figured out accurately.

4 Conclusion

In this paper, we have attempt to give a good display mode to the terahertz security image database (THSID), which contains 181 sets of images containing 200 vertical slices and each with resolution of 127×380. For a certain coordinate (x_0, y_0), the pixels on Z-axis whose value account for the highest 1%, 10%, 20%, 30% are taken out for averaging. Then a two-dimensional image was formed by this averaging operation. The subjective evaluation shows that the second display mode, namely averaging the highest 10% pixel values in Z-axis, gets the best MOSs. Various no-reference IQA algorithms were implemented on the display modes to pick out a relatively good one. The existing algorithms used in this study include 4 opinion-aware approaches, viz. GMLF, NFERM, BLIINDS2, BRISQUE, as well as 7 opinion-unware approaches viz. CPBD, FISBLIM, NIQE, QAC, SISBLIM, S3, Fish_bb. The result of objective evaluation demonstrates that BLIINDS2 and CPBD performs relatively good among the other objective IQA algorithms for the chosen display mode, namely averaging highest 10% pixel intensity in Z-axis. These results demonstrate that the present objective evaluation algorithms are hardly suitable for THz security image. Thus in the future study, new objective methods that performs well on THz image should be explored.

Acknowledgements. The authors would like to acknowledge the financial support from the National Science Foundation of China under Grant Nos. 61422112, 61371146, and 61221001, and the China Postdoctoral Science Foundation funded project (No. 2016M600315).

The authors would like to acknowledge the staffs working in BOCOM Smart Network Technologies Inc., who assisted in acquiring the THz images.

References

1. Sung-Hyeon, P., et al.: Non-contact measurement of the electrical conductivity and coverage density of silver nanowires for transparent electrodes using Terahertz spectroscopy. Measur. Sci. Technol. **28**, 025001 (2017)
2. Xin, F., Su, H., Xiao, Y.: Terahertz imaging system for remote sensing and security applications. In: Antennas and Propagation IEEE, pp. 1335–1338 (2014)
3. Hou, L., et al.: Enhancing Terahertz image quality by finite impulse response digital filter. In: International Conference on Infrared, Millimeter, and Terahertz Waves, pp. 1–2 (2014)
4. Trofimov, V.A.: New algorithm for the passive THz image quality enhancement. In: SPIE Commercial + Scientific Sensing and Imaging, p. 98560L (2016)
5. Trofimov, V.A., Trofimov, V.V.: New way for both quality enhancement of THz images and detection ofconcealed objects. In: SPIE Optical Engineering + Applications, p. 95850R (2015)
6. Fitzgerald, A.J., et al.: Evaluation of image quality in terahertz pulsed imaging using test objects. Phys. Med. Biol. **47**, 3865 (2002)
7. Zhai, G., et al.: Cross-dimensional quality assessment for low bitrate video. In: IEEE International Symposium on Circuits and Systems IEEE, pp. 400–403 (2008)
8. Zhai, G., et al.: A psychovisual quality metric in free-energy principle. IEEE Trans. Image Process. **21**(1), 41–52 (2011)
9. Zhai, G., et al.: Three dimensional scalable video adaptation via user-end perceptual quality assessment. IEEE Trans. Broadcast. **54**(3), 719–727 (2008)
10. Min, X., et al.: Unified blind quality assessment of compressed natural, graphic and screen content images. IEEE Trans. Image Process. **PP**(99), 1 (2017)
11. Min, X., et al.: Saliency-induced reduced-reference quality index for natural scene and screen content images. Signal Process. (2017)
12. Min, X., et al.: Blind quality assessment of compressed images via pseudo structural similarity. In: IEEE International Conference on Multimedia and Expo, pp. 1–6. IEEE (2016)
13. Sheikh, H.R., et al.: A statistical evaluation of recent full reference image quality assessment algorithms. IEEE Trans. Image Process. **15**, 3440–3451 (2006)
14. Gu, K., et al.: The analysis of image contrast: from quality assessment to automatic enhancement. IEEE Trans. Cybern. **46**, 284–297 (2016)
15. Hu, M., et al.: Terahertz security image quality assessment by no-reference model observers. arXiv preprint arXiv:1707.03574 (2017)
16. Gonzalez, R.C., Woods, R.E.: Digital Image Processing. Publishing House of Electronics Industry, Beijing (2010)
17. Xue, W., et al.: Blind image quality assessment using joint statistics of gradient magnitude and Laplacian features. IEEE Trans. Image Process. **23**, 4850–4862 (2014)
18. Gu, K., et al.: Using free energy principle for blind image quality assessment. IEEE Trans. Multimedia **17**, 50–63 (2015)
19. Saad, M.A., et al.: Blind image quality assessment: a natural scene statistics approach in the DCT domain. IEEE Trans. Image Process. **21**, 3339–3352 (2012)
20. Mittal, A., et al.: No-reference image quality assessment in the spatial domain. IEEE Trans. Image Process. **21**, 4695–4708 (2012)

21. Narvekar, N.D., Karam, L.J.: A no-reference image blur metric based on the cumulative probability of blur detection (CPBD). IEEE Trans. Image Process. **20**(9), 2678–2683 (2011)
22. Gu, K., et al.: FISBLIM: a five-step blind metric for quality assessment of multiply distorted images. In: 2013 IEEE Workshop on Signal Processing Systems, pp. 241–246 (2013)
23. Mittal, A., et al.: Making a "completely blind" image quality analyzer. IEEE Signal Process. Lett. **20**, 209–212 (2013)
24. Xue, W., et al.: Learning without human scores for blind image quality assessment. In: IEEE Conference on Computer Vision and Pattern Recognition, pp. 995–1002 (2013)
25. Gu, K., et al.: Hybrid no-reference quality metric for singly and multiply distorted images. IEEE Trans. Broadcast. **60**, 555–567 (2014)
26. Vu, C.T., et al.: S-3: a spectral and spatial measure of local perceived sharpness in natural images. IEEE Trans. Image Process. **21**, 934–945 (2012)
27. Vu, P.V., Chandler, D.M.: A fast wavelet-based algorithm for global and local image sharpness estimation. IEEE Signal Process. Lett. **19**, 423–426 (2012)

Fast Noisy Image Quality Assessment Based on Free-Energy Principle

Yadan Zhao, Yutao Liu$^{(\boxtimes)}$, Feng Jiang, Xianming Liu, and Debin Zhao

Department of Computer Science, Harbin Institute of Technology, Harbin, China
2091954231@qq.com, {yt.liu,fjiang,csxm,dbzhao}@hit.edu.cn

Abstract. In this work, we propose a fast noisy image quality assessment approach under the theory of free-energy principle. The free-energy principle accounts for that the brain tries to predict the input image with an internal generative model. While there exists a discrepancy between the image and its model-predicted version and this discrepancy is believed to be closely related to the perceptual quality of the image. Accordingly, we devise the method for evaluating the quality of the noisy image, in which the internal generative model is first generalized from AR simulation and then instantiated with simple but effective median function. The quality-related discrepancy denoted by the entropy of the predicted residuals is defined to measure the whole quality of the image. Experimental results on LIVE, TID2013 and CSIQ databases demonstrate that the proposed method earns comparable prediction performance to the specialized noise level estimation methods while greatly reduces the running time.

Keywords: Image quality assessment (IQA)
Blind/No-reference (NR) · Noise · Free energy

1 Introduction

Nowadays, abundant digital images flood into people's life and become the important media for conveying information. While the quality of these images varies a lot. In other words, digital images are vulnerable to various distortions in reality, e.g. blur, noise, blockiness etc., which lead to degradation of the image quality [1,2]. Therefore, to effectively measure the image quality and quantify the quality degradation become indispensable for image-related applications for providing users with high quality images. That's the main concern of image quality assessment (IQA). Generally, the image quality can be evaluated by subjective and objective methods. Subjective methods refer to asking viewers to rate the image quality directly, which is the most reliable way of obtaining the image quality since human beings are usually the ultimate receivers in image processing applications [3]. However, subjective methods are always expensive, cumbersome and unable to be embedded into real-time systems.

© Springer Nature Singapore Pte Ltd. 2018
G. Zhai et al. (Eds.): IFTC 2017, CCIS 815, pp. 290–299, 2018.
https://doi.org/10.1007/978-981-10-8108-8_27

Hence, researchers endeavor to study objective IQA methods aiming to substitute subjective assessment methods. Through great efforts of researchers, many objective IQA approaches have been builded, which can be classified into full reference (FR), reduced-reference (RR) and no-reference (NR) methods according to the availability of a reference image. Specifically, for FR methods, the reference or distortion-free image is referred when assessing the image quality. While RR methods evaluate the image quality with partial information of the reference image. Different from FR and RR methods, NR methods give the image quality without any information of the reference image, which is closest to reality as there're always no corresponding reference images for us to perform quality estimation.

Most widely-used IQA method is the peak signal-to-noise ratio (PSNR) because of its low computational cost, high portability and clear physical meaning. Another representative model is the structural similarity index (SSIM) [4], whose philosophy behind is that the human visual system (HVS) is highly adapted to extract the structural information from the visual scene. Zhang et al. employed the low-level features gradient magnitude (GM) and phase congruency (PC) to construct the feature similarity index (FSIM) for IQA [5]. By introducing information theory into IQA, Sheikh et al. proposed a visual information fidelity (VIF) in [6]. These methods all belong to FR methods. While Zhai et al. [7] designed an RR IQA model named free-energy based distortion metric (FEDM), which is based on the recent discovery of free-energy principle in brain theory and neuroscience. In [8], a generic method was proposed for RR IQA by comparing a set of reduced-reference statistical features extracted from divisive normalization transformation (DNT) domain representations of the reference and distorted images. Representative NR IQA methods always follow two steps, feature extraction and training a regression module using the extracted features [9,10]. There are still some effective IQA methods proposed to deal with specific distortions [11,12].

In this paper, we focus on the quality assessment of images that suffer from noise, which is often introduced during image acquisition or transmission. In the literature, the quality of noisy images can be assessed through noise level estimation methods [13,14] based on the conception that the higher the noise level is, the poorer the quality of the image is. That really works as those methods earn high prediction performance for evaluating the quality of the noisy images. However, their time complexity is also high. For example, in [14], calculating the matrix eigenvalues or the iterative framework for noise level estimation all cost much computational time, which is undesirable to the applications that require low computational time. Toward this end, in this work, we propose a fast noisy image quality assessment approach inspired by the free-energy principle. Generally, the free-energy principle models the perception and understanding of an image as an active inference process, in which the brain tries to predict the input image through an internal generative model. While there exists a discrepancy between the image and its model-predicted version, this discrepancy is believed to be closely related to the perceptual quality of the image [7]. Therefore, the free-energy principle provides a new perspective for us to view the issue of noisy image quality evaluation. In the proposed method, the internal generative model is first generalized from AR simulation and then instantiated with the simple but effective median function. The quality-related discrepancy between the image and its prediction is defined as the whole quality of the noisy image, which can be denoted by the entropy of the predicted residuals. Experimental results on LIVE, TID2013 and CSIQ databases demonstrate the proposed method earns comparable prediction performance with the specialized noise level estimation methods while reduces the time complexity greatly.

2   The Proposed Method

2.1   The Free-Energy Principle

Our method is based on the free-energy principle. Therefore, it is needed to specify the formulation of the free-energy principle at first. As mentioned before, the fundamental assumption in free-energy principle is that the cognitive process is governed by an internal generative model in the brain. With the model, the brain is able to actively infer predictions of meaningful information from visual scenes and reduce residual uncertainty at the meantime.

For operational amenability, it is assumed that the internal generative model $\mathcal{G}$ for visual perception is parametric, which explains visual scenes by adjusting the parameter vector $\mathbf{g}$. Specifically, given an image I, its 'surprise' can be calculated by integrating the joint distribution $P(I, \mathbf{g})$ over the space of the internal model parameters $\mathbf{g}$ as:

$$- \log P(I) = - \log \int P(I, \mathbf{g}) d\mathbf{g}. \tag{1}$$

Then a dummy term $Q(\mathbf{g}|I)$ is integrated into both the denominator and numerator of the right part of Eq. (1) as follows:

$$- \log P(I) = - \log \int Q(\mathbf{g}|I) \frac{P(I, \mathbf{g})}{Q(\mathbf{g}|I)} d\mathbf{g}. \tag{2}$$

Here, $Q(\mathbf{g}|I)$ is an auxiliary posterior distribution of the model parameters given the image, which can be thought of as an approximate posterior to the true posterior of the model parameters $P(\mathbf{g}|I)$ calculated by the brain. The brain minimizes the discrepancy between the approximate posterior $Q(\mathbf{g}|I)$ and the true posterior $P(\mathbf{g}|I)$. Through Jensen's inequality, Eq. (2) can be written as:

$$- \log P(I) \leq - \int Q(\mathbf{g}|I) \log \frac{P(I, \mathbf{g})}{Q(\mathbf{g}|I)} d\mathbf{g}. \tag{3}$$

Afterwards, the right side of Eq. (3) is defined as the free energy as follows:

$$F(\mathbf{g}) = - \int Q(\mathbf{g}|I) \log \frac{P(I, \mathbf{g})}{Q(\mathbf{g}|I)} d\mathbf{g}. \tag{4}$$

Obviously, the free energy defines an upper bound of 'surprise' for image I. For intuitive understanding, with $P(I, \mathbf{g}) = P(\mathbf{g}|I)P(I)$, we further derive Eq. (4) as:

$$\begin{aligned}
F(\mathbf{g}) &= \int Q(\mathbf{g}|I) \log \frac{Q(\mathbf{g}|I)}{P(\mathbf{g}|I)P(I)} d\mathbf{g} \\
&= -\log P(I) + \int Q(\mathbf{g}|I) \log \frac{Q(\mathbf{g}|I)}{P(\mathbf{g}|I)} d\mathbf{g} \quad (5) \\
&= -\log P(I) + \mathbf{KL}(Q(\mathbf{g}|I)\|P(\mathbf{g}|I)),
\end{aligned}$$

where $\mathbf{KL}(\cdot)$ refers to the Kullback-Leibler divergence between the approximate posterior and the true posterior distributions and it's nonnegative. It is clearly seen that the free energy $F(\mathbf{g})$ is greater than or equal to the image 'surprise' $-\log P(I)$. The brain tries to lower the divergence $\mathbf{KL}(Q(\mathbf{g}|I)\|P(\mathbf{g}|I))$ between the approximate posterior and its true posterior distributions when perceiving image I. That's the main conception in free-energy principle. More details can be referred to [7,15–17].

2.2   Approximation of the Brain Generative Model

To quantitatively define the quality of the noisy images, assuming the brain generative model $\mathcal{G}$ should be firstly considered. With the model, the brain is able to generate the prediction of the input image. In [7], the linear AR model was employed to approximate $\mathcal{G}$ for its ability to represent a wide range of natural scenes by varying its parameters, denoted as:

$$x_n = \mathcal{X}^k(x_n)\mathbf{a} + e_n \quad (6)$$

where x_n is a pixel in the image, $\mathcal{X}^k(x_n)$ is the vector consist of k nearest neighbors of x_n, $\mathbf{a} = (a_1, a_2, ..., a_k)^T$ is the vector of the AR coefficients and e_n represents the additive Gaussian noise. In this regard, the pixel in question is linearly approximated by its neighbor pixels. In other words, the AR prediction manner denotes a linear method to estimate the current pixel by its surrounding pixels. While we may extend this representation manner to a more general form with a function $\mathcal{F}$ that maps surrounding pixels to current pixel as:

$$x_n = \mathcal{F}\{\mathcal{X}^k(x_n)\} + e_n \quad (7)$$

where x_n is the pixel to be predicted, $\mathcal{X}^k(x_n)$ is the vector consist of k nearest neighbors of x_n, e_n represents the additive Gaussian noise and $\mathcal{F}$ represents the mapping function, which denotes the general prediction of x_n with its neighbor pixels. Here, we extend the AR approximation of the internal generative model to a more general form in $\mathcal{F}$. If $\mathcal{F}$ represents linear prediction, then Eq. 7 can be implemented with Eq. 6. In other words, Eq. 6 is the special case of Eq. 7. Certainly, $\mathcal{F}$ can also be implemented by some other linear prediction models or more complex prediction methods. In fact, the accurate approximation of the internal model in the brain is still unknown and keeps an open issue to be explored [7]. In implementation, here we instantiate $\mathcal{F}$ with the simple but effective median function which means the prediction in Eq. 7 is to take the median value of the surrounding pixels, namely,

$$x_n = \mathcal{M}(\mathcal{X}^k(x_n)) + e_n \tag{8}$$

where $\mathcal{M}(.)$ represents the median function. Experimental results in Sect. 3 will show this instantiation for quality estimation of the noisy images is effective and time-saving.

2.3   Quality Index for the Noisy Image

As the free-energy principle indicates, the discrepancy between the image and its model prediction is believed to be closely related to the perceptual quality of the image. Therefore, we utilize this discrepancy to define the quality index for the noisy image. Specifically, the discrepancy between the image and its prediction is defined with the prediction residual between the noisy image I and its predicted version I_p, namely:

$$R = |I - I_p| \tag{9}$$

where R represents the prediction residual and $|\cdot|$ refers to the absolute operation to guarantee the results nonnegative, I_p is obtained through Eq. 7. Then we pool the prediction residual R with its entropy to define the image quality index as follows:

$$Q = -\sum_{i=1}^{N} p_i \log p_i \tag{10}$$

where Q gives the quality of the noisy image, p_i is the probability of each pixel value in R and N gives the total number of the pixel values. It's needed to point out that our method belongs to NR methods.

3   Experimental Results

3.1   Protocols

As suggested by VQEG [18], before measuring the prediction performance of the objective assessment methods, the objective results given by the quality models are firstly mapped to subjective human ratings through nonlinear regression in the form of a five-parameter logistic function as follows:

$$q(z) = \beta_1 \left(\frac{1}{2} - \frac{1}{1 + \exp(\beta_2 \cdot (z - \beta_3))} \right) + \beta_4 \cdot z + \beta_5 \tag{11}$$

with z and $q(z)$ being the input objective score and the mapped score, respectively. β_j (j = 1, 2, 3, 4, 5) are free parameters to be determined during the curve fitting process. To evaluate the prediction performance of the proposed method, we employed two commonly used statistic indexes which are Pearson Linear Correlation Coefficient (PLCC) and Spearman Rank-Order Correlation Coefficient (SROCC). Both of PLCC and SROCC indicate the correlation between subjective scores and objective results given by the objective IQA methods, PLCC evaluates the IQA method's prediction accuracy, while SROCC evaluates the prediction monotonicity. The higher values in PLCC and SROCC imply the superiority of the objective method. SROCC and PLCC are respectively calculated as follows (Supposing N as the total number of images in the testing database):

$$SROCC = 1 - \frac{6}{N(N^2 - 1)} \sum_{i=1}^{N} d_i^2 \qquad (12)$$

where d_i represents the distance between the i-th image's ranks in objective and subjective scores.

$$PLCC = \frac{\sum_{i=1}^{N}(q_i - \bar{q}) \cdot (s_i - \bar{s})}{\sqrt{\sum_{i=1}^{N}(q_i - \bar{q})^2 \cdot \sum_{i=1}^{N}(s_i - \bar{s})^2}} \qquad (13)$$

where s_i and $\bar{s}$ are the i-th image's subjective rating and the mean of the overall s_i. q_i and $\bar{q}$ are the i-th image's mapped objective score through nonlinear regression and the mean value.

Table 1. SROCC and PLCC values of the objective methods on LIVE, TID2013 and CSIQ databases.

Database	Index	PSNR	SSIM	BIQI	BRISQUE	NIQE	NFEDM	SINE	[14]	Proposed
LIVE	SROCC	0.9853	0.9694	0.9903	0.9911	0.9716	0.9680	0.9836	0.9863	0.9524
	PLCC	0.9880	0.9829	0.9928	0.9929	0.9758	0.9721	0.9797	0.9859	0.9495
TID2013	SROCC	0.9291	0.8671	0.7842	0.8523	0.8194	0.8569	0.8456	0.9316	0.8705
	PLCC	0.9544	0.8684	0.8052	0.8510	0.8271	0.8685	0.8926	0.9499	0.8754
CSIQ	SROCC	0.9363	0.8974	0.8794	0.9253	0.8097	0.8381	0.9541	0.9471	0.9397
	PLCC	0.9532	0.8983	0.8910	0.9333	0.8110	0.8518	0.9563	0.9533	0.9488
AVG	SROCC	**0.9502**	0.9113	0.8846	0.9229	0.8669	0.8877	0.9278	**0.9550**	0.9209
	PLCC	**0.9652**	0.9165	0.8963	0.9257	0.8713	0.8975	0.9429	**0.9630**	0.9246

3.2   Overall Prediction Performance Comparison

The subsets of noisy images in three widely-adopted image databases, LIVE [19], TID2013 [20] and CSIQ [21] serve as the test bed for evaluating the prediction performance of the objective IQA methods.

We list the performance results of all the compared objective methods in Table 1. Among them, PSNR and SSIM [4] are the two most representative FR methods, BIQI [10], BRISQUE [9] and NIQE [22] are the state-of-the-art NR IQA methods, NFEDM [7] is the free-energy induced NR method, SINE [13,14] are the specialized noise level estimation methods. **AVG** means directly taking the average values of PLCC and SROCC over the three databases respectively, where the two best IQA metrics are highlighted in boldface. As we can observe that PSNR performs better than SSIM, this is because noise is a kind of content-independent distortion which lowers the evaluation ability of SSIM on the noisy images. While PSNR is more powerful to deal with these images. By training on LIVE database, BIQI and BRISQUE earn the top performance on LIVE, which also explains that the performance of NIQE on LIVE is superior to that on TID2013 and CSIQ. On the average values of SROCC and PLCC, BRISQUE is still better than BIQI mainly due to the features extracted by BRISQUE are more effective than that of BIQI for quality estimation. It's obvious to see that [14] is comparable to PSNR as their average performance are very close, which is in expectation as [14] is the specialized method to noise level estimation and verifies that noise level of the noisy image indeed determines its quality. While our method earns moderate prediction accuracy as comparable to SINE and BRISQUE over the three databases.

Besides high prediction accuracy for the objective IQA methods, low computational time is also crucial for their practical use. Therefore, we check the running speeds of the selected IQA algorithms as desired. Specifically, we choose one standard noisy image (i01_01_4.bmp) from TID2013 database and test all the involved methods on this image, then record their running time. It should be pointed out that the hardware configuration is a Thinkpad X220 computer with a 2.5GHz CPU and 4G RAM. The software platform is Matlab R2012a. We list the experimental results clearly in Table 2. As can be observed that, PSNR cost the least time for quality evaluation. BIQI, BRISQUE and NIQE have no big gap on the time cost. While the running time of NFEDM is much longer than other methods because the AR coefficients estimation in it is very time-consuming. Comparing the specialized noise level estimation algorithms, [14] is apparently

Table 2. Time cost of the objective IQA methods

Methods	Time cost (seconds)
PSNR	0.0099
SSIM	0.0313
BIQI	0.6257
BRISQUE	0.2293
NIQE	0.3133
NFEDM	42.4917
SINE	2.2428
[14]	0.8884
Proposed	0.0328

better than SINE. It is noted that our proposed method is comparable to SSIM and runs much faster than all of the NR methods and specialized noise level estimation methods.

3.3   Effect of the Window Size on Quality Estimation

In the proposed method, we instantiate the approximation of the brain generative model in Eq. 7 with median function, which is to take the median value of a local window centered at the current pixel as its prediction. However, the window size has an influence on the final quality evaluation. Therefore, we conduct this experiment by changing the window size on the noisy image dataset of LIVE and show the experimental results in Fig. 1, where the horizontal axis is the window size and the vertical axis points out the prediction performance in terms of SROCC. As can be seen that the prediction performance consistently degrades as the window size increases. This is because the negative effect of the approximation with median function, which destroys the image details and cause excessive smooth within a larger window. Therefore, the default value of the window size is set to 3×3 in our proposed method.

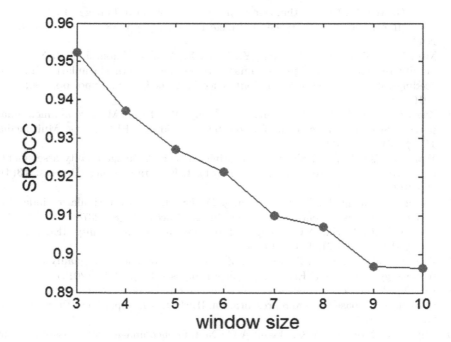

Fig. 1. Prediction performance with different window sizes on LIVE image database. In the horizontal axis, for example, 3 means the window size is 3×3.

4   Conclusion

In this paper, we devise a dedicated noisy image quality evaluation method under the exploration of the free-energy principle. Specifically, we generalize the approximation of the internal generative model and instantiate it with the simple but efficient median function. The discrepancy denoted by the entropy of the prediction residual is defined as the final quality index for the noisy image. Experimental results on LIVE, TID2013 and CSIQ confirm the effectiveness of the proposed method. The most notable point of our method is that it cost little computational time which is very desirable for real-time applications. This work is also an illustration that the exploration for the human brain is the fountain to design objective IQA methods.

Acknowledgement. This work was supported by the Major State Basic Research Development Program of China (973 Program 2015CB351804), the National Science Foundation of China under Grant 61672193.

References

1. Zhai, G., Wu, X.: Noise estimation using statistics of natural images. In: 2011 18th IEEE International Conference on Image Processing, pp. 1857–1860, September 2011
2. Min, X., Zhai, G., Gu, K., Fang, Y., Yang, X., Wu, X., Zhou, J., Liu, X.: Blind quality assessment of compressed images via pseudo structural similarity. In: Proceedings of IEEE International Conference Multimedia and Expo, pp. 1–6, July 2016
3. Zhai, G., Cai, J., Lin, W., Yang, X., Zhang, W., Etoh, M.: Cross-dimensional perceptual quality assessment for low bit-rate videos. IEEE Trans. Multimedia **10**(7), 1316–1324 (2008)
4. Wang, Z., Bovik, A.C., Sheikh, H.R., Simoncelli, E.P.: Image quality assessment: from error visibility to structural similarity. IEEE Trans. Image Process. **13**(4), 600–612 (2004)
5. Zhang, L., Zhang, L., Mou, X., Zhang, D.: FSIM: a feature similarity index for image quality assessment. IEEE Trans. Image Process. **20**(8), 2378–2386 (2011)
6. Sheikh, H.R., Bovik, A.C.: Image information and visual quality. IEEE Trans. Image Process. **15**(2), 430–444 (2006)
7. Zhai, G., Wu, X., Yang, X., Lin, W., Zhang, W.: A psychovisual quality metric in free-energy principle. IEEE Trans. Image Process. **21**(1), 41–52 (2012)
8. Li, Q., Wang, Z.: Reduced-reference image quality assessment using divisive normalization-based image representation. IEEE J. Sel. Top. Signal Process. **3**(2), 202–211 (2009)
9. Mittal, A., Moorthy, A.K., Bovik, A.C.: No-reference image quality assessment in the spatial domain. IEEE Trans. Image Process. **21**(12), 4695–4708 (2012)
10. Moorthy, A.K., Bovik, A.C.: A two-step framework for constructing blind image quality indices. IEEE Signal Process. Lett. **17**(5), 513–516 (2010)
11. Min, X., Ma, K., Gu, K., Zhai, G., Wang, Z., Lin, W.: Unified blind quality assessment of compressed natural, graphic, and screen content images. IEEE Trans. Image Process. **26**(11), 5462–5474 (2017)

12. Zhai, G., Zhang, W., Yang, X., Yao, S., Xu, Y.: GES: a new image quality assessment metric based on energy features in Gabor transform domain. In: 2006 IEEE International Symposium on Circuits and Systems, May 2006
13. Zoran, D., Weiss, Y.: Scale invariance and noise in natural images. In: IEEE International Conference on Computer Vision, pp. 2209–2216. IEEE (2009)
14. Liu, X., Tanaka, M., Okutomi, M.: Noise level estimation using weak textured patches of a single noisy image. In: 2012 19th IEEE International Conference on Image Processing (ICIP), pp. 665–668. IEEE (2012)
15. Gu, K., Zhai, G., Yang, X., Zhang, W.: Using free energy principle for blind image quality assessment. IEEE Trans. Multimedia $17(1)$, 50–63 (2015)
16. Liu, Y., Zhai, G., Gu, K., Liu, X., Zhao, D., Gao, W.: Reduced-reference image quality assessment in free-energy principle and sparse representation. IEEE Trans. Multimedia (2017)
17. Liu, Y., Zhai, G., Liu, X., Zhao, D.: Perceptual image quality assessment combining free-energy principle and sparse representation. In: 2016 IEEE International Symposium on Circuits and Systems (ISCAS), pp. 1586–1589. IEEE (2016)
18. Rohaly, A.M., Libert, J., Corriveau, P., Webster, A., et al.: Final report from the video quality experts group on the validation of objective models of video quality assessment. In: ITU-T Standards Contribution COM, pp. 9–80 (2000)
19. Cormack, L., Sheikh, H.R., Wang, Z., Bovik, A.C.: Live Image Quality Assessment Database Release 2 (2006)
20. Ponomarenko, N., Jin, L., Ieremeiev, O., Lukin, V., Egiazarian, K., Astola, J., Vozel, B., Chehdi, K., Carli, M., Battisti, F., et al.: Image database TID2013: peculiarities, results and perspectives. Signal Process. Image Commun. 30, 57–77 (2015)
21. Larson, E.C., Chandler, D.: Categorical image quality (CSIQ) database (2010). http://vision.okstate.edu/csiq
22. Mittal, A., Soundararajan, R., Bovik, A.C.: Making a completely blind image quality analyzer. IEEE Signal Process. Lett. $20(3)$, 209–212 (2013)

No-Reference Quality Index for View Synthesis Based on Multi-scale Texture Naturalness

Yu Zhou, Leida Li$^{(\boxtimes)}$, Xiaoping Yuan, and Jiansheng Qian

School of Information and Control Engineering,
China University of Mining and Technology, Xuzhou 221116, China
reader1104@hotmail.com

Abstract. View synthesis plays an important role in Free-Viewpoint Television (FTV). The quality of view synthesis directly affects the user experience. Therefore, the quality assessment of view synthesis is of great significance. Distortions in the texture/depth map and distortions caused by imperfect rendering methods can cause the loss of texture naturalness in the synthesized views. The human visual system exhibits multi-scale property when perceiving visual scenes. Inspired by these facts, we propose a blind quality evaluation metric for the Synthesized Views based on multi-scale Texture naturalness (SVT). We first build the scale space of the synthesized view. Then the Gray level Gradient Co-occurrence Matrix (GGCM) map at each scale is computed for texture extraction. Two groups of texture features are calculated from the GGCM maps to quantify the texture naturalness. Finally, the Random Forest (RF) regression model is used to emulate the mechanism of human brain to learn the synthesized view quality model based on the extracted features. The learned model is then employed for the quality prediction of synthesized views. The experimental results on the MCL-3D database demonstrate the superiority of the proposed SVT method.

Keywords: View synthesis · Quality assessment
Gray level Gradient Co-occurrence Matrix (GGCM)
Texture naturalness

1 Introduction

Free-Viewpoint Television (FTV) has been increasingly popular, which allows users to choose any arbitrary view to watch. The realization of free-viewpoint experience depends on a great number of views. In reality, due to the limitation of hardware and the bandwidth efficiency, only limited number of views can be captured. The remaining views need to be generated by view synthesis using the texture and depth signals. Unfortunately, the texture and depth maps are usually subject to compression and transmission errors in practice, which result

L. Li—This work is supported by National Key R&D Program of China (2016YFC 0801800), National Natural Science Foundation of China (61379143, 61771473) and the Qing Lan Project.

© Springer Nature Singapore Pte Ltd. 2018
G. Zhai et al. (Eds.): IFTC 2017, CCIS 815, pp. 300–309, 2018.
https://doi.org/10.1007/978-981-10-8108-8_28

in degraded texure/depth maps. Besides, in the view synthesis process, most rendering algorithms are imperfect [1]. Therefore, the distortions in synthesized views are mainly from three aspects, i.e., distortions from texture maps, depth maps and synthesis process, which together lead to the loss of texture naturalness in the synthesized images. In particular, the texture and depth maps are usually contaminated by common distortions, e.g., Gaussian blur introduced during the image acquisition stage, blockiness caused by the compression, and transmission distortions. The distortions produced in the synthesis process usually cause the edge/texture destructions [2]. With these considerations, quality assessment of view synthesis is highly needed and it plays an important role in benchmarking and optimizing the compression approaches and the rendering methods. Recently, quality assessment has been used in many fields, e.g., information hiding [3] and forensics [4,5].

So far, several works have been done for the quality assessment of synthesized images. Bosc et al. [6] first detected the distorted regions by computing the difference between the synthesized and reference images. Then the quality score of the synthesized image was generated by calculating the mean structure similarity of the extracted distorted regions. Stankovic et al. [7,8] computed Peak Signal-to-Noise Ratio (PSNR) at multi-scales, which were achieved by Morphological Wavelet decomposition and Morphological Pyramids decomposition, respectively. As such, the MW-PSNR and MP-PSNR metrics were produced. Afterwards, the Reduced versions of MW-PSNR and MP-PSNR, namely RMW-PSNR and RMP-PSNR [7,9] were proposed, which only used the details on higher decomposition scales. In [10], the reference and synthesized images were first divided into blocks and block matching was conducted. Then the Kolmogorov-Smirnov distance between the histograms of the matching blocks was computed to produce the quality score of the synthesized image. All these synthesized Image Quality Assessment (IQA) metrics are specifically designed to quantify the distortions produced by the rendering methods in the synthesis process, while ignoring the distortions introduced by the unclean texture/depth maps. As a result, their performances are limited on evaluating the overall synthesized image quality. Moreover, all the synthesized IQA methods in the literature are full-reference (FR), which means that they depend on the corresponding reference image for the synthesized IQA [11,12]. However, due to the difficult access to reference images in practice [13], the applications of these FR metrics are usually limited. Therefore, a no-reference (NR) quality method for view synthesis is highly desirable.

Inspired by these, a NR method for Synthesized Views by computing multi-scale Texture naturalness (SVT) is proposed in this paper. Since the distortions in the synthesized images cause the loss of texture naturalness, we propose to calculate the Gray level Gradient Co-occurrence Matrix (GGCM) to evaluate the texture naturalness, which has been demonstrated to be effective in texture analysis [14]. Furthermore, considering the fact that the Human Visual System (HVS) is a multi-scale device in nature [15], scale space of the synthesized image is first built. Then two groups of texture features are exacted from

Fig. 1. Illustration of the loss of texture naturalness in synthesized images. (a) A reference image; (b) A synthesized image with both texture and depth maps polluted by JPEG2000 compression distortions; (c) A synthesized image with depth map polluted by additional white noise; (d) An image synthesized by a rendering algorithm using clean texture and depth maps.

the GGCM maps. Finally, to combine these features, we propose to use the Random Forest (RF) to learn a quality prediction model for synthesized views. Experimental results show the superiority of the proposed method over both the existing view synthesis quality models and general-purpose IQA methods.

2   Proposed Synthesized View Quality Metric

To predict the quality score that is more consistent with the subjective rating, the multi-scale characteristic of the HVS is considered in the proposed method. Moreover, as aforementioned in Sect. 1, the degradation of synthesized images are mainly caused by the distortions in texture/depth maps, and distortions produced by the imperfect rendering algorithms. All these distortions can result in the loss of texture naturalness in the synthesized images. Figure 1 shows a reference image and a set of synthesized images contaminated by different distortions, respectively. The local patches with obvious texture unnaturalness are marked and zoomed in. We can see that compared with the reference image (a), whether

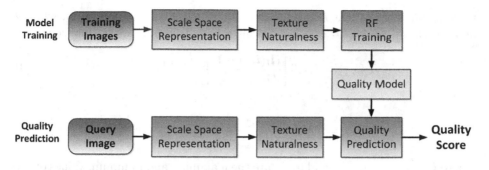

Fig. 2. Flowchart of the proposed quality metric for synthesized views.

the synthesized images (b)-(c) caused by texure/depth distortions, or the synthesized image (d) produced by imperfect rendering, show obvious texture unnaturalness, which can be clearly viewed from the local patches. Figure 2 illustrates the flowchart of the proposed metric, which is composed of model training and quality prediction. The scale space of a synthesized image is first built. Then the features that represent texture naturalness are extracted at multi-scales. These features are fed into the RF regression model to train the quality model, which is then used for the quality prediction of synthesized views.

2.1 Image Scale Space

Gaussian low-pass function has been demonstrated to be the only filter that has the reasonable kernel to generate image scale space [16]. For a synthesized image $\mathbf{I}(x,y)$, its scale space $\mathbf{L}(x,y,\sigma)$ can be obtained as follows:

$$\mathbf{L}(x,y,\sigma) = \mathbf{I}(x,y) * \mathbf{G}(x,y,\sigma), \tag{1}$$

where σ and * denote the standard deviation of Gaussian model and the convolution operator, respectively. The Gaussian kernel is defined as:

$$\mathbf{G}(x,y,\sigma) = \frac{1}{2\pi\sigma^2 e^{-(x^2+y^2)/2\sigma^2}}. \tag{2}$$

In this work, we build the scale space with five scales $(\mathbf{L}_1, ..., \mathbf{L}_5)$, where $\mathbf{L}_1$ denotes the reference scale. The filter size is 3×3 and σ is set to 0.5.

2.2 Textural Naturalness in Synthesized Images

As shown in Fig. 1, the distortions in the synthesized images result in the loss of texture naturalness. It has been demonstrated that GGCM is effective in texture analysis [14], which reflects the joint distribution relation of pixel gray level and edge gradient. Motivated by this, we exploit texture features to represent texture naturalness from the GGCM map in this work. First, we use the Sobel operator to calculate the gradient map at each scale, which is represented by $\mathbf{g}_l$, where l denotes the lth scale ($l = 1, 2, 3, 4, 5$). Then both $\mathbf{I}_l$ and $\mathbf{g}_l$ are normalized as:

$$\widehat{\mathbf{I}}_l(i,j) = INT\left[\frac{(\mathbf{I}_l(i,j) - \mathbf{I}_{l_{min}})}{(\mathbf{I}_{l_{max}} - \mathbf{I}_{l_{min}})}(N_{\mathbf{I}_l} - 1)\right], \tag{3}$$

$$\widehat{\mathbf{g}}_l(i,j) = INT\left[\frac{(\mathbf{g}_l(i,j) - \mathbf{g}_{l_{min}})}{(\mathbf{g}_{l_{max}} - \mathbf{g}_{l_{min}})}(N_{\mathbf{g}_l} - 1)\right], \tag{4}$$

where $\mathbf{I}_{l_{max}}$, $\mathbf{I}_{l_{min}}$, $\mathbf{g}_{l_{max}}$, and $\mathbf{g}_{l_{min}}$ are the maximum and minimum values of the original intensity and gradient values at the lth scale, respectively, INT denotes the integer operator. $N_{\mathbf{I}_l}$ and $N_{\mathbf{g}_l}$ are the maximum gray level and gradient level after normalization, respectively. Here, we set both $N_{\mathbf{I}_l}$ and $N_{\mathbf{g}_l}$ to 32.

The GGCM model, denoted as $\mathbf{M}_l(x,y)$, represents the number of pixel p that simultaneously satisfys $\widehat{\mathbf{I}}_{l_p} = x$ and $\widehat{\mathbf{g}}_{l_p} = y$. Then we calculate the normalized $\mathbf{M}_l(x,y)$, which is defined as:

$$\widehat{\mathbf{M}}_l(x,y) = \frac{\sum_{x=0}^{N_{\mathbf{I}_l}-1}\sum_{y=0}^{N_{\mathbf{g}_l}-1}\widehat{\mathbf{M}}_l(x,y)y^2}{\sum_{x=0}^{N_{\mathbf{I}_l}-1}\sum_{y=0}^{N_{\mathbf{g}_l}-1}\widehat{\mathbf{M}}_l(x,y)}. \tag{5}$$

With the GGCM map, fifteen textural features can be obtained [14]. In this paper, we propose to use the big gradient superiority and gradient entropy to quantify the loss of texture naturalness in the synthesized image:

(1) Big Gradient Superiority (BGS):

$$T_1^l = \frac{\mathbf{M}_l(x,y)}{\sum_{x=0}^{N_{\mathbf{I}_l}-1}\sum_{y=0}^{N_{\mathbf{g}_l}-1}\mathbf{M}_l(x,y)}. \tag{6}$$

BGS measures the leap speed of the gray pixels. Images with higher quality generate higher BGS values, vice versa.

(2) Gradient Entropy (GE):

$$T_2^l = -\sum_{x=0}^{N_{\mathbf{I}_l}-1}\sum_{y=0}^{N_{\mathbf{g}_l}-1}\widehat{\mathbf{M}}_l(x,y)log\sum_{x=0}^{N_{\mathbf{I}_l}-1}\widehat{\mathbf{M}}_l(x,y). \tag{7}$$

GE measures the amount of information in the GGCM map. Higher-quality images generate higher GE values.

We totally obtain two sets of texture features at five scales, namely $\mathbf{T}_1 = [T_1^1, T_1^2, ..., T_1^5]$ and $\mathbf{T}_2 = [T_2^1, T_2^2, ..., T_2^5]$, amounting to ten features.

2.3   Model Training and Quality Prediction

To integrate all features to predict the quality score of synthesized images, we use the RF regression model [17] to learn the synthesized IQA model. Then the trained model is employed to predict the quality score of the query images.

3   Experimental Results

The performance of the proposed method is evaluated on the MCL-3D database
[1], which consists of 684 synthesized image pairs, i.e. 684 left views and 684
right views, together with the MOS values. Among them, 648 image pairs are
polluted by the distortions in their texture/depth maps, which are contaminated individually or simultaneously by six kinds of distortions. The distortions
in the rest 36 image pairs are from the synthesis process generated by four
different rendering algorithms. In particular, the six distortions added into the
texture/depth maps are Gaussian blur, additive white noise, downsampling blur,
JPEG and JPEG-2000 (JP2K) compression and transmission error, while four
rendering algorithms are Depth-Image-Based-Rendering (DIBR) without hole
filling, DIBR with filtering [18], inpainting [19] and hierarchical hole filling [20].

Since the distortions in the left- and right- views are symmetric, the quality
scores of two views predicted by a specific IQA metric are averaged to produce
the overall quality score. Four popular criteria are employed to quantitatively
evaluate the performance of the proposed method, including Pearson Linear Correlation Coefficient (PLCC), Root Mean Square Error (RMSE), Spearman Rank
order Correlation Coefficient (SRCC) and Kendalls Rank Correlation Coefficient
(KRCC). The former two are used to measure the prediction accuracy, while the
latter two are used to measure the prediction monotonicity [21–23]. These criteria are calculated following the five-parameter logistic function [24, 25]:

$$f(x) = \tau_1 \left(\frac{1}{2} - \frac{1}{1 + e^{\tau_2(x-\tau_3)}} \right) + \tau_4 x + \tau_5, \tag{8}$$

where x and $f(x)$ denote the predicted score and corresponding subjective score,
respectively, and $\tau_i, i = 1, 2, 3, 4, 5$, are the parameters to be fitted.

3.1   Performance Evaluation

In this part, we compare the performance of the proposed method with six IQA
methods specially designed for synthesized images, including Bosc's method [6],
MW-PSNR [7], RMW-PSNR [7], MP-PSNR [8], RMP-PSNR [9] and 3Dswim
[10]. The experimental results are summarized in Table 1, where the best results
are highlighted in boldface. In the experiments, 80% images in the database are
randomly selected for the model training and the remaining 20% images are used
for test. To avoid bias, the training-test process is conducted 1000 times and the
median performance values are presented.

It can be seen from Table 1 that even though the existing metrics are all FR
metrics, their performances are still worse than the proposed method, which is
the only NR method. Specifically, among the six existing FR synthesized IQA
metrics, the MP-PSNR [8] method achieves the best performance. However, the
four performance values are only 0.7858, 0.7923, 0.5923 and 1.6092, respectively.
By contrast, the performances of the proposed metric are much higher, i.e.,
0.8555, 0.8613, 0.6800, and 1.3267, respectively.

Table 1. Performance comparison of the proposed method with six existing view synthesis IQA methods.

Metrics	Types	PLCC	SRCC	KRCC	RMSE
Bosc [6]	FR	0.4405	0.4094	0.3066	2.3356
MW-PSNR [7]	FR	0.7654	0.7721	0.5738	1.6743
RMW-PSNR [7]	FR	0.7799	0.7852	0.5901	1.6283
MP-PSNR [8]	FR	0.7858	0.7923	0.5923	1.6092
RMP-PSNR [9]	FR	0.774	0.7802	0.5831	1.6474
3Dswim [10]	FR	0.6364	0.5697	0.4088	2.0067
Proposed method	**NR**	**0.8555**	**0.8613**	**0.6800**	**1.3267**

Table 2. Performance comparison of the proposed method with six general-purpose NR IQA methods.

Metrics	PLCC	SRCC	KRCC	RMSE
BIQI [26]	0.3347	0.3696	0.2504	2.4516
BLIINDS-II [27]	0.5243	0.4976	0.3427	2.2154
BRISQUE [28]	0.6636	0.6283	0.4435	1.9463
DIIVINE [29]	0.6507	0.6482	0.4467	1.9755
NIQE [30]	0.7356	0.6863	0.511	1.7625
DESQUE [31]	0.5306	0.465	0.3272	2.2053
Proposed method	**0.8555**	**0.8613**	**0.6800**	**1.3267**

To further demonstrate the performance of the presented metric, we compare it with six general-purpose NR IQA metrics, namely BIQI [26], BLIINDS-II [27], BRISQUE [28], DIIVINE [29], NIQE [30], DESQUE [31]. These metrics are designed to predict image quality without knowing specific distortion types, such that it is necessary to compare the proposed method with them [32,33]. The results are shown in Table 2. It can be observed that the majority of the general-purpose NR quality metrics have worse performances than existing synthesized IQA methods. By contrast, the proposed metric outperforms them significantly.

The above two experiments not only show the superior performance of the proposed method, but also demonstrate the effectiveness of the extracted texture features in predicting the distortions of the synthesized images.

3.2   Contributions of Two Components

In this work, we propose to extract two kinds of features based on GGCM to predict the quality of synthesized images, including the big gradient superiority (T_1) and gradient entropy (T_2). To investigate their individual contributions, they are separately tested on the database. Table 3 summarizes the experimental results.

Table 3. Contributions of two components in the proposed method.

Feature	PLCC	SRCC	KRCC	RMSE
T_1	0.7856	0.7887	0.6003	1.5941
T_2	0.7755	0.7804	0.5915	1.6364
T_1, T_2 (Proposed)	**0.8555**	**0.8613**	**0.6800**	**1.3267**

It is observed from the table that component T_1 makes slightly greater contributions than component T_2. By using them together, the performance of the proposed metric improves significantly. This demonstrates the reasonability and necessity of the combination of T_1 and T_2.

4 Conclusion

In this paper, we have proposed a no-reference quality index for view synthesis. This method has been inspired by the loss of texture naturalness in the synthesized images and the multi-scale property of the HVS. Based on these, we have extracted two groups of texture features for texture representation at multiple scales to train a synthesized view quality prediction model. The experimental results conducted on the MCL-3D database have demonstrated the advantages of the proposed method over the existing view synthesis and general-purpose image quality metrics.

References

1. Song, R., Ko, H., Jay Kuo, C.C.: MCL-3D: a database for stereoscopic image quality assessment using 2D-image-plus-depth source. J. Inf. Sci. Eng. **31**(5), 1593–1611 (2015)
2. Zhou, Y., Li, L.D., Gu, K., Lu, Z.L., Chen, B.J., Tang, L.: DIBR-synthesized image quality assessment via statistics of edge intensity and orientation. IEICE Trans. Inf. Syst. **E100–D**(8), 1929–1933 (2017)
3. Li, L.D., Guo, B.L., Pan, J.S.: Robust image watermarking using feature based local invariant regions. Int. J. Innovative Comput. Inf. Control **4**(8), 1977–1986 (2008)
4. Liang, Z.S., Yang, G.B., Ding, X.L., Li, L.D.: An efficient forgery detection algorithm for object removal by exemplar-based image inpainting. J. Vis. Commun. Image Rep. **30**, 75–85 (2015)
5. Li, L.D., Li, S.S. Wang, J.: Copy-move forgery detection based on PHT. In: Proceedings 2nd World Congress on Information and Communication Technologies (WICT 2012), Dalian, October 25–26, pp. 1061–1065 (2012)
6. Bosc, E., Pépion, R., Callet, P.L., Koppel, M., Nya, P., Morin, L., Pressigout, M.: Towards a new qualtiy metric for 3-D synthesized view assessment. IEEE J. Sel. Top. Signal Proces. **5**(7), 1332–1343 (2011)
7. Stankovic, D.S., Kukolj, D., Callet, P.L.: DIBR synthesized image quality assessment based on morphological wavelets. In: IEEE International Workshop on Quality of Multimedia Experience, Lisbon, Portugal, pp. 1–6 (2015)

8. Stankovic, D.S., Kukolj, D., Callet, P.L.: DIBR synthesized image quality assessment based on morphological pyramids. In: The True Vision-Capture, Transmission and Display of 3D Video, Lisbon, Portugal, pp. 1–4 (2015)

9. Stankovic, D.S., Kukolj, D., Callet, P.L.: Multi-scale synthesized view assessment based on morphological pyramids. J. Electr. Eng. **67**(1), 3–11 (2016)

10. Battisti, F., Bosc, E., Carli, M., Callet, P.L.: Objective image quality assessment of 3D synthesized views. Signal Process. Image Commun. **30**, 78–88 (2015)

11. Li, L.D., Lin, W.S., Wang, X.S., Yang, G.B., Bahrami, K., Kot, A.C.: No-reference image blur assessment based on discrete orthogonal moments. IEEE Trans. Cybern. **46**(1), 39–50 (2016)

12. Li, L.D., Lin, W.S., Zhu, H.C.: Learning structural regularity for evaluating blocking artifacts in JPEG images. IEEE Signal Proces. Lett. **21**(8), 918–922 (2014)

13. Li, L.D., Zhu, H.C., Yang, G.B., Qian, J.S.: Referenceless measure of blocking artifacts by Tchebichef kernel analysis. IEEE Signal Process. Lett. **21**(1), 122–125 (2014)

14. Lam, W.: Texture feature extraction using gray level gradient based co-occurence matrices. In: IEEE International Conference on Systems, vol. 1, pp. 267–271 (1996)

15. Gu, K., Wang, S.Q., Zhai, G.T., Lin, W.S., Yang, X.K., Zhang, W.J.: Analysis of distortion distribution for pooling in image quality prediction. IEEE Trans. Broadcast **62**(2), 446–456 (2016)

16. Lowe, D.G.: Distinctive image features from scale-invariant keypoints. Int. J. Comput. Vis. **60**(2), 91–110 (2004)

17. Breiman, L.: Random forests. Mach. Learn. **45**(1), 5–32 (2001)

18. Fehn, C.: Depth-image-based rendering (DIBR), compression and transmission for a new approach on 3D-TV. In: Proceedings of SPIE - The International Society for Optical Engineering, vol. 5291, pp. 93–104 (2004)

19. Telea, A.: An amage inpainting technique based on the fast marching method. J. Graph. Tools **9**, 23–34 (2004)

20. Solh, M., Alregib, G.: Hierarchical hole-filling for depth-based view synthesis in FTV and 3D video. IEEE J. Sel. Top. Signal Process. **6**(5), 495–504 (2012)

21. Li, L.D., Cai, H., Zhang, Y.B., Lin, W.S., Kot, A.C., Sun, X.M.: Sparse representation based image quality index with adaptive sub-dictionaries. IEEE Trans. Image Process. **25**(8), 3775–3786 (2016)

22. Gu, K., Zhai, G.T., Yang, X.K., Zhang, W.J.: Using free energy principle for blind image quality assessment. IEEE Trans. Multimedia **17**(1), 50–63 (2015)

23. Gu, K., Li, L.D., Lu, H., Min, X.K., Lin, W.S.: A fast reliable image quality predictor by fusing micro- and macro-structures. IEEE Trans. Ind. Electron. **64**(5), 3903–3912 (2017)

24. Li, L.D., Xia, W.H., Lin, W.S., Fang, Y.M., Wang, S.Q.: No-reference and robust image sharpness evaluation based on multi-scale spatial and spectral features. IEEE Trans. Multimedia **19**(5), 1030–1040 (2017)

25. Li, L.D., Yan, Y., Lu, Z.L., Wu, J.J., Gu, K., Wang, S.Q.: No-reference quality assessment of deblurred images based on natural scene statistics. IEEE Access **5**, 2163–2171 (2017)

26. Moorthy, A.K., Bovik, A.C.: A two-step framework for constructing blind image quality indices. IEEE Signal Process. Lett. **17**(5), 513–516 (2010)

27. Saad, M.A., Bovik, A.C.: Blind image quality assessment: a natural scene statistics approach in the DCT domain. IEEE Trans. Image Process. **21**(8), 3339–3352 (2012)

28. Mittal, A., Moorthy, A.K., Bovik, A.C.: No-reference image quality assessment in the spatial domain. IEEE Trans. Image Process. **21**(12), 4695–4708 (2012)

29. Moorthy, A.K., Bovik, A.C.: Blind image quality assessment: From natural scene statistics to perceptual quality. IEEE Trans. Image Process. **20**(12), 3350–3364 (2011)

30. Mittal, A., Soundararajan, R., Bovik, A.C.: Making a completely blind image quality analyzer. IEEE Signal Process. Lett. **20**(3), 209–212 (2013)

31. Zhang, Y., Chandler, D.M.: No-reference image quality assessment based on log-derivative statistics of natural scenes. J. Elect. Imaging **22**(4), 451–459 (2013)

32. Li, L.D., Wu, D., Wu, J.J., Li, H.L., Lin, W.S., Kot, A.C.: Image sharpness assessment by sparse representation. IEEE Trans. Multimedia **18**(6), 1085–1097 (2016)

33. Li, L.D., Zhou, Y., Lin, W.S., Wu, J.J., Zhang, X.F., Chen, B.J.: No-reference quality assessment of deblocked images. Neurocomputing **177**, 572–584 (2016)

Compression-Based Quality Predictor of 3D-Synthesized Views

Sanyi Li, Junfei Qiao, Maoshen Liu[✉], and Li Wu

Beijing Key Laboratory of Computational Intelligence
and Intelligent System, Faculty of Information Technology,
Beijing University of Technology, Beijing 100124, China
LMSbjut@163.com

Abstract. Depth-Image-Based-Rendering (DIBR) is a fundamental technique used in free Viewpoint Videos (FVVs) to create new frames from existing adjacent frames, which can decrease the cost of camera set up. However, it is unavoidable to introduce geometric distortions in the synthesized images because of the warping and rendering operations in DIBR. Only a few Image Quality Assessment (IQA) methods have been proposed for such images and they are all Full-Reference (FR) methods. Nevertheless, reference DIBR-synthesized image is not accessible in real application scenarios, so No-Reference (NR) methods are more valuable than FR methods. In this paper, we propose an effective and efficient NR method based on Joint Photographic Experts Group (JPEG) image compression technology. The proposed method utilizes the difference of the amount of detail information between undistorted areas and geometry distortions areas, which can be achieved by comparing original images and JPEG images. Experiments validate the superiority of our no-reference quality method as compared with prevailing full-, reduced- and no-reference models.

Keywords: Depth-Image-Based-Rendering · Quality prediction
Natural scene statistics · No reference
Joint photographic experts group

1 Introduction

With the development of science and technology, free Viewpoint Videos (FVVs) and 3D television have received considerable attention and been applied in many areas in the past years [1]. A large amount of cameras are needed to shoot FVVs, which greatly increase shooting cost. To reduce the cost, Depth-Image-Based-Rendering (DIBR) techniques are introduced. DIBR techniques can create new frames from existing adjacent frames, which largely decreases the cost and complexity of camera set up. However, distortions (actually geometry distortions)

This work was supported in part by National Natural Science Foundation of China under Grants 61533002.

© Springer Nature Singapore Pte Ltd. 2018
G. Zhai et al. (Eds.): IFTC 2017, CCIS 815, pp. 310–319, 2018.
https://doi.org/10.1007/978-981-10-8108-8_29

are ineluctably existed in these new synthesized frames that seriously affect the quality of video and visual effect. So an efficient and effective image quality evaluation technique is very necessary.

Many Image Quality Assessment (IQA) methods, such as Full-Reference (FR) and No-Reference (NR) models, have been developed to evaluate natural images. FR IQA methods build IQA models based on the information of the reference image. For example, Wang et al. built an IQA model named Structural Similarity (SSIM) based on the luminance, contrast and structural similarity between a distorted image and its reference image [2]. Wang et al. improved the SSIM based on the statistical information theory and the natural scene statistics (NSS) model [3]. Gu et al. recently improved the SSIM with a valid pooling scheme and proposed the Analysis of Distortion Distribution-based SSIM (ADD-SSIM) metric [4]. Zhai et al. proposed a psychovisual quality metric of images based on the free-energy principle [5]. Gu et al. proposed a local-tuned-global model induced IQA metric based on the theory that the human visual perception to image quality depends on salient local distortion and global quality degradation [6,7].

In contrast to the FR methods, NR methods (also named blind IQA) do not require the information of the reference image. Such as, Gao et al. constructed a new universal NR quality indicator using three types of NSS and incorporating the heterogeneous property of multiple kernel learning [8]. Gu et al. proposed a six-step blind metric (SISBLIM) based on the early human visual model and recently revealed free energy based brain theory [9]. Zhang et al. learned a multivariate Gaussian model of image patches based on NSS and then used Bhattacharyya-like distance to measure the quality of each image patch, the overall quality score is obtained by average pooling [10]. Gu et al. proposed a new NR IQA metric using the free energy based brain theory and classical human visual system (HVS) inspired features [11], and further extended to the screen content images [12]. Based on the autoregressive (AR) parameter space, Gu et al. proposed a new blind sharpness metric via the analysis of AR model parameters and the inevitable effect of color information on visual perception to sharpness [13].

These FR and NR IQA methods mentioned above establish effective assessment models of natural images. However, DIBR-synthesized images have some characters different from natural images. The DIBR technology is to deploy a view and the corresponding per-pixel depth information to synthesize 'virtual' views from a slightly distinct viewing perspective. Generally, a new view is created along with (1) re-projecting the texture information into the 3-D world via the per-pixel depth information and (2) producing the 'virtual' camera by projecting the 3D space points into the 2D image plane. Based on the above process, the key target of DIBR is towards transferring the occluded regions (mainly occurred at the contour of the foreground objects) in the original view to be visible in the 'virtual' view. The depth information can be used to solve the occlusion problem to some extent, yet inevitably introducing the geometry distortions due to the imperfect 3D reprojection. It is very likely that the geometry distortion devastates the semantic structures, which leads to a stronger influence on the image quality than the typical distortions. The general FR and NR IQA methods only use classical low-level visual features which are sensitive to the typical distortions, the new high-level features specific to the geometry distortion are neglected. So these IQA methods cannot yield reliable quality predictions when assessing DIBR-synthesized images.

For DIBR-synthesized image evaluation, only a few works have been done. Vosc et al. proposed the first IQA algorithm for DIBR-synthesized images; they analyze the shifts of the contours of the synthesized view and compute the mean Structural SIMilarity (SSIM) score in the critical areas. Conze et al. designed a View Synthesis Quality Assessment (VSQA) metric, in which the orientation, texture and contrast backed weighting maps were computed to adapt to the characteristics of Human Visual System (HVS) [14]. Battisti et al. proposed an approach based on the comparison of statistical features extracted from wavelet subbands of original and distorted DIBR- synthesized views [15]. Sandic-Stankovic et al. proposed a FR algorithm based on morphological wavelet decomposition to tackle the evaluation of DIBR-synthesized images [16]. Later, the same authors improved their algorithm by replacing the morphological wavelet decomposition with the morphological pyramid decomposition [17]. Lately, Sandic-Stankovic et al. further improved their algorithm by reducing morphological Pyramid Peak signal-to-noise ratio metric and only taking mean squared errors between pyramids' images at higher scales into account [18]. Those algorithms perform better than the algorithms designed for typical distortions and they are all FR methods. Nevertheless, reference DIBR-synthesized image is not accessible in real application scenarios, so NR methods are more valuable than FR methods.

So far, few studies have been done on NR IQA method for DIBR-synthesized image. This paper proposes a NR IQA method for DIBR-synthesized images based on Joint Photographic Experts Group (JPEG) image compression technology. In the process of compression, JPEG images lost some detail information (high-frequency information) which is not sensitive by Human eyes. So the amount of lost information can be achieved by comparing original images and JPEG images. For an image, there are rich details contained in undistorted areas and not in geometry distortions areas, which means the amount lost information in undistorted areas is much more than geometry distortions areas. The algorithm proposed by us is mainly depends on the difference of the amount of lost information between undistorted areas and geometry distortions areas. We apply the algorithm on the IRCCyN/IVC database [1] dedicated to the DIBR-synthesized images, experiment results show that the no-reference quality method proposed by us is better than the compared prevailing full-, reduced- and no-reference models.

The rest of the paper is organized as follows. Section 2 describes the detailed process of the proposed algorithm. Section 3 conducts comparisons of our blind metric with state-of-the-art FR, RR and NR IQA methods on the specific IRCCyN/IVC database [1]. Section 4 concludes the whole paper.

2   Proposed Algorithm

In this section, we describe the detailed process of the proposed algorithm. The proposed NR quality assessment metric for DIBR-synthesized images using compression technique followed by the thresholding.

2.1   JPEG Image Compression

Firstly, use JPEG image compression technology to compress an image need to be evaluated. The pixel values of the input image are first subtracted by 128. Then partition the processed image into non-overlapping 8 × 8 blocks. Transform each block with discrete cosine transformation (DTC) techonlgy and then quantify each block by using element-wise division with the corresponding entries in the quantization table according to the quality factor. Direct Current (DC) coefficients are encoded with differential pulse code modulation (DPCM) which can reduce the coding bit rate. Alternate Current (AC) coefficients are subject to the zigzag ordering, and encoded in the form of Run/Size and Value (RSV) pairs. Entropy encoding all the DC difference values and RSV pairs and store them in JPEG format.

The decompression process is the reverse of the compression process. Assume a JPEG encoded image I is need to be decoded. The dimension of pixel of I is $8M \times 8N \in G$, where (G is the set of natural numbers), the entropy decoded DTC coefficients are reconstructed by

$$EC_{u,v}(i,j) = \chi \times \mathtt{I}_{u,v} \times QT_{u,v} \tag{1}$$

where χ is a constant, $\mathtt{I}_{u,v}$ is the (u,v)th quantized DCT coefficients in the (i,j)th block in I, $QT_{u,v}$ denotes the (u,v)th entry in QT, $1 \leq u, v \leq 8$, $1 \leq i \leq M$ and $1 \leq j \leq N$. The reconstructed coefficients are inversely transformed to the spatial domain, and the process is repeated for each 8 × 8 coefficient block, and all the pixel values are increased by 128 at the end.

2.2   Quality Assessment Metric

When an image is compressed, the error difference map between the input image and the compressed image can be obtained. Because the JPEG image lost some detail information in the process of compression, the error difference map can reflect the lost detail information. The absolute value of the error difference map can be used to evaluate the amount of detail information. There is rich detail information contained in natural images or natural image patches, while few detail information in geometry distortions image patches. That means the amount of lost information in undistorted areas is much more than geometry distortions areas. In other words, the absolute value of the error difference map corresponds to geometric distortion areas is small and to nature areas is large.

Based on the analyses above, we propose to use error difference map between input image and compressed image to judge the quality of a DIBR-synthesized image. We set a threshold λ_t to binarize the filtered error map:

$$E_d = \begin{cases} 0, & \text{if } E_e < \lambda_t \\ 1, & \text{otherwise} \end{cases} \tag{2}$$

where E_e is the error map processed by Gaussian filter; λ_t is a constant threshold (it takes 66 in this paper).

Next, it needs to find a method to pool the binary map E_d generated based on Eq. (2) to obtain the final quality score. Majority of existing IQA metrics were developed based on the NSS model. Some FR-IQA methods were proposed by analyzing the structural variations of a distorted image and its associated reference image. In NR-IQA models, one certain statistic regulation is obtained by analyzing the natural images first, and then the quality score of a distorted image can be estimated based on its deviation from the natural statistic regulation. So, comparing the structure of a distortion image and its associated natural image is a reliable way to assess image quality. Note that, using Eq. (2), the small values in the error difference map, which are associated to the geometric distortion image parts, are set as zero. In comparison, those large values corresponding to natural image parts are set as the unit. This means that the values of a distortion-free natural image in the binary map should be all one. We can compare the binary map of a DIBR-synthesized image E_d with the binary map of natural images E_r to predict its image quality. So the quality score can be calculated by compare the number of one in E_d and E_r. With this view, we set a binary reference map E_r which has the same size with E_d and all the values in E_r are all one. Then the quality measure formula for DIBR-synthesized images can be defined as:

$$Y_s = \frac{N_1}{N} \tag{3}$$

where N is the number of the pixels in image; N_1 is associated to the regions that all the values in which are one.

The quality score can be readily achieved by calculating the ratio of the number of one value pixels to the overall map size, which reflect the similarity between the binary maps of a distorted DIBR-synthesized image and natural images. From Eq. (3), we can see that the score Y_s of a DIBR-synthesized image with high quality is close to 1. For such images, most of the values in the binary map E_d are one, which means those images have fewer amounts of geometric distortions (pixels in N_0 regions). We can also see that the Eq. (3) does not depend on any information about the reference image, so the proposed algorithm is completely blind/referenceless.

3   Experimental Results

In this paper, we proposed a quality assessment metric based on JPEG compression technology, specifically to evaluate the quality of DIBR-synthesized images.

To check the effectiveness of the proposed method, we apply it on the IRC-CyN/IVC database [1] which was dedicated to the DIBR-synthesized images. There are 96 images in this database, 12 of them are original images and the rest 84 images are synthesized images. The 84 synthesized images contain geometric distortions and used for verifying the proposed quality assessment metric.

3.1   Competing IQA Metrics and Evaluation Methodology

There are two kinds of quality assessment methods used to compare with the proposed algorithm. The algorithms in the first kind were designed for natural images and in the second kind were designed to evaluate DIBR-synthesized images specially. The IQA methods in the first category include full-reference algorithms (such as, PSNR, SSIM [2], VSNR [19], MAD [23], IW-SSIM [3], PSIM [7], ADD-SSIM [4]), reduced-reference (such as, RRED [20], FEDM [5], FTQM [21], and referenceless (such as, NIQE [22], SISBLIM [9], IL-NIQE [10], ASIQE [24]). The methods belong to the second category are full-reference algorithms (such as, VSQA [14], 3D-SWIM [15], MW-PSNR [16], MP-PSNR [17], MP-PSNR-reduc [18]).

For the purpose of performance evaluation, we use two common criteria, namely Perason Linear Correlation Coefficient (PLCC) and Spearman Rank order Correlation Coefficient (SRCC). PLCC reflects the prediction accuracy and SRCC reflects the monotonicity of the prediction. A better quality assessment algorithm should attain a higher value of PLCC and SRCC. It needs to reduce the nonlinearity of objective prediction scores before conducting PLCC and SRCC. So the objective prediction scores need to be mapped to subjective human ratings with the following nonlinear logistic function beforehand:

$$f(Y_s) = \gamma_1(0.5 - \frac{1}{1 + e^{\gamma_2(Y_s - \gamma_3)}}) + \gamma_4 Y_s + \gamma_5 \tag{4}$$

where Y_s and $f(Y_s)$ represent the predicted scores and its corresponding mapped scores. $\gamma_i(i \in 1, 2, 3, 4, 5)$ are the parameters which can be obtained during the nonlinear regression. Then we use the converted objective predictions $f(Y_s)$ and subjective quality scores to compute the two criteria (PLCC and SRCC).

3.2   Performance Comparison

The experimental results of the proposed algorithm and existing IQA algorithms (both the first and second categories) are presented in Table 1. The proposed algorithm achieves 0.7006 and 0.6974 of PLCC and SRCC, respectively, which is much better than all the competing IQA methods belong to the first categories and all the full-reference algorithms belong to the second categories. From Table 1, we can get the following two important conclusions:

(1) Those existing IQA algorithms that were designed for natural images (in the first category) are unable to perform effectively. The MAD algorithm [23] performs the best among FR IQA methods tested and it obtains 0.6007

and 0.5994 of PLCC and SRCC, respectively. Across eight RR and NR IQA metrics, the FTQM and SISBLIM methods separately lead to the optimal results in their personal types, more than 0.5 of PLCC. These simulation results confirm our claim that those existing algorithms in the first category cannot catch the geometric distortions, which are the predominant artifacts contained in the DIBR-synthesized images.

(2) Despite the fact that the FR IQA methods designed for the DIBR-synthesized images (in the second category) implement better than those designed for natural images while the performance indices of those algorithms are not sufficient yet. For example, the MP-PSNR-reduc metric performs the best among the FR IQA models designed for DIBR-synthesized views and it attains 0.6772 of PLCC, which is still smaller than the PLCC value obtained by the NR APT algorithm. And furthermore, in those IQA approaches, it requires the complete information about the reference synthesized views, which are generally not accessible in most real application scenarios. The performance of the NR

Table 1. Performance comparison of the proposed algorithm with recently developed metrics (quality assessment metrics for both images and DIBR). The best performance in each type is highlighted with the bold-faces.

Metric	PLCC	SRCC	Designed for	Category
PSNR	0.3976	0.3095	Monoscopic views	Full-reference
SSIM	0.4850	0.4368	Monoscopic views	Full-reference
VSNR	0.4370	0.3851	Monoscopic views	Full-reference
MAD	**0.6007**	**0.5994**	Monoscopic views	Full-reference
IW-SSIM	0.5831	0.4053	Monoscopic views	Full-reference
PSIM	0.5040	0.4120	Monoscopic views	Full-reference
ADD-SSIM	0.5512	0.4672	Monoscopic views	Full-reference
RRED	0.4072	0.3090	Monoscopic views	Reduced-reference
REDM	0.2252	0.1817	Monoscopic views	Reduced-reference
FTQM	**0.5628**	**0.5543**	Monoscopic views	Reduced-reference
NIQE	0.4374	0.3739	Monoscopic views	No-reference
SISBLIM	0.5225	0.3832	Monoscopic views	No-reference
IL-NIQE	0.4936	0.5262	Monoscopic views	No-reference
ASIQE	**0.5854**	**0.4948**	Monoscopic views	No-reference
VSQA	0.5742	0.5233	DIBR-synthesized views	Full-reference
3D-SWIM	0.6584	0.6156	DIBR-synthesized views	Full-reference
MW-PSNR	0.5622	0.5757	DIBR-synthesized views	Full-reference
MP-PSNR	0.6174	0.6227	DIBR-synthesized views	Full-reference
MP-PSNR-reduc	**0.6772**	**0.6634**	DIBR-synthesized views	Reduced-reference
Proposed algorithm	**0.7006**	**0.6974**	DIBR-synthesized views	No-reference

APT algorithm is better than the methods designed for natural images (in the first category) and the FR IQA methods designed for the DIBR-synthesized images (in the second category).

Overall, the proposed metric is completely referenceless and it achieves the similar results of PLCC and SRCC with the existing NR APT algorithm. What's more, the proposed algorithm improves the calculation speed dramatically.

3.3 Discussions

In comparison to existing studies, there include some spotlights in our work. First, based on JPEG compression technique, we have proposed a new NSS model which can capture the geometric distortion appeared in DIBR-synthesized images. Second, this work has achieved superior performance as compared with state-of-the-art IQA models. Third, this work is a NR IQA model designed for DIBR-synthesized views, which does not require reference DIBR-synthesized image.

4   Conclusions

The 3-D synthesized views are the backbone of freeview point videos (FVV), virtual reality (VR), augmented reality (AR), and mixed reality (MR). In the literature, several algorithms were proposed to generate the 3-D synthesized view but referenceless quality assessment metrics are missing. The referenceless metrics are essentially required to evaluate and monitor the synthesized views, as reference synthesized views are generally not available. With this view, in this work, we have proposed an effective and referenceless quality assessment algorithm for DIBRsynthesized views using the proposed new natural scene statistics (NSS) model. The residual error between a DIBR-synthesized image and its compressed image can validly capture the geometry distortions. The visual saliency is then leveraged to modify the proposed blind quality metric to a sizable margin. Experiments validate the superiority of our noreference quality method as compared with prevailing existing full-, reduced-, and no-reference approaches, which includes both type of algorithms specifically designed for the natural and DIBR-synthesized images.

References

1. Bosc, E., Pepion, R., Callet, P.L., Koppel, M., Nya, P.N., Cedex, R.: Towards a new quality metric for 3-D synthesized view assessment. IEEE J. Select. Top. Signal Process. **5**(7), 1332–1343 (2011)
2. Wang, Z., Bovik, A.C., Sheikh, H.R., Simoncelli, E.P.: Image quality assessment: from error visibility to structural similarity. IEEE Trans. Image Process. **13**(4), 600–612 (2004)
3. Wang, Z., Li, Q.: Information content weighting for perceptual image quality assessment. IEEE Trans. Image Process. **20**(5), 1185–1198 (2011)

4. Gu, K., Wang, S., Zhai, G., Lin, W., Yang, X., Zhang, W.: Analysis of distortion distribution for pooling in image quality prediction. IEEE Trans. Broadcast. **62**(2), 446–456 (2016)
5. Zhai, G., Wu, X., Yang, X., Lin, W., Zhang, W.: A psychovisual quality metric in free-energy principle. IEEE Trans. Image Process. **21**(1), 41–52 (2012)
6. Gu, K., Zhai, G., Yang, X., Zhang, W.: An efficient color image quality metric with local-tuned-global model. In: Proceedings of the IEEE International Conference on Image Processing, pp. 506–510, October 2014
7. Gu, K., Li, L., Lu, H., Min, X., Lin, W.: A fast reliable image quality predictor by fusing micro- and macro-structures. IEEE Trans. Industr. Electron. **64**(5), 3903–3912 (2017)
8. Gao, X., Gao, F., Tao, D., Li, X.: Universal blind image quality assessment metrics via natural scene statistics and multiple kernel learning. IEEE Trans. Neural Netw. Learn. Syst. **24**(12), 2013–2026 (2013)
9. Gu, K., Zhai, G., Yang, X., Zhang, W.: Hybrid no-reference quality metric for singly and multiply distorted images. IEEE Trans. Broadcast. **60**(3), 555–567 (2014)
10. Zhang, L., Zhang, L., Bovik, A.C.: A feature-enriched completely blind image quality evaluator. IEEE Trans. Image Process. **24**(8), 2579–2591 (2015)
11. Gu, K., Zhai, G., Yang, X., Zhang, W.: Using free energy principle for blind image quality assessment. IEEE Trans. Multimedia **17**(1), 50–63 (2015)
12. Gu, K., Zhai, G., Lin, W., Yang, X., Zhang, W.: Learning a blind quality evaluation engine of screen content images. Neurocomputing **196**, 140–149 (2016)
13. Gu, K., Zhai, G., Lin, W., Yang, X., Zhang, W.: No-reference image sharpness assessment in autoregressive parameter space. IEEE Trans. Image Process. **24**(10), 3218–3231 (2015)
14. Conze, P.H., Robert, P., Morin, L.: Objective view synthesis quality assessment. In: Electronic Imaging - International Society for Optics and Photonics, p. 8288-56, February 2012
15. Battisti, F., Bosc, E., Carli, M., Le Callet, P.: Objective image quality assessment of 3D synthesized views. Signal Process. Image Commun. **30**, 78–88 (2015)
16. Sandic-Stankovic, D., Kukolj, D., Callet, P.L.: DIBR-synthesized image quality assessment based on morphological wavelets. In: Proceedings of the IEEE International Workshop on Quality of Multimedia Experience, pp. 1–6, January 2015
17. Sandic-Stankovic, D., Kukolj, D., Le Callet, P.: DIBR-synthesized image quality assessment based on morphological pyramids. In: The True Vision-Capture, Transmission and Display of 3D Video, pp. 1–4, October 2015
18. Sandic-Stankovic, D., Kukolj, D., Le Callet, P.: Multi-scale synthesized view assessment based on morphological pyramids. J. Electr. Eng. **67**(1), 1–9 (2016)
19. Chandler, D.M., Hemami, S.S.: VSNR: a wavelet-based visual signal-to-noise ratio for natural images. IEEE Trans. Image Process. **16**(9), 2284–2298 (2007)
20. Soundararajan, R., Bovik, A.C.: RRED indices: reduced-reference entropic differencing for image quality assessment. IEEE Trans. Image Process. **21**(2), 517–526 (2012)
21. Narwaria, M., Lin, W., McLoughlin, I.V., Emmanuel, S., Chia, L.T.: Fourier transform-based scalable image quality measure. IEEE Trans. Image Process. **21**(8), 3364–3377 (2012)
22. Mittal, A., Soundararajan, R., Bovik, A.C.: Making a 'completely blind' image quality analyzer. IEEE Signal Process. Lett. **22**(3), 209–212 (2013)
23. Larson, E.C., Chandler, D.M.: Most apparent distortion: full-reference image quality assessment and the role of strategy. J. Electron. Imaging **19**(1), 011006 (2010)

24. Gu, K., Zhou, J., Qiao, J., Zhai, G., Lin, W., Bovik, A.C.: No-reference quality assessment of screen content pictures. IEEE Trans. Image Process. **26**(8), 4005–4018 (2017)
25. Gu, K., Tao, D., Qiao, J., Lin, W.: Learning a no-reference quality assessment model of enhanced images with big data. IEEE Trans. Neural Netw. Learn. Syst. (2017)

24. Ch. K., Zhou J., Chen J., Zhu C., Lin W., Bu C., Cai C.: Wu S.: Perceptual assessment, Thesisgei compression. IEEE Trans. Image Process. 20(2), pp. 1018 (2017)

25. Ch. K., Bao D., Chan H., Fan W., Lin J., Lu P.: Perceptual quality assessment for 3D animated meshes with hot split. IEEE Trans. Vis. Comput. Graph. (TVCG)

Social Media

Research on Sparse Problem of Personalized Recommendation System

Maocai Dong[1]([✉]), Yuan Zhang[2], and Jinyao Yan[3]

[1] School of Information Engineering, Communication University of China, Beijing, China
819712753@qq.com
[2] Computer NIC Center, Communication University of China, Beijing, China
yuanzhang@cuc.edu.cn
[3] Laboratory of Media Audio and Video, Communication University of China, Beijing, China
jyan@cuc.edu.cn

Abstract. Recommendation system is an intelligent business platform which bases on users' interests and historical purchase behavior to recommend users the information and commodities that they are interested. One challenge problem in current recommendation system is the sparse problem of dataset. Users usually evaluate a few items on website, which result in extremely sparse dataset and low-quality recommendation. Though solutions such as average value filling and genetic clustering are formulated, poor recommendatory efficiency and accuracy exist as before when users' rating dataset is extremely sparse. A new method called CF-average filling algorithm is proposed in this paper to optimize the problem of data sparsity. And three kinds of clustering algorithms that include k-means clustering, hierarchical clustering and spectral clustering are used for community discovery on real dataset from the MovieLens to evaluate our CF-averaging filling algorithm. Experimental results show that the proposed algorithm is highly effective and generally applicable to solve the problem of data sparsity in personalized recommendation system.

Keywords: Recommendation system · Sparse dataset · Collaborative filtering
Clustering · Filling algorithm

1 Introduction

With the rapid development of the Internet, the situation of information redundancy and overload is becoming more and more serious. Therefore, personalized recommendation system which can improve users' efficiency of searching for their own needed information from the massive data has drawn a lot of attention. IMDB and Douban film are movie rating websites which based on the personalized recommendation system with E-commerce and social network functions. Users could leave their comments and gradings on those websites and see other people's reviews. If we regard these users as a community, then divide it into many smaller communities which have different characteristics with the tactics of community discovery, it will be easy to make personalized recommendation effectively for users. But limitation of the information referred to users

© Springer Nature Singapore Pte Ltd. 2018
G. Zhai et al. (Eds.): IFTC 2017, CCIS 815, pp. 323–333, 2018.
https://doi.org/10.1007/978-981-10-8108-8_30

lead to the users' evaluation of items which is rather sparse. A lot of the missing rating data of users makes it difficult to find a similar user set for the target users. As a result, data sparsity not only lower the search accuracy of the nearest neighbor users, but also lower the coverage rate of recommendation, which have a direct effect on the quality and efficiency of recommendation. Therefore, the problem of data sparsity has always been the focus of the research on personalized recommendation system.

In this paper, we propose an algorithm called CF-average filling algorithm base on the collaborative filtering algorithm and the average filling method. The CF-average filling algorithm not only fills more missing values so that greatly reduces the sparseness of dataset, but also improves the accuracy of filling values. It makes community division more reasonable and effective as well as improves personalized recommendation system a better recommendation performance.

The remaining part of this paper is recognized as follows: in the second part, we introduce related works about the problem of data sparsity; in the third part, we explain the theoretical process of the CF-average filling algorithm; in the fourth part, there are some experiments about the efficiency and applicability of the CF-average filling algorithm to verify its better performance; we summarize our work and discuss the future work in the last part.

2 Related Work

A lot of work has been done to solve the problem of data sparsity of personalized recommendation system. These methods can be basically divided into two types [1]. The first type uses optimized algorithm to improve the accuracy of the personalized recommendation system without changing the sparse degree of the dataset. The second type reduces the sparse degree of dataset through disposing the missing data in some ways. In this work we focus on the second direction by leveraging filling value method, clustering method and dimension reduction method [2].

Filling method [2] uses a fixed value to fill the missing scores of dataset to solve the problem of data sparsity. The commonly used method of picking fixed value is the average value filling method, which means that the missing data are filled with average value of the same kind of data. Thus, the average value filling method takes advantage of the average value of rating and make users' rating matrix more integral. This method improves the accuracy of personalized recommendation system, but it can not radically solve the problem of similarity measure on the condition that the users' rating data is extremely sparse.

Clustering method [3] uses clustering algorithms to classify users into different groups according to user' interests. This method takes the central value of group where users belong to as the predicted value of items that users have not been rated. Major clustering algorithms including K-means clustering and genetic clustering [4]. Clustering method takes advantage of rating information of similar group and improves the accuracy of prediction, but it can't show the differences of users' hobbies. Therefore, the accuracy of recommended results of the personalized recommendation system has not been greatly advanced.

Dimensionality reduction method [4] aims to reduce the dimension of dataset to eliminate redundant data as the problem of sparse data is always caused by high dimension of dataset. At present, this method mainly including simple dimension reduction, matrix decomposition and principal component analysis. Though dimensionality reduction method can lower the sparse scale of dataset, it loses part of users' rating of items. And it is difficult to ensure the effect to reduce dimension under condition of high dimensionality as this method is closely related to dataset.

3 CF-Average Filling Algorithm

The above methods in related work can be applied to optimize the problem of data sparsity of personalized recommendation system, which improve the accuracy of the recommendation system as well. However, there still exist some disadvantages, which result in poor solution of the problem of recommendatory efficiency and accuracy when the users' rating dataset is extremely sparse. To better solve the problem of data sparsity of personalized recommendation system and improve the quality of recommendation, we propose a method called CF-average filling algorithm base on the collaborative filtering algorithm and the average filling method. We will describe the details in this section.

3.1 Collaborative Filtering Algorithm

Collaborative filtering algorithm [5] uses collective intelligence to predict and recommend for users. Its basic idea is that the similar users have a similar hobby or the similar items can be preferred by the same user. Accordingly, the collaborative filtering can be classified into the user-based collaborative filtering and the item-based collaborative filtering. But whatever the kind of collaborative filtering is, both of them need to ascertain the similarity of analyzing targets (users or items), then analyse the affection according to the similarity of the target, finally a properly recommend will be given based on the degree of affection.

Steps of the user-based collaborative filtering is showed in the following Fig. 1.

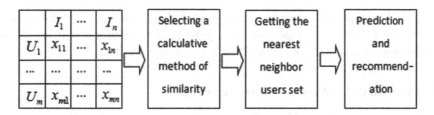

Fig. 1. Steps of the user-based collaborative filtering

Mainly divided into the following four steps:

(1) Construction of user-item rating matrix: according to information of users' rating dataset to establish the user-item rating matrix, m represents the number of users, n represents the number of items, x_{ij} represents the score that user i scores for item j, and the score is usually a positive integer. When there is no score of a item, 0 is used to replace the missing score, which is known as zero filling.

(2) Appropriate method for similarity: currently, many frequently used methods can compute the value of similarity. Such as correlation similarity (Pearson correlation coefficient), cosine similarity and modified cosine similarity. In this paper, the correlation similarity [6] is selected to compute the value of similarity.

Assuming that I_{uv} is the item which is scored by both user u and user v. Then the Pearson correlation coefficient of them, that is correlation similarity, can be expressed as:

$$\text{sim}(u, v) = \frac{\sum_{i \in I_{uv}} \left(x_{ui} - \bar{x}_u\right)\left(x_{vi} - \bar{x}_v\right)}{\sqrt{\sum_{i \in I_{uv}} \left(x_{ui} - \bar{x}_u\right)^2 \sum_{i \in I_{uv}} \left(x_{vi} - \bar{x}_v\right)^2}} \tag{1}$$

(3) Get the nearest neighbor users set for a specified user: in this paper we specify a similarity threshold. The user whose Pearson correlation coefficient is larger than the similarity threshold will be added to set of the nearest neighbor users. Otherwise, users are unvalued to the target user when the Pearson correlation coefficient of them is smaller than the similarity threshold, in other words, it's no relevance between those users and the target user.

(4) Prediction and recommendation: according to scores of the neighbor users to predict score of the target users and list the Top-N recommendation of item. Assuming that P_{ui} represents the predicted score of the user u for unrated item i, then P_{ui} is calculated as:

$$P_{ui} = \bar{x}_u + \frac{\sum_{v \in N(u)} \text{sim}(u, v)\left(x_{vi} - \bar{x}_v\right)}{\sum_{v \in N(u)} |\text{sim}(u, v)|} \tag{2}$$

Where $N(u)$ represents the nearest neighbor set of target user u, x_{vi} represents actual score of user v to item i, $\bar{x}_u$ represents average score of target user u in all rated items, $\bar{x}_v$ represents average score of the neighbor user v in all rated items.

3.2 Program of CF-Average Filling Algorithm

In order to optimize the problem of data sparsity, we propose the CF-average filling algorithm base on the average filling method and the collaborative filtering algorithm. Firstly, the collaborative filtering algorithm is used to predict and fill missing values of user-item rating matrix which is transformed from the original sparse dataset. After that, we continue to fill the newly acquired user-item rating matrix by average filling method. The CF-average filling algorithm not only fills more missing values so that greatly reduces the sparseness of dataset, but also improves the accuracy of filling values. It makes the community division more reasonable and effective.

```
Algorithm. CF-average Filling Algorithm
  Input:  User-item rating matrix:  D_{m×n};
          Similarity threshold:  k;
  Output: Optimized user-item rating matrix by CF-Average
          Filling D"_{m×n};
  Process:
  repeat
     for any two users u and v in D_{m×n} do:
        computing similarity: sim(u,v);
     end for
  until calculate the similarity between any two users;
  obtain the similarity matrix of all users T_{uu}; return;
        for sim(u,v) of the target user in T_{uu} do:
           if sim(u,v) > k:
              add user v to N(u); return;
           else:
              continue;
           end if
        end for
     for v in N(u) do:
        for u in N(u) do:
           predict score of target user u to item i: P_{ui};
           fill P_{ui} in the corresponding vacancy of D_{m×n};
        end for
     end for
  D'_{m×n}; return;
  tor item i in D'_{m×n} do:
     the mean value of scores to item i: m_i;
     fill m_i in the corresponding vacancy of D'_{m×n};
  end for
  D"_{m×n}; return.
```

4 Experiments and Results

In experiment, we choose clustering algorithm as the recommendation algorithm of personalized recommendation system. Three kinds of clustering algorithms, including k-means clustering [7], hierarchical clustering [8] and spectral clustering, are used for community discovery base on the optimized datasets. Users are clustered into several classes of common properties, then personalized recommendation system generates recommendations base on these smaller clustering data.

The experiment is divided into two parts. The first part verifies the effectiveness of CF-average filling algorithm. In this part, we select the number of community division for the follow-up experiment and use the dataset whose missing values are filled by CF-average filling algorithm to do community discovery. Evaluation of the results of community discovery is given to prove that the CF-average filling algorithm is efficient.

In second part, we use experiments of community discovery on 6 datasets of different sparsity to prove the applicability of CF-average filling to solve the problem of data sparsity in personalized recommendation system.

4.1 The MovieLens Dataset

The experimental data derives from the MovieLens dataset [9], which is formed by evaluation data of films on the MovieLens website. The selected MovieLens dataset contains more than one million scores of 3706 movies in total from 6040 users and the size of which is 1 Mb. The scores range from 1 to 5 directly proportional to the user's affection to film. In experiment that verifies the effectiveness of optimized algorithm, the dataset we select is the scores of the top-1200 films, and the sparsity of which is 80.94%. On the other hand, five other datasets with different sparsity are used in the contrast experiment to prove the applicability of optimized algorithm.

4.2 Evaluation Criteria

The evaluation criterion of community discovery is data-dependent [9]. As the experimental dataset is determined, the results of three different algorithms are compared with the comparative evaluation method. The MovieLens dataset used in experiment is widely used in collaborative filtering research, hence we use the result of collaborative filtering as the evaluation criterion of community discovery. We use accuracy as the evaluation criterion of collaborative filtering [10].

Accuracy of personalized recommendation system refers to the difference between predictive score and actual score, computing methods of which mainly including mean absolute error (MAE), mean square error (MSE), and root mean squared error (RMSE). Compared with the mean absolute error, the other two methods have more severe penalties for a relatively large absolute errors because they take the square of each absolute error as the magnitude of difference. Thus we use MAE to measure the accuracy, the smaller the MAE is, the higher the accuracy of collaborative filtering is, and the higher the quality of community discovery is. Suppose r_{uv} represents the user's actual score to item, r'_{uv} represents the user's predictive score to item, and E^P represents the test set, then the mean absolute error can be expressed as:

$$\text{MAE} = \frac{1}{\left| E^P \right|} \sum_{(u,a \in E^P)} \left| r_{ua} - r'_{ua} \right| \tag{3}$$

The specific steps: we need to do community discovery firstly, then each user randomly selects a known film score and collaborative filtering algorithm is used to find users who have the highest correlation with the target user to do the prediction. We use Pearson correlation coefficient as the criterion of correlation between users and users whose Pearson correlation coefficient is larger than 0.1 will be selected as the neighbor of target users.

4.3 Experiments of Effective

Base on the theoretical basis and data analysis above, we use three kinds of clustering algorithms for community discovery on the same dataset whose missing values are filled by different filling methods. Then, by comparing experimental results of different filling methods to prove high efficiency of the CF-average filling algorithm.

Number of communities
To use clustering algorithms for community discovery, we need to determine the number of community firstly. When the number of communities is too small, the MAE value will be high because some neighbor users are worthless to the target users. When the number of communities is too large, the MAE value will be high because the reference scores are few. Results of collaborative filtering evaluation of the three clustering methods are shown in Fig. 2.

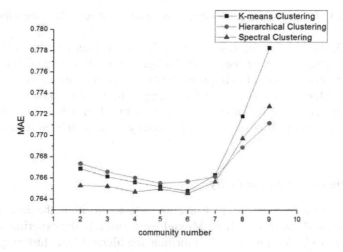

Fig. 2. Community number VS. MAE

In Fig. 2, the abscissa represents number of community division and the ordinate represents MAE values. From the figure,we know that the three kinds of community discovery method have similar results. And the MAE value attains a minimum when it is 6. So the number of community will be 6 in following experiments and analysis.

Comparison of filling methods
Many filling methods are effective as the user-item rating matrix is extremely sparse. Therefore, we use different methods to fill missing values and compare results of each method to prove that the CF-average algorithm is more effective. The first method is the average-filling, which fills missing value with the average score of corresponding film. The second method is the CF-filling, which uses collaborative filtering to predict partial missing values, and remainder missing values will be filled with 0. The last method is the CF-average filling. Results of each method are shown in Fig. 3.

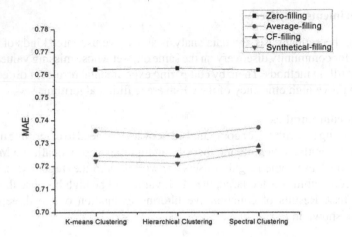

Fig. 3. Results of community discovery by using different filling algorithms

In Fig. 3, the abscissa represents clustering algorithms and the ordinate represents MAE values. It can be seen from the figure, the CF-average filling algorithm is the most effective method to improve the quality of community discovery among these filling algorithms. Thus, the CF-average filling algorithm proposed has a significant effect on the optimization of sparsity problem, which improve both the quality of community discovery and the accuracy of personalized recommendation system.

4.4   Experiments of Applicability

In experiment of effectiveness of CF-average filling algorithm, the dataset we use is scores of the top-1200 movies from MovieLens dataset. In the experiment about the applicability of CF-Average filling algorithm, the hierarchical clustering algorithm is selected to do clustering with other 5 datasets of different sparsity by the same way as the experiment does above. Then, results of both the 5 datasets and the experiment of effectiveness are compared with each other to verify that the CF-Average filling algorithm is equally applicable and effective in data sets of different sparsity. The results are shown in Fig. 4, Tables 1 and 2.

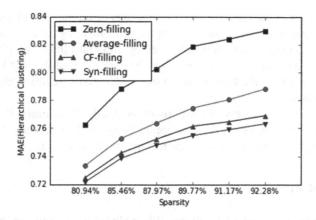

Fig. 4. Community discovery by using different sparse datasets and filling algorithms

Table 1. Hierarchical clustering by using different sparse datasets and filling algorithms.

Data set	Sparsity	Zero-filling	Average-filling
①	80.94%	[86,466,117,244,60,227]	[344,200,172,219,237,28]
②	85.46%	[220,79,125,81,225,470]	[321,180,130,447,23,99]
③	87.97%	[133,142,685,29,124,87]	[44,587,214,143,102,110]
④	89.77%	[61,791,36,28,39,245]	[220,65,568,327,90,32]
⑤	91.17%	[488,348,1,170,2,191]	[411,210,462,8,104,5]
⑥	92.28%	[110,141,8,931,3,7]	[690,10,353,14,127,6]

Table 2. Hierarchical clustering by using different sparse datasets and filling algorithms.

Data set	Sparsity	CF-filling	Synthetical-filling (CF-Average-filling)
①	80.94%	[98,380,114,144,101,363]	[137,198,161,220,318,166]
②	85.46%	[222,92,128,211,82,465]	[109,118,329,296,159,189]
③	87.97%	[118,402,71,192,369,49]	[96,175,285,149,331,164]
④	89.77%	[252,85,62,109,532,140]	[184,129,319,69,230,269]
⑤	91.17%	[531,94,117,328,70,40]	[142,301,82,131,410,134]
⑥	92.28%	[638,63,233,46,95,125]	[370,73,28,181,443,105]

In Fig. 4, the abscissa represents the sparsity of dataset and the ordinate represents MAE values. From the figure we can know that the MAE value of experimental result increased with the increase of sparsity of dataset. Comparison of the experimental results of different filling algorithms by using the same data set shows that CF-Average filling algorithm is the most effective method to improve the quality of community discovery among the three filling algorithms. This conclusion is consistent with the experimental results above.

As can be seen from Tables 1 and 2, the results of community discovery become worse and worse with the increase of data sparsity. Comparing the experimental results of using the same data set which is optimized by different filling algorithms, it can be found that the size of community discovery is the most homogeneous and the quality of community discovery is the best when we use the CF-Average filling algorithm to fill the missing values.

To sum up, for the data sets with different sparsity, the CF-average filling algorithm proposed in this paper has the extensive applicability and Effectiveness for optimizing the data sparsity problem of personalized recommendation system.

5   Conclusion

In this paper, we propose the CF-average filling algorithm to optimize the sparse data set of personalized recommendation system based on the collaborative filtering algorithm and the average filling method. Three kinds of clustering algorithms, including K-means clustering, hierarchical clustering and spectral clustering, are used for community discovery based on the optimized data sets. Results reveal that the problem of data sparsity of the personalized recommendation system is optimized and its accuracy is improved by 7.53% averagely when compare with other methods, and the CF-Average filling algorithm is universally applicable and effective in solving the problem of data sparsity of the personalized recommendation system. We would like to study the cold start problem of collaborative filtering and the community finding and evaluating the quality of communities on the basis of all users in future work.

Acknowledgement. This work was supported by National Natural Science Foundation of China (61472389) and the National Key Technology R&D Program of China under Contract (2015BAK22B02).

References

1. Little, R.J.A., Rubin, D.B.: Statistical Analysis with Missing Data. Wiley, New York (2014)
2. Sun, X.: Research on Sparsity and Cold-Tart Problem in Collaborative Filtering. Zhejiang University, Hangzhou (2005)
3. Deng, A., Zuo, Z., Zu, Y.: Collaborative filtering recommendation algorithm based on item clustering. Mini-Micro Syst. **25**(9), 1665–1670 (2004)
4. Yang, Y.: Research on Item-based Clustering of Collaborative Filtering Recommendation Algorithm. Northeast Normal University, Jilin (2005)
5. Breese, J.S., Heckerman, D., Kadie, C.: Empirical analysis of predictive algorithms for collaborative filtering. In: Proceedings of the Fourteenth Conference on Uncertainty in Artificial Intelligence. Morgan Kaufmann Publishers Inc. (1998)
6. Benesty, J., Chen, J., Huang, Y., Cohen, I.: Pearson correlation coefficient. In: Noise Reduction in Speech Processing. Springer Topics in Signal Processing, vol. 2, pp. 1–4. Springer, Heidelberg (2009). https://doi.org/10.1007/978-3-642-00296-0_5
7. Huang, F., Zhang, S., Zu, X.: Discovering network community based on multi-objective optimization. J. Softw. **24**(9), 2062–2077 (2013)

8. Lei, X., Xie, K., Lin, X.: An efficient clustering algorithm based on K-Means local optimality. J. Softw. **19**(7), 1683–1692 (2008)
9. Ng, A.Y., Jordan, M.I., Weiss, Y.: On spectral clustering: Analysis and an algorithm. Adv. Neural. Inf. Process. Syst. **2**, 849–856 (2002)
10. Newman, M.E.J., Girvan, M.: Finding and evaluating community structure in networks. Phys. Rev. E **69**(2), 1–15 (2004). 026113

Cold-Start Group Profiling
with a Clustering-Coupled Topic Model

Zhijian Jiang[1], Yanfeng Wang[1(✉)], Weiyuan Chen[1], Xie Wang[2], Ya Zhang[1],
Jianping Mei[3], and Zhuowei Huang[3]

[1] Cooperative Medianet Innovation Center, Shanghai Jiao Tong University,
Shanghai, China
wangyanfeng@sjtu.edu.cn
[2] National Engineering Research Center of Digital Television, Shanghai, China
[3] China Central Television, Beijing, China

Abstract. While interactive television enables a new user-centered TV
mode, catering to the tastes of TV users is one of the most critical tasks
in delivering interactive TV experience. It faces two key challenges. First,
the user behaviors on TV are much sparser than those of the internet
users, thus making the modeling of user preferences more challenging.
Second, an TV account is usually associated with multiple individuals
in a family, making it difficult to discriminate the preferences of individual family members. In this paper, we thus propose a novel Clustering-
Coupled Topic Model (CCTM), which characterizes user profile only by
analyzing user viewing behaviors without any program metadata. This
model clusters the users into different groups, then access the group
preference for program recommendation by coupling the interest of different users in the same cluster group. We validate the performance of
the CCTM with real-world data from a national interactive TV program.
The experimental results have demonstrated that the CCTM can reasonably extract the users' potential preference, which is further leveraged to
recommend programs to the users.

Keywords: User profile · Group recommendation
Interactive television · User view behaviours
Clustering-Coupled Topic Model

1 Introduction

Digital interactive television provides more interactive experience in terms of
applications, services and interactions, compared to traditional television [1]. It
also raises the opportunity of delivering personalized content to the viewer [2].
Thus, television suppliers need to identify model user behavior by analyzing user
log [3–5]. However on user profile there are 2 key challenges - data sparsity and
multi-user mix problem. The inconvenient operations on television remote control limit user's viewing resulting in the Sparse user behavior. On the contrary,

© Springer Nature Singapore Pte Ltd. 2018
G. Zhai et al. (Eds.): IFTC 2017, CCIS 815, pp. 334–342, 2018.
https://doi.org/10.1007/978-981-10-8108-8_31

the convenience of Internet page jumps is accompanied by a lot of clicks. Multi-user mix problem means that an TV account is usually shared by more than one members in a family who may have different preferences, which make it difficult to model each member. In practice, user behavior logs are usually treated as documents, in which user is analogous to document and each viewing content is analogous to words in corresponding documents. Thus, topic model [6] can be applied to the documents to model the user preferences and content in vectors. In addition, document clustering [7] can also be utilized to organize similar users into groups, which is significant for user modeling and user preference visualization. Basically, we can perform user clustering method, such as K-means and spectral clustering [8], based on user vectors generated by topic model. Applying them separately fails to capture the coherence between topic and cluster. Recent work [9] shows that applying topic model for document clustering significantly improves the performance of topic model.

The assumption is reliable that correlation the programs a user frequently watches reveal the his/her preference. The analysis for interactive television users' behaviour will be helpful for catering to the tastes of TV users. However, there are some difficulties brought by the sparse user log and the constitutional complexity of an TV account. In this paper, we propose a novel Clustering-Coupled Topic Model (CCTM) in order to model interactive television users' behaviour. Our chief contribution are as follows: (1) We develop a novel Clustering-Coupled Topic Model which incorporate topic model and document clustering. And we derive approximate inference for the model. (2) Based on the proposed model, we extract the user preference from user log and then recommend programs to users.

We experiment the proposed model with a real-world data set provided by a national interactive TV in China. Our analysis has revealed that proposed CCTM is able to cluster users with coherent interest into groups. There is a promising improvement in evaluation index when we further leverage the proposed CCTM for personalized program recommendation.

The rest of the paper is organized as follows. Section 2 introduce the LDA model and the Clustering-Coupled Topic Model. Section 3 introduce the real data and the experiments analysis. Finally, Sect. 4 conclude the paper.

2   Clustering-Coupled Topic Model for Group Profiling

In this section we will introduce the Clustering-Coupled Topic Model for Interactive television user behaviors, which leverages the viewing behaviors to give user profile. Firstly, We introduce how LDA and kmeans may be used to cluster users as well as group profiling. Then we present the structure of the proposed clustering-coupled topic model, including the generative process of the model and the variational inference method.

2.1   LDA Model and Cluster Algorithm Help Group Profiling

A hypothesis is proposed that user viewing process is the embodiment of user interest, an interactive account responding to a family with various interests, and each interest may be expressed as the distribution of television programs. Based on such hypothesis, the LDA model will be adapted to fit the process of user viewing which can be divided into two-step. First, a single interest is selected based on an interest distribution that is sampled from a Dirichlet distribution. Second, a TV program is chosen according to the multinomial distribution that the chosen interest over programs. As result, the generative process for each viewing behaviour is presented below:

(1) Choose $\theta_d \sim Dir(\alpha)$, where the $Dir(\alpha)$ is the Dirichlet distribution of the parameter α.
(2) For each viewing n, where $\forall 1 \leq n \leq N_d$.
    (a) choose an interest $z_{d,n} \sim Multinomial(\theta_d)$.
    (b) choose a TV program $w_{d,n}$ from $p(w_{d,n}|z_{d,n}, \beta)$, a multinomial conditional probability where the interest is $z_{d,n}$.

The Fig. 1 shows the details of the graphical model of LDA. With the LDA model, each family account will be represented by a vector by the distribution over the interests, where each interest is responsible for generating the TV programs.

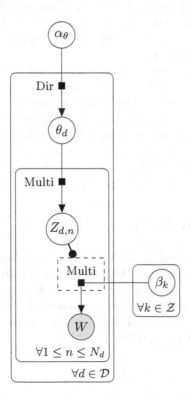

Fig. 1. Latent Dirichlet Allocation (LDA) topic model

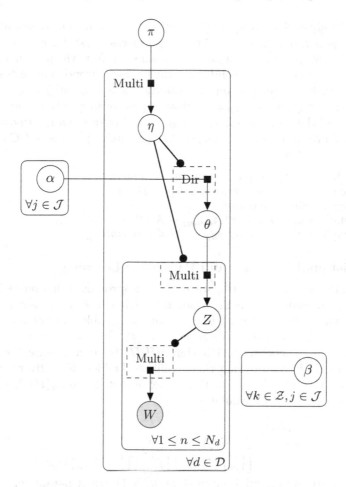

Fig. 2. Clustering-coupled topic model

The results of LDA model facilitate clustering, the K-means algorithm can be using in the interest space to obtain clusters. As result, the group profiling is characterized under the help of LDA model and K-means. However, this strategy that performing LDA model and cluster separately ignores their interaction and the chicken-and-egg relationship. Performing the topic models and clustering jointly contributes to promote each other to realize the global optimal.

2.2 Clustering-Coupled Topic Model

The clustering-coupled topic model is shown in Fig. 2. Given a corpus containing $\mathcal{D}$ user accounts $d \in \mathcal{D}$, there is a assume that user accounts inherently belong to $\mathcal{J}$ groups $j \in \mathcal{J}$. Each group j possess a group-specific Dirichlet prior parameter α_j as well as K group-specific local topics $\beta_{j,k}$.

With the clustering-group LDA model, the viewing behaviors of a family account are generated through a three-step process. First, for each family, associated with a group indicator, a group η_d is sampled from the multinomial distribution parametrized by π. Second, we sample a local proportion vector θ_{η_d} from the group Dirichlet prior α_{η_d} on the condition where group $j = \eta_d$. Third, for each viewing n, an interest z_{d,n,η_d} is picked up according to the local proportion vector θ_{η_d}, and then a program $w_{d,n}$ is generated from the a multinomial conditional probability $p(w_{d,n}|z_{d,n,\eta_d}, \beta_{j,k})$. The generative process of CCTM can be summarized as follows:

(1) For each account, sample a group $\eta_d \sim Multi(\pi)$.
(2) Sample group interest proportion $\theta_{\eta_d} \sim Dir(\alpha_{\eta_d})$.
(3) For each viewing behaviour.
    (a) sample a group interest $z_{d,n,\eta_d} \sim Multinomial(\theta_{\eta_d})$.
    (b) sample a TV program $w_{d,n} \sim Multinomial(\beta_{j,k})$

2.3   Variational Inference and Parameter Learning

Using variational inference [10], we perform approximate inference help solve the critical inference problem what estimating the posterior distribution $p(H|w, \Pi)$, where $H = \{\eta, \theta, z\}$ refer to latent variables, w are observed variables and model parameters are $\Pi = \{\pi, \alpha, \beta\}$. The basic idea of variational inference is emply another distribution $q(H|\Omega)$ to approximate the true posterior $p(H|w, \Pi)$ by minimizing their Kullback-Leibler (KL) divergence, where model parameters $\Omega = \{\zeta, \mu, \phi\}$. The model of distribution $q(H|\Omega)$ is shown in Fig. 3, the mathematical formulation is

$$
\begin{aligned}
&q(H|\Omega) \\
&= q(\eta, \theta, z|\zeta, \mu, \phi) \\
&= q(\eta|\zeta) \prod_{j=1}^{J} q(\theta_j|\mu_j) \prod_{i=1}^{N} \prod_{j=1}^{J} q(z_{i,j}|\phi_{i,j})
\end{aligned}
\tag{1}
$$

where ζ, $\phi_{i,j}$ are multinomial parameters, μ_j is Dirichlet parameter.

The process of variational inference is divided into E-step and M-step, and the result are shown as follows.

In E-step, we optimize the variational parameters while keeping model parameters fixed

$$
\begin{aligned}
\zeta_j \propto \pi_j exp\{log\Gamma(\textstyle\sum_{k=1}^{K} \alpha_{j,k}) - \sum_{k=1}^{K} log(\Gamma\alpha_{j,k}) \\
+ \textstyle\sum_{k=1}^{K}(\alpha_{j,k} - 1)[\Psi(\mu_{j,k}) - \Psi(\sum_{t=1}^{K} \mu_{j,t})]\}
\end{aligned}
\tag{2}
$$

$$
\mu_{j,k} = \zeta_j(\alpha_{j,k} - 1) + \textstyle\sum_{n=1}^{N} \zeta_j \phi_{j,i,k} + 1
\tag{3}
$$

$$
\phi_{j,i,k} \propto exp\{\Psi(\mu_{j,k}) - \Psi(\textstyle\sum_{t=1}^{K} \mu_{j,t}) + \sum_{v=1}^{V} w_i^v log\beta_{j,k}^v\}
\tag{4}
$$

In M-step, the variational parameters is fixed, we optimize the model parameters by maximizing the lower bound

$$
\pi_j \propto \textstyle\sum_{d=1}^{D} \zeta_{d,j}
\tag{5}
$$

$$
\beta_{j,k,v} \propto \textstyle\sum_{d=1}^{D} \sum_{i=1}^{N_d} \zeta_j \phi_{d,i,j,k} w_{d,i}^v
\tag{6}
$$

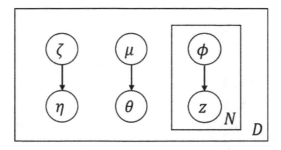

Fig. 3. Approximate model of clustering-coupled topic model

3 Datasets and Experiments

We validate our model on a real-world data set provided by a national interactive TV in China. The entire data covers the user from January 2017 to July of the viewing behaviour, and contains 200,025 families and 9,580 TV programs.

The Fig. 4 and Table 1 show the user viewing curve, less than 20% users posses more than 6 viewings and more than half of the user's viewing behavior is less than twice. Then the Fig. 5 and Table 2 describe the times that the program is viewed, more than half of programs posses less than 50 clicks. These tables and curves clearly illustrate that most people view few program and most programs possess lower click times. In fact, the user's behaviour in this data set is much sparser than the Movielens, with the sparsity of 0.000618, which is a serious problem to analyze user preference.

The Clustering-Coupled Topic Model is proposed here to model the sparse user log. Table 3 shows some actual interactive activities. Each record contains the family account ID (CAID), the program ID (PID), the program title (TITLE) and the program channel (CHANNEL), while only user account and program ID are needed in the Clustering-Coupled Topic Model.

In experiments, the number of groups J is set to 20 and the number of topics every group K is set to 10. Meanwhile other parameters are randomly initialized. The CCTM clusters the users into different group: Fig. 6 shows some group profiling by the form of presenting the most associated programs. Obviously, different groups have different preferences for different types of programs. For example, the group on the right side of the picture consists of the programs that most are provided from channel CCTV8. However, the group users represented on the upper-lift corner are more likely to be related to the programs from CCTV1 channel.

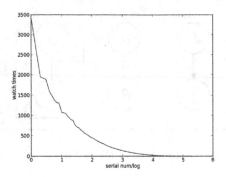

Fig. 4. The curve about the user viewing counts

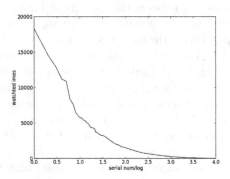

Fig. 5. The curve about the viewed times of every program

Table 1. User average viewing counts

Segment ratio	View counts
0% - 10%	43.11
10% - 20%	6.91
20% - 30%	3.72
30% - 40%	2.51
40% - 50%	2.01
50% - 60%	1.26
60% - 70%	1.23
70% - 80%	1.12
80% - 90%	1.03
90% -100%	1.01

Table 2. Watched times of program

Segment ratio	Watched times
0% - 10%	830.4
10% - 20%	189.8
20% - 30%	112.2
30% - 40%	73.7
40% - 50%	50.8
50% - 60%	33.1
60% - 70%	19.3
70% - 80%	10.1
80% - 90%	4.1
90% -100%	1.4

Table 3. Example records of interactive activities

	CAID	PID	TITLE	CHANNEL
1	0x12324321348953	VIDA1468554199296462	Journey to the West	CCTV8
2	0x12893223432134	VIDA1468567043464536	Tale of White Snake	CCTV11
3	0x13424238957845	VIDE1468566577362380	Snooker	CCTV5

Table 4. Recommendation classical evaluation index

	Precision	Recall	F-Measure
CCTM	0.046308	0.093905	0.047008
LDA	0.027296	0.062598	0.028389
Hot	0.002301	0.005536	0.002387
Random	0.000791	0.001570	0.000747

Fig. 6. Group profiling represented by program title

Furthermore, we apply the result of group profiling for program recommendation. The Table 4 shows that the CCTM has a good improvement on the classical evaluation index including precision, recall or F-Measure when compared to the baseline. Random means the random program recommendation, and the Hot is defined that providing the most popular programs for everyone. LDA refers to the personalized recommendation according to the classical topic model [6]. Apparently, the CCTM achieves the best performance in program recommendation.

4 Conclusion

We propose a novel Clustering-Coupled Topic Model, which takes into account various user interactive viewing behaviours to access implicit user preferences. The largest advantage of this model is the compatibility that only user behaviours are required. Even with the lack of any program metadata or family structure, this model would still obtain user interests from their viewing, and then cluster different users into different group and characterize group profiling by the vector of interests or programs. Furthermore, we validate the performance of the CCTM with real-world data from a national interactive TV. The experimental results have demonstrated that the CCTM can reasonably extract the users' potential preference, which can be further leveraged to recommend programs to the users.

In the future, one direction of this study is extend our model to semi-supervised or supervised clustering settings, for the reason the prior knowledge on family structure is sometimes available.

References

1. Jan, D.V., Peters, O., Heuvelman, A.: Interactive television or enhanced television? The Dutch users interest in applications of ITV via set-top boxes. In: Annual Meeting of the International Communication Association ICA (2017)
2. Cho, J.H., Sah, Y.J., Ryu, J.: A new content-related advertising model for interactive television. In: IEEE International Symposium on Broadband Multimedia Systems and Broadcasting, pp. 1–9. IEEE (2008)
3. Branch, P., Egan, G., Tonkin, B.: Modeling interactive behavior of a video based multimedia system. In: Proceedings of the IEEE International Conference on Communications, pp. 978–982 (1999)
4. Gopalakrishnan, V., Jana, R., Knag, R., Ramakrishnan, K., Swayne, D., Vaishampayan, V.: Characterizing interactive behavior in a large-scale operational IPTV environment. In: Proceedings IEEE INFOCOM 2010, pp. 1–5 (2010)
5. Zhang, Y., Chen, W., Zha, H., et al.: A time-topic coupled LDA model for IPTV user behaviors. IEEE Trans. Broadcasting **61**(1), 56–65 (2015)
6. Blei, D.M., Ng, A.Y., Jordan, M.I.: Latent dirichlet allocation. J. Mach. Learn. Res. **3**, 9931022 (2003)
7. Aggarwal, C.C., Zhai, C.: A survey of text clustering algorithms. In: Aggarwal, C., Zhai, C. (eds.) Mining Text Data. Springer, Boston (2012). https://doi.org/10.1007/978-1-4614-3223-4_4
8. Ng, A.Y., Jordan, M.I., Weiss, Y., et al.: On spectral clustering: analysis and an algorithm. In: Advances in Neural Information Processing Systems, vol. 2, pp. 849–856 (2002)
9. Xie, P., Xing, E.P.: Integrating document clustering and topic modeling. In: Proceedings of the 29th International Conference on Uncertainty in Artificial Intelligence (2013)
10. Wainwright, M.J., Jordan, M.I.: Graphical models, exponential families, and variational inference. Found. Trends@ Mach. Learn. **1**(1–2), 1–305 (2008)

Predicting Relative Popularity via an End-to-End Multi-modality Model

Hongxiang Cai[1]([✉]), Ya Zhang[1], Yanfeng Wang[1], Xie Wang[2], Jianping Mei[3], and Zhuowei Huang[3]

[1] Cooperative Medianet Innovation Center, Shanghai Jiao Tong University, Shanghai 200240, China
{chxtc001,ya_zhang,wangyanfeng}@sjtu.edu.cn
[2] National Engineering Research Center of Digital Television, Shanghai, China
seaname@outlook.com
[3] China Central Television, Beijing, China
{meijianping,huangzhuowei713}@cctv.com

Abstract. Popularity prediction is important for many applications such as service design, network management and so on. Among several factors affecting popularity, content plays a key role, especially when we lack the time sequence data of historical consumption. However, exploring the influence of content-factors on popularity is not easy because of the increasing heterogeneous modalities and their sophisticated inner interplay. In this paper, we utilize several modes to predict popularity. In the meanwhile, considering that it is difficult and little significant to predict the exact number of popularity, we aim to rank pairs of content which is called relative popularity prediction. We cast the relative popularity prediction problem as a classification task and propose an end-to-end multi-modality model with the help of deep neural network. This model combines visual and textual information, maps them to a common feature space and implicitly constructs the interaction between them. Experimental result on real-world data has demonstrated the effectiveness of our model.

Keywords: Relative popularity · Multi-modality
Deep neural network · End-to-End

1 Introduction

With the rise and development of the Internet, thousands of user-generated content is uploaded to the web every minute. The overwhelming amount of content makes it difficult for users to find their interest. Meanwhile, it is also a great challenge for service providers as content services have high demand on transmission bandwidth due to the increasing consumption behavior on user-generated content. Therefore, effective and timely discovery of popular content is a key to solve these problems. It can also help users reduce the clutter and

© Springer Nature Singapore Pte Ltd. 2018
G. Zhai et al. (Eds.): IFTC 2017, CCIS 815, pp. 343–353, 2018.
https://doi.org/10.1007/978-981-10-8108-8_32

focus their attention on the most valuable and relevant content. Moreover, the optimization of network management, delivery strategies and other applications all require knowledge of content popularity.

Popularity of UGC (User Generated Content) is affected by multiple factors such as content itself, time effects, social factors (e.g., which authors are already popular) and so on. Previous work has demonstrated that popularity can be strongly dependent on those non-content factors. Yet content-factors should not be dismissed in popularity prediction, especially when we lack the historical time sequence data of content consumption. And this is a common situation in real world. In addition, content consists of many modes like images, text, videos and audio. These modes influence popularity under interaction with each other. Having better understanding on the sophisticated interplay between these modes can help content providers provide more attractive content to users.

In this paper, we focus on the influence of content-factors on popularity and aim to rank pairs of content in the consideration that it is difficult and unnecessary to predict the exact number of popularity. This problem is called relative popularity prediction. We cast this problem as a classification task and propose an end-to-end multi-modality model based on deep neural network. This model maps image and text to a shared feature space, and implicitly constructs the interplay between them. We conduct experiments on real-world data and results show the effectiveness of our proposed model.

The reminder of this paper is organized as follows: related work is introduced in Sect. 2. Section 3 presents our proposed model in predicting relative popularity. Experiments and results are detailed in Sect. 4. Finally, Sect. 5 concludes this paper.

2   Related Work

In this section, we briefly review some existing work on popularity prediction. Szabo et al. [17] proposed S-H model to predict long-term popularity after observing a strong linear correlation between early and long-term popularity when they are log-transformed. Pinto et al. [16] extended this model with taking early dynamics into consideration and proposed ML and MRBF model. In [18], Support Vector Regression (SVR) was adopted with combining time series features, visual features and social features. Except for methods based on regression model, there are other techniques to predict popularity. Hidden Markov Model (HMM) was used to predict the peak day in [12]. Wu et al. [19] proposed a stochastic fluid model to capture information spreading process and user reaction process. In [2], influence-based self-excited Hawkes process was used to build a probabilistic model.

All above works are based on the observation of historical time series, and could not be used when user generated content is just uploaded or even not uploaded. Consequently, content is particularly important and needs to be used to predict popularity when we lack time series data. [9] excluded non-content factors and explored the influence of content-factors on popularity. But [9] simply concatenated features extracted from image and text, and did not consider interplay between these two modes. In addition, [9] did not use an end-to-end model to predict popularity. To solve these problems, we build an end-to-end model and constructs interaction between these two modes to predict popularity.

3   Our Proposed Model

In this section, we will detail our end-to-end multi-modality model. Our model consists of two branches for representing image and text separately, in the meanwhile, it establishes shared representation and implicitly constructs the interaction between these two different modalities. Moreover, we adopt shared parameters to generate representations for pair content and use these two representations to predict relative popularity. Figure 1 shows the overall framework of our proposed model.

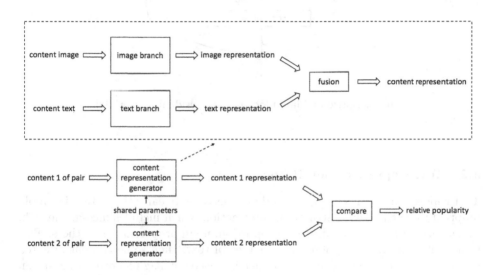

Fig. 1. Overall framework of our proposed model

3.1   Image Representation Branch

Recently, deep convolutional neural networks have gained great success in a range of vision tasks such as classification [13], object detection [6] and so on. Compared with traditional methods generating features like HOG [4], GIST [15] and SIFT [14], CNNs can learn robust and high-level semantic features for images, moreover, they can be trained end-to-end. Thus we choose one of widely used CNN architectures to be the component of our image representation branch.

The basic architecture we used is called Deep Residual Network [8] and the prominent characteristics is its "bottleneck" building blocks (shown in Fig. 2) which form a deep residual learning framework. This architecture addresses the degradation problem and greatly increases the depth of network. The family of deep residual network has 18, 34, 50, 101 and 132 layers' architectures, we choose ResNet50 and remove the last fully connected layer which is for classification task on ImageNet [5]. In addition, we add a random initialized fully connected layer to the average pool layer to generate image feature. Figure 3 shows the architecture of our image representation branch. The left number in Fig. 3 equals to the number of bottle building blocks.

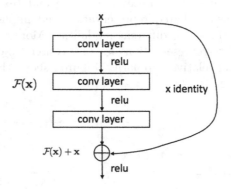

Fig. 2. Bottle building block of deep residual network [8]

3.2 Text Representation Branch

Text representation has been explored over decades. In early times, text is simply mapped to features with structural information which includes message length, punctuation proportion, adjective proportion, noun proportion and others. This representation entirely ignores the content of text, then some content-oriented models were proposed. Unigram model is based on bag-of-words assumption and maps each text to a vector of binary indicator variables. [10] has shown the effectiveness of bag-of-words assumption for some benchmarks. Another popular no-order text representation model is topic model, and it learns topic distribution in text with the help of variants of LDA [3]. Recently deep recurrent neural network has been applied widely in natural language processing, and these models take the order information of words into consideration. LSTM [11] and Bi-LSTM [7] are some successful examples based on RNN architecture.

According to the results of [9] comparing multiple text representations and inspired by the architecture proposed in [20], we decide to use unigram features as text descriptor. In the meanwhile, n stacked triplets of fully connected (FC) layer is adopted for text representation branch. The architecture is depicted in Fig. 4.

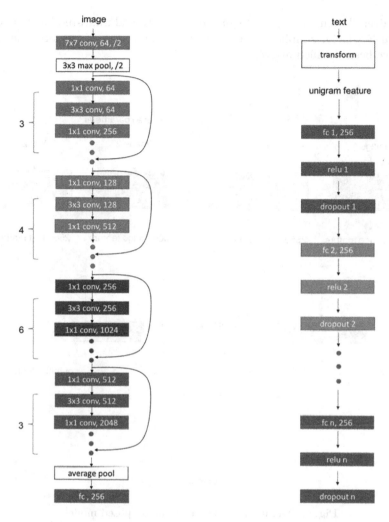

Fig. 3. Image representation branch   **Fig. 4.** Text representation branch

3.3   Pairwise Model

After detailing branches for image and text, we then use these two branches
to complete our final end-to-end multi-modality model. Firstly, we concatenate
output features of the two branches directly. Then we add a fully connected layer
to the concatenated output with the aim to construct a shared and discriminative representation for the two different modalities, in the meanwhile, this layer
implicitly models the interaction between image and text. After that, since we
get the shared representation of content, we adopt the way of pairwise learning-
to-rank and use the difference of pair content representations to accomplish our
relative popularity prediction task. In the end, we cast the task as a classification
task and use hinge loss to train our model.

The overall architecture of our proposed end-to-end multi-modality model is shown in Fig. 5, for simplicity, we omit the architectures of two branches since they have been detailed above.

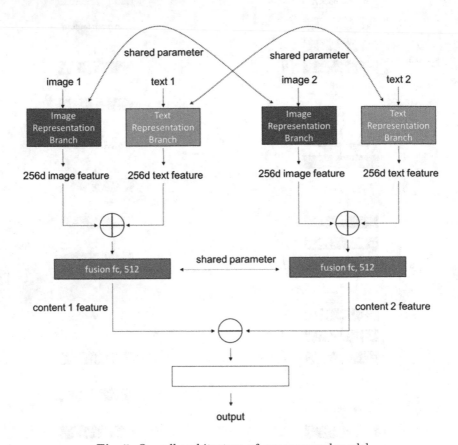

Fig. 5. Overall architecture of our proposed model

4   Experiment

4.1   Datasets

We conduct experiments on real-world datasets released by [9]. These datasets collect pairs of posts submitted to the same Reddit community in close time and each post has a score based on the number of upvotes minus the number of downvotes. This quantity is widely used as the measure of popularity. We choose some of communities covered by raw datasets and they are **aww**, **pics**, **cats**, and **RedditLaqueristas**. Figure 6 shows some examples of posts in these communities. As can be seen, images and captions differ from each other in different communities.

Fig. 6. Random selected samples from communities

We download raw images from imgur since they are not provided directly by the datasets. After removing corrupt and duplicated images, we do some statistics like [9] to check the quality of the clean datasets. Tables 1 and 2 show the statistical results of the datasets before and after clean. The statistical content includes the maximum and average window sizes, the median and average difference, along with the number of posts in every community. We can see that there is little difference between these two results, and the datasets maintain high quality.

In the meanwhile, [9] presents the human annotation accuracy results (shown in Table 3.) to validate that relative popularity prediction task is neither trivial nor impossible. Besides, [9] provides a baseline for the task.

Table 1. Before clean

	Max/Avg Win	Med/Avg Diff	Pairs
pics	30/15 s	117/478	44 K
aww	30/15 s	90/393	33 K
cats	15/7 min	69/231	15 K
RL	30/14 min	56/118	9 K

Table 2. After clean

	Max/Avg Win	Med/Avg Diff	Pairs
pics	29/15 s	117/476	44 K
aww	29/15 s	90/393	33 K
cats	15/7 min	69/231	15 K
RL	30/14 min	56/118	9 K

Table 3. Human annotation accuracy

	aww	pics	cats	RL
Humans	60.0	63.6	59.6	67.2

4.2 Implementation

For datasets, we adopt random 80/20 train/test split, and use scores of pairs to generate ground truth. In addition, we withhold 10% of training data as a validation set to monitor overfitting and stop training in early time.

For model training, we use parameters of pretrained ResNet50 on ImageNet to initialize our image representation branch, and randomly initialize other parameters. Due to different initialization methods, we set different learning rates to different layers. The learning rate of image representation branch is relatively low and ranges from 0.00001 to 0.0001 since this branch has a good start point. As consisting of upper layers and initialized randomly, text representation branch needs relatively high learning rate ranging from 0.001 to 0.01 according to specified datasets. Learning rate in other parameters is set from 0.001 to 0.005. To avoid overfitting, we add dropout layers and a weight decay of 0.0001 into our model.

All architectures are implemented with an open-source deep learning library [1], and we use NVIDIA GeForce Titan X 12 GB GPU to accelerate training speed.

4.3   Results

Since we cast the relative popularity prediction as a classification task, we use accuracy to measure the performance of our proposed model. [9] has conduct several experiments on this task and we use these results as our baseline. Table 4 shows all results.

Table 4. Accuracy results

	aww	pics	cats	RL
Unigram in [9]	59.7	58.6	59.5	60.8
ResNet50 in [9]	64.8	60.0	62.6	64.2
Text + Image in [9]	67.1	62.7	65.9	66.4
Our model	**68.3**	**63.2**	**66.3**	**68.8**

As can be seen in Table 4, our model has better performance than baseline model in these datasets. And it should be noted that this task is challenging and worth exploring deeper.

Moreover, previous work has observed that image can be more predictive than text for predicting relative popularity, and this is demonstrated in [9] too (see ResNet50 in [9] compared with Unigram in [9]). We would like to see the ability of our image representation branch in predicting relative popularity. Table 5 shows the performance of our image representation branch. Surprisingly, we find our image branch performance also surpasses the baseline image model.

Table 5. Image representation branch performancel

	aww	pics	cats	RL
ResNet50 in [9]	64.8	60.0	62.6	64.2
Image representation branch	**65.8**	**60.2**	**63.5**	**66.9**

In addition, we modify the pairwise architecture and score a post directly (shown in Fig. 7). It is noted that this score is different from real score received in Reddit, but we can have intuitionistic understanding on what our model has learned from these specified datasets through this method. Here we select **aww** dataset and Fig. 8 shows examples of high, median, and low scores calculated by our model. As we can see, high score is not simply obtained with high quality image and long text. Interaction has been considered in our model. Moreover, community-specific preference has also been learned by our model and we think dogs are more popular in aww.

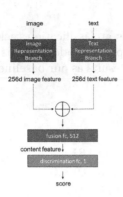

Fig. 7. Our modified model to score post

Fig. 8. Top, middle, low rows represent examples with high, median and low scores.

5   Conclusion

In this paper, we propose an end-to-end multi-modality model to predict relative popularity. Our model consists of two branches for representing image and text. For image representation branch, we use the residual network architecture to map image to high-level semantic feature. For text representation branch, we adopt n stacked triplets of fully connected (FC) layer to represent text. In the meanwhile, our model implicitly constructs the interaction between these two different modalities and outputs a shared and discriminative representation for content. In the end, we use the difference of two content representations to predict relative popularity. Experiments on real-world datasets have shown the effectiveness of our proposed model, and demonstrate the importance of taking interplay into consideration.

References

1. Abadi, M., Agarwal, A., Barham, P., Brevdo, E., Chen, Z., Citro, C., Corrado, G.S., Davis, A., Dean, J., Devin, M., et al.: Tensorflow: large-scale machine learning on heterogeneous distributed systems. arXiv preprint arXiv:1603.04467 (2016)
2. Bao, P.: Modeling and predicting popularity dynamics via an influence-based self-excited hawkes process. In: Proceedings of the 25th ACM International on Conference on Information and Knowledge Management, pp. 1897–1900. ACM (2016)
3. Blei, D.M., Ng, A.Y., Jordan, M.I.: Latent dirichlet allocation. J. Mach. Learn. Res. **3**, 993–1022 (2003). http://dl.acm.org/citation.cfm?id=944919.944937
4. Dalal, N., Triggs, B.: Histograms of oriented gradients for human detection. In: IEEE Computer Society Conference on Computer Vision and Pattern Recognition, CVPR 2005, vol. 1, pp. 886–893. IEEE (2005)
5. Deng, J., Dong, W., Socher, R., Li, L.J., Li, K., Fei-Fei, L.: Imagenet: a large-scale hierarchical image database. In: IEEE Conference on Computer Vision and Pattern Recognition, CVPR 2009, pp. 248–255. IEEE (2009)

6. Girshick, R., Donahue, J., Darrell, T., Malik, J.: Rich feature hierarchies for accurate object detection and semantic segmentation. In: Proceedings of the IEEE Conference on Computer Vision and Pattern Recognition, pp. 580–587 (2014)
7. Graves, A., Schmidhuber, J.: Framewise phoneme classification with bidirectional lstm and other neural network architectures. Neural Netw. **18**(5), 602–610 (2005)
8. He, K., Zhang, X., Ren, S., Sun, J.: Deep residual learning for image recognition. In: Proceedings of the IEEE Conference on Computer Vision and Pattern Recognition, pp. 770–778 (2016)
9. Hessel, J., Lee, L., Mimno, D.: Cats and captions vs. creators and the clock: comparing multimodal content to context in predicting relative popularity. In: Proceedings of the 26th International Conference on World Wide Web, pp. 927–936. International World Wide Web Conferences Steering Committee (2017)
10. Hill, F., Cho, K., Korhonen, A.: Learning distributed representations of sentences from unlabelled data. arXiv preprint arXiv:1602.03483 (2016)
11. Hochreiter, S., Schmidhuber, J.: Long short-term memory. Neural Comput. **9**(8), 1735–1780 (1997)
12. Jiang, L., Miao, Y., Yang, Y., Lan, Z., Hauptmann, A.G.: Viral video style: a closer look at viral videos on Youtube. In: Proceedings of International Conference on Multimedia Retrieval, p. 193. ACM (2014)
13. Krizhevsky, A., Sutskever, I., Hinton, G.E.: Imagenet classification with deep convolutional neural networks. In: Advances in neural information processing systems, pp. 1097–1105 (2012)
14. Lowe, D.G.: Object recognition from local scale-invariant features. In: The Proceedings of the Seventh IEEE International Conference on Computer Vision, vol. 2, pp. 1150–1157. IEEE (1999)
15. Oliva, A., Torralba, A.: Modeling the shape of the scene: a holistic representation of the spatial envelope. Int. J. Comput. Vis. **42**(3), 145–175 (2001)
16. Pinto, H., Almeida, J.M., Gonçalves, M.A.: Using early view patterns to predict the popularity of Youtube videos. In: Proceedings of the Sixth ACM International Conference on Web Search and Data Mining, pp. 365–374. ACM (2013)
17. Szabo, G., Huberman, B.A.: Predicting the popularity of online content. Commun. ACM **53**(8), 80–88 (2010)
18. Trzcinski, T., Rokita, P.: Predicting popularity of online videos using support vector regression. IEEE Trans. Multimed. **19**, 2561–2570 (2017)
19. Wu, J., Zhou, Y., Chiu, D.M., Zhu, Z.: Modeling dynamics of online video popularity. IEEE Trans. Multimed. **18**(9), 1882–1895 (2016)
20. Yan, F., Mikolajczyk, K.: Deep correlation for matching images and text. In: Proceedings of the IEEE Conference on Computer Vision and Pattern Recognition, pp. 3441–3450 (2015)

Telecommunications

Low Latency MPEG-DASH System Over HTTP 2.0 and WebSocket

Xiaona Wu[1,2](✉), Cheng Zhao[1], Rong Xie[1,2], and Li Song[1,2](✉)

[1] Institute of Image Communication and Network Engineering,
Shanghai Jiao Tong University, Shanghai, China
{youli206,xierong,song_li}@sjtu.edu.cn, zhaocheng100a@163.com
[2] Cooperative Medianet Innovation Center,
Shanghai Jiao Tong University, Shanghai, China

Abstract. Dynamic Adaptive Streaming over HTTP (MPEG-DASH) is an adaptive bitrate streaming technique that breaks the video contents into some sequences of small HTTP-based file segments in different bitrates. With enough bandwidth now, live latency has become the most serious problem. MPEG has discussed two core experiments Server and Network-assisted DASH (SAND) and Full Duplex HTTP-compatible Protocols (FDH) to improve performance of video streaming. In this paper, we refer the two ideas and complete a low delay streaming system over HTTP 2.0 and WebSocket. Based on our experiments, we could adaptively choose which bitrate of segments to push according to the network condition. With the smaller header size, utilization of bandwidth has been improved and there is 40.22% start-up time saved and 57.96% transmission latency saved averagely in all situations.

Keywords: MPEG-DASH · FDH · SAND · HTTP 2.0 · WebSocket
Live latency

1 Introduction

Live video streaming has become more and more popular recently. Along with the increasing demand for better user experience, we need to solve problem of live latency in live situations. Compared with traditional protocols and transmission methods [1], MPEG-DASH standard supposed two core experiments FDH and SAND using HTTP 2.0 and WebSocket.

MPEG-DASH was developed under MPEG (The Moving Picture Experts Group) which contains the manifest file Media Presentation Description File and video segments with data in different bitrates. Studies on DASH started in 2010 and DASH became a Draft International Standard in January 2011, and an International Standard in November 2011. The MPEG-DASH standard [2] was published in April, 2012. The media description file defines the media information including adaptation sets, representations and so on. Segments are defined based on two kinds of formats, ISO Base Media File Format [3] and

© Springer Nature Singapore Pte Ltd. 2018
G. Zhai et al. (Eds.): IFTC 2017, CCIS 815, pp. 357–367, 2018.
https://doi.org/10.1007/978-981-10-8108-8_33

MPEG-2 Transport Stream [4]. In 2014 DASH standard was updated to version 2 and proposed FDH [5] and SAND [6] in 2015.

FDH defines full duplex HTTP-compatible protocols which both allows server-initiated and client-initiated transactions. The idea can be applied over HTTP 2.0 and WebSocket. In a DASH session the client requests the MPD file first and then requests video segments with corresponding segment URL and a push strategy. Then the server responses with the requested segments following the given push strategy. PushDirective is used to signal the push strategy that the client wants the server to use, while PushAck is used to inform the client which strategy the server follows. The whole structure can reduce the transmission delay by decreasing the number of requests in live streaming. However, all the push strategies only support pushing segments from a single representation.

SAND enables a bidirectional messaging plane between the clients and other DASH aware network elements (DANE) to carry any kind of operational information and assistance information. SAND messages includes Parameters Enhancing Delivery (PED) messages exchanged between DANEs, Parameter Enhancing Reception (PER) messages sent from DANEs to DASH clients and Metrics and Status messages sent from clients to DANEs. These messages are delivered over HTTP via a URL in a HTTP header or a SAND channel (e.g. WebSocket).

In this work, we implement a low latency DASH system over HTTP 2.0 and WebSocket [7]. HTTP 2.0 supports function of server push. While using the HTTP 2.0 protocol in adaptive streaming, another problem we need to solve is how to select the quality of segments pushed. Of course, we can push definite amount of segments and change the selection after receiving a new request. In this article, we implemented a system using WebSocket to feedback SAND messages from the client and make server determine which kind of content to be pushed.

The remainder of the paper is organized as follows. In Sect. 2, we summarize the recent and related work on MPEG-DASH. Section 3 discusses our own system including the push scheme and implementation of WebSocket to send SAND messages to the server from the client. In Sect. 4, we describe the structure of our system and its corresponding open source tools. The results of experiments and comparison with traditional design are also shown. Section 5 concludes the paper.

2   Related Work

MEPG-DASH is becoming the popular transmission protocol and many people research on it. Some use cases have been presented in [8] for hybrid broadcasting and it explained how the MPEG-DASH standard performed. Datasets composed of segments with different representations are provided in [9]. Comparisons of HTTP 1.1 and HTTP 2.0 are provided both in terms of functionalities and page download time in [10]. As to the researches on low latency, [11] conducted a number of practical experiments on latency for protocols of HTTP 1.1, SPDY and HTTP 2.0. [12] explored WebRTC in a streaming transport process to carry video data and observed its contribution in low delay streaming with fast channel switching.

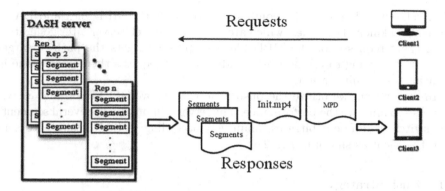

Fig. 1. Traditional MPEG-DASH streaming system

One experiment demonstrated how a DASH client could use Quality of Server (QoS) information to achieve faster quality convergence at start up in [13]. The optimal quality is reached much faster when the DASH client is assisted in estimating the available bandwidth via SAND messages. In this paper, we not only consider push technology from FDH idea, but also explore how to control the quality switch in server side. We finally establish our SAND system based on HTTP 2.0 and WebSocket.

3   Low Latency MPEG-DASH System

In this section, we will introduce our system using push technology and Web-Socket in details.

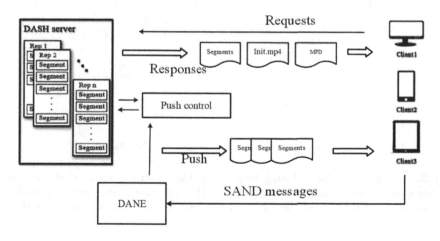

Fig. 2. Low latency MPEG-DASH streaming system

As shown in Fig. 1, media contents are composed of MPD files and DASH segments in kinds of qualities, which are stored in the web server after generated. Then client requests for the MPD file first, parses it, gets the path of target segments according to the network conditions and requests them one by one in traditional streaming system.

In our system, we utilize the push idea in FDH over HTTP 2.0 and SAND messages to improve the performance. The server will push next several segments and switch to different bitrates adaptively according to SAND messages sent from the client as shown in Fig. 2.

3.1   Push Strategy

In our system, we use the HTTP 2.0 protocol to implement push function. The server will push the corresponding resources to the client before it sends its requests for needed certain segments, which can reduce the live and start-up delay. This method can also decrease the number of connections to server and the size of header sent by the client.

In this section, we mainly talk about two methods for media push in our system.

As we said before, push technology can reduce both live latency and start-up latency. For the first purpose, we need to push several media segments to the player not wasting time for the connection establishment between them again and again as shown in Fig. 3(a). And for the start-up delay, we need to do some changes in the beginning of playback for a video as shown in Fig. 3(b).

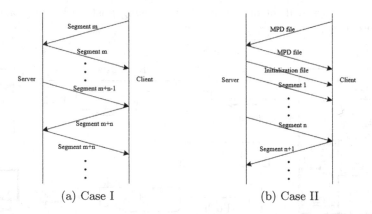

(a) Case I   (b) Case II

Fig. 3. Two methods for reducing time delay. Case I in (a) shows that the server pushes n segments for each request and Case II in (b) shows the server pushes MPD file, initialization file and all the following segments to start playback more quickly.

After receiving the manifest file, the client parses the file and requests for the segments in proper bitrates. The web server will push not only the requested one but also a certain number of following segments in the same quality. After reading from the buffer the client will repeat the request process. This can obviously reduce the Round Trip Time (RTT) in live streaming. Considering that push strategy will mostly be used in live streaming, users watch videos continuously. So there will be no data redundancy because all resources will be provided to users.

For the purpose of decreasing start-up delay, we can just push resources after the server receives the request for MPD. Once web server detects the request, it pushes the initialization mp4 file and several video segments and the client can start to play video immediately. Although we may not play the segments in most appropriate quality to make full use of the bandwidth at first, we reduce the start-up latency to get better experience for users.

3.2 Messages Feedback Over WebSocket

Using pull technology the client would choose the required quality of segments according to the bandwidth calculated by the downloading bitrate. Then when we use the push technology, we need to consider the selection of the proper quality. We attempted several ways to transfer the bandwidth message from client to server. WebSocket has a high real-time performance so we choose it to transfer the SAND messages.

Algorithm 1. Feedback SAND messages using WebSocket

The client:
 Input: current downloading bitrate A, previous bitrate B
  while $\|A - B\|$ is more than 500bps **do**
    send SAND messages M (M=A) to server
    let B = A
    detect downloading bitrate and update A

The server:
 Input: SAND messages M
   Pushing repA
   if M accepted **then**
     if server has repM **then**
        Push repM in new quality
     else
        Push highest quality segments
   else
     Push repA

The basic idea is making the client to estimate the network conditions at all time. Algorithm 1 gives the detailed description. When there is a large enough change the client will send the current downloading bitrate to server. Then the server can judge the message and change to push segments in another bitrate to avoid the network choked or bandwidth wasted. Obviously this scheme proposed a more robust rate adaption method for live streaming. However, we did not take the sharp changing of network into consideration and we will discuss how to improve robustness of the system in the future.

4 Experiments and Comparisons

We implement the low latency MPEG-DASH system based on HTTP 2.0 protocol and WebSocket. The datasets Big Buck Bunny [14] we use are from ITEC-Dynamic Adaptive Streaming over HTTP [15]. The corresponding parts with different segment durations we use are shown in Table 1. We choose Node.js [16] as the web server implementing our push strategy and open source project openssl to generate the key and certificate in the server to establish HTTPS connection for that is the need of HTTP 2.0 protocol. For the client side, dash.js [17], an opensource library, acts as the player developed by DASH Industry Forum and supported by many industry media companies. It also supports the push technology and we only need to add some marks to do our experiments.

Table 1. Datasets with different durations

Index	Duration	FrameWidth	FrameHeight	Bitrate (kbps)
1	1 s	854	480	409
2	2 s	854	480	1236
3	6 s	854	480	3583
4	15 s	854	480	9517

4.1 Adaptive Switch Over WebSocket

First, we test adaptive switches according to SAND messages over WebSocket.

The 1 s segments are used as MPEG-DASH video sources with bitrates of $226106bps$, $270316bps$, $352546bps$, $424520bps$, $537825bps$, $620705bps$, $808057bps$ and $1071529bps$ shown in Table 2. Using $SimpleHTTPServer$ module in Python to start a server for the dash.js player interface and node server for the video resources, we can get all the information of network transmission in the Chrome devtools [18]. A WebSocket connection is established between the server and client.

When network condition is changed large enough, the client will send the current downloading bitrate message to media source server. Then the server judges the message and chooses segments to push. The results of adaptive switch are shown in Fig. 4.

Table 2. Datasets for adpative switch

Name	FrameWidth	FrameHeight	Bitrate (kbps)
bunny_226106bps	480	360	187
bunny_270316bps	480	360	206
bunny_352546bps	480	360	241
bunny_424520bps	480	360	243
bunny_537825bps	854	480	409
bunny_620705bps	854	480	454
bunny_808057bps	1280	720	579
bunny_1071529bps	1280	720	751

From the above figure, we can see that the bandwidth of network is changing along with time. For example, if the server finds out that the condition becomes worse, it will push lower bitrate segments to client to avoid the playback freezes due to the slow downloading speed of high quality resources. On the contrary, when network gets better, the server will choose higher bitrate segments to push in order to improve the bandwidth utilization.

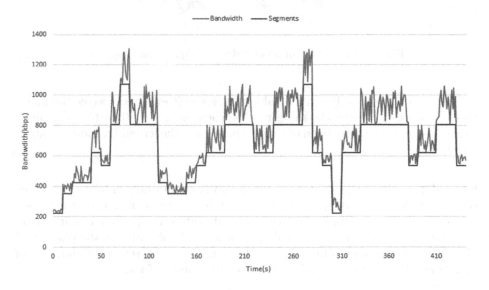

Fig. 4. Adaptive switches over WebSocket with SAND messages

4.2   Key Indicators

In this part we test the performances of our own system. For the experiments, we mainly talk about three main indicators: header sizes of requests and responses, start-up delay and transmission latency.

Header Size. First, we consider the difference of header sizes. Using the 1 s segments we find that header size of requests is 514 and 446 bytes respectively and the response header size is 299 and 142 bytes for traditional and our systems. We get the new result of 259 and 80 bytes when we add the push technology in HTTP 2.0.

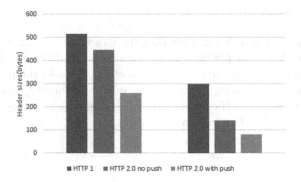

Fig. 5. Comparison of header sizes of request and response

The size is apparently reduced about 50% and it eventually saves the bandwidth resources. We get the same results when using 2 or 6 or 15 s segments. Figure 5 shows the comparison of request headers in the left and response headers another side intuitively.

Start-Up Delay. The start-up delay is another important indicator for video streaming. We test start-up delay using different segments and receive the following results in Fig. 6. The line above represents the start-up delay in our system and the other is for the traditional transmission. As we can see, the player will playback video contents more quickly. The time saved for segments' duration of 1, 2, 6 and 15 s is about 45.46%, 26.7%, 43.21% and 45.51%.

Transmission Latency. The last indicator we need to consider is the transmission latency. When we are stuck in a bad network, it is pretty significant to keep downloading resources to avoid playback freezing. Under the consideration of the segments' sizes, we compare the latency of same one in two systems each time. In the situation for 1 s segments, the results are shown in Fig. 7(a) and compared for each one.

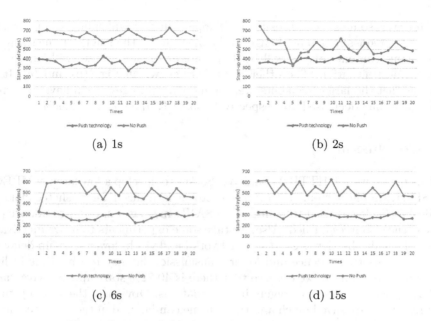

Fig. 6. Start-up delay for 1 s, 2 s, 6 s and 15 s segments.

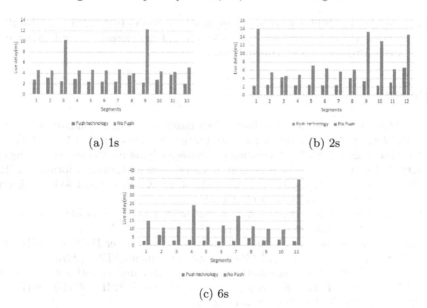

Fig. 7. Transmission delay for 1 s, 2 s and 6 s segments.

However, some sudden breaks may happen when downloading segments and we have to request again or change to the next one. If the length of one segment is too long, contents played will be dulplicate or missing. So we will ignore the 15 s segment situation. The other results are shown in Fig. 7(b) and (c). It is obvious that the larger segments are, the more advantages it will have in saving time. The time decreased are respectively 43.82%, 57.11% and 72.96%.

5   Conclusion

In this paper, we use HTTP 2.0 and WebSocket to develop a low latency MPEG-DASH streaming system. HTTP 2.0 protocol is utilized for push technology, while WebSocket is used to transfer the SAND messages in order to adaptively choose the resources pushed. Also, we take some experiments to prove its advantages of smaller header sizes to save network bandwidth, lower start-up delay to give better user experience and lower transmission latency to save time in live streaming. To sum up, we observe that there is 40.22% start-up time saved and 57.96% live delay saved averagely in all situations. Obviously the start-up time and live delay are saved much and this scheme can be used in the live streaming. It can provide users a more comfortable experience for live broadcasting.

Acknowledgement. This work was supported by NSFC (61671296 and 61521062), the 111 Project (B07022 and Sheitc No. 150633) and the Shanghai Key Laboratory of Digital Media Processing and Transmissions.

References

1. Stockhammer, T.: Dynamic adaptive streaming over http: standards and design principles. In: ACM Conference on Multimedia Systems, pp. 133-144 (2011)
2. ISO/IEC 23009–1:2012, Information technology - dynamic adaptive streaming over http(dash) - part 1: Media presentation description and segment formats (2012)
3. ISO/IEC 14496–12:2015, Information technology - Coding of audio-visual objects - Part 12: ISO base media file format (2015)
4. ISO/IEC 13818–1:2015, Information technology - generic coding of moving pictures and associated audio information - part 1: Systems (2015)
5. Information Technology Dynamic adaptive streaming over HTTP(DASH) - Part 6: DASH over Full Duplex HTTP-compatible Protocols(FDH) (2015)
6. ISO/IEC 23009–5:2017, Information Technology Dynamic adaptive streaming over HTTP(DASH) - Part 5: Server and network assisted DASH (SAND) (2017)
7. RFC 6455, The WebSocket protocol (2011)
8. Feuvre, J.L., Concolato, C.: Hybrid broadcast services using mpeg dash
9. Lederer, S., Timmerer, C.: Dynamic adaptive streaming over http dataset. In: ACM Sigmm Conference on Multimedia Systems, Mmsys 2012, pp. 89–94, Chapel Hill, Nc, Usa (2012)
10. Corbel, R., Stephan, E., Omnes, N.: Http/1.1 pipelining vs http2 in-the-clear: performance comparison. In: International Conference on New Technologies for Distributed Systems, pp. 1–6 (2016)

11. Naik, N., Jenkins, P.: Web protocols and challenges of web latency in the web of things. In: Eighth International Conference on Ubiquitous and Future Networks, pp. 845–850 (2016)
12. Zhao, S., Li, Z., Medhi, D.: Low delay mpeg dash streaming over the webrtc data channel. In: IEEE International Conference on Multimedia Expo Workshops, pp. 1–6 (2016)
13. Thomas, E., Deventer, M.O.V., Stockhammer, T., Begen, A.C., Famaey, J.: Enhancing mpeg dash performance via server and network assistance. In: Ibc (2015)
14. BigBuckBunny. http://www-itec.uni-klu.ac.at/ftp/datasets/DASHDataset2014/ BigBuckBunny/
15. ITEC. http://www-itec.uni-klu.ac.at/dash/
16. Node.js. https://nodejs.org/en/
17. Dash.js. https://github.com/Dash-Industry-Forum/dash.js
18. Chrome DevTools. https://developer.chrome.com/devtools

Performance Enhancement of NAND Flash Using Unequal Error Protection

Dawei Lu, Yiling Xu$^{(\boxtimes)}$, Hao Chen, Zhiqian Jiang, Wenjun Zhang,
and Ning Liu

Shanghai Jiao Tong University, 800 Dongchuan Road, Shanghai, China
{luerer,yl.xu,chenhao1210,zhiqjiang,zhangwenjun,ningliu}@sjtu.edu.cn

Abstract. NAND flash memories are not error-free. The Program/Erase cycles and retention time are two major factors affecting the reliability of NAND flash memories. Most error control codes (ECC) used in a flash memories provide a uniform protection regardless of the different raw bit error rate (RBER) of different storage cells, which fails to take full advantage of the limited available redundancy. To optimize the redundancy and take the unequal RBER into account, an unequal error protection scheme is proposed in this paper to improve the performance of NAND flash. Simulation shows that UEP method is more flexible and performs better in most condition.

Keywords: Unequal-error-protection · Raptor codes
Error-correction-code · NAND flash

1 Introduction

NAND flash is a kind of non-volatile storage technology, i.e., NAND flash memory is capable of storing data without power. Nowadays, NAND flash memory has been widely used in storage devices such as solid-state drives and memory cards thanks to its compactness, low power, low cost and high reliability. However, NAND flash memories are not error-free. There are two major types of errors, namely, retention errors and program interference errors [1]. A widely used method to enhance the reliability of NAND flash memories is applying error correcting codes (ECC). Large amount of researches focusing on the improvement of performance of ECC have been done and there still leaves much room to improve.

MLC (multi-level cell) NAND flash, which store 2 or more bits per cell by supporting 4 or more voltage states [1], suffers more from bit errors because of the large storage density [2] compared with the SLC (single-level cell) NAND flash. On the other hand, different bits within each memory cell belong to different pages, which makes different types of pages have largely varying bit error rates [3]. Meanwhile, with the flash cells continue to scale down in size and storage density continues to increase, there will be stricter requirement on reliability.

© Springer Nature Singapore Pte Ltd. 2018
G. Zhai et al. (Eds.): IFTC 2017, CCIS 815, pp. 368–380, 2018.
https://doi.org/10.1007/978-981-10-8108-8_34

For example, the uncorrectable bit error rate during usage should be less than 10^{-15} and stored data should be available for 5–10 years [4]. Efforts should be done to cope with the errors influencing the reliability of NAND flash and extend the lifetime.

Many kinds of code words have been attempted in NAND flash. At the very beginning, Hamming codes are used as linear error-correcting codes in NAND flash, however the single-error correction capacity of Hamming code is no longer sufficient since the emergent of MLC NAND flash [5]. Long linear block codes with higher error correction capacities, such as BCH and RS code, are applied to the flash memories [6,7]. In recent years, LDPC code has been proposed [8].

Compared with the FEC codes applied in the network transmission, the ECCs for the flash memories have some different properties. The spare region in flash memories is limited so that the ECCs used in NAND flash should have a high code rate [12]. On the other hand, flash memories are composed of multiple blocks and pages, different memory array may move to different process corners [10], which leads to the situation that different storage cells share different RBER (raw bit error rate, the error rate before applying ECC). Each blocks reliability will continuously decrease with the increment of P/E cycle counts and retention time. So the error-correcting requirement is dynamic and can be influenced by the effect factors persistently. A uniform ECC protection for all memory blocks fails to provide the error correction for the distribution of vulnerability across blocks and can cause a great waste if ECC allocation is accordance with worst-case reliability [11]. As is known to us, regular ECC methods are designed on the worst reliability cases and have a great waste of computations [12]. In [3], the author mentioned that available redundancy in NAND flash memory is not fully utilized. How to optimize the available redundancy for the best performance of ECC, combined with the unequal RBER of different storage cells in NAND flash memory, is the major concern of this paper.

[13] proposed a concatenated Raptor Codes in NAND flash memory to cope with the extra protection for the contaminated pages that cannot be corrected by the deployed ECC. Raptor code provides protection against failed pages with a very small extra coding overhead with efficient encoding and decoding by tagged the intersections of failed row and column codes as erasure symbols. The strategy using relative small BCH codes as inner codes and Raptor codes as outer codes offers a considerable performance boost to the regular ECC applied in the NAND flash memory. However, paper [13] only provides several fixed redundancy rate for Raptor codes and cannot deal with the varied error rate in different blocks well.

On account of the two major reasons mentioned above, the unequal error protection (UEP) method, based on Raptor codes, is designed to provide more adaptive and flexible protection. To be brief, UEP method is designed to apply to the NAND flash memories and help to achieve the maximum utilization and optimal performance.

The rest of paper is organized as follows. Section 2 introduces the background of this paper, the NAND memory flash composed of multiple blocks and the two

Table 1. Parameters for the exponential growth models

5x nm MLC	Value	Std Err	95% Confidence
A	2.6953E-09	1.97E-10	2.31E-09
B	0.0001608	4.12E-06	0.000153
C	5.4685E-09	7.77E-10	3.94E-09

factors that impact the RBER are mentioned. Section 3 states the UEP scheme in detail and how it is applied the UEP scheme to NAND flash with Raptor codes. Section 4 demonstrates the simulation results. Finally, this whole paper is concluded in the last section.

2   Preliminary

2.1   Factors Influencing the Reliability

Program/Erase cycle counts and retention time are considered as the two major factors leading to errors. The storage cells itself is a floating-gate avalanche injection MOS transistor. Data is stored or erased in the NAND flash memory in the form of different threshold voltage by changing the charge trapped in the floating-gate transistor [14]. It is easy to understand the causes of cell storage distortion noise sources and errors:

– Electrons capture and emission events is the direct cause of threshold voltage shift and fluctuation, which is referred to as random telegraph noise. Frequent Program or Erase operations cause an accumulating damage to the tunnel oxide of floating gate transistors over time.
– Except for the reason of threshold voltage shift and fluctuation causing errors during the data retention time, electron tunneling current through the gate oxide would cause the gate oxide breaks down, errors may occur when the gate oxide breaks down as a result of long-time application of relatively low electric field.

In the previous study on NAND flash, an exponential growth model is proposed to characterize the impact of wear-out on bit error rate based on detailed error measurement. About 60,000 erase blocks for each type of flash devices were used to exercise and wear out in [15]. It shows that the curve-fit of RBER versus P/E counts can be approximated by:

$$RBER = Ae^{Bx} + C$$

x is P/E cycle counts, the precise parameters of a 5x nm MLC product for the fitting of this experiment is listed in Table 1.

Figure 1 shows the RBER increases with the growth of P/E cycle counts and retention time. If the data retention is not long, the effect of time-dependent

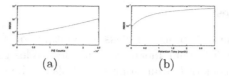

(a)   (b)

Fig. 1. RBER vs. P/E counts and RBER vs. Retention time

gate oxide breakdown is not very obvious and the RBER grows slowly with the P/E cycle counts increased, so at the beginning, P/E counts is the dominating factor for RBER. However, with the past of time, data retention errors show a significant effect on RBER, normally the retention time becomes the dominating factor when retention time is longer than 3 days.

The influence of P/E counts and retention time is better visualized in a 3x nm MLC product in Fig. 2. According to [16], the RBER in relation of P/E counts and retention time fits the formula in general:

$$RBER(c,d) = d_r(c) \cdot d$$

where $d_r(c)$ is the rate at which RBER deteriorates per d(day), c represents the P/E counts and $d_r(c) = 10^{-13} \cdot c^{1.71}$.

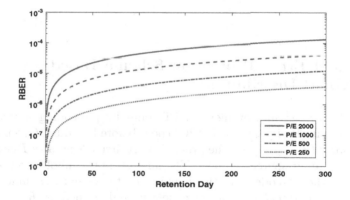

Fig. 2. RBER in 3x nm MLC

Actually, the P/E cycle counts and retention time do not affect the reliability of NAND flash memory independently, actually they both bring errors in. So if the model of RBER growth with P/E cycle counts and retention time during the lifetime is clear, it is possible to apply optimized redundancy allocation to Raptor codes by evaluating the real running time condition with certain sensors. An optimized redundancy allocation would lead to a higher coding efficiency and utilize limited redundancy.

2.2   Raptor Codes

Raptor codes are the first practical class of fountain codes. Fountain codes are a class of rateless codes. That means the encoded codes generated by function codes form a given block of k input source symbols can be unlimited. One source symbol can be consisted of any bits of data or blocks of data in bytes. The most significant feature of function codes is that decoder can recover original source symbols ideally from any subset of the encoding symbols with size k', where k' is just slightly larger than k [17].

Based on the feature of fountain codes stated above, Raptor codes can be designed as erasure codes in NAND flash memories. To handle with the failed pages and bad blocks, suitable redundancy are allocated according to the real running time environment of flash memories instead of wasting massive storage units. Figure 3 is the process of ECC protection applied in flash memories in general.

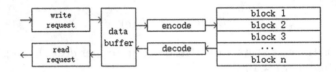

Fig. 3. The process of ECC in NAND flash

3   Unequal Error Protection Scheme Based on RBER Distribution

Raptor codes are an improvement of LT codes by pre-coding source symbols with Low Density Parity Check (LDPC) codes before LT codes. Given a size of k source symbols $(x_1, x_2, ..., x_k)$, the pre-code part firstly generates I intermediate symbols from input source symbols. The final output symbols are the symbols generated by the LT-code from the I intermediate symbols. Assume N output symbols, then the rate(R) of Raptor code can be described as: $R = \frac{k}{N}$, and the overhead redundancy rate of Raptor code is $E = \frac{N-k}{k}$.

The pre-code part of Raptor code relaxes the condition that all input symbols need to be recovered by LT-code. The low boundary constraint of average node degree for LT-code is not $O(klog(k))$, it can now be $O(k)$ instead, because the original source symbols can still be recovered by decoding the intermediate symbols, which is decoded by LT-code firstly, with pre-code. The average node degree is determined by the degree distribution of LT-code when the intermediate symbols are encoded. The generator polynomial can be simply described as: $\Omega(x) = \sum_{i=1}^{k} \Omega_i x^i$, where Ω_i is the probability that the degree of an output node is i.

In this paper, the storage environment of NAND flash is made an analogy to an erasure channel with erasure probability σ. If the decoder is guaranteed to collect m symbols through an erasure probability σ erasure channel, where m must be slighter larger than k for a successful decoding, the following equation should be satisfied: $\sigma = 1 - R(1 + \varepsilon)$, where $\varepsilon > 0$. In a word, if the erasure probability is σ, to protect data against the errors and recover source symbols successfully with a high probability, the rate of Raptor code when encoding source symbols should be approximately

$$R = \frac{1 - \sigma}{1 + \varepsilon}$$

and the allocated redundancy rate:

$$E = \frac{N - k}{k} = \frac{1}{R} - 1$$

Unequal Error Protection (UEP) method focuses on the performance improvement of ECC codes applied on NAND flash. In NAND flash, the page is the storage cell of NAND flash for date programming or reading. It can be known from the introduction that Raptor code is applied to cope with contaminated pages, which fail to recover the data when the inner ECC like BCH code is applied. NAND flash memories consist of several blocks, and each block consist of multiple pages. Assumed that there are N symbols in a page, to provide the best protection and make sure that the probability of successful decoding of Raptor code is sufficiently large, it is important to find the best encoding rate R.

In this paper, the length of source symbols is set as k, the Raptor code generates N symbols at last for one page. That means the total N encoded symbols consist of t repair symbols, where $t = N - k$ in standardized Raptor codes. The correction capability of Raptor code can be defined as t, it can be known from above knowledge that symbols can be decoded only if the number of lost or error symbols is not larger than t. For each symbol stored in the flash, the probability that it will be lost or become erroneous is σ (erasure probability σ can be estimated by the P/E counts (c) and the retention time (d)), it follows a binomial distribution. Supposed that there are N in one page, so the probability that one page can be decoded when x symbols get error is given by the following cumulative distribution function (CDF):

$$P_D(x, \sigma) = \Sigma_{i=0}^{x} \binom{N}{i} \cdot \sigma^i \cdot (1 - \sigma)^{N-i} \tag{1}$$

The erasure probability of each single symbol is independent and follows binomial distribution, this CDF of independent random variables will be approximately equal to a normal distribution according to the central limit theorem (CLT). If error symbols are less than correction capability t, the page can be decoded in a high probability, so the probability that one page can be decoded successfully is:

$$P_{decode}(t, \sigma) = P_D(0 \leq x \leq t)$$

If the given $N\sigma$ is sufficiently large, function (1) can be described as the CDF of a normal distribution:

$$P_{decode}(t,\sigma) \approx \Phi(\frac{t-N\sigma}{\sqrt{N\sigma(1-\sigma)}}) - \Phi(\frac{0-N\sigma}{\sqrt{N\sigma(1-\sigma)}})$$

$$= \Phi(\frac{t-N\sigma}{\sqrt{N\sigma(1-\sigma)}}) + \Phi(\frac{N\sigma}{\sqrt{N\sigma(1-\sigma)}}) - 1$$

(2)

where the mean of normal distribution is $N\sigma$ and the finite variance is $N\sigma(1-\sigma)$. From function (2), it is easy to know that $\Phi(\geq 0) \in [0.5, 1]$, so: $0 \leq P_{decode}(t,\sigma) \leq 1$.

When decoding, suppose that there are m collected symbols. Considering the feature of Raptor code that it does not encode source symbols with LT code directly but encodes the intermediate symbols generated by some pre-code, the performance of Raptor code is not like an ideal fountain code that it can decode the symbols with zero failure probability when $m = k$, the decode failure probability of Raptor code [18] when collected m symbols can be modeled by:

$$P_{fail}(m,k) = \begin{cases} 1 & (m < k) \\ 0.85 \times 0.567^{m-k} & (m \geq k) \end{cases}$$

(3)

It is the main task to find the best encoding rate R, so that the maximum numbers of source symbols (max k) can be stored in the N-symbol page. According to the analysis above, a successful recovery of k source symbols must meet two requirements: (1) collect no less than k symbols ($m \geq k$). (2) succeed in decoding, the probability of a successful page recovery is therefore:

$$P_{sr} = P_{decode}(t,\sigma) \cdot (1 - P_{fail}(t-i))$$

Combining the result with function (1), (2) and (3) yields when $N\sigma$ is sufficiently large:

$$P_{sr}(t;\sigma,N) = \Sigma_{i=0}^{t}\binom{N}{i}\sigma^i(1-\sigma)^{N-i}(1-0.85 \times 0.567^{t-i})$$

$$= P_{decode}(t;\sigma) - 0.85 \times 0.567^t(\Sigma_{i=0}^{t}\binom{N}{i}(\frac{\sigma}{0.567})^i(1-\sigma)^{N-i})$$

(4)

$$= P_{decode}(t;\sigma) - 0.85 \times O(t)$$

$$\approx \Phi(\frac{t-N\sigma}{\sqrt{N\sigma(1-\sigma)}}) + \Phi(\frac{N\sigma}{\sqrt{N\sigma(1-\sigma)}}) - 1$$

To make sure that the source symbols can be recovered with a high probability, set $P_{sr}(t;\sigma,N) = 1 - 10^{-8}$. Since σ can be estimated when P/E counts (c) and retention time (d) is known, the appropriate t could be found to make sure P_{sr} is no less than $1 - 10^{-8}$. As for k, the bigger the better, because it represents the source symbols in one page. Note that $N = k + t$, so the lower bound of t that satisfies the following inequality should be found:

$$\Phi(\frac{t - N\sigma}{\sqrt{N\sigma(1 - \sigma)}}) + \Phi(\frac{N\sigma}{\sqrt{N\sigma(1 - \sigma)}}) - 1 \geq 1 - 10^{-8}$$

$$\Phi(\frac{t - N\sigma}{\sqrt{N\sigma(1 - \sigma)}}) \geq 2 - 10^{-8} - \Phi(\sqrt{\frac{N\sigma}{1 - \sigma}}) \tag{5}$$

the lower bound t^* can be described as:

$$t^* = \lceil N\sigma + \sqrt{N\sigma(1 - \sigma)} \cdot arg\Phi(2 - 10^{-8} - \Phi(\sqrt{\frac{N\sigma}{1 - \sigma}}))\rceil$$

note that $\Phi(\sqrt{\frac{N\sigma}{1-\sigma}}) \rightarrow 1$ as $N\sigma$ is sufficiently large:

$$t^* = \lceil N\sigma + 5.1993 \cdot \sqrt{N\sigma(1 - \sigma)}\rceil \tag{6}$$

the best encoding rate for a N-symbol page when the erasure probability is σ can be:

$$R = 1 - \frac{t^*}{N} = 1 - \sigma - 5.1993 \cdot \sqrt{\frac{\sigma(1 - \sigma)}{N}} \tag{7}$$

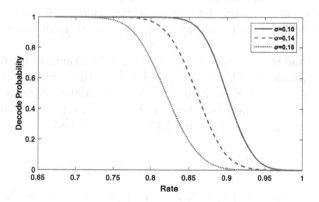

Fig. 4. Rate of encoding vs. decode probability

Figure 4 shows the trend of successful probability when decoding with the increase of encoding rate R over different erasure channel with erasure probability σ_i when N is quite large. The curve shifting to the right as σ decreases in this figure is consistent with the common sense that a lower σ causes less errors so that the needed redundancy is less.

UEP method applied on NAND flash would improve the performance of outer Raptor codes by using the adaptive R according to N and σ. Normally, one block in NAND flash consists of p pages and there could be ω inner ECC codeword in each page. Suppose that each codeword of inner ECC code contains exactly N_r Raptor code symbols, so the total Raptor symbols in one block can be $N = p\omega \cdot N_r$. Different blocks may suffer from different page failure rates, set their failure rate as σ_i and the most suitable R could be calculated with equation (7). In most NAND flash, one block contains 64 pages with 8 codewords, so the Raptor symbols in a block is $N = p\omega \cdot N_r = 64 \times 8 \cdot N_r = 512N_r$, meanwhile σ is about 10^{-3} to 10^{-2}, so $N\sigma$ is sufficiently large to use (7). Section 4 shows the performance of UEP method with the adaptive encoding rate.

4 Simulation Results

The performance of Raptor codes have been analyzed in last section. Figure 4 shows how R changes with σ, however equation (7) also shows the relationship of R and N, they are positively correlated, R gets bigger as N increases. In this simulation, the erasure probability σ_i is set slightly exaggerated from 0.10 to 0.18 to get an obvious simulation result. Curves in Fig. 5 are quite similar to those in Fig. 4. They show that the decoding probability gets higher with R decreasing, for the capability of Raptor code getting larger, when the source symbols length is $k = 128$. It is also easy to find that if the erasure probability increases, encoding rate should become smaller for a relative high decode probability. Figure 6 repeats the simulation but with $k = 512$, compared with Fig. 5 (k = 128), the result shows a better performance. The encoding rate curve moves to the right side of original curve, to protect data over the same σ channel, the encoding rate getting larger as k increases, which means the overhead redundancy rate is getting lower.

It can be found that the rate in Fig. 4 is larger than that in Figs. 5 and 6 under the same circumstance. This happens because of the feature of Raptor code. Raptor code will show good performance when the number of source symbols in a codeword is large. In the previous study in [19], it is known that the uncorrectable bit error rate (UBER) after applying ECC can be defined as:

$$UBER = \frac{1 - P_{decode}}{User\ data\ per\ codeword}$$

combined with the result of Figs. 4, 5 and 6, it can be concluded that the Raptor code gets a good performance when the codeword is large in size.

In this simulation, it is assumed that 9 different blocks suffering from different page failure rate. The σ of 9 blocks is set from 0.01 to 0.05 with step 0.002. Supposed each block contains $p = 64$ pages and each page consists of $\omega = 8$ inner ECC codeword, now the Raptor symbols in one block is $N = p\omega \cdot N_r = 512N_r$. To show the advantage of UEP method, the simulation is set to present the decode failure rate of all these 9 different blocks with the increase of N under three conditions: UEP method with adaptive encoding rate is used, fixed redundancy

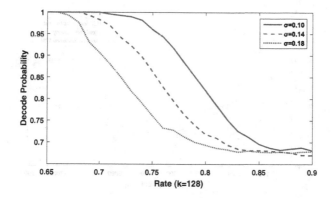

Fig. 5. Rate of encoding vs. decoding probability (k = 128)

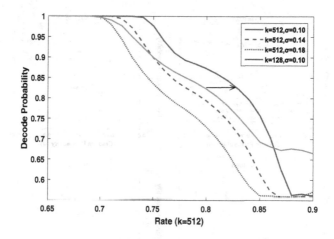

Fig. 6. Rate of encoding vs. decoding probability (k = 512)

rate 1.56% is used and fixed redundancy rate 2.34% is used. In Sect. 3, the probability of a successful recover in a block is defined as $P_{sr}(t, \sigma, N)$, so the decode failure rate of these 9 blocks can be described as:

$$P_{df} = 1 - \prod_{i=1}^{9} P_{sr}(t_i, \sigma_i | N) \tag{8}$$

Figure 7 is the simulation result according to (8). The solid curve in this figure is below two dotted curves, it shows that the failure rate of UEP method is smaller than fixed rate, and it proves that UEP method performs better. Meanwhile, the curves drop slightly with the increase of N ($1 \leq N_r \leq 16$), which supports the result that Raptor codes get a good performance when the codeword is large in size again.

Despite of the decode failure rate of 9 blocks together, Fig. 8 shows the performance of each one block with the σ of blocks varies from 0.01 to 0.05. These four

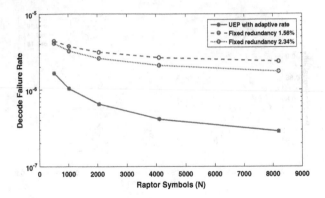

Fig. 7. Decode failure rate of all 9 blocks with the raptor symbols (N) increasing

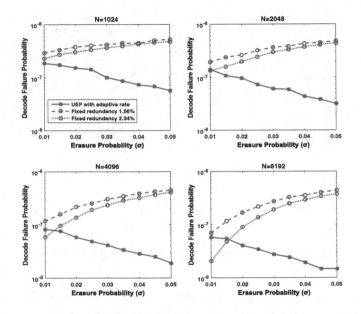

Fig. 8. Decode failure rate of each block

figures shows the simulation when different N_r $(2, 4, 8, 16)$ is chosen. It can be seen from the figure that if the redundancy rate is fixed, it is easy to know that there would be more errors when decoding as σ getting large, so the decode failure rate is increasing. However the UEP method keeps the failure rate at a low level and the failure is even decreasing with the increase of σ because formula (4) will be more accurate as $N\sigma$ is sufficiently large. In the last two figures, the decode failure probability of UEP method shows a little higher than ECC method when $\sigma < 0.02$, the two main reasons may be: (1) The calculation error in formula (4). (2) The probability $(P_{sr} = 1 - 10^{-8})$ set for formula (4) is not high enough, and we can set a higher standard to get better performance. Nevertheless, UEP method get a better recovery in most conditions. The simulation shows the outstanding performance of UEP method compared with normal ECC protection method.

5   Conclusion

In this paper, we investigated the bit errors in NAND flash memories and located the factors that may have obvious effects on RBER. The detailed information about NAND flash and the test statistics was reviewed. Distinguished from regular EEP methods, the UEP scheme proposed in this paper is implemented in the software layer based on Raptor code. It provides a more flexible and resource-saving protection for flash memories. Simulations confirmed the advantages of proposed method especially when the redundancy is limited. And it shows that the proposed method can make full use of the redundancy and get a good performance compared with fixed redundancy rates. Meanwhile, it is proved in this paper that UEP method based on Raptor code can perform far better when the source symbols length is getting larger. In conclusion, compared with regular EEP methods, the UEP scheme based on RBER proposed in this paper helps NAND flash memories with the data loss problems and get an improved performance of NAND flash.

Acknowledgement. This paper is supported in part by National Natural Science Foundation of China (61650101), National High Technology Research and Development Program (863 Program: 2015AA015802), Scientific and Innovative Action Plan of Shanghai (15DZ1100100). Yiling Xu from Shanghai Jiao Tong University is the corresponding author of this paper.

References

1. Yang, C., Muckatira, D., Kulkarni, A., Chakrabarti, C.: Data storage time sensitive ECC schemes for MLC NAND flash memories. In: 2013 IEEE International Conference on Acoustics, Speech and Signal Processing (ICASSP), pp. 2513–2517. IEEE (2013)
2. Yuan, L., Liu, H., Jia, P., Yang, Y.: Reliability-based ECC system for adaptive protection of NAND flash memories. In: 2015 Fifth International Conference on Communication Systems and Network Technologies (CSNT), pp. 897–902. IEEE (2015)
3. Li, J., Zhao, K., Ma, J., Zhang, T.: Realizing unequal error correction for nand flash memory at minimal read latency overhead. IEEE Trans. Circuits Syst. II Express Briefs **61**(5), 354–358 (2014)
4. Cai, Y., Haratsch, E.F., Mutlu, O., Mai, K.: Error patterns in MLC NAND flash memory: measurement, characterization, and analysis. In: Proceedings of the Conference on Design, Automation and Test in Europe, pp. 521–526. EDA Consortium (2012)
5. Xiao-Bo, J., Xue-Qing, T., Wei-Pei, H.: Novel ECC structure and evaluation method for NAND flash memory. In: 2015 28th IEEE International System-on-Chip Conference (SOCC), pp. 100–104. IEEE (2015)

6. Liu, W., Rho, J., Sung, W.: Low-power high-throughput bch error correction VLSI design for multi-level cell NAND flash memories. In: IEEE Workshop on Signal Processing Systems Design and Implementation, SIPS 2006, pp. 303–308. IEEE (2006)
7. Sun, F., Devarajan, S., Rose, K., Zhang, T.: Design of on-chip error correction systems for multilevel NOR and NAND flash memories. IET Circuits Devices Syst. 1(3), 241–249 (2007)
8. Kim, J., Cho, J., Sung, W.: A high-speed layered min-sum LDPC decoder for error correction of NAND flash memories. In: 2011 IEEE 54th International Midwest Symposium on Circuits and Systems (MWSCAS), pp. 1–4. IEEE (2011)
9. Lee, Y.: Hardware optimizations of hard-decision ECC decoders for MLC NAND flash memories. In: 2015 International SoC Design Conference (ISOCC), pp. 133–134. IEEE (2015)
10. Mutyam, M., Wang, F., Krishnan, R., Narayanan, V., Kandemir, M., Xie, Y., Irwin, M.J.: Process-variation-aware adaptive cache architecture and management. IEEE Trans. Comput. 58(7), 865–877 (2009)
11. Paul, S., Cai, F., Zhang, X., Bhunia, S.: Reliability-driven ecc allocation for multiple bit error resilience in processor cache. IEEE Trans. Comput. 60(1), 20–34 (2011)
12. Yuan, L., Liu, H., Jia, P., Yang, Y.: An adaptive ECC scheme for dynamic protection of NAND flash memories. In: 2015 IEEE International Conference on Acoustics, Speech and Signal Processing (ICASSP), pp. 1052–1055. IEEE (2015)
13. Geunyeong, Y., Moon, J.: Concatenated raptor codes in nand flash memory. IEEE J. Sel. Areas Commun. 32(5), 857–869 (2014)
14. Di Carlo, S., Fabiano, M., Piazza, R., Prinetto, P.: Exploring modeling and testing of NAND flash memories. In: 2010 East-West Design & Test Symposium (EWDTS), pp. 47–50. IEEE (2010)
15. Sun, H., Grayson, P., Wood, B.: Quantifying reliability of solid-state storage from multiple aspects. Proc. SNAPI 11 (2011)
16. Park, H., Kim, J., Choi, J., Lee, D., Noh, S.H.: Incremental redundancy to reduce data retention errors in flash-based SSDS. In: 2015 31st Symposium on Mass Storage Systems and Technologies (MSST), pp. 1–13. IEEE (2015)
17. Shokrollahi, A.: Raptor codes. IEEE Trans. Inf. Theory 52(6), 2551–2567 (2006)
18. Kokkinos, V., Papazois, A., Bouras, C., Kanakis, N.: Evaluating RaptorQ FEC over 3GPP multicast services. In: 2012 8th International Wireless communications and mobile computing conference (IWCMC), pp. 257–262. IEEE (2012)
19. Mielke, N., Marquart, T., Wu, N., Kessenich, J., Belgal, H., Schares, E., Trivedi, F., Goodness, E., Nevill, L.R.: Bit error rate in NAND flash memories. In: IEEE International Reliability Physics Symposium, IRPS 2008, pp. 9–19 (2008)

A Perceptual Optimization Approach to Adaptive HTTP Streaming

Huaying Xue[✉], Yuan Zhang, Jinyao Yan, and Dejun Cai

Information Engineering School, Communication University of China, Beijing 100024, China
aimmeexue@outlook.com, {yzhang,jyan,caidejun}@cuc.edu.cn

Abstract. This paper presents a perceptual optimization scheme for the adaptive HTTP streaming services. It is well-known that the content features have deep influence on the user's quality of experience (QoE). However, most of the existing algorithms only consider bandwidth and buffer in quality control. This paper integrates the video-saliency-based adaptation to improve the perceptual quality for end users. The saliency cues, the network condition and the buffer status are jointly considered to manage the resources (e.g., buffer) efficiently. In particular, both the saliency cues of current segment and segments from adjacent shots are taken into consideration. The heuristic adaptation algorithms are implemented on top of the open-source DASH platform—dash.js to demonstrate our superiority compared with the default throughput-based adaptation and well-known BOLA method. Our work has high potential to enhance the current DASH standard by offering the smooth and perceptually optimized adaptive streaming in mobile networks.

Keywords: HTTP adaptive streaming · Video rate adaptation · MPEG-DASH
Visual perceptual model · QoE optimization

1 Introduction

In recent years, media streaming services make up a significant portion of the overall Internet traffic [1]. The development of WiFi/4G/5G technologies enable the mobile terminals to be the key drivers for this growing popularity. The user-perceived quality of experience (QoE) [2] becomes a major factor to evaluate the end user's acceptance of the service. Unreliable network throughput and network heterogeneity become real challenges for the service providers to provide high-quality streaming services with a universal scheme. Using adaptive streaming technologies is one of the solutions to solve the problem. The main challenge is the client decision engine, which raises great interest in the research fields with the advent of the first open standard called ISO/IEC MPEG Dynamic Adaptive Streaming over HTTP (DASH) [3].

The research on DASH client adaptation algorithms could be divided into two categories. In throughput-based approach, the available bandwidth of the link is estimated so that the predicted network resources could be used to determine the affordable bitrate of the next segment to avoid the buffer underrun. A rate adaptation algorithm based on smoothed bandwidth changes measured through the segment fetch time was proposed

© Springer Nature Singapore Pte Ltd. 2018
G. Zhai et al. (Eds.): IFTC 2017, CCIS 815, pp. 381–391, 2018.
https://doi.org/10.1007/978-981-10-8108-8_35

in [4]. The DASH reference player [5] uses the throughput-based heuristic adaptive algorithm as the default adaptive bitrate logic, which adjusts the estimated bandwidth based on the latency.

The second category is the buffer-based approach, which only uses the amount of data stored in the buffer of a video player without predicting the throughput. Spiteri et al. [6] has formulated the rate adaptation as a utility maximization problem and proposed an online control algorithm called BOLA, which only requires the knowledge of the buffer status. They use the Lyapunov optimization technique to minimize the rebuffering and maximize the average video quality. It has also been a common idea to jointly consider buffer and throughput. In the literature, Miller et al. [7] has proposed an adaptation engine based on the actual buffer level with the auxiliary information about the dynamics of the available throughput.

Most of the above HTTP-based adaptive video strategies only conduct the bitrate switching according to the network resources, without a consideration of the video contents. Some dedicated studies on the impact of adaptation strategies and adaptation dimensions (e.g. image quality adaptation, spatial adaptation, temporal adaptation) have shown that the influence on QoE varies greatly depending on the spatiotemporal properties of the different contents [8]. The CPANDA [9] has implemented a content-aware adaptation algorithm based on the original PANDA [10]. However, it only considers the temporal structure of the video contents which cannot properly reflect the perceived quality of human's eyes.

In our previous work, we adopt a spatiotemporal saliency detection model to predict the amount of human visual attentions on different regions in a video [11]. The saliency curve of the frames was mapped to the attention of each segment. In a perceptual optimized decision scheme, more resources (both buffer and bitrate resources) could be assigned to the content with higher saliency. However, it only considers the saliency of the current segment. For some videos with fluctuated saliency cues, it cannot always perform consistently well in buffer allocation, which leads to some big errors in rate allocation. In this paper, we design the algorithm to include saliency cues from both the current segment and the adjacent segments, which are used together with the network conditions and buffer status. The new algorithm performs consistently well for different videos under different network conditions. The proposed algorithm is integrated with the dash.js player. The experiments show that the algorithm can adapt to the visual saliency of the content as well as avoiding stalling and irrational quality oscillation. Being compared with the dash.js default throughput algorithm and the BOLA, our schemes can make effective use of the buffer and network bandwidth to achieve better perceived quality for high saliency contents, and hence improve the overall QoE of on-demand video service.

The remainder of the paper is organized as follows. In Sect. 2, content pre-processing methods are presented. Section 3 describes the visual perception-driven adaptation scheme for DASH. Section 4 presents the evaluation results. Finally, Sect. 5 concludes the paper.

2   Content Pre-processing

In this section, we present how to define the attention of each video segment and integrate this property with the original DASH content. The proposed framework is improved based on the basic DASH system, as shown in Fig. 1.

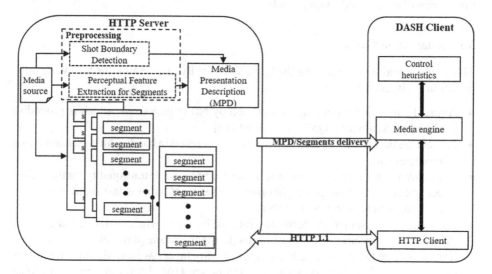

Fig. 1. Visual perception-driven DASH system framework.

2.1   Shot Boundary Detection

The shot segmentation is processed at two goals. First is to achieve the saliency of each segment. To be specific, we average the saliency of frames in a shot and select the saliency of the shot which the segment belongs to as its saliency value. Second is to avoid unnecessary quality shifts in the same shot. We adopt the method in [12] to segment videos into groups of consecutive shots.

2.2   Perceptual Feature Extraction for Segments

The appropriate content features are the key parameters in a content-aware video scheme [13]. The researches have indicated that both spatial and temporal features should be considered in a DASH adaptation scheme. Accordingly, we use a spatiotemporal perceptual model [14] to compute the saliency of each pixel of the frame, ranging from zero to one. Then we get the frame-level saliency values by averaging all pixels' saliency values. By combining the shot information, we obtain the saliency value (ranging from [0, 10]) of each shot. The saliency for each segment is the value of its attached shot. Then we add two properties associated with the content features to the segment element, marked by 'scene = "shotID" and importance = "saliency"' into the MPD file.

3 Proposed Rate Adaptation Algorithm

The challenge for an adaptation algorithm arises from the fact that the available throughput considerably fluctuates due to multiple reasons. Rather than sticking to raise the accuracy of bandwidth estimation, we use the buffer to smooth the estimation errors. First, we will give the adaptation goals.

3.1 Adaptation Goals

The adaptation aims at improving the QoE. Specifically, we identify the following optimization goals as critical.

- Avoid the interruption of playback caused by buffer underruns, which is proved to be the most dominating QoE impairment [15].
- Prevent the buffer from overflow, because it may result in bandwidth waste and frame dropping events.
- Maximize the average quality as well as to ensure higher bitrate quality for the higher saliency content within the neighboring two segments (one is last segment and the other is the first segment of next shot).
- Avoid frequent oscillations between available qualities. The existing schemes solve this problem by minimizing quality shifts during the whole playback time. However, it turns out that the time on each individual quality layer has more significant impacts on the QoE rather than the switching frequency [16]. Therefore, we try to keep constant quality in the same shot in our scheme.

The difficulties lie in how to achieve the trade-offs among the above goals. In our work, we assign the first goal with the highest priority, and thus, some minimum buffer level needs to be maintained all the time. We try to reduce the risk that higher bitrate for higher saliency content may cause the buffer underrun by adopting the buffer reserving scheme. The last goal to keep the constant quality in the same shot also need to take the current buffer and network status into consideration. Thus, we try to change the quality at the beginning of a shot.

3.2 Online Adaptation Algorithm for DASH Client

Bandwidth Estimation. The bandwidth estimation algorithm is preserved from dash.js. The current bandwidth is probed by the last segment downloading and smoothed by three samples. Also, it considers the latency of the internet link.

Bitrate Selection Algorithm. The average latency and estimated bandwidth reveal the available network capacity, being used in the bitrate selection algorithm. The main idea of the algorithm is to consider the saliency of the adjacent two segments within two different shots in each decision stage. Figure 2 shows the flow chart of the bitrate selection process. The whole process can be divided into three parts.

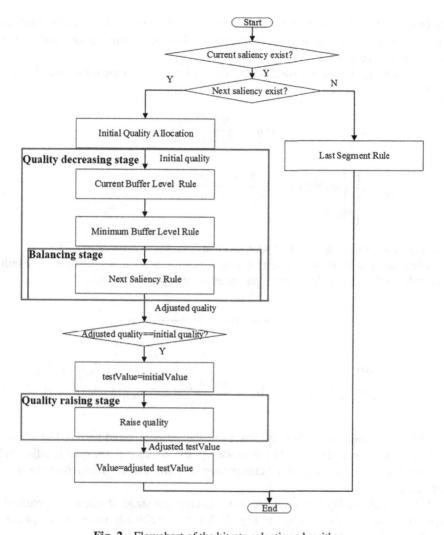

Fig. 2. Flowchart of the bitrate selection algorithm.

We first allocate initial quality according to the saliency difference between the current segment and last segment. The segment granularity ensures low quality oscillations within the same shot. The allocation is denoted as:

$$m_0(n) = \begin{cases} m(n-1) & S(n) = S(n-1) \\ m(n-1) + l[S(n)] - l[S(n-1)] & S(n) > S(n-1) \\ m(n-1) - \{l[S(n-1)] - l[S(n)]\} & S(n) < S(n-1) \end{cases} \quad (1)$$

where $m(n-1)$ is the quality level of the last segment. $l[S(n)]$ is the saliency class of nth segment. $m_0(n)$ is the allocated initial quality level of the current segment and $q_{m0}(n)$ is the actual allocated bitrate.

In the quality decreasing stage, the initial quality is constrained by several rules as Eq. (2).

$$b(n) = \frac{q_{m_0}(n) \times p}{\tilde{w}_n \times B_{cur}(n)}$$

$$q_{m_1}(n) = \begin{cases} \left\{ q(n) \middle| q(n)_{max} \leq \dfrac{\tilde{w}_n \times B_{cur}(n)}{p}, \ q(n) \in \mathcal{R} \right\} b(n) > 1 \\ q_{m_0}(n) \hspace{5cm} b(n) \leq 1 \end{cases} \quad (2)$$

where p denotes the duration of a segment and $\mathcal{R}$ is the representation set.

The minimum buffer level rule (Eq. (3)) which bases on the estimation of the buffer level adjusts the quality to ensure smoothness of the video playback.

$$B_{m_1}(n) = B_{cur}(n) - \frac{q_{m_1}(n) \times p}{\tilde{w}_n} + p$$

$$q_{m_2}(n) = \begin{cases} q_{m_1}(n) \hspace{4.5cm} B_{m_1}(n) \geq B_{min} \\ \left\{ q(n)_{max} \middle| B_{m_2}(n) = B_{cur}(n) - \dfrac{q(n) \times p}{\tilde{w}_n} + p \geq B_{min} \right\} B_{m_1}(n) < B_{min} \end{cases} \quad (3)$$

Balancing stage is to adjust quality to fit the saliency trend among last segment, current segment and next shot. In this process, we don't change the quality adjusted by the above two rules $(q_{m2}(n))$ until it cannot meet with the lowest buffer requirement from next saliency.

If the initial quality is not altered in the decreasing stage, it infers the potential to increase ('Quality raising stage' in Fig. 2). So, we continually increase the quality to test the endurance of the aforementioned constraints.

Schedule. The schedule scheme is the conventional bimodal downloading scheduling, in which the engine might delay for a while to prevent buffer from overflows in case that the buffer reaches some upper limit.

$$\hat{T}[n] = \begin{cases} 0, B[n-1] < B_{stable} \\ 500 \, ms, \quad otherwise \end{cases} \quad (4)$$

4   Simulation Results

To evaluate the performance of the proposed algorithms in real-world scenarios, we have implemented it into the player prototype included in dash.js. The network is simulated by DummyNet [17]. We put this network emulator on the client host to control the downstream available bandwidth. The test video sequence is a concatenated combination of seven YUV sequences [18], arranged as Forman->Waterfall->Stephan->Tempete->Soccer->Highway->Football, and circulated for four times. It ensures the presence of saliency variation in the short testing video. The parameters used in above algorithms are set as Table 1.

Table 1.   Default client parameters.

Parameters	Default values	Parameters	Default values
Frames	6396	Resolution	352×288
Segments	156	p	2 s
GOP	48	B_{min}, $B_{insufficient}$	4 s, 2 s
Frame rate	24fps	B_{stable}, B_{rich}	12 s, 32 s
Resolution	352×288	B_{arget}	[4 s, 12 s]

To prove the effectiveness of the saliency-aware characteristics, we set the network to limited constant available bandwidth of 600 kbps and 300 kbps, respectively, which are typical for the wireless/mobile networks. We compare our algorithm with the dash.js throughput-based algorithm (abbreviated as dashJS) and the BOLA.

4.1   Scenario1: 600 kbps

Figure 3 illustrates how the dashJS, the BOLA and the proposed algorithm select the qualities for each segment. Figure 4 presents the buffer status with the bandwidth of

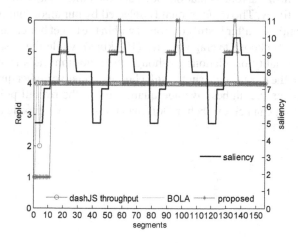

Fig. 3.   Representation index running on the bandwidth of 600 kbps.

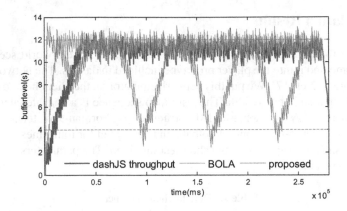

Fig. 4. Buffer status running on the bandwidth of 600 kbps.

600 kbps. The black line in Fig. 3 is the saliency curve of the test sequence. The results show that our algorithm chooses the quality well according to the saliency.

Also, the proposed algorithm has the highest average quality (higher than 450 kbps). It tries to keep constant in the same shot so as to extend the time spent on the same quality level. The reason for the drop in the most salient shot is that the algorithm doesn't reserve buffer for the next whole shot. The BOLA and the dashJS choose quality nearest the average level (450 kbps) of the bandwidth. The fluctuation on buffer status of the proposed algorithm is inevitable for the buffer reserving scheme. However, it can control the buffer within a constant target (4 s to 12 s). Both the buffer status of BOLA and dashJS are kept constant at the stable buffer size, failing in choosing a higher quality. As a result, the proposed algorithm makes better use of network and buffer resources.

4.2   Scenario2: 300 kbps

Figures 5 and 6 show the representation index and the buffer status on the bandwidth of 300 kbps, respectively. The trend of quality selected by our algorithm is similar to that of the 600 kbps and the buffer is still controlled within the target buffer range. The BOLA and the dashJS still choose average quality (150 kbps), while the dashJS also suffers from the severe quality oscillations. Although the algorithm fails in maintaining the highest quality in the most salient shot, it still chooses a relative higher quality (300 kbps) and it also achieves the highest average quality. From the overall point of view, the proposed algorithm can achieve better QoE than the saliency-agnostic algorithms.

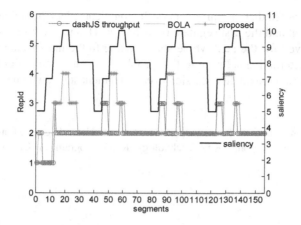

Fig. 5. Representation index running on the bandwidth of 300 kbps.

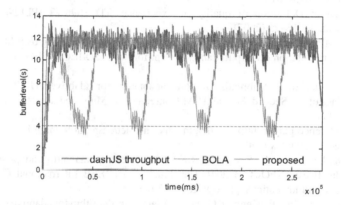

Fig. 6. Buffer status running on the bandwidth of 300 kbps.

5 Conclusions

In this paper, we have explored the temporal and spatial features of the video contents for the video streaming with optimized QoE in the DASH streaming services. In particular, we have adopted the state-of-the-art saliency detection method in computer vision and image processing and integrated it in the DASH server to preprocess the DASH contents. The saliency-aware client adaptation algorithm can make the corresponding decisions driven by the visual perceptual features, which really reflects the expected quality perceived by humans.

When compared with the dash.js throughput-based algorithm and the BOLA, the proposed algorithm not only reaches the highest average quality but also chooses quality according with the attention of each segment. Meanwhile, it has a more robust scheme to minimize the quality shifts in the same shot, which makes a balance among buffer overflow, buffer underflow and requirement for higher quality.

It should be noted that the current algorithm only considers the saliency relationship with last segment and the first segment of next shot. This may cause insufficient buffer resources reserved for the next whole shot, leading to the unexpected quality drop in next shot. An alternative solution to this problem is to use some global optimization methods to program the quality decision in each segment stage, which will be our future work.

Acknowledgement. This work was supported by National Natural Science Foundation of China (61472389) and the National Key Technology R&D Program of China under Contract (2015BAK22B02).

References

1. Cisco: Cisco visual networking index: Forecast and methodology, 2015–2020. CISCO White paper, 2016: 2015-2016
2. ITU-T SG12: Definition of quality of experience. TD 109rev2 (PLEN/12), Geneva, Switzerland, pp. 16–25 (2007)
3. ISO/IEC MPEG: Information technology-dynamic adaptive streaming over http (dash)-part 1: Media presentation description and segment formats. ISO/IEC MPEG, Technical report (2012)
4. Liu, C., Bouazizi, I., Gabbouj, M.: Rate adaptation for adaptive HTTP streaming. In: Proceedings of the Second Annual ACM Conference on Multimedia Systems, pp. 169–174. ACM (2011)
5. DASH reference player: http://mediapm.edgesuite.net/dash/public/nightly/samples/dash-if-reference-player/index.html
6. Spiteri, K., Urgaonkar, R., Sitaraman, R.K.: BOLA: near-optimal bitrate adaptation for online videos. In: IEEE INFOCOM 2016-The 35th Annual IEEE International Conference on Computer Communications, pp. 1–9. IEEE (2016)
7. Miller, K., Quacchio, E., Gennari, G., et al.: Adaptation algorithm for adaptive streaming over HTTP. In: 2012 19th International Packet Video Workshop (PV), pp. 173–178. IEEE (2012)
8. Seufert, M., Egger, S., Slanina, M., et al.: A survey on quality of experience of http adaptive streaming. IEEE Commun. Surv. Tutorials **17**(1), 469–492 (2015)
9. Hu, S., Sun, L., Gui, C., et al.: Content-aware adaptation scheme for QoE optimized DASH applications. In: 2014 IEEE Global Communications Conference (GLOBECOM), pp. 1336–1341. IEEE (2014)
10. Li, Z., Zhu, X., Gahm, J., et al.: Probe and adapt: rate adaptation for HTTP video streaming at scale. IEEE J. Sel. Areas Commun. **32**(4), 719–733 (2014)
11. Xue, H., Zhang, Y., Yan, J.: Perceptual optimized adaptive HTTP streaming. IEEE Visual Communication and Image Processing (2017, accepted)
12. Apostolidis, E., Mezaris, V.: Fast shot segmentation combining global and local visual descriptors. In: 2014 IEEE International Conference on Acoustics, Speech and Signal Processing (ICASSP), pp. 6583–6587. IEEE (2014)
13. Hu, S.H., Yu, J.Q.: Content-based adaptive transmission for soccer video. Adv. Sci. Lett. **10**(1), 478–485 (2012)
14. Wang, W., Shen, J., Shao, L.: Consistent video saliency using local gradient flow optimization and global refinement. IEEE Trans. Image Process. **24**(11), 4185–4196 (2015)

15. Dobrian, F., Sekar, V., Awan, A., et al.: Understanding the impact of video quality on user engagement. ACM SIGCOMM Comput. Commun. Rev. **41**(4), 362–373 (2011)
16. Moorthy, A.K., Choi, L.K., Bovik, A.C., et al.: Video quality assessment on mobile devices: Subjective, behavioral and objective studies. IEEE J. Sel. Top. Sign. Proces. **6**(6), 652–671 (2012)
17. Rizzo, L.: Dummynet: a simple approach to the evaluation of network protocols. ACM SIGCOMM Comput. Commun. Rev. **27**(1), 31–41 (1997)
18. YUV Video Sequences. http://media.xiph.org/video/derf

Dynamic Multi-tree Switching for Multimedia Multicast in an OpenFlow-Based Fat-Tree Network

Liyue Zhu[1]([⊠]), Yongyi Ran[2], Long Sun[2], and Han Hu[3]

[1] Academy of Broadcasting Science, SAPPRFT, Beijing, China
zhuliyue@abs.ac.cn
[2] University of Science and Technology of China, Hefei, China
yyran@ustc.edu.cn, sunlong@mail.ustc.edu.cn
[3] Nanyang Technological University, Singapore, Singapore
hhu@ntu.edu.sg

Abstract. In data center networks, multicast paradigm is significant for multimedia data transmission, e.g. distributed video transcoding [13]. However, single multicast tree generally cannot cope with network congestion and failures well. Although multi-tree multicast is able to achieve load balance and failure recovery by applying dynamic multi-tree switching mechanisms, it is hard to be deployed and implemented in the conventional networks. OpenFlow separates the control plane and data plane, and thus has better controllability and programmability. Therefore, in this paper, we aim to propose an adaptive filter based dynamic multi-tree switching algorithm for multimedia multicast in an OpenFlow-based Fat-Tree data center network. Firstly, for each multicast session, we select several multicast trees as candidates and calculate a priority value for each multicast tree by using the monitored network status. Secondly, adaptive filter is used to predict the priority value of the next time slot which is then used to design the dynamic hierarchical multi-tree switching strategy and the data distribution policy. Finally, experiments are carried out in Mininet to verify the feasibility and performance of our proposed algorithm.

Keywords: Multi-tree multicast · Fat-Tree · OpenFlow
Hierarchical multi-tree switching · Adaptive filter

1 Introduction

A data center plays an instrumental role in data computing, storage and exchange, and provides a plenty of computing and storage resources for Internet services and applications including social networks, web search, distributed multimedia processing, and so on. In modern cloud computing data centers, multicast communication is an important communication mode. For example, social services such as Facebook and Twitter are running on a data center architecture

© Springer Nature Singapore Pte Ltd. 2018
G. Zhai et al. (Eds.): IFTC 2017, CCIS 815, pp. 392–406, 2018.
https://doi.org/10.1007/978-981-10-8108-8_36

that supports multicast [17]. The benefits of supporting multicast services in data center networks include (1) avoiding duplication data to reduce unnecessary network traffic and improve bandwidth utilization; (2) balancing workload by distributing data and tasks among different servers. In order to meet the following requirements: high scalability, low configuration overhead, high bandwidth between servers, flexible topology and link capacity control, some new network topology schemes are being put forward. Fat-Tree [1] is one of these emerging schemes, which presents a switch-centric and three-tier data center network structure and can well meet the high bandwidth and multi-path demands [4] of data centers.

However, due to the increasing internal traffic of the data center network, e.g. multimedia data transmission, the aggregation traffic of the core layer switches in the Fat-Tree network architecture also becomes very large and there exist packet loss and long transmission latency in single-tree multicast [3]. In order to solve these problems, the authors [2,9,15,16,19] used multi-tree multicast for one-to-many data transmission. Most of these existing algorithms mainly rely on centralized computing, but the traditional IP multicast routing is based on routers and has no centralized computing functions. In addition, the overhead would be very large for the routers in a traditional network due to very frequent multicast member join and departure. Therefore, it is difficult to achieve multi-tree multicast transmission over the traditional networks.

Researchers at Stanford University proposed OpenFlow technology [10] in 2008. The core idea of OpenFlow is the separation of logic control and data forwarding. The controller can obtain the global network topology and link states and can decide the transmission path of each data flow, the switches only focus on forwarding data packets according to the forwarding rules. By applying Open-Flow technology in data center to support multicast services, we can not only manage multicast group efficiently and reduce the management overhead, but also can design multicast routing algorithm based on multicast members and link states. More importantly, multi-tree multicast algorithm can be achieved in such an OpenFLow-based fat-tree data center network.

In this paper, we address the aforementioned challenges in an OpenFlow-based Fat-Tree data center network. We design a dynamic multi-tree multicast hierarchical switching mechanism for multimedia multicast based on adaptive filter. This scheme makes full use of the controllability and programmability of OpenFlow network and the multi-path feature of Fat-Tree network structure. In this proposed mechanism, the OpenFlow controller will generate multiple multicast trees according to the network topology and the locations of group members, monitor the real-time states of each link in each multicast tree, and calculate a priority value for each multicast tree according to the monitored link status. Then, the OpenFlow controller will predict the priority value of the next time slot for each multicast tree based on adaptive filter. Finally, we design a dynamic hierarchical multi-tree switching strategy and decide the data distribution ratio of each multicast tree based on the predicted priority values and the Fat-Tree structure. By using the proposed dynamic multi-tree multicast hierarchical switching mechanism, we can steer away from the congestion link in advance, reduce the packet loss as well as the transmission delay. At the same time, it is efficient for us to achieve network load balancing, improve the utilization of network bandwidth and reduce packet loss caused by link failures by employing multi-tree multicast transmission. To verify the performance of our proposed algorithm, experiments are carried out in Mininet. Specifically, our main contributions are as follows.

- We present how to calculate the priority value for a multicast tree according to the monitored link status and predict the priority value of the next time slot for each multicast tree based on adaptive filter.
- We design a dynamic hierarchical multi-tree switching strategy according to the features of OpenFlow and FAT-Tree structure to decide which multicast tree will be used to transmit data packet as well as the amount of data packets for each multicast tree.
- Finally, experiments are carried out in Mininet to verify the feasibility and performance of our proposed algorithm.

The rest of this paper is structured as follows. Section 2 reviews the related work. In Sect. 3, we present the multi-tree multicast in a Fat-Tree network. Section 4 presents the dynamic hierarchical multi-tree switching strategy. The evaluation results are detailed in Sects. 5 and 6 concludes this paper.

2   Related Work

In this section, we investigate relevant research for multi-tree multicast.

Generally, people use a single multicast tree [8] to achieve one-to-many data transmission, but they cannot well solve the problem of delay and packet loss caused by network link congestion or failures. The reason is that the reconstruction of a good multicast tree will consume a lot of time, which is bound to bring a certain delay and packet loss. In order to solve the above problems, multi-tree multicast transmission [2,9,15,16,19] is becoming more and more significant and has been studied in the literature.

In paper [2], the authors introduced a problem formulation with tree-flow conservation constraints and presented a backpressure algorithm for the utility maximization problem for multi-tree multicast. DPMT (Dual-path Multicast Tree) [18] establishes multiple multicast trees for each multicast group. Experiments show that the multicast reliability is improved compared with a single multicast tree. Rahimi et al. [12] study how to maximize the multicast throughput of several multicast sessions, while the network bandwidth is fairly distributed across multicast sessions. Several distributed round-robin algorithms are proposed, and one of the algorithms achieves up to 90% of the theoretic bound on the throughput. The major drawback of these proposed algorithms in [2,12,18] and other similar work is their high maintenance overhead. In contrast, our work leverages OpenFlow for a logically centralized algorithm that is friendly to network administrators. In addition, the prediction algorithm based on adaptive filter presented in our paper can avoid congested links in advance and more efficiently.

There are very few recent papers on multi-tree multicast in SDNs [5,7]. Lee et al. [7] studied the problem of multipath multicast routing for MDC videos, and strived to be robust against switch/link failures, load-balanced across all links, compatible to SDNs, and adaptive to topology changes. They proposed two algorithms, RMMR* and RMMR, to solve the problem which employ multipath multicast for robustness, mathematical optimization for load balancing and SDN compliance, and lightweight routing heuristics for adaptability. Kotani et al. [5] presented a design of OpenFlow controller to handle IP multicast and a method to switch multicast trees with little packet loss. They achieved multicast tree switching with the combination of redundant trees by assigning unique ID for each tree, embedding IDs in the packets, and setting up flow entry to rewrite packet header to the ID-embedded one in the sender switch. DYNSDM(Dynamic Software-Defined Multicast) [14] also used a round-robin mechanism to poll multi-tree, but not fully combined with the network status. In contrast, our work will make full use of the features of OpenFlow group table to achieve an efficient and fast multi-tree switching mechanism.

In summary, although the use of multi-tree multicast for multimedia transmission in data center can lead to higher network throughput, balanced link utilization, etc., the existing work does not make full use of the features of OpenFlow and network architecture. In this paper, we use OpenFlow technology to monitor the network link status in real time, and define the multicast tree priority according to the network states. At the same time, an adaptive filter based prediction algorithm will be presented to predict the priority for each candidate multicast tree. Finally, multi-tree switching strategy is proposed to dynamically decide which multicast tree is used to transmit multimedia data.

3   Multi-tree Multicast in Fat-Tree

In this section, we firstly introduce the primary background of multi-tree multicast in a Fat-Tree data center network, and then propose the system architecture for multimedia multicast with dynamic hierarchical multi-tree switching mechanism. Finally, we discuss the generation of multiple multicast trees in Fat-tree data center network.

3.1   OpenFlow-Based Fat-Tree Networks

Fat-Tree is a switch-centric data center network structure. The switches in Fat-Tree networks can be divided into three layers: the core layer, the aggregation layer and the edge layer switches.

The switch ports in the core layer all connect down to the aggregation switches, half of the switch ports in the aggregate layer go up to the core layer and half go down to the edge layer, and half of the switch ports in the edge layer go up to the aggregate layer and half connect to the servers. The distinctive feature of a fat-tree is that for any switch, the number of links going down to its siblings is equal to the number of links going up to its parent in the upper level. Therefore, the links get fatter towards the top of the tree, and switch in the root of the tree has most links compared to any other switch below it. The set of switches in the dashed box in Fig. 1 is called pod (Point of Delivery). For K-port switches, there would be total K pods, and Fig. 1 is a $K = 4$ Fat-Tree network structure. each pod contains two levels of $K/2$ switches, i.e., the edge level and the aggregation level. Each K-port switch at the edge level uses $K/2$ ports to connect the servers, and uses the remaining $K/2$ ports to connect the aggregation-level switches in the pod. At the core level, there are $(K/2)^2$ K-port switches, and each switch has one port connecting to one pod. Therefore, the total number of servers supported in Fat-Tree is $K^3/4$. In this paper, all switches support the OpenFlow v1.1 protocol, which is responsible for forwarding the data layer and communicating with the Open-Flow controller. The OpenFlow controller maintains basic information about the entire network, such as topology, network elements, and available services. The application running on the OpenFlow controller manages the entire network by controlling the OpenFlow switches according the network-wide information.

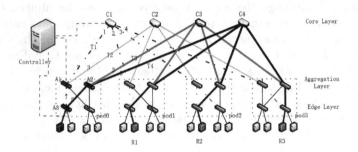

Fig. 1. OpenFlow-based Fat-Tree data center network.

3.2   Multicast Architecture

As shown in Fig. 2, the multi-tree multicast system architecture consists of four major parts on OpenFlow controller and three parts on OpenFlow switches. The "link state monitor" periodically collects the network topology and the link states from OpenFlow switches, the "multi-tree generation" module run multicast tree generation algorithm according to the collected topology information and multicast group member information, the "priority calculation and prediction" module calculates the priority of each multicast tree according to the collected link state information and then predicts the next time-slot priority for each multicast tree based on adaptive filter, and the "AHMS" (dynamic Adaptive filter based Hierarchical Multi-tree Switching strategy) module makes decisions based on the predicted priority values and configures the decision results into the group table with "select" type (OpenFlow version $\geqslant$ v1.1) on OpenFlow switches. The switches on each level will forward multimedia packets according to the rules in

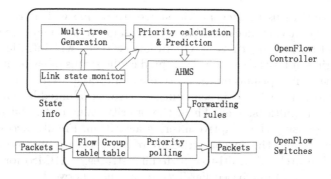

Fig. 2. Muti-tree multicast system architecture

flow tables and group table. In particular, a polling algorithm is designed for the group table on the OpenFlow switches to decide which multicast tree would be employed.

3.3 Multi-tree Generation

At present, the shortest path tree algorithm is a commonly used method to calculate the multicast routing path which aims to generate a shortest path tree from the multicast source to the multicast destinations. In this paper, we use the shortest path algorithm presented in [11] to generate multiple multicast trees. There exist several characteristics of multiple multicast trees in a Fat-Tree data center network due to the three-layer structure. First, each multicast tree must pass through a core layer switch, the path from the core layer switch to the end sever is unique, and there exist **fork nodes** between multicast trees, e.g. A1, A2 and A3 shown in Fig. 1. Second, fork nodes only appear in the pod where the multicast source resides, that is, the switches in the edge layer and aggregation layer of a pod. It is beneficial for making multi-tree switching strategy to clarify the the fork nodes. Based on OpenFlow technology, the OpenFlow controller collects network topology and link information, and establishes multiple multicast trees via the shortest path tree algorithm. As illustrated in Fig. 1, four multicast trees T1, T2, T3 and T4 are generated (plotted in different format line), which go through the core layer switches C1, C2, C3 and C4 respectively.

4   Adaptive Filter Based Hierarchical Multi-tree Switching Mechanism

As descried before, multi-tree multicast for multimedia transmission in data center can effectively avoid congestion and single-multicast tree failure, achieve load balance and improve bandwidth resource utilization. However, because the available bandwidth of the each link is randomly and time-varying, we need to evaluate the status of each multicast tree to decide which tree is the most appropriate one at each decision time. At the same time, monitoring link states and distributing routing rules to OpenFlow switches will introduce a certain delay and bring in hysteresis, so we can predict the status of each multicast tree, and then select the optimal multicast tree based on the predicted values.

In this paper, the status of each multicast tree is evaluated by calculating the priority of each multicast tree. Then, the priority value of the future time slot is predicted by using the adaptive filtering algorithm. Finally, according to the predicted values and the special structure of Fat-Tree, we propose an adaptive filter based Hierarchical Multi-tree Switching strategy (AHMS) for multimedia multicast in a OpenFlow based Fat-Tree data center network.

4.1   Priority Value of a Multicast Tree

In this paper, we define a priority value to represent the status of a multicast tree. Firstly, for a single link, we can derive the weight value according to its current used bandwidth and delay [6]:

$$w_l = \alpha D + (1 - \alpha)B^{1/X} \tag{1}$$

where $1/X = B_{used}/B_{total}$ indicates the proportion of used bandwidth to total bandwidth, B_{used} and B_{total} represent the current used bandwidth and the total bandwidth, D denotes the current delay of this link (unit: ms), α is a weight factor and $\alpha \in (0,1)$, B is a constraint factor used to limit the contribution of the bandwidth to the link weight in the range of $[0, B]$ $(B > 0)$.

Assuming that a multicast session has M available multicast trees, the links of the mth multicast tree can be expressed as a set $L_m = \{l_{m1}, l_{m2}, ..., l_{m|l_m|}\}$, and the weight of l_{mi} is w_{mi}, then the average weight of the mth multicast tree can be defined as:

$$W_m = avg([w_{m1}, w_{m2}, ..., w_{m|l_m|}]) \tag{2}$$

Obviously, the transmission capacity of the mth multicast tree would be worse with a greater W_m and the transmission capacity is better with a smaller W_m.

Definition 1. The priority of the mth multicast tree is defined as:

$$P^m = \begin{cases} \frac{1}{W_m}C & W_m \geqslant 1 \\ C & W_m < 1 \end{cases} \tag{3}$$

In formula (3), C is used to limit the priority in the range of $[0, C]$ $(C > 0)$. It can be observed from formula (3) that the priority of the multicast tree is inversely proportional to the average weight of the multicast tree. A higher priority will lead to a lower the average weight, and vice versa.

4.2   Priority Prediction Based on Adaptive Filter

In this paper, we consider a time-slotted system indexed by $t = \{0, 1, \cdots\}$ where the length of a time slot is δ. At the beginning of each time slot, the multicast tree priority of different time slots can be calculated according to the above formula 3. However, monitoring link states and distributing routing rules to OpenFlow switches will introduce a certain delay and bring in hysteresis, so we can predict the status of each multicast tree, and then select the optimal multicast tree based on the predicted values.

Adaptive filter is a typical method for predicting the signal values at a given time based on the filter adaptation coefficients and historical signal values. This method improves the accuracy of the prediction by adjusting the filter coefficients and adapting it to the statistical characteristics of the signal by obtaining the historical parameters. Therefore, this paper uses adaptive filter to predict the priority of a multicast tree.

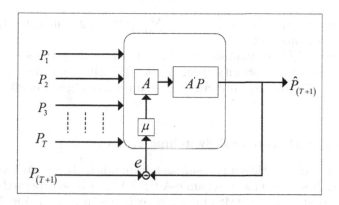

Fig. 3. Structure of the adaptive filter.

Figure 3 shows the structure of adaptive filter. This method is to use the filter adaptation coefficients A and T historical priority values to predict the $(t+1)$th priority value. By calculating the error e between the actual priority values and the predicted priority values, we can adjust the filter coefficients of to make the prediction of the priority at the next time slot. The prediction algorithm consists of two steps: one is to predict the priority value, the second is to adjust the filter adaptation coefficient.

In detail, the first step is to predict the $(t+1)$th priority value of a multicast tree. First, we calculate t historical priority values $P = [P_1, P_2, ..., P_t]'$, where the cardinality t is the number of samples, and the value of t depends on the empirical value (generally, the value range is between 25 and 100). Then, the predicted priority value $\hat{P}_{(t+1)}$ can be calculated:

$$\hat{P}_{(t+1)} = A' P \tag{4}$$

where the filter adaptation coefficients $A = [A_1, A_2, ..., A_t]'$. A will be initialized when we run the prediction system, e.g.

$$A_k = \frac{2k}{t(t+1)}, \; k \in [1, t] \tag{5}$$

The initial value would affect the first round prediction, but we can adjust these coefficients to improve the prediction accuracy.

The second step is to corrects the filter adaptation coefficient A. A is the key factor that affects the prediction result. For the sake of a more accuracy result, in this paper, we use the error e between the actual priority values and the predicted priority values to correct A gradually. The modified filter adaptation coefficients A can be represented as:

$$e = P_{(t+1)} - \hat{P}_{(t+1)} \tag{6}$$

$$A^* = A + 2\mu e P \tag{7}$$

where the convergence factor $\mu = 2/(3\sum_{j=1}^{T}(P_j)^2)$, P_j indicates the priority value at the jth time slot.

The corrected filter adaptation coefficient obtained by the second step can be used to predict the priority value at the $(t + 2)$th time slot. Through the continuous prediction and correction, we can achieve a good prediction with a small error.

4.3 Dynamic Hierarchical Switching Strategy

In order to realize multi-tree transmission in parallel, the OpenFlow controller shown in Fig. 2 will provide a dynamic Adaptive filter based Hierarchical Multi-tree Switching strategy (AHMS) for multimedia multicast in a OpenFlow based Fat-Tree data center network according to the predicted priority values of multiple multicast trees and the Fat-Tree network structure.

In a Fat-Tree network, there exist "fork nodes" between multiple multicast trees according to the aforementioned generation algorithm. The switching is executed exactly on these fork nodes. Here we define two level switching according to the locations of the fork nodes. If the multi-tree switching occurs on aggregation switches, we call this as **"First Level Switching"**. If the multi-tree switching occurs on edge switches, we call this as **"Second Level Switching"**.

At the first level switching, there is only one multicast tree for an egress link on the aggregation layer switch. The primary multi-tree switching strategy is to poll the predicted priority values of the available multicast trees to decide which multicast tree would be used and how many packets would be transmitted. For example, as shown in Fig. 1, the predicted priority $\hat{P}_{T1} = 7, \hat{P}_{T2} = 3, \hat{P}_{T3} = 2, \hat{P}_{T4} = 5$, The "AHMS" module on OpenFlow controller will configure the weight values in group table on OpenFlow switch $A1$ as 7 and 3. When $A1$ receives 10 multimedia packets, it will forward 7 packets from the multicast tree with priority value 7 and forward 3 packets through the multicast tree with priority value 3.

At the second level switching, there exist multiple multicast trees for an egress link on the edge layer switch. Therefore, the second level switching will firstly find a optimal multicast tree with maximum priority for each egress link, and then decide which egress link would be used to transmit packets as well as how many packets should be forwarded by using the polling algorithm presented in the following subsection. For example, as shown in Fig. 1, the switch $A3$ is configured with a group weight of 7 and 5. When the switch receives 12 packets, 7 packets will be forwarded from the port connected to $A1$ and 5 to $A2$.

4.4 Weight Polling Algorithm

In the dynamic hierarchical switching strategy, the controller will send "select" group tables to OpenFlow switches dynamically. In order to realize a polling algorithm to achieve multi-tree switching and packet forwarding on OpenFlow switches, this scheme needs to design a Weighted Round-Robin Scheduling (WRR) algorithm on the switches. WRR algorithm is an important algorithm for real load balancing. The basic idea is to allocate the traffic to each port in turn according to the weight values in the group table. This algorithm takes into account the priority of each multicast tree, i.e., the status of the network, ensures that the multicast tree with higher priority processes more data packets and avoids the overload on one multicast tree. In WRR algorithm, we assume that the "select" group table has multiple action buckets and assign a weight value to each bucket, $bucket[i]$ represents the i-th bucket whose current weight value is $weight[i]$ (i is the Index), Num_bucket is the total number of buckets in the group table, Max_weight is the maximum weight of all buckets, and Gcd_weight is the maximum common divisor for the weight of all buckets. Here we also assume that the index i of the bucket in the group table starts at 0 and

---

Algorithm 1. The Weighted Round-Robin Scheduling (WRR).

Require: select_group_table
Ensure: bucket
1: **if** add or mod select_group_table **then**
2:      Index←1, Weight←0,
3:      Num_bucke←sumbucket[0]...bucket[m],
4:      Max_weight←maxweight[0]...weight[m],
5:      Gcd_weight←gcdweight[0]weight[m].
6: **end if**
7: **for** j ← 0 to Num_bucket **do**
8:      Index←(Index+1) % Num_bucket,
9:      **if** Index == 0 **then**
10:          **if** Weight ⩽ Gcd_weight **then**
11:              Weight←Max_weight,
12:          **else**
13:              Weight←Weight-Gcd_weight,
14:          **end if**
15:      **end if**
16:      **if** weight[Index] ⩾ Weight **then**
17:          **return** bucket[Index].
18:      **end if**
19: **end for**

the weight values are positive integers. The group table weight polling algorithm is summarized in Algorithm 1.

5   Evaluation

In order to verify the performance of the proposed dynamic adaptive filter based hierarchical multi-tree switching algorithm b, we use Mininet to simulate the Fat-tree network topology with $K = 4$ in Linux OS system. The OpenFlow switch in the topology is designed with the group weight polling algorithm (i.e. WRR), and the Ryu controller is used to connect and control each OpenFlow switch, as shown in Fig. 1. In order to simulate the real data center network, we use Ostinato to generate random traffic.

5.1   Performance of Adaptive Filter Based Prediction Algorithm

The traffic size in the network directly affects the available bandwidth and transmission delay, and determines the priority of the multicast tree. Because of the ubiquitous similarity among different network flows, the adaptive filter based prediction algorithm can update and correct the coefficients to make the priority prediction has the ability of dynamic adaptive update, and the algorithm has the advantages of fast convergence and high precision. So we firstly design an adaptive filter based prediction algorithm in the Ryu controller, then calculate and predict the priority for each multicast tree according to the link states.

In the prediction algorithm, we set $B = C = 10$ and use $t = 70$ historical samples to predict the priority value of the next time slot. The length of a time slot is $\delta = 10\,\text{s}$. In our experiment, we record the true priority value and predicted priority value of multicast tree $T2$ illustrated in Fig. 1. It can be observed from the results in Fig. 4 that the predicted curve based on the adaptive filter is almost the same as the true value curve, the root mean square error is 0.28 and the prediction error is small. Therefore, the adaptive filter based prediction algorithm is suitable for predicting the multicast tree priority value.

5.2   Performance of AHMS

In order to verify the performance of the proposed AHMS, we compared AHMS with two other algorithms in terms of transmission delay and packet loss rate of the multimedia multicast service. One comparing algorithm is using a single multicast tree to achieve one-to-many transmission. We use Dijkstra algorithm to generate a SPT (shortest path tree) as a multicast tree. Another comparing algorithm is DYNSDM which is mentioned in Sect. 2. DYNSDM also employ polling algorithm to select an appropriate multicast tree for data transmission, but does not consider the network status.

As illustrated in Fig. 5, when the network is congested, the proposed AHMS gains lower delay obviously compared with the other two methods. Especially at the time 1000 s, 1500 s and 2300 s, SPT has the largest transmission delay.

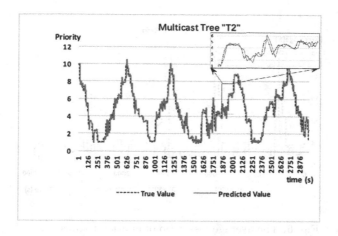

Fig. 4. True and predicted value of multicast tree priority.

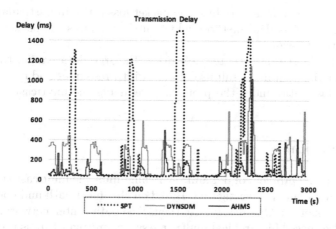

Fig. 5. The average delay of multicast transmission.

The main reason is that when there is a congested link in a single multicast tree, the SPT method can not avoid this congestion. On the other hand, compared with DYNSDM, our proposed AHMS can further reduce the transmission delay. The first reason is that the DYNSDM can not avoid congested tree according to the network status. Instead, it will distribute the multicast data to multiple multicast trees on average which also includes the congested multicast tree. The second reason is that AHMS not only evaluates the priority of the multicast tree in combination with the network status, but also makes accurate prediction, so it can effectively avoids congestion in advance based on the prediction results.

Figure 6 shows the results of packet loss ratio by comparing three algorithms. It can be observed that at the time point 250 s, 1000 s, 1500 s and 2300 s, due to the too large network traffic, SPT-based method can not effectively avoid the congestion links which caused high packet loss ratio. While DYNSDM and our

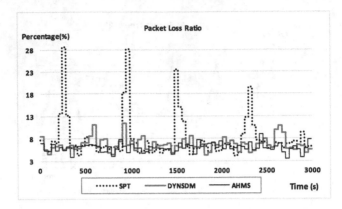

Fig. 6. The average loss ratio of multicast transmission.

proposed AHMS can hugely reduce the packet loss ratio. In particular, AHMS is better than the DYNSDM method, which further reduces the packet loss during multicast transmission.

Therefore, in the data center network with large data traffic, the proposed AHMS algorithm can make full use of bandwidth resources and can guarantee a low packet loss ratio under the premise of reducing the multicast transmission delay.

6   Conclusion

In this paper, the problem of dynamic switching multiple multicast trees for multimedia multicasting is investigated. Based on the multi-path and controllability characteristics of the OpenFlow-based Fat-Tree data center network, a dynamic adaptive filter based hierarchical multi-tree switching algorithm is proposed. The proposed algorithm uses adaptive filter to predict the priority for each multicast tree and then dynamically decides the switching strategy according to these predicted priority. The experimental results show that the proposed algorithm can accurately predict the priority of a multicast tree and can obviously reduce the packet loss as well as the transmission delay.

References

1. Al-Fares, M., Loukissas, A., Vahdat, A.: A scalable, commodity data center network architecture. SIGCOMM Comput. Commun. Rev. **38**(4), 63–74 (2008). http://doi.acm.org/10.1145/1402946.1402967
2. Cho, C., Xia, Y.: Multi-tree multicast with a backpressure algorithm. In: 49th IEEE Conference on Decision and Control (CDC), pp. 655–660, December 2010
3. Guo, Z., Duan, J., Yang, Y.: On-line multicast scheduling with bounded congestion in Fat-Tree data center networks. IEEE J. Sel. Areas Commun. **32**(1), 102–115 (2014)

4. Jo, E., Pan, D., Liu, J., Butler, L.: A simulation and emulation study of SDN-based multipath routing for Fat-Tree data center networks. In: Proceedings of the 2014 Winter Simulation Conference, WSC 2014, pp. 3072–3083. IEEE Press, Piscataway (2014). http://dl.acm.org/citation.cfm?id=2693848.2694235
5. Kotani, D., Suzuki, K., Shimonishi, H.: A design and implementation of OpenFlow controller handling IP multicast with fast tree switching. In: 2012 IEEE/IPSJ 12th International Symposium on Applications and the Internet, pp. 60–67, July 2012
6. Laga, S., Cleemput, T.V., Raemdonck, F.V., Vanhoutte, F., Bouten, N., Claeys, M., Turck, F.D.: Optimizing scalable video delivery through OpenFlow layer-based routing. In: 2014 IEEE Network Operations and Management Symposium (NOMS), pp. 1–4, May 2014
7. Lee, M.W., Li, Y.S., Huang, X., Chen, Y.R., Hou, T.F., Hsu, C.H.: Robust multi-path multicast routing algorithms for videos in software-defined networks. In: 2014 IEEE 22nd International Symposium of Quality of Service (IWQoS), pp. 218–227, May 2014
8. Li, D., Li, Y., Wu, J., Su, S., Yu, J.: ESM: efficient and scalable data center multicast routing. IEEE/ACM Trans. Netw. 20(3), 944–955 (2012). http://dx.doi.org/10.1109/TNET.2011.2169985
9. Long, N.T., Thuy, N.D., Hoang, P.H.: Building multiple multicast trees with guaranteed QOS for service based routing using artificial algorithms. In: Vinh, P.C., Alagar, V. (eds.) ICCASA 2015. LNICST, vol. 165, pp. 354–369. Springer, Cham (2016). https://doi.org/10.1007/978-3-319-29236-6_34
10. McKeown, N., Anderson, T., Balakrishnan, H., Parulkar, G., Peterson, L., Rexford, J., Shenker, S., Turner, J.: Openflow: enabling innovation in campus networks. SIGCOMM Comput. Commun. Rev. 38(2), 69–74 (2008). http://doi.acm.org/10.1145/1355734.1355746
11. Narváez, P., Siu, K.Y., Tzeng, H.Y.: New dynamic algorithms for shortest path tree computation. IEEE/ACM Trans. Netw. 8(6), 734–746 (2000). http://dx.doi.org/10.1109/90.893870
12. Rahimi, M.R., Bais, A., Sarshar, N.: On fair and optimal multi-source IP-multicast. Comput. Netw. 56(4), 1503–1524 (2012)
13. Ran, Y., Yang, J., Yang, E., Chen, S.: Network as a service for next generation internet. In: Naas-Enabled Service Composition in SDN Environment, p. 243 (2017)
14. Rückert, J., Blendin, J., Hark, R., Wächter, T., Hausheer, D.: An extended study of DYNSDM: Software-defined multicast using multi-trees. Technical report, Peer-to-Peer Systems Engineering Lab, TU Darmstadt, Germany (2015)
15. Sun, M., Zhang, X., Wang, L., Shi, H., Zhang, W.: A multiple multicast tree optimization solution based on software defined network. In: 2016 7th International Conference on Information and Communication Systems (ICICS), pp. 168–173, April 2016
16. Tan, X., Li, H., Zhu, Z., Yu, C., Qin, L.: Lmtm: Multi-tree multicast with inter-layer network coding for layered multimedia streaming. In: 2013 8th International Conference on Communications and Networking in China (CHINACOM), pp. 871–876, August 2013
17. Vigfusson, Y., Abu-Libdeh, H., Balakrishnan, M., Birman, K., Burgess, R., Chockler, G., Li, H., Tock, Y.: Dr. Multicast: Rx for data center communication scalability. In: Proceedings of the 5th European Conference on Computer Systems, pp. 349–362. EuroSys 2010, ACM, New York (2010). http://doi.acm.org/10.1145/1755913.1755949

18. Xiao-fei, L., Zhuan, S., De-rain, L., et al.: Improve application layer mulficast stability using dual-path multicast tree. J. Chin. Comput. Syst. **5**(5), 979–982 (2013)
19. Zheng, X., Cho, C., Xia, Y.: Content distribution by multiple multicast trees and intersession cooperation: optimal algorithms and approximations. Comput. Netw. **83**, 100–117 (2015). http://www.sciencedirect.com/science/article/pii/S1389128615000900

Video Surveillance

Current Situation and Research on Consumer Video Surveillance Standards at Home and Abroad

Yi Cheng[1]([✉]), Weicheng Guo[2], and Tao Du[3]

[1] China Electronics Standardization Institute, Beijing 100176, China
cy.c.ok@163.com
[2] Beijing Institute of Technology, Beijing 10080, China
[3] Tianjin University, Tianjin 300072, China

Abstract. In recent years, video surveillance technology has been developing. The application of video surveillance has extended from national and social security to daily life, and a number of consumer-grade video surveillance products have been created. However, the problem also becomes obvious, since the domestic market is still in non-standard stage. The consumer-grade video surveillance does not have specific standards, which seriously affect consumers' awareness of consumer-grade video surveillance products. In this paper, we introduce the video surveillance system and compare the standards of existing video surveillance system. Simultaneously, some suggestions for the standardization of consumer video surveillance are put forward.

Keywords: Video surveillance · Standardization · Consumer

1   Introduction

Video surveillance system is an electronic network system in which the video technology is used to monitor the protected areas. Generally, professional video surveillance products widely existing in industrial environments and especially suitable for running on somewhere with few or unmanned management. Different from the professional video surveillance products, consumer surveillance products should be easier to installation, more practical and higher confidentiality. In recent years, with the change of consumer demand in video surveillance, the reformation of video surveillance technology, and the policy government announced, companies have increased their investment in video surveillance research and continuously some Consumer - oriented video surveillance products launch market. It has aroused great concern from all sectors of the industry, and has become a hot topic of current technical research and standardization.

In this paper, we introduce five components of the video surveillance system, and compare the consumer-grade video surveillance system with the professional-grade

Note: The paper gets subsidized of the 'Test and Verification of Critical Application Standard for Intelligent Manufacturing Model of Color TV Industry' of the Ministry of Industry and Information Technology of the People's Republic of China (MIIT).

© Springer Nature Singapore Pte Ltd. 2018
G. Zhai et al. (Eds.): IFTC 2017, CCIS 815, pp. 409–417, 2018.
https://doi.org/10.1007/978-981-10-8108-8_37

video surveillance system. By analysis, we can see there are significant differences between the two systems. In order to find a solution to the problem, we did followings:

First, we analyzed the consumer demands for video surveillance products. Second, we combined the statistics of Chinese video surveillance, and it shows that the domestic market is not regulated and we need some corresponding standards to regulate the market. Finally, we also analyzed the main content of current domestic and international video surveillance system standards. It is concluded that just simply borrowing professional-grade video surveillance standards cannot meet the demand of reality. As a result, we give some suggestions of establishing consumer-grade video surveillance standards.

2   The Structure of Video Surveillance System

Typically, video surveillance system consists of five parts: camera, transmission, controller, memorizer, and display, as shown in Fig. 1.

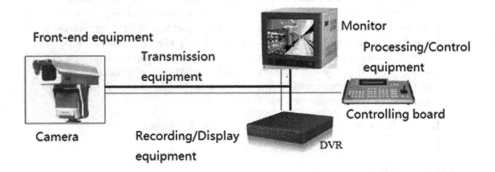

Fig. 1. Basic structure of video surveillance system

Camera. To obtain the external image signal, cameras are installed on the scene with some auxiliary equipment, such as: lenses, shields, scaffolds and platforms. In terms of consumer-grade video surveillance products, the structure of traditional cameras has not been able to meet the demand in appearance, structure and function.

Transmission. The video signal captured by cameras need to be transferred to the back-end equipment. Traditional video signal transmission medium includes coaxial cable, twisted pair and optical fiber. With the development of technology, the way of transmitting video information has changed greatly. Today, consumer-grade video surveillance mainly uses network video surveillance or IP surveillance, and the digital video information is transmitted through wired or wireless IP networks [1].

Controller. The entire control system of cameras includes a decoder, a screen splitter and a video matrix. But in family use, the function request is relatively unitary and the operator's professional ability is different. Therefore, the equipment should be easier to use. The traditional control way has not been able to satisfy the demand.

Memorizer. According to different monitoring environment and requirements, there are several kinds of storage methods: DVR storage, encoder direct connection storage, centralized storage, NVR storage. For the current market of consumer-grade video surveillance products, video storage mainly includes SD card, cloud storage, NVR storage.

Display. Common display devices are monitors and displays. The image signals of all cameras in front system and the recorded replay image signals will be displayed on monitor. Nowadays, consumer video surveillance products have put forward new requirements for display devices. Due to the rapid development of smart phones, consumers prefer to remotely monitor on smart phones and other mobile phones in real time.

3   Standardization of Video Surveillance

3.1   International Standardization

ONVIF Standard. Open Network Video Interface Forum (ONVIF) is an open industry standard jointly developed by companies such as AXIS, BOSCH, SONY etc. This standard describes the network video model, interface, data type and data interaction model, and reuses some existing standards, such as WS series standards [2].

PSIA Protocol. PSIA protocol is an interface protocol developed by the Physical Security Interoperability Alliance that can standardize communications between video management systems and various network media devices [3]. PSIA standard adopts the REST architecture. The implementation of PSIA protocol enables network cameras to meet the uniform standards, which improves the compatibility of network cameras between different manufacturers in the same system. It can recognize the equipment without installing driver to identify the device.

HDCCTV Standard. HDCCTV is a new standard proposed by several chip and system vendors in 2009 for the development of High Definition Surveillance Systems [4]. This standard is a physical electrical interface standard for coaxial cable transmission of uncompressed lossless HD video signals and is the only electrical standard for the world's comprehensive HD surveillance video.

3.2   Differences Between ONVIF, PSIA and HDCCTV

While all of these criteria are issue for network surveillance, there are also many differences. HDCCTV is a compatibility specification for closed-circuit HD cameras, while PSIA and ONVIF are compatible specifications for IP cameras. Compare with ONVIF, PSIA are applicable to the entire security hardware device including access control, but not limited to IP video surveillance. ONVIF was more focused on IP video surveillance at the beginning of the standard setting, but it has since expanded the scope of the standard protocol to include anti-theft and fire-fighting. Besides, the device management and control section defined in ONVIF are provided in the form of Web Services, while PSIA adopted a REST architecture [5].

In addition to the above three standards, there are other relevant standards, such as the following criteria defined by ITU in the communications aspect of video surveillance system [6–12]:

- ITU-T F.743 Requirements and service description for visual surveillance
- ITU-T F.743.1 Requirements for intelligent visual surveillance
- ITU-T F.743.2 Requirements for cloud storage in visual surveillance
- ITU-T F.743.3 Requirements for visual surveillance system interworking
- ITU-T H.626 Architectural requirements for visual surveillance
- ITU-T H.626.1 Architecture for mobile visual surveillance
- ITU-T H.627 Signalling and protocols for visual surveillance

3.3 Domestic Video Surveillance Standards

In China, with the development of video surveillance industry, a number of video surveillance standards have been formed, and the typical standard is GB/T 28181-2016 *Technical requirements for information transport, switch and control in video surveillance network system for public security*. The standard specifies the interconnection structure, communication protocol structure, security requirements and interface protocols of information transmission, exchange and control in the city monitoring alarm network system. This standard is applicable to the scheme design, system test, acceptance and related equipment research and development, production and other information system can be used.

Currently, the main existing national standards in video surveillance are these following six [13–18]:

- GB/T 33778-2017 *RF technical requirements and testing methods for the wireless transceiver of video monitoring system*
- GB/T 25724-2017 *Technical specifications for surveillance video and audio coding for public security*
- GB/T 28181-2016 *Technical requirements for information transport, switch and control in video surveillance network system for public security*
- GB/T 31488-2015 *Technical requirements for face identification of video surveillance in security systems*
- GB/T 30147-2013 *Technical requirements for real time intelligent video analysis devices in surveillance system*
- GB 20815-2006 *Digital video record equipment of video surveillance system in security & protection systems*

At present, the market of consumer-grade video surveillance products is in chaos. In order to solve this problem, the Audio and Video Multimedia System Commission (AVMSC) is establishing a video surveillance standard of 2017-0288T-SJ *Technical Requirements of Cloud Video Storage for Video Surveillance* with major domestic manufacturers. This standard specifies the overall requirements of cloud storage technology of video surveillance, and applicable to video cloud storage system. The formulation work on standardization is underway.

4   Thoughts on Standardization of Consumer-Grade Video Surveillance

4.1   Application of Consumer-Grade Video Surveillance

With the progress of urbanization and the improvement of residents' security needs, the market share of consumer-grade video surveillance products has increased year by year. The video surveillance equipment in many fields is shown in Fig. 2.

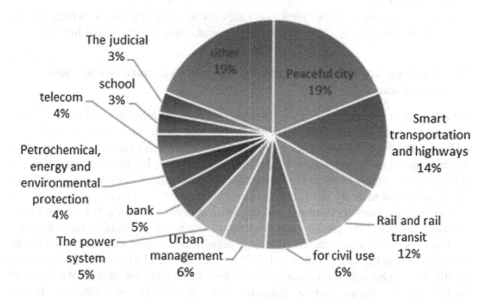

Fig. 2. Application of video surveillance equipment in many fields

In consumer-grade applications, video surveillance is mainly used in these two aspects:

- To family-based applications: Such applications are generally used in residential areas, ranging from dozens of square meters to several hundred square meters. It mainly plays a role of remote video surveillance, remote alarm and night burglar alarm.
- To small micro-enterprise applications: Such applications are generally used for small commercial businesses, and the scope of monitoring is generally the full range of business place. It mainly plays a role of anti-theft, anti-robbery, remote management and supervision of employees.

4.2   Consumer Demand for Video Surveillance

Compared with the professional application, the demand of video surveillance products has also changed greatly, which are mainly reflected in these following aspects:

- Storage methods: Common storage methods include TF card storage, cloud storage and NVR storage.
- Information transmission method: Most of the products on the market offer dual-band Wi-Fi, while few products adopt wired transmission mode. as far as we can see, wireless transmission is a trend in the future.
- Installation and control: Most of the products on the market support the plug-and-play approach, and the camera can be configured and controlled just by downloading a mobile app.
- Privacy protection: Most of the use cases involve privacy issues, which require certain technical means to be protected in transmission, storage and other links.

4.3   The Necessity of Improving the Standards of Consumer-Grade Video Surveillance

We can see that the consumer-grade video surveillance products and professional video surveillance products differ greatly in application site, application and product design, such as Hikvision's fluorite series products, Haier's wireless camera, and Anniewill's wireless monitor. These products are related to video surveillance electronic products in the Internet. Simply learning from the traditional professional-level video surveillance standards cannot meet the needs of the current industry development.

In China, the market of consumer-grade video surveillance products is still in a non-standard stage, and the professional product standards are not suitable for consumer-grade products, caused the fake products are popular on the market. Compared with the products of regular manufacturers, the fake products are cheaper, but the quality is greatly discounted, which causes consumers' fears and affects the survival of the normal market. Besides, the products of different companies are also very different, such as installation mode, indicator light, communication mode, power interface, etc.

With the improvement of people's living standards, ordinary consumers become an important force in promoting the development of consumer security market. Small and medium enterprises, shops and families gradually become the backbone of conventional security needs. According to current statistics, domestic civil security monitoring accounts for only 6% of the market share, far behind the developed countries (for example, American civil security surveillance output accounts for more than 30% of the total), so it has very strong development potential. Compared with the video surveillance permeability in some developed countries and first-tier cities in China, the comparison is shown in Fig. 3.

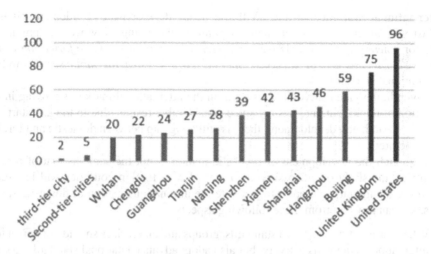

Fig. 3. Comparison of the video surveillance permeability in some developed countries and first-tier cities in China

The continuous development of the family market will make the product more convenient and more orderly. Home monitoring will integrate mobile surveillance, cloud storage, privacy protection and integrated operation services to meet and share personal values, not just to ensure security. Consequently, there is no uniform specification, and special standards should be put forward for consumption grade products.

4.4 Suggestions for Standardization of Future Video Surveillance Areas

Domestic Standardization. The consumer-grade video surveillance is developing rapidly, and to develop the consumer-grade video surveillance, we can proceed from these following aspects:

- Standardize the top-level design to solve the problem, establish and improve the integrated standardization system.
- Focus on the development of standards in key areas, such as cloud computing/cloud storage, UHD technology and high dynamic range.
- Focus on consolidating the technological layout and improving the voice of industry.
- Implementing standards, and spreading the concept of video surveillance products to consumers through standard implementation.
- Promote product consumption, eliminate the concept of confusion and low-quality products to ensure a healthy develop environment in industry.
- Clearly define the technical requirements which closely related to consumers, such as viewing angle, clarity and data security.
- Carry out product testing business to ensure the user experience and promote a reasonable product competition, promote the healthy and orderly development of the market.

International Standardization. With the steady development of video surveillance industry in our country, the international status is also rising. Now we are applying to IEC for converting GB/T 28181-2016 *Technical requirements for information transport, switch and control in video surveillance network system for public security* to IEC international standards.

Overall, the video surveillance system in the international market is moving in the direction of intelligent, and has achieved considerable results. due to the late start and lack of research and development, there is still a big gap between domestic and foreign manufacturers.

Although the development of domestic market is not the same as that of foreign countries, the study of video surveillance market in foreign countries still has some reference significance. In order to promote the internationalization of domestic standards, we can proceed from these following aspects:

- When formulating their own standards, groups and enterprises should not only adopt international standards actively, but also adopt advanced national standards, association standards and enterprise standards in developed countries.
- Follow the trends of international standardization development, and do the collection, collation, analysis and transmission of standardization information at home and abroad.
- Participate of international standardization activities actively, follow the latest development of international standardization and strive to turn Chinese standards into international standards.

5 Conclusion

This paper studies the market and standardization of consumer-grade video surveillance products, and finds out that the relevant market is in chaos and the product quality is uneven, so it is urgent to establish standards and regulate the market. By analyses the demand of consumer-grade video surveillance products and the relevant standards, it is necessary to set specific standards for consumer-grade video surveillance products. Finally, suggestions of relevant standards are given.

References

1. Nazare Jr., A.C., Schwartz, W.R.: A scalable and flexible framework for smart video surveillance. Comput. Vis. Image Underst. **144**, 258–275 (2016)
2. ONVIF. http://www.invif.org. Accessed 30 July 2017
3. PSIA[EB/OL]. http://www.psialliance.org. Accessed 30 July 2017
4. HDCCTV[EB/OL]. https://hdcctvalliance.org. Accessed 30 July 2017
5. Huang, J., Hong, L.: Analysis on standards of IP base video surveillance - ONVIF and PSIA. Video Eng. **37**(1), 175–177 (2013)
6. Recommendation ITU-T F.743: Requirements and service description for visual surveillance (2009)
7. Recommendation ITU-T F.743.1: Requirements for intelligent visual surveillance (2015)

8. Recommendation ITU-T F.743.2: Requirements for cloud storage in visual surveillance (2016)
9. Recommendation ITU-T F.743.3: Requirements for visual surveillance system interworking (2016)
10. Recommendation ITU-T H.626: Architectural requirements for visual surveillance (2011)
11. Recommendation ITU-T H.626.1: Architecture for mobile visual surveillance (2013)
12. Recommendation ITU-T H.627: Signalling and protocols for visual surveillance (2012)
13. SAC: Technical requirements for information transport, switch and control in video surveil-lance network system for public security. GB, Beijing (2016)
14. SAC: RF technical requirements and testing methods for the wireless transceiver of video monitoring system. GB, Beijing (2017)
15. SAC: Technical specifications for surveillance video and audio coding for public security. GB, Beijing (2017)
16. SAC: Technical requirements for face identification of video surveil-lance in security systems. GB, Beijing (2015)
17. SAC: Technical requirements for real time intelligent video analysis devices in surveillance system. GB, Beijing (2013)
18. SAC: Digital video record equipment of video surveillance system in security & protection systems. GB, Beijing (2006)

Bidirectional Markov Chain Monte Carlo Particle Filter for Articulated Human Motion Tracking

Anan Yu, Chuanzhen Li, Long Ye[✉], Jingling Wang, and Qin Zhang

Key Laboratory of Media Audio and Video, Communication University of China,
Ministry of Education, Beijing 100024, China
{yaa,lichuanzhen,yelong,wjl,zhangqin}@cuc.edu.cn

Abstract. A novel framework of particle filter, named bidirectional Markov chain Monte Carlo particle filter (BMCMCPF), has been proposed to estimate articulated human movement state and action category jointly. Owing to the reason that we regard action category as the estimated state in our framework, firstly the motion models for every possible action are built via autoregressive modeling for the captured motion data with minimum distance. Meanwhile, the dynamic model and observation model also get coupled so that tracking and recognition can achieve synchronously. Then, the state estimation is completed by using the bidirectional Marko chain Monte Carlo sampling. BMCMCPF can not only improve the tracking performance as its global optimization property, but also smooth the joint's movement trajectories to ensure the motion coordination. The experimental results on HumanEva datasets show that the effectiveness of BMCMCPF with unknown motion modality in solving the tracking problem.

Keywords: Bidirectional Markov Chain Monte Carlo Particle Filter
Video space-time volume · Joint estimation
Articulated human motion tracking

1 Introduction

Articulated human motion tracking is and continues to be a research hotspot in artificial intelligence area and computer vision area. Recent years, many methods for tracking, particle filter (PF) in particular, have been proposed and achieved good performance. Among all the methods, PF stands out because it can be applied to any nonlinear and non-Gaussian system. But in PF system, the accuracy of posterior probability density depends on particle efficiency. A valid method for improving efficiency is to conduct global search. However, global search leads to high computational complexity.

To solve this problem, one effective way is using human motion prediction model. With the guide of motion model, the search space can be constrained or the state space dimension can be reduced. Generally, the model can be classified into two categories: weak prediction model and strong prediction model. The weak prediction model, such as constant velocity model (CV), constant acceleration model (CA) [1] and some particle filtering variants [2, 3], employs a universal model with unknown action category.

© Springer Nature Singapore Pte Ltd. 2018
G. Zhai et al. (Eds.): IFTC 2017, CCIS 815, pp. 418–428, 2018.
https://doi.org/10.1007/978-981-10-8108-8_38

Lin and Chang [2] presented a progressive particle filter for hierarchical searching to increase searching effectiveness. Lin and Chang [3] reduced the number of iterations by using dynamic kernel-based progressive particle filter (DKPPF). Shi [4] assigned particles around true solutions with higher weights using the improved annealed particle filter. However, such models are not the optimal choice for all motions because of the universality of model. As a consequence, it is possible to get trapped in a local optimum easily and lead to inaccurate tracking results. The strong prediction models usually integrate the mathematical training model into the particle filter when action category is known. The form of each model is special, its effect is also special and good for the improvement of tracking performance. So these models are widely used and show great success in various datasets. These models include 3D strong prediction models containing Linear Kinematic Models, Nonlinear Kinematic Models and Newtonian (Physics-Based) Models etc. [5]. Agarwal and Triggs [6] took advantage of the technique of linear regression to establish the walking prediction model. Furthermore, the walking prediction model was obtained with the method of Nonparametric Belief Propagation (NBP) [7]. Saboune et al. [8] represented human walking as Dynamic Bayesian Network (DBN) with an Interval Particle Filter (IPF). Gonczarek and Tomczak [9] modeled the dynamics of the pose using low-dimensional manifold and a nonlinear dependency based on the application of GPLVM with back constraints. Li et al. [10] applied a learned model of the globally coordinated mixture of factor analyzers (GCMFA) in a Bayesian tracking method. In spite of the intuitive of motion model, these models are too rigid to cope with abrupt changes in motion. So, the target could be lost when its movement can not following models. What's more, strong prediction model is not applicable to a set of different motions since the form of each model is special.

To cope with various motion, the interacting multiple mode (IMM) has been applied to motion tracking [11]. Madrigal and Hayet [12] combined IMM with PF to form a new filter, the interacting multiple mode particle filter (IMMPF), for tracking. The Implicit Mixture of Conditional Restricted Boltzmann Machines (imCRBM) model [13] handled different scenarios including transitions among motions and multiple motions. Khalili et al. [14] proposed three modes: the stop mode, the walking mode and the running mode. Our work also belongs to this category.

In this paper, we present a novel framework PF based on multiple strong prediction models for the case of unknown action category. Firstly, we propose a novel model named video space-time volume model and utilize multiple models for global search. Then, the system estimates state variables and action category variable jointly by using BMCMC method. Therefore, the category of action has got involved in tracking bringing about an improvement in efficiency and accuracy. Furthermore, the unceasing estimation of motion models in tracking process finally is used not only for motion tracking, but also for the purpose of action recognition.

The rest of paper is organized as follows. In Sect. 2, BMCMCPF theory is presented. Section 3 describes the articulated human motion tracking using the proposed PF framework. The experiments are described in Sect. 4 and conclusions are drawn in Sect. 5.

2   Bidirectional Markov Chain Monte Carlo Particle Filter

Based on Bayesian estimation, human motion tracking is usually a two-step process: prediction and update, as shown in Eqs. (1) and (2).

$$g_t^i = f^i\left(g_{t-1}^i, w_{t-1}^i\right) \tag{1}$$

$$I_t^i = h\left(g_t^i, v_t\right) \tag{2}$$

where g_t^i, I_t^i respectively represent the motion state parameters to be estimated and the video sequence with model i ($i = 1, 2, \cdots M$) at time t. When $i > 1$, the state transition probability matrix between M models is signified with a Markov chain:

$$P\{m(t) = j | m(t-1) = i\} = p_{ij}, i, j = 1, 2, \cdots M \tag{3}$$

Using PF for tracking aims to quantify the posterior density $p(g_t | I_{1:t})$, that is the Monte Carlo sampling is used to obtain the solution of Eq. (4).

$$p\left(g_t | I_{1:t}\right) = \alpha_t p\left(I_t | g_t\right) p\left(g_t | I_{1:t-1}\right) \tag{4}$$

Although the multi-model PF solves the problem that single model fails to meet the change in the movement, it still has disadvantages: high calculation cost and lack of motion temporal information. To address these problems, video sequence is separated to many space-time volumes, then a bidirectional Markov chain Monte Carlo particle filter to estimate motion state and action category jointly is adopted in this paper.

Assume that bidirectional Markov properties and observational independence are still tenable, as Eqs. (5) and (6).

$$p\left(g_t | g_1, \cdots \cdots, g_{t-1}, g_{t+1}, \cdots \cdots, g_N\right) = p\left(g_t | g_{t-1}, g_{t+1}\right) \tag{5}$$

$$p\left(I_1, \cdots \cdots, I_\tau | g_1, \cdots \cdots, g_\tau\right) = \prod_{t=1}^{\tau} p\left(I_t | g_t\right) \tag{6}$$

So we can get the posterior probability, as Eq. (7).

$$p\left(g_t | g_1, \cdots \cdots, g_{t-1}, g_{t+1}, \cdots \cdots, g_N, I_1, \cdots \cdots, I_N\right) = \alpha_t p\left(g_t | g_{t-1}, g_{t+1}\right) p\left(I_t | g_t\right) \tag{7}$$

With the video space-time volume, it can be extended to a more general form, as Eq. (8).

$$p\left(g_t | g_1, \cdots \cdots, g_{t-1}, g_{t+1}, \cdots \cdots, g_N, I_1, \cdots \cdots, I_N\right) = \alpha_t p\left(g_t | g_{\partial t}, I_{\partial t}, I_t\right) \tag{8}$$

where ∂t are the neighboring frames of time t. At the same time the action category as a variable is estimated with motion state, as Eqs. (9), (10) and (11).

$$g_t^i = f^i\left(g_{\partial t}^i, c_{t-1}^i, w_{\partial t}^i\right) \tag{9}$$

$$I_t^i = h\left(g_{\partial t}^i, v_{\partial t}\right) \tag{10}$$

$$c_t^i = u\left(g_t^i, g_{\partial t}^i, I_t^i, I_{\partial t}^i\right) \tag{11}$$

where u is the model probability function, $c^i (i = 1, 2, \cdots M)$ represents action category of model i. After that, the coupling of dynamic model and observation model has been established. It forms a bidirectional Markov chain Monte Carlo sampling video space-time volume filter and jointly estimates the motion parameters and category parameter.

3   Articulated Human Motion Tracking

The framework is illustrated in Fig. 1. The system comprises three parts: video space-time volume model building, tracking and recognition. The motion models for every possible action are built via autoregressive modeling for the training motion data with minimum distance. For each query video sequence, we use BMCMC for prediction and feature matching for updating. The feedback of action category implements the coupling of tracking and recognition.

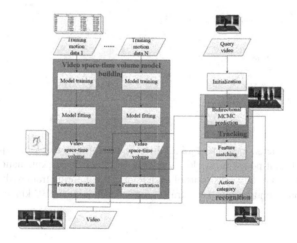

Fig. 1. Framework of the proposed method for tracking.

3.1   Video Space-Time Volume Model

Video space-time volume model is a method by which each motion can be represented in few motion trajectories of joint. Each trajectory contains the spatial change information of the joint point over a period of time.

As is common in the literature [13], we model the body as a 3D kinematic chain consisting of 15 joint points, as shown in Fig. 2(I). They are 2 torso points, 4 arm points, 4 leg points, 2 hand points, 2 foot points and a head point. To achieve invariance, we model the relative positions and joint angles, instead of the absolute position in the ground plane. The formation of video space-time volume model is shown in Fig. 2(II).

Firstly, the original joint points in world coordinate {x, y, z} of every possible action are processed to discrete points with joint angles (Fig. 2(II)a-b). The 3D kinematic chain in each frame is built by this step. After that, the relative positions of each joint in neighboring frames over a period of time are trained (Fig. 2(II)b-c). For simplicity, the minimum-distance model is employed in the model training process. Model training aims to obtain the movement law of each joint over a period of time. After training, the universal relative positions of each joint in neighboring frames for every action are got. Then these relative positions over a period of time are treated as control points for AR fitting so that a group of trajectories of joint is generated (Fig. 2(II)c-d). At last, video space-time volume model is formed (Fig. 2(II)d).

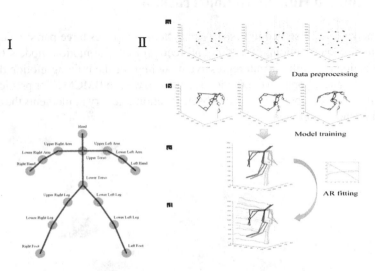

Fig. 2. I: Human skeleton model and joint labels, II: the formation of video space-time volume model (a: original joint points in world coordinate {x, y, z}, b: 3D kinematic chain with joint angles, c: the universal relative positions of each joint in neighboring frames, d: video space-time volume model which contains a group of trajectories of each joint and 3D kinematic chain of each frame)

3.2   BMCMC Sampling

After having obtained video space-time volume model, the prediction of parameters g_t ($g = [x, y, z]$) for each frame in a video space-time volume can be implemented effectively. With regard to the prediction of g_t, the resampling step is different from traditional particle filter and Gibbs sampling. We need to consider the different combinations of particles in neighboring frames before and after combined sampling.

Since having multiple alternative solutions $\left\{\left(g_t^{(m)}, w_t^{(m)}\right)\right\}_{m=1}^{M}$ with weights for each frame t, a comprehensive method for particle filter and Gibbs sampling is developed. First of all, take advantage of the particle filter to initialize, then get the particle and its weight in each frame. Next, select a frame t circularly or randomly, and fix its neighboring frames. After that, carry out the process of bidirectional particle filtering, and maintain the connected relation between each particle with other particles in neighboring frames. After this process converges, a set of particles that obey the posterior distribution $p(g_1, \cdots\cdots, g_N | I_1, \cdots\cdots, I_N)$ is achieved.

It is worth noting that the $(g_1, \cdots\cdots, g_N)$ is implicit in the particles of all frames and their associated graphs (see Fig. 3b), that is, each route connecting the particles in the first frame and the N frame is an analytic graph. For the sake of gaining a typical solution, particles are sampled again, and finally a set of available solutions can be found. The state parameter of any joint n for each frame $(I_t, I_{\partial t})$ in a video space-time volume is fitted out with the state parameter of video space-time volume model. Fitting error is the energy function. It is natural that the probability function $p(g_t | g_{\partial t}, I_{\partial t}, I_t)$ can be decomposed into the mixed distribution of the joint n, as Eq. (12).

$$p(g_t | g_{\partial t}, I_{\partial t}, I_t) = \prod_{n \in I_t} \sum_{i=1}^{M} p(i|n, g_t, g_{\partial t}) p(\varepsilon^{(i)}_{\partial(t,\vec{x}_n)} | i, I_{\partial(t,\vec{x}_n)}) \qquad (12)$$

where $\vec{x}_n$ denotes the center of node n, M is the number of models. Here $p(i|n, I_t, I_{\partial t})$ refers to a priori of the ith video space-time volume model, which is served to constrain the consistency along time axis of the state parameter. The higher value of the probability indicates the more consistent parameter state between the node and its neighbors. $p(\varepsilon^{(i)}_{\partial(t,\vec{x}_n)} | i, I_{\partial(t,\vec{x}_n)})$ is the error distribution function emerged from the parameter in ith video space-time volume model to space-time region $I_{\partial(t,\vec{x})}$.

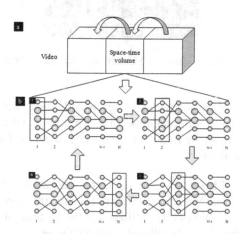

Fig. 3. Joint estimation with BMCMC Sampling (a: intra-volume prediction, b: inter-volume prediction)

As shown in Fig. 3b, along with continuous growth of the number of frames N, the total number of particles rises linearly, while the number of solutions is in an exponential increase. Just because of multiple connections, more permutations and combinations are generated.

3.3   Joint Estimation

Joint estimation increases the opportunity to find global optima. The local optimization is predicted by combination sampling, and then the task of predicting of the action category state c is performed. Thereinto, the ∂t in $p(l_t | l_{\partial t})$ means neighboring frames in a video space-time volume. In fact it is in reference to neighboring space-time volumes in $p(c_t | c_{\partial t})$. After that, the action category parameter c predicted by current video space-time volume is fed back to the previous space-time volume for updating to result in a satisfactory effect of recognition (see Fig. 3a).

4   Experiments and Discussions

Datesets. We conduct some experiments to measure our approach on a real-life benchmark dataset HumanEva [15] which is well known for 3D human motion tracking and recognition and allows quantitative evaluation of performance. The dataset consists of six different actions and its synchronized motion capture data of three different subjects (S1-S3). (Some examples are shown in Fig. 4). Originally, for each subject and action, the dataset is broken down into three disjoint sub-sets: training, validation and testing. The pity is that all testing sequences are not publicly available. Accordingly, a different data division is of help to perform an evaluation in most cases, e.g., in literature [9, 16].

Fig. 4. Some examples of the action in HumanEva dataset: (a) Walking, (b) Jog, (c) Box, (d) ThrowCatch.

Training. The "Train" partition with all subjects performing walking, jog, throwcatch and box actions is used to train, then the "Test" partition and the 200 frames of the "Validation" partition in above four action sequences are used for testing according to Gonczarek and Tomczak [9].

Initialization and Likelihood. In the experiments the size of video space-time volume model is set to 100 frames. We adopt 100 particles and 100 trajectories for one camera view. Likelihoods based on HSV are utilized for the purpose of simplicity and effectiveness, but that using richer likelihoods can obtain better results is admitted. The dimension of HSV feature is 1×193.

Evaluation. Because the motion capture data of the "Test" partition is withheld for evaluation, we carry out experiments on the "Validation" partition to evaluate the difference between the true values with tracking values by the following Eq. (13), which computes an average Euclidean distance between 15 joints.

$$D\left(X, \widehat{X}\right) = \frac{1}{K} \sum_{i=1}^{K} \left\| x_i - \widehat{x}_i \right\| \tag{13}$$

where $x \in R^3$ is location of 3D joint i, and $X = \{x_1, x_2, \cdots, x_K\}$. Measured in millimeters (mm). K is 15 in our experiment.

The proposed approach is compared against three methods: CVPF (weak prediction model), PF with jog model (strong prediction model) and IMMPF (multi models). Each of them is tested with 100 particles.

Results and Discussions. The averaged tracking results presented in Table 1 allow us easily compare our performance with other approaches. The results indicate that the proposed method is slightly better than others. The tracking performance can be intuitively shown in Fig. 5. It shows that our method can deal with self-occlusion problem to some extent and has satisfactory tracking accuracy as well.

Table 1. Mean predictive error over subject S1, S2 and S3 (results are in millimeters).

	Baseline [15]	2010 [13]	2016 [9]	Ours
S1	129.18	48.75	75.50	38.52 ± 2.99
S2	162.75	47.43	90.00	37.84 ± 7.61
S3	180.11	49.81	74.50	39.95 ± 8.25

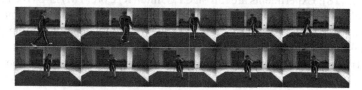

Fig. 5. Tracking results from S3-Walking test sequence (top) and S1-Box validation sequence (bottom) (every 50 frames)

Figure 6 shows the tracking error of comparative experiments in each frame. It indicates that our approach is precise in calculation and stable in performance, i.e., the method tides over error accumulation. CVPF is the worst-performing method, which might be because of inadequate particles or falling into local optimum. If a large number of particles are adopted, there would be another new problem, huge calculations. It should be noted that the results of PF with jog model are relatively better. This is the effect of strong prediction model. However, it is unable to accommodate motion changes. Figure 7 shows that our method is able to adapt to motion changes and performs well. The video sequence is the transition from "Walking" to "Jog". Frames 600–800 are shown.

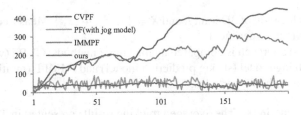

Fig. 6. Tracking error over S2-Jog validation sequence

Fig. 7. Tracking results from S2-Combo sequence (every 20 frames)

Table 2 is the computation time of comparative experiments. Computation time is a major concern in tracking. Generally, it takes from seconds to minutes for tracking in a single frame [18]. Experiments are run on CPU, Intel(R) Core(TM) i5-2410M 2.30 GHz. No particular effort has been made to optimize the code to improve performance. Note that PF with jog model is faster than CVPF due to the efficiency of strong prediction model. In the case of using strong prediction models, our method is superior to PF (with jog model) even if we use the multi model theory which leads to larger computations. This shows the feasibility of BMCMC framework to solve time problem by permutations and combinations.

Table 2. Average runtimes per frame (sec.)

	CVPF	PF (with jog model)	IMMPF	Ours
Runtime	108.26	14.70	27.86	1.82

The average recognition rate of our method is 92.50% (Table 3). As shown in Table 3, the coupling PF is effective to attain satisfied effect, but a little worse than HybridCNN. Since the recognition process proposed is different from the other methods on account of action category iterative estimation.

Table 3. Comparison of recognition algorithms on HumanEva dataset [17]

	CRF	LDCRF	LPCRF	HybridCNN	Ours
Walking	95.0%	96.3%	95.5%	90.0%	93.75%
Jog	89.7%	97.3%	94.6%	85.6%	87.50%
Box	79.4%	75.0%	79.5%	100.0%	96.88%
Gesture	73.4%	77.4%	82.8%	94.5%	93.75%
Throwcatch	–	–	–	–	90.63%
Average	84.5%	86.5%	88.1%	92.5%	92.50%

5   Conclusion

This paper proposes a novel PF framework that regards action category as a prediction variable for human motion tracking. After getting video space-time volume model, a new sampling method based on bidirectional Markov chain Monte Carlo is performed. By means of joint estimation, not only the tracking results but also the action category is obtained. The experimental results on HumanEva datasets illustrate our method achieves good performance of tracking as well as high recognition accuracy. However, there is still room for further improvement. The model proposed is not yet general due to training the experimental dataset under certain conditions. When many similar actions are used, the wrong model is very likely to be tracked so that action category predictive error will be accumulated and tracking error will be increased because of the high similarity among actions. In addition, the tracking effect is easily affected for multiple people. So, future work will cover the universality and interactivity of human model.

Acknowledgment. This work is supported by the National Natural Science Foundation of China under Grant Nos. 61201236 and 61371191, and the Project of State Administration of Press, Publication, Radio, Film and Television under Grant No. 2015-53.

References

1. Li, X.R., Jilkov, V.P.: Survey of maneuvering target tracking. Part I. Dynamic models. IEEE Trans. Aerosp. Electron. Syst. **39**(4), 1333–1364 (2004)
2. Lin, S.Y., Chang, I.: 3D human motion tracking using progressive particle filter. Pattern Recogn. **43**(10), 3621–3635 (2010)
3. Lin, S.-Y., Chang, I.-C.: Dynamic kernel-based progressive particle filter for 3D human motion tracking. In: Zha, H., Taniguchi, R.-i., Maybank, S. (eds.) ACCV 2009. LNCS, vol. 5995, pp. 257–266. Springer, Heidelberg (2010). https://doi.org/10.1007/978-3-642-12304-7_25
4. Shi, X.G.: 3D Human Motion Tracking Based on Single Video Input and Particle Filtering. National Chung Cheng University, Taiwan (2013)
5. Fleet, D.J.: Motion models for people tracking. In: Moeslund, T., Hilton, A., Krüger, V., Sigal, L. (eds.) Visual Analysis of Humans, pp. 171–198. Springer, London (2011). https://doi.org/10.1007/978-0-85729-997-0_10
6. Agarwal, A., Triggs, B.: Tracking articulated motion using a mixture of autoregressive models. In: Pajdla, T., Matas, J. (eds.) ECCV 2004. LNCS, vol. 3023, pp. 54–65. Springer, Heidelberg (2004). https://doi.org/10.1007/978-3-540-24672-5_5
7. Lan, S.-F., Ho, M.-F., Huang, C.-L.: Human motion parameter capturing using particle filter and nonparametric belief propagation. In: IEEE Southwest Symposium on Image Analysis and Interpretation, pp. 37–40 (2008)
8. Saboune, J., Rose, C., Charpillet, F.: Factored interval particle filtering for gait analysis. In: IEEE Engineering in Medicine and Biology Society, pp. 3232–3235 (2007)
9. Gonczarek, A., Tomczak, J.M.: Articulated tracking with manifold regularized particle filter. Mach. Vis. Appl. **27**(2), 275–286 (2016)
10. Li, R., Tian, T.P., Sclaroff, S., et al.: 3D human motion tracking with a coordinated mixture of factor analyzers. Int. J. Comput. Vis. **87**(1), 170 (2010)

11. Blom, H.A.P., Barshalom, Y.: The interacting multiple model algorithm for systems with Markovian switching coefficients. IEEE Trans. Autom. Control **33**(8), 780–783 (1988)
12. Madrigal, F., Hayet, J.B.: Evaluation of multiple motion models for multiple pedestrian visual tracking. In: IEEE International Conference on Advanced Video and Signal Based Surveillance, pp. 31–36 (2013)
13. Taylor, G.W., Sigal, L., Fleet, D.J., et al.: Dynamical binary latent variable models for 3D human pose tracking. In: IEEE Computer Society Conference on Computer Vision and Pattern Recognition, pp. 631–638 (2010)
14. Khalili, A., Soliman, A.A., Asaduzzaman, M.: Quantum particle filter: a multiple mode method for low delay abrupt pedestrian motion tracking. Electron. Lett. **51**(16), 1251–1253 (2015)
15. Sigal, L., Black, M.J.: HumanEva: Synchronized Video and Motion Capture Dataset for Evaluation of Articulated Human Motion. Int. J. Comput. Vision **87**(1–2), 4–27 (2006)
16. Daubney, B., Xie, X.: Tracking 3D human pose with large root node uncertainty. In: IEEE Conference on Computer Vision and Pattern Recognition, pp. 1321–1328. IEEE Computer Society (2011)
17. Lei, J., Li, G., Li, S., et al.: Continuous action recognition based on hybrid CNN-LDCRF model. In: International Conference on Image, Vision and Computing, pp. 63–69 (2016)
18. Peursum, P., Venkatesh, S., West, G.: A study on smoothing for particle-filtered 3D human body tracking. Int. J. Comput. Vis. **87**(1–2), 53–74 (2010)

An Adaptive Multi-scale Tracking Method Based on Kernelized Correlation Filter

Qiling Xu[1,2] and Hua Yang[1,2(✉)]

[1] Institue of Image Communication and Network Engineering,
Shanghai Jiao Tong University, Shanghai, China
{xuqiling0906,hyang}@sjtu.edu.cn
[2] Shanghai Key Laboratory of Digital Media Processing and Transmission,
Shanghai, People's Republic of China

Abstract. Visual tracking is a fundamental computer vision task with a wide range of applications. Kernelized Correlation Filter (KCF) is an excellent algorithm with high tracking speed. However, the target tracking scale in the KCF algorithm is a fixed value which might cause tracking failure or target drifting problem when the target scale changes significantly. In this paper, we present an adaptive multi-scale tracking algorithm based on the KCF algorithm by estimating the scale of the target. Our method builds upon the correlation filter with a Gaussian kernel and reasonable prediction of the target size. In order to verify the effectiveness of the proposed algorithm, 9 sets of complex video sequences of a commonly used tracking benchmark were selected and the results were compared with other tracking methods (KCF, CSK, CT, TLD, Struck, CNN-SVM and MDNet). The results show that the proposed method has high accuracy. The method in this paper has strong robustness in the complex scenes with challenges of scale variation, illumination variation, occlusion, in-plane rotation, out-of plane rotation and deformation.

Keywords: Visual tracking · Kernelized Correlation Filter
Adaptive scale

1 Introduction

Visual tracking is one of the core problems with applications in video processing. A number of tracking algorithms occurred over the past decades of years. The methods of target tracking are usually divided into methods based on generative model and methods based on discriminative model. The classical tracking method can be classified as a generative model [1,2]. By 2010, some classical tracking methods had been commonly used in the tracking fields, such as Meanshift, Camshift, Particle Filter and Kalman Filter.

The methods based on the discriminative model refer to the methods of using the classification to do the tracking, a crucial component of many computer vision systems, with online learning or offline training to distinguish the foreground target and background [3]. Target can be tracked in consecutive frames

© Springer Nature Singapore Pte Ltd. 2018
G. Zhai et al. (Eds.): IFTC 2017, CCIS 815, pp. 429–439, 2018.
https://doi.org/10.1007/978-981-10-8108-8_39

by learning the bounding boxes in the first frame. Every new detection of the subsequent frames provides a new image patch which can be used to update the model. Although the general detection rate is very low at this time, the discriminant tracking methods are more adaptable to the complex changes in the tracking process by presenting the model of the newly updated detector and the various underlying features. Tracking-by-detection has gradually become mainstream.

The authors of the correlation filter algorithm proposed a kernel tracking method based on the cyclic matrix, and solved the problem of dense sampling perfectly. The Fourier transform was used to realize the detection process with high speed. When training the classifier, it is generally believed that the positive samples are closer to the target location and the ones far from the target are negative samples. TLD or Struck will randomly select some patches for training in each frame [4,17]. The learning features are the characteristics of these random sub-windows, and the author of CSK designed a dense sampling framework that can learn all the image patches. The method of correlation filter series developed rapidly. The author of CSK cited MOSSE and he also proposed KCF method based on HOG feature [7–9]. KCF is a discriminant tracking method which trains a target detector in the tracking process. The detector will be used to confirm whether the next frame is a target, and then use the new test results to update the training model and the target detector. In the trained target detector, the target area is selected as a positive sample, and the surrounding area of the target is a negative sample.

However, the existing majority of these trackers based on detection do not solve the problem of scale change. Tracking performance is greatly limited when target scale changes significantly. Therefore, an adaptive multi-scale target tracking algorithm based on kernel correlation filter is proposed by us. We add the process of the estimation of scale which can realize adaptive multi-scale target tracking. Image patches of different sizes in the vicinity of the target are selected and we can get the multi-scale target by finding the maximal value of the responses in the new frame among different scales. In order to verify the effectiveness of the proposed method, 9 sets of complex video sequences are selected from the paper and the other 7 kinds of tracking methods are compared with. It can be proved that our method has strong robustness in the complex scenes.

The rest of this paper is organized as follows. In Sect. 2 we analyze the high-speed tracking algorithm based on Kernelized Correlation Filter in detail. Section 3 describes our improved method specifically. In addition, the experiments and conclusions are presented in Sects. 4 and 5.

2   Tracking with Kernelized Correlation Filter

Kernelized Correlation Filter tracking algorithm is a kind of discriminative tracking methods based on detection, and the tracking method of correlation filter series has obvious advantages in realtime. The algorithm utilizes dense sampling and the cyclic matrix theory. The problem of the redundancy can be solved by

Fourier domain, which can avoid the inverse of the matrix process, to a large extent reduce the complexity of the algorithm. Therefore, KCF have better tracking performance and speed. The process of KCF algorithm is shown in Fig. 1.

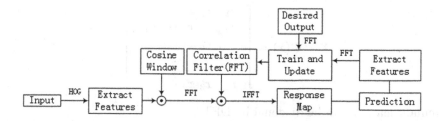

Fig. 1. KCF Algorithm

2.1   Linear Regression

The core task in tracking-by-detection is a classifier. We can give a set of training patterns and labels $(x_1, y_1), ..., (x_m, y_m)$. The purpose of ridge regression is to find a classifier $f(z) = w^T z$ which can minimizes the squared error over training samples and regression targets (x_i, y_i). The minimization problem is

$$\min_w \sum_i (f(x_i - y_i))^2 + \lambda \|w\|^2 \tag{1}$$

The λ is a regularization parameter that controls overfitting ($\lambda \geq 0$). Since we will have to work in Fourier domain, the minimizer of complex-valued is [10]

$$w = (X^H X + \lambda I)^{-1} X^H y \tag{2}$$

2.2   Non-linear Regression

Mapping the inputs of a linear problem to a non-linear feature-space, we have to express the solution w as a linear combination of the samples [11].

$$w = \sum_i \alpha_i \varphi(x_i) \tag{3}$$

Therefore, the non-linear regression function comes into

$$f(z) = w^T z = \sum_{i=1}^{n} \alpha_i \kappa(z, x_i) \tag{4}$$

We use matrix K which is a circulant matrix given by a gaussian kernel with elements $K_{ij} = \kappa(x_i, x_j)$ and the solution to the kernelized version of ridge regression can be given by [10],

$$\alpha = (K + \lambda I)^{-1} y \tag{5}$$

where α is the vector of coefficients α_i.

2.3   Circulant Matrix

Circulant matric $C(x)$ is obtained from the vector x. We can use $(P^u x | u = 0, ...n - 1)$ as the rows of a data matrix X:

$$X = C(x) = \begin{bmatrix} x_1 & x_2 & x_3 & \cdots & x_n \\ x_n & x_1 & x_2 & \cdots & x_{n-1} \\ x_{n-1} & x_n & x_1 & \cdots & x_{n-2} \\ \vdots & \vdots & \vdots & \ddots & \vdots \\ x_2 & x_3 & x_4 & \cdots & x_1 \end{bmatrix} \tag{6}$$

Circulant matrixs can be diagonal by DFT:

$$X = F diag(\hat{x}) F^H \tag{7}$$

where $\hat{x}$ denotes the DFT of the generating vector. F is a constant matrix which is known as the DFT matrix. From the conclusion above, we can get the eigendecomposition of a general cirulant matrix. Therefore, we can simplify the regression when training data is circulant matrix.

2.4   Fast Detection

We can compute all the responses simultaneously and efficiently with the usage of the properties of circulant matrix discussed earlier. We can diagonalize Eq. (5) and take advantage of the feature of circulant, obtaining

$$\mathcal{F}(\alpha) = \frac{\mathcal{F}(y)}{\mathcal{F}(k^{xx}) + \lambda} \tag{8}$$

where $\mathcal{F}$ denotes the Discrete Fourier Transform. From Eq. (4), we can get the classifier with $f(x) = (K^z)^T \alpha$. K^z can be defined with the first row which is gaussian correlation of x and z. The output of the full detection response can be diagonalized, and we obtain

$$\mathcal{F}(\hat{y}) = \mathcal{F}(k^{z\hat{x}}) \bigodot \mathcal{F}(\alpha) \tag{9}$$

where $\hat{y}$ is the output response for all the testing patches. The target position located in the maximal value of the full detection responses $\hat{y}$. Using the cyclic shift, the complexity for the full kernel correlation is bound by the FFT operations and is only $O(n \log(n))$.

3   Adaptive Multi-scale Tracking Method

The core component of discriminative tracker is mainly about the task with distinguishing between the target and the environment. Since the KCF algorithm does not solve the problem of scale change, in this paper, on the basis of KCF tracker, we complete the process of the estimation of scale which can realize adaptive multi-scale target tracking. Image patches of different sizes in the vicinity of the target are selected and transform into the size of initial size according to the bilinear interpolation. Then, the different image patches are extracted and detected by the kernel correlation filter. The kernel correlation filter can learn according to the detection method of the target position in Sect. 2. The scale of detection response exists with the maximal value of the target in the new frame at different scales. At the same time, the position of the target and the model of the relevant parameters in the new frame is obtained.

Algorithm 1. Adaptive Multi-scale Tracking based on Kernelized Correlation Filter.

---

inputs:
x, The current frame image patch;
y, Gaussian shape centered on the target;
z, The next frame image frame;

outputs:
scale, The scale factor of the next frame compared to the current frame
responses, Detection score for all position of different scales;

function GAUSSIANCORRELATION($x1, x2, \sigma$)
    $c \leftarrow$ **ifft2**(**sum**(**conj**(**fft2**($x1$)). $*$ **fft2**($x2$), 3));
    $d \leftarrow x1(:)' * x1(:) + x2(:)' * x2(:) - 2 * c$;
    $k \leftarrow$ **exp**($-1/\sigma^2 *$ **abs**(d)/**numel**(d));
    return k
end function

function TRAIN(x, y, σ, λ)
    $k \leftarrow$ GAUSSIANCORRELATION(x, x, σ);
    $\alpha \leftarrow$ **fft2**(y)./(**fft2**(k) $+ \lambda$);
    return α
end function

for $scale = 0.95 : 0.05 : 1.05$ **do**
    $z1 \leftarrow x * scale$;
    $z2 \leftarrow$ **imResample**($z1$, **size**(x),'bilinear');
    $k \leftarrow$ GAUSSIANCORRELATION($z2, x, sigma$);
    $responses \leftarrow$ **real**(**ifft2**($\alpha.*$ **fft2**(k)));
end for
return $responses, scale$;

We work on HOG descriptors with a cell size of 4 pixels, in particular Felzenszwalb's variant [12,14] which has 31 HOG features per spatial. Working in the dual has the advantage of allowing multiple channels by simply summing over them in the Fourier domain. A dot-product can be computed by simply summing the individual dot-products for each channel, we can apply this rea-soning to the Gaussian kernel and merely have to sum over the channels and obtain [13]

$$k^{xx'} = \exp(\frac{1}{-\sigma^2}(\|x\|^2 + \|x'\|^2 - 2\mathcal{F}^{-1}(\sum_c \hat{x}_c^* \odot \hat{x}'_c))) \tag{10}$$

The tracking model then will obtain a new position and target size of the next frame. The kernel correlation filter will update with a learning rate η as

$$\hat{x}^t = (1 - \eta)\hat{x}^{t-1} + \eta x^t \tag{11}$$

$$\mathcal{F}(\alpha^t) = (1 - \eta)\mathcal{F}(\alpha^{t-1}) + \eta\mathcal{F}(\alpha) \tag{12}$$

Through the continuous updating of the model, we can continue this process to complete the tracking of the target. As a result of the scale of the adaptive process, tracking can be more accurate.

4   Evaluations of the Tracking Performance

This algorithm is written in Matlab. In our system, the specifications of hardware are as follows, Core Intel i7-3770U 3.4 GHz and 8 GB RAM. In the experiment, the parameters in the algorithm remain unchanged for all test videos.

In order to evaluate the performance of our tracking algorithm, we selected 9 sets of complex video sequences from paper [15] to test, and with the other 7 kinds of excellent tracking method were compared [4,6–8,17–19]. The test sequences and challenges in our experiments are shown in Table 1.

Table 1. Test sequences in our experiments.

Video	Frames	Challenges
Car4	659	IV SV
CarScale	252	SV OCC FM IPR OPR
David3	252	OCC DEF OPR BC
Dog	127	SV DEF OPR
Freeman1	326	SV IPR OPR
Girl	500	SV OCC IPR OPR
Toy	271	SV FM IPR OPR
Twinnings	472	SV OPR
Vase	271	SV FM IPR

Our algorithm is mainly for the limitations of scale to improve, so the main challenges in the test video for the scale variation (SV), while also covering the illumination variation (IV), occlusion (OCC), fast motion (FM), background

(a) Car4   (b) CarScale   (c) David3

(d) Dog   (e) Freeman1   (f) Girl

(g) Toy   (h) Twinnings   (i) Vase

Fig. 2. The result of our method, compared with the other seven tracking algorithm. The black dashed box represents our adaptive multi-scale tracking method, black dotted box represents KCF, blue box represents TLD, green box represents CT, red box represents Struck, pink box represents CSK, yellow box represents MDNet and cyan box represents CNN-SVM. (Color figure online)

clutters (BC), in-plane rotation (IPR), out-of plane rotation (OPR) and deformation (DEF). The results of 8 tracking methods are shown in Fig. 2.

The single scale algorithm will accumulate the background interference information introduced by the tracking window, and finally the tracking error will occur. From the test results below, we can see that our algorithm can do the scale adaptation of the tracking target. When the target scale becomes smaller, the tracking box follows the change of the target scale, which can reduce the interference of the background feature to the tracking process and it is more accurate for the feature extraction. When the target scale becomes larger, the extraction of the feature can be better extended to the full range of the target.

In order to analyze the performance of the tracking method quantitatively, we take use of two performance evaluation indicators which are the distance precision (DP) and the overlap score (OS) of the predicted target and the ground truth. DP refers to percentage of frames where the predicted location is within the threshold of the ground truth. We can obtain OS by

$$OS = \frac{R_i \bigcap R_g}{R_i \bigcup R_g} \tag{13}$$

where R_i is the area of target window we predict and R_g is the area of the window that we can get from the ground truth.

The following table shows the distance of frames where the predicted location is within 20 pixels. This threshold was used by Babenko et al. [16].

Table 2. Distance Precision compared with other algorithm with a threshold of 20 pixels.

Video	CT [5]	TLD [4]	Struck [17]	CSK [8]	CNNSVM [18]	MDNet [19]	KCF [7]	OURS
Car4	0.281	0.863	0.992	0.355	**1.000**	**1.000**	0.950	**1.000**
CarScale	0.718	0.817	0.647	0.651	0.702	0.687	0.806	**0.905**
David3	0.413	0.111	0.337	0.659	0.996	1.000	1.000	1.000
Dog	0.992	1.000	0.945	1.000	0.953	1.000	0.992	1.000
Freeman1	0.396	0.540	0.801	0.555	0.985	1.000	0.393	1.000
Girl	0.608	0.918	1.000	0.554	1.000	0.970	0.864	1.000
Toy	0.380	0.934	0.897	0.491	0.934	0.956	**0.985**	0.900
Twinnings	0.744	0.621	0.998	0.977	0.593	1.000	0.905	0.998
Vase	0.679	0.531	0.513	0.760	0.583	0.749	0.793	**0.875**

For single scale algorithms, many of the tracking results introduce too much interference of the background or the characteristics of the target can not be extracted very well which means only part of the characteristics of the target can be extracted. Although the distance precision of KCF and our algorithm results are not very different in some of the above-mentioned results, the accuracy of the tracking results is quite different due to the size difference of the target frame. We can get the Overlap Sate between the tracking target and the ground truth of each frame in the following figure.

By analyzing the experimental results shown in Table 2 and Fig. 3, we can see that the two indexes(DP and OS) of this method can be improved in most test videos we present, especially in the test videos with obvious scale change. In the case of extremely blurred conditions in the experiment videos, there may be still a loss of tracking, but there has been a significant improvement over the KCF algorithm.

In spite of our algorithm is not as good as MDNet which is based on deep learning in terms of Overlap Score, the traditional tracking method still has many advantages over the deep learning method. The main problem of deep learning is the lack of training data and tracking based on deep learning costs a lot of training to achieve satisfaction with increased amount of calculation. Deep learning model requires effective learning of a large number of annotated training data and there is a huge possibility that many problems can not find

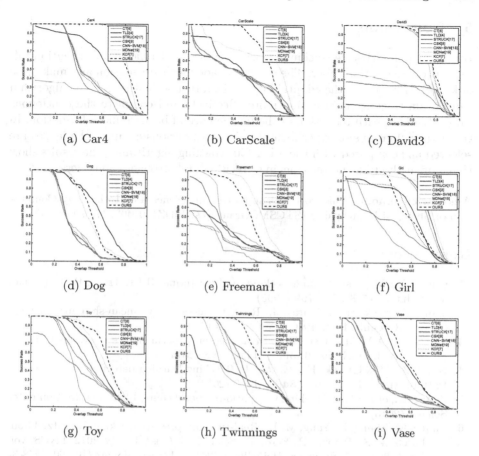

Fig. 3. Curves of Overlap Score compared with other algorithms.

enough data. The target tracking task usually only provides the first frame of the bounding-box as training data. In this case, it is more difficult to tracking for the current target. In addition, the depth of the network training process also requires GPU support and the learning process of deep learning takes a long time. However, the tracking based on correlation filtering only needs to provide the first frame of the bounding-box as the training data, so this method has the advantages of fast tracking speed and simple network structure.

Our method can adjust the tracking window automatically according to the scale change, so that the target position and scale can be estimated. The method improves the drifting problem in the KCF algorithm due to the scale change. At the same time the method is still able to deal with tracking a variety of complex situations better.

5   Conclusion

An adaptive multi-scale tracking algorithm based on Kernelized Correlation Filter is proposed in this paper. The algorithm adds scale estimation and makes use of kernel trick. Due to the adaptability of the target scale, the tracking algorithm can obtain tracking information more effectively and complete the continuous target tracking with reduction of the interference of background information. In this paper, 9 groups of experimental video with various complex challenges are selected and compared with the other four tracking algorithms. The results show that our method has better tracking precision and stronger robustness.

Acknowledgement. This work was supported in Science and Technology Commission of Shanghai Municipality (STCSM, Grant Nos. 15DZ1207403, 17DZ1205602).

References

1. Cheng, Y.: Mean shift, mode seeking, and clustering. IEEE Trans. Pattern Anal. Mach. Intell. **17**(8), 790–799 (1995)
2. Vojir, T., Noskova, J., Matas, J.: Robust scale-adaptive mean-shift for tracking. Pattern Recognit. Lett. **49**(C), 250–258 (2013)
3. Smeulders, A.W.M., et al.: Visual tracking: an experimental survey. IEEE Trans. Pattern Anal. Mach. Intell. **36**(7), 1442–1468 (2014)
4. Kalal, Z., Mikolajczyk, K., Matas, J.: Tracking-learning-detection. IEEE Trans. Pattern Anal. Mach. Intell. **34**(7), 1409 (2012)
5. Zhang, K., et al.: Fast Tracking via spatio-temporal context learning. In: Computer Science (2013)
6. Zhang, K., Zhang, L., Yang, M.-H.: Real-time compressive tracking. In: Fitzgibbon, A., Lazebnik, S., Perona, P., Sato, Y., Schmid, C. (eds.) ECCV 2012. LNCS, vol. 7574, pp. 864–877. Springer, Heidelberg (2012). https://doi.org/10.1007/978-3-642-33712-3_62
7. Henriques, J.F., et al.: High-speed tracking with kernelized correlation filters. IEEE Trans. Patt. Anal. Mach. Intell. **37**(3), 583 (2015)
8. Henriques, J.F., Caseiro, R., Martins, P., Batista, J.: Exploiting the circulant structure of tracking-by-detection with kernels. In: Fitzgibbon, A., Lazebnik, S., Perona, P., Sato, Y., Schmid, C. (eds.) ECCV 2012. LNCS, vol. 7575, pp. 702–715. Springer, Heidelberg (2012). https://doi.org/10.1007/978-3-642-33765-9_50
9. Bolme, D.S., et al.: Visual object tracking using adaptive correlation filters. In: Computer Vision and Pattern Recognition IEEE, pp. 2544–2550 (2010)
10. Rifkin, R., Yeo, G., Poggio, T.: Regularized least-squares classification. Nato Sci. Ser. Sub Ser. III **190**, 131–154 (2003)
11. Scholkopf, B., Smola, A.: Learning with Kernels: Support Vector Machines, Regularization, Optimization, and Beyond. MIT Press, Cambridge (2002)
12. Felzenszwalb, P., Girshick, R., McAllester, D., Ramanan, D.: Object detection with discriminatively trained part-based models. IEEE Trans. Pattern Anal. Mach. Intell. **32**(9), 1627–1645 (2010)
13. Gonzalez, R.C., Woods, R.E.: Digital Image Processing. Prentice Hall, Upper Saddle River (2008)
14. Dollar, P., Appel, R., Belongie, S., Perona, P.: Fast feature pyramids for object detection. IEEE Trans. Pattern Anal. Mach. Intell. **36**(8), 1532–1545 (2014)

15. Wu, Y., Lim, J., Yang, M.H.: Object tracking benchmark. IEEE Trans. Pattern Anal. Mach. Intell. **37**(9), 1834–1848 (2015)
16. Babenko, B., Yang, M.-H., Belongie, S.: Robust object tracking with online multiple instance learning. TPAMI **33**(8), 1619–1632 (2011)
17. Hare, S., Saffari, A., Torr, P.H.S.: Struck: structured output tracking with kernels. In: IEEE International Conference on Computer Vision, pp. 263–270. IEEE (2012)
18. Hong, S., You, T., Kwak, S., Han, B.: Online tracking by learning discriminative saliency map with convolutional neural network. In: ICML (2015)
19. Nam, H., Han, B.: Learning multi-domain convolutional neural networks for visual tracking. In: CVPR (2016)

Virtual Reality

Rhombic Mapping Scheme for Panoramic Video Encoding

Chengjia Wu[✉], Haiwu Zhao, and Xiwu Shang

Shanghai University, Shanghai 200444, China
q1565149320@163.com

Abstract. Since modern video coding standards are not designed for processing panoramic videos, the spherical videos are mapped onto a rectangular plane before encoding. Usually the mapping scheme includes two steps: sampling points on the sphere and arranging the points into a rectangle. Traditional mapping schemes, such as equirectangular and cubic mapping, have different sampling densities on the sphere, which creates many non-information-carrying pixels. Besides, the cubic mapping leads to some discontinuous (adjacent but uncorrelated) pixels, which are not conducive to inter and intra prediction of the encoding, when arranging the six cube faces into one rectangle before encoding. In this paper, we propose a novel rhombic mapping scheme that not only solves the issue of oversampling, but also arranges the points into a compression-friendly rectangle without discontinuous pixels. Experimental results demonstrate that the proposed mapping scheme can save more bitrate compared to the state of the art mapping schemes.

Keywords: Rhombic mapping · Panoramic video · Oversampling

1 Introduction

Panoramic videos, which are also known as omnidirectional video, are captured by vision sensors with a 360-degree field of view [1, 2]. Early techniques for capturing panoramic video [3, 4] utilized a camera and a parabolic mirror. To obtain higher quality panoramic videos, the frames captured by multiple high definition cameras are stitched [5]. Then users can change our viewpoints interactively via the immersive virtual reality (VR) displays [6, 7] when watching panoramic videos. As the panoramic videos store the pixels of all viewpoints' scene, the frames have a quite high resolution. Therefore, it is necessary to propose an effective mapping scheme to transmit and code the numerous pixels.

The common mapping schemes are the equirectangular mapping (ERM) and cubic mapping [8] (CBM). As shown in Fig. 1, the ERM uses constant spacing latitude and longitude to divide the sphere into several regions, samples one pixel for each region, and arranges all the pixels into a $2M \times M$ rectangle. This scheme has the problem of oversampling that result in wasteful pixels when the sampling areas close to the poles. The CBM fills the whole sphere via six cube faces with the same resolution $L \times L$, then uses the method proposed in [9] to rearrange the six cube faces into one rectangle, shown

© Springer Nature Singapore Pte Ltd. 2018
G. Zhai et al. (Eds.): IFTC 2017, CCIS 815, pp. 443–453, 2018.
https://doi.org/10.1007/978-981-10-8108-8_40

as Fig. 2. The CBM scheme reduces the sampling density on the two poles, but leads to oversampling in the edge of each cube face.

Fig. 1. ERM illustration.

Fig. 2. CBM illustration.

Besides the ERM and CBM, there are some studies on panoramic video mapping. In [10, 11], Wan et al. proposed isocube mapping that uniformly samples the unit sphere (uniformly distributed), and all samples span the same solid angle (equally important). In [12], Bauermann et al. warped and resampled the raw video via a cylindrical projection. Similar to the cubic, in [13] Fu et al. place the sphere at the center of a rhombic dodecahedron, in [14] Lin et al. place the sphere at the center of an octahedron, and in [15] SRI et al. place the sphere at the center of an icosahedron. In [16], Yu et al. proposed tiles scheme, which divided the video vertically into tiles and rearranged the tiles into a rectangle. Then in [17], Li et al. improved the scheme by redevising the tiles around the poles and set overlapping areas between tiles.

In this paper, we proposed a novel rhombic mapping (RBM) scheme to sample points on sphere and combine the points to a rhombus. Then we reshape and rearrange the rhombus into rectangular frame before the encoding processing.

The pixels in panorama videos are generally stored by the equirectangular format that leads to much residue especially on the poles of the sphere. The traditional PSNR objective quality metric measures the pixels in the same weight that cannot reveal the distortion between two panorama frames. In [18], Yu et al. proposed four quality metrics for sphere (Sph) video:

- WeightSph: S-PSNR (spherical peak signal-to-noise ratio) with sphere points weighted by point access frequency.
- LatSph: S-PSNR with sphere points weighted by the corresponding latitude access frequency.
- Sph: S-PSNR where all points are weighted equally.
- Quad: PSNR calculated by mapping both the ground truth and the coded videos to the same 6K × 3K Equirectangular projection.

In this paper, we use the Sph: S-PSNR to evaluate the objective quality, as considering the points on the sphere have the same weight.

2   Proposed Mapping

2.1   Sampling Points

Since the sphere is a closed curved surface, to simplify sampling, we divide it into several curved surfaces.

Firstly, as Fig. 3 shows, we divide one sphere into N annular curved surfaces, from top to bottom, labeled O_0~O_{N-1}. Then, we use constant spacing longitude lines to divide O_i (i is the index of annular curved surface) into T_i square curved surfaces, and one square curved surface is one points sampling area.

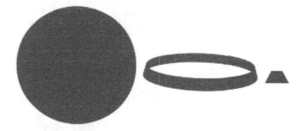

Fig. 3.   Divide sphere to square curved surfaces illustration. Left (sphere). Middle (annular curved surface). Right (square curved surface).

The sampling density is determined by the T_i. We design a T_i formula to reduce the sampling density at high latitudes and uniformity sampling density at middle-low latitudes.

On the unit sphere, the O_i's (i is the index of annular curved surface) circumference is $2\pi\cos(y)$, where y is latitude. We unfold all the annular curved surfaces (O_0~O_{N-1},), as the gray region shows in Fig. 4. Then we use $\triangle ABC$ to approximate the sphere. The value of T_i should be proportional to the annular curved surface's circumference. So, T_i is related to the $\triangle ABC$, as the formula (1) shows.

$$T_i = \begin{cases} 2 + 4 * i, \ 0 \leq i < N/2 \\ \\ T_{N-1-i}, \ N/2 \leq i < N \end{cases} \tag{1}$$

$$T_i = 16N, \ 0 \leq i < N \tag{2}$$

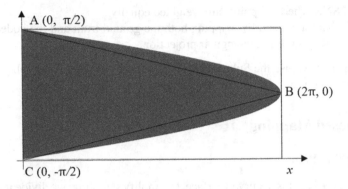

Fig. 4. $O_0 \sim O_{N-1}$ unfolding illustration.

When the value of T_i is calculated by formula (2), the mapping scheme is the ERM. On unit sphere, O_i's square curved surface's width is $\dfrac{2\pi\cos(y)}{T_i}$, where y is latitude. When $N = 1024$, the Fig. 5 shows the O_i's square curved surface's width curve.

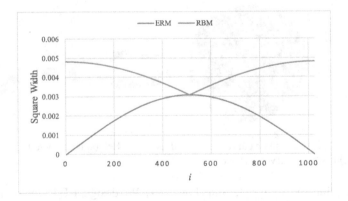

Fig. 5. Square width curve when $N = 128$.

In Fig. 5, RBM has wider square width and flatter curve. Therefore, RBM has lower sampling density at high latitudes and more uniformity sampling density at middle-low latitudes.

As the CBM samples points through rectilinear projection instead of sampling points on annular curved surfaces, we sample equal points respectively on sphere by the ERM, CBM and RBM schemes to compare sampling density. According to the formula (1), we can calculate the sum of sampling points is N^2. And for the ERM, the sum of sampling points can be $2M^2$, M is the vertical resolution. $6L^2$ is the sum of the CBM sampling points when the resolution of the cube face is $L \times L$.

Setting the value of M to 16, correspondingly, the value of N is $\left(\text{round} \sqrt{2M^2} \right) \approx 22$, L is $\left(\text{round} \sqrt{\dfrac{2M^2}{6}} \right) \approx 8$. The distribution of each scheme's points on the sphere is shown in Fig. 6. The ERM scheme has a very high sampling density on the poles. And the points in the center is much less than in edge of the cube face in CBM. Point's distribution is more uniform on RBM sphere.

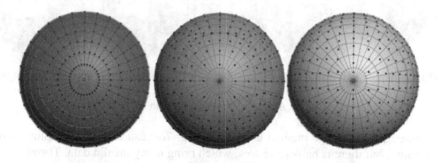

(a) Vertical view. Left (ERM). Middle (CBM). Right (RBM).

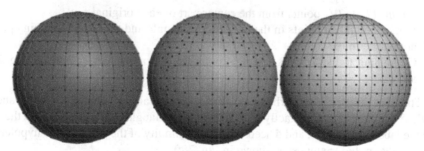

(b) Front view. Left (ERM). Middle (CBM). Right (RBM).

Fig. 6. Sampling points illustration.

2.2 Arranging Points

In RBM, there are N annular curved surfaces, and the most points on the annular curved surfaces is $2N - 2$. Therefore, we firstly arrange the points in a rectangle with the size of $2N \times N$. The points on annular curved surfaces O_i are arranged in i row of the rectangle, and the first point's column coordinate is $(N - T_i/2)$. All the points combine into a rhombus shown in Fig. 7(a), and the white area indicates no points.

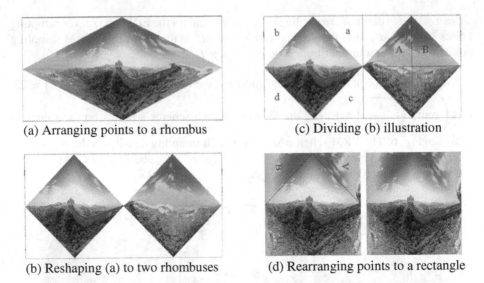

(a) Arranging points to a rhombus   (c) Dividing (b) illustration

(b) Reshaping (a) to two rhombuses   (d) Rearranging points to a rectangle

Fig. 7. Arranging points illustration of RBM

Although the arrange method used in the Fig. 7(a) can keep the sampling points continuous, but there is half-white area, which bring many invalid data. Therefore, we need to rearrange the sampling points based on Fig. 7(a). Firstly, we reshape the rhombus area by dividing the points into two part:

(1) Taking $(T_i + 2)/2$ points from the center part of each original row.
(2) Placing the taken points in the left of the rectangle and the other remaining points are placed in the right.
(3) Combining the left points and right points into rhombus respectively as Fig. 7(b) shows.

Then, we divide the right rhombus into four identical right-angled triangles labeled A, B, C and D. There are exactly four right-angled triangles with no points on the left, and we label them a, b, c, and d according the continuity of the pixels in the hypotenuse of the right-angled triangles, as shown in Fig. 7(c).

Finally, we splice A, B, C, D to a, b, c, d by translation and rotation. All the parts are rearranged into a rectangle with the size of $N \times N$, as shown in Fig. 7(d), and the rotated capital letters indicates the direction of rotation.

As the Fig. 7(d) shows, we can find that the final layout has no discontinuous pixel. We use this scheme to arrange the sampling points into rectangle frames with the resolution of N * N. In addition, those rectangle frames are compression-friendly.

3   Experimental Results

We do two contrast experiments to verify the mapping performance and encoding compression performance of the proposed mapping scheme. The first experiment called

PD-Rate (Points Distortion Rate) experiment is designed to compare the distortion created by the different mapping schemes. The second experiment called BD-Rate (Bit Distortion Rate) is designed to compare the distortion created by mapping and coding.

As the Fig. 8 shows, the PD-Rate experiment steps are shown as green arrows, and the red arrows show the BD-Rate experiment steps. As the original test sequences is the equirectangular form, we map the higher precision original date to the sphere firstly. Lanzcos interpolation is used in these two experiment. PD-Rate is the rate between sampling points number and the distortion after mapping. In this experiment, we use different mapping schemes to sample the equal points on the sphere, then map back to the sphere and calculate the objective quality metric S-PSNR. BD-Rate is the rate between bitrate and the distortion after mapping-coding. We map the spheres points to the rectangular frames and coding these frames, then map back to the sphere and calculate S-PSNR.

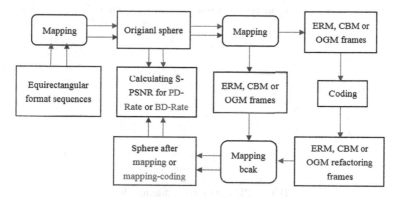

Fig. 8. Experimental flow chart (Color figure online)

The twelve test sequences, which frames number is 300 and including eight sequences with the 4096 × 2048 resolution and four sequences with the 8192 × 4096 resolution, are from [19]. In PD-Rate experiment, there are four kind of points number, the first eight sequences' points numbers are from $1.2 M (2^{20})$ to $3.6 M$, and the last two sequences are from $2.4 M$ to $14.4 M$. The experiment results are shown in Fig. 9 and Table 1, including cubic mapping PD-Rate (CPD), ISP [15] PD-Rate (IPD) and RBM PD-Rate (RPD). The contrast method is ERM in the PD-Rate calculations.

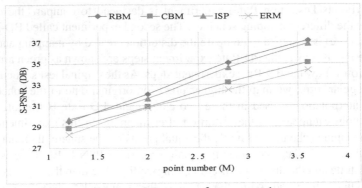

(a)   PD curve of sequence. 1

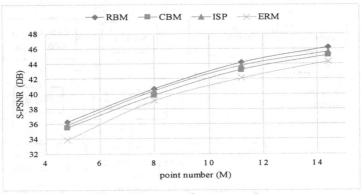

(b)   PD curve of sequence. 9

Fig. 9. PD curve of two sequences.

Table 1. PD-Rate experimental result.

Sequence	CPD	IPD	RPD
1	−6.2%	−20.4%	−24.3%
2	−7.5%	−32.2%	−41.1%
3	−7.0%	−21.3%	−20.7%
4	−11.0%	−12.5%	−9.4%
5	−3.2%	−21.9%	−24.7%
6	−17.1%	−32.6%	−35.1%
7	−11.2%	−25.6%	−31.4%
8	−4.3%	−10.7%	−19.9%
9	−9.5%	−12.3%	−18.6%
10	−5.1%	−12.8%	−13.4%
11	−2.4%	−8.9%	−12.5%
12	−11.5%	−15.6%	−9.8%
Average	−8.0%	−18.9%	−21.7%

The BD-Rate experiments are conducted with the open source AVS encoder RD16.1 on its default settings. And the QPs used for computing the BD-rate are 27, 32, 38, and 45. The first eight sequences sample 2 M points, the last two sequences sample 8 M points when mapping. The results are shown in Fig. 10 and Table 2, including cubic mapping BD-Rate (CBD), ISP BD-Rate (IBD) and RBM BD-Rate (RBD). The contrast method is ERM in the BD-Rate calculations.

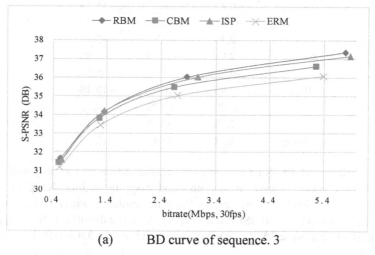

(a)   BD curve of sequence. 3

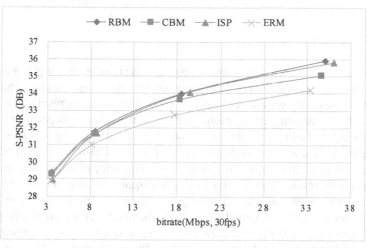

(b)   BD curve of sequence. 10

Fig. 10. BD curves of two sequences.

Table 2. BD-Rate experimental result.

Sequence	CBD	IBD	RBD
1	3.4%	−11.6%	−16.5%
2	5.8%	−32.6%	−50.8%
3	−16.7%	−19.8%	−24.90%
4	−24.4%	−27.9%	−16.8%
5	−6.7%	−10.8%	−15.3%
6	−7.9%	−12.8%	−14.0%
7	−2.3%	−6.8%	−2.5%
8	4.0%	−0.9%	−1.8%
9	−0.6%	−3.2%	−5.3%
10	−10.6%	−18.9%	−19.4%
11	−8.2%	−13.2%	−17.2%
12	2.5%	−2.7%	−3.4%
Average	−5.1%	−13.4%	−15.7%

The PD-Rate and BD-Rate experiments results all show the proposed mapping scheme have a good improve in mapping and mapping-coding. Keeping the same mapping distortion, RBM can save 21.7% PD-Rate compared with ERM and save more 2.8% PD-Rate compared with ISP. And keeping the same distortion after mapping and encoding, RBM can save 15.7% BD-Rate while ISP save 13.4% BD-Rate, compared with ERM.

4   Conclusion

In this paper, we propose a rhombic mapping (RBM) scheme for panoramic video coding, which decreases the number of oversampling points and arranges the pixels to a compression-friendly rectangular frame without discontinuous pixels. The proposed mapping scheme sampling points more uniform on the sphere compared to the typical mapping scheme. To compare the distortion of different mapping schemes, PD-Rate performance experiments are conducted firstly. Then, the BD-Rate performance experiments are performed to compare the compression efficiency of different schemes.

Experimental results show that the proposed mapping scheme can save up to 21.7% of PD-rate and 15.7% BD-rate on average compared to traditional equirectangular mapping scheme. When compared to the ISP scheme, the proposed mapping scheme save up to more 2.8% PD-rate and 2.3% BD-rate on average. As the proposed mapping scheme is highly uniform and compression-friendly, it can be exploited to map panoramic images and videos.

References

1. Kang, S.B.: Catadioptric self-calibration. In: Proceedings of the Computer Vision and Pattern Recognition Conference, pp. 201–207 (2000)
2. Huang, K.C., Chien, P.Y., Chien, C.A., et al.: A 360-degree panoramic video system design. In:2014 International Symposium on VLSI Design, Automation and Test (VLSI-DAT), pp. 1–4. IEEE (2014)
3. Szeliski, R., Shum, H.-Y.: Creating full view panoramic image mosaics and environment maps. In: Proceedings of the 24th Annual Conference on Computer Graphics and Interactive Techniques, pp. 251–258. ACM Press/Addison Wesley Publishing Co. (1997)
4. Zorin, D., Barr, A.H.: Correction of geometric perceptual distortions in pictures. In: Proceedings of the 22nd Annual Conference on Computer Graphics and Interactive Techniques, pp. 257–264. ACM (1995)
5. Alface, P.R., Macq, J.-F., Verzijp, N.: Interactive omnidirectional video delivery: a bandwidth effective approach. Bell Labs Tech. J. 16(4), 135–147 (2012)
6. Neumann, U., Pintaric, T., Rizzo, A.: Immersive panoramic video. In: Proceedings of the 8th ACM International Conference Multimedia, pp. 493–494 (2000)
7. Tang, W.-K., Wong, T.-T., Heng, P.-A.: A system for real-time panorama generation and display in tele-immersive applications. IEEE Trans. Multimedia 7(2), 280–292 (2005)
8. Ng, K.-T., Chan, S.-C., Shum, H.-Y.: Data compression and transmission aspects of panoramic videos. IEEE Trans. Circuits Syst. Video Technol. 15(1), 82–95 (2005)
9. IEEE 1857.9 working group: Syntax Design of Cubic Face Layout, 1857.9-03-M0020, Haerbin, China, May 2016
10. Ho, Y., Wan, L., Lam, P.M., Leung, C.S., Wong, T.T.: Unicube for Dynamic Environment Mapping. IEEE Trans. Visual Comput. Graph. 17(1), 51–63 (2011)
11. Wan, L., Wong, T.T., Leung, C.S.: Isocube: exploiting the cubemap hardware. IEEE Trans. Vis. Comput. Graph. 13(4), 720–731 (2007)
12. Bauermann, I., Mielke, M., Steinbach, E.: H.264 based coding of omnidirectional video. In: Proceedings of the International Conference on Computer Vision and Graphics, pp. 22–24 (2004)
13. Fu, C.-W., Wan, L., Wong, T.-T., Leung, C.-S.: The rhombic dodecahedron map: An efficient scheme for encoding panoramic video. IEEE Trans. Multimedia 11(4), 634–644 (2009)
14. Lin, H.C., Huang, C.C., Li, C.Y., et al.: AHG8: inter Digital's projection format conversion tool Joint Video Exploration Team of ITU-T SG16 WP3 and ISO/IEC JTC1/SC29/WG11, JVET-D0021. In: 5th Meeting, Geneva (2017)
15. Sri, N.A., Anubhav, S., Amith, D., et al.: AHG8: efficient frame packing for Icosahedral Projection Joint Video Exploration Team of ITU-T SG16 WP3 and ISO/IEC JTC1/SC29/ WG11, JVET-D0015. In: 5th Meeting, Geneva (2017)
16. Yu, M., Lakshman, H., Girod, B.: Content adaptive representations of omnidirectional videos for cine-matic virtual reality. In: Proceedings of the 3rd International Workshop on Immersive Media Experiences, pp. 1–6. ACM (2015)
17. Li, J., Wen, Z., Li, S., Zhao, Y., Guo, B., Wen, J.: Novel tile segmentation scheme for omnidirectional video. In: 2016 IEEE International Conference on Image Processing (ICIP), Phoenix, AZ, USA, pp. 370–374 (2016)
18. Yu, M., Lakshman, H., Girod, B.: A framework to evaluate omnidirectional video coding scheme. In: 2015 IEEE International Symposium on Mixed and Augmented Reality (ISMAR), pp. 31–36. IEEE (2015)
19. IEEE 1857.9 working group: Mapping Core experiment description, 1857.9-04-N0008, Guizhou, China, June 2016

Research of the Ear Reconstruction Based on the Poisson Image Blending

Yang Li, Qiangqing Zhang, Bicheng Wang, Xiang Li, and Jianling Hu[⊠]

School of Electronic and Information Engineering,
Soochow University, Suzhou 215006, Jiangsu, China
jlhu@suda.edu.cn

Abstract. Due to the undesirable reconstruction result of the ear part in the 3D face reconstruction which based on single image, we propose an ear reconstruction approach based on the Poisson image blending method. First of all, the 3D face shape is reconstructed from the single frontal image by fitting the sparse morphable model. Then the cylindrical expansion approach and the elliptical skin color criterion are combined in order to utilize for the texture reconstruction and correction process. Finally, the Poisson image blending method is selected to carry out the second recovery for the ear part. The experiment results demonstrate that our approach not only ensure a fast and simplified reconstruction process but also efficiently improve the undesirable reconstruction result in the face profile especially the ear part, which has existed in some 3D face modeling technologies. Meanwhile, it further enhances the sense of reality of the reconstruction result.

Keywords: 3D face reconstruction · Sparse morphable model · TPS
Poisson image blending

1 Introduction

Three-dimensional (3D) face reconstruction has always been a hot and difficult issue in the fields of computer vision, image processing and pattern recognition. As one of the key technology, 3D face reconstruction can be widely used in face recognition, video surveillance, security, augmented reality (AR), and so on. So the research of 3D face reconstruction has important theoretical significance and practical value [1]. The key performance indicators of 3D face reconstruction are reconstruction efficiency and reconstruction fidelity. In recent decades, various algorithms and methods have been developed to improve these performances, which can be classified into two main kinds, image based facial modeling method and morphable model method.

According to the 2D face image information, image based facial modeling method mainly uses vision method added with face geometry and anthropometry to reconstruct the 3D face [2]. Although image based facial modeling method

© Springer Nature Singapore Pte Ltd. 2018
G. Zhai et al. (Eds.): IFTC 2017, CCIS 815, pp. 454–465, 2018.
https://doi.org/10.1007/978-981-10-8108-8_41

has relative high flexibility, it has high complexities because manual interactive labelling is needed to extract the feature points of faces. Morphable model method is based on statistical theory, which divides facial information into two parts: shape and texture. By making statistical analysis of facial data in the 3D face database, the 3D face of the input image will be reconstructed automatically [3]. However, the construction of the model is very time consuming and the model matching algorithm has to process a large amount of data. It also has some drawbacks like unsatisfactory reconstruction of face profile and ear features.

In order to improve the reconstruction fidelity, we introduce an ear reconstruction approach based on Poisson image blending method into the morphable model method. In this paper, we realize the reconstruction of the 3D face shape from the single frontal image by fitting the sparse morphable model [4], and then the Poisson image blending method is selected to carry out the second recovery for the ear part. Firstly, we construct the sparse morphable model by manually labeling the 3D face samples in the BJUT 3D facial dataset. Secondly, the model is further fitted by the 2D facial image feature points extracted through active shape model (ASM) method. Then 3D thin plate spline (TPS) [5] function is selected to realize the facial model deformation. In order to solve the problem of unsatisfied face profile and ear part reconstruction in the texture mapping, cylindrically unfolding method combined with Poisson image blending algorithm is introduced. Comparing to the traditional morphable model method, the proposed algorithm reduce the scale of data processing and solve the complex alignment problem. The experiment results illustrate that our approach has a better sense of reconstruction fidelity especially in the ear part.

2   Algorithm Framework

Its an ill-condition problem to reconstruct the 3D structure of the object from one single image. The traditional morphable model method has to solve the problem of dense alignment of the facial data which leads to high computation complexity. Because one single frontal facial image cant provide adequate information about the face profile in the texture mapping, the reconstruction result of ear part is usually not satisfactory. In order to solve above two issues, a two-step reconstruction method is introduced in this paper. Firstly, sparse morphable model with TPS function is selected to reconstruct the initial 3D face, which doesnt need the dense alignment of face samples and therefore can reduce the computation complexity effectively. Secondly, Poisson image blending algorithm [6] is introduced to refine the texture of the ear parts, which refines the reconstruction effect of the ear part and then improves the overall reconstruction fidelity. Figure 1 presents a comprehensive description of the proposed 3D face reconstruction system, which is composed of following five steps. (1) 2D feature points are extracted using ASM method aided with manual refinement. (2) The manually labeled 3D feature points is combined with the general model selected form BJUT-3D face database. (3) TPS function is used to realize the

deformation of the particular input and the shape of 3D face will be generated.
(4) Vertical texture mapping and cylindrically unfolding texture inpainting is
performed according to the frontal input image to reconstruct the texture of the
3D face. (5) Poisson image blending algorithm is introduced to refine the texture
of ear parts and then the final reconstructed 3D face will be obtained.

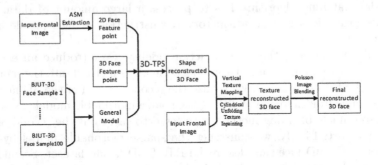

Fig. 1. Framework of proposed 3D face reconstruction system

3   Shape Reconstruction of 3D Face

3.1   Sparse Morphable Model

Sparse morphable model is constructed by manually labelling the feature points
of the 3D face samples. 50 male samples and 50 female samples from the BJUT-
3D database [7] are selected by this paper. For each face sample, 64 feature points
are selected as shown in Fig. 2(a). The feature points should contain facial organs
as many as possible, such as eyes, nose, etc. Moreover, the feature points should
have correspondingly accurate description of the contour of the frontal face.
Figure 2(b) shows a 3D sparse face model constructed from the selected feature
points of the face shown in Fig. 2(a).

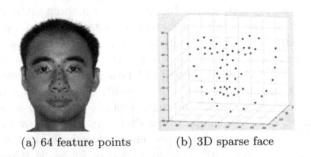

(a) 64 feature points   (b) 3D sparse face

Fig. 2. 3D sparse morphable model

Assuming that a 3D face has N spatial vertices, it can be described as:

$$S_1 = (X_1, Y_1, Z_1, \cdots, X_N, Y_N, Z_N)^T \tag{1}$$

where X, Y, Z are the 3D coordinates of the vertices in the rectangular coordinate system. Defining a vector α as combination coefficient, so that we can use 100 facial samples to represent or approximate a new face as shown in (2).

$$S_{new} = [S_1, S_2, \cdots, S_{100}] \alpha \tag{2}$$

In order to obtain good approximation, N should be as large as possible. But larger N will need higher computation complexity. As the sparse model used in this paper, it's shown that N of 64 can offer good overall performance. As shown in (2), the key problem for sparse morphable model is to find the optimum linear combination coefficients α for any input face.

3.2   Fitting Sparse Feature Points for Specific Face

The 2D sparse model of the input 2D facial image extracted by ASM method aided with manual refinement can be defined as $S_{2D} = (x_1, y_1, \cdots, x_{64}, y_{64})^T$. And the 3D sparse model extracted from BJUT-3D database can be defined as $S = (X_1, Y_1, Z_1, \cdots, X_{64}, Y_{64}, Z_{64})^T$. Because the Y axis of BJUT-3D database corresponds to the depth of the nose tip, so we should project S to the X-Z plane and get the 2D projection model as:

$$S_{prj} = (X_1, Z_1, \cdots, X_{64}, Z_{64})^T \tag{3}$$

Assuming the input 2D sparse model can be represented by the combination of the projection models generated from 3D database, according to Sect. 3.1, we have (4).

$$S_{2D} = \left[S_{prj}{}^1, S_{prj}{}^2, \cdots, S_{prj}{}^{100} \right] \alpha \tag{4}$$

Usually the input face image has different coordinate system and different size with sample faces in the BJUT-3D database, so translation and scaling are needed before model fitting. Using c to represent the scaling factor and d to represent the translation parameter, (4) can be rewritten as (5).

$$c(S_{2D} + d) = \left[S_{prj}{}^1, S_{prj}{}^2, \cdots, S_{prj}{}^{100} \right] \alpha \tag{5}$$

Let O_{2D} be the geometric center of 2D sparse model S_{2D} of input face and O_{3D} be the geometric center of 2D projection model S_{prj} generated from BJUT-3D database as illustrated in (6) and (7) respectively.

$$O_{2D} = (\overline{x}, \overline{y}) = \frac{1}{N} \left(\sum_{i=1}^{N} x_i, \sum_{i=1}^{N} y_i \right) \tag{6}$$

$$O_{3D} = (\overline{X}, \overline{Z}) = \frac{1}{kN} \sum_{j=1}^{k} \left(\sum_{i=1}^{N} x_i, \sum_{i=1}^{N} z_i \right) \tag{7}$$

where N is the number of facial feature points, k is the number of face samples selected to construct the sparse morphable model (in this paper, $N = 64$, $k = 100$). Then the scaling factor and translation parameter can be derived by as follows:

$$c = \frac{\frac{1}{k}\sum_{j=1}^{k}\sum_{i=1}^{N} \| (X_{ji}, Z_{ji}) - O_{3D}\|}{\sum_{i=1}^{N} \| (x_i, y_i) - O_{2D}\|} \tag{8}$$

$$d = O_{3D} - O_{2D} \tag{9}$$

The (5) is a overdetermined equation, so the optimum estimation of α can be deduced using least square method as shown below.

$$\alpha' = (S_t^T S_t)^{-1} S_t^T (c(S_{2D} + d)) \tag{10}$$

where $S_t = [S_{prj}{}^1, S_{prj}{}^2, \cdots, S_{prj}{}^{100}]$.

Substituting the solution of (10) into (2), then we can achieve the fitting result. Keep the depth coordinate Y unchanged and replace the coordinates X, Z with the coordinates of the input 2D face after scaling and translation, and we can get the feature point model S_f which can be further used in TPS.

3.3 Model Deformation Using TPS

The selection of the general model is based on the minimal distance principle. Assuming that S_{ave} is the average coordinate value of all samples that constitute the 3D sparse model. According to the minimal distance principle, the minimal distance between S_i and S_{ave} is:

$$\varepsilon_{min} = \min_{1 \leq i \leq 100} \|S_i - S_{ave}\| \tag{11}$$

where $\| \cdots \|$ represents the Euclidean distance. When ε_{min} is found, the corresponding face sample can be used as the general model G and the corresponding 3D feature point model is S_g. The TPS correspondence between S_g and S_f obtained from previous section can be established, and then the deformation from the general model to the specific model by TPS equation can be realized.

Using (X_i, Y_i, Z_i) to represent the coordinate of 3D feature point of the general model and $f(X_i, Y_i, Z_i)$ to represent the TPS function between S_g and S_f and we have following expression:

$$f(X_i, Y_i, Z_i) = a_0 + a_X X_i + a_Y Y_i + a_Z Z_i + \sum_{j=1}^{64} \omega_j U(r_{i,j}) \tag{12}$$

where $r_{i,j}$ is the Euclidean distance between any two 3D feature points in the general model and $U(\cdot)$ is the radial basis function.

$$U(r_{i,j}) = (r_{i,j})^2 \log (r_{i,j})^2, \quad U(r_{i,i}) = 0 \tag{13}$$

We need to get the parameters a_0, a_X, a_Y, a_Z and ω_j which represent the constant term, weight vectors in X, Y, Z directions and weight coefficient respectively. These parameters have to satisfy following constraints:

$$\sum_{j=1}^{64} \omega_j = 0, \quad \sum_{j=1}^{64} \omega_j X_j = 0$$
$$\sum_{j=1}^{64} \omega_j Y_j = 0, \quad \sum_{j=1}^{64} \omega_j Z_j = 0$$

(14)

After obtaining the above parameters, the TPS equation can be used to realize the deformation from the general model to the specific model, and the 3D shape information of the input face can be reconstructed.

4   Texture Reconstruction of 3D Face

4.1   Texture Restoration Based on Vertical Projection

Vertical projection method can achieve real-time and effective texture inpainting and can provide higher reconstruction fidelity. This method is based on the corresponding relationship between the 3D coordinate point and the 2D unfolded map. Assuming that the corresponding 2D unfolded coordinate of the point $P(X, Y, Z)$ is (h, φ), we can obtain the corresponding texture array according to the corresponding relationship and further realize texture mapping of projection points. Figure 3 shows the vertical texture mapping result.

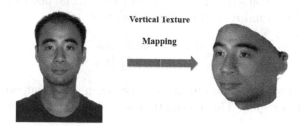

Fig. 3. Vertical texture mapping

4.2   Texture Inpainting Based on Cylindrical Unfolding and Elliptical Skin Model

The texture information obtained through vertical mapping method may not be correct especially in the face profile and ear part where there is less information. As shown in Fig. 3, the cheek and ear part of the reconstructed face has some white regions which is not in conformity with the reality. So further texture inpainting based on cylindrical unfolding and elliptical skin model is introduced to refine these reconstructed non-skin regions.

Firstly, the face image is cylindrically unfolded. Assuming that P is one point of the input face, its rectangular coordinate is (X_P, Y_P, Z_P), texture value is (R_P, G_P, B_P), and its cylindrical coordinate is (h_P, φ_P, d_P). So the cylindrical coordinate can be calculated as:

$$\varphi_p = \begin{cases} \tan^{-1}\left(\frac{X_P}{Y_P}\right), & Y_P > 0 \\ \cos^{-1}\left(\frac{Y_P}{d_P}\right), & X_P > 0, Y_P < 0 \\ -\cos^{-1}\left(\frac{Y_P}{d_P}\right), & X_P < 0, Y_P < 0 \end{cases} \tag{15}$$

$$h_p = Z_p \tag{16}$$

$$d_p = \sqrt{X_p^2 + Y_p^2} \tag{17}$$

The cylindrically unfolded image $f(h, \varphi)$ should be further discretized. In this paper, 285 levels uniform discretization is adopted in both dimensions. Using u, v to represent the discretized angle and height values, we have:

$$u_i = 285 - round\left\{\frac{284 * \varphi_i - \min(\varphi_i)}{\max(\varphi_i) - \min(\varphi_i)}\right\} \tag{18}$$

$$v_i = 285 - round\left\{\frac{284 * h_i - \min(h_i)}{\max(h_i) - \min(h_i)}\right\} \tag{19}$$

After unfolding and discretization, the non-skin regions are refined according to the ellipse skin model proposed by Rein-Lien Hsu [8]. Firstly the color space of the face image is converted from RGB to YC_bC_r. The pixel values C_b, C_r are transformed into m and n by the following matrix:

$$\begin{bmatrix} m \\ n \end{bmatrix} = \begin{bmatrix} \cos\theta & \sin\theta \\ -\sin\theta & \cos\theta \end{bmatrix} \begin{bmatrix} C_b & -C_x \\ C_b & -C_y \end{bmatrix} \tag{20}$$

If m and n are in the same elliptical region, then this point can be recognized as a point of skin region. This means that m and n should satisfy:

$$\frac{(m - ec_x)^2}{a^2} + \frac{(n - ec_y)^2}{b^2} = 1 \tag{21}$$

where c_x, c_y, θ, ec_x, ec_y, a and b can be derived from the skin clustering space [8].

Only the pixels satisfying the elliptic equation will be reserved (except the pixels which RGB values are all zeros), otherwise, interpolation method will be used to update the original RGB values. This texture inpainting will perform through all pixels of the unfolded image. Figure 4 shows the effect of proposed texture inpainting.

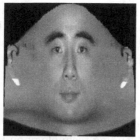
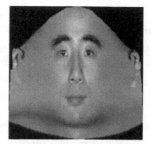

(a) Before inpainting   (b) After inpainting

Fig. 4. Comparison of cylindrically unfolded face image before and after texture inpainting

4.3   Ear Refinement Based on Poisson Image Blending

Many frontal face image based the 3D face reconstruction algorithms cant reconstruct the ear part satisfactorily. The main reason is that the frontal image cant provide sufficient information of face profile and the vertical projection method cant reconstruct the ear part well. We can extract ear part information from the general model (the ear part information can also be extracted from the cylindrically unfolded image of the BJUT face sample according to the size and shape of the ear), and then attach the ear part to the cylindrical unfolded image of the reconstruction result. However, as shown in Fig. 5, such attaching method will generate serious artifacts. So Poisson image blending algorithm is introduced to refine the attached ear part.

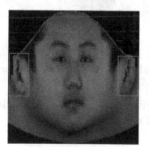
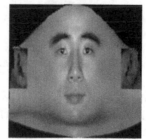

(a) Extracting ear part   (b) Reconstruction result
with artifacts

Fig. 5. Attaching ear part to the cylindrically unfolded image

Using g to represent the selected ear region, v is the gradient field of g. Ω represents the region covered by Poisson image blending, its boundary is $\partial\Omega$. The blended image should be as smooth as possible, so the gradients in Ω should be as small as possible. The minimization of the gradient can be formulated as:

$$\min_{f} \iint \|\nabla f - v\|^2 \quad \text{and} \quad f|_{\partial x} = f^*|_{\partial x} \tag{22}$$

where ∇ is gradient operator, $\| * \|$ is L2-norm of the vector $*$, f and f^* represent the pixel value inside and outside the region Ω respectively. Using Euler-Lagrangian equation, we can get its optimal solution which is a Poisson equation satisfying the Dirichlet boundary condition:

$$\nabla^2 f = \nabla \cdot v \quad \text{amd} \quad f|_{\partial x} = f^*|_{\partial x} \tag{23}$$

where $\nabla^2 f = \frac{\partial^2 f}{\partial x^2} + \frac{\partial^2 f}{\partial y^2}$ is Laplace operator, $\nabla \cdot v$ is the divergence of v, therefore $\nabla \cdot v = \frac{\partial v}{\partial x} + \frac{\partial v}{\partial y}$. Performing Poisson image blending technology on Fig. 5(b), and further mapping the cylindrically unfolded face image back to the 3D model, we can get the results as shown in Fig. 6.

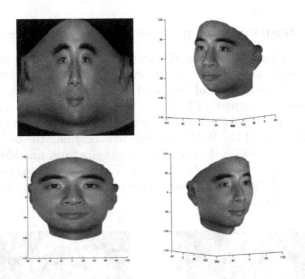

Fig. 6. Poisson image blended image and multi-view 3D face reconstruction results

Figure 6 shows that Poisson image blending can solve the problems of ear texture blur and incomplete reconstruction of ear part effectively, and can improve the reconstruction fidelity.

5   Simulation and Analysis

In this paper, MATLAB is selected as the programming tool to implement the proposed 3D reconstruction algorithm. The fidelity of 3D reconstruction can be used to evaluate the overall performance of the 3D reconstruction algorithm. Figure 7 shows different input frontal face images and their multi-view reconstruction results. The experimental results show that good reconstruction result of face profile and ear part can be achieved by the Poisson image blending method and the proposed algorithm can offer good reconstruction fidelity.

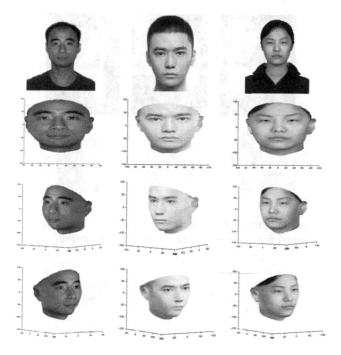

Fig. 7. Poisson image blended image and multi-view 3D face reconstruction results

The performance of the proposed reconstruction algorithm is compared with those of other algorithms illustrated in literatures as shown in Fig. 8. The first and second line of Fig. 8(a) show the reconstruction results of [9] and this paper respectively. And the first and second line of Fig. 8(b) show the reconstruction results of [10] and this paper respectively. It shows that the face profile reconstruction results of [9] are unsatisfactory because of the inadequate vertices of CANDIDE-3 model. After rotating to the side part, the missing ear part deceases the overall reconstruction fidelity. The reconstruction result of [10] is slightly insufficient for ear part, especially the reconstruction of ear texture is inaccurate. In contrast, the reconstruction results of the proposed method can get full face contours, more delicate details, complete shape and clear texture of the ear parts.

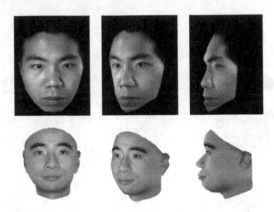

(a) First line: reconstruction results of [9]
Second line: reconstruction results of this paper

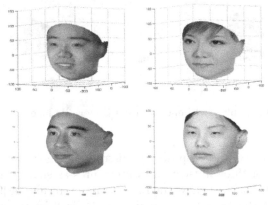

(b) First line: reconstruction results of [10]
Second line: reconstruction results of this paper

Fig. 8. Reconstruction results comparison

6   Conclusions

Trying to solve the unsatisfactory reconstruction results of face profile and ear part based on one single frontal face image, we proposed a 3D reconstruction algorithm which used sparse morphable model to reconstruct the shape of the 3D face and Poisson image blending algorithm to reconstruct the ear part. Firstly, 2D facial feature points of the frontal image were extracted, and the general model was selected according to the minimum distance criterion. Secondly, the transformation relation between the 2D and 3D feature points was established through the TPS function, and the deformation from the general model to the specific face model was realized. Then after vertical texture mapping, texture inpainting based on cylindrical unfolding and elliptical skin model was performed. Finally, Poisson image blending algorithm was used to refine the ear part and then the final 3D reconstruction face was obtained. The experimental results show that our reconstruction results not only have full contours and delicate details, but also have adequate information about the shape and texture of the ear part. Compared with other 3D face reconstruction algorithm, the proposed algorithm can offer better overall reconstruction fidelity.

References

1. Xu, C.H., Wang, Y.H., Tan, T.N.: Overview of research on 3D face modeling. J. Image Graph. **9**(8), 893–903 (2004)
2. Horn, B.K.P.: Height and gradient from shading. Int. J. Comput. Vis. **5**(1), 37–75 (1990)
3. Blanz, V., Vetter, T.: Face recognition based on fitting a 3D morphable model. IEEE Trans. Patt. Anal. Mach. Intell. **25**(9), 1063–1074 (2003)
4. Li, X.: Research of 3D Modeling Based on the Single Frontal Image. Soochow University (2016)
5. Bookstein, F.L.: Principal warps: thin-plate splines and the decomposition of deformations. IEEE Trans. Patt. Anal. Mach. Intell. **11**(6), 567–585 (2002)
6. Rez, P., Gangnet, M., Blake, A.: Poisson image editing. ACM Trans. Graph. **22**(3), 313–318 (2003)
7. Yin, B., Sun, Y., Wang, C., et al.: BJUT-3D large scale 3D face database and information processing. J. Comput. Res. Dev. **46**(6), 1009–1018 (2009)
8. Ran, H.Z., Zhou, J.L., Wang, L.: Face detection in color image. Asia Pac. J. Anthropol. **10**(1), 56–58 (2009)
9. Tian, Y.: 3D Face Reconstruction Based on Single Frontal Face Image. Chongqing University (2011)
10. Deng, Q.P.: 3D Face Reconstruction Based on a Single Image and Statistical Model. Shanghai Jiao Tong University (2010)

An Efficient 3-D Mapping Algorithm for RGB-D SLAM

Jiadong Yu, Zhixiang You, Ping An[✉], and Jie Xia

Key Laboratory of Advanced Displays and System Application, Shanghai Institute for Advanced Communication and Data Science, Ministry of Education, Shanghai University, Shanghai 200444, China
anping@shu.edu.cn

Abstract. Mapping algorithm is the beginning of SLAM, having a significant influence on the design of the follow-up SLAM system and final results. However, the popular mapping algorithms are not robust enough. These algorithms most are based on feature detection but can't effectively eliminate false matches under challenging circumstances. In addition to this, there is a need for faster algorithms to process higher pixel images with the development of RGB-D sensors. This paper presents a new mapping algorithm to solve the problems. The approach converts the smoothness constraints to offer ultra-robust feature matching. Then, it takes the image smoothness as a statistical likelihood to sore the feature points' adjacent region. Finally, we use Bi-direction KD-Tree to improve the ICP algorithm. Experiments are carried out with nyuv2 data set. It is challenging enough to test the performance of the new algorithm.

Keywords: SLAM · RGB-D · Feature matching · Smoothness constraints
Bi-direction KD-Tree

1 Introduction

Simultaneous localization and mapping (SLAM) needs to obtain the 3D modules of environment and track the corresponding robot's pose over long trajectories quickly and accurately. It is the key algorithm of mobile robot autonomous navigation [1]. With the application of Augmented Reality (AR) and Virtual Reality (VR) spread into the mass market, the simultaneous localization and 3D reconstruction have become increasingly popular in the field of computer vision.

The current SLAM systems mainly use two kinds of sensors: one is laser scanner which provides the high-precision information of environment. Scene reconstruction of some studies [2] can even achieve millimeter accuracy in recent years. But this kind of sensor has following disappointed shortcomings: expensive, heavy, poor robustness under challenging circumstances. So it is difficult to be used for mobile robotics or consumer robotics. The other is visual sensor. This kind of SLAM system is named Visual SLAM. Visual SLAM extracts features from camera images directly. But it costs heavily to compute the depth information of environment, regardless of monocular or binocular. Thanks to the emergency of the Kinect which is a kind of RGB-D camera, we now have another powerful and attractive alternative. Kinect V1 obtains RGB images

© Springer Nature Singapore Pte Ltd. 2018
G. Zhai et al. (Eds.): IFTC 2017, CCIS 815, pp. 466–477, 2018.
https://doi.org/10.1007/978-981-10-8108-8_42

with 640 × 480 pixels and depth images with 320 × 240 pixels in 30 Hz. As the RGB and depth information of environment obtained easily, it can be used to build the dense 3D maps [3].

The purpose of SLAM is to solve the problems of localization and mapping in robot navigation. When a SLAM system uses Kinect to obtain the RGB images and depth images for building the 3D maps, we call this kind of SLAM system as RGB-D SLAM. Recent years, many scholars began to study Kinect applied in the robot 3-D SLAM. Great achievements have been made in this field. Henry first proposed the RGB-D mapping in 2012 [4]. He used Kinect for modeling indoor environments, which directly extracted SIFT (Scale Invariant Feature Transform) [5] in combination with ICP (Iterative Closest Point) [6]. In the same year, Hu *et al.* proposed a robust RGB-D SLAM algorithm based on the work of Henry [7]. Henry's approaches must need enough depth information. But due to the unsatisfactory sunlight or distance limitations of Kinect, sometimes will lack of depth information. Hu overcomes this by combining RGB-D SLAM with monocular SLAM. This new RGB-D SLAM technique can switches between BA (Bundle Adjustment) [8] with or without available depth. The drawback is that it will slow down the process. In [9], Yang *et al.* proposed a 3D modeling algorithm in the household environment for robot's hand-eye coordinated grasping. In order to accelerate the system, the SIFT algorithm is implemented by using GPU. The algorithm uses RANSAC (RANdom SAmple Consensus) based on three points [10] to compute the pose transformation between adjacent frames. Experimental results show that it is very useful for small objects modeling. The error is just about 1 mm, which fully satisfies the requirements for the coordinate determination in robot grasping. But it is not useful for large-scale scenes. In [11], the famous Computer Vision Group of Technical University of Munich (TUM) completed the first state-of-art RGB-D SLAM system. It is designed specifically for the RGB-D sensor. The system's frontend is similar to the previous work. Endres *et al.* still extracted features to calculate the camera poses, but they employed RANSAC to eliminate the false matches. It has been proved to be useful, but not perfect. RANSAC itself greatly depends on the number of false matches. Most false matches must to be pre-eliminated. In [12], Mur-Artal *et al.* designed the ORB-SLAM which is the first open-source SLAM system for monocular, stereo and RGB-D cameras together. They overcame the limitation that the map is only used to compute the poses of the camera. Map can also localise a different camera or to relocalise the same camera from different viewpoints based on bags of binary words [13] with ORB features.

As described above, mapping of RGB-D SLAM needs to extract features from RGB images. This method has a significant influence on the design of the follow-up system and final results. In [11], ORB with RANSAC is a good choice, for it can eliminate a certain number of false matches. But it is not useful under challenging environment. Too much false matches make RANSAC less effective. We need a more robust way. Furthermore, RGB-D sensors have made a great development. For example, Kinect V2 can obtain RGB images with 1920 × 1080 pixels and depth images with 512 × 424. It is a huge upgrade compared with V1. Current algorithms are too slow to keep up with the pace. A faster mapping algorithm can not only accelerate the SLAM system, but also reduce the computational limits of the backend. It is also good for achieving more accurate results.

This paper presents an efficient 3-D mapping algorithm to solve these problems. First, we convert the smoothness constraints (adjacent pixels share similar motion) into feature matching. It can offer ultra-robust feature matching even on intractable scenes [14]. Afterwards, as the smoothness constraints are complex to implement, we use the GMS (Grid-based Motion Statistics) which takes the image smoothness as a statistical likelihood to sore the Feature points' adjacent region. Finally, we improve the ICP point cloud registration using Bi-direction KD-Tree [15]. ICP is a precise algorithm but the time consumer is high. Traditional nearest neighbor searching method with KD-Tree can only accelerate the ICP Iterative process, the robustness is not satisfied when it is used in small point clouds. Bi-direction KD-Tree can make the results be more accurate in a limited number of iterations.

2   The Efficient 3-D Mapping Algorithm

This section mainly introduces the proposed mapping algorithm. The overview of the system framework is showed in Fig. 1.

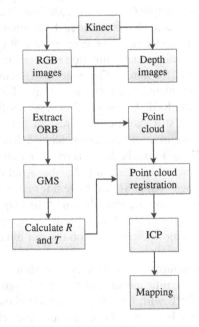

Fig. 1. Overview of the system

Six primary modules comprise the system, including Extract ORB, Point cloud, GMS, Calculate R and T, Point cloud registration, ICP. Same as other RGB-D SLAM, the method starts with the Kinect. Firstly, we can calculate the three-dimensional coordinate of each point in the scene according to camera imaging principle. These points comprise the point cloud. At the same time, feature detection is executed using ORB. Then, GMS is used to eliminate the false matches. The rest of the matches are used in pose transformation estimation between previous frame and last frame. After calculating the R and T, it is used as an importation to point cloud registration. Point cloud registration just adds the new point cloud to the original point cloud. The new point cloud has a pose transformation relative to the original point cloud. Finally, we use the ICP based on Bi-direction KD-Tree to optimize the registration result. With continuous scan of Kinect, we process the new RGB images and depth images following the previous steps until the mapping work is finished.

2.1 Feature Detection Using ORB

The detection of features is to find feature points in the image and confirm its position. The feature detection algorithms in visual SLAM are mainly SIFT, SURF, FAST and ORB et al. SIFT matches the images well by finding the same features despite of differences in location, rotation, scale, 3D viewpoint, illumination or noise. It has been proposed for many years. However, it needs a large quantity of computation. SURF is too sensitive to light. It is a huge short board in computer vision. FAST is very fast because it just compares the brightness difference between pixels. On the other hands, it leads to its poor performance in SLAM which contains a large number of rotation and translation. ORB is a combination of BRIEF and FAST. It has been demonstrated one of the most effective descriptors in SLAM systems.

FAST doesn't produce multi-scale features. By making the image pyramid, ORB can generate features at every level of the pyramid. This solves the problem of scale invariance. Furthermore, ORB adds extra orientation information for FAST based on the intensity centroid. It is the prerequisite to solve the rotation invariance. Firstly, defining the moments of an image as follows:

$$M_{ij} = \sum_y \sum_x x_i y_j I(x, y) \tag{1}$$

Where $I(x, y)$ means the image gray scale at (x, y). The centroid of the moment is:

$$C = \left(\frac{m_{10}}{m_{00}}, \frac{m_{01}}{m_{00}} \right) \tag{2}$$

The angle of the vector is the orientation of the feature. It is calculated as follows:

$$\theta = \arctan \left(\frac{m_{10}}{m_{00}} \bigg/ \frac{m_{01}}{m_{00}} \right) = \arctan \left(m_{10} / m_{01} \right) \tag{3}$$

Next, ORB extracts BRIEF descriptors along the orientation of (3). The point sets are represented by matrix as:

$$S = \begin{pmatrix} x_1 , \ldots, x_n \\ y_1 , \ldots, y_n \end{pmatrix} \tag{4}$$

Giving the rotation matrix:

$$R = \begin{pmatrix} \cos\theta & -\sin\theta \\ \sin\theta & \cos\theta \end{pmatrix} \tag{5}$$

So the new points set containing orientation can be calculated as $S_o = RS$. The ORB descriptor can be represented as:

$$ORB(p,\theta) = BRIEF(p) \mid (x_i, y_i) \in S_o \tag{6}$$

2.2   Grid-Based Motion Statistics for Feature Matching

As described in the previous section, converting smoothness constraints into feature matching can offer ultra-robust feature correspondence even on intractable scenes. It can be seen in Fig. 2, the false and true matches can be differenced clearly with GMS.

(a). ORB+RANSAC   (b). ORB+ GMS

Fig. 2.   A comparison between GMS and RANSAC

Smoothness constraints reflected in feature matches is that the neighborhood around a true feature match views the same 3D location while the neighborhood around a false match views different 3D locations. Here neighborhood is defined as a pair of regions $\{n_1, n_2\}$ showed in Fig. 3. In other words, there will have many similar features around a true match with many supporting matches. Likewise, there will have fewer supporting matches around a false match. These factors are applied into a statistic called GMS.

As shown in Fig. 3. Assume that there is a pair of images $\{I_1, I_2\}$ with $\{N, M\}$ features and there are some feature matches between I_1 and I_2. $K = \{k_1, k_2, \ldots, k_N\}$ is a set of the all matches in regions $\{n_1, n_2\}$ between I_1 and I_2. f_i is one of the features in region n_1. f_i has a probability of C to match correctly. If the match is false, f_i may match with any of the M possible features in I_1. This can be represented as:

$$p(f_i^j \mid f_i^F) = \beta m / M \tag{7}$$

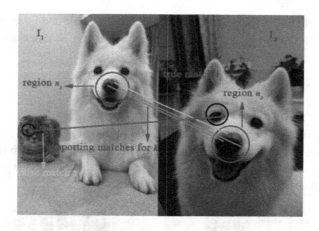

Fig. 3. True matches and its supporting matches in $\{n_1, n_2\}$

Where f_i^F means f_i matches wrongly, $f_i^F = 1 - C$. f_i^j means f_i's supporting matches lie in n_2. β is factor added to accommodate violations that f_i may not match with the M possible features because of the repeated structures.

Our goal is to derive the rate of matches in regions $\{n_1, n_2\}$ when view the same or different 3D locations. When $\{n_1, n_2\}$ view the same locations, p_C is derived as follows:

$$
\begin{aligned}
p_C &= p\left(f_i^j \mid T_{ij}\right) = p\left(f_i^C \mid T_{ij}\right) + p\left(f_i^F, f_i^j \mid T_{ij}\right) \\
&= p\left(f_i^C \mid T_{ij}\right) + p\left(f_i^F \mid T_{ij}\right) p(f_i^j \mid f_i^F, T_{ij}) \\
&= p(f_i^C) + p(f_i^F) p(f_i^j \mid f_i^F) \\
&= C + (1 - C)\beta m / M
\end{aligned}
\tag{8}
$$

Where T_{ij} means $\{n_1, n_2\}$ view the same 3D locations. The first line of Eq. (8) is based on that event f_i^j consists of event f_i^C and event $f_i^F \cdot f_i^j$. $f_i^F \cdot f_i^j$ means f_i matches wrongly but its neighborhood matches lies in n_2. According to the Bayes theorem, we derive the second line. Because $p(f_i^F)$ and $p(f_i^j)$ are independent of T_{ij}, T_{ij} is eliminated. Substituting the (7) into the third line gives the final expression.

When $\{n_1, n_2\}$ view the different locations, p_F is similar to (8):

$$
\begin{aligned}
p_F &= p\left(f_i^j \mid D_{ij}\right) = p\left(f_i^F, f_i^j \mid D_{ij}\right) \\
&= p\left(f_i^F \mid D_{ij}\right) p(f_i^j \mid f_i^F, D_{ij}) \\
&= p(f_i^F) p(f_i^j \mid f_i^F) \\
&= (1 - C)\beta m / M
\end{aligned}
\tag{9}
$$

Where D_{ij} means $\{n_1, n_2\}$ view the different 3D locations.

Now, we define S_i as the neighborhood support of f_i. True and false matches can be differentiated by the score-S_i. Based on a threshold, it can be calculated as binomial distribution:

$$S_i \sim \begin{cases} B(n, p_C), & \text{if } f_i \text{ is true} \\ B(n, p_F), & \text{if } f_i \text{ is false} \end{cases} \tag{10}$$

The time complexity of S_i is O(N), N means the number of features. It can't meet the real-time needs. We overcome this by dividing the image into grids showed in Fig. 4. Scores of grid-pairs are computed only once. This make scores computation independent of features numbers. Time complexity is reduced to O(1).

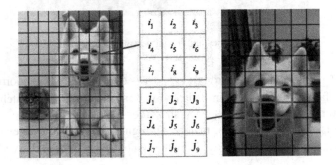

Fig. 4. Grid-based statistics

2.3   ICP with Bi-direction KD-Tree

KD-Tree (K-Dimensional Tree) is a kind of data structure that divides the k-dimensional data space, mainly used for accelerating the data searching process. A Two-Dimensional Tree is showed in Fig. 5. Database of points is recursively bisected in order to build a search tree. Yellow node is the root node, the next layer is red, then the third layer is green, the fourth layer is blue.

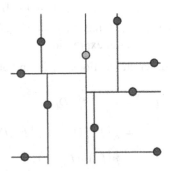

Fig. 5.   Two-Dimensional Tree (Color figure online)

ICP algorithm with the nearest neighbor searching based on Bi-direction KD-Tree is an Bi-directional registration method. The registration algorithm generally includes following steps:

1. There are a source point cloud P and a target point cloud Q. For every point in P, searching the nearest neighbor points in Q. Repeat searching until the corresponding point set S_1 is build.
2. Similar as above, search the nearest neighbor points in P of Q and build the corresponding point set S_2.
3. Find the intersection S_3 of point set S_1 and S_2.
4. According to the corresponding point set S_3, the rotation matrix R and the translation vector T can be calculated.
5. Repeat the steps 4, until the ICP reaches the established number of iterations or it is convergent.

We use the famous Bunny model from Stanford University Computer Graphics Laboratory to test performance of this algorithm. The maximum number of iterations in the test is set to 100 and the maximum corresponding distance is set to 1.5. Then the threshold of the convergence is set to 0.01 (Fig. 6).

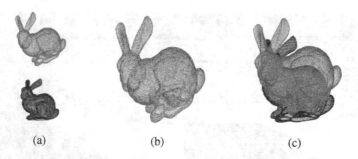

(a)   (b)   (c)

Fig. 6. The test for Bi-direction KD-Tree

As can be seen that (a) is the initial position of source point cloud and target point cloud, (b) is the registration result of traditional ICP, (c) is the registration result using ICP based on Bi-direction KD-Tree. With the Bi-direction KD-Tree, the corresponding point set S_3 can be estimated accurately. It can offer a good importation for the iteration. Of course, ICP based on Bi-direction KD-Tree can achieve a better result.

3   Experimental Results

The experiment is implemented in Ubuntu 14.04. We use some dataset (Slam_nyuv, Freiburg1_room, Living_room) [16] to test performance of the mapping algorithm. The dataset Slam_nyuv is a scan of kitchen. It contains about 782 RGB images and 782 depth images. There is a lot of furniture in the kitchen. The cabinet and table are filled with all kinds of items. There is even a moving man in the scene when the Kinect is scanning.

So it is challenging enough to test the performance. The Dataset Freiburg1_room is a scan of office which contains about 800 RGB images and 800 depth images. It is also challenging to test the performance. Dataset Living_room is a scan of living room, it is not as challenging as the first two scenes.

As showed in Fig. 7. The GMS still keeps its ultra-robustness. It still works very well under the challenging scene.

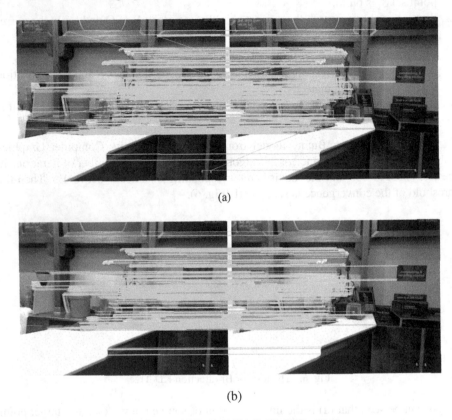

(a)

(b)

Fig. 7. (a) ORB+RANSAC, (b) ORB+GMS

The final 3D maps of the Slam_nyuv is showed in Fig. 8(a), (b). Figure 8(a) is the result of our algorithm, and Fig. 8(b) is the result of the popular algorithm proposed by Endres [11]. Module (b) has two big drifts marked with red circle. One is the wall of the scene, the beams on the wall have been staggered. The other is corner, the upper part of the corner and the lower part obviously have malposition. These seriously affected the quality of the model. Figure 8(a) has a more accurate module. There are no any obviously drifts. Because we converting the smoothness constraints into feature matching and improve the ICP with Bi-direction KD-Tree. Of course, it can be seen in both (a) and (b) that the reconstruction of the moving man is not perfect. The reconstruction of dynamic objects has always been difficult in the SLAM. It needs to be further improved. The final 3D maps of the Freiburg1_room is showed in Fig. 8(c), (d). The results of the two are generally same. Only the computer boundary in (d) has a drift. The result of Living_room is showed in Fig. 8(e), (f). There aren't any obvious drifts difference in the two maps. All in all, it can be seen that our algorithm is more robust under challenging environment. And when it is used in simpler circumstance, its performance is similar to Endres's algorithm.

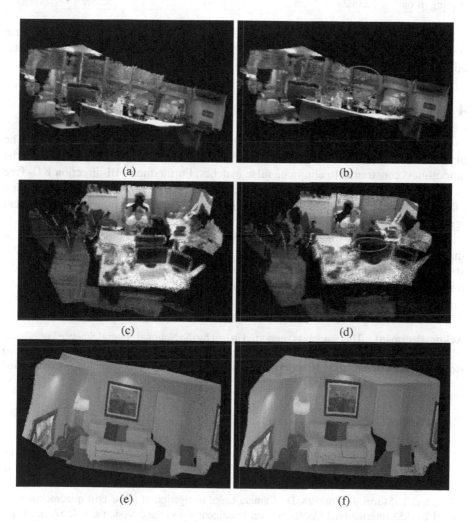

(a)   (b)

(c)   (d)

(e)   (f)

Fig. 8. Comparison of the final 3D map

Time consumption of the mapping algorithm under different dataset is recorded in Table 1. Our algorithm is compared with the [11].

Table 1. Comparison of the final 3D map

Dataset	Total time cost of (a)/s	Total time cost of (b)/s	Change percentage
Slam_nyuv	111.971	121.529	7.86%
Freiburg1_room	172.841	180.785	4.6%
Living_room	238.2	251.381	5.53%

The new algorithm reduces the time-consuming by 4%–7%. This is expected because we take the image smoothness as a statistical likelihood to sore the Feature points' adjacent region. The Bi-direction KD-Tree also accelerates the framework.

4   Conclusion

In this paper, we propose an efficient 3-D mapping algorithm for RGB-D SLAM. The algorithm has improvements on both robustness and speed. For robustness, we use the smoothness constraints to eliminate false matches. Furthermore, Bi-direction KD-Tree is used to improve the ICP. To improve the algorithm speed, we use the GMS which takes the image smoothness as a statistical likelihood to sore the feature points' adjacent region.

For future work, we need to solve the problem of dynamic object reconstruction in the SLAM. In dynamic environment, the surface features are rapidly changing. We should not depend on the features any more. To avoid using the feature-based methods, it may be a good choice to directly optimize on the gray-scale image geometric information.

Acknowledgment. This work was supported in part by the National Natural Science Foundation of China under Grants 61571285 and U1301257, Construction Program of Shanghai Engineering Research Center under Grant 16dz2251300, and Shanghai Science and Technology Commission under Grant 17DZ2292400.

References

1. Endres, F., Hess, J., Engelhard, N., et al.: An evaluation of the RGB-D SLAM system. In: IEEE International Conference on Robotics and Automation, vol. 162, no. 4, pp. 1691–1696 (2012)
2. Engel, J., Sturm, J., Cremers, D.: Camera-based navigation of a low-cost quadrocopter. In: IEEE/RSJ International Conference on Intelligent Robots and Systems, vol. 57, no. 1, pp. 2815–2821 (2013)
3. Han, J., Shao, L., Xu, D., et al.: Enhanced computer vision with Microsoft Kinect sensor: a review. IEEE Trans. Cybern. **43**(5), 1318–1333 (2013)
4. Henry, P., Krainin, M., Herbst, E., et al.: RGB-D mapping: using Kinect-style depth cameras for dense 3D modeling of indoor environments. Int. J. Robot. Res. **31**(5), 647–663 (2012)
5. Lowe, D.G.: Distinctive image features from scale-invariant keypoints. Int. J. Comput. Vis. **60**(2), 91–110 (2004)
6. Besal, P.J., McKay, H.D.: A method for registration of 3-D shapes. IEEE Trans. Pattern Anal. Mach. Intell. **14**(2), 239–256 (1992)

7. Hu, G., Huang, S., Zhao, L., et al.: A robust RGB-D SLAM algorithm. In: IEEE/RSJ International Conference on Intelligent Robots and Systems, vol. 7198, no. 6, pp. 1714–1719 (2012)

8. Triggs, B., McLauchlan, P.F., Hartley, R.I., Fitzgibbon, A.W.: Bundle adjustment — a modern synthesis. In: Triggs, B., Zisserman, A., Szeliski, R. (eds.) IWVA 1999. LNCS, vol. 1883, pp. 298–372. Springer, Heidelberg (2000). https://doi.org/10.1007/3-540-44480-7_21

9. Yang, Y., Cao, Q.X., Zhu, X.X., et al.: A 3D modeling method for robot's hand-eye coordinated grasping. Robot 35(2), 151–155 (2013)

10. Fischler, M.A., Bolles, R.C.: Random sample consensus: a paradigm for model fitting with applications to image analysis and automated cartography. Commun. ACM 24(6), 381–395 (1981)

11. Endres, F., Hess, J., Sturm, J., et al.: 3-D mapping with an RGB-D camera. IEEE Trans. Robot. 30(1), 177–187 (2014)

12. Mur-Artal, R., Tardos, J.D.: ORB-SLAM: tracking and mapping recognizable features. IEEE Trans. Robot. 31(5), 1147–1163 (2015)

13. Galvez-Lopez, D., Tardos, J.D.: Bags of binary words for fast place recognition in image sequences. IEEE Trans. Robot. 28(5), 1188–1197 (2012)

14. Wang, J.B., Yan, W.L., Yasuyuki, M., et al.: GMS: grid-based motion statistics for fast, ultra-robust feature correspondence. In: Conference on Computer Vision and Pattern Recognition (CVPR) (2017)

15. Wen, F.Z., Jun, S.L., Peng, Z.Y.: Small point cloud matching based on bi-direction random KD-tree. In: Asia International Symposium on Mechatronics, pp. 1517–1521 (2015)

16. Silberman, N., Hoiem, D., Kohli, P., Fergus, R.: Indoor segmentation and support inference from RGBD images. In: Fitzgibbon, A., Lazebnik, S., Perona, P., Sato, Y., Schmid, C. (eds.) ECCV 2012. LNCS, vol. 7576, pp. 746–760. Springer, Heidelberg (2012). https://doi.org/10.1007/978-3-642-33715-4_54

Indoor Localization System for Individuals with Visual Impairment

Yi Zeng[✉], Duo Li, and Guangtao Zhai

Institute of Image Communication and Information Processing,
Shanghai Jiao Tong University, Shanghai, China
{zy_sjtu,zhaiguangtao}@sjtu.edu.cn, liduoee@gmail.com

Abstract. There are millions of people with visual diseases around the world, most of whom are suffering from inconvenience in their daily lives. In this paper, we demonstrated an indoor localization system for people with visual impairments to help them finding out the right directions without others' assistance. The system contains three main parts, the hidden display module, the localization module and direction-giving component. Based on temporal psychovisual modulation, hidden display module enables the system to obtain the information required without disturbing normal people. Localization is based on a pair of wearable smart glasses that captures and analyses the surrounding environment. The direction-giving function works by feeding direction back to the user with haptic signals. We test our system by simulating indoor environment and collecting location data. We find out in the same situation, using our system can make subjects find the right places in shorter time compared with random guess.

Keywords: Indoor localization · Visual impairment · Scene analysis
Augmented reality · Hidden display

1 Introduction

According to findings from the 2015 National Health Interview Survey (NHIS) data [1], an estimated 23.7 million adult Americans (or 10% of all adult Americans) reported they either "have trouble" seeing, even when wearing glasses or contact lenses, or that they are blind or unable to see at all. Throughout the world, there are millions of people suffering in visual diseases. People with visual diseases can see the outside world, but have to bear the partial damage of the image that their eye see. For people with night blindness, they tend not to be adapted to the weak light in the night. For people with color blindness, they will mistake some one color for another. For people with age-related macular degeneration (AMD), the image that they receive tend to be distorted. For people with low vision, people tend to feel difficult to read, because the letters are too small for them. There are also other kinds of visual diseases that make patients life uncomfortable. To help guiding people who cannot see contains two main problems. First, how to locate

© Springer Nature Singapore Pte Ltd. 2018
G. Zhai et al. (Eds.): IFTC 2017, CCIS 815, pp. 478–491, 2018.
https://doi.org/10.1007/978-981-10-8108-8_43

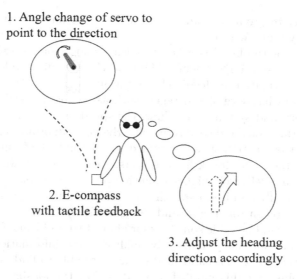

1. Angle change of servo to point to the direction

2. E-compass with tactile feedback

3. Adjust the heading direction accordingly

Fig. 1. Work flow of the direction-giving component

the person in a given environment. Second, how to feed the direction information back to the user in a more natural way (Fig. 1).

In the past decades, augmented Reality (AR) has been a popular topic. Researchers work hard to explore the potential of AR to make human's life better [2–6]. There are already many researchers studying in the possibility of AR techniques to be introduced to medical treatment, such as 3D imagery in laparoscopic surgery [5], a see-through HMD (head mounted device) to overlay MR scans on heads and provide views of tool manipulation hidden beneath tissue and surfaces [6]. Bajura et al. [7] set up a vision enhancement system that can be used in image guided surgical procedures and location 3D interactive architecture preview. And some researchers try to explore AR through visual attention [8–10].

To the best of the author's knowledge, some researchers have been paying attention to the possible approaches to improve people's vision recently [11]. Peli [12,13] has created a new kind of glasses using vision multiplexing techniques to vision rehabilitation. He applied vision multiplexing to restore the interplay of central and peripheral vision using eye movements. Hicks et al. [14] has created a HMD to aid navigation in partially sighted individuals with the help of a depth camera. Using the depth camera, they can detect the distance to nearby objects and thus achieve obstacle avoidance.

As the increase of computing speed of smart phones and HMD such as Google Glass, Epson Moverio BT-200 [15,16], as well as the development of head mounted display techniques, such as Sony HMZ-T3W [17] and Cardboard [18], it is becoming easier to develop a system to assist people with visual impairments. These devices are mainstream platforms to develop visual applications.

They are easier to promote than those specifically produced devices because of their simplicity and low price.

Navigation for the blind is a key problem for developing assistance devices for people with visual impairments. Many previous studies explored the potential of voice information as feedback for the users [19,20]. However, this kind of feedback form has several shortages, such as feedback speed, naturalness of user experience, and system cost. First, the speed of reaction is not real time, since it takes time for the device to display the voice information. If we use tactile feedback, the reaction speed is immediate. Second, the form of voice is less intuitive than tactile feedback for the users. Third, the hardware cost of voice feedback system is relatively higher than that of tactile feedback. The voice feedback system usually requires a speech generation module, while tactile feedback only need a servo control circuit, and the latter is cheaper.

There are several possible solutions for above two problems. Localization has been a hot topic for many years. By analysing the information contained in electromagnetic radiations, hand held devices are able to find out the location. The main problem of this kind of method is that the localization precision is not high enough for indoor applications. For instance, the wifi-based indoor localization works with a precision of over one meter. For majority of situations, a meter's location error may lead users who cannot see to danger. More precise locating methods are studied for a long time in the area of Robots. To guide the Robots move around in an environment, while mapping the surrounding scenes, a series of algorithm called SLAM is proposed. Combining SLAM and object recognition algorithms, we can locate the user and give the right guidance. However, this requires a lot of computing resources, which is not practical for low cost wearable devices. Fortunately, we can decline the computing cost for SLAM and object recognition algorithms by introducing markers with special features into the system. In [21], authors have introduced a powerful tool for augmented reality applications called ArUco. In [22,23], authors use Aruco markers [24] for locating, which is a promising method for our system. The main problem for traditional Aruco marker based locating system is that the markers confuses people with normal vision. In this paper, we propose a system that uses Aruco to localize for people with vision impairments while hiding the markers to people with normal vision. The algorithm to hide markers is based on a recent work called TPVM which makes use of temporal and spatial redundancy of modern display devices.

The other problem is means of feeding back. For people who cannot see clearly, their sense to the environment mainly depends on haptics, hearing, and smalling. Recently, there are new tactile feedback called visual prostheses to help the blind to reconstruct vision. The protheses feeds back surrounding information in the form of a matrix of stimulating points. This kind of feedback usually requires high dimensional capturing devices, such as RGB camera, and depth camera. Moreover, to match the captured information to the feedback protheses, algorithms to process the images [25] are important for the navigation effects. The cost of visual protheses are too high for ordinary people to use in daily life.

In our work, we proposed a low cost, straightforward, real-time direction feedback for people with visual impairments. The direction feeding back stage consists of three parts, a electrical compass, control module, and a servo driven pointer. The electrical compass captures the strength of the magnetic field, then the control module computes the corresponding angle of the target direction. Finally, the control module drives the servo to point to the consequent angle. Through this process, the pointer points to the target direction continuously.

We compare our system with other kind of ways to guide people with vision impairments. Through experiments, we find that our proposed system gives directions more quickly and accurately. During the process of indoor localization and guidance for people with visual impairments, subjects reflect to us that the system is of better user experience.

Reminder of the paper is as follows: Sect. 2 introduces the design principle of the system and correspondingly proposed possible solutions the visual impairments, Sect. 3 shows the experimental results and discusses the performance of the system, Sect. 4 is the conclusion.

2   Design and Implementation of the System

The indoor localization system is a synthetic auxiliary system for visual impairments which consists of three main parts. In this section, the design and implementation of the system is introduced respectively by consecution.

2.1   Hidden Display Module

(1) Philosophy of TPVM
Temporal psychovisual modulation (TPVM) [26,26] is proposed as ingenious interplay of signal processing, optoelectronics and psychophysics [27]. With the rapid development of display technology, most of modern display and projection equipments support the refresh rate of 120 Hz. However, the research shows that the human visual system (HVS) can hardly distinguish fast-changing optical signals beyond flicker fusion frequency [28] (about 60 Hz for most people), which means that the high refresh rate of these equipments may cause visual redundancy. As a result, HVS will merge adjacent frames together. Building on this fact, the redundant frames of the equipments could be made the most of to convey addition information to different viewers through personal watching equipments.

Here we use an equation of three matrixes to describe the implementation of TPVM:

$$Y_{N \times K} = X_{N \times M} \bullet W_{M \times K} \tag{1}$$

where K is the number of display channels, M is the number of atom frames, N is the total pixels of the displayer. For $N \times K$ matrix Y, column vector $y_1, y_2 \ldots y_K$ represent syncretic frames of channel $1, 2 \ldots K$, which is the final result formed in HVS. Column vector $x_1, x_2 \ldots x_M$ of the $N \times M$ matrix X are atom frames, which have been defined as a series of frames in a period that HVS cannot resolute. The $M \times K$ matrix W is a coefficient matrix whose column vectors mean different modulation type on the atom frames and every element is the transmittance of corresponding atom frame which is subjected to $0 < W < 1$.

With matrix Y known generally, we use non-negative matrix factorization(NMF) [29] to obtain matrix X and matrix Y.

(2) Difference between HVS and digital Camera in sampling

Digital camera works with a shutter which cannot keep opened in order to avoid overexposure. Furthermore, it takes time to convert an optical signal into an electrical signal. Since shutter closing is necessary and has a minimum time for converting, the camera obtains the optical signal by discrete sampling, resulting that camera cannot record all information of the optical signal especially when the signal transforms with high frequency. For a camera sampling interval, the information recorded by camera can be presented as:

$$V_{camera} = \int_0^{t_1} f + \int_{t_1}^{t_2} 0 \bullet f = \int_0^{t_1} f \tag{2}$$

where t_1 is the time point when the shutter turns to be closed, t_2 is the time point when the shutter turns to be open again, f is the information of the optical signal and V_{camera} is the information the camera sampled during a camera sampling interval.

Due to a different working principle, HVS can carry on a continuous sampling to the optical signal, accounting for sampling intact signal. For the same period, the information recorded by HVS can be denoted as:

$$V_{HVS} = \int_0^{t_2} f \tag{3}$$

Since $t_1 < t_2$ and they cannot be extremely close, it makes sense that if the refresh rate of displayer is so high that the frames change more than once during t_2, the information recorded by HVS and digital camera could be of a great difference.

(3) Formation of Atom Frames

Based on *(1)* and *(2)* above, in order to hide the ArUco marker boards, what we need is two display channels, one is for normal people, the other is for the indoor localization system. Thus, we materialize the basic matrix equation of TPVM into following form with a displayer of 120 Hz:

$$(Y_0 \; Y_1) = (X_1 \; X_2)\begin{pmatrix} 1 & W_1 \\ 1 & W_2 \end{pmatrix} \tag{4}$$

A set of solutions of equations above can be denoted as:

$$\begin{cases} X_1 = S \\ X_2 = T - X_1 \\ W_1 = 1 \\ W_2 = 0 \end{cases} \tag{5}$$

Fig. 2. Given outline of marker board comparing with original board

where X_1 means atom frame 1, X_2 means atom frame 2, Y_0 is the channel for normal people, Y_1 is the channel for the system.

So atom frame 1 displays frame S, which convey general information as common public screens do or project image with zero in R, G and B, reducing the impact of the system on normal people. And atom frame 2 displays frame $T - X_1$, where T is the image of ArUco marker board. Subject to $X_2 = T - X_1$ and $X_2 > 0$, we map gray scale of T from original $[0, 255]$ to $[128, 255]$, which means $I' = I/2 + 128$. In the meantime, X_1 is mapped to $[0, 127]$. Finally, the two atom frames can be denoted as:

$$
\begin{cases}
X_1 = S/2 \\
X_2 = T/2 + 128S/2
\end{cases}
\tag{6}
$$

Based on TPVM, we could take advantages of screens or projections in the indoor pubic place to display ArUco marker boards while normal people cannot see it directly.

2.2 Localization Module

The localization module consists of recognizable marker maps and corresponding camera pose estimation algorithm. The OpenCV library provides a kind of useful markers named ArUco, which is a great option for camera to detect. Furthermore, ArUco could append location information to the marker. So once we demarcate the location of a marker in world coordinate system, it can be recorded in the marker that more marker boards can be placed indoor without confusing their location parameters. The methods of generating and detecting markers has been released in ArUco library [21].

As the marker board detected successfully by camera, we need to process the image to get the coordinates of the camera in the world coordinate system. What we can obtain is a set of 2D images with outline of markers given by function in ArUco, as shown in Fig. 2.

We can extract four vertices from a marker, and the four vertices are rotated invariant. Thus, the problem is abstracted as a process of estimating the 3D posture of an object by a set of 2D points. Here, we use orthogonal projection iteration [30] to solve this problem. For any pose in a three-dimensional space coordinate system, it can be determined by rotation and translation. Thus, camera pose can be defined as:

$$R = \begin{pmatrix} R_{11} & R_{12} & R_{13} \\ R_{21} & R_{22} & R_{23} \\ R_{31} & R_{32} & R_{33} \end{pmatrix} = \begin{pmatrix} R_1^T \\ R_2^T \\ R_3^T \end{pmatrix} \tag{7}$$

$$T = \begin{pmatrix} T_x \\ T_y \\ T_z \end{pmatrix} \tag{8}$$

where R is rotation matrix and T is translation vector. Row i of R represents the coordinates of the unit vector in the ith coordinate axis direction in the camera coordinate system in the world coordinate system; column j of R represents the coordinates of the unit vector in the ith coordinate axis direction in the world coordinate system in the camera coordinate system. T is the coordinates of the origin of the world coordinate system in the camera coordinate system. Particularly, T_z represents the depth of the origin of the world coordinate system in the camera coordinate system.

Meanwhile, perspective projection transformation is denoted as:

$$\begin{cases} x = \dfrac{f}{Z_c} X_c \\ y = \dfrac{f}{Z_c} Y_c \end{cases} \tag{9}$$

where (x, y) is the coordinate in millimeters in the image coordinate system, (X_c, Y_c, Z_c) is the coordinate in millimeters in the camera coordinate system. f is the focal length of the camera, whose value is not vital in the field. On the contrary, the ratio between f and (x, y) is important which can be determined according to f_x and f_y in the camera intrinsic matrix. As the basic parameters of the camera, the intrinsic matrix uses the following format: $\begin{bmatrix} f_x & s & c_x \\ 0 & f_y & c_y \\ 0 & 0 & 1 \end{bmatrix}$, where the coordinates $[c_x, c_y]$ represent the optical center (the principal point), in pixels. When the x and y axis are exactly perpendicular, the skew parameter, s, equals 0. f_x and f_y represent the normalized focal length on the x-axis and y-axis respectively.

Suppose the point in the world coordinate system is (X_w, Y_w, Z_w), then Eq. 9 can be extended as:

$$\begin{pmatrix} Z_c x \\ Z_c y \\ Z_c \end{pmatrix} = \begin{pmatrix} f X_c \\ f Y_c \\ Z_c \end{pmatrix} = \begin{pmatrix} f R_1^T & f T_x \\ f R_2^T & f T_y \\ R_3^T & T_z \end{pmatrix} \begin{pmatrix} X_w \\ Y_w \\ Z_w \\ 1 \end{pmatrix} \tag{10}$$

Both side divided by T_z, Eq. 10 transforms into:

$$\begin{pmatrix} wx \\ wy \\ w \end{pmatrix} = \begin{pmatrix} sR_1^T & sT_x \\ sR_2^T & sT_y \\ R_3^T/T_z & 1 \end{pmatrix} \begin{pmatrix} X_w \\ Y_w \\ Z_w \\ 1 \end{pmatrix} \tag{11}$$

$$\text{with} \begin{cases} w = Z_c/T_z \\ y = f/T_z \end{cases}.$$

When the origin of the world coordinate system is near the center of the object, it can be considered that the average depth is T_z in the translation vector T, that is, the average of Z_c for each point is T_z. While Z-coordinate range of the surface on object in the camera coordinate system is much smaller than the average depth of the object in the Z-axis direction, fluctuation of w is much smaller than w itself, which means:

$$w = Z_c/T_z \approx 1 \tag{12}$$

Since we have given an estimate of w, it can be treated as a known amount. To simplify the calculation, we can delete the third row in Eq. 10:

$$\begin{pmatrix} wx \\ wy \end{pmatrix} = \begin{pmatrix} sR_{11} & sR_{12} & sR_{13} & sT_x \\ sR_{21} & sR_{22} & sR_{23} & sT_y \end{pmatrix} \begin{pmatrix} X_w \\ Y_w \\ Z_w \\ 1 \end{pmatrix} \tag{13}$$

The iterative equation has eight unknowns which can be composed of three vectors:

$$sR_1 = \begin{pmatrix} sR_{11} \\ sR_{12} \\ sR_{13} \end{pmatrix}, sR_2 = \begin{pmatrix} sR_{21} \\ sR_{22} \\ sR_{23} \end{pmatrix}, sT = \begin{pmatrix} sT_x \\ sT_y \end{pmatrix} \tag{14}$$

Given a pair of coordinates (one is the coordinates of the world coordinate system, the other is the coordinates of the image coordinate system, they correspond to the same point), we can get two independent equations. As we can obtain four pairs from marker detection and extraction, the eight unknowns can be determined. Since R_1 and R_2 are unit vectors with modulus 1, we can compute s and T_z approximately as:

$$s = \sqrt{|sR_1| \bullet |sR_2|} \tag{15}$$

$$T_z = f/s \tag{16}$$

Furthermore, R_3 is the cross product of R_1 and R_2:

$$R_3 = R_1 \times R_2 \tag{17}$$

Fig. 3. A simple model of direction-giving component

Thus, rotation matrix and translation vector have been determined. However, these are only approximations, because we have assumed $w = 1$ at the beginning. Now that we have an approximate translation matrix, it can be used to calculate a new depth for each point, which is more accurate than T_z. Since each point has a different depth, they also have a different iteration coefficient w. Because w (characterizing the depth information) is more accurate than the last iteration, it will generate a more accurate translation matrix, which will in turn to generate a more accurate w. Reciprocating feedback, we can gradually approximate the exact solution.

2.3 Direction-Giving Component

The direction feeding back stage consists of three parts, a electrical compass, control module, and a servo driven pointer, as shown in Fig. 3. The electrical compass captures the strength of the magnetic field, then the control module computes the corresponding angle of the target direction. Finally, the control module drives the servo to point to the consequent angle. Through this process, the pointer points to the target direction continuously.

The system tracks directional information and convey this information to users by changing angle of the servo. Consequently, the servo will always point to the same direction. Users can get the direction by touching the servo. Visually impaired people can use this system to obtain direction guidance in their daily lives.

3 Experiment

In order to verify the feasibility and robustness of the system, we use a simplified usage scene to observe the result of hidden display. Further, we use the camera to take pictures to simulate the process of smart phones scanning ArUco

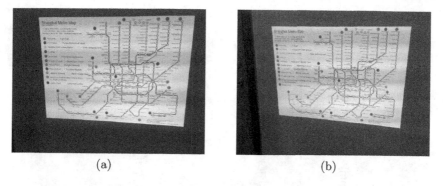

Fig. 4. Since camera cannot catch the metro map if we had hidden the marker board, the map is taken purely only to show the image that human eyes can obtain

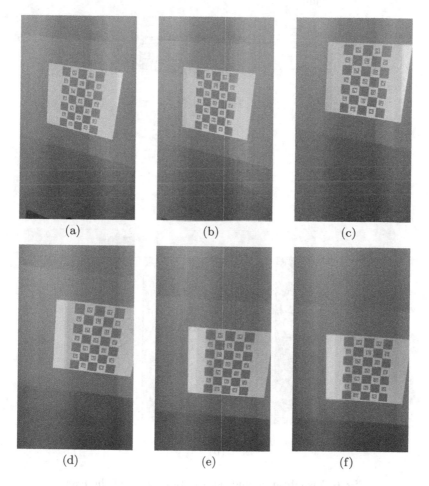

Fig. 5. The camera takes ArUco from diverse locations

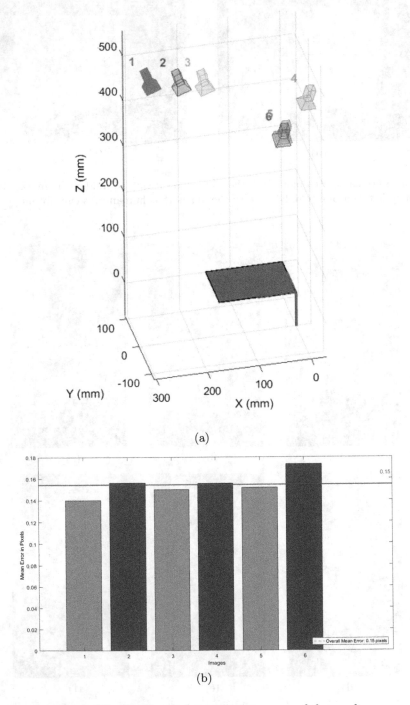

(a)

(b)

Fig. 6. Visualization and reprojection errors of the result

marker boards. Possible interference factors which should be taken account of are shake and distortion of camera, asperous surface of wall and inadequate iterations.

In our experiment, we use a projector with a refresh rate of 120 Hz to simulate the indoor screen playback or projection environment. We project a metro map (Fig. 4), which could be useful for normal people in a way. Then, we hide an ArUco marker board under the map with TPVM. Thus, human eyes can see the map only, and in the meantime, camera can photo the marker board directly. Here is the result of photoing marker board from different location in Fig. 5.

Then the figures are processed and analyzed by a laptop with an Intel Core i7-4720HQ 2.60 GHz processor and 8192 MB of RAM. And the results are showed in Table 1. A visualization of the localization and reprojection errors of the camera pose estimation is showed in Fig. 6(a) and (b) respectively.

Table 1. Result of translation and rotation parameters of each picture

Image no	T_x(mm)	t_y(mm)	T_z(mm)	R_x(rad)	R_y(rad)	R_z(rad)
1	95.33	40.59	605.87	0.100	0.340	0.082
2	63.59	97.74	548.31	0.163	0.293	0.131
3	54.34	126.68	507.31	0.201	0.215	0.164
4	45.51	98.65	459.03	0.32	−0.139	0.130
5	70.59	82.49	434.64	0.426	−0.0620	0.0430
6	73.84	82.69	427.24	0.430	−0.065	0.036

4 Conclusion and Future Work

Our system can offer accurate localization for visual impairments with influencing normal people slightly, which make the most of redundancy of refresh rate. Addtionally, we have proposed a new usage mode of marker boards, which may save a lot of space. Furthermore, our system feeds back tactile information in real-time. In the future, we will conduct subjective experiments where people with visual impairments go through disordered spaces with guidance of our system. This helps us to measure and improve the quality of experience of the system. We will also use this tactile feedback into situations such as simultaneous navigation with help of mobile devices.

References

1. American foundation for the blind. http://www.afb.org/info/blindness-statistics/2
2. Azuma, R.T., et al.: A survey of augmented reality. Presence **6**(4), 355–385 (1997)
3. Van Krevelen, D.W.F., Poelman, R.: A survey of augmented reality technologies, applications and limitations. Int. J. Virtual Real. **9**(2), 1 (2010)

4. Wohlgemuth, W., Triebfürst, G.: Arvika: augmented reality for development, production and service. In: Proceedings of DARE 2000 on Designing Augmented Reality Environments, pp. 151–152. ACM (2000)
5. Fuchs, H., et al.: Augmented reality visualization for laparoscopic surgery. In: Wells, W.M., Colchester, A., Delp, S. (eds.) MICCAI 1998. LNCS, vol. 1496, pp. 934–943. Springer, Heidelberg (1998). https://doi.org/10.1007/BFb0056282
6. Willers, D.: Augmented reality at airbus. In: International Symposium on Mixed & Augmented Reality (2006)
7. Bajura, M., Fuchs, H., Ohbuchi, R.: Merging virtual objects with the real world: seeing ultrasound imagery within the patient. In: ACM SIGGRAPH Computer Graphics, vol. 26, pp. 203–210. ACM (1992)
8. Min, X., Zhai, G., Gao, Z., Gu, K.: Visual attention data for image quality assessment databases. In: Proceedings of IEEE International Symposium on Circuits System, pp. 894–897, June 2014
9. Min, X., Zhai, G., Gu, K., Yang, X.: Fixation prediction through multimodal analysis. ACM Trans. Multimed. Comput. Commun. Appl. 13(1), 61–623 (2016)
10. Min, X., Gu, K., Zhai, G., Hu, M., Yang, X.: Saliency-induced reduced-reference quality index for natural scene and screen content images. Signal Process. 145, 127–136 (2017)
11. Min, X., Zhai, G., Ke, G., Liu, J., Wang, S., Zhang, X., Yang, X.: Visual attention analysis and prediction on human faces. Inf. Sci. 420, 417–430 (2017)
12. Peli, E.: Vision multiplexing: an engineering approach to vision rehabilitation device development. Optom. Vis. Sci. 78(5), 304–315 (2001)
13. Peli, E., Luo, G., Bowers, A., Rensing, N.: Development and evaluation of vision multiplexing devices for vision impairments. Int. J. Artif. Intell. Tools 18(03), 365–378 (2009)
14. Hicks, S.L., Wilson, I., Muhammed, L., Worsfold, J., Downes, S.M., Kennard, C.: A depth-based head-mounted visual display to aid navigation in partially sighted individuals. PloS One 8(7), e67695 (2013)
15. Epson Moverio BT-200. http://www.epson.com/cgi-bin/Store/jsp/Product.do?sku=V11H560020
16. Epson Moverio BT-200. http://www.epson.com/cgi-bin/Store/jsp/Landing/moverio-bt-200-smart-glasses.do
17. Sony HMZ-T3W. http://www.sonystyle.com.cn/products/hmd
18. Google cardboard. https://cardboard.withgoogle.com/
19. Loomis, J.M., Golledge, R.G., Klatzky, R.L.: Navigation system for the blind: auditory display modes and guidance. Pres. Teleoper. Virtual Environ. 7(2), 193–203 (1998)
20. Holland, S., Morse, D.R., Gedenryd, H.: AudioGPS: spatial audio navigation with a minimal attention interface. Pers. Ubiquit. Comput. 6(4), 253–259 (2002)
21. Garrido-Jurado, S., Muñoz-Salinas, R., Madrid-Cuevas, F.J., Marn-Jimnez, M.J.: Automatic generation and detection of highly reliable fiducial markers under occlusion. Pattern Recogn. 47(6), 2280–2292 (2014)
22. Ecklbauer, B.L.: A mobile positioning system for android based on visual markers. Mobile Comput., 91 (2014)
23. La Delfa, G.C., Catania, V.: Accurate indoor navigation using smartphone, bluetooth low energy and visual tags. In: Proceedings of the 2nd Conference on Mobile and Information Technologies in Medicine (2014)
24. Madrid-Cuevas, F.J., Garrido-Jurado, S., Muñoz-Salinas, R., Marn-Jimnez, M.J.: Automatic generation and detection of highly reliable fiducial markers under occlusion. Pattern Recogn. 6(47), 2280–2292 (2014)

25. Jung, J.H., Aloni, D., Yitzhaky, Y., Peli, E.: Active confocal imaging for visual prostheses. Vis. Res. **111**, 182–196 (2015)
26. Zhai, G., Xiaolin, W.: Multiuser collaborative viewport via temporal psychovisual modulation [applications corner]. IEEE Signal Process. Mag. **31**(5), 144–149 (2014)
27. Xiaolin, W., Zhai, G.: Temporal psychovisual modulation: a new paradigm of information display [exploratory dsp]. IEEE Signal Process. Mag. **30**(1), 136–141 (2012)
28. Hecht, S., Shlaer, S.: Intermittent stimulation by light : V. The relation between intensity and critical frequency for different parts of the spectrum. J. Gen. Physiol. **19**(6), 965 (1936)
29. Lee, D.D., Seung, H.S.: Learning the parts of objects by non-negative matrix factorization. Nature **401**(6755), 788 (1999)
30. Deutsch, F.: The method of alternating orthogonal projections. In: Singh, S.P. (ed.) Approximation Theory, Spline Functions and Applications. NATO ASI Series, vol. 356, pp. 105–121. Springer, Dordrecht (1992). https://doi.org/10.1007/978-94-011-2634-2_5

Construction of an Indoor Topological Map of a Robot Based on Prunable Self-Organizing Map

Cheng Li, Xiao-gang Ruan, Ke Gu, and Xiao-qing Zhu[✉]

Faculty of Information Technology, Beijing University of Technology,
Beijing 100124, China
alex.zhuxq@bjut.edu.cn

Abstract. Environmental map building is an important premise of robot navigation, Self-Organizing Map (SOM) or Growing Self-Organizing Map (GSOM) can establish the topological map of the indoor environment through the environmental cognition. Aimed at the problem of traditional SOM containing error structure in constructing topological map while long time consuming of GSOM, this paper proposes a Prunable Self-Organizing Map (PSOM) algorithm which can prune wrong connections between neurons from the environmental structure, thus proving accurate topology while greatly reducing the implementation cost of the program compared to the Growing Self-Organizing Map. The proposed method (PSOM) is verified by experimental of environment map building based on physical indoor environment.

Keywords: Self-Organizing Map · GSOM · PSOM · Topological map

1 Introduction

The environment map construction robot is one of the basic links for navigation, there are many scholars research on robot map building problems, common environmental map representation of geometric feature map and grid map, the topological graph, the grid map can be more vivid characterization of environmental space and uncertainty, but limited to the environment size; geometry map can express simple environment for complex environment is difficult to say; topological map does not need to know the scale of specific information, which can be characterized as a connection between the specific points in the environment and specific location, suitable for robot path planning and navigation, but the process of constructing the topological map is relatively complex. There are many shortcomings are trying to map building method to characterize the mixed environment to make up a single environment map representation methods, such as Thrun S and grid map topology combined with the grid construction of indoor topological graph [1], completes the construction of Hybrid Map [2] solemn and Xu Xiaodong according to the geometry and topology of the environment model, but to accurately describe the environment the structure requires a large amount of data in the robot navigation process will produce a lot of search and data storage of [3].

© Springer Nature Singapore Pte Ltd. 2018
G. Zhai et al. (Eds.): IFTC 2017, CCIS 815, pp. 492–500, 2018.
https://doi.org/10.1007/978-981-10-8108-8_44

Self-organizing feature map (Self-Organizing Map, SOM [4] can imitate the human brain map) feature mapping function, has the high dimensional input space to a low dimensional space compression mapping neural computing function and keep the input space topological invariant features. Vlassis [5] using the robot position as samples, topological map building indoor environment using SOM and its application in robot path planning, but the topological map errors that exist neuronal connections between neurons through the connecting wire obstacles may mislead the robot into the obstacle in the navigation process. Derived from SOM GCS (Growing Cell Structure) [6], GSOM (Growing Self-Organizing Map), [7] (Growing Neural Gas, GNG [8]) without prior design of the number of nodes, and will expand as the input of the network scale grows. The network structure and node generation control conditions adopted by them are different, but they are trained by the best matching and neighborhood weight correction method. The author in previous work can increase the self-organizing map GSOM algorithm is applied to the algorithm in [9] modeling environment, constantly adding new neuron self drawn topological map, and on the desktop robot maze physical experiment system is verified on the [3]. Yan et al. [10] use GNG neural networks (Growing Neural Gas) to build indoor environmental cognitive maps, and obtain topological maps which can describe environment accurately. Both GSOM and GNG can determine the optimal number of SOM neurons describing the environmental features under the condition that the number of samples is unknown, and a more accurate environment map can be established. But the growth of their neurons is very slow, and it is not suitable for occasions with high time requirements.

In view of the problem of the connection between neurons and neurons in the map created by the fixed SOM neural network, a SOM graph algorithm with PSOM structure is proposed. The algorithm first uses SOM neural network to create a topological map of the environment preliminary, then the wrong neurons and neurons connect line topology map to find, finally removing errors of neurons and segment may be an accurate description of the topological map of the environment. Compared with the GSOM diagram, the SOM graph and the GSOM algorithm can accurately represent the environment topology, but the convergence time is greatly reduced.

2   Relating Work

2.1   SOM Algorithm

In 1982, Kohonen proposed an organization feature map called simply SOM, SOM, or SOM neural networks. Figure SOM neurons with structure of feedforward and feedback the dimension of the input vector is arbitrary, the dimension of the output layer usually has only one or two dimensional form, operation mechanism of SOM graph contains 3 important aspects: competition, collaborative links and synaptic adaptive link.

Algorithm 1. SOM

Initialization: Setting neural numble of SOM is N, Random initial SOM neuron feed forward weight vector WJ (j=1,2,... N). Make t=0 the initial value of the discrete time, and i=1 is the discrete sequence. Set the maximum number of iterations T.

　for $t = 1{:}1{:}T$ do
　　for each sample S(corresponding sample vector$x$) do
　　Step1 Competition stage:

$$o_{i(x)}(x) = \min \| x - w_{win}^T \|$$

　　Step2 Coordination stage:

$$\omega_{jwin} = \exp\{-\frac{d_{jwin}^2}{2\sigma^2}\}(j = 1, 2, ..., N)$$

　　Step3 Synaptic adaptive stage:

$$\begin{cases} \Delta w_j(t) = \alpha(t)\omega_{jwin}(t)(x - w_j(t)) \\ w_j(t+1) = w_j(t) + \Delta w_j(t)(j = 1, 2, ..., N) \end{cases}$$

　end for
　⋮

$$\sigma(t) = \sigma_0 \exp(-\kappa_\sigma t)$$
$$\alpha(t) = \alpha_0 \exp(-\kappa_\alpha t)$$

　⋮
end for

In If the sample collection Sample = {S_1, S_2, …, S_n} has been previously obtained, where $S_i(i = 1, 2, …, N)$ is the i sample point, then the algorithm using SOM chart algorithm, see Algorithm 1.

From the implementation of the algorithm, we can see that the self-organizing process of SOM diagram can be divided into a "competition, coordination and adaptation" process.

2.2　Environment Representation with SOM

Figure 1 is the indoor environment at Beijing University of Technology's 1101 laboratory. The black area in the diagram is the barrier area.

The indoor mobile robot has a ranging sensor, and the robot body is equipped with an indoor positioning system to obtain the position information of the mobile robot.

First let the robot traverse the interior, and the robot will return its position coordinates at intervals of sampling time as Si(i = 1, 2, …, N) and finally get the set of sample points S = {S1, S2, …, Sn}. Figure 2 is the sketch map of sample set.

The computer used in the experiment simulation is HP dc5850, and the processor is AMD Athlon (TM) Dual core processor 5200B 2.70 GHz, and the simulation software is MATLAB2013b.

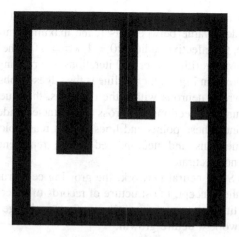

Fig. 1. Indoor environment

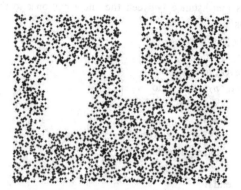

Fig. 2. Sketch map of sample set

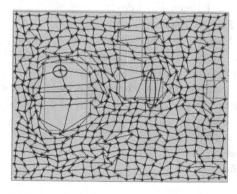

Fig. 3. Topological environment map with SOM (Color figure online)

The set neuron number is $N = 23 * 23 = 529$, and the feed forward weight of the neuron takes the random value between $0 \sim 1$, the maximum number of iterations is $T = 400$. When $t = 0$, the effective radius $\sigma 0 = 4$, $\kappa\sigma = 0.01$, the learning rate $\alpha 0 = 1$, $\kappa\alpha = 0.01$. Using SOM algorithm, after 400 iterations, the running time of the program for the 65.02 s. As shown in Fig. 3, the red line is the edges of obstacles, the small blue circle point out the wrong neurons within the obstacles, the blue line within a ellipse point out a wrong neural connections that cross the obstacles. Indeed, there are 13 such points and 15 such lines, these points and lines are not reachable for the robot. Those errors neuronal connections and neurons led to the representation of topological environment map is not accurate.

Fritzke based on SOM neural network, the growing cell structures (Growing Cell Structures, GCS) of the concept, the structure of records of all cells in the competitive learning in winning times, by comparing the number to change the number of nerve cells, can realize network structure growth.

Algorithm 2. Adjacent neuron finding algorithm

Initialization: Setting the value of n_1, n_2, max_d

d_i is the distance between the new neuron and the other neurons.

    $num\_n_1 = 0$

    $num\_n_2 = 0$

    for every neuron do

        if $d_i < n_2 * max\_d$ do

            index_n2[num_n_2]=i

            num_n_2 += 1

            if $d_i < n_1 * max\_d$ do

                index_n1[num_n_1]=i

                num_n_1 += 1

            end if

        end if

    end for

    for $j_1 = 1:1:num\_n_1$ do

        for $j_{21} = 1:1:num\_n_2 - 1$ do

            for $j_{22} = 1:1:num\_n_2 - 1$ do

            if the line between the new neuron and $v_{index\_n1[j1]}$ and the line between neuron vindex_n2[j21] and vindex_n2[j21] do not intersect do

                making the new connection between the new neuron and neuron $v_{index\_n1[j1]}$

                end if

            end for

        end for

    end for

The author in the previous work of GSOM (Growing Self-Organizing Map) to construct the topological map for the algorithm, and the results were compared with the SOM algorithm, compared with SOM algorithm; GSOM algorithm can better express the environment. GSOM algorithm has the input samples in each input, to judge the input samples and win SOM neurons weights of the Euclidean distance is greater than a given value of max_d, if it is, is that the SOM map of the size of the current is not sufficient to describe the characteristics of the sampling points, an increase of SOM neurons, and in the near range search can be established the connections between neurons, neurons called adjacent neurons. The adjacent neurons finding Algorithm is shown in Algorithm 2.

The algorithm requires $f(n) = num(N1) * (num(N2)-1)2$ cycles, and the time complexity of the algorithm is $T(n) = O(f(n))$. As GSOM runs, the number of neurons increases, and the number of neurons N1 and neuron N2, num(N1) and num(N2) will become larger and larger, which will inevitably cause new neurons to look for their neighboring neurons for longer periods of time.

When the GSOM growth process is over, two training sessions are required to achieve the optimal sample distribution structure description.

The same GSOM algorithm is used to express the environment shown in Fig. 1, set the parameters of growth process: the initial number of neurons was 1, max_d = 0.03, when t = 0, the effective radius $\sigma0 = 0$; set the second training process parameters: t = 0, the effective radius $\sigma0 = 0.01$, $\kappa\sigma = 0.01$, learning rate $\alpha0 = 0.01$, $\kappa\alpha = -0.001$. When the program runs for 13.1 h at the end, the environment topology map is shown, as shown in Fig. 4, when the number of neurons is 519. As can be seen from the results, GSOM is more accurate in expressing the environment. Only when the diameter of the obstacle is less than n1*max_d is it possible to pass through the connection between the neurons, which greatly reduces the error. However, as the number of neurons increases, the search for new neurons becomes longer and closer to the neuron, resulting in a long running time for the entire GSOM algorithm.

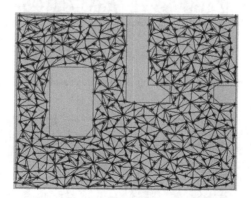

Fig. 4. Topological environment map with GSOM

3 Prunable Self-Organizing Map (PSOM)

GSOM algorithm can describe the environment very well, but its program running time is too long, and the environment represented by SOM diagram is not accurate, but the program running time is much faster than GSOM. You can see from Fig. 3, there are obstacles where the SOM graph is relatively sparse, expressed in neurons and neurons around the Euclidean distance and large, another obstacle in sample neurons distance is far, line length longer neurons connection through the obstacles. According to these features, SOM can be found between the error figure error structure, neurons and neuron connections, the SOM structure is wrong, you can delete the error structure, get the topological map is more precise. Specific algorithms see Algorithm 3.

Based on 1.2 experiments, using the above graph cut SOM error structure algorithm, the threshold parameters DistSumThre = 0.118, DistNeuronSampleThre = 0.004, DistLineThre = 0.1, get the result shown in Fig. 5, with the deletion of SOM map error structure algorithm to find the wrong neuron topology (figure in the "×" mark) and neuron connections (error the blue line), finally cut the final topology error environment map structure is obtained as shown in Fig. 6, we can see that the use of the algorithm to find the number of neurons in error is 13, the error is 12 root connections between neurons, this topology can better express the environment. The running time of the whole algorithm is 68.14 s, which shows that the algorithm runs faster than the GSOM algorithm.

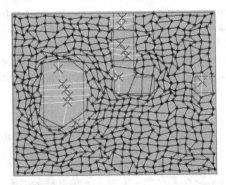

Fig. 5. Wrong neurons and wrong connections result (Color figure online)

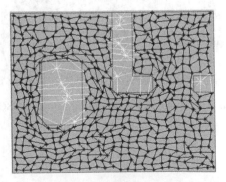

Fig. 6. Topological environment map with PSOM

Algorithm 3. Prunable Self-Organizing Map (PSOM)

Initialization: Setting the threshold of sum of given distance DistSumThre, the threshold of distance between the selecting neuron and sample DistNeuronSampleThre, the threshold of distance between selecting neuron and its adjacent neuron DistLineThre.

Where Dist is the sum of Euclidean distances between the selecting neuron and its adjacent neuron; DistNeuronSample is Euclidean distance between the selecting neuron and each sample, min(DistNeuronSample) is the minimum Euclidean distance between the selecting neurons and samples; DistLine is the distance between the selecting neuron and its adjacent neuron

for every neuron do
   if Dist>DistSumThre
      Record this neuron as susceptive neuron NS
   end if
   end for
for every susceptive neuron do
   if min(DistNeuronSample)>DistNeuronSampleThre
      Record this neuron as wrong neuron NSO
   end if
   end for
for every susceptive neuron do
   if DistLine>DistLineThre
      Record this connection between this neuron and its a
djacent jth neuron as wrong connection<NSL , j>
   end if
   end for
Delect the wrong neuron and wrong connections

---

4   Conclusion

(1) The traditional SOM algorithm and GSOM algorithm have advantages and disadvantages in the topological map building environment, SOM map containing the error structure, can not accurately describe the environment, GSOM algorithm can be a good description of the environment, but its time complexity is too large, causing the program running time is too long, not high efficiency and quick access to the topology map the environment.

(2) In the SOM graph, this paper proposes a pruning algorithm of SOM graph structure (PSOM), this algorithm can obtain the environment topology accurately, but compared to the GSOM greatly reduces the running time of the program, is a method for constructing an efficient and accurate environment map.

References

1. Thrun, S.: Learning metric-topological maps for indoor mobile robot navigation. Artif. Intell. **99**(1), 21–71 (1998)
2. Yan, Z., Xiaodong, X., Wei, W.: Mobile robot geometrictopological map building and selflocalization. Control Decis. **20**(7), 815–818 (2015)
3. Xiaogang, R., Xutao, X., Xinyuan, L.: A desktop robot system and its autonomous mapping algorithm. Control Eng. **17**(6), 856–860 (2010)
4. Kohonen, T.: Self-organized formation of topologically correct feature maps. Biol. Cybern. **43**(1), 59–69 (1982)
5. Vlassis, N.A., Papakonstantinou, G., Tsanakas, P.: Robot Map Building by Kohonen's Self-Organizing Neural Networks (1998)
6. Fritzke, B.: Growing cell structures — a self-organizing network for unsupervised and supervised learning. Neural Netw. **7**(9), 1411–1460 (1994)
7. Choi, D.I., Park, S.H.: Self-creating and organizing neural networks. IEEE Trans. Neural Netw. **5**(4), 561–575 (1994)
8. Fritzke, B.: A growing neural gas network learns topologies. In: Advances in Neural Information Processing Systems, pp. 625–632. MIT Press, Cambridge, USA (1995)
9. Xiaogang, R., Shaomin, X., Xinyuan, L.: Mapping based on the growing self-organizing map (GSOM). J. Syst. Simul. **20**(1), 81–84 (2008)
10. Yan, W., Weber, C., Wermter, S.: A neural approach for robot navigation based on cognitive map learning. In: International Joint Conference on Neural Networks, pp. 1–8. IEEE (2012)

Computer Vision

Nest Detection Using Coarse-to-Fine Searching Strategy

Nianwang Wan[1], Zhenyu Duan[2(✉)], Yongdong Hua[1], Qingbin Wang[3], and Weihai Li[4]

[1] NARI-TECH SANNENG INSTRUMENT (NANJING) CO., LTD.,
Nanjing, China
{wannianwang,huayongdong}@sgepri.sgcc.com.cn
[2] Shanghai Jiao Tong University, Shanghai, China
o17650@sjtu.edu.com
[3] Yunfu Power Supply Bureau of Guangdong Power Grid Co., Ltd.,
Yunfu, China
wqbity@163.com
[4] 91998 troop, Binzhou, China
lwh666@126.com

Abstract. Nest on pylon is a great threat to the safety and function of electric power system. Thus detection of nest has been considered as a vital task when checking transmission line through intelligent surveillance system. Traditional detection methods for nests are basically based on artificial identification, resulting a lot of time consumption and human waste. In addition, it's impractical to apply this method to the situation with massive pending data. In this paper, we propose an automatic framework for nest detection. This work firstly locates the pylon, then detects nest on it through color analysis. To boost the speed of pylon location, our work combines the technology of detection and tracking after extracting HOG features of pylons. In addition, building on the observation that most pylons are standing out from background for the sake of their sharp outlines and unique color patterns, a number of filtering operations in this work are designed to significantly decrease the number of candidate boxes. Experiments have been conducted to show that this framework could achieve promisingly precise and robust detection for nest in complex environment.

Keywords: Nest detection · Tracking · Computer vision

1 Introduction

Inspection of the safety of electricity transmission is an important task to guarantee the normal work of electricity power system. It plays a vital role in daily life to prevent the accidents and accompanying loss from occurring. Traditional methods used to check are mainly accomplished by workers, which is dangerous

© Springer Nature Singapore Pte Ltd. 2018
G. Zhai et al. (Eds.): IFTC 2017, CCIS 815, pp. 503–512, 2018.
https://doi.org/10.1007/978-981-10-8108-8_45

as well as of low efficiency. Modern checking framework, which is called intelligent surveillance system, is thus designed to automatically checks the state of the pylons and specify the existed problems. In this framework, image information is collected through UAV. And potential dangers are then found by analyzing these image information.

Nest detection is one of most fundamental tasks of this surveillance system, while very few methods are proposed for automatic detection of nest. Nest is a critical factor in the pylon's accident. The fallen wire, damp weeds and other conductive material from nests could result in dangerous short and breakdown of transmission line. In addition, flashover caused by the birds droppings on insulator is one of the main cause of transmission lines cascading trips. Statistically, from Januray 2007 to the end of December 2011, over hundreds of tips occurred in transmission line of one province with 220 kV and above. Of these trips, about 14% are caused by nests. The proportion reached 16% in 2011, meaning nest is the biggest threat to the safety of power system after lightning (47%) and external forces (22%) [13]. Though serious harm has been caused because of existence of nest, there are few efficient detecting methods except manual detection.

In this paper, we propose a computer vision technology based framework to realize automatic detection of nest. The general scheme could be seen at Fig. 1. Building on the motivation that to find nests lying above pylons, our work firstly locates and tracks pylons in image sequences collected by UAV. Then nests are detected on pylons, where color characteristic feature are used to screen out non-nest region.

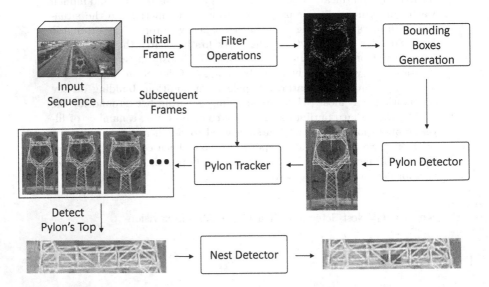

Fig. 1. General introduction of the proposed framework. The first frame of a sequence is used to initialize the pylon's detector. To reduce the number of candidate bounding boxes, filtering operations are applied. Then tracker use the given coordinates to track pylons in subsequent frames. Note that to reduce false positive of nest, the detection area for nests is narrowed down to the pylon top.

The rest of the paper is structured as follows: Sects. 2 and 3 will respectively introduce the methods used to detect and track pylons, the algorithm used to detect the nest is then narrated in Sect. 4. In Sect. 5, experiments and analysis of nest detection will be given. Section 6 is the final conclusion.

2   Detection Framework of Pylons

In this section, the detection framework of pylons is introduced in detail. It will wrap in 3 part. The first part is the HOG feature extraction of pylons. Then we use gentle AdaBoost as the classifier to recognize pylons. To further boost the detection speed, our work applies multiple filter operations to screen out candidate bounding boxes which contains no pylons.

2.1   Feature Extraction and Classifier

The first step of feature extraction process is to generate a lot of bounding-box candidates which probably contain pylons from the image. In the bounding boxes, HOG (Histrogram of Oriented Gradient) feature [2] in this work is used to describe pylons in feature space. Considering that HOG feature does not take into consideration the changeable scale of object, so we adjust the size of candidate boxes with fixed aspect ratio, through which the dimension of feature is also fixed. HOG is a feature descriptor used in computer vision and image processing field for object detection. This feature is based on statistical information that counts the total occurrence of gradient orientation from multiple portions of a given image. The calculation process of HOG starts from computing gradient value. It is realized through applying simple convolutional kernel to image, such as $[-1, 0, 1]$ and $[-1, 0, 1]^T$. Then histogram is utilized to count orientation information from every single patch chosen from the image. Considering the change in illumination and contrast, gradient value in histogram are then locally normalized by following equation (L2-norm).

$$f = \frac{v}{\sqrt{||v||_2^2 + e^2}} \tag{1}$$

where v is the gradient value of one bin, and f is the normalized value. e is a small floating number used to prevent divide-by zero errors.

HOG feature was widely used in pedestrian detection task for its generalization ability and robustness for geometric and photometric deformation. In this work, we use HOG feature as the descriptors of pylons.

After HOG feature has been extracted from the image, AdaBoost classifier is applied to do classification of the candidate bounding boxes. AdaBoost [8] is strong classifier which has combined a number of different types of algorithms (weak classifiers). For each sample to be classified, the decisions of every week classifiers are integrated in a weighted sum way to determine final result, which significantly increases the performance of this classifier. The combination of HOG feature and AdaBoost has shown a competitive performance and efficiency in detection for pedestrians [9, 10].

In this paper, HOG feature could perfectly characterize the pylons. When the feature combined with AdaBoost, the special structure of pylons could be efficiently learned and detected.

2.2   Filter Operations

The HOG+AdaBoost classifier could process a single patch in a relatively fast speed. However, the massive generated bounding boxes slow down the detection speed. So we take a lot of filter operations to screen out bounding boxes with low probabilities of pylons' occurrences. These operations consist of 3 parts: by scale, by color filter operation and by edge detection.

Scale. Addressing on the problem of nest detection, it could be found that only if the scale of pylon is big enough, the nests on pylon will be possible to be detected. Sometimes the pylons are too small to be recognized and it's impossible to precisely tell nests apart. So we set a searching threshold of pylons to make sure the tiny objects will not be chosen.

Color Filter Operation. Building on the observation that the metal material used for pylon is usually gray or white and has a high brightness, we use color property to screen out non-pylon region. Aforementioned color characteristics is expressed as below:

$$var(i) < threshold\_var \qquad (2)$$

$$mean(i) > threshold\_mean \qquad (3)$$

where i is the RGB values of a pixel, $var(\cdot)$ is the variance of RGB values of the pixel, $mean(\cdot)$ is the mean value of RGB values. $threshold\_var$ and $threshold\_mean$ are the thresholds values for variance and mean value. The first equation determines that the pixels are white or gray without considering the brightness. The second equation ensure that the pixels are bright enough to belong to metal pylons. Above operations with thresholds for RGB value will roughly select pixels which belong to pylon.

Edge Detection. It could be observed that the pylon region is the one with a lot of regular edges, so we use edge detector as additional filter. In this work, we apply canny edge detector [1] framework to accompany the mentioned color filtering operation to further remove non-pylon regions. The canny detector starts from removing noise and smoothing image by Gaussian filter, this could prevent that the detected edges are partly from noise. Then canny detector uses 4 masks to detect horizontal, vertical and diagonal edges. After that, the intensity gradient image and direction of each pixel are generated and used to track edges. In tracking process, 2 thresholds are used. The higher threshold is to label edges which have a high probability, while the lower one is used to link labeled edges where the border-line is hazy (Fig. 2).

In this paper, we use these 3 operations to coarsely screen out the regions without pylons. However, it's still imperfect because of the slow detection speed and the detection failures caused by partially invisibility of pylons.

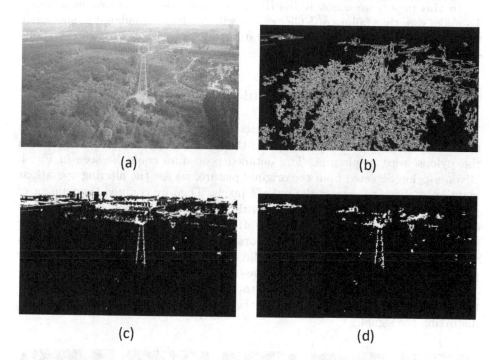

Fig. 2. Example of pixel filter. (a) is the original image. (b) is the result picture after canny edge detection. (c) is the result picture after filtering by color and (d) is the result of combination of (b) and (c).

3   Tracking Framework of Pylons

As said in last section, detection of pylons shows a relatively slow speed and low robustness when pylons are partly invisible. Considering that the image data collected by UAV is continuous sequences, so we adopt tracking framework to improve the detection accuracy (Fig. 3).

The algorithm we used to track pylons is kernelized Correlation Filter tracker (KCF) [6], which is known as an efficient and very fast tracker in computer vision field. KCF was primarily famous for its fast speed and outstanding tracking performance compared with a set of traditional methods (such as TLD [7] and Struck [5]). Instead of performing classification in spatial domain, KCF tracker adopts circular matrix to transform it into a dot production in frequency domain.

In OTB-50 tracking benchmark [12], KCF+HOG could achieve 73.2% in mean precision at a speed of 172 fps. As for KCF+Raw-pixels, the mean precision is 56.0% while the speed is 154 fps. It is more efficient compared with TLD (60.8% at a speed of 28 fps) and Struck (65.6% at a speed of 20 fps).

Though KCF is known for its efficiency, it shows a lack of robustness for deformation and variation of scale. For the continuous frames taken by UAV, these problems hardly occur so that KCF performs perfectly in this situation.

In this paper, we adopt KCF+HOG to track pylons occurred in pictures. To make sure that failure of KCF tracker will not be accumulated in successive frames, we use the same filtering operations of detection process to determine whether to halt the tracking process.

4   Nest Detection Sub-module

The nests are searched from the detected and tracked pylon areas. It could be found that nests are usually located on the top of the pylons, so we first search the pylons' tops in pictures. The detailed procedure could be seen in Fig. 4. Given a pylon detected from the original picture, we use the filtering operations mentioned above to extract the pylon's pixels. Then we counted the number of pixels in each horizontal row (the statistic result which is denoted as blue lines could be seen at the right side of Fig. 4). Then we apply Savitzky-Golay filter [4,11] to smooth the data (denoted as orange line in Fig. 4). Then the first peak value and corresponding vertical coordinate is found in the smoothed data. The peak's vertical coordinate is seen as the center of pylon's top.

The Savitzky-Golay filter is a digital filter designed to smooth the discontinuous data points, which increases the signal-to-noise ratio without greatly distorting the signal.

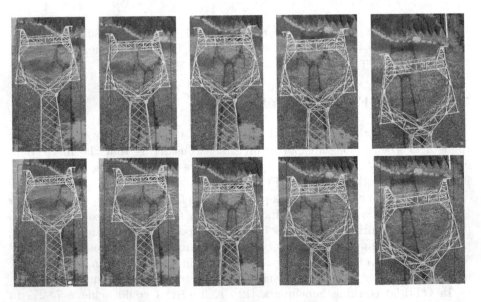

Fig. 3. The demo of tracking continuous pylons V.S. detecting pylons separately. With the distance from UAV to pylon getting closer, detector fails to find pylons while tracker could perfectly locate pylons.

Note that to make it more robust, the peak value selected need to surpass all the values of neighboring region with a width of 14 pixels. There are also few conditions where the selected region is slightly above the real pylon top, so we adopt the following equation to select pylon top region:

$$pixels \in \{p|v(p) < peak + 30 \,\&\&\, v(p) > peak - 20\} \tag{4}$$

where $v(p)$ is the vertical coordinate of pixel p and $peak$ is the selected peak value. Considering that the shapes of nests are unfixed, so we adopt color statistical feature to locate where the nest is.

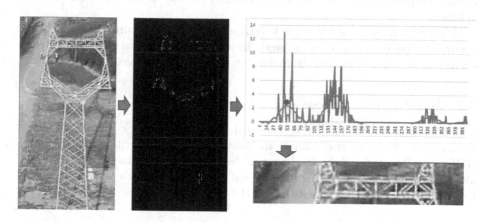

Fig. 4. The flowchart of detection of pylon top. After filtering operations, Savitzky-Golay filter is adopted to smooth the data which is collected from each horizontal pixel row. The vertical coordinate where the first peak value (denoted as red circle) occurred is chosen as the center of pylon top's region. (Color figure online)

The nest is mainly made of branches and wires and soil, thus the color property of the nest is usually the same as soil (in khaki) which has a fixed ratio of RGB values. Through statistical analysis for 1000 pixels of nests, the R/B ratio is between 1.17 and 1.4 and the R/G ratio is between 1.1 and 1.15. Thus for each pixel, we use following function to judge whether a selected pixel i belongs to nests:

$$R(i)/B(i) \in [1.17, 1.4] \tag{5}$$

$$R(i)/G(i) \in [1.1, 1.15] \tag{6}$$

where $R(i)$ means the R-channel value of the pixel i. The same to $G(i)$ and $B(i)$. Note that we use the ratio of the values of different color channels, which could avoid the impact of brightness variation.

5 Experiments

5.1 Implementation Detail

In this paper, the image data about pylons and nests are collected by UAV in real world with a frame rate of 25 fps and a resolution of 1920 × 1080. Implementation of this framwork is based on OpenCV. To train the HOG+AdaBoost detector, we use 300 different pylons taken from the dataset and additional pylons' pictures from pylon synset of ImageNet dataset [3] as the positive examples. As for negative examples, we randomly select 600 patches from aforementioned dataset where the patches are then manually checked to ensure they does not contain pylons.

We set a maximum tracking length as 150 to make sure that the newly occurred objects will not be ignored. In addition, when two and more pylons occurs in a single frame, this framework will chose the closer object to track.

5.2 Results and Analysis

To test the performance of the proposed framework, Harr Feature+AdaBoost is adopted as the traditional method to compare with the proposed HOG+AdaBoost framework. These 2 frameworks both use color threshold method to detect nests. This experiment is conducted on a sequence of continuous frames which include totally 1118 frames (Table 1).

Table 1. Result of experiment on nest detection.

	Nests	Detected nest	Detected non-nest	Undetected nest
Haar+AdaBoost	661	277	75	384
HOG+AdaBoost	661	598	61	63

Table 2. Statistic result of experiment.

	True positive	False positive	False negative
Haar+AdaBoost	41.91%	11.3%	58.09%
HOG+AdaBoost	90.46%	9.23%	9.54%

According to this experiment, compared with Haar feature, HOG feature performs a better generalization ability for pylons' feature and greatly improve the detection performance. Compared with other traditional nest detection methods, the proposed framework narrows down the searching region and use KCF tracker to realize the fast and robust updates of pylons' coordinates (Table 2).

6   Conclusion

In this paper, we propose a nest detection method which is based on color filter operation. The framework starts from searching for pylons by HOG+AdaBoost detector and KCF tracker to greatly reduce searching range of nests. To further boost the speed of detection, multiple operations are utilized to minimum the number of bounding-box candidates. Given a series of continuous frames taken by UAV, this work could offer a quicker and safer solution of detection for nests on pylons (a potential safety-threat for power system). Thus it could be predicted that this framework will play an important role in applications of intelligent surveillance system. There are still space for this work to be perfect in future, for example a quicker detector based on deep learning technology with massive training data.

Acknowledgment. The work was supported by State Key Research and Development Program (2016YFB1001003). This work was also supported by NSFC (U1611461, 61502301, 61527804, 61671298) and STCSM17511105401, China's Thousand Youth Talents Plan, the 111 Project under Grant B07022, and the Shanghai Key Laboratory of Digital Media Processing and Transmissions.

References

1. Canny, J.: A computational approach to edge detection. IEEE Trans. Pattern Anal. Mach. Intell. **8**(6), 679–698 (1986)
2. Dalal, N., Triggs, B.: Histograms of oriented gradients for human detection. In: 2005 IEEE Computer Society Conference on Computer Vision and Pattern Recognition, CVPR 2005, vol. 1, pp. 886–893. IEEE (2005)
3. Deng, J., Dong, W., Socher, R., Li, L.-J., Li, K., Fei-Fei, L.: Imagenet: a large-scale hierarchical image database. In: IEEE Conference on Computer Vision and Pattern Recognition, CVPR 2009, pp. 248–255. IEEE (2009)
4. Guest, P.G.: Numerical Methods of Curve Fitting. Cambridge University Press, London (2012)
5. Hare, S., Golodetz, S., Saffari, A., Vineet, V., Cheng, M.-M., Hicks, S.L., Torr, P.H.S.: Struck: structured output tracking with kernels. IEEE Trans. Pattern Anal. Mach. Intell. **38**(10), 2096–2109 (2016)
6. Henriques, J.F., Caseiro, R., Martins, P., Batista, J.: High-speed tracking with kernelized correlation filters. IEEE Trans. Pattern Anal. Mach. Intell. **37**(3), 583–596 (2015)
7. Kalal, Z., Mikolajczyk, K., Matas, J.: Tracking-learning-detection. IEEE Trans. Pattern Anal. Mach. Intell. **34**(7), 1409–1422 (2012)
8. Kégl, B.: The return of AdaBoost.MH: multi-class hamming trees. arXiv preprint arXiv:1312.6086 (2013)
9. Liu, Q., Qu, Y.: Hog and color based adaboost pedestrian detection. In: 2011 Seventh International Conference on Natural Computation (ICNC), vol. 1, pp. 584–587. IEEE (2011)
10. Wang, Z.-R., Jia, Y.-L., Huang, H., Tang, S.-M.: Pedestrian detection using boosted hog features. In: 2008 11th International IEEE Conference on Intelligent Transportation Systems, ITSC 2008, pp. 1155–1160. IEEE (2008)

11. Whittaker, E.T., Robinson, G., et al.: The Calculus of Observations, vol. 8. Blackie, London (1924)
12. Wu, Y., Lim, J., Yang, M.-H.: Online object tracking: a benchmark. In: Proceedings of the IEEE Conference on Computer Vision and Pattern Recognition, pp. 2411–2418 (2013)
13. Zhu, C., Wang, T.: Analysis and prevention of bird damage in transmission line. Cent. China Electr. Power **22**(4), 46–49 (2009)

Image Compression

A Deep Learning Based Perceptual Bit Allocation Scheme on Conversational Videos for HEVC λ-Domain Rate Control

Lisha Zhu[✉], Guozhong Wang, Guowei Teng, Zhenglong Yang, and Liliang Zhang

School of Communication and Information Engineering,
Shanghai University, Shanghai, China
2385470012@qq.com,18355311758@163.com

Abstract. The newest λ-domain rate control in High efficiency video coding (HEVC) adaptively allocates bit per pixel (bpp) without considering the visual importance. A perceptual bit allocation scheme based on deep learning for conversational videos is proposed. Firstly, a multitask cascaded convolutional network is employed to detected facial region in the encoding videos. Then, instead of the predefined bit ratio for frame level bit allocation, an adaptively bit rate ratio, mainly according to variation of inter frames, is used to allocate bit rate more reasonable for every frame. Finally, the quality parameters (QP), belonging to the facial regions, will be clipped in a smaller interval to get a better visual quality. The experimental results show that the quality of facial region is improved significantly with a good rate control performance.

Keywords: HEVC · Rate control · Deep learning
Perceptual video coding

1 Introduction

Rate control is a crucial module in High efficiency video coding (HEVC) [1], which aims to improve the quality of reconstructed video at a target bit rate. Recently, lots of excellent rate control algorithms are proposed for HEVC. In [2], a pixel based unified Rate-Quantization (URQ) rate control model is proposed. In the URQ model, QP is regarded as the most important factor to control the bit rate. While, Li *et al.* suggest that only when all the other coding parameters except QP are not too flexible, the bit rate is influenced by QP. So the λ-domain rate control [3] is proposed and gets a better performance than URQ model. To further improve the rate control performance, an adaptive bit allocation scheme [4] is proposed. In this scheme, bit rate ratio is decided by frame λ, α and β. For the traditional rate control scheme, bits allocated for every pixel without considering the visual characteristics. In [5], human attention can be guided by bottom-up attention and top-down attention, which can be described

© Springer Nature Singapore Pte Ltd. 2018
G. Zhai et al. (Eds.): IFTC 2017, CCIS 815, pp. 515–524, 2018.
https://doi.org/10.1007/978-981-10-8108-8_46

as the natural reflection and outside stimuli. The typical bottom-up and top-down attention is human face and moving objects respectively. Tang *et al.* [6] improve the quality of moving objects. In [7], a perceptual URQ rate control algorithm based on hierarchical face model is proposed to improve the subjective quality of face or facial feature regions. Then, Li *et al.* [8] propose a weight-based R-λ rate control for improving quality of facial regions. Both of them get a good coding performance based on machine learning, but have a weak ability for half-facial or multi-facial detection.

Deep learning approaches can achieve impressive performance on classification and recognition. Recently, convolutional neural networks (CNNs) achieve remarkable progresses in a variety of computer vision tasks, such as image classification and face recognition. Inspired by the significant successes of deep learning methods in computer vision tasks, several studies utilize deep CNNs for face detection. In [9], the trained ImageNet LSVRC-2010 can classify 1000 different classes with five convolutional layers and three fully-connected layers. However, due to its complex CNN structure, this approach is time costly in practice. Zhang *et al.* [10] propose a multitask cascaded convolutional networks for joint face detection. It uses three convolutional neural networks (CNNS) to go on the coarse search, fine search and facial decision respectively. The mean facial detection ratio can achieve 93.1%. By given the cascade structure, the method can achieve high speed in joint face detection and alignment, meanwhile using this method, the quality of the face is high, and some of the wrong point of the judge will be reduced, some of the details of the human face compared to other existing methods have a better deal. So we combine the deep learning and rate control for improving quality of the facial regions on conversational videos. Different from previous works, the half-facial and multi-facial regions in the videos can be detected accurately, and this is very useful for bit allocation of different regions.

The rest of this paper is organized as follows. Section 2 will introduce the related works. The proposed perceptual bit allocation scheme is described in Sect. 3. Then, Sect. 4 will illustrate the experimental results. The conclusions will be given in Sect. 5.

2   Related Works

(a) The employed CNN model

The overall framework, in [10], is shown in Fig. 1:

The network (P-Net) is a fully convolutional network which is to obtain the candidate facial windowsand and their bounding box regression vectors. All candidates are fed to another CNN, which is called refinenetwork (R-Net). It further rejects a large number of false candidates, performs calibration with bounding box regression, and conducts non maximum suppression (NMS). Finally all the datas will be sent to the finally network which is similar to the R-Net. Using the net, it can identify face regions with more supervision meanwhile and get five facial landmarkspositions.

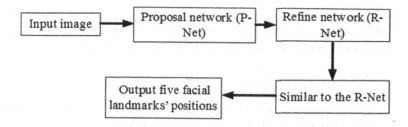

Fig. 1. The flowchart of the employed CNN model.

Nowadays, multiple CNNs have been designed for face detection. However the performs of CNN are limited by the following facts: (1) In convolution layers some filters may limit their discriminative ability because the filters lack diversity; (2) compared to other multiclass objection detection and classification tasks, face detection is a challenging binary classification task. So it may need less numbers of filters per layer to get a better result. In the new cascaded CNN Architectures, it reduces the number of filters, uses 3×3 filter, and increases the depth to reduce the computing. The facial detection results are shown in Fig. 2 with four sequences.

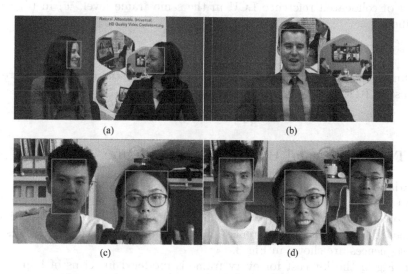

Fig. 2. Facial detection results for (a) *KristenAndSara* at 5th frame, (b) *Johnny* at 20th frame, (c) *Two-People* at 40th frame and (d) *Three-People* at 70th frame

(b) Overview the λ-domain rate control

In [3], the R-D relationship is modeled by the Hyperbolic function, which is defined as

$$D = a \cdot R^{-b} \tag{1}$$

Where a and b are model parameters. R is modeled in terms of bpp, and D is modeled in terms of mean square error (MSE) of luma component. As is well known, λ is the slop of R-D curve and (1) can be calculated by

$$\lambda = -\frac{\partial D}{\partial R} = a \cdot b \cdot bpp^{-b-1} \triangleq \alpha \cdot bpp^{\beta} \tag{2}$$

Where $\alpha = a \cdot b$ and $\beta = -b - 1$. Now, the R-D model is built for rate control. Then, the target bit rate T of the frame is calculated by

$$T = \frac{T_{GOP} - \sum R_i}{\sum \hat{w}_i} \cdot \hat{w}_k \tag{3}$$

Where T_{GOP} is target bit for current GOP. $\sum R_i$ is the sum of used bits. $\sum \hat{w}_i$ is the sum of the bit ratio for left encoding frames, which is predefined. $\hat{w}_k$ is the bit ratio for current frame. Finally, the target bit per pixel is calculated by

$$bpp = \frac{T - \tilde{T}}{n \sum \overline{w_i}} \cdot \overline{w_j} \tag{4}$$

Where $\tilde{T}$ is the estimated header bits. $\sum \overline{w_i}$ is the sum bit ratio of all LCU. $\overline{w_j}$ is the bit ratio of current LCU. n is the pixel number in LCU. Then, according to [4], the bit ratio of current LCU is calculated by the current frame λ, the α and β of collocated reference LCU in the same frame level. $\overline{w_j}$ in (5) will be modified as

$$\overline{w_j} = n \cdot \left(\frac{\lambda}{\alpha}\right)^{\frac{1}{\beta}} \tag{5}$$

During the adaptive process, bit rate will be allocated adaptively. Instead of exhaustive RDO process, the optimal QP is determined by the given λ as

$$QP = c \cdot \ln(\lambda) + d \tag{6}$$

3   The Perceptual Bit Allocation Scheme

(a) Adaptively bit ratio decision

As mentioned in (4), $\hat{w}_k$ is predefined. This may be unreasonable for frame level bit allocation. We carry out the experiment to search the relationship between the inter frame difference and the frame bit cost. The results from four sequences are shown in Fig. 3.

In Fig. 3, the bit cost for every frame is modeled in terms of bpp (bit per pixel), and the inter frame difference is modeled in terms of difference per pixel. From the results, we can see that there is an approximately linear relationship between Diff and bpp. So if the large variation between inter frames is assigned with a small bit rate ratio and vice versa, this will lead to the whole frame quality decreasing or bits waste.

According to the experimental above, we adopt a mean inter frame difference based adaptive bit rate ratio for frame level bit allocation. The mean inter frame difference is defined as

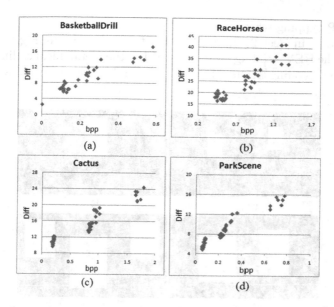

Fig. 3. The relationship between the mean inter frame difference value and bit cost for (a) *BasketDrill*, (b) *RaceHorses*, (c) *Cactus* and (d) *ParkScene*.

$$MD^f = \frac{1}{W \cdot H} \sum_{x=1}^{W} \sum_{y=1}^{H} \left| P_{x,y} - P_{x,y}^f \right| \tag{7}$$

$$MD^b = \frac{1}{W \cdot H} \sum_{x=1}^{W} \sum_{y=1}^{H} \left| P_{x,y} - P_{x,y}^b \right| \tag{8}$$

Where MD^f and MD^b are forward difference and backward difference of current frame respectively. $P_{x,y}$, $P_{x,y}^f$ and $P_{x,y}^b$ are the pixel values of current frame, forward reference frame and backward reference frame respectively. W and H are the width and height of current frame. Then, the adaptive bit rate ratio for every frame is defined as

$$\overline{\overline{w}} = \frac{\left(MD^f + MD^b \right)}{2} \tag{9}$$

So the (3) is redefined as

$$T = \frac{T_{GOP} - \sum R_i}{\sum \overline{\overline{w}}_i} \cdot \overline{\overline{w}}_K \tag{10}$$

From (9) and (10), the bits are allocated mainly according to the variation of inter frame, this will be more effective for coding.

(b) LCU QP clipping scheme

As mention in Sect. 2(a), the facial detection maps, in Fig. 2, should be mapped as the HEVC coding structure which is the hierarchical coding structure based on CTU (coding tree unit). The corresponding results are shown in Fig. 4.

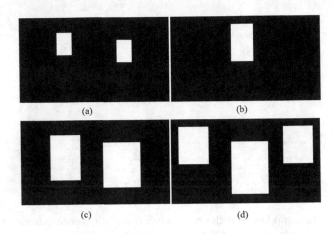

Fig. 4. Facial mapping results for (a) *KristenAndSara* at 5th frame, (b) *Johnny* at 20th frame, (c) *Two-People* at 40th frame and (d) *Three-People* at 70th frame

In Fig. 4, the facial regions are marked with white boxes, and the smallest mapping unit is LCU (largest coding unit). As the smaller QP will get a smaller distortion, and bring a higher coding quality, the LCU, belonging to the facial regions, should be assigned with a small QP. So the calculated LCU QP, obtained from (6), should be smoothed by frame QP and the collocated reference LCU QP. The QPs, belonging to facial LCUs, will be clipped by

$$
Clip\left(\max\left(\frac{(QP^F - 3)}{2}, \frac{(QP^{LCU} - 2)}{2} \right), \min\left(QP^F + 3, QP^{LCU} + 2 \right), QP \right)
$$
(11)

Others will be clipped by

$$
Clip\left(\max\left(QP^F - 3, QP^{LCU} - 2 \right), \min\left(QP^F + 3, QP^{LCU} + 2 \right), QP \right)
$$
(12)

where QP^F is the current frame QP and QP^{LCU} is the collocated referenc LCU QP.

4   The Experimental Results

The proposed algorithm is implemented in the test model HM16.9. The default rate control scheme of HM16.9 is utilized as the reference scheme with random access configuration for 100 frames. In the sequence set, three videos are captured by HIKVISION NETWORK CAMERA at 1280×720 25 Hz, which are named as *One-People*, *Two-People* and *Three-People*.

(a) Objective performance

The bit rate accuracy formula is defined as

$$M\% = \frac{|T_{actual} - T_{target}|}{T_{target}} \cdot 100\% \tag{13}$$

Where T_{actual} and T_{target} are the actual and target bit rate for encoding current sequence, The PSNR formula for facial regions and the whole sequence are defined as

$$PSNR = 10 \cdot \log_{10} \frac{255^2}{msd} \tag{14}$$

Where msd is the mean square error of all pixel values belonging to facial regions or the whole sequence respectively.

$$\triangle P = PSNR_{PROPOSED} - PSNR_{HM16.9} \tag{15}$$

The experimental results are shown in Table 1.

Table 1. The experimental results

Seq.	Proposed			HM16.9		Proposed	HM16.9	ΔP total	ΔP face	BDRate total	BDPSNR total
	Target bit rate	Total PSNR	Facial PSNR	Total PSNR	Facial PSNR	M%	M%				
One-People	5000	34.05	33.79	33.68	33.44	0.588	0.022	0.37	0.35	−3.20%	0.25
	16000	41.05	40.76	40.71	40.27	0.676	0.003	0.34	0.49		
	20000	43.00	42.77	42.70	42.20	0.312	0.003	0.30	0.57		
Two-People	5000	35.22	34.89	34.77	34.50	0.186	0.160	0.45	0.39	5.28%	0.21
	7000	36.57	36.23	36.26	35.88	0.401	0.000	0.31	0.35		
	20000	43.85	43.50	43.38	42.92	0.037	0.000	0.47	0.58		
Three-People	7000	37.99	37.36	37.60	36.93	0.287	0.143	0.40	0.43	−5.97%	0.41
	16000	43.44	42.79	42.93	42.19	0.098	0.000	0.50	0.59		
	20000	45.31	44.69	44.74	44.00	0.000	0.000	0.57	0.69		
Johnny	15000	45.25	44.39	44.92	43.80	0.003	0.001	0.32	0.59	−15.01%	0.33
	20000	45.90	45.24	45.51	44.65	0.001	0.002	0.39	0.59		
	25000	46.47	45.98	46.04	45.35	0.001	0.002	0.43	0.63		
yvidyo4	15000	45.53	44.28	45.22	43.69	0.073	0.018	0.31	0.59	−9.67%	0.29
	20000	46.41	45.30	46.10	44.60	0.043	0.029	0.31	0.69		
	25000	47.19	46.22	46.90	45.49	0.118	0.052	0.29	0.74		
Average						0.118	0.029	0.38	0.55	−5.71%	0.30

From Table 1, we most concern about the bit rate accuracy, which are 0.188% for proposed algorithm and 0.029% for HM16.9. Although the proposed algorithm decreases the accuracy, it is still kept at a high accurate level. The $\triangle P$ values for total sequence and facial regions are 0.38 dB and 0.55 dB, which mean we not only improve the quality of facial regions but the total regions are also

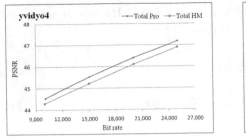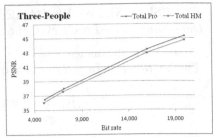

Fig. 5. R-D curves for *yvidyo4* and *Three-People*

increased. At last, the BDRate and BDPSNR for total regions are −5.71% and 0.30 dB respectively. So we improve the quality of face in the sequence with a good rate control performance. The R-D curves for *yvidyo4* and *Three-People* are shown in Fig. 5.

(b) Subjective performance

   The subjective performance is shown in Fig. 6, the left picture is obtained from HM16.9 and the right picture is obtained from proposed algorithm.

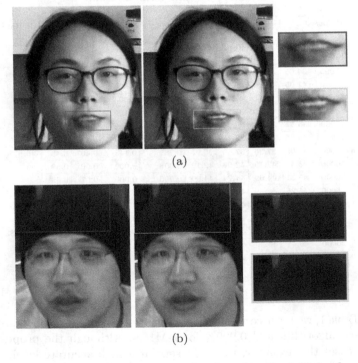

Fig. 6. Subjective performance from *One-People* and *yvidyo4* (Color figure online)

In (a), they are obtained from *One-People* at 34th frame @1000 kbps and (b) are obtained from *yvidyo4* at 16th frame @1000 kbps.

From (a), we can see the mouse part which is marked with red box is blurrier than the part marked with yellow box. In (b), the difference can be seen from the man' hat. The hat in yellow box is clearer than the hat of HM16.9. As the adaptive bit rate ratio is used, bit rate is allocated reasonable to every frame. On the other hand, smaller QP is assigned to facial regions which will lead smaller distortion. So we improve the quality of facial regions efficiently.

5   Conclusion

In this paper, we bring an employed CNN model to rate control for conventional videos. Considering human visual characteristics and the CNN model can detect the facial regions accurately, we propose an adaptive bit rate ratio for frame level bit allocation and a narrow interval for facial LCU QP clipping to improve quality of the facial regions at the target bit rate. The experimental results show that we improve the facial quality efficiently at a good rate control performance. Although the CNN model has improved performance, the model has a high cost of construction, and there are some problems in the process of building, such as when the training data is not sufficient, the model can not work, even if the model can be established, but the accuracy is very low; the establishment of the model at the same time need to cost a lot of time, the hardware configuration requirements are higher. In the future work study, we will continue to study the working principle of CNN, improve the database and improve its accuracy so that we can get better detection and recognition of the facial regions.

Acknowledgment. This work is supported by National Science Foundation of China under Grant No. 61271212. National High-tech R&D Program (863 Program) under Grant No. 2015AA015903. National Science Foundation of Shanghai under Grant No. 14ZR1415200.

References

1. Sullivan, G.J., et al.: Overview of the high efficiency video coding (HEVC) standard. IEEE Trans. Circ. Syst. Video Technol. **22**(12), 1649–1668 (2012)
2. Choi, H., Yoo, J., Nam, J., Sim, D., Bajic, I.: Pixel-wise unified rate-quantization model for multi-level rate control. J. Sel. Top. IEEE Signal Process. **7**(6), 1112–1123 (2013)
3. Li, B., Li, H., Li, L., Zhang, J.: λ domain rate control for high efficiency video coding. IEEE Trans. Image Process. **23**(9), 3841–3854 (2014)
4. Li, B., Li, H., Li, L.: Adaptive bit allocation for R-lambda model rate control in HM. In: JCT-VC of ITU-T SG16 WP3 and ISO/IEC JTC1/SC29/WG11 13th Meeting, Incheon, Republic of Korea, Doc JCTVC-M0036 (2013)
5. Lee, J.-S., Ebrahimi, T.: Perceptual video compression: a survey. IEEE J. Sel. Top. Signal Process. **6**(6), 684–697 (2012)

6. Tang, C.-W.: Spatiotemporal visual considerations for video coding. IEEE Trans. Multimedia **9**(2), 231–238 (2007)
7. Xu, M., et al.: Region-of-interest based conversational HEVC coding with hierarchical perception model of face. IEEE J. Sel. Top. Signal Process. **8**(3), 475–489 (2014)
8. Li, S., et al.: Weight-based R-rate control for perceptual HEVC coding on conversational videos. Signal Process. Image Commun. **38**, 127–140 (2015)
9. Krizhevsky, A., Sutskever, I., Hinton, G.E.: Imagenet classification with deep convolutional neural networks. In: Advances in Neural Information Processing Systems (2012)
10. Zhang, K., Zhang, Z., Li, Z., et al.: Joint face detection and alignment using multitask cascaded convolutional networks. IEEE Signal Process. Lett. **23**(10), 1499–1503 (2016)
11. Chen, D., Ren, S., Wei, Y., Cao, X., Sun, J.: Joint cascade face detection and alignment. In: European Conference on Computer Vision, pp. 109–122 (2014)

Author Index